Lecture Notes in Computer Science 11592

Commenced Publication in 1973
Founding and Former Series Editors:
Gerhard Goos, Juris Hartmanis, and Jan van Leeuwen

More information about this series at http://www.springer.com/series/7409

Jia Zhou · Gavriel Salvendy (Eds.)

Human Aspects of IT for the Aged Population

Design for the Elderly and Technology Acceptance

5th International Conference, ITAP 2019
Held as Part of the 21st HCI International Conference, HCII 2019
Orlando, FL, USA, July 26–31, 2019
Proceedings, Part I

 Springer

Editors
Jia Zhou
Chongqing University
Chongqing, China

Gavriel Salvendy
University of Central Florida
Orlando, USA

ISSN 0302-9743   ISSN 1611-3349 (electronic)
Lecture Notes in Computer Science
ISBN 978-3-030-22011-2   ISBN 978-3-030-22012-9 (eBook)
https://doi.org/10.1007/978-3-030-22012-9

LNCS Sublibrary: SL3 – Information Systems and Applications, incl. Internet/Web, and HCI

This Springer imprint is published by the registered company Springer Nature Switzerland AG
The registered company address is: Gewerbestrasse 11, 6330 Cham, Switzerland

Foreword

The 21st International Conference on Human-Computer Interaction, HCI International 2019, was held in Orlando, FL, USA, during July 26–31, 2019. The event incorporated the 18 thematic areas and affiliated conferences listed on the following page.

A total of 5,029 individuals from academia, research institutes, industry, and governmental agencies from 73 countries submitted contributions, and 1,274 papers and 209 posters were included in the pre-conference proceedings. These contributions address the latest research and development efforts and highlight the human aspects of design and use of computing systems. The contributions thoroughly cover the entire field of human-computer interaction, addressing major advances in knowledge and effective use of computers in a variety of application areas. The volumes constituting the full set of the pre-conference proceedings are listed in the following pages.

This year the HCI International (HCII) conference introduced the new option of "late-breaking work." This applies both for papers and posters and the corresponding volume(s) of the proceedings will be published just after the conference. Full papers will be included in the *HCII 2019 Late-Breaking Work Papers Proceedings* volume of the proceedings to be published in the Springer LNCS series, while poster extended abstracts will be included as short papers in the HCII 2019 *Late-Breaking Work Poster Extended Abstracts* volume to be published in the Springer CCIS series.

I would like to thank the program board chairs and the members of the program boards of all thematic areas and affiliated conferences for their contribution to the highest scientific quality and the overall success of the HCI International 2019 conference.

This conference would not have been possible without the continuous and unwavering support and advice of the founder, Conference General Chair Emeritus and Conference Scientific Advisor Prof. Gavriel Salvendy. For his outstanding efforts, I would like to express my appreciation to the communications chair and editor of *HCI International News,* Dr. Abbas Moallem.

July 2019   Constantine Stephanidis

HCI International 2019 Thematic Areas and Affiliated Conferences

Thematic areas:

- HCI 2019: Human-Computer Interaction
- HIMI 2019: Human Interface and the Management of Information

Affiliated conferences:

- EPCE 2019: 16th International Conference on Engineering Psychology and Cognitive Ergonomics
- UAHCI 2019: 13th International Conference on Universal Access in Human-Computer Interaction
- VAMR 2019: 11th International Conference on Virtual, Augmented and Mixed Reality
- CCD 2019: 11th International Conference on Cross-Cultural Design
- SCSM 2019: 11th International Conference on Social Computing and Social Media
- AC 2019: 13th International Conference on Augmented Cognition
- DHM 2019: 10th International Conference on Digital Human Modeling and Applications in Health, Safety, Ergonomics and Risk Management
- DUXU 2019: 8th International Conference on Design, User Experience, and Usability
- DAPI 2019: 7th International Conference on Distributed, Ambient and Pervasive Interactions
- HCIBGO 2019: 6th International Conference on HCI in Business, Government and Organizations
- LCT 2019: 6th International Conference on Learning and Collaboration Technologies
- ITAP 2019: 5th International Conference on Human Aspects of IT for the Aged Population
- HCI-CPT 2019: First International Conference on HCI for Cybersecurity, Privacy and Trust
- HCI-Games 2019: First International Conference on HCI in Games
- MobiTAS 2019: First International Conference on HCI in Mobility, Transport, and Automotive Systems
- AIS 2019: First International Conference on Adaptive Instructional Systems

Pre-conference Proceedings Volumes Full List

1. LNCS 11566, Human-Computer Interaction: Perspectives on Design (Part I), edited by Masaaki Kurosu
2. LNCS 11567, Human-Computer Interaction: Recognition and Interaction Technologies (Part II), edited by Masaaki Kurosu
3. LNCS 11568, Human-Computer Interaction: Design Practice in Contemporary Societies (Part III), edited by Masaaki Kurosu
4. LNCS 11569, Human Interface and the Management of Information: Visual Information and Knowledge Management (Part I), edited by Sakae Yamamoto and Hirohiko Mori
5. LNCS 11570, Human Interface and the Management of Information: Information in Intelligent Systems (Part II), edited by Sakae Yamamoto and Hirohiko Mori
6. LNAI 11571, Engineering Psychology and Cognitive Ergonomics, edited by Don Harris
7. LNCS 11572, Universal Access in Human-Computer Interaction: Theory, Methods and Tools (Part I), edited by Margherita Antona and Constantine Stephanidis
8. LNCS 11573, Universal Access in Human-Computer Interaction: Multimodality and Assistive Environments (Part II), edited by Margherita Antona and Constantine Stephanidis
9. LNCS 11574, Virtual, Augmented and Mixed Reality: Multimodal Interaction (Part I), edited by Jessie Y. C. Chen and Gino Fragomeni
10. LNCS 11575, Virtual, Augmented and Mixed Reality: Applications and Case Studies (Part II), edited by Jessie Y. C. Chen and Gino Fragomeni
11. LNCS 11576, Cross-Cultural Design: Methods, Tools and User Experience (Part I), edited by P. L. Patrick Rau
12. LNCS 11577, Cross-Cultural Design: Culture and Society (Part II), edited by P. L. Patrick Rau
13. LNCS 11578, Social Computing and Social Media: Design, Human Behavior and Analytics (Part I), edited by Gabriele Meiselwitz
14. LNCS 11579, Social Computing and Social Media: Communication and Social Communities (Part II), edited by Gabriele Meiselwitz
15. LNAI 11580, Augmented Cognition, edited by Dylan D. Schmorrow and Cali M. Fidopiastis
16. LNCS 11581, Digital Human Modeling and Applications in Health, Safety, Ergonomics and Risk Management: Human Body and Motion (Part I), edited by Vincent G. Duffy

17. LNCS 11582, Digital Human Modeling and Applications in Health, Safety, Ergonomics and Risk Management: Healthcare Applications (Part II), edited by Vincent G. Duffy
18. LNCS 11583, Design, User Experience, and Usability: Design Philosophy and Theory (Part I), edited by Aaron Marcus and Wentao Wang
19. LNCS 11584, Design, User Experience, and Usability: User Experience in Advanced Technological Environments (Part II), edited by Aaron Marcus and Wentao Wang
20. LNCS 11585, Design, User Experience, and Usability: Application Domains (Part III), edited by Aaron Marcus and Wentao Wang
21. LNCS 11586, Design, User Experience, and Usability: Practice and Case Studies (Part IV), edited by Aaron Marcus and Wentao Wang
22. LNCS 11587, Distributed, Ambient and Pervasive Interactions, edited by Norbert Streitz and Shin'ichi Konomi
23. LNCS 11588, HCI in Business, Government and Organizations: eCommerce and Consumer Behavior (Part I), edited by Fiona Fui-Hoon Nah and Keng Siau
24. LNCS 11589, HCI in Business, Government and Organizations: Information Systems and Analytics (Part II), edited by Fiona Fui-Hoon Nah and Keng Siau
25. LNCS 11590, Learning and Collaboration Technologies: Designing Learning Experiences (Part I), edited by Panayiotis Zaphiris and Andri Ioannou
26. LNCS 11591, Learning and Collaboration Technologies: Ubiquitous and Virtual Environments for Learning and Collaboration (Part II), edited by Panayiotis Zaphiris and Andri Ioannou
27. LNCS 11592, Human Aspects of IT for the Aged Population: Design for the Elderly and Technology Acceptance (Part I), edited by Jia Zhou and Gavriel Salvendy
28. LNCS 11593, Human Aspects of IT for the Aged Population: Social Media, Games and Assistive Environments (Part II), edited by Jia Zhou and Gavriel Salvendy
29. LNCS 11594, HCI for Cybersecurity, Privacy and Trust, edited by Abbas Moallem
30. LNCS 11595, HCI in Games, edited by Xiaowen Fang
31. LNCS 11596, HCI in Mobility, Transport, and Automotive Systems, edited by Heidi Krömker
32. LNCS 11597, Adaptive Instructional Systems, edited by Robert Sottilare and Jessica Schwarz
33. CCIS 1032, HCI International 2019 - Posters (Part I), edited by Constantine Stephanidis

34. CCIS 1033, HCI International 2019 - Posters (Part II), edited by Constantine Stephanidis
35. CCIS 1034, HCI International 2019 - Posters (Part III), edited by Constantine Stephanidis

http://2019.hci.international/proceedings

5th International Conference on Human Aspects of IT for the Aged Population (ITAP 2019)

Program Board Chair(s): **Jia Zhou,** *P.R. China* **and Gavriel Salvendy,** *USA*

- Julie A. Brown, USA
- Bessam Abdulrazak, Canada
- Ning An, P.R. China
- Marc-Eric Bobillier Chaumon, France
- Jessie Chin, USA
- Francesca Comunello, Italy
- Hua Dong, UK
- Hirokazu Kato, Japan
- Shehroz Khan, Canada
- Masatomo Kobayashi, Japan
- Chaiwoo Lee, USA
- Jiunn-Woei Lian, Taiwan
- Eugene Loos, The Netherlands
- Yan Luximon, Hong Kong, SAR China
- Andraž Petrovčič, Slovenia
- Marie Sjölinder, Sweden
- Hwee-Pink Tan, Singapore
- António Teixeira, Portugal
- Wang-Chin Tsai, Taiwan
- Ana Isabel Veloso, Portugal
- Terhi-Anna Wilska, Finland
- Fan Zhang, Canada
- Yuxiang Zhao, P.R. China
- Martina Ziefle, Germany

The full list with the Program Board Chairs and the members of the Program Boards of all thematic areas and affiliated conferences is available online at:

http://www.hci.international/board-members-2019.php

HCI International 2020

The 22nd International Conference on Human-Computer Interaction, HCI International 2020, will be held jointly with the affiliated conferences in Copenhagen, Denmark, at the Bella Center Copenhagen, July 19–24, 2020. It will cover a broad spectrum of themes related to HCI, including theoretical issues, methods, tools, processes, and case studies in HCI design, as well as novel interaction techniques, interfaces, and applications. The proceedings will be published by Springer. More information will be available on the conference website: http://2020.hci.international/.

General Chair
Prof. Constantine Stephanidis
University of Crete and ICS-FORTH
Heraklion, Crete, Greece
E-mail: general_chair@hcii2020.org

http://2020.hci.international/

Contents – Part I

Aging and the User Experience

Contents – Part II

Games and Exergames for the Elderly

Ambient Assisted Living

Design with and for the Elderly

Employing Interdisciplinary Approaches in Designing with Fragile Older Adults; Advancing ABLE for Arts-Based Rehabilitative Play and Complex Learning

Paula Gardner[1]([⊠]), Caitlin McArthur[2], Adekunle Akinyemi[3], Stephen Surlin[1], Rong Zheng[4], Alexandra Papaioannou[2], Yujiao Hao[4], and Jason Xu[4]

[1] Communication Studies and Multimedia, McMaster University, Hamilton, ON, Canada
{gardnerp, surlins}@mcmaster.ca
[2] Health Sciences, McMaster University, Hamilton, ON, Canada
{mcarthurc, papaioannou}@hhsc.ca
[3] WBooth School of Engineering Practice and Technology, McMaster University, Hamilton, ON, Canada
akinyema@mcmaster.ca
[4] Computing and Software, McMaster University, Hamilton, ON, Canada
{zheng, haoy21}@mcmaster.ca, Jason.xu1260@gmail.com

Abstract. ABLE is a gesture-based interactive platform that transforms physical therapy into game play and art creation – movement creates a virtual painting, digital music creation or engages users in game play with others. ABLE offers a menu of scalable physical therapy exercises designed to enhance strength, balance, and agility for variable populations with frailty and dementia presenting with low to severe impairments. It is designed for older adults with dementia and fragility, aiming to harness the incentivizing ability of art and gaming to encourage playful, physical interactions. The project aims to establish synergy between physical interaction and creative engagement to reduce boredom, agitation and social isolation while enhancing physiological, affective and cognitive health. This paper reviews how our interdisciplinary team of software engineers, medical scientists and artist/designers work to adapt design thinking in this research, to create participatory roles for older adults and caregivers that take into account the limits to participation posed by various barriers and their differing interests and investment in participation. We discuss how participant feedback can be integrated into the software interface, app design and user experience to meet the diverse and variable needs of users, for both independent use and supported use in residence. As well, to meet the diverse needs of this complex population, we draw on HCI gaming research as well as neuroplasticity research to formulate interaction experiences that seek to teach learning that can translate across the physical, cognitive and affective needs of this population. In seeking to enhance both pleasure and learning, we speculate that users will engage in sustained use of the platform over time and translate learnings into everyday life, to improve their opportunities to achieve health and wellness objectives. This design approach recognizes the need to incorporate diverse

© Springer Nature Switzerland AG 2019
J. Zhou and G. Salvendy (Eds.): HCII 2019, LNCS 11592, pp. 3–21, 2019.
https://doi.org/10.1007/978-3-030-22012-9_1

research findings into our approach. It also requires we adjust participatory approaches to accommodate less able-bodied participants, and adopt techniques for integrating participant data into all elements of design work, to ensure a coherent interdisciplinary team approach.

Keywords: Participatory design · User interaction design ·
Interdisciplinary practice · Geriatrics · Physical therapy ·
Human computer interaction · Prevention · Fragility · Dementia ·
Neuroplasticity · Complex learning theory

1 Introduction

ABLE is a gesture-based interactive platform that transforms physical therapy into game play or art creation – through exercise, older adults, for example, create virtual paintings or music feedback. ABLE targets older adults with dementia and fragility, employing art and gaming to encourage playful, physical interactions with family members, peers and care providers. This population experiences a range of barriers to participation including lack of motivation, lack of access and exercise support and cognitive deficits due to dementia. ABLE hypothesizes that such barriers can be overcome via technological solutions devised with careful consideration of the needs of diverse users. Yet, design thinking and user interaction methods often do not take into account barriers to participatory research experienced by frail adults.

Design thinking approaches can be limited in assuming an able population who can participate regularly and intensively in research; we augment critical and affective user interaction methods to accommodate participants' barriers to such participation. Reviewing various useful methods, we imagine a platform befitting a health and wellness future as imagined by older adults, taking into account their varying expectations for mobility, and art and exercise experiences across different settings. Specifically we plan to adjust the user interaction design to assess the specific physiological, affective and practical needs of diverse users in our design of: wearable biometric sensors for data capture; art-based biofeedback experiences; the tablet-based app employing a user-friendly interface; and optimizing the entire ABLE platform for use in diverse residential and home spaces.

As well, this paper recognizes the struggles of working in a university research setting, with researchers from distinct disciplines with divergent research methods. Our team of computer scientists, physiotherapists, geriatricians, and artist/designers, bring different approaches to framing problems, creating research experiment protocols and objectives, testing, and evaluating of findings and conclusions. Design thinking approaches often fail to nuance the processes by which teams cohere research methods to integrate user testing data comprehensively and iteratively, and consistently, while also producing results that satisfy the different expectations of our academic fields. At the same time, focus on limited literature resources can narrow the field of potential research findings. The paper engages multiple disciplinary approaches by referencing research from HCI as well as neuroscience and design methods to build a research method that can best engage participants and research to create a research apparatus that can meet the formidable goals of this interface to create both physical and aesthetic interaction experiences that meet a myriad of linked affective, physical and cognitive health and wellness goals.

2 Background: The Benefits of Physical Therapy and ABLE Design

Frailty is a clinical syndrome characterized by decreased reserves (energy, cognition, physical ability, health) resulting in vulnerability and adverse outcomes (e.g., falls, fractures, death) [1]. It's many consequences include: reduced functional abilities, social interaction, mood, and quality of life, and cognitive impairment [2]. Frailty is related with older age, however, not all older adults are frail [3]. Exercise, including strength and balance training, is one part of recommended multicomponent interventions to decrease the negative consequences associated with frailty [4]. As well, research suggests that negative psychological states may worsen physical and cognitive decline that occurs as people age, decreasing older adult's sense of well being and quality of life [5, 6].

Physical therapy provides targeted therapeutic exercise aimed at improving mobility for older adults who are frail to improve functional independence, such as the ability to risk out of a chair or maintain balance while walking. Physical therapy employs targeted therapeutic exercises to improve balance and strength which in turn improve mobility [5]. However, the provision of physical therapy is constrained by financial resources. Publicly funded physical therapy is often limited to three to five visits where the physical therapist will leave written instructions for the exercises. Older adults and their caregivers (e.g., personal support workers, spouses, family members, friends) are then expected to continue exercising independently. Without support, older adults may cease to complete their exercises as they do not know how to do them, are not motivated, or do not know how often to do them to gain maximum benefits. Older adults residing in institutional settings like nursing or retirement homes increasingly experience significant cognitive and physical impairments [7], further limiting their ability to participate in routine exercise.

The ABLE platform deploys physical therapy in playful engagements aiming to keep older adults independent while maximizing quality of life. ABLE design responds to research showing that physical activity and movement reduce functional decline. A systematic review showed that using interactive technology games (e.g., Wii Fit, XBox Kinect) significantly improved balance, mobility, and muscle strength and reduced fear of falling and reaction time compared to traditional exercise programs [8]. However, most interactive technology to date focuses on sports-based interactions, such as heading a soccer ball or slalom skiing [9], while ABLE focuses on an arts-based interaction. ABLE invites older adults with physical and cognitive impairments to engage in therapeutic exercise as meaningful art experience that produces a virtual painting or sound score. Recent research suggests a synergistic effect from combined movement, social engagement and art practice. For example, engaging clients in dance and movement has been shown to improve emotional wellbeing, depression or anxiety [10]. Art and dance stimulate memories in people with dementia, minimizing feelings of distress and disorientation, and improving health outcomes [11]. Making art creates more dramatic outcomes than simply viewing [12], enhancing agency and lessening social withdrawal and poor communication [13]. As well, creative and social engagements improve depressed mood and quality of life and decrease social isolation. ABLE confronts these problems by offering this arts-based exercise platform that facilitates socialization, including playful and enhanced interactions with family members and care providers, and reduces boredom and agitation which are chronic problems associated with dementia.

To date, we have tested our ABLE prototype in various settings including Baycrest Hospital, Toronto and more recently with older adults living at home and receiving physical therapy at St. Peter's hospital in Hamilton, ON. Thus far, users have been enthusiastic to engage with ABLE's playful digital feedback. In our next development phase it is crucial that our methods carefully include participants in the design process as we advance it toward greater usability, and appeal to diverse expectations of mobility and play for different users. The advancements we are working toward include: enhancing the networking interface to improve usability (i.e., advancing the consumer-friendly plug and play form); increasing social interactions (e.g. with care-givers and family members); and customizing the experiences to the distinct physical needs of older adults (e.g., those who can stand versus those using a wheelchair), and users' goals (e.g., purposeful exercise to prevent falls versus playful group physical activity). In these considerations, we recognize the value of affective and emotional user interaction design, as well as speculative design approaches to ensure that ABLE meets practical needs and desires of users but also ensures that the technology impacts social, affective, and ideological- are desired and useful to participants.

3   The ABLE Platform: Creating Opportunities for Mobility, Play, and Socialization for Fragile Older Adults

As described, the Able platform is being designed to encourage older adults with dementia or frailty to take part in physical therapy exercises or playful movement, alone or with a caregiver or family member, that reward participants with audio-visual feedback. The ABLE platform is highly responsive—it tracks lower extremity movements used in exercise, such as standing up or walking a line, producing visual effects and sounds that correspond to the movement. In response to standing up, the user may create a coinciding musical score or a painterly footpath appears on screen, tracking a subject walking a straight line. Multiple players (e.g. user and family members) may engage in collaborative movements in order to navigate a game, for example, a trek through a jungle (currently an early prototype). We are currently advancing design elements to produce artistic creations, gaming, movement, and interactions that suit user's diverse goals for mobility and wellness, diverse physiological and cognitive needs and diverse aesthetic and gaming preferences. Our goal is to make ABLE so pleasurable that participants are likely to use it sustainably over time to achieve their self-defined health results.

The ABLE app (also designed with physical therapy experts) provides a menu of scalable physical therapy exercises designed to enhance strength, balance, and agility for variable populations with frailty and dementia presenting with low to severe impairments. In developing the platform with a range of older adult participants (hospital patients, supported housing residents and home residents) we have sought to create a first prototype that is pleasurable and provides us a model for future development of the hardware and software interface, the app, and the user interaction experiences. The prototype currently under development invites grander, gross motor engagement (e.g. dancerly movements) alone or in pairs, that provide art-based feedback. The aim of this iterative development is to create successful experiences that will encourage sustained use of over time in a range of residential spaces for personals with varying physical abilities and health goals.

3.1   ABLE Technical Specs and the ABLE Experience

ABLE is a platform consisting of shoe-based wearable sensors and an app that is operated on a microsoft tablet. One wearable sensor module is worn on each foot, fastened to the users' shoe/footwear using a metal clip attached to the back of the module. The module is a 3D printed (PLA non-toxic filament) enclosure with an illuminated button on the top that indicates the battery is charged and can be pressed to reset the connection to the ABLE application. There are 2 USB ports on the back of the module: a USB 2.0 port used to connect the insole sensors, and a Micro USB port for charging the module's battery (rechargeable Lithium Ion, LiPo, 400 mAh battery). The modules can be charged when not in use. Inside the module there is an Arduino powered Bluetooth Low Energy (BLE) circuit board (Adafruit M0 BLE Feather Board, Open-Source software and hardware). This board processes the sensor data and BLE data that is sent to the ABLE application on the tablet.

Two pressure sensors (round force sensitive resistor, FSR) are installed near the toe and heel of each insole and attached to the wearable sensor module using a ribbon cable with a USB 2.0 plug attached to the end. The sensors are sandwiched between a layer of felt for comfort and the cotton canvas provides traction. They detect the weight of the user as they shift from their heels to toes on both feet. The weight of the user is translated into voltages by the sensors and read by the Arduino, resulting in 12-bit values between 0 and 1023.

The ABLE application is a web-based app that runs using a Node.JS server, based on Javascript, to connect the BLE wearable sensor modules and run the app; it can be viewed in a Chrome browser window by clicking on the app icon on the desktop of the tablet, which is a Microsoft Surface GO running Windows 10.

The ABLE app allows physiotherapists (or users) to program a series of exercises, using the "physio" menu. All components of the platform are designed to be user friendly including to users– both health professionals and fragile older adults– who may not have had experience in the past with such technology. The physiotherapist can enter and save prescribed exercises, based on their initial in person visit with the user. These exercises have accompanying instructions and video tutorials offering the exercise lists, and demonstrating proper form and movement for each exercises. Written instructions for the exercise are depicted below the video demonstration.

The app is operated on a tablet that can, if desired, be connected to a television or computer screen via an HDMI connection. This allows the user to see visual feedback on a larger screen, while maintaining the convenience of navigating the app on the tablets' touch screen. When connected to a screen with built-in speakers, users can adjust the app's volume on the screen, and the audio will automatically be sent to the screens' speakers.

To begin, the user presses the "Start" button on the app, which begins the interactive audio visual experience responding to movement. Movement data is captured by the wearable sensor; pressure on the users' feet are mapped in the X and Y axis planes of the art canvas. Visual art work is displayed on the screen, generated by the users' movements in real time. Exerting more pressure on the left or right foot, heels or toes and combinations of these cause the painting cursor to move around the screen translating the users' centre of mass into a virtual computer mouse or joystick, which moves the drawing cursor around the screen. In one iteration, as the cursor travels, it splatters the screens with coloured circles, creating a pattern responding to movement over time; this iteration produces a colorful plotted path mapping the users' movements. Additionally, movement creates an audio response. The algorithm codes the x-axis exercise space canvas into 5 distinct sections. Each section represents a chord in the C major music scale. When the user moves, causing the cursor to travel over at least one portion (left foot to right foot), a chord is triggered. In the conduct of the exercise, then, users colourful path creation is accompanied by a pleasing musical score produced in real time.

The user navigation is illustrated in the rendering below (Fig. 1).

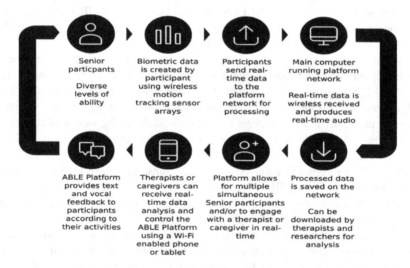

Fig. 1. User navigation of the ABLE system

Through this real-time feedback design that returns both audio and visual effects, ABLE seeks to create an embodied experience that seamlessly conjoins movement to the art feedback in real time. Via this embodied experience, the platform seeks to create generative experiences that, because it is both rewarding and surprising, motivates participants to exercise. These dual reward and surprise crafts user's desires to engage in the exercise because it feels like art creation or gaming in producing surprising and pleasing results. The research questions then must inquire into participant's discrete functional needs and interaction and aesthetic interests– those that are so pleasurable and satisfying that they may encourage sustained use over time.

To produce our early functional ABLE prototype, our team has to date focused on developing the hardware and software, and app in manners that are user friendly, easy to understand, and functional to use. We have concentrated first on developing the app, tutorials in manners that meet functional needs; this includes ensuring language and communication on the app and tutorial are clear and intuitive. As such, the above described hardware and software interfaces as non-transparent, and user's instructions for turning the system on, putting wearables in shoes and engaging with the experience are easy to understand and successfully complete– either with or without assistance.

Research Method Needs. To date we have focused on practical needs (making the platform responsive and legible) and creating an interaction that is highly responsive and legible– e.g. a path of plotted footsteps that is both recognizable (reminiscent of a stone path or footprints made in the mud) and pleasurable. As well, we created a musical score in the (non-offensive, pleasurable) key of C responding to our expectations of a baseline user.

As we move toward the creation of our next iteration, we recognize and confront a number of new challenges. First, we recognize the barriers to participation to date by fragile adults with dementia, and the need to consider alterations to our design method to more fully integrate participant's desires and needs into the design of the aesthetic experiences, the interaction design and the computer learning components. We challenge ourselves to take up design methods that enable us to install dynamics to encourage learning and incentive to enhance experiences of play and interaction among players.

Beyond practical issues of accessibility, our team, in our next iteration seeks to understand how art-based feedback and interaction can most effectively craft experiences that cause learning, interest and engagement particularly in fragile populations. We seek to unpack the role played by the combination of physical and art activity, and the role of learning therein in order to better strategize engagements that might achieve goals of sustained use by fragile adults, and in turn physiology, affective and socialization benefits.

In the remaining of the paper, then we create a new methodological blueprint for our research that draws from diverse design methods as well relevant research on gaming that seeks to bring physical, cognitive and/or affective enhancements to fragile populations.

4 Fragile Participants and Methodological Design Challenges

In our research to date we recognize barriers to the intense and regular participation of older adults in our research testing. This has led us to reconsider the problems (e.g. ableist assumptions) embedded in many user interaction design approaches and how we might adjust those to ensure the integration of older adults as fully as possible in all stages of our iterative design process.

We have tested early prototypes of ABLE with both healthy (highly mobile) and less mobile older adults in the fragility clinic at St Peter's hospital, where the latter receive physiotherapy. In order to enhance our understanding of clinical practices and expectations, we have provided demos of ABLE and interviewed physiotherapists working at this clinic, capturing their experience and understandings of the particularly physiological needs and incentive needs and barriers of older adults with fragility. We have also conducted observation during field visits to a long term residence's supported living and (higher level) Memory Care living spaces, which provide scaled support for mobility and cognitive care needs. This has included witnessing older adults with significant cognitive impairment due to dementia and limited mobility- in their leisure time at the residence, and taking an exercise class, all engaging from a seated position.

We are currently testing the ABLE in home settings to assess users' abilities to set up and use the ABLE platform independently, and their pleasure in this iteration providing a digital painting and musical feedback experience in response to physical therapy exercise and desires for changes to the interactions or different game/art experiences. Via this observation, field testing and extended interviews with older adults and physiotherapists, we have assessed a number of key needs and barriers of at home participants.

First, we note that older adults, across these spectrums of mobility and cognitive abilities, have widely different expectations for mobility, habits of and interest in exercise, interests in art and gaming platforms. At the same time, we have found widespread interest in engaging in this digital platform and pleasure in doing so– across these diverse participants. Geriatricians and physiotherapists express need for supportive technologies that can encourage sustained use of physiotherapy exercises for this population in order to provide physiological, cognitive and socialization benefits– all of which improve mood and combat depression. To this end, it has become clear that all elements of the ABLE platform need to be designed with the goal of making the platform: universally accessible, customizable, offering diverse and numerous art and gaming options, and the possibility to play alone or in pairs or groups, and finally, affordable, easy to use and appropriate to various residential and medical environments.

Because older adult users have diverse mobility expectations, physiological and cognitive needs and differing desires for art and game experiences, it is imperative we adopt user interaction techniques that capture these diverse needs, desires, interests and barriers of this diverse population. The methods must be respectful and foreground, at all times, the needs of participants. This requires as well that captured data is, relayed to the entire team, and integrated into all phases of project creation and design, as they occur in independent (sequential) design work, and in our iterative design work. This is a formidable challenge in two key ways: first, older adults are unable to participate in sustained research practice due to their health and mobility barriers. Secondly, a successful iterative process requires we adopt a method of data translation and integration that is effective for all team members' disciplinary expectations.

Our goal is to incorporate user-defined needs, goals and desires in each element of the project from software design, app design, and user experience to overall platform design that suits multiple spaces of use. It also requires assessing the aesthetic engagements, interactions and play that incentivizes different participants, including preferences for independent versus shared peer or intergenerational experiences. In so doing, we seek to design the system not only in terms of its components and efficacy but geared toward participant's preferences for play and art experiences hypothesizing that participants are most likely to be incentivized by self-defined goals and interests. This assumption is also grounded in literature suggesting that exercise or movement, art practice, and socialization, each enhance pleasure and mood in older adults, and we hypothesize are also likely to incentivize sustainable cycles of use and play. Research shows for example that positive psychological states are closely intertwined with enhanced physical and mental health outcomes [14]. There are, however, major barriers to incorporating older adults into a regular design research process who experience fatigue or gaps in knowledge while participating in testing, or due to health problems, are will be unable to at regular research meetings. In pursuit of these goals and mindful of these barriers, we discuss below, our emerging design thinking method, which seeks to: integrate participants fully in each element of design; draft a method enabling our designers, physiotherapists and engineers to integrate user data into their research methods and design interface.

5   Barriers in the Design Thinking Approach and Methodological Alternatives

While many teams attempt to employ user interaction design, doing so in everyday practice poses numerous challenges. In our early attempts to employ user interviews, field observation, platform tests, we recognize issues must be overcome in two areas: the practices by which we collect user inputs and data and the practices by which our team integrates these data systematically into to design elements and the overall platform. In reviewing our use of interaction design, we target the problematic normative and ableist assumptions of many design thinking practices that might reinforce the designer as expert and in so doing disempower participants, particularly those who are already vulnerable or fragile.

5.1   Challenges in Design Thinking Approaches

Our team came to this research project employing a standard 5 step design thinking approach that includes empathizing, defining, ideating, prototyping and testing in a iterative process. It became clear early on that this design model, which required constant feedback from "users" was ableist in assuming that "users" could in fact participate in regular sessions, held in regular intervals and could use their bodies in similar ways over each research session. In reality, older adults with fragility and cognitive impairments have a range of health factors (fatigue, hearing, vision and cognitive limitations) that complicate and limit testing and interviewing sessions. As well, regular attendances is not possible for a range of reasons including changing health and mobility status, cognitive challenges, and practice restraints including inconsistent personal care support and transportation enabling participants to attend sessions at testing spaces. A key challenge then is to create a method to integrate diverse participants into our process that accommodates their barriers to participation. It is useful to draw from critical ethnography approaches that foreground the creation of methods that level instances of power imbalances that can occur in health and medical relationships as well as in academic-participant research practices.

We also recognize that due to participant's changing health and mobility, it is important to return to defining the problem and to the empathizing stage, in order to capture changing participant needs and concerns. This requires adjusting the five step model which returns designers, in each iteration, to the definition rather than the empathy stage. A second challenge then is to shift our focus to observe and understand the everyday life activities in empathize more acutely.

The university environment poses another barrier to this 5-step method in that our differing work schedules and responsibilities create time and space barriers; these make it challenging for the entire team to assess the meaningfulness of captured data, discuss its integration into all phases of the project and then integrate it immediately following data capture sessions- before the next test phase is conducted. A third challenge, then, is to create a method by which we can iterate effectively and quickly, integrating collectively defined interpretations of user data into each element of design and the overall platform design.

The Promise of Critical Ethnographic, Speculative and Affective Design Approaches. Critical ethnography, speculative and affective design approaches outline methods and practices to meet the challenges posed by design thinking approaches for less mobile and able populations and challenges to deep interdisciplinary team collaboration.

To begin, it is useful to reference critical design approaches, which draw upon anthropological ethnography, that seek to overcome power disparities in all phases of participatory research. [16], cite four key stages in this effort; first, researchers should engage in participant observation to develop a 'thick' understanding and description' of user realities and needs and to begin to blur the observer/observed dynamic, followed by co-constructing an understanding of the problem, in this case, aging, and decreased mobility and its meaning. These two key understandings– the problem, and the meaning of the problem are crucial to moving toward solutions, but crucially, this participatory design process is never complete and must be revisited throughout the research. This objective to reassess with participants and in team process– empathy, problem naming and meaning in an ongoing manner poses a challenge to the standard design thinking and iterative design models.

Relatedly, as team members from diverse disciplines, we also must recognize how our disciplinary-centric expectations and assumptions can restrain interdisciplinary collaboration. To encourage self-reflexive evaluation of our disciplinary assumptions, [17], who suggests we fine tuning principles of design thinking by first, identifying the what (problem) and the how (techniques), to imagine the frame (approach) that will achieve desired values [4]. At a macro manner we need to adjust our lens from so-called 'healthism', the assumption that health and medical authorities define for users a definition of health that good citizens unproblematically adopt and self-apply. [17], Healthism is problematic in two ways– it instills authority for defining health in governmental and scientific "experts", reducing the agency of the individual, or the potential for communities to self-define self and set goals and methods by which health is achieved. As well, it puts in place an individualist ethos, making the self responsible to attain health goals determined by others.

To counter the ethos of healthism that can slip into institutional, medical and design research practices with older adults, we are inspired by critical ethnography, which calls for a method to continually assess the problem and its meaning with participants. This might be accomplished in part by employing the critical design ethos articulated in the speculative design approach of Dunn and Raby [10]. Indeed, in their provocative call to imagine the future one wishes for via speculation, the pair caution us *against* seeking advisement from 'experts'. As so-called experts ourselves, we take this critique as an opportunity to check our assumptions about health and the values and desires of older adults (whom Dunn and Raby would uncomfortably term 'non experts', decrying the expert/non-expert binary) by inviting participants instead to speculate on an imagined health future for fragile adults. The authors propose we speculate about imagined futures not only in the service of design, but to instigate design as a practice encouraging more social engagement with 'what if' questions, so that we might collectively speculate and build toward popularly imagined futures. By incorporating this approach, we would invite older adults to speculate on the near future of mobility they imagine for themselves, but also the longer range future for aging populations who will live through similar challenges of fragility and cognition. Speculative design incorporates critical ethnographic concerns by asking: what should that future look like, what is health in that future, who defines it, how do we achieve it, what tools or resources are there to assist?

Affective user interaction approaches also can assist designers to attend to the broader needs and interests of participants. For ABLE this means ensuring we focus not only on the limitations of frail adults with dementia, but also attending to their affective desires for technology of movement, and social engagement in addition to their functional needs (e.g. to remain mobile in order to maintain control of self-care and hygiene). In his design approach approach, [18], Norman proposes the ABC model, which targets the visceral, behavioral and reflective impact of technology on participants. The approach calls on designers to ensure the experience brings not only functional results but a rich and pleasurable experience to participants. Similarly useful is Jordan's 4 pleasures model [19], that calls on designers to address the physical, psychological, social and ideological interests of participants. Such an approach refocuses the design endeavour as one that provides practical support (e.g. offering exercise, socialisation) while recognizing those practices as fully loaded with psychological, social and ideological import that impact user's everyday life experiences.

For example, we have designed our shoe sensor to sit in the shoe itself; some participants may require assistance to place the sensor inside the shoe or may be unable to read even the large font we have used on the app housed on the tablet. Such participants may find such levels of assistance to be disempowering or even humiliating; inquiry into the level of independence users expect in ABLE then is crucial to ensuring the affective impact of the technology is positive. As another example, individuals from non-western cultures may find ABLE's musical choices to be foreign to them, and not interesting, and those with dementia may find the music to be disarming and unfamiliar. Inquiring into user's affective and personal desires for aesthetic feedback is crucial to ensuring interest in the platform. Inserting this level of empathy into the design process signals that we respect personal and cultural differences, and seek to avoid elevating certain styles of art, music or movement as normal or universally desirable.

Research has suggested that psychological well being and respect are crucial to older adults and can improve physiological wellness, as demonstrated by the "Happiness Project" [20]. This project queried whether working to enhance psychological well-being in community-residing older adults, could enhance mood and in turn, trigger physiological and wellness potentials. Participants were invited reflect on the meaning of happiness and compassion and connection, activating approaches to inciting it, including practices of foreignness, mindfulness and humour. Research results showed significant improvements in mood, and depression, increased mindfulness and decreased stress levels among participants. Participant comments suggest they were empowered by their newly honed abilities to define and manage their happiness for example, by locating it in small, everyday events. The study, while not yet replicated, suggests the great potential of building personal agency in the simple act of self-defining participant expectations for happiness, and perhaps wellness or mobility.

In seeking a method that can address struggles in working with populations with disabilities and in an interdisciplinary team, we are intrigued by the persistent collaboration methodology of [21]. This team creatively adapted a method to enable their research with children with autism who had limitations to engagement. Like our research process, the authors recognize participant engagement as a key challenge for developing suitable technology for this population ably managing the diverse and divergent perspectives of all the disciplines and stakeholders involved. The team foregrounds users as a participant in the design process, instantiating a method of 'persistent and consistent' integration of user testing data into four phases of research: observation, reflection, design and action.

This model demonstrates the importance of integrating user data, again which should be "thick" and negotiated among the team, into each phase of an iterative process. Importantly, [21], insist this methodological labour and documentation is significant not only to create research tools that serve users well, but to contribute to theory and practice advancements.

5.2   Toward Fragile-Friendly Participatory Design Methods

In reflecting upon our research achievements and struggles and our review of these methodological studies, we seek to inject the following additions into our critical design approach. Methodological advancements, often cited as obligations in research are, we contend, crucial elements that advance technological research help us to meet the needs as defined by participants and advance theory and practice learnings that move research forward. Toward this mission, in the following, we incorporate learnings from affective and speculative design into our methodological revision for the ABLE project.

First, in addition to enhancing our participant observation phase of research, a speculative design component should be incorporated into our dialogues with participants. As will be discussed, a new tool will be devised to ensure full team dialogue and integration of user participant feedback, and to include user response to iterative alterations.

Significant barriers, however, are posed by ablest elements of standard design thinking methods. Some fragile and vulnerable participants will not be able to give routine feedback on design updates. In response, we propose to expand our research testing participants to a broader and evolving participant group. We further empower participants by positioning them as designers, which means empowering them to co-define our understand of the current problem we are solving for, the meaning of the dilemmas, and to assess our integration of their feedback at each stage. We will add speculative questions to our ideation interviews, asking participants to discuss their personal (short term future) goals for mobility and wellness, and also, to imagine wellness for their children (or upcoming generations) as they age. In this speculative research, we will invite participants to engage in a range of activities as designers–including visualising and sketching spaces, technologies, resources and daily regimes that they find would enhance their physiological, cognitive and mood health. In response to the cognitive impairments limiting participant engagement, with their consent, we will interview medical caregivers and loved ones to obtain further information regarding needs or interests previously articulated by older adult participants. We will ask participants their opinion on those suggestions, and integrate recommended feedback.

We recognize time/space challenges as key problematics in university research environments that can prohibit the cohesive integration of all user data and feedback by team members in each phase of iterative design, despite best intentions. As solution, agreed upon team processes are required where all members discuss the meaning and value of participant feedback. This dialogue ideally takes place in face to face team meetings because they engage members in dialogue and processing. This method, common in critical ethnography, encourages dialogue such that the team collectively unpacks the "thick" discourse of participant observation and feedback, and evaluate its meaning and value as a team [16]. This should be the gold standard, but it not always possible due to conflicting researcher schedules. Problematically, project management and communication platforms such as Trello or Slack are not routinely used by all team members. To address these issues, we will seek to devise a discussion tool (e.g. a blog) that creates threads of discussion from face to face team dialogue, and solicits input from team members (not present at the meeting) on the blog. This blog will process or "digest" in order to not only summarize but to create collective understandings of the meaningfulness of data, and then plug those 'findings' iteratively into design plans, and chart changes employed to platform components and the entire platform. To ensure subteams have both digested and integrated data, teams will log these digestion and integration efforts into the team digestion blog in regular intervals. This research tool ensures we have, in our individual work and in our collective design of the platform, integrated data in a coherent and systematic manner. In turn, the tools will allow us to track progress, successes and hiccups, to contribute back to theory and practice findings.

6 Solutions from Emerging Research on Complex Gaming and Generative Design

The challenge to meet diverse needs and interests of participants with effective art and gaming experiences is limited when researchers use research drawn primarily from their own disciplines. Research is advanced when teams draw in diverse, relevant research that addresses research questions and challenges. In the case of ABLE, emerging research on digital movement gaming techniques (specifically) helps us to frame exercise and art interactions toward enhanced learning. As well, recent neuroscience research on brain plasticity helps us to craft the ABLE platform to trigger a range of cognitive and physical learning that might in turn create desired physiological, cognitive and affective benefits in our older adults population. We review that research briefly below.

Digital Movement Gaming Research. The potentials of digital gaming to meet varied needs of older adults is a small but growing area of research. Researchers [22] have found that older adults are keen to engage in gesture-based and digital movement games, and that these often enhance mood and emotional well being. The researchers note the relative deficit of research with older adults. Research has shown the natural movements in games, such as steering, locomotion and walking, cause help participants older adults to learn to match learned game movements to real world activities [23]. Of note, it has been shown to be helpful to provide older adults taking part in such movement interaction research, with guided tutorials and on-screen instruction to support learning in digital environments [24].

It appears that much research with older adults has focused on designing to physical constraints, rather than creating desirable challenges or employing interaction and aesthetics to encourage older adults' interest or risk taking. There is little research focusing on the combined role of art and exercise in digital movement experiments, nor the benefits of participatory research and how each of these might incentive older adults' sustained use and the potential of these to enhance mood, physical health, socialization.

Learning Through Generative Experiences. There is great potential in drawing upon learning findings from movement game design research in our investigations of potentials for older adults to incorporate physical therapy learning (gained from ABLE experiences) into their everyday activities.

Much learning research in gaming environments has focused on video gaming. It suggests that learning might be enhanced for a broad range of ages, via experiences with complex gaming interfaces. Drawing from theories of complexity thinking, researchers surmise that video gaming enables learning due to the complex and emergent process experienced; specifically, players negotiation of their role in the game while observing the experiences of others players, resulting in transformations that are both physical and behavioural. [25] Where rules-based systems cause players to learn patterns and actions by 'coupling' information to their actions, emergent systems are different. As complex environments, they structure rules or limit possibilities, but also offer engagement that is interactive, dynamic and flowing, providing the potential for infinite interaction possibilities [26]. Citing Davis and Sumara [27], the authors explain that learning arises in adaptive, self-organizing systems when the learner is transformed by the experience. Hopper et al., find that users become agents in such 'distinct semiotic systems', thriving on the instability and the unknown which heightens the coupling of perception and action, generating user interest and engagement.

To encourage this type of transformation and attendant agency, the authors urge game designers to create complex systems of learning that befit the interests of diverse players. To achieve this, design methods must ensure that game platforms include 3 features: allowing diverse (among players) to generate different experiences; providing 'liberating' restraints that create common vocabulary among players; and finally allowing play scenarios or contexts to produce local (or individual) understandings.

Attention to the links between learning and game engagement, then, is crucial to creating an ABLE experience that will offer gaming that is engaging but also transformative and thus works to build agency. In creating these opportunities for complex learning, we enhance the potential that the older adults will return to the gaming, and garner a range of benefits that will also transmit learnings into everyday life experiences.

Cognitive Enhancements and Gaming. Much can be learned from gaming research that investigates how learning occurs via cognitive processes. Video gaming has been shown to enhance attention control, cognitive flexibility and learning for different types of users, thought little has focused on older adults. Specifically, gaming can positively impact perception, attention, task switching, spatial cognition and mental rotation. Research suggests that complex training environments (e.g. video games) seem to foster brain plasticity, that teaches users to 'learn to learn' [28, 29]. While much research assume that real life experiences (e.g. aerobic activity, working memory and action video gaming) cause learning, other research claims that gaming instead more generally teaches us how to learn skills. Real life game play testing, in contrast to lab testing, engages users in complex visual scenes, producing enthralling feeling, and moving toward varying goals, at different timescales [29]. Engagement in such complex tasks results, researchers find, in learning that transfers to different tasks and environments with different goals. In other words, action game play doesn't train people in particular skills but rather increases the ability to extract patterns or regularities in the environment. The authors also evaluate neuroscience literature demonstrating that action video game play leads to enhanced cognitive resources, but also an 'intelligent allocation' of resources in response to the game's goals.

These finds suggest great promise in research, such as with the ABLE platform, to investigate how learning occurs in movement-based (digital/video) gaming. Specifically, ABLE can investigate how embodied (wearable) action-based gaming might take different forms, including competitive or cooperative game play or art creation. As well, in focusing on this older adult population we have the opportunity to investigate how players might learn to learn for example by extracting and transferring distinct needs (e.g. spatial memory, and cognitive memory processing, physical benefits such as balance and agility) into everyday life practices.

Next research steps for ABLE, then, include designing a testing platform of art and movement exercises to test to determine if complex game training might impacts the varying physical and cognitive abilities of older adults with frailty and dementia and to set up testing scenarios that gauge the transfer to skills to other learning in everyday life.

7 Incorporating Diverse Research to Improve Physical and Cognitive Learning in Older Adults with Fragility and Dementia

The point of this review has been to probe and employ a variety of research to advance our design research methods to best suit our research population and objectives, and fully integrate these methods into our team based practices. In the first round of prototyping, teams often seek to achieve a functioning tool. In a true and rich iterative approach, we suggest that with this experience behind them, teams are positioned to then reflect upon their initial research questions, successes, mishaps, and barriers, to reframe their method in responses to arising demands and gaps, and to integrate solutions from relevant research obtained from multiple disciplines.

The problems our team seeks to address in the next phase include engaging in critical participatory design with a population deep diversity (differing abilities, mobilities and ages, as well as divergent cultural backgrounds and health goals) creating diverse needs. Our methods must respect these needs and find techniques to capture these needs, reflecting users differences, while also respecting their inability to engage in long term regular participatory process. Finally we must return, cyclically, to inquire into the limitations, goals and meaningfulness of the research for users, which evolve over time. The platform goals to incite interest must be complicated to consider the types of learning that can be accomplished (e.g. how learning to learn might be facilitated) and can be transferred to everyday life. We must expand our design methods to consider the value not only of creating recognizable and intuitive experiences, but also those that challenge users with changing scenarios and risk and a potential for rich experiences and complex learning. Models must be created to test these outcomes and the potential synergistic contributions of art plus exercise to achieve sustained user engagement and positive impacts on physiology, cognition and affect.

For ABLE this mean altering the standard design thinking method, incorporating speculative and affective design components that centre older adults with fragility and dementia as designers. This also requires incorporating their visions of an imagined future for themselves and the next generation, as well as foregrounding the distinctive mobility, cognitive and affective needs outlined by older adults, with attention to the meaningfulness of these objectives in their everyday lives. This approach requires we conduct this research with care given to reflecting participants' diverse ideological views and affective needs. We are also cognizant that we must integrate this participant input with consistency across our iterative process and because users needs change.

Through our diverse interdisciplinary research, it has become apparent that the question of creating engaging gaming that produces physical and affective benefits are questions well informed by research on movement learning and brain plasticity. This area of research is currently sparse requires more researchers to contribute. Advanced research will test how embodied learning occurs through the distinct practices of gaming that require both cognitive and physical engagement and produce learning that translates into everyday life activities that produce pleasure and fitness. Scenarios will need to vary tasks, and test learning scenarios, and how these build personal interest and agency.

There are great potentials to employ artificial intelligence in a various ways. First, we are currently capturing data from diverse bodies to train the ABLE AI system to respond to the different abilities, needs and baseline movements of differently aging bodies. In the next iterative phase, AI will be employed to capture learning data, to understand under what conditions and in what scenarios (physical practice alone or with art feedback) the participants learned. This captured data can then be used to level up exercise and interaction challenges for users to ensure they are engaging in complex challenging scenarios that are more likely to increase engagement and interest. These data can then be incorporated into post testing design models, to query if users have translated physical and cognitive learning into everyday life mobility practices such as dressing, walking, and non-digital exercise.

Cognitive ability data captured via AI and via field testing and observation can be combined in the next iteration of game design for participants with dementia; these game scenarios can aim to help users to maintain ability levels across time, and test if cognitive successes in the gaming scenarios translate to everyday life.

In our approach, we have, to date worked in a cooperative and user-focused rather than participatory manner to assess how stakeholders define mobility goals, the barriers posed by diverse environments, and exercise and interaction techniques that could be effective for subjects in diverse residential and hospital spaces. Armed with experience and approaches learned in this research review, our enhanced participatory model integrates participant goals and desires more meaningfully and regularly. Planned tools and methods for capturing and integrating data seek to create an enhanced iterative process. A renewed focus on 'learning to learn' and offering challenges in play to heighten interest will be employed as we test potentials in wearable action-based gaming attempting to couple perception and action in players.

Research testing will seek to understand how these new gaming and art scenarios incentive older adults, whether learning translates into everyday life, and whether any or both of these results produces sustained use of the platforms. In later research stages, we will be prepared to test the potential synergistic impact of art and exercise, and how these produce cognitive, physical and affective benefits for older adults with dementia and fragility.

We have conducted this review of our own methods to highlight the complex problems posed to researchers seeking to understand how complex interactions (such as art and exercise) can be employed to stimulate synergistic physical, cognitive and affective benefits. Researchers sometimes restrain their research questions and programs to practices that are more narrow, have fewer variables and are easier to test. This is not practical nor possible when dealing with the complex frailty and cognition problems experienced by these older adults, who experience complexly linked physical, cognitive and affective barriers. Research in the areas of brain plasticity and action gaming research, usefully examines complexity in digital learning and gaming as complex processes; such scholarship outfits researchers with tools and methodological findings enabling us to iterate our own methods. It is essential that that we continue to ideate, test and discuss our research methods and struggles, to encourage more research tackling complex problems (such as fragility and dementia in older adults) in order to innovate understandings and solutions to such growing social health dilemmas.

References

1. Rockwood, K., et al.: A global clinical measure of fitness and frailty in elderly people. CMAJ **173**, 489–495 (2005). https://doi.org/10.1503/cmaj.050051
2. Rockwood, K., Mitnitski, A.: Frailty defined by deficit accumulation and geriatric medicine defined by frailty. Clin. Geriatr. Med. **27**, 17–26 (2011). https://doi.org/10.1016/j.cger.2010.08.008
3. Mitnitski, A.B., Graham, J.E., Mogilner, A.J., Rockwood, K.: Frailty, fitness and late-life mortality in relation to chronological and biological age. BMC Geriatr. **2**, 1 (2002)
4. de Labra, C., Guimaraes-Pinheiro, C., Maseda, A., Lorenzo, T., Millán-Calenti, J.C.: Effects of physical exercise interventions in frail older adults: a systematic review of randomized controlled trials. BMC Geriatr. **15**(1), 154 (2015)
5. Corcoran, J., Brown, E., Davis, M., Pineda, M., Kadolph, J., Bell, H.: Depression in older adults: a meta-synthesis. J. Gerontol. Soc. Work **56**(6), 509–534 (2013). https://doi.org/10.1080/01634372.2013.811144
6. Shtompel, N., Whiteman, K., Ruggiano, N.: Negative feelings and help seeking among older adults with chronic conditions. J. Gerontol. Soc. Work **57**(8), 810–824 (2014). https://doi.org/10.1080/01634372.2014.898008
7. Poss, J., Sinn, C.-L., Grinchenko, G., Blums, J., Peirce, T., Hirdes, J.: Location, location, location: characteristics and services of long-stay home care recipients in retirement homes compared to others in private homes and long-term care homes. Healthc. Policy | Polit. Santé **12**(3), 80–93 (2017). https://doi.org/10.12927/hcpol.2017.25025
8. Neri, S.G., Cardoso, J.R., Cruz, L., et al.: Do virtual reality games improve mobility skills and balance measurements in community-dwelling older adults? Systematic review and meta-analysis. Clin. Rehabil. **31**(10), 1292–1304 (2017)
9. Warburton, D., Bredin, S., Horita, L., et al.: The health benefits of interactive video game exercise. Appl. Physiol. Nutr. Metab. **32**(4), 655–663 (2007). https://doi.org/10.1139/H07-038
10. Dunn, A., Raby, F.: Speculative Everything: Design, Fiction and Social Dreaming. MIT Press, Boston (2013)
11. Lawton, P.M., Van Haitsma, K., Klapper, J., Kleban, M.H., Katz, I.R., Corn, J.: A stimulation-retreat special care unit for elders with dementing illnesses. Int. Psychogeriatr. **10**(4), 379–395 (1998)
12. Stewart, E.G.: Art therapy and neuroscience blend: working with patients who have dementia. Art Ther.: J. Am. Art Ther. Assoc. **21**(3), 148–155 (2004)
13. Bar-Sela, G., Atid, L., Danos, S., Gabay, N., Epelbaum, R.: Art therapy improved depression and influenced fatigue levels in cancer patients on chemotherapy. Psycho-Oncology **16**(11), 980–984 (2007)
14. Chida, Y., Steptoe, A.: Positive psychological well-being and mortality: a quantitative review of prospective observational studies. Psychosom. Med. **70**(7), 741–756 (2008). https://doi.org/10.1097/PSY.0b013e31818105ba

15. Dam, R., Siang, T.: 5 Stages in the Design Thinking Process. The Interaction Design Foundation   (n.d.).   https://www.interaction-design.org/literature/article/5-stages-in-the-design-thinking-process

16. Barab, S.A., Thomas, M.K., Dodge, T., Squire, K., Newell, M.: Critical design ethnography: designing for change. Source: Anthropol. Educ. Q. **35**(2), 254–268 (2004). Published by: Wiley on behalf of the American Anthropological Association Stable. http://www.jstor.org/stable/3651405

17. Dorst, K.: The nature of design thinking. Interpreting design thinking. In: Dorst, K., Stewart, S., Staudinger, I., Paton, B., Dong, A. (eds.) Proceedings of the 8th Design Thinking Research Symposium (DTRS8), 19–20 October 2010, Sydney, pp. 131–144 (2010). https://www.researchgate.net/publication/299456548_Design_Thinking_An_overview

18. Norman, D.A.: Emotional Design. Basic Books, New York (2005). ISBN 0-465-05136-7

19. Jordan, P.: Designing Pleasurable Products: An Intro to the New Human Factors. Taylor & Francis, London (2010). ISBN 978-0415298872

20. Turner, J., Greenawalt, K., Goodwin, S., Rathie, E., Orsega-Smith, E.: The development and implementation of the Art of Happiness intervention for community-dwelling older adults. Educ. Gerontol. **43**(12), 630–640 (2017). https://doi.org/10.1080/03601277.2017.1380894

21. Porayska-Pomsta, K., et al.: Developing technology for autism: an interdisciplinary approach. Pers. Ubiquit. Comput. **16**, 117–127 (2012). https://doi.org/10.1007/s00779-011-0384-2

22. Gerling, K.M., Livingston, I.J., Nacke, L.E., Mandryk, R.L.: Full-body motion-based game interaction for older adults. In: CHI 2012, 5–10 May 2012, Austin, Texas, USA (2012)

23. Payne, J., et al.: Gameplay issues in the design of spatial 3D gestures for video games. In: Proceedings of CHI 2006, pp. 1217–1222. ACM (2006)

24. Gerling, K.M., Schild, J., Masuch, M.: Exergame design for elderly users: the case study of silver balance. In: Proceedings of ACE 2010, pp. 66–69. ACM (2010)

25. Sanford, K., Hopper, T.: Videogames and complexity theory: learning through game play. Loading… **3**(4) (2009)

26. Hopper, T., Sanford, K., Clarke, A.: Game-as-teacher and game-play: complex learning in TGfU and Videogames. In: Hopper, T., Butler, J., Storey, B. (eds.) TGfU…Simply Good Pedagogy: Understanding a Complex Challenge, p. 246. Physical Health Education, Ottawa (2009)

27. Davis, B., Sumara, D.: Complexity and Education: Inquiries into Learning, Teaching and Research. Lawrence Erlbaum, London (2006)

28. Cardosa-Leite, P., Bavelier, D.: Video game play, attention, and learning: how to shape the development of attention and influence learning? Curr. Opin. Neurol. **27**, 185–191 (2014). https://doi.org/10.1097/wco.0000000000000077

29. Bavelier, E., Green, C.S., Pouget, A., Schrater, P.: Brain plasticity through the life span: learning to learn and action video games. Ann. Rev. Neurosci. **35**, 391–416 (2012). https://doi.org/10.1146/annurev-neuro-060909-1528322012.35:391-416

Study on the Persuasive Design Method of Health Education for the Elderly Adults

Yongyan Guo$^{(\boxtimes)}$ and Wei Ding$^{(\boxtimes)}$

School of Art Design and Media,
East China University of Science and Technology, Shanghai, China
g_gale@163.com, dw.6789@163.com

Abstract. In the aging society, it will play an effective role in preventing chronic diseases that the elderly adults improve the health knowledge and form a healthy lifestyle with health education. At present, people did not pay enough attention to the health education, because of some reasons. This paper explores the persuasive design method of health education in accordance with the PSD model and health behavior theory. Through literature review, questionnaire survey and focus group interviews, user's motivation and ability are studied and the corresponding persuasive design method and design principles are put forward.

Keywords: Aging health education · Persuasive design method ·
Healthy behavior theory

1 Introduction

1.1 Current Situation and Demand of Health Education for Aging

Health education is defined by the World Health Organization as "Consciously constructed opportunities for learning involving some form of communication designed to improve health literacy, including improving knowledge, and developing life skills, which are conducive to individual and community health.", "fostering the motivation, skills and confidence (self-efficacy) necessary to take action to improve users' health……" [1].

This paper summarizes the status quo of community health education on elderly adults through literature review and user survey: (1) Lack of health education professionals. (2) The working platform of health education is not perfect. (3) The existing records and data of health education activities in the community are incomplete. (4) The form of community health education is out of date. (5) The content of community health education is simple and outdated, lacking uniform health education materials and systematic and individualized content.

Yang et al. [2] proposed that the appropriate difficulty of health education contents should be matched for users. The evaluation dimension of the level of textbooks should be difficulty, readability, content appropriateness and culture. Wang and Li [3] believe that the diversified demand of health education for empty nesters in community is needed. Modern technology should be combined to the health education with rich

© Springer Nature Switzerland AG 2019
J. Zhou and G. Salvendy (Eds.): HCII 2019, LNCS 11592, pp. 22–33, 2019.
https://doi.org/10.1007/978-3-030-22012-9_2

knowledge, strong practicability and easy acceptance traits. Shan et al. [4] and Jiang et al. proved that exposure to health knowledge in We-chat can improve control level of blood pressure and ability of self-management in patients with hypertension [5].

The above research shows that the elderly group lacks effective health education services. The focus of this paper is to study the design strategy of health education for the elderly according to their learning motivation and learning ability, combined with the interactive characteristics of mobile phones, and to establish a set of persuasive design method of health education for the aging society through user research.

1.2 Persuasion Design Model and Health Education Theory

Health education persuasive design method combines persuasive design model, healthy behavior theory, and cognitive theory. There are two persuasion models that have the greatest impact in design. One is the Fogg Behavior Model (FBM) [6] proposed by Professor BJ Fogg, in which the user's behavior is mainly affected by motivation and ability, and the trigger of design. The other is the persuasion design model of interactive system proposed by Oinas-Kukkonen and Harjumaa [7]. Interactive design persuasion system model is divided into four parts: task support, dialogue support, system reliability support and social support according to different persuasive strategies.

American scholar Prochaska holds that different motivations and needs are corresponded to people's behavior at different stages. People's behavioral patterns can be changed gradually due to different behavioral stimulus factors [8]. In carrying out these activities, we should pay attention to long-term effectiveness, systematisms and continuity of the health education, guiding people to change their lifestyle actively. There are many health behavior theories, such as rational model, health belief model, extended parallel process model, trans-theoretical model of change, planned behavior theory, activation health education model, communication theory, innovation diffusion theory, etc. In different designs, these theoretical methods should be selected reasonably.

Cognitive Behavior Theory is a kind of psychological and behavioral therapy which aims at eliminating negative emotions and unhealthy behaviors by means of reconstructing cognition, counselling psychology, solving problems and correcting behavior [9]. Daud et al. (2013) proposed a preliminary model of persuasion design based on Web Learning environment [10]. The persuasive design method is based on the above theories and models.

Motivation Study of Health Education Objects. Yang compared the traditional propaganda health education mode with health belief education mode, and concluded that health belief mode can significantly improve the compliance behavior of patients with coronary heart disease in community [11]. The object of health education should include users themselves and their relatives and friends [12]. Scholar Guilera et al. [13] concluded that the effect of comprehensive intervention group was better than that of traditional propaganda group. Laslett et al. [14] think that the long-term improvement of health behavior needs more efforts and self-control of users. Therefore, health education needs to be carried out regularly in order to strengthen users' health literacy, and to promote users' healthy knowledge and memory for a long time.

Study on the Ability of Health Education Objects. Xu et al. [15] believed that the factors affecting health education for the elderly included changes in sensory organs, memory, reaction speed, physical strength and personality. Mechanical memory and unfamiliar content memory should be avoided in the health education activities. Health education should respect the autonomous willingness of the elderly, and gradually expand from their known areas to the unknown areas [16]. According to the old people's past experience and knowledge, a learning plan should be established to stimulate their interest and create a suitable learning environment. Health content should meet the individual's different needs in different stages of life. Establishing task- or problem-oriented learning methods can help elderly users apply what they have learned and improve their motivation for learning (Table 1).

Table 1. Ability of elderly to receive health education - design strategies

Ability	Characteristics	Principles of health education product design
Sensory	Psychological ability	As to users' anxiety, fear, social isolation, low self-confidence, low activity ability, change of perception, impaired language communication ability and impaired self-protection ability, elderly users' interest and motivation should be stimulated
	Hearing loss	In health education, the speaking speed should be slower than usual and the tone be lower. At the same time, facial expressions, gestures, body language and audio-visual textbooks should be used to assist the explanation
	Vision change	Large font and the color with high contrast should be used. Blue, green and purple should be Avoid in design. Because of changes in crystals, it is not easy for the elderly to distinguish these shorter wavelength colors. In addition, keeping the environment quiet and full of light is very important
Memory	Information processing	The health content should be organized and processed for easy to remember. The situational logic strategy should be used to enhance memory with the fully developed of the user's experience
	Memory strategy	In order to grasp the learning content easily, relevant memory methods should be adopted, such as association, categorization and repetition, location method and image card method
	Emotional preservation	According to health belief model, the elderly should be helped to pay attention to self-care, maintain emotional stability, happy mood and confidence to delay memory decline

(*continued*)

Table 1. (*continued*)

Ability	Characteristics	Principles of health education product design
Reaction rate	Slow down of the reaction rate	Educators should speak slowly so that the elderly have enough time to absorb what they have learned
	Change of thinking process	The time of health education should not exceed half an hour each time. Don't give too much information at a time. Health contents should be divided into multiple introductions, and the information should be simplified
	Language communication barriers	Use body language to communicate, and mostly use the click-and-choose
	Solidification of thinking mode	Let the elderly adults recall past life experiences and link those with new knowledge and skills
Physical strength	Spasm and soreness of Muscle, stiffness of joint	Old people often need to spend more time to complete every movement. It is need to prevent the occurrence of musculoskeletal diseases or minimize their impact on the elderly
	Total sleep time is Reduced	The rest time can be appropriately provided to maintain the appropriate physical strength of the elderly people
Character	Caution, conservatism, decreased in interest of life	Safety, Familiarity, Ease of use, Entertainment, To ensure that the operation of health education is simple and easy to use, and has a pleasant emotional experience [17]

Study on the Content of Health Education. Zhao summarized the content structure of health education needed by the elderly as follows: strengthening health education and behavioral intervention for chronic diseases, developing health education to establish a good lifestyle, take care of psychological nursing, popularizing knowledge of health care and disease prevention, and introducing the dietary structure [18]. The content of health education mainly involves establishing healthy lifestyle, maintaining stable and optimistic dietary structure [19]. The single factor analysis study of Jiang showed that smoking, drinking, inadequate intake of protein food, inadequate intake of vegetables and fruits, heavy diet, lack of physical exercise and excessive intake of seafood were the causes of chronic diseases [20]. The survey of Zhang et al. [21] showed that the subjective needs of the elderly for health education were mainly health diet, prevention and treatment of chronic diseases, medication, psychological health care and first aid. Some knowledge, such as sports, fall prevention, sleep and so on, are important but with inadequate attention. Wang [22] formed five parts of community health education system network by analyzing user needs: health information management module, doctor consultation and answering module, hospital doctor management module, personal health service module and health knowledge testing module (Table 2).

Table 2. System architecture of health education content

Major Categories	Subcategories	Contents
(1) Medical knowledge	Knowledge of Chronic Diseases	Knowledge modularization, knowledge systematization, knowledge customization, learning effect testing, etc.
	Medication knowledge	Main and side effects of drugs, methods of taking drugs, increase or decrease of dosage of drugs, first aid knowledge, etc.
	Psychological health knowledge	Focus on Alzheimer's disease and depression knowledge, counseling of mental health in the elderly
	Healthy Lifestyle	Diet: Dietary structure, focusing on intake of oil, salt, vegetables, fruits, alcohol; Sports: Recommend types of sports, focusing on speed and time; Knowledge of sleep
(2) Elderly health records	personal data	General sociological data of patients
	Record of Medical Drugs	Records of physical examination, medical treatment and use of drugs in past years
	Intervention follow-up records	Diet and exercise intervention, follow-up records, etc.
(3) Stakeholders	Family members	Actively encourage, urge and cooperate with patients
	Community workers and Volunteers	Enhance communication with old people and their families by means of online interaction, and understand the implementation effect of users' good living behavior
	Community hospital	Medical consultation and lecture guidance by medical experts

Persuasive Design Strategies of Health Education

Zhuang and Lv put forward various innovative ways of health education, such as setting up stations of community health life guidance and health counseling service, issuing health guide of health and disease prevention, conducting health education lectures and knowledge competitions, and setting up health training classes in senior activity centers [23]. Hua and Chen put forward health education methods, including establishing follow-up card, conducting regular group discussions and regular testing [24]. The suggestion of health education of Wen [25] is customize the training plan according to the education level, age and related health knowledge of elderly patients, and form a multi-batch, regular and diversified health education mode. Hu [26] studied the health education tool of picture-reading dialogue, that is, to let users participate in the interactive learning experience of pictures and text, and to discuss the topics and pictures that users are most interested in.

2 The Persuasive Design Method of Health Education for the Aged

According to Fogg model, on the basis of researching users' motivation and ability, following design strategies are built: first, to stimulate users' motivation through interesting interaction, social interaction, incentive system and other design strategies; second, to reduce users' difficulty in using product according to usability design strategy; third, to maintain users' behavior of accepting health education through timely reminder strategies.

The persuasive design method of health education for elderly adults can be summarized as follows: (1) user motivation and ability survey; (2) choice of health behavior theory; (3) decomposition of health education content as self-health status inquiry, health knowledge popularization and cultivation of healthy lifestyle; (4) consultation of health experts on system architecture; (5) learning tools design of easy-to-use: e.g. video learning method, game learning, dialogue graphics, etc. (6) Compare different persuasive design strategies; (7) Establish design prototype.

3 Research Process

3.1 Questionnaire Survey

(1) *Questionnaire star* was used to survey the health education status of the elderly adults. A total of 300 questionnaires were distributed and 287 valid questionnaires were collected, with a recovery rate of 95.7%. (2) Questionnaire analysis. The content of the questionnaire was formulated according to Fogg's persuasive model. The motivation, ability, interest and media of users' acceptance of health education were analyzed. (3) The focus group method and literature analysis method were combined to analyze the existing health education methods and media interaction characteristics, and the advantages and disadvantages of the existing health education are obtained through user interviews. (4) Combining the research results and the content of literature analysis, the expected structure and design strategy of health education system are confirmed, which will provide guidance for the interactive system design of health education that meets the needs of the elderly in the future.

3.2 Survey Result

Description	Classification	Frequency	Percentage
Gender	Male	137	47.74%
	Female	150	52.26%
Age	51–60	60	20.91%
	61–70	197	68.64%
	71 and above	10	10.45%
Education	Junior high school and below	135	47.04%

(*continued*)

(continued)

Description	Classification	Frequency	Percentage
	Senior High School	116	34.49%
	Undergraduate	25	8.71%
	Master and above	11	3.83%
Occupation	Retire	68	23.69%
	Management	22	7.67%
	Ordinary staff	125	43.55%
	Workers/Farmers	72	25.09%

According to the data of health survey, 9.76% of users said they never did exercise, 28.22% said they did regular and quantitative exercise every week, and 62.02% said they only did sport occasionally. The situation of health check-up is that 8.36% of the respondents never do health check-up, 57.14% of the respondents do health check-up when they feel uncomfortable, and 34.49% of the respondents have at least one physical check-up every year. When answer the question "If you were ill, what would you do?", 11.85% chose to "do nothing and wait for to be good by itself", 43.9% chose to "buy medicine in pharmacy", and 44.25% chose to "see a doctor in time in a hospital or other medical institution". In response to the attitude of "participating in health education activities to improve their health status", 36.59% of the people chose to be very willing, 45.64% chose to be willing, 12.89% chose to be indifferent, and 4.88% chose not to be willing, indicating that most people had the motivation to accept health education.

According to the proportion of users' choices, the order of users' concern about the content of health education is: doctor consultation, disease treatment, daily health care, chronic disease prevention, personal health records, etc. (Fig. 1).

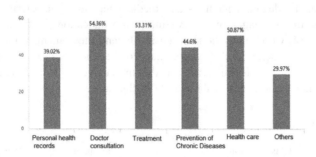

Fig. 1. Survey of health education concerns

Surveys on "common chronic diseases that need to be prevented in the elderly" showed that hypertension and cardiovascular and cerebrovascular diseases account the highest proportion (Fig. 2).

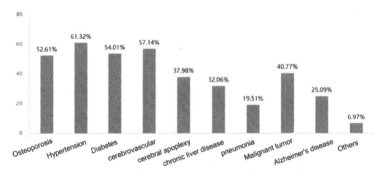

Fig. 2. Common chronic diseases in the elderly

According to the survey of "acceptance mode of health education", many elderly people have a higher acceptability of the health education on network and mobile phone. 47.74% of the respondents chose the affirmative answer to the question whether they had ever used the medical health APP in mobile phones. To sum up, the advantages of various media should be fully used for reference in the design, so as to conform to the usage habits of the elderly (Fig. 3).

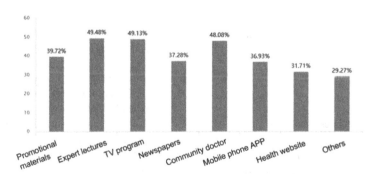

Fig. 3. Expected methods of health education

According to the survey on the purpose of receiving health education, self-health management is the strongest motivation, followed by improvement of existing diseases, prevention and health care, self-learning to treat and so on. The ranking results should be reflected in the system design of health education for the elderly (Fig. 4).

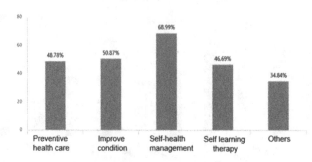

Fig. 4. Purpose of health education learning

3.3 Focus Group Interview

Fifteen elderly people aged 60 to 75 (8 females and 7 males) were invited to participate in the focus group discussion. Users were asked to compare the advantages and disadvantages of the existing community health education with the online health education to inspire design principles of health education on the mobile phone (Tables 3 and 4).

Table 3. Problems and needs of community health education

Type	Status	Design strategy
Memory effect	It is difficult to recall without deep memory	Provide long-term, high-frequency and systematic health education to Deep memory; reduce mistake of drugs and missed medication; limit the length of content, and avoid redundant information
Publicity	Less publicity	Long-term, repeatedly, coherent
Propaganda form	Banners, leaflets and brochures, propaganda boards, promotional films, Experts provide lectures and advisory services etc.	Content is refined, propaganda form is life-like and easy to remember, content is updated in time and keep up with the times
Content	Content is scattered and unsystematic	Content should be relevance, persistence and coherence
Easy to apply	Difficult to remember and apply in life	Different health education information is customized for different needs of elderly adults, and mobile health memorandums are provided to be consulted at any time

Table 4. Problems and needs of the online health education

Type	Status	Design strategy
Health Education Website	Self-regulated learning is supported, but the content of the interface column is too much, and the information is not organized effectively. The elderly has less chance to log in the website with the computer	Clear display to provide a better learning environment for the elderly. To overcome the disadvantage of inconvenience use
Application of Health Education Mobile Phone	*Chunyu Doctors APP*: Focus on online fee-based consultation with many advertisements *Renwei MOOC*: Video courseware is abundant for professional doctors, and the content is not easy to understand for ordinary people *WeChat Subscription of health*: content with daily push, rich and concentrated content, lack of user interaction and action promotion strategy. The authority and credibility of information cannot be guaranteed	Easy to use; Simplified content and easy to browse; Daily push; Easy to retrieve and apply; Convenient to record data; Have self-detection; Study at any time by Keeping it with you; Support multimedia format; Rich content; Select the content of health education according to user's need…

Through focus group interviews and Research on existing health education websites and APPs, the persuasive design principles of health education for elderly adults are as follows:

(1) The principle of demand-driven design: health education for the users should adapt to the cognitive characteristics of the elderly, and pay attention to the knowledge, science, interest and Understandability in content and form. Investigation and research confirmed that the main needs of the elderly for health education are doctor consultation, disease treatment, daily health care, chronic disease prevention, personal health records, etc.

(2) Easy-to-use design principle: Health education should conform to the learning ability and health literacy level of the elderly adults. As every old person has different life background, acceptance ability of new technology and health literacy, health education should give effectively support according to users' different characteristics. User' s health literacy level and difficult level of the health education should be assessment, so as to provide the appropriate health education content for users. Older people with higher education level is suitable to learn health information by reading, while those with lower education level are suitable for a simple and intuitive way of education, such as face to face explanation and watching videos.

(3) Design principle of personalized customization: Serialized and targeted health education should be adopted according to the characteristics of individual diseases. Design strategies of personalized customization is a good way to improve user experience.

4   Result Discussion

According to the health behavior theory, the important strategy of health education is to disseminate health information systematically, promote people to accept, believe and voluntarily adopt healthy behaviors. On this study, Fogg's persuasion theory was used to investigate the motivation and ability of elderly. Focus group method was used to analyze the existing problems of health education, and corresponding persuasive strategies of the health education for the elderly was established.

In the follow-up study, we will study the relationship between different motivations and abilities of the elderly users in the selection of persuasive strategies. The user's satisfaction of various persuasive strategies will be discussed based on the prototype design method.

Acknowledgement. This paper is supported by the Humanities and Social Sciences Fund of the Ministry of Education, No. 17YJCZH055. This paper is supported by the Shanghai Peak Plateau Fund Project.

References

1. Health promotion glossary, p. 14. WHO, Geneva (1998). http://www.who.int/hpr/NPH/docs/hp_glossary_en.pdf. Accessed 23 Mar 2011
2. Yang, G., Jin, Y.: Health literacy status of the elderly influencing factors and health education strategies. Chin. J. Gerontol. **1**(36), 250–252 (2016)
3. Wang, H., Li, Y.: Investigation and analysis of health education needs and influencing factors of empty nesters in community. Contemp. Nurses **12**, 160–163 (2017)
4. Shan, X., Feng, Ai.: Evaluation of the intervention effect of Wechat health education mode on health literacy. Health Educ. Health Promot. **11**(02), 98–99+102 (2016)
5. Jiang, F., Zhang, Y.: Application of Wechat support in health education of hypertension. Shanghai Med. **39**(20), 50–52 (2017)
6. Fogg, B.J.: Creating persuasive technologies: an eight-step design process. In: Proceedings of the 4th International Conference on Persuasive Technology (Persuasive 09), Claremont, CA, pp. 1–6 (2009)
7. Oinas-Kukkonen, H., Harjumaa, M.: A systematic framework for designing and evaluating persuasive systems. In: Oinas-Kukkonen, H., Hasle, P., Harjumaa, M., Segerståhl, K., Øhrstrøm, P. (eds.) PERSUASIVE 2008. LNCS, vol. 5033, pp. 164–176. Springer, Heidelberg (2008). https://doi.org/10.1007/978-3-540-68504-3_15
8. Spencor, L., Adams, T.B., Malone, S., et al.: Applying the transtheoretical model to exercise: a systematic and comprehensive review of the literature. Health Promot. Pract. **7**(4), 428–443 (2006)

9. Han, Y.: Chinese guidelines for percutaneous coronary intervention 2012. Chin. J. Crit. Care Med.: Electron. Ed. **40**(3), 18–26 (2012)

10. Daud, N.A., Sahari Ashaari, N., Muda, Z.: An initial model of persuasive design in web based learning environment. Procedia Technol. **11**, 895–902 (2013). ICEEI 2013

11. Yang, W.: The effect of different health education methods on compliance behavior of community patients with coronary heart disease. Contemp. Nurses **17**(5), 82–83 (2009)

12. Yan, X., Zhang, H., Deng, S.: The effect of family health education on lifestyle and drug compliance of hypertension patients. Qilu Nurs. **15**(7), 22–23 (2009)

13. Guilera, M., Fuentes, M., Grifols, M., et al.: Does an educational leaflet improve self-reported adherence to therapy in osteoporosis? The OPTIMA Study. Osteoporos. Int. **17**, 664–671 (2006)

14. Laslett, L.L., Lynch, J., Sullivan, T.R., et al.: Osteoporosis education improves osteoporosis knowledge and dietary calcium: comparison of a 4 week and a one-session education course. Int. J. Rheum. Dis. **14**, 239–247 (2011)

15. Xu, L., Wen, H.: Brief analysis on improving the efficiency of health education for the elderly. Med. Equip. **29**(7), 148–149 (2015)

16. Keister, K.J., Blixen, C.E.: Quality of life and aging. J. Gerontol. Nurs. **24**(5), 22–28 (1998)

17. Du, H., Xia, S., Li, M.: Learning characteristics and health education methods for the elderly in community. Clin. Nurs. **5**(4), 71–72 (2006)

18. Zhao, G.: Approach to health education methods and effects for the elderly in community. Zhongyuan Med. J. **33**(6), 87–88 (2006)

19. Lu, H.: Study on health education mode of chronic diseases among middle-aged and elderly people in urban community. Nurs. Res. **18**(7), 1211–1212 (2004)

20. Jiang, H.: The correlation between lifestyle and chronic diseases of the elderly in community and the influence of health education on lifestyle of patients. Prim. Health Care China **31**(8), 39–40 (2017)

21. Zhang, L., Yin, Z., Geng, G.: Survey on the needs of elderly families in community for health education content. PLA J. Nurs. **31**(16), 21–28 (2014)

22. Wang, Y.: Design and implementation of community health education system. Hebei Yanshan University (2014)

23. Zhuang, Y., Lv, L.: Discussion on the ways of community health education promoting elderly health. China Geriatr. Health Care Med. **10**(2), 61–63 (2012)

24. Hua, X., Chen, H.: The effect of two health education methods on blood pressure and cognitive behavior of hypertension patients in community. Chin. Gen. Pract. **10**(2), 248–249 (2012)

25. Wen, C.: Study on the effect of health education for elderly patients with hypertension in Yancheng community. Nanjing Southeast University (2016)

26. Hu, J.: Study on the effect of dialogue health education tool in health education for patients with coronary heart disease. Jilin University (2013)

Ontology Construction for Eldercare Services with an Agglomerative Hierarchical Clustering Method

Peng Han[1], Yulong Li[1], Yue Yin[2(✉)], and Ning An[1]

[1] School of Computer and Information,
Hefei University of Technology, Hefei, China
[2] Institute of Industrial and Equipment Technology,
Hefei University of Technology, Hefei, China
frank.y.yin@qq.com

Abstract. A high-quality ontology for eldercare service can help deliver high quality eldercare services in increasingly aged and digitized societies because it can serve as a reference for formulating eldercare service standards and exchanging information pertain to eldercare services over the Internet. Improving upon previous work, we proposed an agglomerative hierarchical clustering method to construct such an ontology. This method incorporates longitudinal denoising and the word bag model to achieve accurate results verified by experiment results.

Keywords: Ontology construction · Eldercare services · Agglomerative hierarchical clustering

1 Introduction

As people live in increasingly aged and digitized societies, many researchers have looked into assisting elders to cope with the digital world [1, 2]. However, little research has studied how to provide standard names for eldercare services that have been growing in both volume and varieties. Many eldercare service names are by convention or coined by service providers. This leads to at least two issues: (1) one service has multiple names and (2) one name means different services at different places. These issues could cause confusion in the marketplace and hinder the information exchange pertain to eldercare services on the Internet.

As shown in other fields [3], an effective way to tackle this problem is to build an ontology for eldercare services. Ontology is the philosophical study of being. More broadly, it studies concepts that directly relate to being, in particular becoming, existence, reality, as well as the basic categories of being and their relations. Traditionally listed as a part of the major branch of philosophy known as metaphysics, ontology often deals with questions concerning what entities exist or may be said to exist and how such entities may be grouped, related within a hierarchy, and subdivided according to similarities and differences. Philosophers can classify ontologies in various ways, using criteria such as the degree of abstraction and field of application [4]:

© Springer Nature Switzerland AG 2019
J. Zhou and G. Salvendy (Eds.): HCII 2019, LNCS 11592, pp. 34–45, 2019.
https://doi.org/10.1007/978-3-030-22012-9_3

Upper ontology, Domain ontology, Interface ontology and Process ontology. Here we choose the domain ontology, for example, information technology, computer languages and the specific branches of science. The ontology defines a common dictionary for researchers to use when sharing information in a particular domain. It contains the basic concepts in the field that can be interpreted by the machine and the relationships between the concepts. Domain experts can leverage many rules for developing standardized ontology. Building an ontology is like defining a set of data and their structure for use by other programs. At present, there are several cases in which other ontology libraries have been successfully constructed in other fields, for example, Ontology Construction for Information Selection [5], Ontology construction for information classification [6] and so on. The use of these tools significantly reduces the complexity of dealing with patients at home [7]. To our best knowledge, we were the first to propose building an ontology for eldercare services in China [8]. The K-means method was used to preliminary studied building an ontology for eldercare service in China, but there is no evaluation of the clustering result and the related names merging. In the previous method, they used the K-means method which used must give an initial cluster number K first, the result of clustering will be different for different K values. When there is noise in the dataset, the k-means clustering proceed will deviate considerably. In this paper, we perform the text denoising before we apply the agglomerative hierarchical clustering method.

The construction of ontology is a systematic project that should follow certain construction guidelines and under the guidance of reasonable methodology, using suitable ontology description language and convenient ontology development tools [9]. There are many methods to build an ontology, for example, Skeletal Methodology, IDEF5 (Integrated Definition for Ontology Description Capture Method), TOVE, Methontology, and seven-step method. In this paper, we use the seven-step method. The seven-step method was developed by Stanford University School of Medicine and is mainly used for the construction of domain ontology, they are determined the scope and scope covered by the ontology, considering multiplexing existing ontology, enumerate all terms, defining the hierarchy of a class, define the properties of the class, define class constraints, create instances. In the seven-step method of ontology construction, the most critical step is the fourth step. There are usually many concepts involved in building ontology, and manually defined methods are often inefficient. Everyone has a different understanding of a particular term may result in multiple classifications. In view of this, many researchers will do preliminary classification through cluster analysis.

2   Clustering Methods

Clustering is to divide a given data set into different clusters according to a specific criterion, so that the similarity between objects in the same cluster is high whereas the dissimilarity between objects in the different clusters is high [10].

Researchers generally categorize clustering algorithms into the following six categories: partition-based methods, density-based methods, network-based methods, model-based methods, fuzzy-based clustering and hierarchy methods.

Partition-based methods [11]: firstly, it is necessary to determine the number of clusters, then select several points as the initial center point randomly, and iteratively reset the points according to the predetermined heuristic algorithm until the target effect is finally achieved. Partition-based methods are simple and efficient for large data sets, furthermore, it has good performance both in time and space. The disadvantage is that the result is easy to be locally optimal when the data set is large, the K value needs to be set in advance and it is very sensitive to the K points selected at the beginning. Such algorithms form the k-means algorithm and its variants, including k-medoids, k-modes, k-medians, kernel k-means, and other algorithms.

Density-based methods [12]: there are two parameters should be defined, one is the maximum radius of the circle, the other is the number of points that the circle should contain at least. As long as the density of adjacent regions (the number of objects or data points) exceeds a certain threshold, the clustering will continue. Finally, each circle corresponds a class. Its advantage is that it is insensitive to noise and can find the arbitrary shapes. The disadvantage is that the result of clustering has a great relationship with parameters. Its typical algorithm is DBSCAN (Density-Based Spatial Clustering of Applications with Noise).

Grid-based methods [13]: the principle of this method is to divide the data space into grid cells, map the data object set into grid cells, and calculate the density of each cell. According to the preset threshold value, each grid cell is judged to be a high-density cell, and a class is formed from a group of adjacent dense cells. The advantage of this type of method is that it is fast because its speed is independent of the number of data objects but only depends on the number of cells in each dimension in the data space. The disadvantages are sensitive to parameters, inability to handle irregularly distributed data.

Model-based methods [14]: this method assumes a model for each cluster and looks for the best fitting of data from the given models. This kind of method mainly refers to probabilistic model-based method and neural network model-based method, especially probabilistic model-based method. Its advantage is that the division of classes is expressed in the form of probability, and the characteristics of each class can also be expressed by parameters. The disadvantage is that the execution efficiency is not high, especially when the distribution quantity is large and the data quantity is small. The most typical and commonly used method is the GMM (Gaussian Mixture Models).

Fuzzy based clustering [15]: a sample belongs to a class with a certain probability. There are some typical fuzzy clustering methods based on objective function, similarity relation and fuzzy relation. The FCM algorithm is an algorithm that determines the degree to which each data point belongs to a certain cluster degree by membership degree. This clustering algorithm is an improvement of the traditional hard clustering algorithm. It is sensitive to isolated points, but it does not ensure that the FCM converges to an optimal solution.

Hierarchical methods are described in more detail in Sect. 3.

Because this paper study the name of eldercare services, we focus on text clustering here. Text clustering is to treat every text as a sample and clustering all the samples. However, the difference from the common clustering operations in machine learning is that the text clustering object is not the direct text itself, but the features extracted from the text. Because the characteristics of the text directly affect the quality of the clustering results, so how to extract features and filter noise is a very important step [16]. There are two kinds of algorithms for text clustering. The first kind is based on layered algorithms, including single links, full links, group averaging, and Ward methods. Using aggregation or division method, one can cluster documents into a hierarchical structure. The other kind contains K-means and its variants. In general, layered algorithms produce more in-depth information for detailed analysis, while algorithms based on variants of the K-means algorithm are more efficient and provide sufficient information for most purposes. Here we build the corresponding text documents by merging the search results of the care service names, and the clustering result of the corresponding service name is obtained by clustering the text documents.

3   Proposed Hierarchical Clustering Method

In this paper, we apply an agglomerative hierarchical clustering method to construct an ontology for eldercare services. We first acquire names of the eldercare service by assigning search engine results as a text document for the corresponding service name. Next, we segment these text documents before denoising and longitudinal denoising them. Then, we use the TF-IDF method to give weights of all word segmentation results of the corresponding name. Subsequently, converts each eldercare service name into a word vector. At last, we apply an agglomerative hierarchical clustering method to cluster the service names in multiple layers. Figure 1 illustrates the follow of the proposed method.

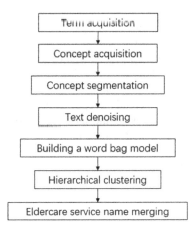

Fig. 1. Eldercare service name clustering method flow

3.1   Term Acquisition

The eldercare service names under study come from two sources. The first group of eldercare services was crawled from the website of the civil affairs department of each province and city. This group of service names include meal service, living service, bathing service, sanitation cleaning service, agency service, preventive health service, medical assistance service, health consultation service, elderly health file filing. The second group of service names came from the official websites of major pension institutions, nursing homes and pension service companies including health assessment services, physical examination services, health knowledge courses, self-health management services, food supplements, cleaning, walking, bathing, lighting, hood cleaning, carpet cleaning, air conditioning cleaning, errands, vegetables and fruits. The total number of names is 412. It is clear that many service names could overlap with others in terms of services they represent, such as babysitters and home sitters, cleaning and sanitation.

3.2   Concept Acquisition

In the Baidu search engine, we crawl the search results for each eldercare service name. The search results include a subtitle of each column and an introduction below the title. We use 20 search results for each service name and merge them together as a text document corresponding to the service name. Because the content of this advertisement may be more relevant to the service, the search results contain the advertisements.

3.3   Concept Segmentation

We use the jieba tokenizer to perform word segmentation on our text dataset. The jieba algorithm for word segmentation uses a prefix-based dictionary to achieve efficient word graph scanning, and generates a directed acyclic graph composed of all possible word generated by Chinese characters in sentences. Dynamic programming is used to find the maximum probability path, and the maximum segmentation combination based on word frequency is found. For the unregistered words, the HMM model based on the ability of Chinese characters is adopted. The jieba tokenizer is used because it is suitable for search engine segmentation. Using the precise model, the long words are divided into words and the recall rate is improved.

The jieba word segmentation actually supports custom word segmentation, so we need to add our care service names to the custom dictionary in advance to avoid splitting our care service names. Finally, more than 1000 kinds of Chinese stop words in the network are used to perform preliminary noise reduction on the processed word segmentation text documents.

3.4   Text Denoising

Through the pre-processing of the previous steps, we have obtained a relatively complete text: the first column of each line is the name of the eldercare service and remaining columns are the search results related to this particular service name. Longitudinal denoising is achieved by comparing the similarity between the service name and each column of word segmentation, then intercept the similarity higher than the set threshold. The word2vec model proposed by Mikolov et al. [17] has attracted a great amount of attention in recent years, and it has shown effectiveness in text mining analysis. In fact, it is a group of related models used to produce word embedding.

Taking a large corpus of text as input, the Word2vec generates a vector space that typically is of several hundred dimensions, before it positions each unique word in the vector space in such way that words that share common contexts in the corpus are located in close proximity to one another in the space [17]. Through the training of a large number of corpora, each word is mapped into a vector of high dimension, that is, the processing of text content is simplified to vector operation in vector space, and the similarity in vector space is calculated to indicate the similarity between words. By setting the similarity threshold, one can delete many unrelated words to improve the clustering effect. In this paper, the result segments with thresholds of 0.6, 0.65, 0.7, 0.75, 0.8, 0.85, and 0.9 are set as new texts, the best clustering results are obtained by comparison.

3.5   Building a Word Bag Model

The next process needs to perform the following steps on the seven data sets obtained in the previous step and compare them for the best results.

The bag-of-words model is a simplifying representation used in natural language processing and information retrieval. In this model, a text (such as a sentence or a document) is represented as the bag of its words (disregarding grammar and even word order but keeping multiplicity). The bag-of-words model is commonly used in methods of document classification where the occurrence of each word is used as a feature for training a classifier. Zellig Harris's 1954 paper on Distributional Structure [18] is an early reference to "bag of words" in a linguistic context. Intuitively, all the word segmentation results in this paper constitute a large word bag, each eldercare services have a corresponding word bag with different value.

The term "Term Frequency–Inverse Document Frequency" (abbreviated as TF IDF) is a commonly used weighting technique for information retrieval and data mining and it intends to reflect how important a word is to a document in a collection or corpus [19]. The importance of words increases with the number frequency appear in the file, but decreases inversely as it appears in the corpus. Various forms of TF-IDF weighting are extensively applied by search engines as a measure or rating of the degree of correlation between a file and a user query.

If a word or phrase appears in an article with a high frequency and rarely appears in other articles, then the word or phrase is considered to have good class distinguishing ability and is suitable for classification. For the word t_i in a particular file, its weight can be calculated as follows:

The word frequency (TF) refers to the frequency at which a given word appears in the file. The value is obtained by the following formula:

$$tf_{i,j} = \frac{n_{i,j}}{\sum_k n_{k,j}} \tag{1}$$

Where: $n_{i,j}$ denotes the number of occurrences of the word in the file d_j.

$\sum_k n_{k,j}$ denotes the sum of the occurrences of all the words in the file d_j.

The inverse document frequency (IDF) is a measure of the universal importance of a word. The value is obtained by the following formula:

$$idf_i = \log \frac{|D|}{|\{j : t_i \in d_j\}|} \tag{2}$$

Where: $|D|$ denotes the total number of files in the corpus

$|\{j : t_i \in d_j\}|$ denotes number of files containing the word t_i (the number of files with $n_{i,j} \neq 0$) will cause the dividend to be zero if the word is not in the corpus.

Then calculate the product of TF and IDF:

$$tfidf_{i,j} = tf_{i,j} \times idf_i \tag{3}$$

The high word frequency within a particular file, and the low file frequency of the word in the entire file set, can produce a high weight of TF-IDF. Therefore, TF-IDF tends to filter out common words to retain important words.

The result is that each service name corresponds to a word vector, and each vector has the same dimension.

3.6 Hierarchical Clustering

It groups a set of data in a way that maximizes the similarity within clusters and minimizes the similarity between two different clusters. Hierarchical clustering methods seek to build a hierarchy of clusters. The strategies for hierarchical clustering generally contain two types:

Divisive: a top-down approach starts from all the texts, and splits the texts according to some rules recursively.

Agglomerative: a bottom-up approach considers each text as a cluster, and merges pair of clusters for each step.

We chose the agglomerative method in this paper. Its basic ideas are as follows. Initially each sample is treated as a cluster, so the size of the original cluster is equal to the number of samples, and then these initial clusters are merged according to certain criteria until a certain condition is reached or the set number of categories is reached. The main steps are as follows:

(1) Get the distance matrix of all samples;
(2) Treat each sample as a separate cluster;
(3) Calculate the cosine similarity between each pair of samples (x,y) according to the following formula, and find a pair of sample points with the smallest cosine similarity (x,y):

$$cos(x, y) = \frac{\sum_{i=1}^{n}(x_i * y_i)}{\sqrt{\sum_{i=1}^{n}(x_i)^2} * \sqrt{\sum_{i=1}^{n}(y_i)^2}} \tag{4}$$

Where: x, y denote any two clusters, also refer to the service name;

x_i denotes the weight corresponding to each word in the word bag after the x cluster;

(4) Combine the two clusters x and y with the largest cosine similarity, then update the distance matrix of the merged samples by calculating the mean of these two matrixes;

(5) Repeat steps (2)–(4) until we merge all samples into one cluster.

The advantage of hierarchical clustering methods is that it does not require specifying the number of clusters in advance. On the contrary, K-means method used in our previous study [8] must first give an initial cluster number K, and the result of clustering will depend on different K values. Hierarchical clustering methods view data having different granularity levels, hence can assist people to visualize and interactively explore large document collections [20], then we cut the clustering tree according to the quality of clusters.

However, the disadvantage of hierarchical clustering is that the amount of computation is large, since hierarchical clustering algorithms require pairwise inter object proximities, the complexity of these clustering procedures is at least $O(N^2)$ [21].

3.7   Eldercare Service Name Merging

Researchers intervene at this step and divide the clustering results into 24 named subcategories. The training model introduced in step 3.4 is then used to calculate the similarity of the two care services in each category. The calculation results will provide a reliable reference to decide whether to merge.

4   Experimental Results and Analysis

4.1   Result Verification

According to the clustering results, the final clustering results have 24 categories. In order to select the optimal clustering results, we calculated the F-measure of 9 corresponding result types in 3.4. We select 2 researchers to manually label the 412 care service names according to the naming results, and calculate the precision, recall and F-Measure. The accuracy rate is the proportion of objects that are clustered in the clustering result, and it is judged whether each service name is correctly classified to the category to which it belongs. The recall rate is the proportion of similar names in the same topic merged into a class, and it is judged whether the name of each category is completely divided into the corresponding class.

F-measure is a composite indicator that is the harmonic average of precision and recall. The larger the value of f-measure is, the better the clustering effect is. The formula is as follows:

$$Precision = \frac{n_{ij}}{n_i} \tag{5}$$

$$Recall = \frac{n_{ij}}{n_j} \tag{6}$$

$$F - \text{Measure} = \frac{2 \times Precision \times Recall}{(Precision + Recall)} \tag{7}$$

where: n_{ij} denotes the number of names in class i manually labeled in cluster j;

   n_i denotes the number of names in manually labeled class I;

   n_j denotes the number of names in cluster j.

Finally, the clustering result obtained when the threshold is set to 0.75 is the best. The F-measure results are shown in Table 1. For the sake of simplicity, we have chosen 1–24 instead of 24 types of services.

Table 1. F-measure

Category code	1	2	3	4	5	6
Researcher 1	0.86	0.96	0.86	0.85	0.81	0.9
Researcher 2	0.9	0.92	0.88	0.8	0.86	0.93
Category code	7	8	9	10	11	12
Researcher 1	0.93	0.91	0.96	0.95	0.94	0.9
Researcher 2	0.98	0.93	0.97	0.86	0.88	0.91
Category code	13	14	15	16	17	18
Researcher 1	0.95	0.98	0.95	0.7	0.94	0.86
Researcher 2	0.91	0.96	0.89	0.9	0.97	0.93
Category code	19	20	21	22	23	24
Researcher 1	0.89	1	0.82	0.84	0.8	0.96
Researcher 2	0.95	1	0.94	0.95	0.91	0.82

According to the results, the proposed method consistently achieves the good F-measure. The eldercare service names with obvious characteristics such as hospital departments and health records have higher accuracy.

4.2   Eldercare Service Names Merging Result

Utilizing domain knowledge, we finally merged the eldercare service names: 23 pairs of service names merged and 28 service names deleted. For example, unlocking locks, repairing locks, changing lock cylinders, changing locks, technical unlocking, cost collection, payment of various fees, spiritual comfort, psychological comfort, family doctors, family doctor services, health file establishment, health files, appointments Registration, registration services, hospital registration and other services.

4.3   Result Analysis and Display

Through aforementioned steps, we finally build a bottom-up ontology with protégé4.3 and generate the output in OWL format. The ontology is divided into four layers, the first layer is the eldercare services; the second layer is the four major categories of life demand service, daily demand service, health care service and hospital service. There are 24 categories in the third floor, which are leisure service, life assistant service, life guidance service for the elderly, life distribution service, errands service, housekeeping service, home cleaning service, payment unlocking service, travel service, home appliance repair service, and elderly rights service, elderly cultural and sports services, elderly care services, health assessment services, health monitoring services, rehabilitation care services, psychological care services, common equipment services, feature testing services, accompanying medical services, health records services, hospital services, elderly data services, hospitals Assistant service. The fourth layer is the name of various eldercare services. Each of these classes and its subclasses are inclusive. Part of the results as shown in Fig. 2.

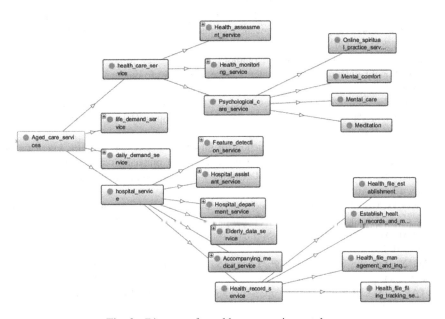

Fig. 2. Diagram of an eldercare service ontology

5 Conclusion

To meet the needs of rapidly aging population, eldercare services continue to grow in both volume and types. While there are new technologies to support this aging population [22], the naming and content of existing, and especially emerging, eldercare services lack of clear specifications. A high quality ontology for eldercare service can help experts categorize these services into standards that not only has their own merits, but also can enable IT technologies to improve the efficiency and quality of eldercare services. Extending our preliminary work on this subject, we propose an agglomerative hierarchical clustering method to improve the quality of the constructed ontology for eldercare services. The experiment results demonstrate the proposed method has a good accuracy. As more work need to be done on this practical and important subject, we plan further optimize our method, especially by looking into reducing the word bag redundancy.

Acknowledgements. This work was supported in part by the Anhui Key Project of Research and Development Plan under Grant No. 1704e1002221 and the National Program of Introducing Talents of Discipline to Universities ("111 Program") under Grant No. B14025.

References

1. Zhou, J., Rau, P.L.P., Salvendy, G.: Use and design of handheld computers for older adults: a review and appraisal. Int. J. Hum.-Comput. Interact. **28**(12), 799–826 (2012)
2. Wang, A., An, N., Lu, X., Chen, H., Li, C., Levkoff, S.: A classification scheme for analyzing mobile apps used to prevent and manage disease in late life. JMIR mHealth uHealth **2**(1), e6 (2014)
3. Li, X., et al.: Building a practical ontology for emergency response systems. In: 2008 International Conference on Computer Science and Software Engineering, vol. 4, pp. 222–225. IEEE (2008)
4. Petrov, V.: Ontological Landscapes: Recent Thought on Conceptual Interfaces Between Science and Philosophy. Acknowledgements (2011). https://doi.org/10.1515/978311031-9811
5. Khan, L., Luo, F.: Ontology construction for information selection. In: IEEE International Conference on Tools with Artificial Intelligence. IEEE Computer Society (2002)
6. Weng, S.S., Tsai, H.J., Liu, S.C., et al.: Ontology construction for information classification. Expert Syst. Appl. **31**(1), 1–12 (2006)
7. Riaño, D., Real, F., Campana, F., Ercolani, S., Annicchiarico, R.: An ontology for the care of the elder at home. In: Combi, C., Shahar, Y., Abu-Hanna, A. (eds.) AIME 2009. LNCS (LNAI), vol. 5651, pp. 235–239. Springer, Heidelberg (2009). https://doi.org/10.1007/978-3-642-02976-9_33
8. An, N., Yin, Y., Shi, H., Han, P., Cheng, S., Li, L.: Building an ontology for eldercare service in China with a hierarchical clustering method. In: Zhou, J., Salvendy, G. (eds.) ITAP 2018. LNCS, vol. 10927, pp. 3–12. Springer, Cham (2018). https://doi.org/10.1007/978-3-319-92037-5_1
9. Li, H., Li, J., Li, M.: Research on modeling method of domain ontology. Comput. Eng. Des. **9**(2), 381–384 (2008)
10. Elhabbash, A.H.: Enhanced k-means Clustering Algorithm (2010)
11. Velmurugan, T., Santhanam, T.: A survey of partition based clustering algorithms in data mining: an experimental approach. Inf. Technol. J. **10**(3), 478–484 (2011)
12. Kriegel, H.P., Kröger, P., Sander, J., et al.: Density-based clustering. Wiley Interdisciplinary Rev.: Data Mining Knowl. Discov. **1**(3), 231–240 (2011)
13. Ma, E.W.M., Chow, T.W.S.: A new shifting grid clustering algorithm. Pattern Recogn. **37**(3), 503–514 (2004)
14. Zhong, S., Ghosh, J.: A unified framework for model-based clustering. J. Mach. Learn. Res. **4**(Nov), 1001–1037 (2003)
15. Yao, J., Dash, M., Tan, S.T., et al.: Entropy-based fuzzy clustering and fuzzy modeling. Fuzzy Sets Syst. **113**(3), 381–388 (2000)
16. Yang, J.M., Liao, W.C., Wu, W.C., et al.: Trend analysis of machine learning-a text mining and document clustering methodology. In: 2009 International Conference on New Trends in Information and Service Science, pp. 481–486. IEEE (2009)

17. Mikolov, T., Chen, K., Corrado, G., Dean, J.: Efficient estimation of word representations in vector space. arXiv preprint arXiv:1301.3781 (2013)
18. Harris, Z.S.: Distributional structure. Word **10**(2–3), 146–162 (1981)
19. Rajaraman, A., Ullman, J.D.: Mining of Massive Datasets. Cambridge University Press, Cambridge (2011)
20. Zhao, Y., Karypis, G.: Evaluation of hierarchical clustering algorithms for document datasets. In: Proceedings of the Eleventh International Conference on Information and Knowledge Management, pp. 515–524. ACM (2002)
21. Murtagh, F.: A survey of recent advances in hierarchical clustering algorithms. Comput. J. **26**(4), 354–359 (1983)
22. U.S. National Science & Technology Council. Emerging technology to support an aging population. USOSTP (2019)

Mobile Experience Sampling Method: Capturing the Daily Life of Elders

Rong Hu[1], Xiaozhao Deng[1], Xiaoning Sun[2], Yuxiang (Chris) Zhao[3], and Qinghua Zhu[4(✉)]

[1] Southwest University, Chongqing 400715, China
[2] Shanxi University of Finance and Economics, Taiyuan 030006, China
[3] Nanjing University of Science and Technology, Nanjing 210094, China
[4] Nanjing University, Nanjing 210023, China
qhzhu@nju.edu.cn

Abstract. The aging of populations worldwide has emerged as an important focus of research and policy. Concomitantly, capturing the daily life of elders is becoming a major task for researchers and service providers. In a mobile internet environment, traditional methods are not adequate to support contextualized information behavior research on the elderly. Based on a comparison of six methods from four perspectives (context, time, user, and data), this paper introduces the mobile experience sampling method (mESM) as an effective approach to the study of elders' everyday information behaviors. An overview of mESM is presented, and a general three-stage framework is proposed to discuss its implementation. We also offer suggestions to improve the efficacy of mESM in addressing the real conditions and characteristics of the elderly and discuss the method's advantages, disadvantages and related problems from the perspectives of researchers, elders, and policymakers. Overall, we find mESM to be an ideal longitudinal method for capturing the contextualized day-to-day information behavior of elders.

Keywords: Mobile experience sampling method · Daily life · Elders · Longitudinal research · Real situation

1 Introduction

The world population is aging rapidly. It is estimated that by 2050, the proportion of the global population aged 65 and over will reach 20% [1]. This demographic shift has emerged as an important focus of both research and policy planning worldwide. Within the field of information behavior research, capturing the daily life of older people has become an overarching task for researchers and service providers, who hope to understand the needs of older people and thus provide more effective information services for them. However, in the emerging mobile internet environment, elders' information behaviors are highly situational, and traditional methods are thus sometimes inadequate to capture the day-to-day information behaviors of elders. This study aims to introduce a new approach—the mobile experience sampling method (mESM)

J. Zhou and G. Salvendy (Eds.): HCII 2019, LNCS 11592, pp. 46–55, 2019.
https://doi.org/10.1007/978-3-030-22012-9_4

—with which to investigate elders' everyday information behavior. Two principal questions guide our research:

1. Why is mESM suitable for capturing the daily life of the elderly in the emerging mobile internet environment?
2. What are the necessary steps to implement the mESM approach? How can mESM be employed to effectively explore elders' information behaviors?

2 Why mESM?

Traditional methods for capturing data from the elderly include interviews [2–8], surveys [9–11], experiments [12], diary-keeping [13], and general ESM [14, 15]. In addition, sensor-based method can provide real-time monitoring of older people [16–18]. Together, these methods have played an important role in collecting qualitative or quantitative data from elders. However, in the current mobile internet environment, elders' information behaviors are always rooted in specific contexts. Accordingly, when we try to go deep into the everyday life of the elderly, we need to capture not only the qualitative or quantitative data of needs, behaviors, experiences and emotions in a given time and place, but also the corresponding real-life situations in which data are generated. Meanwhile, if a method can easily support repeated measurements of daily life and build cumulative data sets for comprehensive and fine-grained analysis, it will help us more accurately understand the rhythm and regularity of elders' day-to-day information behavior. These research requirements prompt us to seek a more suitable longitudinal method of capturing intensive information from the real-life situations faced by the elderly.

The criteria for selecting such a method can, we suggest, be viewed from four perspectives: context, time, user and data. Such an analysis suggests that traditional methods may not be adequate for current daily-life research. The pertinent issues are summarized in Table 1. First, in terms of ecological validity, interview, survey, experiment and diary methods each face great limitations in collecting real-situational data. Researchers using these methods obtain only fuzzy recall data, not a real-time sample. Although a diary may help the respondents recall incidents and situations, it can hardly capture the real situation in the moment. The general experience sampling method (ESM) is designed to facilitate data collection concerning both the context and content of individuals' daily life [18]. The sensor-based method likewise derives greater ecological validity from its provision of context-sensitive raw sensor data in real time.

From the perspective of time, interviews, surveys and experiments usually collect transverse data at a specific point of time. They are implemented only once and are typically classified as one-shot evaluation methods. Diary, general ESM, and sensor-based methods, in contrast, permit repeated measurements of variables and collect data cumulatively; they can be grouped as intensive longitudinal methods [19, 20]. With respect to the user's participation and perception, most of these methods (interview, survey, experiment, diary and general ESM) require active participation or self-reporting, and the whole process is made explicit to the users. An exception is the sensor-based method, which collects data directly without user's participation and can thus be characterized as implicit and passive, reducing the interruptions experienced by users.

Table 1 also presents five aspects of data as they apply to each method: data characteristics, data size, the collection of emotional or experiential data, the data's semantic richness, and the presence of retrospective bias. In general, data collected via interviews and diaries will be qualitative, whereas surveys, experiments, and sensor-based methods usually collect quantitative data. Notably, general ESM can capture both [18, 21]. In terms of data size, surveys usually allow for a large sample, whereas interviews, experiments, diaries, and general ESM are often restricted to a small sample size; the sampling size of sensor-based methods can be large or small. Diary, general ESM and sensor-based methods can collect cumulative data, while the other methods obtain one-shot data. Sensor-based methods yield raw sensor data without semantics, which gives rise to a problem of interpretation. Such methods, unlike the others, cannot supply information about individuals' experiences and emotions per se. Since sensor-based methods and general ESM can capture real-time data, these two methods have a smaller retrospective bias.

The above comparison shows that traditional methods, such as interviews, surveys, experiments and diary-keeping, cannot effectively capture real-situation data or facilitate longitudinal research. Although sensor-based methods can be applied to large or small samples with implicit data collection, the data obtained by this method is only raw sensor data, lacking semantic information. General ESM provides a good methodological framework for studying daily life, helping to capture real situations and supplying intensive longitudinal data; it can collect both qualitative and quantitative data and supply semantically rich descriptions of experiences and emotions, but it is complicated and inconvenient to implement (a point developed further below), especially when being used to study the elderly, and a small sample size is typical. Thus, in a mobile internet environment, it is necessary to improve general ESM to allow for the effective and convenient study of elders' day-to-day information behaviors.

Information and communication technology (ICT) offers tremendous opportunities for both researchers and the elderly. As mobile technology gradually integrates into our lives, a mobile phone has become a necessity, not a luxury. Increasingly, older adults use mobile phones or smartphones to satisfy their everyday health, social, and leisure needs. The corresponding information behaviors have been of great interest to researchers. Meanwhile, more and more researchers have adopted mobile technology to facilitate their elderly-related studies. In this paper, mobile experience sampling method (mESM) is proposed as highly suitable for research on the day-to-day information behavior of the elderly within this emerging mobile internet environment. mESM is a longitudinal method that uses mobile technology to study behaviors and experiences occurring naturally in people's everyday life. It is, in essence, an experience sampling method that inherits the implementation framework of ESM and improves upon it with mobile technology. Herein, we aim to introduce mESM and its implementation framework, and to contemplate potential improvements to mESM for studying the daily life of the elderly.

Table 1. Comparison of six data capture methods

			Interview	Survey	Experiment	Diary	General ESM	Sensor-based method
Context	Ecological validity		Low	Low	Low	Low	High	High
Time	Transverse		✓	✓	✓			
	Longitudinal					✓	✓	✓
User	Participation	Active	✓	✓	✓	✓	✓	
		Passive						✓
	Perception	Implicit						✓
		Explicit	✓	✓	✓	✓	✓	
Data	Characteristics	Qualitative	✓			✓	✓	
		Quantitative		✓	✓		✓	✓
	Size	Sampling	Small	Large	Small	Small	Small	Large or small
		Cumulative				✓	✓	✓
	Emotional or experiential		✓	✓	✓	✓	✓	
	Semantic richness		High	High or low	High or low	High	High	Low
	Retrospective bias		Large	Large	N/A	Large	Small	Small

3 How to Use mESM

3.1 Make Good Use of the Implementation Framework

mESM is a descendant of the *experience sampling method* (ESM), a systematic phenomenology approach proposed at the University of Chicago in the 1970s [18]. Typically, general ESM uses a tool to signal participants, allow them to answer questions at random moments every day or complete a report following a particular event of interest, achieving the purpose of data collection. It is essentially a self-report method. Because participants voluntarily and spontaneously perform their reports in a real and natural situation, ESM is ecologically valid. Through repeated measurement, ESM can help to explore people's dynamic and complex behaviors, experiences and emotions.

Generally, the signaling tool and experience sampling form (ESF) are the two important components of ESM [18], as shown in Fig. 1. Early ESM studies used a setup known as paper-based ESM (ESMp), with pagers for signaling and paper ESFs for data collection. After receiving a signal, ESMp participants filled out the paper ESF immediately and mailed it back to the researcher as soon as possible (e.g. at the end of the day) [22]. It was understandably difficult for ESMp researchers to control this cumbersome process, and participants may have felt inconvenienced as well. Computerized ESM (ESMc) was welcomed by researchers because it alleviated some of these problems, allowed researchers to better understand the process of participants' completion of the forms, and reduced the cost of data transcription. The ESM programs ESP and iESP, for example—both developed by Intel Research [23]—used a PDA to signal participants and collect data. However, researchers still needed to download and aggregate data from every participant's PDA after finishing their research. This created problems with data synchronization and prevented ESMc from attaining popularity as a tool for large-scale field research. The development of mobile devices, the proliferation of wireless networks, and the growing popularity of online surveys led to the creation of mESM, which highlights the advantages of using mobile technology. Modern mESM software usually runs on smartphones, supports both signaling and ESF completion, and has servers to support real-time synchronization of data. Some mESM tools can even support context awareness and signaling based on sensors (e.g. GPS sensors). Therefore, mESM greatly improves the convenience of everyday-life research and makes it possible to enlarge the sample size. In addition, a mESM tool with sensors may collect both explicit self-report data and implicit sensor data, thereby obtaining more richly contextualized data and semantics. In short, mESM is an ideal method for everyday-life research.

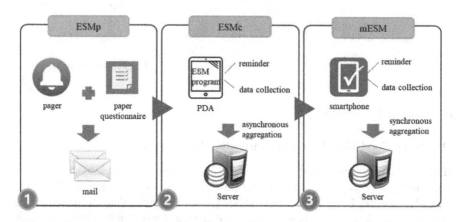

Fig. 1. Evolution of ESM tools

Table 2 shows a detailed implementation framework for mESM. It can be divided into three stages: before implementation (BI), during implementation (DI) and after implementation (AI). In the BI stage, researchers need to select a sampling method, determine a timeframe, choose an mESM tool, and design the ESF. Next, they must recruit, select, and orient participants. Within ESM, there are generally three classes of sampling method from which to choose (Table 2). In *time-contingent sampling*, participants are signaled at random times or at different time intervals every day [19]. For example, researchers may send a certain number of signals randomly between 7:00 am and 10:00 pm every day. The *event-contingent sampling* method solicits self-reports following a specific event of interest [18] (e.g. an interaction in social media). *Mixed sampling* usually combines time-contingent sampling with event-contingent sampling; for example, researchers may signal readers to complete self-reports at specific times; at the same time, the readers may complete their reports once they have finished reading an e-book.

The timeframe decision concerns how many days participants will be asked to report (*research cycle*) and how many times per day they will be signaled to provide these reports (*daily sampling frequency*). Together, these two criteria determine the sampling schedule. Some guidance can also be obtained from researchers' long experience with general ESM: studies shows that a seven-day cycle is likely to yield a fairly representative sample of the various activities individuals engage in and to elicit multiple responses from many of these activities [18]. The most common daily sampling frequency is three times per day (e.g. in the morning, at noon and at night) [24]. Sampling for longer than seven days or more frequently than six times per day may place an excessive burden on some participants [18, 25].

Although there are some ready-made mESM-style tools (e.g. *Ohmage*, *Open Data Kit*, *Paco*, *LifeData*, *Ilumivu*, *MetricWire*, *Movisens*, *Expimetrics*, *Aware*, *ESM capture*, and *Piel Survey*) [21], researchers must still decide between a ready-made tool and a custom tool according to the needs of research. It is also necessary to design an ESF that can be completed within five minutes or less to reduce the burden borne by participants.

In principle, anyone who can read and operate a smartphone can participate in a mESM study. It is essential, however, that individuals voluntarily participate in the study and can guarantee their completion of the entire research process. Because of the richness of the data, studies with as few as 5 or 10 participants can produce enough data to be used reliably in simple statistical analysis [18]. Certainly, with the support provided by an mESM tool, a larger sample size is possible. However, before actually going into the field, researchers should have an orientation meeting and implement a pilot test. Orientation will provide instruction about the procedure and strengthen the research alliance by providing further explanation of the study's goals and answering any questions.

In the DI stage, participants first receive SMS or other signals, then fill in and submit ESF anytime and anywhere. Researchers should track the research every day to find missing data and send reminders to corresponding participants. Incentivization (whether material or nonmaterial) and retention of participants are necessary; to realize the latter, it is beneficial to provide a thorough and honest explanation of the study and establish a relationship of trust. In this stage, researchers are highly recommended to write memos every day, because memos provide more extensive and in-depth data and thinking for mESM research.

In the AI stage, a debriefing interview may help researchers get more extensive information. For example, participants are often asked whether they felt that the period of signaling represented a "normal week" in their lives and whether any specific activities or situations caused them to fail to answer the signal. After data cleaning, the process of data analysis includes both *response-level* and *person-level* analysis [18]. The former involves the raw data submitted after each individual signaling, while the latter involves summarizing and analyzing the raw data for each individual. According to the underlying purpose of the research, this analysis may be qualitative (e.g. case analysis) or quantitative (e.g. ANOVA, ordinary least squares (OLS) or hierarchical linear modeling (HLM)) [18].

Table 2. Implementation framework for mESM

Stage	Contents	Details
BI	Determine sampling method	• Time-contingent sampling • Event-contingent sampling • Mixed sampling
	Determine framework of time	• Research cycle • Daily sampling frequency • Signaling schedule
	Decide on mESM tool	• Choosing a ready-made or customized tool
	Design ESF	• Controlling items of ESF
	Recruit, select and orient participants	• Basic requirements for participants • Prerequisites of participation • Number of participants • Orientation
DI	Send signals	• SMS or other signals
	Participants fill in and submit ESF	• Anytime, anywhere
	Track the research	• Anytime, anywhere
	Reminder participants to fill in	• Timing and frequency of reminders
	Incentives and retention	• Material or nonmaterial incentives • Explain the study and establish relationship of trust
	Create memo	• Provide extensive data
AI	Interview	• Debriefing interview
	Process and analyze data	• Data cleaning • Response-level analysis • Person-level analysis

Note: BI: before implementation; DI: during implementation; AF: after implementation

3.2   Improvements for the Elderly

The above implementation framework provides basic guidance for mESM field studies. However, there are some specific improvements to consider in studying the day-to-day life of elderly people (those who use smartphones). First, older participants may not be comfortable reading text in small fonts, so picture, voice, and video channels may be a good choice. For example, items in the ESF may be displayed as pictures or videos, and participants may complete their report as a voice recording. Second, researchers should consider allowing elderly respondents to capture their experiences by taking photos, which can also assist in recollection after the fact [26]. Third, the cognitive load of the elderly should be taken into account: it is recommended to use mESM tools with a simple interface and a simple feature set. Fourth, it should be acknowledged that health problems are prevalent among the elderly; a large amount of sensor data involving position, movement, etc., can be integrated into health information behavior research conducted on elderly subjects. Fortunately, all of these criteria can be satisfied with smartphone-based mESM; accordingly, our team are developing a mESM tool tailored to the elderly. In addition, the sampling method, timeframe, orientation, sampling schedule, incentives, and retention practices should be tailored both to the age of the participants and to the purpose of the research.

4   Discussion

From a researcher's perspective, mESM has become an ideal method for capturing the day-to-day information behaviors of the elderly. Compared with general ESM, mESM is more convenient and can capture qualitative or quantitative data explicitly or implicitly for a large or small sample size. In addition, mESM tools are readily combined with other methods, such as ethnography or field experiments [21]. Therefore, widespread adoption of mESM is expected in various fields, including clinical medicine, healthcare and pharmaceutical research, mobile health management, mobile social and mobile education. However, repeated signaling inevitably disturbs the elderly, and the development or selection of a tool, combined with orientation and the provision of a monetary incentive, will tend to increase the cost of this method. Additionally, if a study integrates sensors, the investigators will face the challenges inherent in dealing with heterogeneous data.

The perspective of the elderly, too, must be taken into account. Researchers should favor reporting methods that are accessible, easy to navigate, and not cognitively burdensome. Moreover, an effort must be made to improve the ICT literacy of the elderly, and the privacy issues arising in an mESM-based study should be managed so as to protect elders' rights.

Policymakers also have a role to play. Given the method's potential value for understanding the needs and challenges of the elderly, the government should encourage mESM studies with elderly respondents. Official guidance for research and related industries is also important, as are clear policies on mESM-related privacy protection.

5   Conclusion

In sum, mESM is an ideal research method that combines the strengths of classic ESM with current mobile technology. Although there are still some challenges in applying the method to the day-to-day life of older people, mESM shows evident promise in this field. With the support of mESM-based studies, we may understand the elderly more accurately, facilitate older adults' self-management of daily life, choose policies that better match the needs and characteristics of elderly citizens, and enable service providers to provide more accurate context-based services for this growing demographic.

Acknowledgements. The authors would like to thank the reviewers for their insightful comments, which have improved the paper. This study has been supported by the Major Project of National Social Science Foundation of P. R. China (Grant No. 15ZDB126), the Humanities & Social Science Youth Foundation of Ministry of Education of P. R. China (Grant Nos. 16XJC870001, 18YJC870018), the Social Science Planning Foundation of Chongqing in

P. R. China (Grant No. 2016PY76), the General Project of Philosophy & Social Science Research in Colleges and Universities in Shanxi Province of P. R. China (Grant No. 201803021), and the PhD Foundation of Southwest University in China (Grant No. swu118021).

References

1. IFA. http://www.ifa-fiv.org/publication/demographics/aging-world-2015/. Accessed 23 Feb 2019
2. Gunnarsson, E.: 'I think I have had a good life': the everyday lives of older women and men from a lifecourse perspective. Ageing Soc. **29**(1), 33 (2009)
3. Imhof, L., Wallhagen, M.I., Mahrer-Imhof, R., et al.: Becoming forgetful: how elderly people deal with forgetfulness in everyday life. Am. J, Alzheimer's Dis. Other Dement. **21** (5), 347–353 (2006)
4. Kwok, J.Y.C., Tsang, K.K.M.: Getting old with a good life: research on the everyday life patterns of active older people. Ageing Int. **37**(3), 300–317 (2012)
5. Dunér, A., Nordström, M.: Intentions and strategies among elderly people: coping in everyday life. J. Aging Stud. **19**(4), 437–451 (2005)
6. Arslantas, D., Unsal, A., Metintas, S., et al.: Life quality and daily life activities of elderly people in rural areas, Eskisehir (Turkey). Arch. Gerontol. Geriatr. **48**(2), 127–131 (2008)
7. Crombie, I.K.: Why older people do not participate in leisure time physical activity: a survey of activity levels, beliefs and deterrents. Age Ageing **33**(3), 287–292 (2004)
8. Elers, P., Hunter, I., Whiddett, D., et al.: User requirements for technology to assist ag-ing in place: qualitative study of older people and their informal support networks. Jmir Mhealth Uhealth **6**(6), e10741 (2018)
9. Ajaj, A., Singh, M.P., Abdulla, A.J.J.: Should elderly patients be told they have cancer? Questionnaire survey of older people. BMJ **323**(7322), 1160 (2001)
10. Harris, T., Cook, D.G., Victor, C., et al.: Predictors of depressive symptoms in older people– a survey of two general practice populations. Age Ageing **32**(5), 510 (2003)
11. Jakobsson, U.: Using the 12-item short form health survey (SF-12) to measure quality of life among older people. Aging Clin. Exp. Res. **19**(6), 457–464 (2007)
12. Dinet, J., Brangier, E., Michel, G., Vivian, R., Battisti, S., Doller, R.: Older people as information seekers: exploratory studies about their needs and strategies. In: Stephanidis, C. (ed.) UAHCI 2007. LNCS, vol. 4554, pp. 877–886. Springer, Heidelberg (2007). https://doi.org/10.1007/978-3-540-73279-2_98
13. Stjernborg, V., Wretstrand, A., Tesfahuney, M.: Everyday life mobilities of older per-sons – a case study of ageing in a suburban landscape in Sweden. Mobilities **10**(3), 383–401 (2015)
14. Myllykangas, S.A., Gosselink, C.A., Foose, A.K., et al.: Meaningful activity in older adults: being in flow. World Leis. J. **44**(3), 24–34 (2002)
15. Hnatiuk, S.H.: Experience sampling with elderly persons: an exploration of the method. Int. J. Aging Hum. Dev. **33**(1), 45–64 (1991)
16. Stefanov, D.H., Bien, Z., Bang, W.C.: The smart house for older persons and persons with physical disabilities: structure, technology arrangements, and perspectives. IEEE Trans. Neural Syst. Rehabil. Eng. **12**(2), 228–250 (2004)
17. Gietzelt, M., Feldwieser, F., Gövercin, M., et al.: A prospective field study for sensor-based identification of fall risk in older people with dementia. Inf. Health Soc. Care **39**(3–4), 249–261 (2014)
18. Hektner, J.M., Schmidt, J.A., Csikszentmihalyi, M.: Experience Sampling Method: Measuring the Quality of Everyday Life. Sage, Thousand Oaks (2007)

19. Duan, J., Chen, W.: Ambulatory-assessment based sampling method: experience sampling method. Adv. Psychol. Sci. **20**(7), 1110–1120 (2012)
20. Li, W., Zheng, Q.: Everyday experience study: a unique and heuristic research method. Adv. Psychol. Sci. **16**(1), 169–174 (2008)
21. Hu, R., Tang, Z., Zhao, Y.: Mobile experience sampling method: facilitating human information behavior research in the real context. J. China Soc. Sci. Tech. Inf. **37**(10), 1046–1059 (2018)
22. Côté, S., Moscowitz, D.S.: On the dynamic covariation between interpersonal behavior and affect: prediction from neuroticism, extraversion, and agreeableness. J. Pers. Soc. Psychol. **75**, 1032–1046 (1998)
23. Fischer, J.E.: Experience-sampling tools: a critical review. In: Proceedings of Mo-bileHCI 2009, Bonn, Germany (2009)
24. Zhang, Y., Luo, N., Shi, W.: Experience sampling: a new method to collect "real" data. Adv. Psychol. Sci. **24**(2), 305–316 (2016)
25. Christensen, T.C., Barrett, L.F., Bliss-Moreau, E., et al.: A practical guide to experience-sampling procedures. J. Happiness Stud. **4**(1), 53–78 (2003)
26. Yue, Z., Litt, E., Cai, C.J., et al.: Photographing information needs: the role of photos in experiences sampling method-style research. In: Proceedings of the SIGCHI Conference on Human Factors in Computing Systems, pp. 1545–1554. ACM Press, New York (2014)

Setting Up and Conducting the Co-design of an Intergenerational Digital Game: A State-of-the-Art Literature Review

Eugène Loos[1](✉), Teresa de la Hera[2], Monique Simons[3], and Dorus Gevers[4]

[1] Utrecht University, Bijlhouwerstraat 6, 3511 ZC Utrecht, The Netherlands
e.f.loos@uu.nl
[2] Erasmus University, Postbus 1738, 3000 DR Rotterdam, The Netherlands
teresadelahera@gmail.com
[3] Utrecht University, Princetonlaan 8a, 3584 CB Utrecht, The Netherlands
M.Simons@uu.nl
[4] Maastricht University Medical Centre, P.O. Box 616, 6200 Maastricht,
The Netherlands
Dorus.gevers@maastrichtuniversity.nl

Abstract. In our ageing society, health and social problems of older people are on the rise. A possible way to deal with these issues is to ensure older people remain actively engaged in society by stimulating social interaction with other generations, such as (grand) children. Playing intergenerational digital games could be a way to achieve this kind of social interaction. The present state-of-the-art literature review aims to provide insight into the factors to take into consideration for setting up and conducting the *co*-design (involving younger and older adults interacting both with one another and with game designers) for an intergenerational digital game. Finally, this paper offers recommendations for the co-design of such games.

Keywords: State-of-the-art literature review · Intergenerational digital games · Co-design · Design recommendations

1 Introduction

Older people are at risk of health issues (e.g., due to mental and physical decline) as well as social problems (e.g., loneliness) (http://www.who.int/about/mission/en/). As the world's population is ageing rapidly, with the number of older people estimated to double to 1.6 billion globally between 2025 and 2050 (U.S. Census Bureau, 2016), this is an important social issue. The ageing of the population is a megatrend that will impact on global society for decades to come. Yet another megatrend that is swiftly changing the world is that of the digitization of society. The number of users of digital media in Western countries has soared over the past few years across all age groups, from young to old (http://www.pewinternet.org/2017/05/17/tech-adoption-climbs-among-older-adults/ and https://ec.europa.eu/eurostat/statistics-explained/index.php/people_in_the_EU_-_statistics_on_an_ageing_society).

© Springer Nature Switzerland AG 2019
J. Zhou and G. Salvendy (Eds.): HCII 2019, LNCS 11592, pp. 56–69, 2019.
https://doi.org/10.1007/978-3-030-22012-9_5

Remaining actively engaged in society, for example, through social interaction with other generations, such as (grand) children, could offer a way to deal with the health issues and social problems confronting older adults. Studies have clearly shown that fostering intergenerational contact can serve as a valuable instrument to achieve such active engagement [1–3]. As play is a necessary human activity (see Huizinga [4] on the "homo ludens"), and playing digital games in our everyday life has become as common as watching television for many of us [5, 6], intergenerational digital games could provide a useful tool in getting or keeping older people involved in our society.

Literature reviews [7, 8] explored the possibilities of intergenerational digital gaming in a broad sense, and examined various characteristics of intergenerational digital games. They did not, however, analyze in detail the process of designing intergenerational digital games. Another literature review [9] provided insight into the attraction of intergenerational digital games and the factors that need to be taken into consideration when setting up and designing digital games targeted at mixed-aged players. But to our knowledge, no state-of the-art literature review has yet focused on how co-design can be used to set up and conduct an intergenerational digital game to enable seniors to become or remain involved in society. This is somewhat remarkable, as involving the future players – in this case, members of both older and younger generations - in the design process is a logical condition to foster meaningful play; gaming is a shared play activity for which the players need each other.

The present state-of-the art literature review, therefore, aims to provide insight into the characteristics and dynamics of setting up and conducting the co-design of an intergenerational digital game. We are aware of the fact that other terms have also been proposed for this type of design, such as player-centered game, participatory design, human-centered game design, and user-centered game design, each of which, however, carries a slightly different meaning. In this article, we use the term co-design to refer to a process in which involving users from the very beginning to the end is crucial. According to Stewart et al. [10], such an approach blurs "the boundary between game player and traditional 'creator'" (p. 20). Following [11–14] we define the co-design of an intergenerational digital game as: A process involving younger and older adults both with one another and with game designers) in the design of a digital game through a participatory approach to enhance meaningful play. And we follow [15] who, after first having argued that "meaningful play in a game emerges from the relationship between player and system outcome" (p. 34), later added in a section about Games as Social Play that for such games, it is not enough to focus only "on the relationship between an individual player and a game, but also on the social experiences that occur when more than one player participates in the same game." (p. 462). We also follow [16] who state that "a thorough understanding of seniors, their expectations, their likes and dislikes, social relationships, etc. is essential to designing meaningful play for elderly citizens". It goes without saying that, in the case of intergenerational digital game design, this applies to younger citizens, as well.

The co-design process is an iterative, cyclic one that consists of the following four phases: analysis, design, development and evaluation [17]. Several techniques may be used during each phase. The analysis phase, for example, may involve performing contextual inquiries and participatory design. Contextual inquiries are observations of persons in their natural environments to understand how people usually behave [17].

Participatory design is a technique that is used to collect qualitative data about the proposed user, As the focus of participatory design is less on game concepts, and more on the user, it is not only part of the design and development phase, but also of the analysis phase [17]. Evaluations are preferably carried out after every phase, to ensure that feedback is received in time to allow modifications to be made to the game. In earlier stages, these user tests might be performed using low-fidelity prototypes, which are low-cost preliminary versions of the game with only limited functionality [17].

As our definition of the co-design of intergenerational digital games makes clear, the creation process should have a participatory character. This implies that game designers should involve the target groups in an active way, i.e., ensuring the full participation of older and younger people in the design process, from the very beginning to the end.

In the present state-of-the-art literature review, we will examine empirical studies to gain insight into factors to take into consideration for the set up and co-design of intergenerational digital games.

2 The Importance of Intergenerational Games

Intergenerational play can serve different purposes, such as fun (leisure), seriousness (learning) or serious fun (see [7, 18]). According to Davis et al. [1] intergenerational play could be instrumental in enhancing intergenerational contact, which could be mutually beneficial to grandparents and grandchildren. De la Hera et al. [19] argue that this kind of social interaction, "must be stimulated, as not only do the generations hold negative age stereotypes about each other, age differences also contribute to a lack of mutual understanding, which may serve to inhibit interactions between the generations [20]".

In our opinion, intergenerational gaming is significant, because it can contribute to an important societal issue: enhancing intergenerational relations. [1] state that "it is well documented that ongoing social connection between the young and the elderly increase the sense of wellbeing of both parties" (p. 191), and [3] argue that: "Inter-generational contact can reduce the prevalence of ageism, and significantly help improve the mental and physical health amongst the elderly [2]. Similarly, within the family, strong intergenerational relationships have been found to increase self-esteem for the young, and provide positive long-term psychological benefits for children as they move into adulthood [21]." (p. 368)." So, intergenerational contact has the potential to reduce the prevalence of ageism, and significantly improve the mental and physical health of younger and older persons. Costa and Veloso [7] and Zhang and Kaufman [8] have pointed out the potential benefits at the cognitive level (e.g. the exchange of information, knowledge and skills [2], attitudinal level (e.g. reducing ageist ideas, e.g. [7]; and the social level (companionship, e.g. [22]). Finally, [2] underlined the importance of family contexts, especially grandparent-grandchild relationships, in this regard (see also [1, 22–25]).

3   The Importance of Co-design

It is important to involve game players in game design, especially when it comes to non-traditional player groups [13, 26]. The following statement, though, made by Vetere et al. [25] in 2005, still applies today:

"One of the crucial critiques of the current state of game development is the apparent lack of originality in design solutions: games are designed to appeal to a rather narrow, already existing player demographic. As long as the design of new games is based on the traditional model of individual game author or small team designing games based on their personal likings and vision, rather than on understanding derived from their potential new audiences, this is unlikely to change" (p. 1).

Game designers are typically young male adults with little understanding of the needs that older adults have [11] Or, as Oudshoorn et al. [27, p. 41]) (citing Akrich ([28], see also [16, 29]) phrases it, the pitfall of I-methodology should be avoided: "The I-methodology refers to a design practice in which designers consider themselves as representative of the users [28]. Akrich [28] describes the I-methodology as the "reliance on personal experience, whereby the designer replaces his professional that by that of the layman" [p. x]."

This is often an unconscious process: the designer is not aware of the fact that the user representation he or she is using resembles himself or herself. In contrast to the images created by designers and what people expect, implicit methods are often more powerful than explicit methods in shaping the design (p. 41).

Co-design in an intergenerational context implies the involvement of two different user groups (younger and older adult), who interact both with one another and with game designers. As we saw in Sect. 1, involving younger and older adults - the future players - in the design process is a logical condition to foster meaningful play, as gaming is a shared play activity for which the players need each other. It follows, therefore, that a co-design process is essential to developing a digital game that fits the motivations and abilities of both older and younger players.

It is also important to be aware of the fact that the motivations to play digital games differ between older and younger individuals. This finding led De la Hera et al. [19] to argue that older players (1) tend to reject reflex-oriented games such as fighting or racing games, as they find such games more difficult, less interesting and therefore less enjoyable to play [30], (2) avoid action and violent games, (3) prefer games with intellectual challenges [30–33], (4) like playing games because of social aspects, in particular when playing with family members, when the social aspect is more important than the game itself [33, 34], and (5) tend to be less competitive and inclined to assume more passive and supportive roles [30, 31, 33, 35]. Common ground should therefore continuously be sought: the need for fun and relaxation, to escape reality and for social interaction and connectedness is shared by both generations [11].

De la Hera et al. [19] also argue that, as older players are generally less competitive than younger adults and children, digital games designed for intergenerational play should preferably take the form of collaborative games or digital games implementing cooperative competition (e.g. Khoo's digital game *Age Invaders*) rather than competitive games [35–37].

Finally, we should keep in mind that there are age-related differences between younger and older players. Loos [11] points to a number of problems confronting senior players, such as age-related decline in vision (difficulties with reading texts on screens and with detecting items in the periphery of the screen), hearing (problems hearing certain sounds), cognition (difficulties with speed) and visual-motor coordination (problems with mouse and key board controls, selecting and scrolling pages on the screen); see also [23, 37–40].

To accommodate these age-related differences, De la Herra et al. [19] have suggested taking the following points into account when co-designing intergenerational digital games regarding:

- older players:
  (1) strive to develop in-game adjustable speeds instead of time restricted games [31];
  (2) allow for the possibility to play according to the players' own abilities (see the digital game *Age Invaders* [23, 24];
- younger players:
  tailor the game technology to their age and abilities [25, 41];
- older and younger players:
  (1) include easy to master physical and tactile controls, because they elicit higher degrees of involvement for both generations, tend to be shorter (attractive for older players) and feature lighthearted themes and characters (attractive for younger players) [36];
  (2) make use of enactive interaction that avoids relying on specific knowledge of how to operate digital games [36, 37].

After having presented the characteristics of intergenerational relations, play and gaming, including implications for game designers, in the next sections we move on to the central theme of our article: the *co*-design of intergenerational digital games.

4   Method State-of-the-Art Literature Review

As our goal is to review empirical studies to get insight into the dynamics of setting up and conducting the co-design of an intergenerational digital game. The focus is on intergenerational game activities in which *game designers collaborated with younger and older players to get insight into their experiences of gaming* together to optimize the design process. So, the goal is not to provide a basis for evidence-informed policymaking and practice, and for this reason we decided against conducting a systematic literature review, opting instead for state-of-the art literature review, including full papers of empirical studies published until the end of 2017, with this focus. We started with the review by Costa and Veloso ([7], and using the snowball method [42], we finally included eight empirical studies.

Please note that we did not include Knudtzon et al. [43] in our state-of-the art literature review as the term 'intergenerational' in their title 'Starting an intergenerational technology design team: a case study', referred to children and game designers and not to older players. Neither did we include Van den Abeele and De Schutter [44] as this publication was not a full paper but a one page description of a design research project based on a framework (called P-III) to facilitate intergenerational play between grandparents and grandchildren (see also a comparable research project, called e-Treasureproject by the same researchers, aiming at developing a digital game by means of a player-centered design process, including seniors and youngsters from the beginning until the end - https://iiw.kuleuven.be/onderzoek/emedia/projects/etreasure).

4.1   The Included Empirical Studies

As explained in Sect. 4, eight articles on the co-design of intergenerational digital games were retrieved from the literature (see Table 1), and discussed in terms of study design, aims and populations, theoretical/methodological approach or design rationales, and the recommendations given for the co-design of intergenerational digital games (see Table 1).

Table 1. Co-designing intergenerational digital games

Article	Study design	Study aim(s)	Study population	Theoretical/methodological approach or design rationales	Recommendations for the co-design of intergenerational digital games
1. Al Mahmud et al. [45]	3 case studies: 1: designing and testing with children, 2: designing and testing with older adults, 3. testing both digital games with both user groups	"(...) we investigated various options for enhancing the gaming experience through augmented tabletop games for children and older adults" (p. 147)	Children aged 7–11 and older adults aged 65–73. Both groups were studied separately and together.	Qualitative and quantitative user test of the digital game Tangible (social) interaction was the starting point for the development of the digital game. Augmented tabletop gaming was found to be suitable by the researchers	• Maximize social interaction. For instance, by including guessing, cooperation, and competition • Create uncertainty within the digital game, such as hidden resources, to introduce new challenges • Theme and game elements should attract children • Maintain a balance between social interaction and immersion • Make sure the digital game is easily followed by both user groups, for instance by gradually introducing technology and use simple game rules • Game rules must encourage cooperation • Keep in mind the preferences of children, rather than the elderly

(continued)

Table 1. (*continued*)

Article	Study design	Study aim(s)	Study population	Theoretical/methodological approach or design rationales	Recommendations for the co-design of intergenerational digital games
2. Derboven et al. [46]	Case study: User tests of an intergenerational digital game	"(…) explore how direct video communication in an inter-generational game influences game experience" (p. 57)	15 couples of one senior (60 or older) and his/her (grand)-child (15 or older) participated in user tests	Qualitative and quantitative user test of the digital game (i.e. evaluation/proto-typing) Observations of older people to understand the kind of digital games usually played (i.e. contextual inquiry) Starting point was that the digital game had to include a social aspect/social interaction	• Use video chat functionality • Moving through game phases should occur simultaneously for all players • Include an exercise mode, preferably in such a way that older and younger players can explore the digital game together • All players should have to opportunity to 'take the lead' • Digital games should have the possibility to play both with and without extra communication functionality
3. Khoo et al. [23]	Case study: a description of the digital game (design) and user tests	"[Highlighting] the general methodologies for designing computer games for the elderly." (p. 15)	5 university employees aged 45–60, and 5 students aged 16–20	"General methodologies followed for designing computer related games for elderly [were followed]." (p. 5) (e.g. assessing how well elderly understand modern technologies, finding out which digital games are currently available, and conducting user studies with target population) Starting points for the digital game included four different aspects: social gaming, physical gaming, a cognitive aspect, and a psychological aspect	• Recommendations for the *Age Invaders* game only
4. Khoo et al. [24]	Case study: a description of the digital game (design)	"This paper presents steps for designing an inter-generational family entertainment system which focuses on physical and social inter-actions using a mixed reality floor system." (p. 76)	User studies: 49 students and 20 persons from the target groups (10 persons 60-80 and 10 children 10–12)	A User-Centered design approach was followed, including: - problem identification - problem exploration (e.g. observation of or focus groups with target groups) - setting design goals - identifying design requirements for prototype of the digital game, including identification of financial resource, time constraints and user needs, and researching the context/setting of use - design idea generation (e.g. brainstorm sessions) - usability studies Design goals: (physical and tangible interaction) Social interaction	• Recommendations for the *Age Invaders* game only

(*continued*)

Table 1. (*continued*)

Article	Study design	Study aim(s)	Study population	Theoretical/methodological approach or design rationales	Recommendations for the co-design of intergenerational digital games
5. Rice et al. [47]	Case study on the co-design of an intergenerational digital game	To explore interests, motivations, and design ideas for digital game applications among young, old, and game designers	50 participants aged 15–21 and 55–74	Three design workshops with 2 to 4 persons within own and mixed age groups performing several activities (e.g. "100 pictures") A co-design approach was applied. Co-design methods and activities were borrowed from [42], among others	• Take advantage of differences in ability between older adults and young persons (e.g. life-skills and experiences, physiological abilities) • Use relevant user group expertise (comparable to previous recommendation); e.g., children/younger adults could support older adults in understanding the digital game, older adults could pass on positive life experiences • Make sure there is long-term motivational interest in the digital game: intergenerational digital games require both complexity and challenge • Explore opportunities within public spaces for community engagement • Recognize local challenges and opportunities for intergenerational digital games
6. Romero and Ouellet [13]	Intergenerational digital game design workshops	Analyzing "the scaffolding process of inter-generational game design activities as a s an instructional learning strategy." (p. 74)	34 18 to 80 years old participants	Participatory activities involving older and younger participants to scaffold a digital game creation process (by using a storyboard and the visual programming tool Scratch (http://scratch.mit.edu). Approach characterized by the fact that "... the final game product is not the objective, but an intergen-erational facilitator." (p. 80)	• "A highly guided approach to scaffold the intergenerational game creation workshop was a key element for its successful development." (p. 80)
7. Vanden Abeele and De Schutter [37]	Case study on the design and user evaluation of existing digital games and user evaluation of the developed mini-game	To verify the design rationales and test the inter-generational digital game	User-evaluation of existing mini-games: 5 pairs of a senior and a younger adult (3 of the pairs had a grand-parent-grandchild relationship, 2 pairs were acquaintances) User-evaluation of developed mini-game: 7 seniors (and one 45-year-old stand-in) and 8 younger adults	Qualitative user test of the developed digital game (i.e. evaluation/proto-typing) and comparable existing digital games Ethnographically inspired research The digital game was developed applying a player-centered design process, but the authors report that "the discussion of the entire player-centered design process is beyond the scope of this paper" (p. 426) Three design rationales were reported. These were produced by the design team and supported by theory	• No general recommendations for co-design of intergenerational digital games mentioned

(*continued*)

Table 1. (*continued*)

Article	Study design	Study aim(s)	Study population	Theoretical/methodological approach or design rationales	Recommendations for the co-design of intergenerational digital games
8. Xie et al. [48]	Case study on the design and user evaluation of existing digital games and user evaluation of the developed mini-game	To understand how older adults and children can work together to co-design technology and to determine what (new) co-design methods are needed	6 older adults aged 68–81 and 7 children aged 6–9 who did not know each other	Co-design activities took place in several stages and included among other, distributed design sessions, sticky note ideas, and brainstorming. One of the methods was called "co-design of co-design" (p. 16) by the authors. A co-design approach was applied. One of the study aims was to "revise and improve methods with co-design partners." (p. 415)	• Children and older adults need time together to start the collaboration and understand each other's needs, but also time apart to advance the collaboration in a less stressful environment • Work primarily in small groups when children and older adults are together • It is important to build and elaborate upon the (shared) ideas of children and older adults • Spend time on a group discussion with older adults only so they can express their needs and wishes • Use art supplies for children • Use sticky notes for children and older adults to share ideas

4.2   Discussion of the Empirical Studies

Although the studies differed substantially as regards study design, aims and populations, all dealt with an empirical study on the co-design of (newly developed) intergenerational digital games involving users form different generations. Most authors reported on one or more case studies and focused on user tests of newly developed intergenerational digital games. Of the eight studies in our state-of the-art literature review, Rice et al. [47] and Xie et al. [48] were the ones that focused most on the co-design process of intergenerational digital games.

Xie et al. [48] explicitly aimed to explore co-design methods that could be employed to involve older adults and children in the use of technologies in intergenerational interaction. This study was specifically set up to develop co-design methods for technology use in an intergenerational context. The authors call one particular activity within their design process 'co-design of the co-design methods', through which important insights were gained as regards setting up and conducting the co-design of an intergenerational digital game. The most pivotal recommendation in this study was that intergenerational collaboration, according to these authors, could best take place in a distributed fashion. Co-located collaboration is not essential; instead, older and younger adults should spend time together (to understand the needs and preferences of each other) as well as apart (to elaborate on ideas). Other recommendations for co-design were to work in small groups, to use art supplies with children, and to make use of sticky notes for both target groups (i.e. older adults and children) to share ideas. An important point to keep in mind about this study is that the older adults and children had never met before taking part in the study. Hence, the extent to which the findings can be generalized to co-design processes with older adults and their (grand) children is unclear.

Rice et al. [47] focused on "the roles games have in fostering relations with strangers, and the extent they differ to a family context" (p. 377). They conducted three workshops with 50 participants, who took part in a range of design activities intended to create an intergenerational digital game. They analyzed videotaped workshop sessions and materials (e.g. game concepts, storyboards) created by the participants. They recommended "to address possible disparities in skill sets, designers should build on the intrinsic qualities and experiences of targeted age groups (p. 376)". For a discussion of age-related differences between younger and older individuals, we refer to Sect. 3.

Although the design process was not the main focus of the other studies, these nevertheless also provided useful insights for designers aiming to set up and conduct the co-design of an intergenerational digital game. Some of the studies used a qualitative approach (#5, 6, 7 and 8), other studies used a mix of qualitative and quantitative users' tests (#1, 2, 3 and 4). The co-design characteristics most often reported were user observations and interviews with user groups, to understand the type of game they play, and user tests of prototype games that have been developed. Al Mahmud et al. [45] for instance, reported that their game design started with an observation of the target groups in their natural environment. These activities can be regarded as contextual inquiries and are obviously part of a player-centered design process [17]. The evaluation of a prototype of the game was part of the design process in several studies (#1, 2, 3, 4 and 8). This method occurs in the player-centered design process as well, preferably following each of the three design phases, i.e., after the analysis phase, design phase, and development phase) [17]. In most empirical studies the design processes were difficult to reconstruct from the information available in the articles and as a result and hard to evaluate in the light of the predetermined criteria. By contrast, [23, 24] published a series of articles on the design process of *Age Invaders*, in which low-fidelity prototypes were followed by higher fidelity prototypes. For example, [23] presented the results of a user study with a preliminary prototype, while in their later article [24], they describe the use of a more advanced prototype for this purpose.

None of the eight articles alluded to the use of theories in the co-design process, nor were any theories, such as the Self-Determination Theory [49, 50], the Uses and Gratifications Theory [51–53] and the Domestication Theory [54, 55] used as a theoretical frame work for co-design. Design methodologies were barely mentioned or only implicitly touched on. Study findings and recommendations were highly dependent on how the (co-)design had been conducted. Exploiting the differences in skills and abilities of both user groups (by studies #2, 4, 5 and 8) were recommendations for the design of intergenerational digital games that emerged a couple of times.

5   Conclusions

Our state-of-the-art literature review clearly showed that empirical studies providing insight into the dynamics of setting up and conducting the co-design of intergenerational digital games are scarce. While the eight studies we discussed critically in our state-of-the-art literature review differed with regard to study design, aims and populations, they all focused on an empirical study on the co-design of intergenerational digital games, or on user tests of such newly developed games. The following Table shows which lessons can be drawn from our state-of-the-art literature review (Table 2).

Table 2. Recommendations for the co-design of intergenerational digital games

• Allow children and older adults to spend time together to start the collaboration and understand each other's needs, but let them also have time apart to advance the collaboration in a less stressful environment. • Work primarily in small groups when children and older adults are together. • Build and elaborate upon the (shared) ideas of children and older adults. • Use relevant user group expertise (e.g., children/younger adults could support older adults in understanding the game, older adults could pass on positive life experiences). • Make sure that the game is easily followed by both user groups (e.g. by gradually introducing technology and use simple game rules). • Moving through game phases should occur simultaneously for all players, use relevant user group expertise (e.g., children/younger adults could support older adults in understanding the game, older adults could pass on positive life experiences). • Make sure there is long-term motivational interest: intergenerational digital games require both complexity and challenge.

We conclude that for setting up and conducting the co-design of intergenerational digital games distributed collaboration is important: children and older adults should spend time together to start the collaboration and to understand one another's needs, but also time apart to advance the collaboration in a less stressful environment, work in small groups, and pay attention to and make use of differences in their skills (including age-related differences). To sum up, we recommend "designing with, rather than for participants ..." ([47], p. 369).

Acknowledgements. This research was supported by the Focus Area Game Research at Utrecht University and the paper was written within the project "Persuasive Gaming in Context. From theory-based design to validation and back" funded by the Netherlands Organization for Scientific Research (NWO). See www.persuasivegaming.nl.

References

1. Davis, H., Vetere, F., Francis, P., Gibbs, M., Howard, S.: "I wish we could get together": exploring intergenerational play across a distance via a 'Magic Box'. J. Intergener. Relat. **6** (2), 191–210 (2008)
2. Lloyd, J.: The State of Intergenerational Relations Today. International Longevity Centre, London (2008)
3. Rice, M., Yau, L.J., Ong, J., Wan, M., Ng, J.: Intergenerational gameplay: evaluating social interaction between younger and older players. In: CHI 2012 Extended Abstracts on Human Factors in Computing Systems, pp. 2333–2338. ACM (2012)
4. Huizinga, J.: Homo Ludens: A Proeve eener bepaling van het spel-element der cultuur. [Homo Ludens: A Study of the Play Element in Culture]. Amsterdam University Press, Amsterdam (1938) (2008)
5. Bogost, I.: Persuasive Games: The Expressive Power of Video Games. MIT Press, Cambridge (2007)
6. Juul, J.: A Casual Revolution: Reinventing Video Games and their Players. MIT Press, Cambridge (2012)
7. Costa, L., Veloso, A.: Being (Grand) Players: Review of Digital Games and their Potential to Enhance Intergenerational Interactions. J. Intergener. Relat. **14**(1), 43–59 (2016)
8. Zhang, F., Kaufman, D.: A review of intergenerational play for facilitating interactions and learning. Gerontechnology **14**(3), 127–138 (2016)
9. De la Hera, T., Paz Aléncar, A.: Collaborative digital games as mediation tool to foster intercultural integration in primary Dutch schools. eLearn. Pap. **43**, 13–23 (2015)
10. Stewart, J., et al.: The potential of digital games for empowerment and social inclusion of groups at risk of social and economic exclusion: evidence and opportunity for policy. Joint Research Centre, European Commission (2013)
11. Loos, E.F.: Designing meaningful intergenerational digital games. In: Proceedings of the International Conference on Communication, Media, Technology and Design, Istanbul, 24–26 April 2014, pp. 46–51 (2014)
12. Romero, M.: Intergenerational learning, life narratives and games. In: Proceedings of the SGISS 2015, vol. 1. Université Laval, Centre de recherche et d'intervention sur la réussite scolaire, Québec (2015)
13. Romero, M., Ouellet, H.: Scaffolding digital game design activities grouping older adults, younger adults and teens. In: Zhou, J., Salvendy, G. (eds.) ITAP 2016. LNCS, vol. 9754, pp. 74–81. Springer, Cham (2016). https://doi.org/10.1007/978-3-319-39943-0_8
14. DeSmet, A., Thompson, D., Baranowski, T., Palmeira, A., Verloigne, M., De Bourdeaudhuij, I.: Is participatory design associated with the effectiveness of serious digital games for healthy lifestyle promotion? A meta-analysis. J. Med. Internet Res. **18**(4), e94 (2016)
15. Salen, K., Zimmerman, E.: Rules of Play: Fundamentals of Game Design. MIT Press, Cambridge (2003)
16. De Schutter, B., Vanden Abeele, V.: Meaningful play in elderly life. In: Paper Presented at the 58th Annual Conference of the International Communication Association "Communicating for Social Impact", Montreal, Quebec, Canada (2008)
17. Vanden Abeele, V., De Schutter, B., Annema, J.H., Husson, J., Desmet, S., Geerts, D.: Van co-design tot playtest: een leidraad voor een player-centered design process. KU Leuven, e-Media Lab van Groep T en het Centrum voor User Experience Onderzoek, Leuven (2009)
18. Uhlenberg, P.: Integration of old and young. Gerontol. **40**(3), 276–279 (2000)
19. De la Hera, T., Loos, E.F., Simons, M., Blom, J.: Benefits and factors influencing the design of intergenerational digital games: a systematic literature review. Societies **7**(3), 18 (2017)

20. Nguyen, H.T., Tapanainen, T., Theng, Y.L., Lundberg, S., Luimula, M.: Fostering communication between the Elderly and the Youth with social games. In: Proceedings of the Pacific Asia Conference on Information Systems (PACIS) (2015)
21. Antonucci, T.C., Jackson, J.S., Biggs, S.: Intergenerational relations: theory, research, and policy. J. Soc. Issues **63**(4), 679–693 (2007)
22. Tomlin, A.M.: Grandparents' influences on grandchildren. In: Szinovacz, M. (ed.), Handbook on Grandparenthood, pp. 159–170. Greenwood Publishing Group Santa Barbara, California, U.S. Census Bureau (2016). An Aging World: 2015 - International Population Reports (1998)
23. Khoo, E.T., Cheok, A.D., Nguyen, T.H.D., Pan, Z.: Age invaders: social and physical intergenerational mixed reality family entertainment. Virtual Reality **12**(1), 3–16 (2008)
24. Khoo, E.T., Merritt, T., Cheok, A.D.: Designing physical and social intergenerational family entertainment. Interact. Comput. **21**(1), 76–87 (2009)
25. Vetere, F., Davis, H., Gibbs, M., Howard, S.: The magic box and collage: responding to the challenge of distributed intergenerational play. Int. J. Hum.-Comput. Stud. **67**(2), 165–178 (2009)
26. Ermi, L., Mäyrä, F.: Player-centred game design: experiences in using scenario study to inform mobile game design. Game Stud. **5**(1), 1–10 (2005)
27. Oudshoorn, N., Rommes, E., Stienstra, M.: Configuring the user as everybody: gender and design cultures in information and communication technologies. Sci. Technol. Hum. Values **29**(1), 30–63 (2004)
28. Akrich, M.: User representations: practices, methods and sociology. In: Managing Technology in Society. The Approach of Constructive Technology Assessment, pp. 167–184. Pinter, London (1995)
29. Oudshoorn, N., Pinch, T.: How Users Matter: the Co-construction of Users and Technology (Inside Technology). MIT Press, Cambridge (2003)
30. Pearce, C.: The truth about baby boomer gamers a study of over-forty computer game players. Games Cult. **3**(2), 142–174 (2008)
31. Nap, H., Kort, Y., IJsselsteijn, W.: Senior gamers: preferences, motivations and needs. Gerontechnology **8**(4), 247–262 (2009)
32. Schultheiss, D.: Entertainment for retirement?: Silvergamers and the internet. Pub. Commun. Rev. **2**(2), 62–71 (2012)
33. Osmanovic, S., Pecchioni, L.: Family matters: the role of intergenerational gameplay in successful aging. In: Zhou, J., Salvendy, G. (eds.) ITAP 2016. LNCS, vol. 9755, pp. 352–363. Springer, Cham (2016). https://doi.org/10.1007/978-3-319-39949-2_34
34. Wen, J., Kow, Y.M., Chen, Y.: Online games and family ties: influences of social networking game on family relationship. In: Campos, P., Graham, N., Jorge, J., Nunes, N., Palanque, P., Winckler, M. (eds.) INTERACT 2011. LNCS, vol. 6948, pp. 250–264. Springer, Heidelberg (2011). https://doi.org/10.1007/978-3-642-23765-2_18
35. Gajadhar, B.J., Nap, H., Kort, Y., IJsselsteijn, W.: Out of sight, out of mind: co-player effects on seniors' player experience. In: Proceedings of the 3rd International Conference on Fun and Games, Fun and Games 2010, pp. 74–83. ACM (2010)
36. Chiong, C.: Can video games promote intergenerational play & literacy learning? In: The Joan Ganz Cooney Center at Sesame Workshop (2009)
37. Vanden Abeele, V., De Schutter, B.: Designing intergenerational play via enactive interaction, competition and acceleration. Pers. Ubiquit. Comput. **14**(5), 425–433 (2010)
38. IJsselsteijn, W.A., Nap H.H., de Kort, Y.A.W, et al.: Digital game design for elderly users. In: Proceedings of the 2007 Conference on Future Play, Toronto, ON, Canada, 14 November 2007, pp. 17–22 (2007). http://dl.acm.org/citation.cfm?id=1328206

39. Charness, N., Jastrzembki, T.S.: Gerontechnology. In: Saariluoma, P., Somäki, H. (eds.) Future Interaction Design II, pp. 1–30. Springer, London (2009). https://doi.org/10.1007/978-1-84800-385-9_1

40. Vasconcelos, A., Silva, P. A., Caseiro, J., Nunes, F., Teixeira, L.F.: Designing tablet-based games for seniors: the example of CogniPlay, a cognitive gaming platform. In: Proceedings of the 4th International Conference on Fun and Games (FnG 2012), pp. 1–10. ACM, New York (2012)

41. Martínez, A.I.G., Morán, A.L., Gámez, E.H.C.: Towards a taxonomy of factors implicated in children-elderly interaction when using entertainment technology. In: Proceedings of the 4th Mexican Conference on Human-Computer Interaction 2012, pp. 51–54. ACM (2012)

42. Ridley, D.: The Literature Review: A Step-by-Step Guide for Students. Sage, Los Angeles (2012)

43. Knudtzon, K., et al.: Starting an intergenerational technology design team: a case study. In: Proceedings of the 2003 Conference on Interaction Design and Children, pp. 51–58. ACM (2003)

44. Van den Abeele, V., De Schutter, B.: Blast of the past: applying the P-III framework. Gerontology 13(2), 163 (2014)

45. Al Mahmud, A., Mubin, O., Shahid, S., Martens, J.B.: Designing social games for children and older adults: two related case studies. Entertain. Comput. 1(3), 147–156 (2010). http://www.sciencedirect.com/science/article/pii/S1875952110000066

46. Derboven, J., Van Gils, M., De Grooff, D.: Designing for collaboration: a study in intergenerational social game design. Univ. Access Inf. Soc. 11(1), 57–65 (2012)

47. Rice, M., Cheong, Y.L., Ng, J., Chua, P.H., Theng, Y.L.: Co-creating games through intergenerational design workshops. In: Proceedings of the Designing Interactive Systems Conference, pp. 368–377. ACM (2012)

48. Xie, B., et al.: Connecting generations: developing co-design methods for older adults and children. Behav. Inf. Technol. 31(4), 413–423 (2012)

49. Ryan, R.M., Deci, E.L.: Intrinsic and extrinsic motivations: classic definitions and new directions. Contemp. Educ. Psychol. 25(1), 54–67 (2000)

50. Ryan, R.M., Rigby, C.S., Przybylski, A.: The motivational pull of video games: a self-determination theory approach. Motiv. Emot. 30(4), 344–360 (2006)

51. Ruggiero, T.E.: Uses and gratifications theory in the 21st century. Mass Commun. Soc. 3(1), 3–37 (2000)

52. Sherry, J.L., Lucas, K., Greenberg, B.S., Lachlan, K.: Video game uses and gratifications as predictors of use and game preferences. In: Vorderer, P., Bryant, J. (eds.) Playing Video Games - Motives, Responses, and Consequences, pp. 213–224. Lawrence Erlbaum Associates, London (2006)

53. De Schutter, B.: Never too old to play: the appeal of digital games to an older audience. Games Cult. 6, 155–770 (2011)

54. Haddon, L.: Empirical studies using the domestication framework. In: Berker, T., Hartmann, M., Punie, Y., Ward, K. (eds.) Domestication of Media and Technologies, pp. 103–122. Open University Press, Maidenhead (2005)

55. De Schutter, B., Brown, J.A., Van den Abeele, V.: The domestication of digital games in the lives of older adults. New Media Soc. 17(7), 1170–1186 (2015)

The *Digital Drawer:* A Crowd-Sourced, Curated, Digital Archive Preserving History and Memory

Scott L. Robertson[1]([✉]), Laura Levy[1]([✉]), Amelia Lambeth[1]([✉]),
and Jesse P. Karlsberg[2]

[1] Interactive Media Technology Center (IMTC),
Institute for People and Technology (IPaT),
Georgia Institute of Technology, Atlanta, GA 30308, USA
{scott,laura,amy}@imtc.gatech.edu
[2] Emory Center for Digital Scholarship, Atlanta, GA 30322, USA
jesse.p.karlsberg@emory.edu

Abstract. While many digital asset management platforms and digital libraries exist, most have been designed for technically savvy users and not the older adults who are a key audience for our *Digital Drawer* platform. In the domain of digital humanities collections, our project is significant in that we are utilizing a participatory design (PD) process wherein all of the stakeholders and potential users of a system are actively involved in the design process to help insure the result meets their needs and is usable. This paper presents a case study on the PD process and the challenges of designing a crowd-sourced media and metadata submission tool for the Historic Rural Churches of Georgia to accommodate older adult users with low technical savvy and disabilities. We report on the PD process to design the user interface and user experience (UI/UX) for this user demographic, present conclusions and plans for future work.

Keywords: Access to education and learning · Design for aging ·
Design for all best practice · Design for all methods · Techniques and tools ·
Evaluation of accessibility · Usability · User experience

1 Introduction

The *Digital Drawer* partnership is a rare collaborative partnership formed to pilot a method of gathering, curating and disseminating crowd-sourced community memory. This effort of the Georgia state library system, universities, humanities and non-profit organizations is testing an online concept through a program permitting Georgians to upload their carefully preserved documents, photographs, images of artifacts and oral memories of historic churches that were the foundation of their community life. The *Digital Drawer* platform, being developed by the Georgia Institute of Technology's Interactive Media Technology Center (IMTC), in collaboration with Emory University's Center for Digital Scholarship (ECDS) and the Historic Rural Churches of Georgia (HRCGA), is unique in that it will be designed to accommodate the limited technical capacity of an anticipated older demographic with disabilities. The platform

© Springer Nature Switzerland AG 2019
J. Zhou and G. Salvendy (Eds.): HCII 2019, LNCS 11592, pp. 70–83, 2019.
https://doi.org/10.1007/978-3-030-22012-9_6

will be a cloud-hosted media and metadata repository with data sharing service available to the public through their public libraries or partner websites.

The goal of the *Digital Drawer* partnership is to create a methodology for gathering, curating and disseminating these crowd-sourced collections of rural church histories, establishing a digital community memory. We intend for the *Digital Drawer* to become an international, open-source platform to be used by humanities scholars and the general public to access collections of these historical and often lost voices in our past.

While many digital asset management (DAM) platforms and publicly accessible digital libraries exist, most have been designed for technically savvy users (to the extent that these systems were designed with the involvement of end-users) and not the older adults who are a key audience for our *Digital Drawer* platform. In the domain of digital humanities collections, our project is significant in that we are utilizing a participatory design (PD) process wherein all of the stakeholders and potential users of a system are actively involved in the design process to help insure the result meets their needs and is usable.

We have engaged our target user community in a series of participatory design activities, including focus groups, UI prototyping interviews and collaborative design exercises.

This paper presents a case study on the participatory design process and the challenges of designing a public-facing media and metadata submission tool for our identified user population. We report on both the PD process and activities as well as our initial findings and conclusions.

Our findings are helping to inform a preliminary report on design guidelines for the public-facing *Digital Drawer* web application that is uniquely innovative in its universal approach to accessibility, accommodating the needs of this older audience. Having recently secured funding from the National Endowment for the Humanities (NEH) to design, implement and deploy the *Digital Drawer*, we plan to continue to employ the PD approach, involving all stakeholders from end-users to public library personnel and humanities researchers, as we refine the UI/UX design and user requirements and implement the *Digital Drawer* platform. Our goal is to develop a platform, including a publicly accessible API and data sharing service, upon which future applications, data visualizations and collection sharing can be developed. We plan to open source the API and documentation to encourage further development of the *Digital Drawer* platform and its use in other domains.

1.1   History and Cultural Importance of the Project

Religion has played an important role in forming America and from its first settlements, rural churches formed the vital core of community life in America [1]. Many of the churches that once functioned as centers of rural life are today physically disintegrating. As congregations disappear and church structures are abandoned, local historical memory of communities that date back to the beginnings of the European occupation of North America are also endangered. In fact, society may lose many of these records that generations before us preserved, but are now at risk.

Churches are often key sites for examining several important strands in American history. In Georgia, rural churches document the settlement of the state in the wake of the forced removal of Native Americans. Churches tell stories of the state's racial history in the post-Civil War era through the long Civil Rights Movement, and they document the rise and fall of population centers as the state's political economy shifted. Church records, replete with names, dates, and descriptions of events large and small, contain information useful in understanding the state's history from the bottom up. Rural churches, scattered across often resource-poor sections of the state, are significant yet under-represented sites preserving components of this history.

1.2   Historic Rural Churches of Georgia

Saving this important part of American history is the mission of Historic Rural Churches of Georgia (HRCGA) [2]. Historic Rural Churches of Georgia was founded in 2012 by Sonny Seals and George Hart with a mission to research, document, and ultimately preserve historic rural churches across Georgia. They initially created a pictorial archive of endangered churches and associated history around Georgia that is featured on their website, launched in 2013 (see Fig. 1). With over 50,000 followers on Facebook, over 30,000 monthly visitors to the website and a Georgia Public Television show broadcast in the Fall of 2018, HRCGA engages a large public audience interested in and involved with Georgia's historic rural churches. Visitor and follower data from HRCGA's web site and social media pages reveals that their primary demographic is older women (65+) living in rural areas of the state.

Friendship Baptist

SUMTER COUNTY | ORG 1839 | PHOTOGRAPHY BY STEVE ROBINSON

Friendship Baptist, built in 1857 and located in northwestern Sumter County, is the oldest standing church in the county. Much of the history of the church would be lost if not for the efforts of Jack F. Cox, of Americus, and Mrs. Scott Hart, of Schley County. Mrs. Hart preserved the original

Fig. 1. Church detail page from hrcga.org.

A key component of preserving these vitally important structures is collecting and disseminating information about their history. The HRCGA's *Digital Drawer* was conceived as a platform and editorial structure to crowd-source the collection of such documents and it has the potential to build an archive of significant historical importance while providing a model to extend such work beyond the state of Georgia. Crowd-sourcing documents also helps build community around historic structures in need of preservation, providing an extensible model for such work. The Digital Drawer platform is being designed to better serve HRCGA's identified primary demographic (elderly, female, rural).

2 Designing the User Experience for Older Adults

Recent survey data shows that technology adoption is steadily rising among older adults, including adults 65 and older, but this population still has lower than average technical savvy and a relatively higher incidence of disabilities, attributes that should inform user interface/user experience (UI/UX) design of apps and web sites [3].

There have been many efforts to improve the accessibility and usability of web sites and web apps, including the development of accessibility guidelines for web content (i.e. the WAI's WCAG 2.1) [4, 5] and authoring tools [6]. The W3C's WAI-AGE project, in fact, concluded that existing web accessibility guidelines such as WCAG 2.0 adequately address the accessibility needs of older web users [7]. Aside from explicit adherence to accessibility guidelines, other possible indirect contributors to improving accessibility include new browser capabilities and page layout technologies, wide application of search engine optimization (SEO) techniques and an increasing need to create cross-device web designs [8].

It is important to adhere to accessibility guidelines when designing and building web pages and apps, especially for older adult users, but as some researchers point out, relying on guidelines alone to improve the accessibility of web sites and apps for older users and users with disabilities doesn't necessarily also result in better usability of those sites and apps [9, 10]. Guidelines for designing systems for older adults often recommend simplifying the graphical UI of a system, increasing the size and visual contrast of fonts and icons to increase accessibility, but it is also important to address the ease-of-use of such systems by employing other techniques such as using a system navigation style which is more familiar to older adults [11]. Castilla et al. (2016) found that when designing software user interfaces for older adults, it is often beneficial to leverage their previous experience with analog media which presents information in a linear format (i.e. books, video) [11]. Their experiments comparing perceived ease-of use, satisfaction and task performance on a web mail application with participants aged 60 or older showed a clear preference for a simplified, linear navigation version of the UI compared with a hypertextual version (i.e. Gmail).

2.1 *Digital Drawer* User Requirements Gathering

In designing the UI and UX of the Digital Drawer content submission web app, we take a user-centered design approach with an emphasis on maximizing usability for our target user demographic. We employ a participatory design (PD) process wherein all of the stakeholders and potential users of a system are actively involved in the design process to help insure the result meets their needs and is usable.

As part of our PD approach, we conducted user requirements gathering activities with members of our target user demographic, expanded to include public library personnel who could provide insights into what typical technology troubles that library patrons experience when using similar tools and how such a tool could be used by the library system.

We conducted two focus groups at the Waycross Public Library in Waycross, Georgia on Thursday May 11, 2017. The first focus group included four library personnel (3 women, 1 man) and the second group for content researchers (i.e. members of the general public who have an interest in historic rural churches, genealogy, Georgia and American history, etc.) included five participants (3 women, 2 men). Overall, participants were enthusiastic about a proposed web-based online content submission system for the facilitation of research on historic rural churches in Georgia. Library personnel made suggestions on the design and feasibility of a dedicated kiosk within a library for content submitters. Researchers described their research methods, use of and familiarity with technology, and design recommendations for the online system.

Focus Group 1 - Library Personnel: Questions for this focus group were designed to assess three main topics: (1) current process in assisting library patrons with technology, (2) acceptance of proposed dedicated space for content submission system, and (3) advice on design of this system based on their experience and expertise.

Currently, these library personnel spend a significant portion of their daily duties assisting library visitors with using computers. Requests include basic computer help (e.g. starting the machine, using a mouse or web browser) and setting up online profiles for banking systems and social media. For a dedicated machine set up for historic rural church content submission, our participants had the following advice:

- If visitors anticipate needing help for any stage (e.g. creating a profile, scanning, uploading content), they should schedule a 30 min time slot through the library website so library personnel can make sure they have the human resources available to assist
- Appointments for assistance using the space would need to be limited to a couple of days a week
- Equipment this library would need and does not currently have is a flat bed scanner
- Particular attention to the accessibility design of a system that is W3C compliant is paramount.

These participants suggested capturing oral histories and this library is equipped with high quality audio equipment they purchased for their maker space. They recommended partnering with local high schools to create a program where students would assist and interview content submitters, then edit the captured media to create short projects (e.g. podcasts, videos). This would satisfy the requirement that high school students complete community service hours to graduate while also teaching them how to interview, as well as media capturing and editing skills. Additionally, this would solve the problem of having sufficient human resource hours to assist content creators while resulting in finished content that can be posted online for the public.

Focus Group 2 - Content Submitters and Researchers: Questions for this focus group were focused on understanding the (1) motivations, (2) research process, and (3) technology familiarity of the demographic involved in researching and submitting information on historic rural churches.

In this group, two were current content submitters/researchers and two were interested in doing so, but had experience with similar projects (e.g. graves). All participants were enthused at the prospect of having a dedicated online system to assist in the research and aggregation of information on Georgia's historic rural churches. Their current research process involves exploring an area by car or on foot, investigating if there is a written history associated with that church by contacting people nearby or those associated with the congregation (if any), examine names in the nearby cemetery (if there is one), and checking with nearby church phone directories. One experienced researcher takes extensive notes on paper in addition to taking video with a point-and-shoot camera while verbally annotating the features he sees around the site. He later transcribes these notes and supplements photos with more information. The most important tool cited was a point-and-shoot camera, though many in the group were beginning to prefer using their smartphone for picture and video taking. This may be a good opportunity for a mobile version of the site, where participants can upload photos directly from their smartphones.

Each current and interested researcher had favorite interests they preferred to begin their research on and continue the focus on throughout their process. This included architecture/church design ("I like to see if the church has a special reinforced floor, suggesting that dancing was important to services"), age of the building and of attached cemeteries ("I like to look for extremes – what is the oldest gravestone in the cemetery, who lived the shortest length, who the longest?"), and longevity/persistence of the church ("If an old church has been well cared for and is still used, that shows the success of a community").

In this small group, the younger participants (40–55 years) were interested in using technology and fairly adept at common activities such as using a smartphone, web browser, and similar online resources like Ancestry.com. An older participant (90 years old) self-described himself as "old-fashioned" and preferred analog tools, though he noted that a video camera was his most important tool and that he had interest in using a web-based content submission system.

Ideas Generated by the Group for Wants in This System Were:

- Easy, concise site use tutorials
- A "general help button" to be connected with a "buddy" that could help them use the site
- Ability to search preferred localities, such as by county
- Ability to view and search by historical maps
- Upload audio recordings
- Ask questions through a board or forum and communicate with other site members
- Ability to organize local events so that researching members of a community can meet together in person: a picnic or clean-up event, for example

- A feature to flag at-risk churches (e.g. slated for demolition, in need of preservation)
- Individual log-ins and profiles so that users can track their progress researching specific church profiles.

Conclusions: Our initial design hypothesis describing a submission system similar to Ancestry.com appears to be on the right track based on the feedback received from our second focus group. The home landing page should be a simple site allowing for two main functions: (1) search the database for current church profiles by location, name, or other tags (e.g. date, architecture), and (2) create a new profile for a new researched church not currently in the database.

The home page may also have a carousel with a "featured church", links to tutorials (e.g. video how-tos), and information on the project. Each church may have a social media-esque profile, like Facebook, to leverage user familiarity with these systems. For example, the most prominent features of a church profile would be the common name (in addition to "also known as" names), date built (if known), a carousel of user submitted photos, fields for other known and submitted information beneath, and possible a Timeline-esque space for comments and questions by community members.

Some Important Design Considerations of This System Include:

- Many churches have many historical names that have changed throughout the years (based on town name changes, re-dedications, etc.). Each church profile should have an "also known as" field with other common names the church has existed under. This may help prevent duplicate submission, as well.
- Community moderators would be a useful addition. These mods may be locally specific (for example they moderate all submissions within a particular county), can review submissions for accuracy and can remove or consolidate duplicate church profiles.

2.2   Prototyping Interviews

Having established that our target user demographic may have a desire for a research and content contribution tool for users interested in historic rural churches, we next conducted one-on-one design prototyping interviews with several potential *Digital Drawer* users. We constructed a series of UI/UX paper prototype screen variants of a hypothetical *Digital Drawer* search and contribute workflows. Our prototype search and contribute workflow screens were designed to have a linear flow and to require or allow a minimum number of branching decisions or options, a navigation style.

Three older men (ranging from very low to moderate technical savvy) met individually with a Georgia Tech researcher to work through paper prototype use cases and usability requirements of a proposed content submission for the Historical Rural Churches of Georgia (HRCGA) Society. Paper prototyping consisted of proceeding through a hypothetical use case of uploading pictures and text information to an online church profile within the proposed system. The researcher asked questions regarding usability (e.g. what would you expect this button to do?), familiarity (e.g. have you uploaded photos to a website before?), acceptability (e.g. is this a process you would be interested in learning how to do?), and their expert research advice (e.g. do you have recommendations for the functioning of a system like this?).

Mockups of the proposed system were created and provided by Amy Lambeth, IMTC's graphic designer. The proposed system is modeled after popular content submission procedures championed by social media sites (e.g. Facebook) to leverage user experience and knowledge of these functions. Over the course of 1 h through a participatory design process, a Georgia Tech researcher led each participant through a hypothetical use case of uploading photo and text to an existing church's profile.

Searching for a Church: In this proposed use case, a user possessing information (e.g. pictures) on a certain church would visit this page to search for the church of interest (see Fig. 2). Our participants greatly enjoyed the textual nature of the search that had them fill in the search terms as blanks within a sentence.

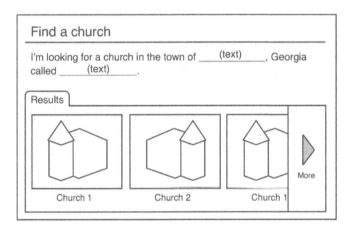

Fig. 2. Searching for a church screen

For users who are more intimidated by technology appreciated that this search function operated within a complete sentence so there was no confusion for what terms to insert. Our participants were familiar with the picture carousel design and understood that their search term results would scroll horizontally.

Selecting the Target Church: Figure 3 represents a search screen with supplementary church profile information, like a map. Our participants were enthused about the map, particularly if it were a Google Maps display, which most participants were already familiar. They cited this was helpful in planning daytrips to churches in their area, knowing if they could get gas or food nearby, and studying the satellite imagery to understand the road terrain and nearby natural features (e.g. forests, rivers). The prominence of the church image, name, and map were most important to our participants in their understanding if this was the correct church they were searching for.

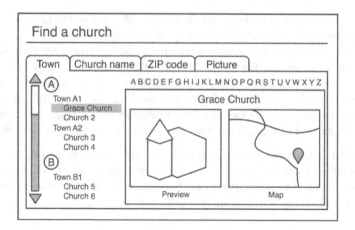

Fig. 3. Selecting the target church screen

Adding Church Information: This screen (see Fig. 4) leverages existing profile display designs utilized by sites like Facebook and Wikipedia. Our participants were most familiar with using Wikipedia for daily research and they appreciated the tab organization and prominent display of summary information beside the main church image. The "add more information" button was more clear to them on its function, as opposed to hyperlink text.

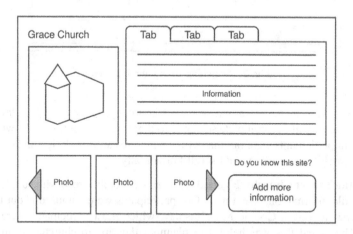

Fig. 4. Church information screen

Uploading Photos: Our participants were not as familiar with a drag-and-drop uploading function, but felt confident they could learn that or use the traditional file system exploring function for the file of interest.

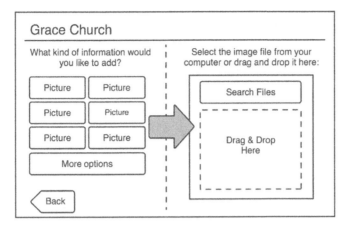

Fig. 5. Uploading photos screen

Adding Metadata to Uploaded Media: Figure 6 shows a screen design wherein users would populate information on the submitted content (here, a picture) such as date of the content, context (i.e. event/occasion), and people. Back, next, and save buttons guide users through the process without overwhelming them with too many actions at once. Participants had no privacy concerns for uploading people's names associated with images, particularly if the image were old and the members of the photo deceased. They felt that including historical names was an important archiving feature to having a complete record.

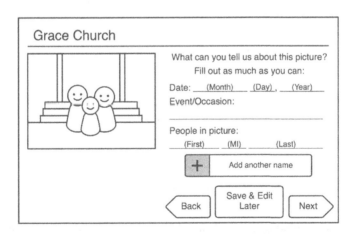

Fig. 6. Adding metadata to uploaded media screen

Adding Tags to Uploaded Media: Our participants were not as familiar with the concept of "tags", but were familiar with keywords. All participants understood and liked that content could be given accompanying tags to help with search for other users. Figure 7 shows a screen design for adding tags/keywords to an uploaded image.

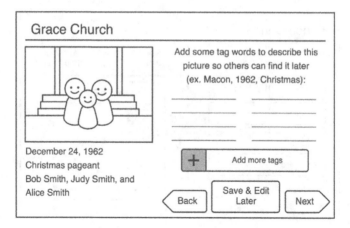

Fig. 7. Adding tags/keywords to uploaded media screen

Adding Freeform Information: Figure 8 shows a screen which allows users to input other information such as stories, anecdotes, and informal notes about the submitted information. Our participants felt this was particularly important to include because so much of this content exists within personal stories that need to be captured.

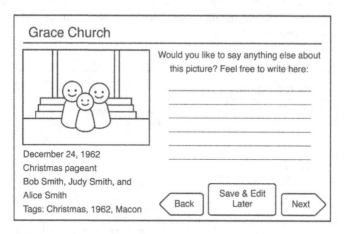

Fig. 8. Adding freeform information screen

Final Review and Submit: Figure 9 shows a screen design where users would review the uploaded content and the information they have provided for final edits before submitting it to the church profile.

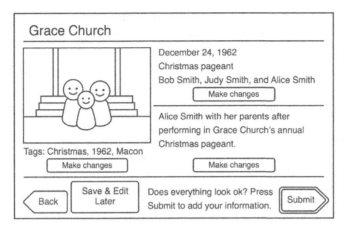

Fig. 9. Final review and submit screen

Design Recommendations: Overall, our initial prototype design seemed appropriate and clear to our three participant users. Incorporating familiar designs provided by Facebook and Wikipedia was useful in supporting their understanding of how such a system would work. All participants said that a system like this exceeds the functionality of other sites, like Find-A-Grave. Even the participant most intimidated by technology said he would be interested in learning to use a system like this, especially if he had some help.

3 Conclusion

Based on our PD activities with target users, we recommend using a conversational style for instructions throughout the site's functions to make the system more intuitive and approachable for this demographic of older, less confident technology users. Gating users through the search, upload and metadata annotation process by dividing the content submission procedure into simple steps, each with only the minimum required choices and decisions, is also recommended. Dividing steps into separate screens also allows more of the display to be magnified and simplified making it easier for older users to operate. This finding, a preference for a simplified, linear navigation style, agrees with results reported by Castilla et al. [11].

Our participants were mostly familiar with how image file types work and how they need to be uploaded. The most complex process by one participant to import photos to his computer was to take a picture with his phone and then fax the photo to his home computer's native faxing application. Our other participants preferred to email the photo taken from their phone and download it to their desktop.

The Google Maps function was particularly important to our participants and they would want to be able to zoom in/out from the church profile page, download or save the location, and complete navigation functions within the church profile tab. Other recommendations for content fields include if the church has a cemetery (active or not), denomination, event calendars, relevant community and newspaper article links, and links to social media pages for that community and church.

4   Future Work

The *Digital Drawer* project is ongoing and at the time of writing we have completed the first two phases of our participatory design process. Beyond the user-facing components of the *Digital Drawer*, the platform will include a web API and back-end database and will be designed to interoperate with other digital libraries and repositories using common metadata schemas (i.e. Dublin Core [12]) and will support 3rd party applications via a public web services API (see Fig. 10).

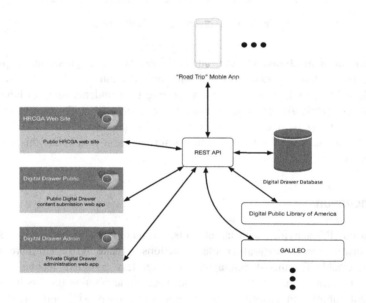

Fig. 10.   Digital drawer platform web services architecture

Future work on the *Digital Drawer* will include implementing a prototype content submission web app based on the sequential screen designs resulting from our UI/UX prototyping interviews. We plan to continue our PD activities by engaging our target users in user testing sessions with the prototype, for example, A/B testing a sequential screen design for the content submission app against a more monolithic design incorporating all of the information and input fields of the sequential design on a single screen (i.e. a design more akin to Gmail, Facebook, Ancestry.com and similar web apps).

References

1. Butler, J., Balmer, R.H., Wacker, G.: Religion in American Life: A Short History. Oxford University Press, Oxford (2011)
2. Historic Rural Churches of Georgia (HRCGA). https://www.hrcga.org. Accessed 22 Jan 2019
3. Anderson, M., Perrin, A.: Tech adoption climbs among older adults. Pew Research Center, 1–22 (2017)
4. Web Accessibility Initiative (WAI). https://www.w3.org/WAI/. Accessed 25 Jan 2019
5. Web Content Accessibility Guidelines (WCAG). https://www.w3.org/WAI/standards-guidelines/wcag/. Accessed 25 Jan 2019
6. Authoring Tool Accessibility Guidelines (ATAG). https://www.w3.org/WAI/standards-guidelines/atag/. Accessed 25 Jan 2019
7. Arch, A., Abou-Zahra, S.: Developing websites for older people: how web content accessibility guidelines (WCAG) 2.0 applies. Web Accessibility Initiative (2010)
8. Richards, J., Montague, K., Hanson, V.: Web accessibility as a side effect, pp. 79–86 (2012)
9. Petrie, H., Kheir, O.: The relationship between accessibility and usability of websites. In: Proceedings of the SIGCHI Conference on Human Factors in Computing Systems, pp. 397–406. ACM (2007)
10. Designing User Interfaces for Older Adults: Myth Busters. https://www.uxmatters.com/mt/archives/2013/10/designing-user-interfaces-for-older-adults-myth-busters.php. Accessed 25 Jan 2019
11. Castilla, D., et al.: Effect of Web navigation style in elderly users. Comput. Hum. Behav. **55**, 909–920 (2016)
12. Dublin Core Metadata Initiative. http://dublincore.org. Accessed 28 Jan 2019

Development of an Age-Appropriate Style Guide Within the Historytelling Project

Torben Volkmann[✉], Amelie Unger, Michael Sengpiel,
and Nicole Jochems

Universität zu Lübeck, Ratzeburger Allee 160, 23562 Lübeck, Germany
{volkmann,unger,sengpiel,jochems}@imis.uni-luebeck.de

Abstract. How can we support the development of age-appropriate system design in a society with new information and communication technologies (ICT) emerging at an ever-increasing rate, making it imperative to consider age-appropriate design to achieve the best possible usability and acceptance for older adults? This paper describes the development of a style guide within the Historytelling Project to increase the consistency and therefore efficiency of the interface and to gain a higher software development efficiency. The implementation of the style guide is based on the preexisting CSS framework Bootstrap because of its high amount of predefined UI elements. The developed style guide consists of two components: the actual implementation of the style guide in the form of CSS customizations and the associated documentation. Both components are freely accessible and editable online. An adjusted interface was tested against a standard Bootstrap interface with 31 older adults aged 51 to 93 (M = 71), of which 15 participants used the standard Bootstrap interface and 16 the age-adjusted interface. Findings indicate a higher task completion rate (effectiveness) across tasks for the adjusted Bootstrap+ version.

Keywords: Aging users · Human-Centered Design (HCD+) · Style guide

1 Introduction

How can we support the development of age-appropriate system design? And how can the demographic change and steadily increasing percentage of older adults be used to create something meaningful for each individuum and for the society? The Historytelling project (HT) addresses these issues by developing a digital social platform for older adults to empower them in recording, visualizing and sharing their life stories. These stories are an anchor to strengthen the ties between different generations and to tie new ones. The research project relies on the strengths of older adults, giving them a voice in the development of the software and seeks positive impact on the societal, group and personal level (for an illustration see Fig. 1). On a personal level, HT offers possibilities for reminiscence, for biographical work and for stronger contact to one's own history and other people. On a group level it can strengthen the ties of existing relationships with friends and family and help establish new ones. And on a societal level, HT offers the possibility to experience history from multiple perspectives and to pass on life experience and knowledge from generation to generation.

© Springer Nature Switzerland AG 2019
J. Zhou and G. Salvendy (Eds.): HCII 2019, LNCS 11592, pp. 84–97, 2019.
https://doi.org/10.1007/978-3-030-22012-9_7

Fig. 1. Illustration of the three levels Historytelling addresses: personal, group and societal

The core of the HT project is an interactive website, creating a digital network on which older adults can document their life stories, enrich them with multimedia content and embed them in a temporal and spatial context. Furthermore, story sharing is possible within a family and public space to help establish vivid interaction between users through the stories, providing a powerful trigger to write even more stories.

For the development of HT, the integration of potential users as participants is crucial. Participants should be integrated in the development process from early on and continuously in preferably all steps of the HCD process. HT uses the HCD+ framework [1], which in turn helps to improve this framework by adding new guidelines for the participatory development with and for older adults. HCD+ is an approach based on Human Centered Design (HCD), to develop information and communication technology for older adults and focuses on "user characteristics and their impact on the design process and results" [1].

1.1 First Development Steps

As stated above, the involvement of older adults throughout the development process is important for HT. Thus, 19 interviews with older adults were conducted already in the ideation phase of the project [1]. Preliminary results can be found in [2]. Interviews were analyzed using the User Centered Design Canvas developed by [3] based on the Business Model Canvas to visualize information about challenges and motives. A project plan was created based on these results, and the HT topic was further narrowed to specific features. This plan was used to simultaneously develop features in a component-based software engineering approach, first described by McIlroy [4]. Although the idea of component-based system engineering is not new, with the advent of (web-) technologies focusing heavily on this approach, it gets easier to reuse and test parts of the source code within different user interfaces, increasing the development speed, yet creating new usability challenges, especially regarding consistency [5–7].

Figure 2 shows resulting interface examples described in [8–10]. They show that there is little consistency among the interface elements, although the usability of each interface tested positively in isolation. Figure 3 emphasizes this fact in detail by displaying all different buttons of the HT interface. One approach to address these challenges and ensure consistency among interfaces is to establish an age-appropriate style guide.

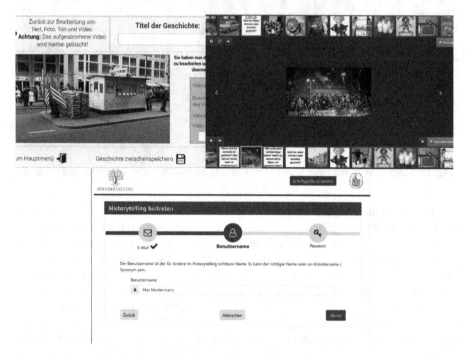

Fig. 2. Example of HT interfaces prior to style guide development

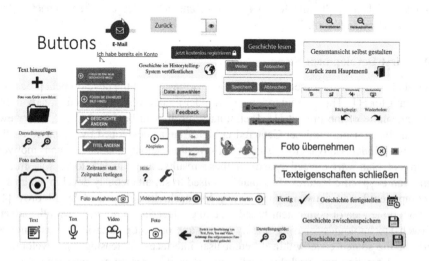

Fig. 3. Interface inventory of all buttons used in the various HT components

1.2 Style Guides

User interface style guides are about as old as user interfaces themselves and were first introduced by Apple for the Macintosh, with IBM and Microsoft following shortly thereafter. The importance and benefits of these style guides were also discussed early on [11]. As Gale [11] stated, the objectives for style guides are to "promote visual and functional consistency within and between different applications", "promote good design practice" and to "reinforce company branding or an organization's public image". Frost [12] and Debenham [13] define style guides as a clearly defined collection for documentation and organization of design materials to provide guidelines, practical application and guidance. In the literature, various motivations for using style guides are mentioned, among them:

- Consistency and therefore efficiency [11, 14, 15]
- Having a clear, tangible output [11]
- Increased user participation in design [14]
- Increased user acceptance [14]
- Higher software development efficiency [14].

With the development and usage of style guides, there are potential pitfalls to consider. Occurring problems can be divided into two groups: "Problems with the contents of a style guide and problems with handling the document" [16]. Some potential problems and challenges regarding style guides are the following:

- Shifting responsibility for design away from the programmers [11]
- User interface and style guide complexity and quantity of guidelines [11, 15]
- Low or no update frequency [11]
- Development process and schedules [15]
- Incorrectness and inconsistencies within the style guide [16]
- Continuous appearance of new style guide tools [16]
- Lacking style guide introduction within the organization [11]
- Access [16].

Some of the problems only occur with offline or paper-based style guides and could be bypassed by using online open source style guides. Vogt [16] discusses some of these challenges in further detail. For example, regarding incorrectness and inconsistencies within the style guide he states that these are solvable intrinsic problems. Concerning the appearance of new tools, Vogt states that the development of new tools will not slow down in the future. Torres [15] sees a solution to the challenges of style guide usage and development in applying HCD principles. He stresses the importance of setting measurable goals, keeping users involved throughout the development process, appealing competitiveness, designing the whole user experience, designing with a multidisciplinary team and evaluating designs and design decisions. Gale [11] also proposes a collaborative approach to style guide development with the following five steps based on the involvement of developers and users throughout style guide creation: (1) "Raising awareness amongst developers and end users. (2) "Building consensus" (3) "Documenting the Style Guide" (4) "Providing training and support material" (5) "Establishing an environment which enables the guide to evolve".

Also, Gale sees advantages in using enriched style guide. He argues that a style guide should not just be a document, but rather an "interactive demonstration to illustrate the look and feel", using "reference tables for quick reference of critical data", and provide source code to "promote sharing user interface code."

Olsson and Gulliksen [14] promote the communication and involvement of users as an inherited feature of style guides. They built a hypertext based online accessible style guide with the capability to communicate opinions and ask questions. The advantage of this approach is, as Olsson and Gulliksen state, the easier maintainability and the possibility to perform revisions.

Looking at the "Website Style Guide Resources" by Anna Debenham [17], it is apparent that the usage of the term "style guide" is nearly extinct in today's use. Instead, terms like "design system" or "pattern library" are used. One example is the carbon design system by IBM [18]. Often, these design systems contain not only design guidelines but also the company's corporate identity. As Debenham [13] states, design systems are an umbrella term for design principles, design of language and tools. Pattern Libraries in contrast focus on the integration of elements and components into a website and address the needs of programmers and less the needs of designers.

For HT, style guides can help on two levels: (1) the consistency of the developed user interfaces and (2) the coordination and efficiency of student's work on theses and other qualifications creating them. Students usually have little programming experience and work only briefly on the HT project due to the nature of qualification work. Therefore, there is little time for onboarding and first steps guidance is critical. Also, with a growing number of components, documentation and source code, the onboarding into the development and the maintainability of the project gets more difficult, impeding the goal of age-appropriate design.

1.3 Age-Appropriate Guidelines

With higher age, limitations in perception, cognition and motor control increase, which are relevant for using digital technology [19]. Also, socio-cultural factors and the acceptance of technology usage among generations and can influence or impair user behavior [20] and it is important to consider the diversity of older adults as a group, especially regarding their limitations, capabilities and experience with technology [19]. To avoid stigmatization, labeling user interfaces as 'specific for older adults' should be avoided [21].

Much has been written about age appropriate guidelines for older adults, mostly based on a combination of literature reviews, focus groups, interviews and user studies and concluding to list age-specific requirements [20–25]. Arch, Abou-Zhara and Henry [22] conducted a literature review based on 150 articles and observed some recurring patterns in user requirements. Information overload was one of the most common challenges, in particular the number of various items on one page, making it hard to focus on relevant information, the usage of advertisements and animated elements which were distracting, non-linear navigation through websites and inconsistency regarding layouts, navigation and interaction. The authors saw a lack of information in three areas: (1) Considering hearing loss and deafness. Although hearing loss was identified as age related, most of the literature did not include recommendations to address hearing limitations. (2) Assistive technology or adaptive strategies were rarely mentioned and thus guidelines regarding these technologies are seldom included. (3) Existing Web accessibility guidelines are mostly not acknowledged or discussed and thus many authors develop redundant recommendations.

2   Development

The implementation of the HT style guide is based on a preexisting CSS framework and uses the component-based approach of the underlying source code. There are many usable frameworks for different purposes. Typical examples for general purpose frameworks are for example Foundation, UI Kit, Semantic UI and Bootstrap [26]. CSS Frameworks have the benefit of providing predefined initial CSS rules, reusable layouts and UI elements, meeting a certain standard [27]. Also, they make differences between general and age specific style guides testable. The style guide developed for HT uses Bootstrap because of its high amount of predefined UI elements, which can be used first and then be adapted to age specific guidelines step by step. In analogy to the development of the underlying HCD+ approach, the adjusted Bootstrap framework will be called Bootstrap+.

2.1   Bootstrap

Bootstrap provides HTML, CSS and JavaScript patterns for layout, typography, forms, buttons, navigation and further user interface elements. These components can be extended and adjusted by using a CSS and JavaScript layer on top the framework. The current version is 4.2.1. Bootstrap describes itself as a CSS framework for "responsive, mobile-first projects on the web" and as "the world's most popular front-end component library" [28]. It comes with good documentation, has an active community with 1059 contributors (as of February 2019) since 2011 and is the most starred CSS framework repository on github with over 130.000 stars. Originally, Bootstrap was developed and published 2011 by Twitter and is by their own account used by NASA, FIFA, Spotify and others.

2.2   Bootstrap+

Bootstrap+ consists of two components: the style guide documentation and the associated implementation (accessible via the node package manager npm named historytelling-styleguide [29]). The recommended way to include the style guide into a project is by installing it via npm. If a module bundler, such as webpack, is used inside a project, the provided SCSS preprocessor files can be included into the project and adapted if required. If no preprocessor is used, also a standard CSS file can be used inside a project. The loadable index file loads bootstrap, adjusted variables and the custom HT styles, such as colors. The second component of Bootstrap+ is the documentation, accessible at [30]. The various UI elements are divided into different categories according to Debenhams design system [13]: Components, Elements, Tokens (See Table 1 for an overview).

Table 1. Overview of the components, elements and tokens used within the style guide documentation

Components	Elements	Tokens
• Progress indicator	• Buttons	• Color
• Process card	• Media buttons	• Logo
• Timeline	• Progress buttons	• Language
• Story card	• Button group	• Icons
• Navbar	• Text area	• Font
• Bottom navigation bar	• Text entry	• Structure and content
• Login indicator	• Headings	• Functionality
• Story Display	• Running text	
• Story Content	• Smileys	
• Media	• Date block	
• Feedback input		
• Emoji input		
• Feedback display		
• Emoji bar		
• Commentary display		

Tokens define basic design bits such as color schemes, fonts and icons. Elements define stand-alone UI elements such as buttons, text areas and headings (See Fig. 4 for an example). Components define combinations of elements which should have one single purpose such as indicating the current login status (see Fig. 5 for an example). The implemented pages typically consist of various components. Each item consists of a heading, an explanation, a graphical representation of the element and copiable code. The documentation exists as a living style guide in an open github repository in which suggestions for improvement can be submitted by the issue tracker or pull requests.

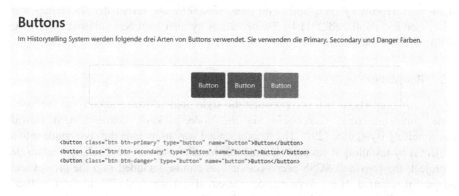

Fig. 4. An example for an element. The element is described, visually represented and source code is provided

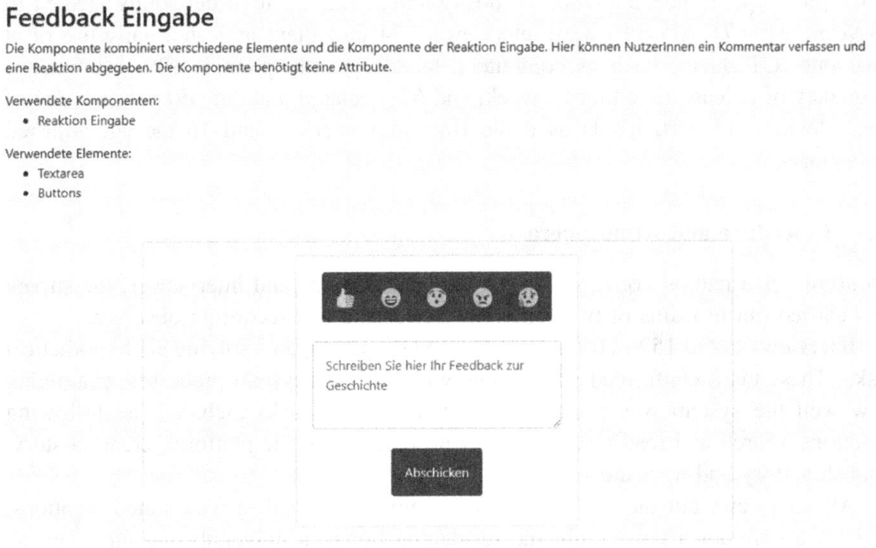
Feedback Eingabe
Die Komponente kombiniert verschiedene Elemente und die Komponente der Reaktion Eingabe. Hier können NutzerInnen ein Kommentar verfassen und eine Reaktion abgegeben. Die Komponente benötigt keine Attribute.
Verwendete Komponenten:
• Reaktion Eingabe
Verwendete Elemente:
• Textarea
• Buttons
Schreiben Sie hier Ihr Feedback zur Geschichte
Abschicken

Fig. 5. An example for a component. The component is described as well as other used components and elements and the component is visualized

3 Empirical Evaluation

To evaluate the developed prototype with age appropriate adjustments, it was tested in an A/B-Test with the standard Bootstrap interface without age appropriation and without style guide adjustments vs. the adjusted interface simply called Bootstrap+, as has been suggested by Torres [15]: “A new style guide should be evaluated against predecessors competitive style guides, just as products are evaluated.” Below, this empirical evaluation is documented regarding participant recruitment, testing atmosphere and procedure as well as methods applied as described in the HCD+ approach [1].

3.1 Recruitment of Participants

Participants were recruited in two ways, one successful, one less so: at first, people were directly approached and asked for participation in spontaneous short interviews at the central train station. The aim was to quickly reach a high number of diverse participants, yet that approach failed leading to merely one participant. Thus, local residencies, care facilities and associations were contacted, based on established connections from previous projects as well as new internet search results. Most of the new care facilities and residential homes dismissed the request due to a stated lack of technology use by older residents. Ultimately, only one residential home with 9 participants and two local women’s associations (Frauenring Lübeck and Lübecker Landfrauen) with 9 and 12 participants could be recruited for the empirical evaluation of the prototype. Hence, a total of 31 mostly female (22 f; 9 m) older adults aged 51 to 93 years (M = 71, SD = 9) were interviewed. 74% of them indicated daily use of at least one ICT device such as computers, tablets or smartphones, 19% estimated a frequency of at least three times a week, and 6% declared that they do not own any of these devices. 15 participants used the Bootstrap interface and 16 the age-adjusted Bootstrap+.

3.2   Procedure and Atmosphere

To allow for a natural conversation between participants and interviewer, the survey was carried out in teams of two: one interviewer and one recording observer.

Interviews lasted 15 to 20 min and focused on participants solving six hypothetical tasks. These tasks confronted participants with different system processes, examining how well the system was perceived and understood. Tasks included the following functions: search and read a story, comment, register for the platform, create a story, publish a story and navigate.

All interviews but the one at the train station were held in well suited locations, such as a common room within the residential home, a university usability lab, an empty café and a private home – all of which allowed for a pleasant conversational atmosphere. In the residential home, interviews were conducted at an afternoon coffee gathering, leading to high noise level and some insecurities among the participants. Also, a number of residents interested in the project did not consider themselves capable enough for participation.

3.3   Methods

For the evaluation, an A/B between subjects design was chosen with an even split between Bootstrap (N = 15) and Bootstrap+ (N = 16) interfaces. A detailed evaluation sheet was used in which the recording observer categorized participants performance for each task, based on an adjusted evaluation scale presented by [31]. The performance on each task was rated as not solved, partly solved (e.g. with help) or completely solved (alone). The evaluation sheet combined quantitative and qualitative data, revealing common problems, misuses or other observations while at the same time including individual opinions and ideas of single participants. Results from the evaluation sheets were aggregated and analyzed in search for patterns or similarities in the distribution of code-frequencies. Qualitative data was aggregated and interpreted using content analysis [32]. Based on this analysis, specific problems and potentials for optimization of the adjusted Bootstrap+ interface were identified and integrated into the developed prototype of the style guide. See Fig. 6 for an exemplary comparison of both interfaces.

Fig. 6. Examples of interfaces used in the evaluation. Standard Bootstrap on the left and Bootstrap+ on the right.

4 Results

The following section provides a description of the results from the collected data in regard to general demographic aspects of the participants, as well as relevant information on differences in participants performance between the two interface versions.

4.1 Quantitative Data

Findings indicate a higher task completion rate (effectiveness) across tasks for the adjusted Bootstrap+ version, see Table 2. Looking at individual tasks, Bootstrap+ showed higher task completion rates in all tasks but the third, concerning the registration process for the platform. Accordingly, there were more tasks solved with help or not solved at all with the unmodified Bootstrap interface.

Table 2. Comparing effectiveness (as task completion rate) for Bootstrap (N = 15) and Bootstrap+ (N = 16) interfaces across all tasks

	Interface	Task1	Task2	Task3	Task4	Task5	Task6	Means
Solved	Bootstrap+	72%	76%	68%	81%	78%	83%	77%
	Bootstrap	68%	67%	73%	78%	72%	48%	**69%**
Solved with help	Bootstrap+	11%	9%	13%	12%	11%	7%	11%
	Bootstrap	11%	18%	27%	16%	18%	16%	**18%**
Not solved	Bootstrap+	17%	15%	18%	7%	11%	10%	12%
	Bootstrap	21%	16%	0%	5%	9%	36%	**14%**

4.2   Qualitative Data

Qualitative data was summarized in task-specific categories and clustered into general themes. In general, they support the improved effectiveness of Bootstrap+, in detail a few findings for the tasks shall be described here as follows:

- **Task 1 (searching for stories)**, difficulties with Bootstrap found with the timeline, as the depiction of two beams (one selecting the year and the other the month) lead to confusion and misinterpretations
- **Task 2 (commenting)**, the emoji-bar was either not noticed or not understood in the Bootstrap interface, suggesting a better visualization in Bootstrap+, which still showed a lack of comprehension regarding the interactivity of the emoji-bar
- **Task 3 (registration)**, common problems across versions, e.g. with the displayed progress bar, understanding the presented information or general attitudes towards user registration
- **task 4 (story creation)**, difficulties with Bootstrap interface regarding text input for the story title and navigation through the process of story-creation, suggesting an improvement in Bootstrap+, which still showed problems with the temporal and spatial classification of stories
- **Task 5 (story completion)** and **6 (navigation)** again show common problems across versions that provide good starting points to improve the existing prototype (see Table 3).

Table 3. Frequencies of participants' difficulties with the style guide's interface elements for Bootstrap (N = 15) and Bootstrap+ (N = 16) interfaces

Style guide item	Bootstrap	Bootstrap+	Total
Timeline	12	2	14
Navigation bar	17	13	30
Emoji bar	12	6	18
Commentary display	3	2	5
Progress indicator	12	7	19
Bottom navbar	4	1	5
Text entry	1	1	1
Date picker	1	0	1
Language/Labeling	15	15	30

Also, participants stated their demands for the interface and potential further development of the style guide and HT: Options to set restriction for stories' visibility to others (6), Sharing stories via email (2), Uploading option for documents (1), Uploading option for externally created stories (1), Keyword integration (1), Freedom of not completing the story creation at once, option to review and revise (1), Enhanced community functionality (1).

5   Discussion

The goal of this paper was to show how the development of age-appropriate system design can be supported. In first iterations of HT, it became apparent that the component-based development process efficiently produces components with high usability scores, but lacks consistency across HT components. The development of a style guide helps to harmonize the development of HT and presents possibilities for other researchers and designers to implement age-appropriate software. Furthermore, new style guide approaches like Debenhams [13] with components, elements and tokens, work well within the component-based development approach of HT.

As Gale [11] stated, one of the reasons why style guides fail is a lack of updates. Thus, as Gale [11] and Torres [15] suggest, a collaborative approach for the development of the HT style guide was used. Also, the style guide has been implemented as a living online document, which can be easily shared and edited. Finally, there are special requirements for the development of HT: Since the nature of student's qualification work brings about short collaboration times, fast onboarding with a short training period is essential for the success of new component development. On the other hand, the setting makes it easier to follow Gales suggestions [11]: (1) "Raising awareness amongst developers and end users" (2) "Building consensus" (3) "Documenting the Style Guide" (4) "Providing training and support material" (5) "Establishing an environment which enables the guide to evolve". For the HT project, we were able to show that both components of the style guide, the documentation and the customized CSS source files, can help to improve the effectiveness measured as task completion rate.

6   Outlook and Future Work

Future development of HT will follow Bootstrap+ to maintain consistency across all components of the interface. Of course, there is still much room for improvement. Over time, new HT components will be developed, and new elements will be added to the HT style guide documentation and the source code to attain an ever more complete style guide for more general purposes. Also, for further development and establishing it will be crucial to formalize the organization and usage of it and parameters for goals and objectives have to be set as for example Kholmatova [33] states. To keep the style guide alive, new functionality will be added to it, such as a feedback loop for developers and an option to edit content without editing the source code.

References

1. Sengpiel, M., Volkmann, T., Jochems, N.: Considering older adults throughout the development process – the HCD+ approach. In: Proceedings of the Human Factors and Ergonomics Society Europe Chapter 2018 Annual Conference, Berlin, Germany (in press)
2. Volkmann, T., Sengpiel, M., Jochems, N.: Historytelling: a website for the elderly a human-centered design approach. In: Proceedings of the 9th Nordic Conference on Human-Computer Interaction, pp. 100:1–100:6. ACM, New York (2016)

3. The Rectangles—UX design studio. https://ucdc.therectangles.com. Accessed 14 Feb 2019
4. McIlroy, M.D., Buxton, J., Naur, P., Randell, B.: Mass-produced software components. In: Proceedings of the 1st International Conference on Software Engineering, pp. 88–98. Garmisch-Partenkirchen, Germany (1968)
5. Vale, T., Crnkovic, I., de Almeida, E.S., da Mota Silveira Neto, P.A., Lemos Meira, S.R.: Twenty-eight years of component-based software engineering. J. Syst. Softw. 111, 128–148 (2016)
6. Greenfield, J., Short, K.: Software factories: assembling applications with patterns, models, frameworks and tools. In: Companion of the 18th Annual ACM SIGPLAN Conference on Object-Oriented Programming, Systems, Languages, and Applications (OOPSLA 2003), pp. 16–27. ACM, New York (2003)
7. Prieto-Diaz, R., Freeman, P.: Classifying software for reusability. IEEE Softw. 4, 6–16 (1987)
8. Volkmann, T., Dohse, F., Sengpiel, M., Jochems, N.: Age-appropriate design of an input component for the historytelling project. In: Bagnara, S., Tartaglia, R., Albolino, S., Alexander, T., Fujita, Y. (eds.) IEA 2018. AISC, vol. 822, pp. 672–680. Springer, Cham (2019). https://doi.org/10.1007/978-3-319-96077-7_73
9. Volkmann, T., Sengpiel, M., Jochems, N.: Altersgerechte Gestaltung eines Registrierungsprozesses für das Historytelling-Projekt. In: Dachselt, R., Weber, G. (eds.) Mensch und Computer 2018 - Tagungsband. Gesellschaft für Informatik e.V, Bonn (2018)
10. Volkmann, T., Grosche, D., Sengpiel, M., Jochems, N.: What can i say?: Presenting stimulus material to support storytelling for older adults. In: Proceedings of the 10th Nordic Conference on Human-Computer Interaction, pp. 696–700. ACM, New York (2018)
11. Gale, S.: A collaborative approach to developing style guides. In: Proceedings of the SIGCHI Conference on Human Factors in Computing Systems, pp. 362–367. ACM, New York (1996)
12. Frost, B.: Atomic Design. Brad Frost, Pittsburgh (2016)
13. Debenham, A.: Front-end style guides: creating and maintaining style guides for websites (2017)
14. Olsson, E., Gulliksen, J.: A corporate style guide that includes domain knowledge. Int. J. Hum.-Comput. Interact. 11, 317–338 (1999)
15. Torres, R.J.: A user centered design based approach to style guides. In: Vanderdonckt, J., Farenc, C. (eds.) Tools for Working with Guidelines, pp. 15–33. Springer, London (2001). https://doi.org/10.1007/978-1-4471-0279-3_2
16. Vogt, T.: Difficulties in using style guides for designing user interfaces. In: Vanderdonckt, J., Farenc, C. (eds.) Tools for Working with Guidelines, pp. 197–208. Springer, London (2001). https://doi.org/10.1007/978-1-4471-0279-3_19
17. Website Style Guide Resources. http://styleguides.io/. Accessed 14 Feb 2019
18. Carbon Design System. https://www.carbondesignsystem.com/. Accessed 14 Feb 2019
19. Fisk, A.D., Rogers, W.A., Charness, N., Czaja, S.J., Sharit, J.: Designing for Older Adults: Principles and Creative Human Factors Approaches, 2nd edn. CRC Press, Boca Raton (2009)
20. Wirtz, S., Jakobs, E.-M., Ziefle, M.: Age-specific usability issues of software interfaces. In: Proceedings of the IEA, vol. 17. Springer, Cham (2009)
21. Seifert, A.: Altersgerechtes Internet durch angepasste Webgestaltung (2012)
22. Arch, A., Abou-Zahra, S., Henry, S.: Older users online: WAI guidelines address older users web experience. User Experience Mag. 8 (2009)
23. Carmien, S., Manzanares, A.G.: Elders using smartphones – a set of research based heuristic guidelines for designers. In: Stephanidis, C., Antona, M. (eds.) UAHCI 2014. LNCS, vol. 8514, pp. 26–37. Springer, Cham (2014). https://doi.org/10.1007/978-3-319-07440-5_3

24. Hodes, R.J., Lindberg, D.A.: Making your website senior friendly. National Institute on Aging and the National Library of Medicine, Baltimore, Maryland, USA (2002)
25. Zaphiris, P., Ghiawadwala, M., Mughal, S.: Age-centered research-based web design guidelines. In: CHI 2005 Extended Abstracts on Human Factors in Computing Systems, pp. 1897–1900. ACM, New York (2005)
26. Github - Awesome CSS Frameworks. https://github.com/troxler/awesome-css-frameworks. Accessed 14 Feb 2019
27. Koshijima, R., Goto, K., Toyama, M.: Generating responsive web pages using SuperSQL. In: Proceedings of the 18th International Conference on Information Integration and Web-Based Applications and Services, pp. 231–240. ACM, New York (2016)
28. Bootstrap. https://getbootstrap.com/. Accessed 14 Feb 2019
29. Historytelling Style guide. https://www.npmjs.com/package/historytelling-styleguide. Accessed 14 Feb 2019
30. Styleguide des Historytelling Systems. http://www.historytelling.net/styleguide/. Accessed 14 Feb 2019
31. Klimmt, C., Sowka, A., Hefner, D., Mergel, F., Possler, D.: Testinstrument zur Messung von Medienkritikfähigkeit: Dokumentation der Testentwicklung und der Testaufgaben, Hannover, Germany (2014)
32. Mayring, P.: Qualitative content analysis: theoretical background and procedures. In: Bikner-Ahsbahs, A., Knipping, C., Presmeg, N. (eds.) Approaches to Qualitative Research in Mathematics Education, pp. 365–380. Springer, Dordrecht (2015). https://doi.org/10.1007/978-94-017-9181-6_13
33. Kholmatova, A.: Design Systems - A Practical Guide to Creating Design Languages for Digital Products. Smashing, Freiburg, Germany (2017)

The Effect of Product Aesthetics
on Older Consumers

Tyan-Yu Wu[(⊠)]

Chang Gung University, Kwei-Shan, Taiwan
tnyuwu@mail.cgu.edu.tw

Abstract. Older consumers are a quickly increasing segment of the consumer market. However, few products have been designed specifically for this group, and little research has been done specifically on their aesthetic perceptions. This study focuses on symmetry and cultural elements related to aesthetics from older persons' points of view. The experiment featured 77 subjects (24 males; 53 females; ages 55–70) who responded to a survey of seven questions. Independent variables included symmetry and asymmetry with and without cultural elements, while dependent variables covered subjective aesthetics, emotions (i.e., valence, arousal), preference attitudes, and purchase intension. A total of 32 stimuli were used to examine (1) high symmetry + a high culture pattern × 8, (2) high symmetry + a low culture pattern × 8, (3) low symmetry + a low culture pattern × 8, and (4) low symmetry + a high culture pattern × 8. The results showed that female participants tend to be more sensitive to products that include cultural elements, and older consumers have greater aesthetic responses to products with symmetry than those marked by asymmetry. Products with cultural elements also had greater responses than products without cultural meanings.

Keywords: Order · Symmetry · Cultural elements · Emotion

1 Products with a Beautiful Appearance Evoke Greater Emotional Responses

The dramatic increase in the population resulting from the baby boom has led to an continuously expanding aging population in the 21st, century; By 2025, Taiwan will be called as a super-aged society since the population of elderly will increase up to 20% (Lin and Huang 2015). The older population in many countries will also have a great impact on society and product markets, which means that marketing efforts of the future will undergo a great change to appeal to these consumers. As is well-known, a good product should offer not only functional satisfaction and an ergonomic fit, but also a beautiful appearance, from the user's perspective. Moreover, a product must fit consumers' tastes (Dhar and Wertenbroch 2000; Hoyer and Stokburger-Sauer 2012; Postrel 2003). Therefore, creating a product that suits the tastes of older consumers, particularly their aesthetic tastes, has become a critical issue in design.

A product with a beautiful appearance often enjoys added value (Blijlevens et al. 2009; Bloch et al. 2003; Hirschman and Holbrook 1982; Hoyer and Stokburger-Sauer

© Springer Nature Switzerland AG 2019
J. Zhou and G. Salvendy (Eds.): HCII 2019, LNCS 11592, pp. 98–106, 2019.
https://doi.org/10.1007/978-3-030-22012-9_8

2012; McDonagh et al. 2002). Moreover, the product may increase consumers' positive emotional responses when they use it. Thus, a good product for the older population should have smart functions, be user-friendly, and have a pleasant aesthetic quality; all of these can enhance the user's experience and further increase positive emotions (Helander and Khalid 2006; Khalid 2001). A product's aesthetic appeal can be very important for its first impression and for evoking consumers' emotions. Despite the importance of product aesthetics on first impressions, there is little research focused on older consumers' sense of aesthetics and emotions. This gap in the research has inspired this study.

2 Products with Symmetrical Forms and Cultural Elements May Enhance Aesthetic Qualities

Aesthetics involve complex characteristics that are affected by a variety of attributes and factors. External aesthetics include principles such as symmetry, unity, contrast, balance, and proportion (Coates 2003; Lauer 1979). These can be visualized and quantified during an experiment. Several past studies have shown that people prefer to observe forms that are symmetrical, compared to forms that are asymmetrical, because of their more stable and balanced look. In other aspects, some studies have shown that older consumers prefer classic decorations and retro style (Marchegiani and Phau 2011). When considering internal aesthetics, responses can be derived from the understanding of a cultural pattern's meaning, which is often connected to the viewer's memory and which can further evoke his or her emotions. For example, when older consumers observe a product made with a familiar and traditional pattern, it may prompt them to recall something meaningful in their past. This, in turn, can lead to the showing of strong responses to these classic patterns, due to the sense of nostalgia they evoke. When an item is associated with a part of someone's memories of the past, it has the chance to resonate emotionally immediately (Holbrook and Schindler 2003). In sum, we can conclude that symmetrical forms and meaningful patterns can enhance a product's aesthetics and evoke consumers' emotions right away. Taking advantage of nostalgia, designers should try to create products specifically targeted at older consumers, in order to satisfy the future of the market. In this study, we focused on symmetry and asymmetry (i.e., an external effect) and cultural patterns (i.e., an internal effect) because of the ease with which we can control such visual elements. We hypothesized that products with a symmetrical shape and those with culturally related patterns would be able to evoke positive emotions strongly among older consumers. The purpose of this study is to test (1) whether older consumers have greater emotional responses to products that are symmetrical and (2) if older consumers have greater emotional responses to products that contain a cultural element.

3 Symmetry as an Aesthetic Factor

One of the principles that can enhance aesthetics most strongly is symmetry. Humans of all nationalities are capable of perceiving and judging symmetrical aesthetics precisely (Evans et al. 2000; Julesz 1971; Tyler 2002; Wagemans 1999; Wenderoth 1994). Washburn and Humphrey (2001) note that people naturally seem to prefer symmetrical objects, even without any professionally guided training. Coates (2003) believes that the characteristics of products' aesthetics are associated with how their elements are assembled in the design process. During the form development process, the principle of symmetry is the simplest way to display objects with a balanced image (Lauer 1979). Symmetrical forms visually convey a sense of order and can relieve tension (Schmitt and Simonson 1997). Creusen et al. (2010) suggest that symmetry is associated with tidiness, uniformity in button shape of the clothes, and placement in space. Murdoch and Flurscheim (1983) have referred to symmetry as a state of order. Designers use the principle of symmetry to create beautiful shapes, so this is often an element of the product form development process. Designers assemble and rearrange visual elements until they are satisfied that they have constructed the most optimal product form. Conversely, asymmetrical forms may conjure up feelings of visual instability. Sometimes, this is done for a creative and/or amusing effect. To date, few studies have focused on aesthetic principles; more research has focused on the simplicity and meaninglessness of artificial nonsense stimuli.

Although older consumers may pay more attention than average to a product's usability, functionality and stability, some studies have shown that ordinary users prefer products with highly consistent and symmetrical forms (Berlyne 1971; Hekkert et al. 1994; Lauer 1979; Lewalski 1988; Veryzer and Hutchinson 1998). Moreover, related research on symmetry has found that people prefer to observe faces that are symmetrical (Rhodes 2006). Generally speaking, prior studies have implied that the symmetry aesthetic is very important to older people's aesthetic judgments, and specifically as they relate to product designs. Therefore, this is an important factor for increasing a product's aesthetic appeal. In short, we hypothesized that products with symmetrical forms would be able to psychologically convey both visual balance and a stable visual perception. We thus assumed that older consumers have a similar preference when it comes to their visual perceptions of products.

As Giannouli (2013) stated, symmetrical arrangements can be classified into three types: translational, rotational, and mirror. In this study, we adopted translational and mirror symmetry when developing the stimuli, because of their popularity in product design. The common ground among facial, body art, and the decorative arts is the symmetry design principle. Surprisingly, facial symmetry studies conducted in a variety of cultures have demonstrated the same results: symmetry enhances physical attraction (Grammer and Thornhill 1994; Hume and Montgomerie 2001; Jones et al. 2001; Koehler et al. 2002; Little et al. 2001; Mealy et al. 1999; Penton-Voak et al. 2001; Perrett et al. 1999; Rhodes et al. 1998; Rhodes et al. 2001a; Rhodes et al. 2001b). In addition, one study on website layout design showed a similar result: that vertical symmetry is the most important factor when designing a website. By contrast, websites with asymmetrical layouts are considered less beautiful (Tuch et al. 2010). Overall, previous works have implied that designs marked by symmetry provide unique means of increasing attraction.

4 Method

This experiment examined the independent variables of symmetry and asymmetry and items with and without cultural elements. The dependent variables were related to subjective aesthetics, emotion, preference, and purchase intension.

4.1 Subjects

The subjects were 75 participants, 35 men and 40 women, between the ages of 55 and 75.

4.2 Stimuli

The stimuli were product pictures collected from websites and magazines depicting familiar objects in the participants' daily lives. Such high involvement products have strong connections with the users' daily lives, because they are used often and seem important to them. Based on this familiarity, participants can be expected to pay close attention during the experiment (Zaichkowsky 1985). Participants may observe the products' information closely, and/or show strong attitude and high levels of purchase intention (Bart et al. 2014; Lutz et al. 1983). Items selected for use in the study included lamps with shades, two cabinets, a contemporary chair, a classic chair, a kettle, a computer monitor, and a radio. A total of 32 stimuli were created. These covered four classifications (two stimuli for each classification): (1) high symmetry + high culture pattern × 8, (2) high symmetry + low culture pattern × 8, (3) low symmetry + low culture pattern × 8, and (4) low symmetry + high culture pattern × 8. The stimuli pictures were edited and displayed with only line work, to bring the profile into a uniform level of quality. Photoshop software was used to edit the stimuli to make them consistently high quality images.

4.3 Questionnaire

The questionnaire contained three dimensions: aesthetic, emotional, and behavioral responses. The aesthetic items included both symmetry and asymmetry and cultural pattern variables, while valence and arousal items were used for assessing emotion; purchase intention or preference items accounted for behavior.

4.4 Experiment Processes

The experiment was conducted in a quiet room without any interruptions. Participants were invited to answer the questionnaire as volunteers. The researcher explained the definitions of the terminology used and the experiment processes before starting the experiment. Each participant received a $7 honorarium upon completion of the survey.

5 Results

One-way ANOVA was used to analyze the results. The statistical analysis demonstrated that there were no significant differences between the male and female participants in terms of aesthetic, preference, or emotional factors. However, the results did reveal that men and women had different perceptions (P < 029; see Table 1) of those products that included a cultural element, which affected their attitudes toward purchasing the products. Female participants (M = 4.4694; SD = 1.60929) had greater responses to those products with cultural elements than those without them (M = 4.3133; SD = 1.68065). This implies that the female participants are more sensitive to products with cultural elements. Moreover, female participants (M = 3.3624; SD = 1.64938) were also willing to purchase more of the products than their male counterparts were (M = 3.6094; SD = 1.68271) (see Table 2).

Table 1. ANOVA results of the influence of cultural factors on men and women

		SS	df	Ms	F	Sig.
Cultural meaning	Between groups	4.785	1	12.749	4.785	.029
	Within groups	6434.010	2415	2.664		
	Total	6615.494	2390			

Table 2. ANOVA results of men's and women's purchase intensions

		SS	df	Ms	F	Sig.
Cultural meaning	Between groups	31.703	1	31.703	11.504	.001
	Within groups	6583.791	2389	2.756		
	Total	6615.494	2390			

The results of the descriptive statistics show that the participants had significant responses related to asymmetry–symmetry and cultural–no cultural elements. First, we examined the participants' responses to the symmetry–asymmetry of the products' forms. The results showed that our participants tended to have higher aesthetic responses to products with symmetrical forms (M = 5.2116; SD = 1.43161), compared to those with asymmetrical forms (M = 4.2541; SD = 1.74078). Our participants also showed greater cultural responses when looking at products with symmetrical forms (M = 4.6374; SD = 1.55090) than when observing asymmetrical products (M = 4.2026; SD = 1.68489). When we asked participants how they felt about the items' aesthetic qualities, they reported that products with symmetrical forms (M = 4.5091; SD = 1.47109) are more beautiful than products with asymmetrical forms (M = 4.1431; SD = 1.62815). Similarly, participants preferred products with symmetrical forms (M = 4.0248; SD = 1.49198), compared to products with asymmetrical forms (M = 3.6988; SD = 1.59673). This indicates that older consumers are likely to prefer products with symmetrical forms. Furthermore, they showed a greater willingness to purchase products with symmetrical forms (M = 3.6346; SD = 1.62803), compared to products with asymmetrical forms (M = 3.2477; SD = 1.67719). The participants consistently showed greater emotional responses (i.e., valence and arousal) when looking at products with symmetrical forms (M = 4.3607/4.1177; SD = 1.40423/1.50883) than when looking at products with asymmetrical forms (M = 4.0315/4.1177; SD = 1.55902/1.57853).

Next, we examined the participants' responses to product with cultural elements. The results indicate that our participants had significant responses to those products with cultural elements. Overall, the participants reported greater levels of feeling regarding the products with cultural elements than products without such elements. The participants agreed that products with cultural elements (M = 4.8659; SD = 1.62832) were more beautiful than those without them (M = 4.5997; SD = 1.68878). The participants also had greater responses to products with cultural elements than to those products without cultural elements. In other words, a product with cultural meaning is more attractive than a product without cultural meaning. Subjectively, participants felt that products with cultural elements (M = 4.6192; SD = 1.56252) were more beautiful than the products without cultural elements (M = 4.0339; SD = 1.50635). Furthermore, they preferred products with cultural elements (M = 4.1020; SD = 1.58218) over products without cultural elements (M = 3.6228; SD = 1.48670). In short, our participants preferred products with cultural elements. Similarly, older consumers are more willing to purchase products with cultural elements (M = 3.6552; SD = 1.72045) than those without cultural elements (M = 3.2285; SD = 1.57754). Finally, the results indicated that products with cultural elements have a greater chance of evoking older consumers' emotions (valence: M = 4.4183/4.1993; SD = 1.50337/1.56865), compared to products without cultural elements (arousal: M = 3.9743/3.7313; SD = 1.44845/1.49826).

6 Discussion

Products with aesthetic qualities can evoke users' emotions affectively. This result is consistent with previous research (Bloch et al. 2003; Creusen et al. 2010). The results of the present study further confirm that both external aesthetics (i.e., symmetry) and internal aesthetics (i.e., cultural meaning) are capable of evoking older participants' emotions. In this case, participants' emotions were evoked by products whose appearances contained Chinese cultural patterns that made sense to them. Most of our Chinese participants obviously perceived the patterns in the stimuli, and somehow these patterns connected to their cognitive processes. It is also possible that these patterns were familiar to the participants. The population studied here had long been familiar with these patterns, as they appear on their furniture and are present in daily television shows.

We determined that older consumers prefer products that have a beautiful appearance, which increases their familiarity, visual adaptation, and satisfaction when observed and used in daily life. Designers should be aware that older consumers prefer both symmetrical forms and cultural elements, as both provide stable images and meaningful content.

In this experiment, we used very traditional patterns in the stimuli, and these were attractive to our participants, but are there any other patterns also associated with these cultural elements in older consumers' minds? Do they have to be visual elements? Might they, instead, be familiar scents, for example? We believe that all aspects of the senses could be the elements to evoke users' emotions, as long as they are capable of recalling users' memories. With this in mind, products' physical appearances should be designed with stable-looking forms, such as those rooted in symmetry. As designers, we should note that older users also prefer beautiful products that include both symmetry and culturally pleasant forms. These designed elements are capable of motivating them to purchase products that, in turn, have a greater chance of satisfying them and making them happy when using them.

References

Bart, Y., Stephen, A.T., Sarvary, M.: Which products are best suited to mobile advertising? A field study of mobile display advertising effects on consumer attitudes and intentions. J. Mark. Res. **51**(3), 270–285 (2014)

Berlyne, D.E.: Aesthetics and Psychobiology. Appleton-Century-Crofts, New York (1971)

Blijlevens, J., Creusen, M.E., Schoormans, J.P.: How consumers perceive product appearance: the identification of three product appearance attributes. Int. J. Des. **3**(3), 27–35 (2009)

Bloch, P.H., Brunel, F.F., Arnold, T.J.: Individual differences in the centrality of visual product aesthetics: concept and measurement. J. Consum. Res. **29**(4), 551–565 (2003)

Coates, D.: Watches Tell More than Time. McGraw-Hill, New York (2003)

Creusen, M.E.H., Veryzer, R.W., Schoormans, J.P.L.: Product value importance and consumer preference for visual complexity and symmetry. Eur. J. Mark. **44**(9/10), 1437–1452 (2010)

Dhar, R., Wertenbroch, K.: Consumer choice between Hedonic and Utilitarian goods. J. Mark. Res. **37**(1), 60–71 (2000)

Evans, C., Wenderoth, P., Cheng, K.: Detection of bilateral symmetry in complex biological images. Perception **29**(1), 31–42 (2000)

Giannouli, V.: Visual symmetry perception. Encephalos **50**, 31–42 (2013)

Grammer, K., Thornhill, R.: Human (Homo sapiens) facial attractiveness and sexual selection: the role of symmetry and averageness. J. Comp. Psychol. **108**(3), 233–242 (1994)

Hekkert, P., Peper, C.E., van Wieringen, P.C.W.: The effect of verbal instruction and artistic background on the aesthetic judgment of rectangles. Empir. Stud. Arts **12**(2), 185–203 (1994)

Helander, M.G., Khalid, H.M.: Affective and pleasurable design. In: Salvendy, G. (ed.) Handbook on Human Factors and Ergonomics, pp. 543–572. Wiley, New York (2006)

Hirschman, E.C., Holbrook, M.B.: Hedonic consumption: emerging concepts, methods and propositions. J. Mark. **46**(3), 92–101 (1982)

Holbrook, M.B., Schindler, R.M.: Nostalgic bonding: exploring the role of nostalgia in the consumption experience. J. Consum. Behav. **3**(2), 107–127 (2003)

Hoyer, W.D., Stokburger-Sauer, N.E.: The role of aesthetic taste in consumer behavior. J. Acad. Mark. Sci. **40**(1), 167–180 (2012)

Hume, D.K., Montgomerie, R.: Facial attractiveness signals different aspects of "quality" in women and men. Evol. Hum. Behav. **22**(2), 93–112 (2001)

Jones, B.C., Little, A.C., Penton-Voak, I.S., Tiddeman, B.P., Burt, D.M., Perrett, D.I.: Facial symmetry and judgments of apparent health: support for a "good genes" explanation of the attractiveness symmetry relationship. Evol. Hum. Behav. **22**(6), 417–429 (2001)

Julesz, B.: Foundations of Cyclopean Perception. University of Chicago Press, Chicago (1971)

Khalid, H.M.: Can customer needs express affective design? In: Helander, M.G., Khalid, H.M., Po, T.M. (eds.) Proceeding of Affective Human Factors Design, pp. 190–198. ASEAN Academic Press, London (2001)

Koehler, N., Rhodes, G., Simmons, L.: Are human female preferences for symmetrical male faces enhanced when conception is likely? Anim. Behav. **64**(2), 233–238 (2002)

Lauer, D.A.: Design Basics. Holt, Rinehart and Winston, New York (1979)

Lewalski, Z.M.: Product Esthetics: An Interpretation for Designers. Design & Development Engineering Press, Carson City (1988)

Lin, Y., Huang, C.-S.: Aging in Taiwan: building a society for activity aging and aging in place. Gerontol. Soc. Am. **56**, 176–183 (2015)

Little, A.C., Burt, D.M., Penton-Voak, I.S., Perrett, D.I.: Self-perceived attractiveness influences human preferences for sexual dimorphism and symmetry in male faces. Proc. Roy. Soc. Lond. Ser. B: Biol. Sci. **270**, 1759–1763 (2001)

Lutz, R.J., MacKenzie, S.B., Belch, G.E.: Attitude toward the ad as a mediator of advertising effectiveness: determinants and consequences. In: Bagozzi, R.P., Tybout, A.M. (eds.), Advances in Consumer Research, vol. 10, pp. 532–539. Association for Consumer Research, Ann Arbor, MI (1983)

Marchegiani, C., Phau, I.: The value of historical nostalgia for marketing management. Mark. Intell. Plan. **29**(2), 108–122 (2011)

McDonagh, D., Bruseberg, A., Haslam, C.: Visual product evaluation: exploring users' emotional relationships with products. Appl. Ergon. **33**(3), 231–240 (2002)

Mealy, L., Bridgestock, R., Townsend, G.: Symmetry and perceived facial attractiveness. J. Pers. Soc. Psychol. **76**(1), 151–158 (1999)

Murdoch, P., Flurscheim, C.H.: Form. In: Flurscheim, C.H. (ed.) Industrial Design in Engineering, pp. 105–131. The Design Council, Worcester, UK (1983)

Penton-Voak, I.S., et al.: Symmetry, sexual dimorphism in facial proportions and male facial attractiveness. Proc. Roy. Soc. Lond. Ser. D. Biol. Sci. **268**, 1617 1623 (2001)

Perrett, D.I., Burt, D.M., Penton-Voak, I., Lee, K., Rowland, D., Edwards, R.: Symmetry and human facial attractiveness. Evol. Hum. Behav. **20**(5), 295–307 (1999)

Postrel, V.: The Substance of Style. HarperCollins, New York (2003)

Rhodes, G.: The evolutionary psychology of facial beauty. Annu. Rev. Psychol. **57**, 199–226 (2006)

Rhodes, G., Proffitt, F., Grady, J., Sumich, A.: Facial symmetry and the perception of beauty. Psychon. Bull. Rev. **5**(4), 659–669 (1998)

Rhodes, G., Yoshikawa, S., Clark, A., Lee, K., McKay, R., Akamatsu, S.: Attractiveness of facial averageness and symmetry in non-Western cultures: in search of biological based standards of beauty. Perception, **30**(5), 611–625 (2001a)

Rhodes, G., Zebrowitz, L., Clark, A., Kalick, S.M., Hightower, A., McKay, R.: Do facial averageness and symmetry signal health? Evol. Hum. Behav. **22**(1), 31–46 (2001b)

Schmitt, B., Simonson, A.: The Strategic Management of Brands, Identity & Image. The Free Press, New York (1997)

Tuch, N.A., Bargas-Avila, A.J., Opwis, K.: Symmetry and aesthetics in website design: it's a man's business. Comput. Hum. Behav. **26**(6), 1831–1837 (2010)

Tyler, C.W. (ed.): Human Symmetry Perception and its Computational Analysis. Erlbaum, Mahwah (2002)

Veryzer, R.W., Hutchinson, J.W.: The influence of unity and prototypicality on aesthetic responses to new product designs. J. Consum. Res. **24**(4), 374–394 (1998)

Wagemans, J.: Parallel visual processing in symmetry perception: Normality and pathology. Doc. Ophthalmol. **95**, 359–370 (1999)

Washburn, D., Humphrey, D.: Symmetries in the mind: production, perception, and preference for seven one-dimensional patterns. Vis. Arts Res. **27**(2), 57–68 (2001)

Wenderoth, P.: The salience of vertical symmetry. Perception **23**(2), 221–236 (1994)

Zaichkowsky, J.L.: Measuring the involvement construct. J. Consum. Res. **12**(3), 341–352 (1985)

Aging and Technology Acceptance

Capturing the Adoption Intention and Interest in InOvUS an Intelligent Oven: Segmenting Senior Users to Evaluate the Technology

Bessam Abdulrazak[1]([✉]), Susan E. Reid[2], and Monica Alas[1]

[1] Université de Sherbrooke, Sherbrooke, QC, Canada
{bessam.abdulrazak,monica.alas}@usherbrooke.ca
[2] Bishop's University, Lennoxville, QC, Canada
sreid@ubishops.ca

Abstract. Cognitive issues associated with aging have become a major concern as it affects how seniors carry on activities of daily living, like cooking. The kitchen has been cited as the key problem area for seniors and it is well cited that almost all senior Americans and Canadians (90%) live independently in their community and wish to remain this way for as long as possible. We propose a solution, InOvUS, which focuses on safety and reducing the risk of fire, burn and intoxication for the rising senior population. We also developed a conceptual adoption model that is specific to the 65+ segment and that is based on existing scales like Consumer Adoption Intention (CAI), Consumer Innovativeness (CI), Technology Acceptance Model (TAM), Perceived Ease of Use (PEOU) and Perceived Usefulness (PU). We evaluate the adoption intention and interest of InOvUS by dissecting seniors' willingness-to-adopt through the application of a cluster analytical procedure. The segments were profiled using K-Means analysis. Our results confirmed that the seniors do not behave like a homogenous group when assessing their need to acquire and use technologies such as InOvUS. Rather, four distinct segments further define the senior population, which differ considerably in terms of their buying intention, perceived usefulness, perceived ease of use, adoption intention and consumer innovativeness.

Keywords: Willingness-to-adopt · Intelligent oven · Safety ·
Cognitive decline · Seniors

1 Introduction

As the rising number of seniors globally doubles from 12% to 22% between 2015 and 2050, all countries will be facing major challenges to ensure that their health and social systems are ready for this major demographic shift [20]. Cognitive issues caused by aging have become a major concern as it affects how seniors carry on activities of daily living, like cooking. As a matter of fact, the kitchen has been cited as the key problem area for seniors and it is well cited that almost all senior Americans and Canadians (90%) live independently in their community and wish to remain this way for the

© Springer Nature Switzerland AG 2019
J. Zhou and G. Salvendy (Eds.): HCII 2019, LNCS 11592, pp. 109–120, 2019.
https://doi.org/10.1007/978-3-030-22012-9_9

longest possible time. More specifically, in seniors aged 65+ burns and fires have been found to be the 5th leading cause of accidental death [1].

As reported in the American Burn Association [6] 43% of these accidental deaths occur from fire/flame, 34% from scald injuries and 9% from a contact with a hot object. Seniors' limited mobility combined with the physical inability to quickly react and reach safety when faced with danger are one of the main factors that impact their vulnerability to burn injuries. In fact, 23.7% of seniors collapse when they are caught in a fire which aggravates their injuries [17]. Moreover, in a recent leading study on senior patients who were discharged from the emergency unit, it was demonstrated that 68% of all burns among seniors were related to cooking, with the majority of these burns originating in the kitchen [12]. When we take into account that 82.6% of all burn injuries reported actually occurred at home [5], the kitchen embodies a very high majority of all cases of burns.

Indeed, the aging process is said to trigger physical, sensorial and cognitive declines, with all of which have severe impacts on Activities of Daily Living (ADL) and not to mention the side effects of medication. Aging is a complex multi-factorial process that is often associated with increased dependence and requirement for assistance with activities [7]. Even more specifically, some cognitive decline in aging, like problems related to attention and memory, limit people in performing their cooking tasks. As a result, seniors and their family members become strongly concerned with cooking-associated risks (e.g., fire, burn or intoxication) [1].

In Canada there are 5.8 million 65+ Canadians and the number of 80+ has been forecasted to more than double to 3.3 million by 2036 based on a medium growth scenario [23] whereas in the United States, by 2060, the number of 65+ (47.8 million) is projected to double (98.2 million) and 19.7 million will be 85+ [25]. All this making the safety management of cooking risk a vital concern and even more so when taking into account that the vast majority of seniors living independently (90%) want to remain in their environment as long as possible [8]. Consequently, one of the moti-vations for assistive technologies research is the significant increase of an aging population around the globe which is projected to increase to 2 billion in 2050 [19]. More specifically, the senior population projected growth pattern places a real burden on healthcare facilities and social services, aside caregivers, as ensuring safety of activities of daily life becomes a critical element in helping seniors remain autonomous. This is even more accentuated when seniors engage with what can become a high-risk activity such as cooking. As a result, today there is an increasing number of tech-nologies that focus on specific assistive needs. However, although there have been advances in the sensing and ambient intelligence technologies, the focus has been on the technology side, rather than on building knowledge and methods to understand seniors' willingness-to adopt such technologies.

The research objectives of this paper are: (1) to research the literature to identify the risks and solutions posed for seniors when cooking; (2) to identify the interest in an intelligent oven, such as the Intelligent Oven at the University of Sherbrooke (InOvUS) a safety kitchen solution which focuses on safety and reducing the risk of fire, burn and intoxication, designed to better manage such risks; and (3) to assess whether there are segments within the senior population and examine the ways in which these segments differ in their willingness-to-adopt InOvUS. In fact, the application of a segmentation strategy to our analysis will deepen our understanding of the dynamics of seniors' needs and requirements regarding assistive technologies.

2 Literature Review

The literature was assessed from 2015 to 2018 by conducting a methodological review analysis, a technique which aims at identifying and appraising relevant research to see how researchers addressed a variety of topics ranging from the needs assessment to the conceptual development of intelligent oven as a response to burns, fire and intoxication among the 65+. The focus was on the proof of concept, quantitative and qualitative work, sampling techniques, data collection and data analysis involving the senior population.

Essentially, there are 3 major risks that can emerge while cooking in the kitchen: fire, burn and intoxication [1, 28]. Although, these 3 risks can result in devastating consequences, current research often addresses only fire as a risk in cooking [9, 14, 18, 27] and no global solution for kitchen safety has been reported. As seen in the literature, most work concentrate on identifying the causes and consequences of home fires without addressing specific populations that may present higher risks than others. Yet, a review of studies from 1990 to 1998 on factors that trigger domestic fires demonstrated a correlation between domestic fire sources and the type of people living in the housing unit [9] still no research work has focused on specific populations.

Additionally, the literature has also demonstrated that unattended cooking is the leading main factor responsible for fire in the kitchen [2, 16] and fires related to the usage of the oven, the use of unattended stove burners and the use of portable devices such as toasters [13] have been reported as the three main causes of fires while cooking. Moreover, a three-decade review of senior burn patients showed that for any given type of burn, among the 75+ age category, more serious consequences were reported including higher mortality rates. And although we can extrapolate that intoxication by inhalation is higher in the senior population, the literature has rarely covered this and instead has focused on injuries caused by carbon monoxide [21].

Although it is undisputable that the consequences of fire risks can be fatal to this date, there is a limited range of solutions that have been designed to reduce cooking-related risks affecting seniors in the kitchen. For instance, Doman et al. [11] devised a system that assists seniors avoid potential cooking hazards in the kitchen. By means of video and audio, the system transmits reminders to senior-users to follow the correct steps when performing a cooking task but this system has not been conceived to react in the advent of a dangerous situation. The literature also brings forth other systems that involve the help of a human. For instance, Sanchez et al. [22] designed a system to aid people when they are engaged in a cooking task. The system works by reacting when a potential dangerous situation is detected through rapid variations in temperature and smoke found in the kitchen. In response to rapid temperature variations, the system will send notifications with camera shots to caregivers and to the fire department, activate exhaust fans and a fire-extinguishing suppression system. Although it can be argued that this type of system can help mitigate risks from cooking activities, systems with camera surveillance are generally not well perceived and adopted by users due to the intrusion into the user's private life [15]. This is a critical issue because in the provision of care high usability and acceptance are essential for a system to be recognized as a practical assisted living system.

Some work has been done involving oven monitoring as a part of larger systems to track ADL. More specifically, Alwan et al. [3] focused on measuring oven usage whereas Wai et al. [26] approach was based on detecting unsafe usage of the oven. In the conception of intelligent systems, the key is to understand the user environments such as the surrounding kitchen temperature and senior activities, in order for the system to provide adaptive assistance to seniors. As such, both of these systems use embedded temperature sensors to measure the burner status, ultrasonic sensors to detect the presence of a pot and electric current sensors to detect the usage of the oven and levels of abnormality in the kitchen [26]. Still, similar with Sanchez et al.'s [22] system, these two systems could be considered intrusive, as they either use visible-light cameras or require modifications to the oven to install sensors.

A study by Yuan et al. [29] investigated an automated top oven-monitoring system that used thermal cameras to track dangerous situations. More precisely, this system alerts users or caregivers when a hazardous situation arises. What differentiates this system from Alwan et al. [3], Wai et al. [26] and Sanchez et al. [22] is that Yuan et al. [29] system is based on thermal imaging instead of visible-light cameras, thereby respecting user privacy. In fact, thermal cameras do not process regular images but are constricted to important limitations: they are sensitive to cooking heat and smoke. Although this system addresses the privacy violation concern by using a thermal camera, which in theory would increase the likelihood of such system to be accepted and used by seniors, the accuracy in detecting a dangerous situation in the kitchen environment that is subject to smoke and cooking heat is an issue. In fact, Demiris et al. [10] work showed that for an assistive living system to be accepted and used by seniors three major concerns need to be removed: privacy violation, sensor visibility and accuracy of the assistive living system.

Moreover, the aim of assistive technologies used in assistive living solutions is to provide hands on support to ensure that seniors live safely and independently in their homes. However, in all related work, it is obvious that the systems designed to manage or reduce cooking risks have major limitations that can impact senior's willingness to use and adopt such systems. Paradoxically, although the risks associated with age-related cognitive decline may positively influence seniors to adopt such systems, the invasion of privacy by the cameras of these systems can severely attenuate the interest and willingness of seniors to adopt them. It is clear that with the rapid rise of an ageing population, the numerous statistics on fires, burns and intoxication risks, as well as the restrained technologies available in the market all call out to the urgent need to develop solutions to improve senior quality-of-life while meeting their needs. Despite the fact that systems could provide the best assistive technology solution, if these systems are not easily accessible and user-friendly and if they do not correspond to the needs and concerns of seniors, such systems would not be accepted.

Moreover, to the best of our knowledge, only a limited number of assistive technologies to assist seniors in the kitchen have been developed. However, these previous studies have shown greater interest on the technology side, rather than on building safety (i.e., reducing the risk of fire, burn and inhaling) and knowledge from the perspective of the user. Indeed, almost all related work focuses more on evaluating the technical mechanisms and validating algorithms than on evaluating the end-user perspective of such systems. There is a greater importance that has been attributed to the accuracy of activity recognition for assistive technologies as the accuracy rate varies depending on the number and type of activities, the number and location of sensors used and the activity recognition models that detect ADLs often achieve lower accuracy than models that detect ambulatory activities [30]. Consequently and most importantly, none of the studies seen in the literature addresses the interest and/or adoption intention from the end-user perspective and the studies that focus on the technology side are mostly conducted by using young adults or rely on simulation which might not represent the true activity and reactions of a senior person [30].

To this end, this study aims at proposing an intelligent oven, or a sensor-based cooking safe system, called 'InOvUS'. InOvUS is designed to identify hazardous situations by monitoring and measuring relevant parameters around the oven to specifically reduce the risks of fire, smoke inhalation and burn. As such, InOvUS' fire parameters include concentrations of Volatile Organic Compound (VOC) and Alcohol gases that are found in the cooking environment. The burn parameters are derived from the relative humidity, utensil temperatures, burner temperature and presence of utensils on the burner for burn by splash and contact. Lastly, the concentration of Carbone monoxide (CO) gas is observed for intoxication by gas/smoke. These parameters are extracted based on an in-depth risk analysis [1]. Additionally, a segmentation strategy is incorporated to our analysis as key insight on the needs, requirements and interests of end-users have the ability to provide decisive information to ensure the effective development and design of assistive technologies.

3 Methodology

As the world senior population is projected to about 2 billion by 2050 [19] attention and a more profound understanding of seniors' complex needs is a necessity. As such, this paper is part of a framework for understanding the various components of seniors' willingness-to-adopt InOvUS.

In a previous exploratory phase, we developed a conceptual model to test senior's willingness-to-adopt, which was defined by five constructs in a past study [24]: *Buying Intention* (BI), *Perceived Usefulness* (PU), *Perceived Ease of Use* (PEOU), *Consumer Adoption Intention* (CAI) and *Consumer Innovativeness* (CI). Consumer Adoption Intention (CAI), a 4-item scale, measures and relates to whether consumer level of understanding of a product is strong enough to potentially lead to purchase. As such it is a good metric to utilize as a base to measure, 'Willingness-To-Adopt'. Consumer Innovativeness (CI) has to do with the level of comfort consumers find with the use of new products, in general. The literature has also consistently shown that both the perception of ease of use (PEOU) and usefulness (PU) on the part of consumers are important aspects of a decision of whether to adopt a new product (CAI) or buy it (BI), and therefore are also incorporated in our model. Our conceptual model is specific to the 65+ segment and it is based on existing scales for each construct. Figure 1 shows our research model.

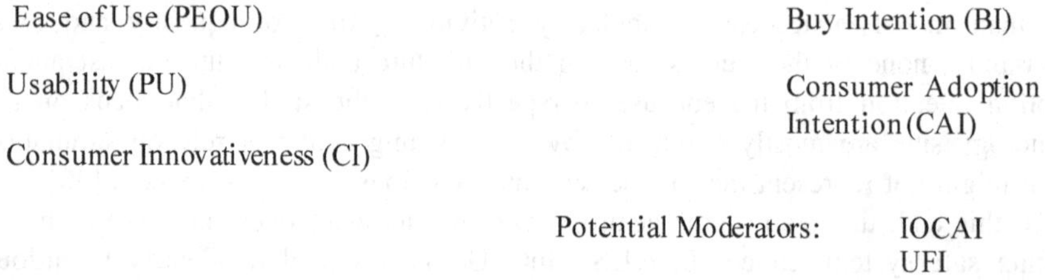

Ease of Use (PEOU)   Buy Intention (BI)

Usability (PU)   Consumer Adoption
                                                              Intention (CAI)
Consumer Innovativeness (CI)

                                    Potential Moderators: IOCAI
                                                               UFI

Fig. 1. Model Used: CAI: Consumer Adoption Intention; PEOU: Perceived Ease of Use; PU: Perceived Usefulness; CI: Consumer Innovativeness; IOCAI: Impact on Consumer Adoption Intention (by family members, caregivers); UFI: Usefulness for Family Influencers; BI: Buying Intention.

In total, these five constructs were captured by 14-items. The reliability for each construct was obtained using Cronbach's α and results show that our scales hold satisfactory internal consistency with all Cronbach's α above 0.750 and the Bartlett's Test of Sphericity has an associated p-value of 0.000 thereby confirming the statistical significance of our model. Participants were asked to rate their agreement with each statement on a 5-point scale anchored by "strongly disagree" and "strongly agree". The questionnaire, the detailed factor analysis, and key statistics can be consulted in our previous study [24].

The main objective of this research is to further investigate the interest and needs on an assistive technology such as InOvUS, to be able to better understand the design and development of intelligent ovens for an aging population. Therefore, our methodology is designed to evaluate the adoption intention and interest of InOvUS by further dissecting seniors' willingness-to-adopt through the application of a cluster analytical procedure. The underlying purpose is to see if there are segments within the senior population and examine the ways in which these segments differ in their willingness-to-adopt InOvUS. As such, we use the K-Means analysis to profile the segments. The applicability of segments in the senior population will derive a clearer understanding of seniors' needs and interest to assist and inform the design, development, and implementation decisions of InOvUS.

4   Results

In total, 57 seniors (65+) aged 65 to 95 participated in our study to test our model on seniors' adoption intention and interest of InOvUS as an innovative safety kitchen system. The key demographics of our sample can be examined in Table 1.

Table 1. Demographics of the sample

Gender	Male	44	Female	13

Driver's License	Yes	50	No	7

A ge	65 - < 70	70 - < 75	75 - < 80	80 - < 85	85 - < 90	90 - < 95	95+
	20 (35.1%)	18 (31.6%)	12 (21.1%)	3 (5.3%)	3 (5.3%)	1 (1.8%)	0 (0%)

General Health	Excellent	Very Good	Good	Fair	Poor
	17	22	16	1	

Physical Health or Emotional Problems Interference with Social Activities	None of the time	A little bit of the time	Some of the time	Most of the time	All of the time
	42	12	1	1	

Marital Status	Single	In couple	Married	Divorced	Separated	Widow
	4	9	22	9	1	12

In come	0 – 10,000	10,001 – 15,000	15,001 – 20,000	20,001 – 25,000	25,001 – 40,000	> 40,001	not disclose
	1 (1,8%)		13 (22.8%)	3 (5,3%)	9 (15,8%)	30 (52,6%)	1

To test the presence of segments in our sample, K-Means analysis was performed on the regressed factorial scores. The minimal sample size to be included in a cluster analysis is 2^k cases, where K is the number of variables [4]. As there are five factorial scores, the minimum sample size require to perform our analysis is 32.

Results confirm that the seniors do not behave like a homogenous group when evaluating their necessity to acquire and use technologies such as InOvUS. Rather, four distinct segments further define the senior population, which differ considerably in terms of their interest and willingness-to-adopt InOvUS (Cluster Mean Square BI $\alpha = 0.000$, Cluster Mean Square PU $\alpha = 0.000$, Cluster Mean Square PEOU $\alpha = 0.000$, Cluster Mean Square CAI $\alpha = 0.000$, Cluster Mean Square CI $\alpha = 0.000$). In other words, the senior population is composed of four distinct segments that differ considerably in terms of their buying intention, perceived usefulness, perceived ease of use, adoption intention and consumer innovativeness.

The results in Table 2 enable us to start profiling our segments. The most predominant segment in terms of size is segment 2, it is composed of 40% (23/57) of the senior population. 28% (16/57) of seniors are in segment 1, 23% (13/57) fall in segment 3 and 9% (5/57) of seniors form part of segment 4.

One of the benefits of conducting a segmentation analysis on InOvUS is to see how seniors' needs, attitudes and beliefs towards an intelligent oven varies. In more technical terms, these differences are explained by distance found between segments, whereby the distance measures how far apart two segments are from each other. Results in Table 2 show that all of our segments have different interests in InOvUS as there is a fair distance that exists between each segment. Specifically, the greatest distance is noted between segment 3 and 4 (3.646), as these are the two groups that are the least similar to each other followed by segment 2 and 4 (2.793). The differences in InOvUS are more accentuated between seniors in segment 1 and 4 (2.581) than between seniors in segment 1 and 2 (2.304).

Table 2. Segment constitution and segment distances between final segment centers

Segment	Number of cases in each segment	1	2	3	4
1	16.000		2.304	2.360	2.581
2	23.000	2.304		2.660	2.793
3	13.000	2.360	2.660		3.646
4	5.000	2.581	2.793	3.646	

Next, results in Table 3 show how the four segments differ according to their buying intention, perceived usefulness, perceived ease of use, adoption intention and consumer innovativeness.

Table 3. Segments scores per willingness-to-adopt construct

	Segments			
	1	2	3	4
BI REGR factor score	.51169	−.67989	.48647	.22528
PU REGR factor score	−.72958	−.00871	1.12250	−.54376
PEOU REGR factor score	.55983	−.95010	.69214	.77946
CAI REGR factor score	−.01527	.19519	−1.12175	2.06754
CI REGR factor score	.75754	−.26440	−.19059	−.71236

Compared to other segments, seniors forming part of segment 1 attribute the higher importance to CI (0.75754) and their willingness-to-adopt InOvUS is the least affected by PU (−0.72958). CI is the most important element for this segment, this is why we called them the *early adopters*. However, PEOU (0.55983) and BI (0.51169) also play a role in their interest level on assistive technologies such as InOvUS. Segment 2 is the segment that is the most difficult to convince in terms of BI (−0.67989), PEOU (−0.9501), and CI (−0.2644) and these seniors are almost indifferent towards PU

(−.00871). The key characteristic that differentiates them from all other segments is how picky they are when it comes to BI, this segment is called the *technology cautious*.

Segment 3 sees the greatest PU potential in what they can do with InOvUS (1.125) than all other segments. Conversely, they are also the ones that are the least concern about CAI (−1.12175). This segment is called the *technology driven*. For that group, PEOU is the other element that they will take into consideration when evaluating assistive technologies to help them mitigate reducing the risk of fire, burn and inhaling. Lastly, CAI (2.06754) is the key criteria, out of the five constructs that define the willingness-to-adopt, that influences segment 4 in their decision to adopt InOvUS but also when compared to all other segments. Therefore, CAI is what this segment values the most. We call them the *technology vigilant*. PEOU (0.77946) also sets apart seniors who belong in segment 4 as benefits is what interests this segment. Segment 4 also includes seniors that will rely the least on CI (−0.71236) and PU (−0.54376) to evaluate InOvUS.

5 Discussion

The results of our study show that to understand the needs of seniors and thus optimize the technology development, there are greater benefits to be achieved by segmenting the senior users as opposed to undertake a general approach to the needs assessment and interest of an assistive technology solution. More precisely, in our past study we demonstrated that PEOU was the driving force behind seniors' buying intention of InOvUS and that PU influences seniors' actual CAI [24]. However, by pursuing a segmentation approach we were able to see that seniors' interests and needs are actually more complex and can only be well defined by profiling each segment that constitutes the seniors. Additionally, this research demonstrates how different variable sets of the willingness-to-adopt (i.e., *Buying Intention* (BI), *Perceived Usefulness* (PU), *Perceived Ease of Use* (PEOU), *Consumer Adoption Intention* (CAI) and *Consumer Innovativeness* (CI)) impact each segment.

Indeed, the observation of the characteristics that differentiate the *early adopters* (segment 1) reveals that for 26% of the senior market being the first in their circle to adopt a technology such as InOvUS is a key driver behind the interest they will have towards such a device and in their desire to adopt it. After all, the early adopters are trendsetters, therefore, it is important for marketers and developers to understand that early adopters are not interested on how an intelligent oven can enhance their cooking effectiveness, improve their cooking performance or productivity, but that they are rather interested on the new technological advancements that an intelligent oven has to offer including its actual technological features and benefits. These are the key elements that will transform an interest into an adoption resolution. Yet, it is important that the early adopters perceive InOvUS as an intelligent oven that is easy to understand and use.

The technology cautious, segment 2, are seniors that have high expectations regarding what an assistive technology can do. Consequently, in order for them to be interested in adopting and using InOvUS requires that developers possess a thorough understanding of their technological needs for their expectations to be surpassed.

Otherwise, the technology cautious will continue to be reluctant to use InOvUS and they constitute 40% of the senior users. Additionally, as technology does not necessarily speak to them, as they need to see that how their needs can be met, they are negative as to how easy it can be to use and understand an assistive technology.

The key technological features for the technology driven, which represent 23% of the senior population, is what InOvUS can do to help them improve their cooking effectiveness, performance and productivity. These are the technological features that will make them seek to adopt an assistive technology when evaluating assistive technologies to help them mitigate reducing the risk of fire, burn and inhaling. For this segment, understanding what are the trade-offs among the costs and benefits of buying and using InOvUS, or knowing how they will have to change their behaviors to attain the potential benefits of such a technology or even what are the benefits they could expect if they bought it, are the least important technological concerns they can have compared to all other segments. For this group, an assistive technology has to be easy to use, clear and understandable as well as easy to get the technology to do what they want it to do for them to be willing to adopt it.

For the technology vigilant, an assistive technology has to be designed in such a way that the relevant trade-offs between the costs and benefits of using it are very apparent including whether or not a senior person has to change their behavior quite significantly to attain its potential benefits of using it. If developers are successful at this, the technology vigilant, which includes 9% of the senior users, will be inclined to adopt and use assistive technologies as that is the main driver influencing their willingness-to-adopt InOvUS and other assistive technology. Compared to other segments, the easiness to use InOvUS will seal their willingness-to-adopt it. Consequently, it is important that technology vigilant see that InOvUS is easy to use, easy to work with for them to get InOvUS to do what they want it to do and that InOvUS is easy to understand, as these seniors tend to pay more attention to features, in terms of usability, than their peers.

As we can see, our results show that there are more practical implications for targeting seniors by applying a segmentation approach than a general approach. Indeed, segmenting the senior users provides better guidelines for developers on how to address the technology development needs.

6   Conclusion and Limitation

Seniors have specific capabilities, limitations and experiences that affect their ADLs. Assistive technologies such as InOvUS have the potential to provide value in providing proactive support in mitigating the safety management of cooking risk. This is a vital importance especially when we consider that there will be two billion seniors in 2050 and that the vast majority want to live independently and remain in their environment as long as possible. The overall goal of our research work is to develop solutions for seniors, such as InOvUS, compensating for cognitive declines associated with aging. Our research instrument was designed to collect seniors' view on the development of the next generation of assistive technology to improve safety and reduce risks in seniors' home environment. However, many challenges remain to develop technologies that meet senior's needs, support them in performing everyday activities such as cooking, protect their independence and security. Indeed, one of the challenges to the effective design and development a technology like InOvUS is the understanding of the conceptual model of seniors and involving them at an early stage of development early enough in the technology development or design process. The present study makes a contribution that addresses this void. Our methodology of developing a willingness-to-adopt conceptual model that is specific for the 65+ population combined with a segmentation approach provides a unique opportunity to develop user needs studies and concept development for technological products while increasing the odds of seniors' willingness-to-adopt and use such products.

There is a limitation with regards to this study that pertain to a response bias that might have occurred as participants completed the questionnaire on a paper format. There was a section that had all of the 22 original willingness-to-adopt items divided in two pages. This type of survey formatting could have introduced an acquiescence response bias. This means that it is likely that a similar response pattern could have resulted in this section.

Moreover, we recommend that this study be repeated with seniors 65+ living in residence with full and partial autonomy as well as with seniors living at home. Furthermore, we will further evaluate our willingness-to-adopt model to develop other metrics aimed at obtaining an in-depth understanding of seniors' needs and requirements regarding in-home safety assistance.

Acknowledgments. The authors would like to acknowledge the generous financial support of the Fonds de recherche du Quebec nature et technologie, awarded through the INTER research team, the University of Sherbrooke and Bishop's University.

References

1. Abdulrazak, B., et al.: Toward pervasive computing system to enhance safety of ageing people in smart kitchen. In: International Conference on Information and Communication Technologies for Ageing Well and e-Health, pp. 17–28, Lisbon, Portugal (2015)
2. Ahrens, M.: Home smoke alarms: the data as context for decision. Fire Technol. **44**(4), 313 327 (2008)
3. Alwan, M., et al.: Impact of monitoring technology in assisted living: outcome pilot. IEEE Trans. Inf. Technol. Biomed. **10**(1), 192–198 (2006)
4. Formann, A.K.: Die Latent-Class-Analyse : Einführung in Theorie und Anwendung [Latent class analysis: Introduction to theory and application]. Weinheim, Beltz [W. Germany] (1984)
5. American Burn Association: Burn Injury Fact Sheet (2018)
6. American Burn Association: National Burn Repository report of data from 2005–2014, Chicago (2015)
7. Burdge, J.J., et al.: Surgical treatment of burns in elderly patients. J. Trauma Inj. Infect. Crit. Care **28**(2), 214–217 (1988)
8. PHA Canada: Healthy Aging in Canada: A new Vision, A Vital Investment, From Evidence to Action [a background paper], Ottawa, ON (2006)
9. D, K.: Reducing Residential Fires Fatalities [Rapport Technique] (1999)

10. Demiris, G., et al.: Senior residents' perceived need of and preferences for "smart home" sensor technologies. Int. J. Technol. Assess. Health Care **24**, 120–124 (2008)
11. Doman, K., Kuai, C.Y., Takahashi, T., Ide, I., Murase, H.: Video CooKing: towards the synthesis of multimedia cooking recipes. In: Lee, K.-T., Tsai, W.-H., Liao, H.-Y.M., Chen, T., Hsieh, J.-W., Tseng, C.-C. (eds.) MMM 2011. LNCS, vol. 6524, pp. 135–145. Springer, Heidelberg (2011). https://doi.org/10.1007/978-3-642-17829-0_13
12. Ehrlich, A.R., et al.: Elderly patients discharged home from the emergency department with minor burns. Burns **31**(6), 717–720 (2005)
13. Hall, J.R.: Home Cooking Fire Patterns and Trends. National Fire Protection Association, Quincy (2006)
14. Istre, G.R., Mallonee, S.: Smoke alarms and prevention of house-fire—related deaths and injuries. West. J. Med. **173**(2), 92–93 (2000)
15. Kim, Y., et al.: A server-based real-time privacy protection scheme against video surveillance by unmanned aerial systems. In: Conference Proceedings of the 2014 IEEE International Conference on Unmanned Aircraft Systems, ICUAS 2014, pp. 684–691 (2014)
16. Lushaka, B., Zalok, E.: Development of a sensing device to reduce the risk from kitchen fires. Fire Technol. **50**(3), 791–803 (2014)
17. Mabrouk, A., et al.: An epidemiologic study of elderly burn patients in Ain Shams University Burn Unit, Cairo, Egypt. Burns **27**(7), 687–690 (2003)
18. Mallonee, S., et al.: Surveillance and prevention of residential-fire injuries. N. Engl. J. Med. **335**(1), 27–31 (1996)
19. World Health Organization (2014). https://www.who.int/features/factfiles/ageing/ageing_facts/en/
20. World Health Organization. Ageing and Health (2018). https://www.who.int/news-room/fact-sheets/detail/ageing-and-health
21. Prockop, L.D., Chichkova, R.I.: Carbon monoxide intoxication: an updated review. J. Neurol. Sci. **262**(1–2), 122–130 (2007)
22. Sanchez, A., Burnell, L.: A smart home lab as a pedagogical tool. Intell. Adapt. Educ. Syst. **17**, 293–314 (2013)
23. Statistics Canada: Seniors (2017)
24. Reid, S.E., et al.: Modelling willingness-to-adopt an intelligent oven: capturing the seniors perspective. J. Health Sci. **6**, 5 (2018)
25. United Census Bureau: Facts for Features: Older Americans Month (2017)
26. Wai, A.A.P., Shanthini Devi, S., Biswas, J., Panda, S.K.: Pervasive intelligence system to enable safety and assistance in kitchen for Home-Alone Elderly. In: Abdulrazak, B., Giroux, S., Bouchard, B., Pigot, H., Mokhtari, M. (eds.) ICOST 2011. LNCS, vol. 6719, pp. 276–280. Springer, Heidelberg (2011). https://doi.org/10.1007/978-3-642-21535-3_41
27. Warda, L.J., Ballesteros, M.F.: Interventions to prevent residential fire injury. In: Doll, L.S., Bonzo, S.E., Sleet, D.A., Mercy, J.A. (eds.) Handbook of Injury and Violence Preventions, pp. 97–115. Springer, Boston (2007). https://doi.org/10.1007/978-0-387-29457-5_6
28. Yared, R., et al.: Cooking risk analysis to enhance safety of elderly people in smart kitchen. In: 8th ACM International Conference on PErvasive Technologies Related to Assistive Environments (PETRA). ACM, Corfu, Greece (2015)
29. Yuan, M.Y., et al.: Thermal imaging for assisted living at home: improving kitchen safety. J. Med. Biol. Eng. **33**(4), 380–387 (2013)
30. Zhu, C., Sheng, W.: Motion- and location-based online human daily activity recognition. Pervasive Mob. Comput. **7**, 256–269 (2011)

Older Users' Benefit and Barrier Perception of Using Ultrasonic Whistles in Home Care

Hannah Biermann[✉], Julia Offermann-van Heek, and Martina Ziefle

Human-Computer Interaction Center, RWTH Aachen University,
Campus-Boulevard 57, 52074 Aachen, Germany
{biermann,vanheek,ziefle}@comm.rwth-aachen.de

Abstract. Against the current development of demographic change, the proportion of older people in Germany increases. To compensate for supply gaps, ambient assisted living (AAL) technologies and systems provide new healthcare services for an aging population to grow old at home. However, the acceptance of assistive devices in the living environment is limited, for instance, by usability and privacy concerns. Hence, the present study examined the use of ultrasonic whistles in home care with special attention given to older adults' benefit and barrier perception. For this purpose, an online questionnaire was conducted ($N = 188$) focusing on people aged 50 years and older. Results revealed significant influences of the participants' health status on the perception and attitudes towards aging. Further, a cluster analysis revealed three groups of participants differing distinctly in their perception of benefits and barriers of the described AAL technology based on ultrasonic whistles. Besides considerable evaluation differences, these groups were further characterized by impacts of gender, attitude towards aging, and a distinct intention to use the described technology. This study's outcomes contribute to a deeper understanding of age and the perception of aging in the context of AAL technology acceptance.

Keywords: Ambient assisted living · Technology acceptance · Age ·
Aging in place · Ultrasonic whistle · Benefit and barrier perception

1 Introduction

Due to continuous shifts in the age structure, elderly people, their needs, and demands, move into the focus of today's society [1]. Regarding the European Union, Germany is one of the countries where demographic change proceeds rapidly, since nearly one in five people is 65 years or older – provided that this number will rise to one-third by 2060 – while the working-age population steadily declines [2, 3]. As aging restricts health and mobility, new care measures are needed to bridge the gap between growing care needs and shortages of skilled workers [4]. To this, ambient assisted living (AAL) technologies and systems, such as the ultrasonic whistle, provide innovative solutions to increase independence in old age and relieve health care.

In general, AAL is referred to as "the use of information and communication technologies (ICT), stand-alone assistive devices, and smart home technologies in a person's daily living and working environment to enable individuals to stay active

© Springer Nature Switzerland AG 2019
J. Zhou and G. Salvendy (Eds.): HCII 2019, LNCS 11592, pp. 121–139, 2019.
https://doi.org/10.1007/978-3-030-22012-9_10

longer, remain socially connected, and live independently into old age" [5]. The ultrasonic whistle is a new assistive device that is to be used as an integrated part of supportive home environments and can be installed at little cost and effort, e.g., in switches fixed to the wall. The user interface is particularly designed for people with motoric disabilities, who can easily access and operate the ultrasonic whistle on a large and robust surface at the push of a button, for example. As a holistic assistance system, the ultrasonic whistle is adaptable to personal needs, such as the automation of domestic tasks, safety prevention, and fall detection.

Though, assistive devices facilitate aging in place, they are not accepted per se due to perceived restrictions, such as privacy concerns within living space [6]. In fact, the perception and evaluation of AAL technologies and systems differ among users [7]. Hence, the willingness to adopt innovative technology strongly depends on user-diverse factors, such as trust when dealing with technology [8], data security and control needs [9], but also personal experience with care and disabilities [10]. Particularly with regard to older adults, a central but heterogeneous user group of AAL, there are different needs and demands on what an assistance system should (not) be able to do [11]. Hence, this study's aim was to examine the assessment of ultrasonic whistles in home care with special regard to older users' benefit and barrier perception, since so far there is only little known about requirements of the elderly in this context.

2   The Acceptance of AAL in an Aging Society

In recent years, the majority of frail and older people in Germany has been cared for by family members at home, since nursing staff decreases [12], but also, because many (care-dependent) people prefer to grow old in their familiar environment [13]. This development opened up other ways of long-term care, besides traditional nursing homes and care wards, leading to "aging in place" as a growing research branch [e.g., 14–19]. In order to support aging in place and relieve those affected, ambient assisted living (AAL) technologies and systems have been investigated in a variety of applications and contexts to meet individual user demands and care needs [e.g., 20–23]. In practice, AAL includes stand-alone devices, which are often visible for others (e.g., stair lift), as well as holistic systems that are unobtrusively integrated into the living environment (e.g., floor sensors for fall detection) to prevent stigmatization, support residents and their relatives in daily life, and enhance caregiving tasks [24–27].

In the present study, the focus was set on the ultrasonic whistle, a new AAL application for home care. The final ultrasonic whistle will be small and made of soft silicone, so it can be installed in user friendly switches and easily retrofitted in different places (e.g., living spaces and objects). Technically, ultrasound is generated mechanically (when the switch is actuated) and transmitted via air towards microphones and receivers for decoding [28, 29]. Receiving devices are installed in ceiling lights or other home devices nearby, which are permanently connected to electricity, to ensure a reliable signal transmission. The ultrasonic signal is frequency coded using different pipe lengths to activate one specific function. In particular, the ultrasonic whistle serves for home automation (e.g., automatic door and window opening or lightning control) and emergency services (e.g., emergency calls to outside assistance).

Against the background of an aging society, the key is to adjust AAL technologies and systems to the needs of older users, as they are at a higher risk for diseases and care [30]. One of the main challenges is, that the adoption of assistive devices in the personal living environment can be limited by perceived barriers (e.g., low usability, technical support, and experience) [31]. This is particularly important with regard to older adults, who are less expertized [9] and may be restricted in the use of technology by memory loss or motoric disabilities, for example [32]. However, disease incidences [33], the way people feel satisfied with their personal aging process [34], as well as the perceived need for technical assistance (e.g., due to disabilities) [10] differ between individuals. Hence, it is essential to address "the elderly" as a heterogeneous user group [17].

To predict the intention to use and usage behavior, age was integrated as a moderating factor into technology acceptance models, here to be mentioned in particular UTAUT (unified theory of acceptance and use of technology) [35] and its extension to UTAUT2 [36]. However, both models lack the possibility of context transfer [37] – as they were not specifically tested in the sensitive context of AAL – and the consideration of age as a multidimensional factor (e.g., including self-perceptions of and attitudes towards aging [34, 38]).

For a deeper understanding, user studies focused on older adults' personal requirements concerning the use of AAL, with special regard to trade-offs between perceived benefits and barriers [e.g., 39–41]. For this purpose, diverse research approaches were conducted, using qualitative and quantitative methods (e.g., interviews [42], focus groups [32], and scenario-based questionnaires [43]) as well as participatory [44] and mixed-method designs [45]. Results showed that older users are aware and appreciate the advantages of AAL as great support for aging in place – but also, that it affects their perception and meaning of home, as the necessity of using assistive devices creates an awareness of own health insufficiencies and users may behave differently because of monitoring systems in their living environment [32, 42].

Major perceived benefits referred to an increased feeling of independence, a stronger sense of security, and the opportunity to reduce burdens on family caregivers [13, 41–43]. In particular, visual and hearing aids, the automation of home infrastructure, and reminder systems for appointment notices were appreciated to cope with everyday tasks [32]. In contrast, privacy concerns, the feeling of losing control over technology and being restricted in one's own behavioral freedom, less human contact as well as usability risks were detected as strong perceived barriers [31, 32, 41–43]. As personal characteristics (e.g., confidence), attitudinal factors (e.g., the perceived usefulness of a technology), and the social environment (e.g., family support) influence the decision to adopt or reject technology assistance at home [31], there is a need to take greater account of user factors, particularly in connection with the technology acceptance of elderly people [46].

Concerning the ultrasonic whistle, previous studies showed that its acceptance depended on different functions and usage locations, provided that emergency applications in the bathroom were appreciated the most – with regard to the users' perspective, biological age and attitudes towards aging seemed to affect the adoption of ultrasonic whistle in home care [47]. As the technology is still under development, there is great potential to iteratively integrate user requirements into the production process to achieve high acceptance levels.

3 Method

The following section presents the study's empirical approach, the design of the online questionnaire, a description of the study's sample as well as detailed insights regarding the relationships between the user factors age, aging, and health status.

3.1 Empirical Design

The current study aimed for (a) an investigation of older people's attitude towards aging and (b) the examination of older people's benefit and barrier perception with regard to AAL technology based on usage of ultrasonic whistles. For both research aims an empirical approach was needed considering individual user factors as potential influencing parameters, e.g., gender, health status, or attitude towards aging (only for benefit and barrier perception).

An overview of the underlying empirical research design is presented in Fig. 1. The items of the online questionnaire based on a literature review (e.g., attitudes towards aging) as well as on a preceding qualitative study [38], in which in particular diverse benefits and barriers were identified with regard to using an AAL system based on ultrasonic whistles within the own home environment.

The first part of the questionnaire referred to independent variables including demographics of the participants such as age, gender, educational level, occupation, income (optional), and living circumstances. Additionally, this part also considered the participants' health status by asking if the participants (answer options: yes/no) suffer from a chronic illness, depend on care, depend on using medical assisting technology, or have a physical impairment. If a participant answered one of these aspects with "yes", he or she was categorized as "ill" and otherwise as "healthy". A last aspect belonging to the independent variables, referred to the participants' attitude towards aging using 10 items focusing on the areas health, active aging, dealing with change, autonomy, and social integration. The items based on a preceding study [38], included potential positive as well as negative aspects of aging, and were assessed on a six-point Likert scale (min = 1: "I strongly disagree"; max = 6: "I strongly agree").

Following this first part of the questionnaire, a scenario was used in order to emphasize the participants with a situation of care needs due to health restrictions. The scenario contained a short explanation of an AAL system based on ultrasonic whistles and described possible functions and applications, i.e. using ultrasonic whistles as emergency button or for fall detection by integrating them into the floor. Within the scenario, the participants were asked to imagine the situation that he/she or a close family member is in need of care and an AAL system based on ultrasonic whistles was integrated unobtrusively in the home environment in order to enable an active and autonomous longer staying at home. The technical description as well as the scenario were evaluated in a pretest with participants of different ages ensuring comprehensibility and clarity.

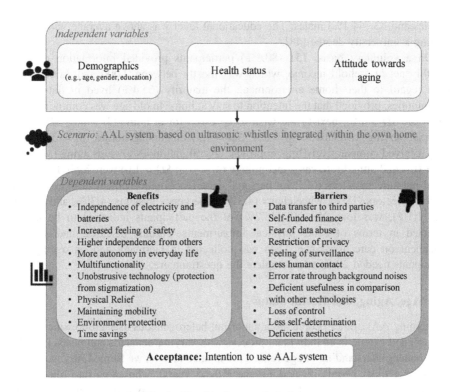

Fig. 1. Empirical research design.

Following the scenario, the participants were asked to evaluate perceived benefits and perceived barriers of the AAL system, as well as their acceptance in terms of their intention to use the described AAL system in their daily routine. As first dependent construct, perceived benefits were evaluated using 10 items (α = .918) focusing on safety, relief, independency, mobility, invisibility, but also on technology-specific aspects in terms of independency of electricity and batteries. As a second construct, perceived barriers were assessed using 11 items (α = .891) reaching from data security and privacy-related aspects to concerns about finances, surveillance, or control. Finally, the acceptance of the described AAL system was evaluated using 4 items (α = .886) referring to the participants' behavioral intention to use the system. All items of the dependent variables were evaluated using six-point Likert scales (min = 1: "I strongly disagree"; max = 6: "I strongly agree").

Overall, evaluations above the mean of the scale (>3.5) indicated acceptance, whereas evaluations below the mean of the scale (<3.5) indicated rejection of a statement or construct.

3.2 Sample Description

In total, 188 (= N) participants completed the questionnaire, aged between 50 and 93 years, with an average of 61.8 years (SD = 9.8). The sample consisted of 105 (55.9%)

females and 83 (44.1%) males. The educational level was above average with 44.1% holding a university degree [48].

On a voluntary basis, 151 (80.3%) participants provided information on their monthly net household income, which was mostly between 2,000 and 3,000 euros. With regard to their home environment, the majority (65.4%) lived in flat-sharing communities, provided that the intention to stay at home in old age was commonly high ($M = 5.2$; $SD = 1.0$), next to the wish to be cared for at home ($M = 4.0$; $SD = 1.5$), whereas moving to relatives ($M = 2.4$; $SD = 1.3$) or nursing homes ($M = 2.3$; $SD = 1.2$) received comparatively little approval. Overall, attitudes towards aging ($M = 4.1$; $SD = 0.7$) and attitudes towards technology ($M = 4.5$; $SD = 1.0$) were high. Except for blood pressure monitors (61.2%), personal experience with medical devices, such as motion detectors (17%), wheelchairs (4.3%), emergency systems (4.3%), and bathtub lifts (1.1%), was low. Yet, 85 (45.2%) of the participants indicated to be health-restricted in terms of acute physical impairments, chronic diseases, and/or being dependent on care assistance. Data was collected in Germany and on average the participants needed 20 min to complete the questionnaire.

3.3 Age, Aging, and Health Status

Concerning AAL, older people are a major but heterogeneous user group, since aging, its onset and extent, is an individual process with varying demands and needs [17, 30]. For a better understanding of age-related acceptance factors, we formed two age groups considering older people in working-age (50–65 years), who came into question as family caregivers, and the elderly (≥ 66 years) as potentially care-dependent patients. Descriptive age group profiles of demographic and attitudinal data are presented in Table 1. With regard to aging perceptions, both age groups were positively inclined. However, slight differences were observable, indicating that people in working-age ($M = 4.1$; $SD = 0.6$) tended to be a little more optimistic concerning issues such as health, dealing with change, active aging, social integration, and autonomy than the elderly ($M = 4.0$; $SD = 0.8$).

Table 1. Descriptive age group profiles of demographic and attitudinal data.

	Older people in working age (50–65 years; $n = 134$)	The elderly (≥ 66 years; $n = 54$)
Age	$M = 56.6$ ($SD = 4.4$)	$M = 74.9$ ($SD = 6.6$)
Gender	female $n = 76$ (56.7%)	female $n = 29$ (53.7%)
	male $n = 58$ (43.3%)	male $n = 25$ (46.3%)
Health status	healthy $n = 75$ (56%)	healthy $n = 28$ (51.9%)
	ill $n = 59$ (44%)	ill $n = 26$ (48.1%)
Attitudes towards aging (min 1; max 6)	$M = 4.1$ ($SD = 0.6$)	$M = 4.0$ ($SD = 0.8$)

Correlation analyses (see Table 2) did not confirm a relation between age and attitudes towards aging ($r_s = -.057$; $p = .441$; n.s.). However, health status correlated with attitudes towards aging ($r_s = .348$; $p < .01$), indicating that people in good health shared more positive aging concepts compared to those who were affected by health restrictions.

Table 2. Correlation analyses of user factors ([**]$p < .01$).

	Age	Gender	Health status	Attitude towards aging
Age	–	.031	−.118	−.057
Gender	–	–	−.073	−.097
Health status	–	–	–	.348[**]
Attitudes towards aging	–	–	–	–

For a closer regard to attitudes towards aging depending on the participants' health status, two health groups were formed: The first group consisted of "healthy" participants ($n = 103$) who were not affected by any health restrictions and thus, also not dependent on nursing services, whereas the second group of "ill" participants ($n = 85$) indicated to suffer from acute or chronic diseases and, partially, being care-dependent. Descriptive health group profiles of demographic and attitudinal data are presented in Table 3.

Table 3. Descriptive health group profiles of demographic and attitudinal data.

	Healthy group ($n = 103$)	Ill group ($n = 85$)
Age	$M = 61.1$ ($SD = 9.0$)	$M = 62.7$ ($SD = 10.6$)
Gender	female $n = 60$ (58.3%)	female $n = 45$ (52.9%)
	male $n = 43$ (41.7%)	male $n = 40$ (47.1%)
Attitudes towards aging (min 1; max 6)	$M = 4.3$ ($SD = 0.6$)	$M = 3.9$ ($SD = 0.7$)

Overall, the group of healthy participants had more positive attitudes towards aging ($M = 4.3$; $SD = 0.6$) compared to the ill ones ($M = 3.9$; $SD = 0.7$). In detail (see Fig. 2), for the healthy group, aging in particular included *staying in contact* ($M = 5.5$; $SD = 0.7$) with others, next to *making plans* ($M = 5.0$; $SD = 0.8$), *being more relaxed* ($M = 4.8$; $SD = 1.0$), and *keep on learning* ($M = 4.6$; $SD = 0.9$), whereas pessimistic aging concepts, especially *less enjoyment* ($M = 2.6$; $SD = 1.2$), did not seem to bother them that much. In contrast, the group of ill participants tended to evaluate negative aging attitudes more strongly, in particular the fear of *being less fit and lively* ($M = 4.4$; $SD = 1.2$) and *decreasing health* ($M = 4.3$; $SD = 1.0$), as well as *being dependent* ($M = 3.8$; $SD = 1.3$) on others, although, their perception of positive aging concepts was still high.

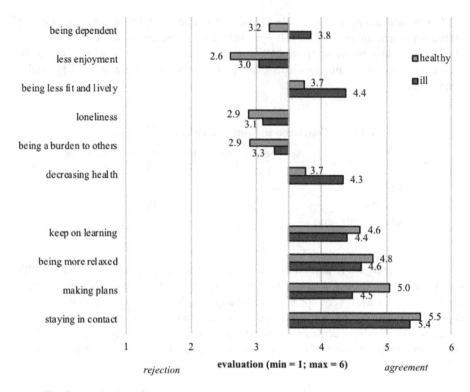

Fig. 2. Evaluation of attitudes towards aging between two health groups (means).

4   Results

The following section presents the study's results starting with the evaluations of benefits and barriers with regard to the whole sample. Afterwards, the results of a cluster analysis are detailed in order to understand user-specific evaluation patterns concerning benefit and barrier perceptions of a specific AAL technology.

4.1   Overall Evaluation of Using Ultrasonic Whistles in Home Care

In general, the acceptance of ultrasonic whistles in home care was rather high ($M = 4.0$; $SD = 1.2$) with minor evaluation differences concerning different usage locations and installation sites. According to this, the participants agreed to use the ultrasonic whistle in the *bathroom* ($M = 4.7$; $SD = 1.2$) rather than in the *bedroom* ($M = 4.5$; $SD = 1.3$) and *living room* ($M = 4.4$; $SD = 1.4$). Besides, the installation on *doors* ($M = 4.2$; $SD = 1.5$), *wall switches* ($M = 3.9$; $SD = 1.5$), and *windows* ($M = 3.8$; $SD = 1.5$) was more acceptable compared with *cupboards* ($M = 3.6$; $SD = 1.5$), *floor mats* ($M = 3.5$; $SD = 1.6$), and *chairs* ($M = 3.5$; $SD = 1.5$).

Concerning **perceived benefits** of using ultrasonic whistles in home care, all items were marked with approval (see Fig. 3). Above all, an *increased feeling of safety* ($M = 4.9$; $SD = 1.1$) and *independence of electricity and batteries* ($M = 4.8$; $SD = 1.3$)

were highly valued within the whole sample, followed by *higher independence from others* (*M* = 4.3; *SD* = 1.3) and *more autonomy in everyday life* (*M* = 4.3; *SD* = 1.3), *multifunctionality* (*M* = 4.2; *SD* = 1.3), *unobtrusive technology* (*M* = 4.2; *SD* = 1.3) as a protection from stigmatization, and *maintaining mobility* (*M* = 4.1; *SD* = 1.3). In comparison, *environment protection* (*M* = 4.0; *SD* = 1.4), *physical relief* (*M* = 3.9; *SD* = 1.4), and *time savings* (*M* = 3.5; *SD* = 1.3) were less decisive.

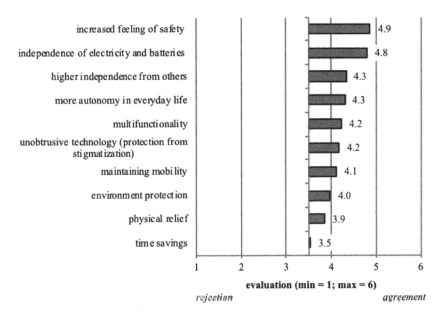

Fig. 3. Evaluation of perceived benefits regarding ultrasonic whistles in home care (means).

With regard to **perceived barriers** (see Fig. 4), in particular the *fear of data abuse* (*M* = 3.6; *SD* = 1.4) and *self-funded finance* (*M* = 3.6; *SD* = 1.4) were assessed as restrictions on the willingness to use ultrasonic whistles in home care. In contrast, *data transfer to third parties* (*M* = 3.5; *SD* = 1.4), the *feeling of surveillance* (*M* = 3.3; *SD* = 1.3), *restriction of privacy* (*M* = 3.2; *SD* = 1.3), and an *error rate* (*M* = 3.1; *SD* = 1.1) due to interfering noises (for example in the background) were not perceived as use-inhibiting. The same applied to *less human contact* (*M* = 2.9; *SD* = 1.3), *deficient usefulness* (*M* = 2.8; *SD* = 1.2) in comparison with other technologies, *loss of control* (*M* = 2.5; *SD* = 1.2), *deficient aesthetics* (*M* = 2.4; *SD* = 1.0), and *less self-determination* (*M* = 2.4; *SD* = 1.2).

4.2   User-Specific Evaluation of Perceived Benefits and Barriers

To get a broader understanding of the perception of perceived benefits and barriers, a deeper analysis and investigation of the participants' evaluation was necessary. For this purpose, a two-step cluster analysis was chosen (hierarchical and K-means cluster analysis) [49] identifying user segments based on their evaluations of (a) perceived benefits and (b) perceived barriers.

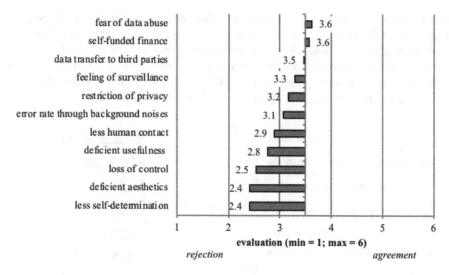

Fig. 4. Evaluation of perceived barriers regarding ultrasonic whistles in home care (means).

Starting with the evaluation of **perceived benefits**, the hierarchical cluster analysis identified a three cluster segmentation as best segmentation solution in the data set. The first cluster contained $n = 76$ (40.4%) participants, the second cluster comprised $n = 88$ (46.8%) participants, and $n = 24$ (12.8%) participants were part of cluster 3. Subsequently, a K-means Cluster analysis was applied and segmented the respondents into three distinct groups based on the evaluation of perceived benefits. In a next step, ANOVAs confirmed the validity of the cluster segmentation, as the three clusters significantly differed (a) with regard to demographic characteristics (see Table 4) and (b) regarding all perceived benefit items.

With regard to the demographic characteristics, inference statistical analyses revealed that the three groups differed significantly regarding their attitude towards aging and gender (see Table 4). In contrast, the clusters were not influenced by the participants' age or health status. Cluster 1 contained a clearly higher proportion of women than men and hold the comparatively least positive attitude towards aging. Cluster 2 was the largest group of participants holding a nearly equal distribution of women and men and also a clearly lower expressed positive attitude towards aging than Cluster 3. Cluster 3 represented the smallest group of participants and was characterized by a slightly higher proportion of men than women as well as the most positive attitude towards aging compared to the other two groups.

As a further criterion, the intention to use the ultrasonic whistle was investigated with regard to the three clusters. The results revealed significant differences ($F(2,187) = 33.449$; $p < .01$) indicating the highest usage intention for Cluster 1, a neutral intention to use for Cluster 2, and a slight negative intention to use for Cluster 3. Based on these differences and in accordance with the evaluation of benefits (see Fig. 5), Cluster 1 was simplified called "*Adopters*", Cluster 2 the "*Undecided*", and Cluster 3 "*Rejecters*".

Table 4. Demographic characteristics and intention to use the ultrasonic whistle of the segmented clusters (perceived benefits).

	Cluster 1 "Adopters" (n = 76)	Cluster 2 "Undecided" (n = 88)	Cluster 3 "Rejecters" (n = 24)	P
Age	$M = 62.4$ $(SD = 11.0)$	$M = 61.1$ $(SD = 8.8)$	$M = 61.7$ $(SD = 7.9)$	n.s.
Gender	female $n = 49$ (64.5%)	female $n = 45$ (51.1%)	female $n = 11$ (45.8%)	$p < .10$
	male $n = 27$ (35.5%)	male $n = 43$ (48.9%)	male $n = 13$ (54.2%)	
Health status	healthy $n = 40$ (52.6%)	healthy $n = 37$ (42.0%)	healthy $n = 8$ (33.3%)	n.s.
	ill $n = 36$ (47.4%)	ill $n = 51$ (58.0%)	ill $n = 16$ (66.7%)	
Attitude towards aging	$M = 4.0$ $(SD = 0.6)$	$M = 4.1$ $(SD = 0.7)$	$M = 4.6$ $(SD = 0.6)$	$p < .01$
Intention to use	$M = 4.7$ $(SD = 0.9)$	$M = 3.7$ $(SD = 1.1)$	$M = 2.9$ $(SD = 1.1)$	$p < .01$

Figure 5 shows the evaluation of benefits differentiating between the three identified clusters. Cluster 1, the "Adopters", clearly evaluated all benefits positively indicating a high acknowledgement of all potential benefits of using the ultrasonic whistle. Thereby, *independence of electricity and batteries* ($M = 5.5$; $SD = 0.7$) as well as *increased feeling of safety* ($M = 5.5$; $SD = 0.6$) represented the most confirmed benefits, while *environment protection* ($M = 4.8$; $SD = 1.1$) and *time savings* ($M = 4.6$; $SD = 1.0$) received lower, but still high agreements from this group.

In contrast, almost all potential benefits were clearly rejected by Cluster 3, the "Rejecters". This indicates that this group did not perceive the evaluated aspects to be "real" benefits. Thereby, *time savings* ($M = 1.9$; $SD = 1.4$) and *environment protection* ($M = 1.9$; $SD = 1.3$) represented the strongest rejected benefits, while *increased feeling of safety* ($M = 3.5$; $SD = 1.8$) received the highest evaluations of this group.

For the "Undecided", Cluster 2, the evaluations showed more heterogeneous patterns: the participants acknowledged an *increased feeling of safety* ($M = 4.7$; $SD = 0.8$) as well as *independence from electricity and batteries* ($M = 4.6$; $SD = 1.0$) as benefits, showed slight agreements towards most of the other aspects, e.g., *more autonomy in everyday life*, and slightly rejected *physical relief* ($M = 3.4$; $SD = 0.9$) and *time savings* ($M = 3.1$; $SD = 0.8$) to be benefits of the ultrasonic whistle's usage.

Considering the evaluation of **perceived barriers**, the hierarchical cluster analysis also identified a three cluster segmentation as optimal segmentation solution in the data set. The first cluster comprised $n = 55$ (26.1%) participants, the second cluster contained $n = 84$ (44.7%) participants, and $n = 49$ (26.7%) participants were part of cluster 3. Similar to the procedure for the perception of benefits items, a K-means Cluster analysis was applied and segmented the respondents into three distinct groups based on the evaluation of perceived barriers. In a next step, ANOVAs again confirmed

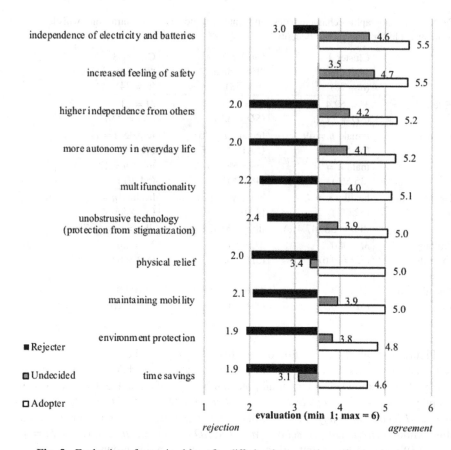

Fig. 5. Evaluation of perceived benefits differing between three clusters (means).

the validity of the cluster segmentation, as the three clusters significantly differed (a) with regard to demographic characteristics (see Table 5) and (b) regarding all perceived barrier items.

Taking demographic characteristics into account, the three identified barrier clusters differed also significantly regarding gender and attitudes towards aging and were not influenced by the participants' age or health status.

Cluster 1 contained a higher proportion of men than women and hold a less positive attitude towards aging compared to Cluster 2. Cluster 2 represented the largest group of participants with a higher proportion of women than men and the comparatively most positive attitude towards aging. Cluster 3 was characterized by the comparatively highest proportion of women and the least positive attitude towards aging.

As a further criterion, the intention to use the ultrasonic whistle was investigated with regard to the three barrier clusters. The results revealed significant differences (F (2,187) = 8.412; p < .01) indicating the highest usage intention for cluster 1, a slight positive intention to use for cluster 2, and a neutral intention to use for Cluster 3. Based

Table 5. Demographic characteristics and intention to use the ultrasonic whistle of the segmented clusters (perceived barriers).

	Cluster 1 "Adopters" (n = 55)	Cluster 2 "Undecided" (n = 84)	Cluster 3 "Rejecters" (n = 49)	P
Age	M = 61.0 (SD = 9.6)	M = 61.8 (SD = 9.1)	M = 62.8 (SD = 11.1)	n.s.
Gender	female n = 21 (38.2%)	female n = 52 (61.9%)	female n = 32 (65.3%)	p < .01
	male n = 34 (61.8%)	male n = 32 (38.1%)	male n = 17 (34.7%)	
Health status	healthy n = 24 (43.6%)	healthy n = 37 (44.0%)	healthy n = 24 (49.0%)	n.s.
	ill n = 31 (56.4%)	ill n = 47 (56.0%)	ill n = 25 (51.0%)	
Attitude towards aging	M = 4.1 (SD = 0.7)	M = 4.3 (SD = 0.7)	M = 4.0 (SD = 0.7)	p < .10
Intention to use	M = 4.4 (SD = 1.1)	M = 4.1 (SD = 1.0)	M = 3.5 (SD = 1.3)	p < .01

on these differences and in accordance with the evaluation of barriers (see Fig. 6), Cluster 1 was simplified called "Adopters", Cluster 2 the "Undecided", and Cluster 3 "Rejecters".

Figure 6 shows the evaluation of barriers differentiating between the three identified clusters. Starting with Cluster 1, a clear rejection of all potential barrier aspects was striking. Thus, this group did not perceive any of the aspects as "real" barriers of using the ultrasonic whistle in home care. Thereby, *loss of control* ($M = 1.5$; $SD = 0.6$) and *less self-determination* ($M = 1.5$; $SD = 0.6$) represented the most rejected aspects, while *fear of data abuse* ($M = 2.8$; $SD = 1.2$) was comparatively least rejected by this group.

In contrast, Cluster 3 showed partly high agreements of some barriers (i.e., *data transfer to third parties* ($M = 4.9$; $SD = 0.8$), *self-funded finance* ($M = 4.7$; $SD = 1.0$), *restriction of privacy* ($M = 4.7$; $SD = 0.8$), and *feeling of surveillance* ($M = 4.6$; $SD = 1.1$)). Further, slight agreements were found for single aspects (e.g., *less human contact* ($M = 4.0$; $SD = 1.3$) and *loss of control* ($M = 3.7$; $SD = 1.3$)). Even Cluster 3 slightly rejected *less self-determination* ($M = 3.4$; $SD = 1.2$) and *deficient aesthetics* ($M = 3.2$; $SD = 1.0$) to be "real" barriers of technology usage.

Similar to the benefit cluster, a more heterogeneous evaluation pattern was found for Cluster 2: *Data transfer to third parties* ($M = 3.6$; $SD = 1.0$), *self-funded finance* ($M = 3.5$; $SD = 1.1$), and *fear of data abuse* ($M = 3.5$; $SD = 1.1$) represented the barriers with the comparatively highest – but still nearly neutral – evaluations, while all other barriers were slightly (e.g., feeling of surveillance ($M = 3.1$; $SD = 1.0$)) to moderately (e.g., *less self-determination* ($M = 2.4$; $SD = 0.9$)) rejected to be real barriers of using ultrasonic whistles in home care.

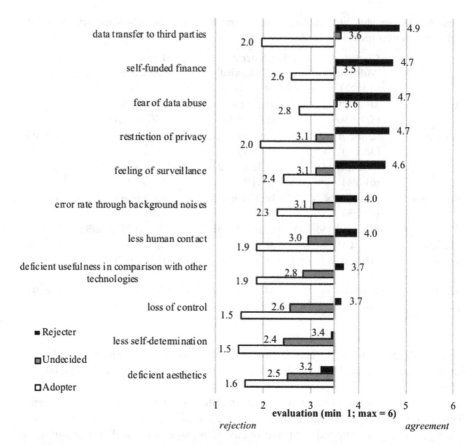

Fig. 6. Evaluation of perceived barriers differing between three clusters (means).

5   Discussion

In the following section, the study's insights are discussed with regard to previous research in the field of AAL, technology acceptance, and aging. In addition, limitations of the study and ideas for future work are outlined.

5.1   Interpreting Perceptions of Aging, Benefits, and Barriers

This study's aim was to achieve deeper insights into the assessment of ultrasonic whistles in home care, with special regard to older users' benefit and barrier perception, as the risk for health restrictions and care needs increase with age. Though, commonly referred to as "the elderly", our study showed that older people represent a heterogeneous user group with subjective aging concepts and visions of life. As new insights, the analysis of evaluation patterns proved an influence of attitudes towards aging on the decision to adopt or reject home care assistance.

In general, the obtained results revealed that the wish to grow old at home was commonly high, confirming corresponding research in the field of aging in place [13] and the importance of AAL studies. The majority of participants had only little experience with AAL technologies and systems (except for blood pressure monitors), presumably, as they were in good health. Overall, attitudes towards aging were positive, indicating an optimistic age frame regardless of predominant age stereotypes, such as of "the old and frail" (cf. [34]). On closer regard to the user characteristics, it was found that health status was related to the attitude towards aging. In detail, healthy participants shared rather positive concepts and expectations of aging, such as social inclusion, active lifestyle, and relaxed mood. In return, ill participants tended to agree more strongly with negative attitudes, such as decreasing health, being less fit and lively, which can be explained by negative experiences they have already made in terms of care dependency, acute and/or chronic diseases. Interestingly, neither gender nor age correlated with the attitude towards aging. Since in this context, personal experience (e.g. through health restrictions) was obviously more decisive, a rethinking of age and aging is required to meet individual needs of an elderly society, especially when it comes to how people imagine and perceive their lives in old age.

Considering the use of ultrasonic whistles as a new assistive device in home care, evaluation patterns were generally positive. With special attention given to the perception of benefits and barriers, an increased feeling of safety (as in many other AAL contexts [32, 42]) as well as independence from electricity and batteries (as a core feature in the present scenario) were considered as major advantages within the whole sample, whereas particularly the fear of data abuse restricted the adoption of ultrasonic whistles, emphasizing the importance of transparency and users' trust in the monitoring system as essential acceptance factors. Besides, potential users were disconcerted by the self-funded finance, which may be explained against the background of an increasing poverty among the elderly [33].

With regard to effects of user diversity, we identified groups of "*Adopter*", "*Undecided*", and "*Rejecter*" in both evaluation contexts (benefits and barriers), summarized as follows: While the *Adopters* agreed with the benefits and rejected the barriers more strongly, the *Rejecters* disapproved of the benefits and supported the barriers, while the *Undecided* did not express a clear opinion in either context. Overall, the results showed a distinct intention to use the ultrasonic whistle in home care (which was highest for *Adopters*) as well as an influence of gender and the attitude towards aging on the perception of benefits and barriers. It was particularly surprising that people who did not appreciate benefits of using ultrasonic whistles (the "*Rejecter*"), had a comparatively very positive attitude towards aging, which may be related to an intrinsic drive for independence and autonomy, regardless of technology use. Hence, with regard to further research, the handling and perception of aging should be focused instead of the consideration of "age groups".

5.2   Limitations and Outlook

Besides new insights into evaluation patterns regarding benefits and barriers of assisting technology and their relationships with different user factors (age and attitude towards aging), there are some limitations of the current study, which should be considered for future work in this research field.

As one methodological limitation, a cluster analysis was used to identify user groups differing in their perception of benefits and barriers. The cluster analysis presents only one approach to investigate user diversity impacts. In order to gain deeper insights into the relevance of user diversity, future research should aim an investigation of standard deviation distributions comparing the whole sample and the clusters. Besides this approach, future studies should investigate other relevant user factors such as attitude towards care and handling of aging.

Further, the knowledge about relationships between benefits and barriers is limited due to isolated evaluation of benefit items on the one and barrier items on the other hand. Current and future work therefore focuses on other approaches such as conjoint analyses [50] in which real life decisions, e.g., considering several benefits and barriers of technology usage can be simulated.

Besides scenario-based approaches, future studies should aim for investigations of the described AAL technology based on ultrasonic whistles in real life settings. This is of major importance as previous research has already shown that the applied methodology probably effects an underestimation of potential benefits and an overestimation of potential barriers [45]. Thus, future studies should aim for hands-on evaluations of the described AAL technology considering diverse user groups.

Another aspect refers to fact that the current study was conducted in Germany and represents a perspective of one single country. In particular with regard to perception of aging and care, other countries and cultures will probably have diverse attitudes and handlings of aging due to different family structures, (feelings of) responsibility, and diverse health care systems. Future studies will therefore focus on cross-national and cross-cultural comparisons of attitudes towards as well as handling of aging and care and their potential relationships with technology acceptance.

With regard to the sample, the sample size was adequate – in particular considering the fact that people aged 50 years and older were under study. While gender was equally spread, the educational level of the sample was above average [48]. Thus, future studies should investigate a more diverse sample with a broader range of educational levels (higher proportions of people with lower education levels) and its potential impact on evaluation patterns of benefits and barriers.

Acknowledgements. The authors thank all participants for their openness to participate in the study and to share their opinions on relevant decisions regarding usage of AAL technologies. Thanks go also to Simon Himmel for ideas, support, and encouragement within the collaboration. This work has been funded partly by the German Federal Ministry of Education and Research projects Whistle (16SV7530) and PAAL (6SV7955).

References

1. United Nations. Ageing. http://www.un.org/en/sections/issues-depth/ageing/index.html. Accessed 06 Sep 2018
2. Destatis: Germany's Population by 2060. Results of the 13th coordinated population projection. Federal Statistical Office of Germany, Wiesbaden (2018)
3. Destatis: Roughly one in five people in Germany is 65 years or older. https://www.destatis.de/EN/Press/2018/09/PE18_370_12411.html. Accessed 16 Oct 2018
4. BMWi (Federal Ministry for Economic Affairs and Energy): Skilled professionals for Germany. https://www.bmwi.de/Redaktion/EN/Dossier/skilled-professionals.html. Accessed 15 Jan 2019
5. Blackman, S., et al.: Ambient assisted living technologies for aging well: a scoping review. J. Intell. Syst. **25**(1), 55–69 (2015)
6. van Heek, J., Himmel, S., Ziefle, M.: Privacy, data security, and the acceptance of AAL-systems – a user-specific perspective. In: Zhou, J., Salvendy, G. (eds.) ITAP 2017. LNCS, vol. 10297, pp. 38–56. Springer, Cham (2017). https://doi.org/10.1007/978-3-319-58530-7_4
7. Wilkowska, W., Ziefle, M.: User diversity as a challenge for the integration of medical technology into future smart home environments. In: User-Driven Healthcare: Concepts, Methodologies, Tools, and Applications, pp. 553–582. IGI Global (2011)
8. Steinke, F., Fritsch, T., Silbermann, L.: Trust in ambient assisted living (AAL) - a systematic review of trust in automation and assistance systems. Int. J. Adv. Life Sci. **4**, 77–88 (2012)
9. Wilkowska, W., Ziefle, M.: Privacy and data security in E-health: requirements from the user's perspective. Health Inf. J. **18**(3), 191–201 (2012)
10. van Heek, J., Himmel, S., Ziefle, M.: Living with disabilities – the many faces of smart home technology acceptance. In: Röcker, C., O'Donoghue, J., Ziefle, M., Maciaszek, L., Molloy, W. (eds.) ICT4AWE 2017. CCIS, vol. 869, pp. 21–45. Springer, Cham (2018). https://doi.org/10.1007/978-3-319-93644-4_2
11. Himmel, S., Ziefle, M., Lidynia, C., Holzinger, A.: Older users' wish list for technology attributes. In: Cuzzocrea, A., Kittl, C., Simos, Dimitris E., Weippl, E., Xu, L. (eds.) CD-ARES 2013. LNCS, vol. 8127, pp. 16–27. Springer, Heidelberg (2013). https://doi.org/10.1007/978-3-642-40511-2_2
12. Destatis: People in need of long-term care. http://www.webcitation.org/6zzhxHuMI. Accessed 12 Jan 2019
13. Peek, S.T.M., Wouters, E.J.M., van Hoof, J., Luijkx, K.G., Boeije, H.R., Vrijhoef, H.J.M.: Factors influencing acceptance of technology for aging in place: a systematic review. Int. J. Med. Inf. **83**, 235–248 (2014)
14. Marek, K.D., Rantz, M.J.: Aging in place: a new model for long-term care. Nurs. Adm. Q. **24**(3), 1–11 (2000)
15. Oswald, F., Jopp, D., Rott, C., Wahl, H.W.: Is aging in place a resource for or risk to life satisfaction? Gerontologist **51**(2), 238–250 (2011)
16. Vasunilashorn, S., Steinman, B.A., Liebig, P.S., Pynoos, J.: Aging in place: evolution of a research topic whose time has come. J. Aging Res. **2012**, 1–6 (2012)
17. Wiles, J.L., Leibing, A., Guberman, N., Reeve, J., Allen, R.E.S.: The meaning of "aging in place" to older people. Gerontologist. **52**(3), 357–366 (2012)
18. Scharlach, A.E., Diaz Moore, K., Bengtson, V.L., Settersten, R.: Aging in place. In: Bengtson, V.L., Settersten Jr., R. (eds.) Handbook of Theories of Aging, pp. 407–425. Springer, Heidelberg (2016)

19. Ahn, M., Kwon, H.J., Kang, J.: Supporting aging-in-place well: findings from a cluster analysis of the reasons for aging-in-place and perceptions of well-being. J. Appl. Gerontol. 1–27 (2017)
20. Cook, D.J.: Health monitoring and assistance to support aging in place. J. Univers. Comput. Sci. **12**(1), 15–29 (2006)
21. Hristova, A., Bernardos, A.M., Casar, J.R.: Context-aware services for ambient assisted living: a case-study. In: First International Symposium on Applied Sciences on Biomedical and Communication Technologies, Aalborg, Denmark, 25–28 October, pp. 1–5 (2018)
22. Skubic, M., Alexander, G., Popescu, M., Rantz, M., Keller, J.: A smart home application to eldercare: current status and lessons learned. Technol. Health Care **17**(3), 183–201 (2009)
23. Rashidi, P., Mihailidis, A.: A survey on ambient-assisted living tools for older adults. IEEE J. Biomed. Health Inf. **17**(3), 579–590 (2013)
24. Kleinberger, T., Becker, M., Ras, E., Holzinger, A., Müller, P.: Ambient intelligence in assisted living: enable elderly people to handle future interfaces. In: Stephanidis, C. (ed.) UAHCI 2007. LNCS, vol. 4555, pp. 103–112. Springer, Heidelberg (2007). https://doi.org/10.1007/978-3-540-73281-5_11
25. Demiris, G., Hensel, B.K.: Technologies for an aging society: a systematic review of "smart home" applications. Yearb. Med. Inf. **17**(1), 33–40 (2008)
26. Lê, Q., Nguyen, H.B., Barnett, T.: Smart homes for older people: Positive aging in a digital world. Future Internet **4**(2), 607–617 (2012)
27. Stone, E.E., Skubic, M.: Fall detection in homes of older adults using the Microsoft Kinect. IEEE J. Biomed. Health Inf. **19**(1), 290–301 (2015)
28. Gerhardy, C.: Ultraschallerzeugende Mikrostrukturen für batterielose Fernbedienungen [Ultrasonic Microstructures for Remote Control Without Batteries]. RWTH Aachen University, Aachen (2009)
29. Ibargüen, J.M., Lewandowski, R., Gerhardy, C., Schomburg, W.K.: Position detection with micro whistles. In: Transducers 2013, Barcelona, Spain, pp. 940–943. IEEE, Piscataway, NJ (2013)
30. Jaul, E., Barron, J.: Age-related diseases and clinical and public health implications for the 85 years old and over population. Front. Pub. Health **5**, 335 (2017)
31. Lee, C., Coughlin, J.F.: PERSPECTIVE: older adults' adoption of technology: an integrated approach to identifying determinants and barriers. J. Prod. Innov. Manag. **32**(5), 747–759 (2015)
32. Demiris, G., et al.: Older adults' attitudes towards and perceptions of 'smart home' technologies: a pilot study. Med. Inf. Internet Med. **29**(2), 87–94 (2004)
33. Destatis: Older people in Germany and the EU. Report 2016. https://www.bmfsfj.de/blob/113952/83dbe067b083c7e8475309a88da89721/aeltere-menschen-in-deutschland-und-in-der-eu-englisch-data.pdf. Accessed 28 Nov 2018
34. Kotter-Grühn, D., Hess, T.M.: The impact of age stereotypes on self-perceptions of aging across the adult lifespan. J. Gerontol. B Psychol. Sci. Soc. Sci. **67**(5), 563–571 (2012)
35. Venkatesh, V., Morris, M.G., Davis, G.B., Davis, F.D.: User acceptance of information technology: toward a unified view. MIS Q. **27**(3), 425–478 (2003)
36. Venkatesh, V., Thong, J.Y.L., Xu, X.: Consumer acceptance and use of information technology: extending the unified theory of acceptance and use of technology. MIS Q. **36**(1), 157–178 (2012)
37. Halbach, P., Himmel, S., Offermann-van Heek, J., Ziefle, M.: A change is gonna come. In: Zhou, J., Salvendy, G. (eds.) ITAP 2018. LNCS, vol. 10926, pp. 52–69. Springer, Cham (2018). https://doi.org/10.1007/978-3-319-92034-4_5

38. Biermann, H., Himmel, S., Offermann-van Heek, J., Ziefle, M.: User-specific concepts of aging – a qualitative approach on AAL-acceptance regarding ultrasonic whistles. In: Zhou, J., Salvendy, G. (eds.) ITAP 2018. LNCS, vol. 10927, pp. 231–249. Springer, Cham (2018). https://doi.org/10.1007/978-3-319-92037-5_18

39. Arning, K., Ziefle, M.: Different perspectives on technology acceptance: the role of technology type and age. In: Holzinger, A., Miesenberger, K. (eds.) USAB 2009. LNCS, vol. 5889, pp. 20–41. Springer, Heidelberg (2009). https://doi.org/10.1007/978-3-642-10308-7_2

40. Mitzner, T.L., et al.: Older adults talk technology: technology usage and attitudes. Comput. Hum. Behav. **26**(6), 1710–1721 (2010)

41. Jaschinski, C., Allouch, S.B.: An extended view on benefits and barriers of ambient assisted living solutions. Int. J. Adv. Life Sci. **7**(2), 40–53 (2015)

42. Beringer, R., Sixsmith, A., Campo, M., Brown, J., McCloskey, R.: The "acceptance" of ambient assisted living: developing an alternate methodology to this limited research lens. In: Abdulrazak, B., Giroux, S., Bouchard, B., Pigot, H., Mokhtari, M. (eds.) ICOST 2011. LNCS, vol. 6719, pp. 161–167. Springer, Heidelberg (2011). https://doi.org/10.1007/978-3-642-21535-3_21

43. van Heek, J., Himmel, S., Ziefle, M.: Caregivers' perspectives on ambient assisted living technologies in professional care contexts. In: 4th International Conference on Information and Communication Technologies for Ageing Well and e-Health (ICT4AWE 2018), pp. 37–48, SCITEPRESS – Science and Technology Publications (2018)

44. Muñoz, D., Gutierrez, F.J., Ochoa, Sergio F.: Introducing ambient assisted living technology at the home of the elderly: challenges and lessons learned. In: Cleland, I., Guerrero, L., Bravo, J. (eds.) IWAAL 2015. LNCS, vol. 9455, pp. 125–136. Springer, Cham (2015). https://doi.org/10.1007/978-3-319-26410-3_12

45. Wilkowska, W., Ziefle, M., Himmel, S.: Perceptions of personal privacy in smart home technologies: do user assessments vary depending on the research method? In: Tryfonas, T., Askoxylakis, I. (eds.) HAS 2015. LNCS, vol. 9190, pp. 592–603. Springer, Cham (2015). https://doi.org/10.1007/978-3-319-20376-8_53

46. Ziefle, M., Wilkowska, W.: Why traditional usability criteria fall short in ambient assisted living environments. In: Boll, S., Köhler, F. (eds.). User-Centered Design. 4th International Workshop on User-Centered Design of Pervasive Healthcare Applications, pp. 218–221. European Alliance for Innovation. Institute for Computer Science, Social-Informatics and Telecommunications Engineering (ICST) (2014)

47. Biermann, H., Offermann-van Heek, J., Himmel, S., Ziefle, M.: Ambient assisted living as support for aging in place: a quantitative users' acceptance study on ultrasonic whistles. JMIR Aging **1**(2), e11825 (2018)

48. Destatis: 17% of the population with academic degree. http://www.webcitation.org/6zzigjeXF. Accessed 09 Mar 2018

49. Hair, J.F.: Multivariate data analysis: an overview. In: Lovric, M. (ed.) International Encyclopedia of Statistical Science, pp. 904–907. Springer, Berlin (2011). https://doi.org/10.1007/978-3-642-04898-2

50. Orme, B.: Interpreting the results of conjoint analysis, getting started with conjoint analysis: strategies for product design and pricing research, pp. 77–89. Research Publications LLC Madison, WI (2010)

An App for Who?

An Exploration of the Use and Adoption of Mobile Ordering Applications Among Aging Populations

Christopher Chagnon[✉], Ryan LaMarche, and Soussan Djamasbi

User Experience and Decision Making Lab, Worcester Polytechnic Institute,
Worcester, MA 01609, USA
cjchagnon@wpi.edu

Abstract. With the ubiquity of smart and connected devices such as smartphones, and the ease of downloading Apps from various marketplaces, it has become standard practice for companies to enhance their service experience by releasing their own mobile apps. In one particular vertical, Fast-Food Restaurants, these applications have started to offer customers a chance to place mobile-orders. While mobile ordering comes with a variety of benefits such as skipping lines, order customization, and personalization features, it is not clear that current design can benefit all users. This study is part of a larger project that attempts to provide a service experience design that includes the needs of older users. As a first step toward this goal, in this study we assess the adoption, user experience (UX) and overall usability of an actual mobile ordering applications in an organization with respect to generational differences.

Keywords: Mobile ordering · Ageing · Handheld devices ·
Human-system interaction · Usability · Engagement

1 Introduction

In 2009 Apple Inc. coined their, now trademarked, "There's an App for that" phrasing. At the time this phrase was intended to be used to illustrate the diversity of applications available for download on the Apple iPhone. With over two-million apps available on the Google Play app store and the Apple App Store, and hundreds of thousands of applications on other marketplaces, there truly is an app for almost everything [1]. The breadth and variety of applications available cover nearly every imaginable niche, and have given way to new means of interaction between companies and consumers.

The proliferation of e-commerce, and now with mobile m-commerce solutions, has elicited a new model for service experience that allows for a new means of interaction [2]. Beyond online shopping, the food and hospitality industry is another area that has seen recent innovations in service experience. With big players such as McDonalds, Dominos, and Starbucks releasing their own mobile applications, the industry has followed suit with many players releasing their own services [3–5].

This increase in mobile commerce is due to the ubiquity of mobile devices. According to PEW, mobile technology usage in 2018 is at an all-time high, with about

J. Zhou and G. Salvendy (Eds.): HCII 2019, LNCS 11592, pp. 140–157, 2019.
https://doi.org/10.1007/978-3-030-22012-9_11

95% of Americans owning a cellphone of some kind, and smartphone ownership at 77%, up from 35% in 2011 [6]. When looking at the access to devices across age-groups the breakdown of ownership starts to diverge. As shown in Table 1, while technology adoption is up among older populations, it has yet to reach the same saturation that can be found among younger groups [6, 7].

Table 1. Breakdown of Cell Phone ownership by Age group [6]

Age group	Any cellphone	Smartphone	Cellphone (not smart)
18–29	100%	94%	6%
30–49	98%	89%	9%
50–64	94%	73%	21%
65+	85%	46%	40%

Generational differences between the named generations, Baby Boomers, Gen X, Gen Y (Millennials) and Gen Z, are an oft discussed topic in news media and academia. The generational definitions were created along the idea of birth-cohorts which allow for grouping of people born within common time-periods and cultural movements [8–10]. With terms such as "Digital Natives" coined to describe those who grew up in a world where technologic ubiquity and the proliferation of mobile devices and the internet were not just common, but expected [11–13]. Prior works have examined the use of new media, and the internet among generations, but have found that, while age may be a factor, there are other important social, and financial factors as well [14, 15]. Further works have looked at habits of web-use, and information gathering on the web and have found differences in use, especially with relation to speed and task time, but not in general patterns [16–18].

While computer and internet usage differences among generations have been studied, the increase in ownership and usage of mobile devices has created an interest in investigating the adoption of mobile applications. Food industry companies use a variety of features exclusive to mobile experiences, such as rewards programs, the ability to skip lines, and coupons brands to get users to adopt their applications. Even with many incentives, our initial observations of daily lines of many dozens of people at an on-campus coffee shop shows that many people forgoing the application. These lines are often comprised of a diverse group of people, however, we observed that those using mobile order pickup skewed younger. This observation was the impetus for the creation of a questionnaire to better understand factors that can impact the usage and adoption of the mobile application for food services in an organization, such as the coffee shop that was the focus of this study.

In addition to questions relevant to consumer behavior, we also focused on capturing user engagement. When a system holds a user's attention, they are attracted to it for intrinsic rewards. Hence, user engagement is likely to be an important factor in successful adoption of a technology [19, 20]. In this study our primary question is to understand if there is indeed a significant generational difference in the adoption and engagement for the use of a coffee shop's mobile app. If there is a difference; what factor(s) contribute to this difference?

2   Method

The primary method used in this study was an anonymous self-reported questionnaire that assessed user engagement. Additionally, we asked users questions to better understand the usage and incentives of the food service application.

2.1   Procedure

The questionnaire started with an informed consent statement and overview of the study before following the conditional logic as illustrated below (Fig. 1).

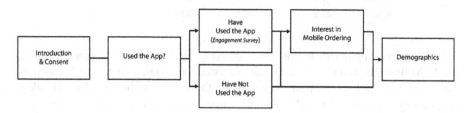

Fig. 1. Process flow for survey logic

Application Usage. To start off the survey we needed to sort respondents into two groups based upon whether or not they had used the mobile application. Respondents were presented with the following options (Table 2):

Table 2. Question 1: Have you ever used the Dunkin' Donuts™ mobile app?

Yes
No
Unsure

Respondents who chose yes or unsure were presented with a set of questions for users who have used the App while those who selected no were presented with a set of questions for users who have not used the app.

Users Who Have Used the App. The first set of questions that users in this group were presented with were regarding frequency of usage. Users were asked how often they use the application and were presented with the following options (Table 3):

Table 3. Question 2a: How often do you use the Dunkin' Donuts™ mobile app?

Several times per day
Several times per week
Several times per month
Several times per year

In order to get a deeper understanding regarding frequency of usage, these users were also asked question 3a, "In a given month, how many days (0–31) do you use the Dunkin' Donuts™ app?"

These users were also asked about the features that they use on a regular basis, and were presented with the following options (Table 4):

Table 4. Question 4a: In the app, which features do you regularly use?

Order On-the-Go (mobile ordering)
Payment
Auto-Reload
DD Perks™ & Offers
Find Locations
Menu & Nutrition

In order to measure engagement among users of the app, questions were adopted from a web-site engagement questionnaire [19]. These users were presented with a seven point Likert scale, and asked to rate their level of agreement with the following statements (Table 5).

Table 5. Question 5a: For the following items, please rate your level of agreement.

The app kept me totally absorbed in using it
The app held my attention
The app excited my curiosity
The app aroused my imagination
The app was fun
The app was intrinsically interesting
The app was engaging

Users Who Have not Used the App. In order to provide some insight to barriers to entry for users who have not previously used the app, these users were first asked why they have not used it and presented with the following options (Table 6):

Table 6. Question 2b: Why have you not used the app?

My phone does not support it
I did not know it was available
I prefer face-to-face interaction
I do not trust it
It seems confusing / complicated
Other

Next we asked the users which features they would be likely to use and presented them with the following list of Dunkin' Donuts mobile application features [21] (Table 7):

Table 7. Question 3b: Which of the following features would you be likely to use?

Order On-the-Go (mobile ordering)
Payment
Auto-Reload
DD Perks™ & Offers
Find Locations
Menu & Nutrition

Users Who Displayed Interest in Mobile Ordering Feature. This set of questions was presented to users who have used the mobile application and regularly use the mobile ordering feature, as well as those who have not used the mobile app but indicated that they would be likely to use the mobile ordering feature.

The first question users were asked was to rank features based on how important the feature was to them, and they were presented with the following features (with a randomized order for each survey participant) (Table 8):

Table 8. Question 6: Drag to rank the following mobile ordering features in order of their importance to you (most to least).

Skip the line
Ordering in advance
Saving favorite orders
Browse the menu
Customize order
Stored payment
DD Perks™ & Offers

Finally, in order to elicit any other feedback, these users were asked question 7, "Do you have any other thoughts or feedback on mobile ordering?"

Demographics. All respondents were asked question 8, "What is your age?" These respondents were then asked about their affiliation to the University, and were presented with the following options (Table 9):

Table 9. Question 9: What is your affiliation to WPI?

| Undergraduate student |
| Graduate student |
| Faculty |
| Staff |
| Alumni |
| Other |

Respondents were also asked about the type of smartphone they primarily use, and were presented with the following options (Table 10):

Table 10. Question 10: What type of smartphone do you primarily use?

| Android |
| iPhone |
| Other |
| I do not have a smartphone |

2.2   Subjects

Participants for this questionnaire were recruited from the campus population of a University in the United States. The university presented an opportunity to focus on a population with a diverse range of ages, all with experience ordering from the on-campus coffee shop. Respondents (n = 150) ranged from age 18–99 with a mean age of M = 37.42 years (SD = 15.84) (Fig. 2).

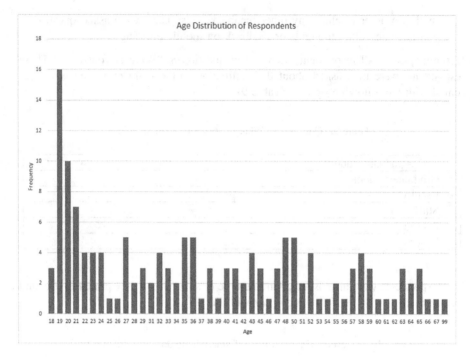

Fig. 2. Age distribution of respondents

For analysis, subjects were classified according to four age groups based on the birth cohort generational construct [8–10].

- "Baby Boomers", aged 56–99, with a population of N = 25 (M = 62.52, SD = 8.29).
- "Gen X", aged 41–55, with a population of N = 36 (M = 47.72, SD = 4.18).
- "Gen Y", aged 27–40, with a population of N = 40 (M = 33.15, SD = 4.17).
- "Gen Z", aged 18–26, with a population of N = 49 (M = 20.53, SD = 1.84).

3   Results

3.1   Application Usage

Application usage among respondents was highest among Gen Y, with similar usage among Gen X, Gen Y and Gen Z between 50–60%, while among Baby Boomers usage was 16% (Fig. 3).

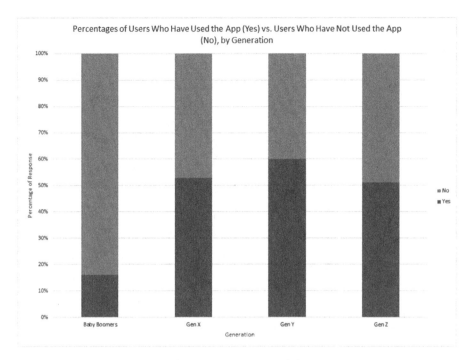

Fig. 3. Question 1: Percentages of Users Who Have Used the App (Yes) vs. Users Who Have Not Used the App (No), by Generation

3.2   Users Who Have Used the App

Most respondents who have used the app indicated that they used it "several times per week" in all four generations. Gen Z, Gen Y, and Gen X each had 1–2 respondents indicate that they use the app "several times per day", and many more who indicated that they use the app "several times per month" or "several times per year." The average number of days per month that the app is used by each generation varies only slightly, with all four averages ranging between 9–12 days per month (Figs. 4 and 5).

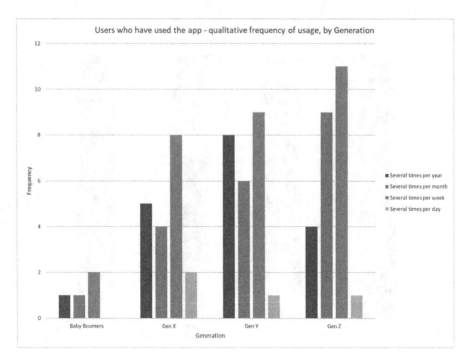

Fig. 4. Question 2a: Users who have used the app - qualitative frequency of usage, by generation

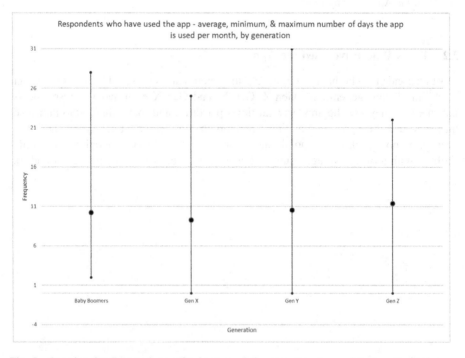

Fig. 5. Question 3a: Respondents who have used the app - average, minimum, & maximum number of days the app is used per month, by generation

Respondents were asked to rate their level of agreement on a scale from [1–7] (strongly disagree - strongly agree) with each of 7 statements. A higher level of agreement with each statement is indicative of a higher level of engagement. Gen X, Gen Y, and Gen Z all seem to have very similar trends among their responses to the statements. Baby Boomers, however, indicated a noticeably stronger level of agreement to all 7 statements, indicating a higher level of engagement (Fig. 6).

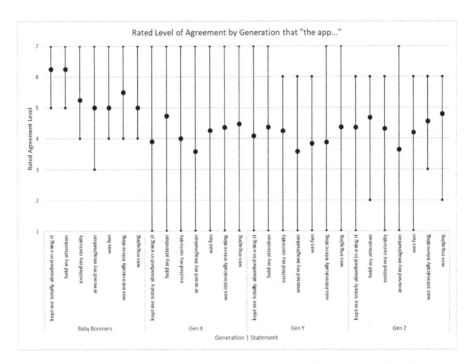

Fig. 6. Question 4a: Rated level of agreement by generation with statements that "the app…"

Respondents who have used the app most frequently used features such as DD Perks & Offers, mobile ordering, and payment. In Gen X and Gen Y, more respondents use payment than mobile ordering. However, in Gen Z, more respondents use the mobile ordering feature than payment. There were 0 Baby Boomers who responded that they use the payment feature, but some of them do use mobile ordering (Fig. 7).

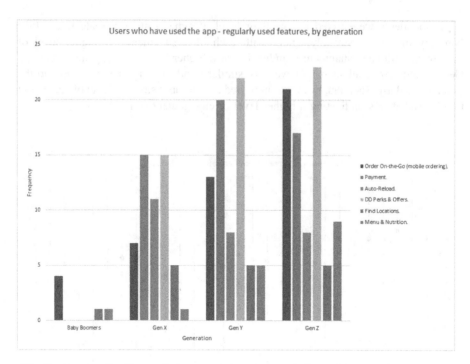

Fig. 7. Question 5a: Users who have used the app - regularly used features, by generation

3.3   Users Who Have not Used the App

Of respondents who have not used the app, many either did not use it because they prefer face-to-face interaction, or they did not know it was available. There was a high response in Gen Z of subjects who did not know that the app was available, and there was a high response in Baby Boomers of those who prefer face-to-face interaction (Fig. 8).

The other option as a fill in was popular among all four generations. Many of the other answers can be summarized using other choices provided as options, however some additional insights provided through the other option include:

- Students on a meal plan using their provided meal plan dollars.
- Not going to the restaurant (enough) or making their own at home.
- Not "getting around to it", with many intending to but not doing so.

Of the respondents who have not used the app, in all four generations there was a high response indicating that they would like to use features such as mobile ordering and DD Perks & Offers. In Gen Z, Gen X, and Baby Boomers, there was a particularly strong response in respondents who would like to use the feature "Find locations." All four generations had a very low response in respondents who would be interested in using the "Auto-Reload" feature (Fig. 9).

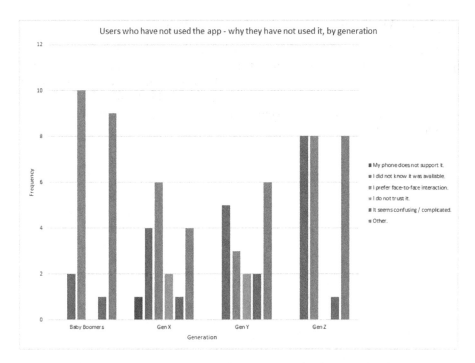

Fig. 8. Question 2b: Users who have not used the app - why they have not used it, by generation

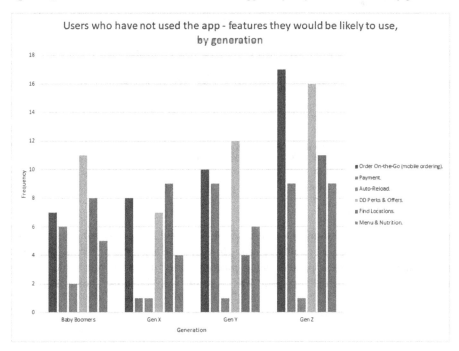

Fig. 9. Question 3b: Users who have not used the app - features they would be likely to use, by generation

3.4 Users Who Displayed Interest in Mobile Ordering

Of the respondents who displayed an interest in mobile ordering, all four generations' highest ranked features in terms of importance were the ability to skip the line and the ability order in advance. Baby Boomers indicated that the least important feature to them was being able to store payment in the app. Gen X, Gen Y, and Gen Z indicated that the least important features to them in the app include saving favorite orders and browsing the menu (Fig. 10).

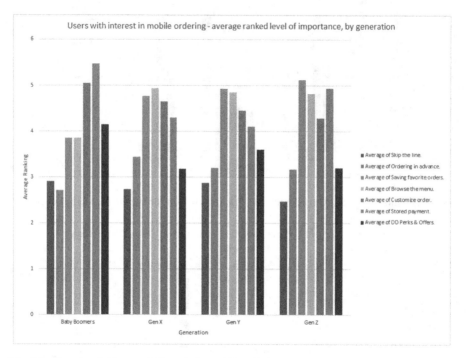

Fig. 10. Question 6: Users with interest in mobile ordering - average ranked level of importance, by generation (lower is better).

3.5 Demographics

Of the demographic questions, the age question was used for sorting subjects, and the affiliation was used only for quality control. However, the results of the device question indicate a trend toward app-users being predominantly iPhone users, while among those who had not used the app, there was more diversity in phone choice (Fig. 11).

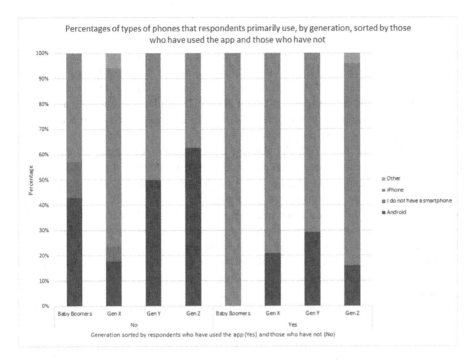

Fig. 11. Question 10: Percentages of types of phones that respondents primarily use, by generation, sorted by those who have used the app and those who have not

3.6 Additional Feedback

The open response field for additional feedback was used by about one third of respondents. Data was cleaned to remove: (a) short responses such as "No", (b) non-sense responses (c) feedback about the survey rather than the app.

After cleaning, the data was then coded to capture the main sentiment of the comment and to group similar comments upon subject. Comment breakdown followed these key topics:

- **Like**: These users like the app and were sharing their happiness with its features, convenience, etc.
- **Dislike**: These users had bad experiences or were not in favor of the app.
- **Buggy**: A subset of dislike, these comments shared experiences with the app not working as expected, or with bugs they had encounters.
- **Trust**: There were many comments about a fear of using the app, or trusting financial data within the app.
- **Face to Face**: These users commented about the workers of the coffee shop, and about wanting to see them, make sure they got tips, or worried for them.
- **No Need**: Several users commented that there just isn't a need for this app, because they have great experiences regularly at the coffee shop.

4 Conclusion

In looking for a significant generational difference in the adoption and engagement for the use of a coffee shop's mobile app, there does appear to be increased adoption among younger generations. A key finding of this questionnaire is that usage of the coffee shop's mobile app aligns well with the general adoption and prevalence of mobile devices, with the youngest generation having the most favorable reaction, and the baby boomers not using the application as often.

In attempting to assess which factor(s) contributed to this generational gap a repeated theme arose across all questions. Technology should serve to enhance or offer new value where it can, perks and rewards, coupons, easy payment, and benefits such as line skipping all do incentivize usage among app users. Not all rewards hold the same sway, while some features like line-skipping may be beneficial to some, to others they remove another benefit, such as social interaction, or the intimacy of a face-to-face interaction with the workers. Among the baby boomers this last point was especially pertinent with much of the enjoyment of their trip to get coffee being in the experience itself. There is a perceived benefit to interacting with the workers, but also a trust in them that to many, an app cannot replace. Older generations were less ready to trust their financial information with the app, while younger generations were much more willing to use the app and its many features.

Among those who were interested in mobile ordering, features were ranked fairly similarly, with features like advanced ordering, line skipping and perks ranking highly. Across all generations the idea of bonuses, coupons and free rewards was nearly universally noted as a good thing. Boomers were consistent with their trust related rankings in that they consistently ranked stored payment as their least wanted feature. A feature that many called out in their open response fields and other boxes was their love of customization. The application allows users to feel confident in customizing their orders and getting exactly what they want. At the same time, users did note that sometimes the customization feature was restrictive, and forced them to order food within a certain construct or limitations, that they can bypass with a human, but the app doesn't allow.

Surprisingly, the Baby boomer generation provided higher average engagement as compared to the other cohorts. This increase in engagement among older populations, is similar to the generational difference in Loos study on use of new media [16, 18]. This may have the do with the novelty of technology as the older generations experience it [22]. The younger generations have lived a larger portion of their lives absorbed in technology, having more time to become accustomed to mobile applications [11, 12]. Because these generations are more used to mobile applications in their everyday lives, the same novelty of experience is not there as it is in the older generations [23–25]. For this study, these factors may have contributed to lower engagement among younger generations.

Across all users it is important for companies to build trust among their users. A mobile application can provide an enriched service experience and even offer users the potential to interact in new ways. However, this experience can't come at the expense of the customer. Part of building out a mobile platform is to extend the company's existing trust and reputation with users into a new environment, and allow for increased engagement. This means having a consistent, secure, and valuable experience.

While this sentiment works for all users, it is especially important when onboarding new users from aging populations. The results of this questionnaire show that while older users found the app engaging, they did not trust the app as their younger counterparts. Trust with boomers is difficult to obtain, and if a company wishes to seek engagement through new channels, they need to make sure that the application gains their trust. While there may be "an app for that" it is important to consider who is actually using those applications, and how an applications design and implementation could affect long-term adoption.

5   Limitations

For the purposes of this study it is important to note the impact that some of our choices have had to potentially inform the results of this research. The most influential factors in that could change these results would be around our sample size and demographics, and for the specific application we chose to study adoption within.

Demographically we focused on generation as a function of age, however our sample was selected entirely from the community of a university within the United States. The impact of this choice means that our results with a sample size of n = 150, all respondents were faculty, staff, students, or alumni of the university. This means that the responses were likely skewed toward the university population more-so than representing a broader, random, sample. The results for a larger sample size selected from the general population could vary.

The second important factor is in choosing a coffee shop for this study. While a large subset of the university community takes advantage of the on-campus coffee shop, not all people buy coffee or meals from this location. If the study had been run focusing on a different type of application the results might have been varied.

In examining the university population, the potential for an intersectional sample was available. The university accepts students globally, and hires positions across many vocations from tradespeople to professionals, to executives, which meant that there would likely be a diversity of responses. The most readily available, consistently utilized on-campus location, with a mobile app was the coffee shop.

6   Future Work

The distribution of this questionnaire is the first step toward addressing the issue of lower adoption among aging populations. The questionnaire has helped to identify that there is a trust-deficit among older app users that needs to be addressed. Users across all generations expressed interest in accessing some of the features and benefits of the application, future work should help identify how we can personalize a service experience within an application to appeal to multiple generations, while instilling trust, but also maintaining a hospitable human-factor in interaction.

In addition to personalization and increased generational accessibility, future work will investigate the application of social presence theory in order to add more intimate, personal, warm and sensible interactions to the application [26–28]. Through the application of human-like agents for ordering, or the use of avatars as an analog for face-to-face interaction, or even telepresence capabilities we can investigate if these human-like factors increase adoption and trust among users, particularly older users who seemed to place a great value on social interaction as part of service experience.

Additional work can investigate the engagement, and trust differences between personal devices and on-site kiosks, to see if the issue is with the application experience or the overall technology augmentation to the traditional service experience. It will be important to establish if the disconnect within generational adoption is due to the specific implementation, or if the adverse trust-relationship is resultant from technology as a whole.

Finally, to address some of the limitations of this study, future work should examine larger and more varied populations, and explore if these results hold true across different verticals for technology adoption. Future studies should endeavor to discover if the type of cuisine impacts results, and if a wider sample modifies the outcome.

References

1. Appfigures & Various sources (n.d.). Number of apps available in leading app stores as of 3rd quarter 2018, 19 December 2018. https://www.statista.com/statistics/276623/number-of-apps-available-in-leading-app-stores/
2. Khalifa, M., Ning Shen, K.: Explaining the adoption of transactional B2C mobile commerce. J. Enterp. Inf. Manag. **21**(2), 110–124 (2008)
3. McDonald's Mobile order and Pay (2018). https://www.mcdonalds.com/us/en-us/mobile-order-and-pay.html
4. Starbuck's App. (2018). https://www.starbucks.com/coffeehouse/mobile-apps
5. Domino's: Technology & Innovation (2018). https://www.dominos.com.au/inside-dominos/technology
6. Pew Research Center. Mobile fact sheet. Pew Research Center: Internet, Science Tech (2018). http://www.pewinternet.org/fact-sheet/mobile/
7. Anderson, M., Perrin, A.: Tech adoption climbs among older adults. Pew Research Center (2017). http://www.pewinternet.org/2017/05/17/tech-adoption-climbs-among-older-adults/
8. Horovitz, B.: After Gen X, Millennials, what should next generation be, USA Today (2012)
9. Owram, D.: Born at the Right Time: A History of the Baby-Boom Generation. University of Toronto Press, Toronto (1997)
10. Strauss, W., Howe, N.: Generations: The history of America's future, 1584 to 2069. William Morrow and Company Inc., New York (2008)
11. Prensky, M.: The emerging online life of the digital native: what they do differently because of technology, and how they do it (2004). http://www.marcprensky.com/writing/Prensky-The_Emerging_Online_Life_of_the_Digital_Native-03.pdf
12. Prensky, M.: Don't Bother Me, Mom, I'm Learning!: How Computer and Video Games are Preparing Your Kids for 21st Century Success and How You Can Help!. Paragon House, St Paul (2006)
13. Prensky, M.: Digital natives, digital immigrants part 1. Horizon **9**(5), 1–6 (2001)

14. Lapa, T., Cardoso, G.: What "digital divide" between generations? A cross-national analysis using data from the world internet project. In: Stephanidis, C., Antona, M. (eds.) UAHCI 2013. LNCS, vol. 8010, pp. 113–122. Springer, Heidelberg (2013). https://doi.org/10.1007/978-3-642-39191-0_13

15. Loos, E.F., Haddon, L., Mante-Meijer, E.A. (eds.): Generational Use of New Media. Ashgate, Farnham (2012)

16. Loos, E.F.: Generational use of new media and the (ir)relevance of age. In: Colombo, F., Fortunati, L. (eds.) Broadband Society and Generational Changes, pp. 259–273. Peter Lang, Berlin (2011)

17. Tullis, T.S.: Older adults and the web: lessons learned from eye-tracking. In: Stephanidis, C. (ed.) UAHCI 2007. LNCS, vol. 4554, pp. 1030–1039. Springer, Heidelberg (2007). https://doi.org/10.1007/978-3-540-73279-2_115

18. Loos, E.: In search of information on websites: a question of age? In: Stephanidis, C. (ed.) UAHCI 2011. LNCS, vol. 6766, pp. 196–204. Springer, Heidelberg (2011). https://doi.org/10.1007/978-3-642-21663-3_21

19. Webster, J., Ho, H.: Audience engagement in multimedia presentations. ACM SIGMIS Database DATABASE Adv. Inf. Syst. 28(2), 63–77 (1997)

20. Kim, Y.H., Kim, D.J., Wachter, K.: A study of mobile user engagement (MoEN): engagement motivations, perceived value, satisfaction, and continued engagement intention. Decis. Support Syst. 56, 361–370 (2013)

21. Dunkin' Donuts: The Dunkin' Donuts App. (2018). https://www.dunkindonuts.com/en/dd-cards/mobile-app

22. O'Brien, H.L., Toms, E.G.: The development and evaluation of a survey to measure user engagement. J. Am. Soc. Inf. Sci. Technol. 61(1), 50–69 (2010)

23. Thompson, P.: The digital natives as learners: technology use patterns and approaches to learning. Comput. Educ. 65, 12–33 (2013)

24. Atack, L.: Becoming a web-based learner: registered nurses' experiences. J. Adv. Nurs. 44(3), 289–297 (2003)

25. Niederhauser, D.S., Reynolds, R.E., Salmen, D.J., Skolmoski, P.: The influence of cognitive load on learning from hypertext. J. Educ. Comput. Res. 23(3), 237–255 (2000)

26. Gunawardena, C.N.: Social presence theory and implications for interaction and collaborative learning in computer conferences. Int. J. Educ. Telecommun. 1(2), 147–166 (1995)

27. Short, J., Williams, E., Christie, B.: The social psychology of telecommunications (1976)

28. Shin, N.: Beyond interaction: the relational construct of transactional presence. Open Learn. 17(2), 121–137 (2002)

Work in Progress: Barriers and Concerns of Elderly Workers Towards the Digital Transformation of Work

Julian Hildebrandt[✉], Johanna Kluge, and Martina Ziefle

Human-Computer Interaction Center (HCIC), Chair of Communication Science,
RWTH Aachen University, Campus-Boulevard, Aachen, Germany
{hildebrandt,kluge,ziefle}@comm.rwth-aachen.de

Abstract. Digital transformation of work is in progress and will force employees to focus on computer related competences, training and flexibility. In addition, elderly workers are less experienced and slightly less efficient in training, will play a key role for labour markets in the near future due to demographic change. To understand elderly workers needs and to further guide this transformation process, this article focuses elderly workers concerns and barriers about the digital transformation at work. In a fist step, we could identify user, technology, and context related factors of importance, such as working effort, lack of competence, unclear responsibility, fear of unemployment, compromised work-life balance, insufficient legal foundation, changing habits, and lack of support in the company. In a second step, we found that elderly workers are most concerned about changing habits, but nevertheless, concern ratings were not high. These results show that it is of high importance to consider employees needs during the digital transformation of work. Results were discussed in order to provide validated instructions on how to supervise and encourage digital transformation, and how to ensure participation of less technology enthusiastic workers.

Keywords: Digital transformation · Future of work · Age · Mixed-method

1 Introduction

The digital transformation of work is in progress, but still, this process is mostly researched by technicians or engineers who aim to optimize technical or economical parameters like efficiency, effectiveness or costs. Nevertheless, since this transformation is a manifold process involving technical innovations (e.g. big data, cloud integration, artificial intelligence, decision support systems etc.) as well as political, economical and social transitions, it is important to understand every shareholder's perspective (i.e. politicians, employers and employees) to ensure societal integrity. Especially elderly workers play a key role in this transformation process for several reasons: First of all, they started to work

J. Zhou and G. Salvendy (Eds.): HCII 2019, LNCS 11592, pp. 158–169, 2019.
https://doi.org/10.1007/978-3-030-22012-9_12

in pre-digital environments and—even if digital transformation is different from previous industrial revolutions—they possess a very experienced perspective and a very elaborated viewpoint on technological change in general. Secondly, they have different needs in terms of technology acceptance [1], making them harder to address by technology developers, and thirdly, industrial countries perform a demographic change, which makes elderly workers the largest working group in the near future. Because the digital transformation of work might profit considerably from understanding their perspective and needs, we aim to identify and validate concerns and barriers using a two-step mixed method approach and conducted two mixed-aged focus groups, followed by an quantitative online survey with an elderly sample.

The outline of this article is as follows: In Sect. 2, we provide an overview about the digital transformation of work (Sect. 2.1), and the domain of elderly workers (Sect. 2.2). In Sect. 3, we describe the method of our focus group study (Sect. 3.1), as well as the results from qualitative content analysis (Sect. 3.2). Correspondingly, we describe method (Sect. 4.1) and results (Sect. 4.2) of our elderly-sampled questionnaire study in Sect. 4. We discuss the results of both studies in Sect. 5, deliberate limitations of our methodology in Sect. 6 and summarize our contribution in Sect. 7.

2   Related Work

2.1   Digital Transformation of Work

The digital transformation of work is an extensive and irreversible process that will change the future of employment tremendously on several dimensions. We use the terms *digitization, digitalization* and *digital transformation* according to [2]: Digitization is the process of making analogue information digital, digitalization the use of digital information in applications and digital transformation the process of increasing interconnection of digital data and processes.

What does it mean for employees? While in the classical analogue industrial employment system—that might be digitalized, but not yet transformed—, the employees fulfilled narrowly defined jobs in an office that is provided by the employer, while being part of a strictly hierarchical decision-making process. The digital employments system provides project-based working, is independent from location, and decision making takes place in teams with flat hierarchies. Furthermore, this shift put an emphasis on workers knowledge, training, skill and intellectual property, while making borders between firms permeable: Workers are hired for shorter tenures, and are instead expected to move horizontally from company to company, rather than climbing a vertical job ladder [3]. However, this is not even the final form of the transformation, since recent developments broke work down into smaller parts than projects, such as clickwork (e.g. tagging items on a website), or crowdwork [4], where smartphone apps are deploying single tasks (e.g. driving) [5]. When considering that—despite the huge potential on digital transformation on wellbeing—most of these new crowdwork jobs are precarious, the need to guide this process becomes a key challenge to retain societal integrity.

Digital transformation of work affects the whole nature of work, it re-shapes established job-roles and workforce-skills; workers have to acquire basic computer skills to be able to interact in a digitalized working environment, and have to develop data-related skills like data monitoring, analysis, and diagnostics, while machinery operation and physical strength will be of decreasing importance [6]. The demand of labour power is shifting towards a competence profile of employees that focusses computer skills as well as creativity and interpersonal skills [7]. Even though concerns about *technological unemployment* are not novel, and technological development had always led to an increase in wealth in intermediate-term, it is important to take employees concerns seriously [6], especially since machines are not just getting stronger, but are also getting artificially intelligent [8].

2.2 Elderly People at Work

Elderly workers are of increasing importance for companies since demographic structures are changing in form of falling birth rates and longer life spans, which leads to an increased median age of workers and an increased proportion of elderly workers in the labour force [9], especially in economically developed countries [10]. However, the process of aging is multidirectional and multidimensional, and its influence of task performance is quite extensively discussed in research: According to a meta-analysis [11] (380 studies), age was not related to core task performance and creativity, but positively associated to social and safety behaviour (e.g. helping co-workers resp. complying with safety rules). Furthermore, age was negatively related to counterproductive work behaviors, but the performance in training programs was found to be slightly lower in elderly workers. In contrast to these empirical findings, stereotypes against older workers are quite persistent: They are considered less adaptable, more costly, at higher health risk, less energetic, and disinterested in training [12].

As a consequence, companies are advised to develop a learning and aging friendly climate, encourage knowledge transfer and provide physical as well as psychological health practices [13]. In addition, aging employees are advised to utilize current strengths and abilities at best and behave proactive in terms of enquiring feedback, altering the view of the job, as well as defeating stereotypes [14], which are otherwise internalized and replicated [15].

In summary, digital transformation is not yet finished and is already putting an emphasis on lifelong learning, especially in computer-related domains. In addition, older workers will be the biggest working group in the labour market and might not have developed those skills yet. Furthermore, working tasks may change to an extend that elderly workers might not benefit from their experience anymore, but are instead suffering under slightly worse learning abilities and unfounded stereotypes. To understand elderly workers concerns and barriers when dealing with digital technology in working context is therefor essential to guide the digital transformation of work.

3   First Study: Exploratory Identification of Relevant Factors

As an initial step into the domain, we conducted two explorative focus groups to get qualitative insights.

3.1   Method

Focus Group Design and Sample Description. Both focus groups were designed as semi-structured guideline-based interviews and had the same moderator to keep experimenter artifacts consistent [16]. The whole session was designed to last about 60 min, and despite snacks and beverages there was no monetary compensation, all participants volunteered. The guideline was divided in 4 sections. Section 1 was about the status quo of digital transformation of the subjects work environment, Sect. 2 about the increasing digitization in general, Sect. 3 about specific challenges, barriers and concerns, and Sect. 4 was designed as mind mapping task to make the participants recap the session. To prevents participants from repeating stereotypes, age factors were not explicitly mentioned the guideline, but unknowingly to them, two members of the group were deliberately sampled to be older than 50. Both groups automatically discussed the topic of elderly workers.

In addition, all subjects were sampled to be employees and both groups were composed to have equally represented gender and work experience. Overall, n = 7 volunteers (3 female), aged from 24 to 58 ($M = 38.14, SD = 15.5$) could be recruited to take part in our focus groups. Both focus groups were held in German language.

Analysis Procedure. To keep the analysis as objective and reliable as possible, we used a consensual approach of thematic qualitative content analysis [17]. The recordings of the two focus groups were transcribed in accordance to the GAT2 standard [18]. As initial step into the analysis, we defined two main categories deductively: *Usage Barriers and Concerns*, and *Factors of Age*. We used our transcriptions as sampling units, the participants contribution to the discussion as recording unit, a single phrase as smallest possible content unit, and a whole coherent statement as context unit.

The whole material was assigned into the two main categories by four experienced coders independently, while memos and headings were written into the material, complying with the *open coding* approach [19] and the guidelines defined in [20]). Inductive sub-categories were developed subsequently. The final consensual category system was elaborated by combining the four independent approaches among several coder-meetings. The final result is unanimous and inter-coder reliable. Anchor examples are translated into English language for Sect. 3.2.

3.2   Qualitative Results

In this section, we report the results of two focus groups. We identified 81 content units and assigned them into 17 sub-categories that were developed inductively.

Main Category 1: Usage Barriers and Concerns. The fist main category contains usage barriers towards the digital technology in professional domains. Our content units could be assigned into three sub-categories: *Technology Factors*, *User Factors*, and *Context Factors*.

Technology Factors. This category contains arguments that were related to digital technology itself. Among these content units, we could furthermore derive two sub-sections: *Working Effort is not Decreasing, but Increasing*, and *IT Security is not Sufficient*.

Working Effort Is not Decreasing, but Increasing. Subjects stated in various cases that the use of digital technology led to more working effort and therefor not to an increase in efficiency. According to our subjects, this is mostly related to poor usability design ("If a customer wants to buy three things, I have to open his account three times and he leaves the shop with three separate slips of paper.") or insufficient scope of functions.

IT Security Is not Sufficient. One participant argued that she wants to use free third party software at work, but she is not allowed to because sufficient IT security could not be granted. Others stated that cybercrime is already a huge threat to the company: "I was advised to pull out all plugs immediately when a specific notification shows up. Otherwise, the company could be forced to close the doors for several months.".

User Factors. This second sub-category contains factors that are quite essential to the research question: User Factors. Among all arguments that contained indicators for transformation of work being delayed for reasons of users barriers or fears, we could examine five sub-categories: *Lack of Competence, Who is Responsible?*, and *Fear of Unemployment, Unbalanced Work-Life Balance*.

Lack of Competence. Participants often argued that a lack of competence is a barrier to deal with. One the one hand, they argued that they "have to deal with more and more information", as well as they need "domain knowledge AND the knowledge about the technology". On the other hand, two participants argued that some workers underestimate the autonomy of analogue work, because some jobs can not be done anymore if services out of reach (e.g. servers) are down. The topic of apprenticeship and schooling was discussed quite controversely, since some subjects stated that there is an urgent need for more digital content, while others argued that some educational material is already digital, but shouldn't be.

Who Is Responsible? Subjects often stated that the question of responsibility is still unsolved. The representation of relevant content on a display might lead to a "responsibility-shift from worker to machine". Users fear to carry not only the responsibility for their actions and decisions, but in addition the responsibility for the maintenance of hardware. Workers often feel urged to give up responsibility, because otherwise they would not be able to work, but on the other hand they would be "made responsible" for faulty technology.

Fear of Unemployment. Some content units contained arguments that reflected the fear of being substituted by technology. Besides "the fact that there is the potential for substitution", participants also minded that "the whole process is driven by short-term improvement of costs instead of human-centered transformation".

Unbalanced Work-Life Balance. When talking about the possibility to work independently from time and location, our subjects stated that it is already a challenge to remain work and life well balanced. Underlying factors were the uncomfortable feeling to be contactable at all time, and the fear of not getting a promotion if taking too much off-time. One participant stated that "it could be positive to be able to work all the time, but i don't want to be obliged to.".

Context Factors. The third sub-category adresses the basic conditions that were mandatory to workers: *Legal Foundation*, and *Support in the Company*.

Legal Foundation. Several participants argued that the actual legal foundation fails to cover the possibilities of a digitally transformed world of employment. Legally limited working times might not be sufficient for projects, even if there is enough off-time as compensation. On the other hand, according to our sample, there is not enough worker protection for newly created jobs like clickworkers. Furthermore, workers in jobs with an increasing amount of sensor information often suffer from regulations from pre-digital area, since they "have to write documentations until they are completely exhausted".

Lack of Support in the Company. Furthermore, subjects identified co-workers or even managers as unsupportive and overcautious in processes of change: "employees use what they are instructed to, but higher levels fear that something goes wrong". In addition, one participant even said that "there are smaller fights from time to time to convince people of technological development".

Main Category 2: Factors of Age. The second main category contains factors that were directly related to workers' age. We could identify *Younger Workers in Disadvantage* and *Elderly People in Disadvantage* as sub-categories. We could furthermore identify two content units that were relevant for our research question, but could not be covered by any of the other categories. We report those as *Additional Findings*.

Younger Workers in Disadvantage. Participants stated that especially younger workers are disadvantaged if technology fails, because they are less experienced in working without technology. Furthermore, one subject argued that "younger workers often struggle to combine classic work with the technical component".

Elderly Worker in Disadvantage. When discussing the topic of elderly workers, participants argued that those workers are often overcharged by digital technology. Underlying factors were inexperience, because they are just not "grown up" with technology, or they are just not considered by technology designers to cope with e.g. visual impairment. In addition it was reported that especially elderly workers struggle to change their habits.

Additional Findings. One of the elder subjects argued that she is not at all concerned about digital transformation because she had no problems with technological progress at work during the last decades. Another subject argued that especially older and more experienced workers are expected to suggest ideas about digital transformation, even if they are less experienced in the use of technology.

4   Second Study: Evaluation with Elderly Sample

To further evaluate our results from the first study (Sect. 3), we conducted a quantitative online survey as a follow up.

4.1   Method

Survey Design and Variables. The survey was designed to have a completion time of 15 min. As demographic data we measured gender, age, highest education degree and self-efficacy towards technology (SET) [21]. As dependent variables we measured the barriers and concerns from the first study by asking a single 6-point likert-item per concern/barrier. The ascertained variables reflected *Habits, Competence, Effort, Age, Unemployment, Work-Life Balance, Responsibility, Legal Foundation,* and *Support.* The wording of the items was chosen accordingly to the results from study 1, e.g. "When thinking about the digital transformation of my job, I am concerned that the usage of digital work equipment leads to higher effort for me, because the application is not easy to use." for the variable *Effort.* All likert items were measured on a scale from 0 ("strongly disagree") to 5 ("strongly agree").

Sample Description. Overall, n = 239 participants (49% female) completed the survey. Age was ranged from 50 to 66 years ($M = 56.31 SD = 4.45$). 34.7% of our sample completed lower secondary school, 36.4% secondary school, and 24.9% had a high school diploma. SET was ranged from 0.5 to 3.5 ($M = 2.33, SD = 0.65, \alpha = 0.85$) on a scale from 0 to 5. All participants were recruited via an online panel and got a small monetary incentive in return.

4.2   Results

Descriptive Statistics. Table 1 shows the descriptive statistics of our dependent variables. Every single items covered the whole theoretical range from 0 to 5. Surprisingly, concerns about habits were rated the highest ($M = 2.35, SD = 1.57$), while concerns about insufficient legal foundation remained the lowest ($M = 0.78, SD = 1.19$). Concerns about the own competences ($M = 1.87, SD = 1.53$) resulted in the same (rounded) mean value as concerns about age ($M = 1.87, SD = 1.58$), while the worry about increasing effort remained slightly lower ($M = 1.81, SD = 1.42$). Furthermore, the fear to be unemployed resulted in a mean value of $M = 1.52$ ($SD = 1.47$), slightly above the concern of unsure responsibility ($M = 0.98, SD = 1.31$), impaired Work-Life Balance ($M = 0.98, SD = 1.31$) and insufficient support by co-workers or management ($M = 0.93, SD = 1.21$).

Table 1. Descriptive statistics of measured concerns and barriers.

	Min	Max	Md	M	SD
Habits	0	5	2	2.35	1.57
Competence	0	5	2	1.87	1.53
Effort	0	5	2	1.81	1.42
Age	0	5	2	1.87	1.58
Unemployment	0	5	1	1.52	1.47
Work/Life-Balance	0	5	0	0.98	1.31
Responsibility	0	5	0	0.98	1.33
Legal Foundation	0	5	0	0.78	1.19
Support	0	5	0	0.93	1.21

Note: Order of rows was chosen according to Diagram 1.

Figure 1 shows the likert plot of the same results. Overall, its rather visible that concerns and barriers are more frequently disagreed than agreed on. Even the most agreed concern, that habits need to be adapted to digital technology, is slightly more often declined (51%) than affirmed.

4.3   Evaluations of Barriers

As could be seen in the previous chapter, concerns and barriers were not that severe in terms of absolute agreement. When considering correlations (Table 2), it can be shown that within our elderly sample, the concern to get unemployed for reasons of digital transformation decreases with age ($R = -.15*, p < .05$). Furthermore, higher SET is associated with lower fear to be left behind by younger coworkers ($R = -.16*, p < .05$). Gender (dummy-coded) is as well

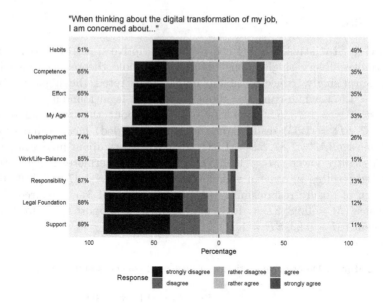

Fig. 1. View of the subject; 2 pillars are out of sight.

correlated to the concern to get unemployed $(R = .19**, p < .01)$, the concern of impaired work-life balance $(R = .18**, p < .01)$, and lack of legal circumstances $(R = .16**, p < .01)$, all with men being more afraid. All three results can be covered by inferential statistics (Mann-Whitney U-Test): Elderly men are more afraid to lose their jobs $(U = 5371.5***, p < .001)$, more afraid that their work-life balance gets impaired $(U = 5534.5***, p < .001)$, and more concerned that legal foundation fails to cover their needs $(U = 5753.5**, p < .01)$. Furthermore, all barriers/concerns are heavily intercorrelated.

5   Discussion

According to our qualitative results, we could replicate some of the previous findings: Workers are concerned about being substituted by technology, are aware of the importance of training and development of data related competences, and consider elderly workers to be less flexible. Surprisingly, we found a gender difference regarding the fear of unemployment with men being more afraid. This might result from different working domains, since men of our sample (recall: age was 50+) might work in more technology driven or even physical strength requiring domains. However, the underlying factor is not sufficiently explored, yet important. In addition to that, we could identify indications that current working technology lacks of usability, which is rendering the desired increase in productivity void. Following that argument, its important to consider the hitherto underrated role of software developers and highly usable products for the digital transformation as well. This is also covered by the finding, that elderly people need to be specifically addressed in terms of e.g. visual impairment.

Table 2. Significant Spearman-Correlation for age, gender, SET and concerns/barriers.

	Age	Support	Habits	Legal Foundation	Work/Life-Balance	Unemployment	Responsibility	Competence	Effort
age						-.15*			
gender				.16*	.18**	.19**			
SET	-.16*								
Age	—	.55***	.35***	.18***	.27***	.31***	.41***	.38***	.46***
Support		—	.28***	.46***	.47***	.57***	.68***	.45***	.47***
Infrastructure			—	.31***	.41***	.45***	.35***	.65***	.61***
Legal Foundation				—	.71***	.45***	.48***	.37***	.41***
Work/Life-Balance					—	.47***	.49***	.52***	.51***
Unemployment						—	.61***	.51***	.44***
Responsibility							—	.51***	.46***
Competence								—	.69***
Effort									—

Note: $*p < .05$, $**p < .01$, $***p < .001$. Gender is dummy-coded: female = 1, male = 2.

The fear to changing habits was rated as the highest concern about digital transformation, which leads us to the conclusion that future training programs should not only foster technical skills, but also flexibility and iterative improvement and adaption of routines. This becomes a key challenge, especially since elderly workers are slightly less effective in training programs, less experienced in the use of technology and are also facing stereotypes according their flexibility. Nevertheless, the concerns were slightly negated in absolute benchmarks, indicating that elderly workers are not only experienced in their domain, but are also experienced in the domain of change, which might include digitization. This is also covered by the qualitative results: Elderly workers are not overly-worried in general, yet underlying factors are not explored sufficiently; we were not able to find a factor that explains inter-individual differences. Future work should address the role of habits on well-being and productivity at work, particularly in the context of computer-related skills, as well as the influence of human factors, such as demography, specific work experience and personality.

6   Limitations

As mentioned in Sect. 3.1, our guideline design was not specifically mentioning age factors to avoid the problem of stereotype replication vs. experience based result. We consider this a valid approach, but especially qualitative designs are very vulnerable in terms of guideline topics and moderator behaviour. Future studies should triangulate our results by choosing a different approach, e.g. by letting the subjects discuss purposely aging stereotypes, or by conducting focus groups with an all-young or all-old sample. Furthermore, our quantitative design is based on the analysis of single items, which is not only sensitive to response biases, but also prohibits parametric analysis. Our second study aims to give a first insight into the topic of concern priority, but these important concerns need to be operationalized into reflective or even formative self-reporting scales for future studies. In addition, we found legal foundations to be of surprisingly low importance in the quantitative results, which might not be transferable to other industrial nations, because the attitude towards legislature might differ among cultures.

7   Conclusion

Since digital transformation of work is in progress and elderly people play a key role for the labour market in the near future, we conducted two exploratory studies—an to examine elderly workers concerns and barriers when dealing with digital technology at work. In our first study, we examined technology, user and context related factors that were of relevance to elderly workers. Our subjects stated that the use of digital technology leads to an increased working effort, while furthermore essential technological competences are not sufficiently developed or educated. Furthermore, the question of responsibility, the fear of unemployment and an impaired work-life balance were topics of high importance, along with insufficient legal foundation, lack of support in the company, and the need to change habits. The need to change habits was found to be rated higher than the other concerns, while the fear of impaired work-life balance, the question of responsibility, while insufficient legal foundation and company support were predominantly negated. This result shows that companies should further focus on training programs and reduction of stereotypes. Furthermore, we found a significant gender difference in men being more concerned about unemployment, work-life balance and legal foundation than women. Future studies should investigate underlying factors to consider user-diversity in training programs.

Acknowledgments. We would like to thank Anna Rohowsky, Verena Grouls and Fabian Comans for sharing their methodological expertise by taking part in our qualitative consensual coding approach. Furthermore, we would like to thank Julian Massau for his contribution to the focus groups, as well as all participants of both our studies.

References

1. Arning, K., Ziefle, M.: Different perspectives on technology acceptance: the role of technology type and age. In: Holzinger, A., Miesenberger, K. (eds.) USAB 2009. LNCS, vol. 5889, pp. 20–41. Springer, Heidelberg (2009). https://doi.org/10.1007/978-3-642-10308-7_2
2. Erfurth, C.: The digital turn: on the quest for holistic approaches. In: Fahrnberger, G., Gopinathan, S., Parida, L. (eds.) ICDCIT 2019. LNCS, vol. 11319, pp. 24–30. Springer, Cham (2019). https://doi.org/10.1007/978-3-030-05366-6_2
3. Stone, K.V.: From Widgets to Digits: Employment Regulation for the Changing Workplace. Cambridge University Press, Cambridge (2004)
4. Cherry, M.A.: A taxonomy of virtual work. Ga. Law Rev. **45**, 951 (2010)

5. Cherry, M.A.: Beyond misclassification: the digital transformation of work. Comp. Labor Law Policy J. **37**, 577 (2015)
6. Gekara, V.O., Thanh Nguyen, V.X.: New technologies and the transformation of work and skills: a study of computerisation and automation of Australian container terminals. New Technol. Work Employ. **33**(3), 219–233 (2018)
7. Prainsack, B., Buyx, A.: The value of work: addressing the future of work through the lens of solidarity. Bioethics **32**(9), 585–592 (2018)
8. Kaivo-Oja, J., Roth, S., Westerlund, L.: Futures of robotics. Human work in digital transformation. Int. J. Technol. Manag. **73**(4), 176–205 (2017)
9. Bowen, C.E., Noack, M.G., Staudinger, U.M.: Aging in the work context. In: Handbook of the Psychology of Aging, 7th edn., pp. 263–277. Elsevier (2011)
10. Fraccaroli, F., Deller, J.: Work, aging, and retirement in europe: introduction to the special issue. Work Aging Retire. **1**(3), 237–242 (2015)
11. Ng, T.W., Feldman, D.C.: The relationship of age to ten dimensions of job performance. J. Appl. Psychol. **93**(2), 392 (2008)
12. Posthuma, R.A., Campion, M.A.: Age stereotypes in the workplace: common stereotypes, moderators, and future research directions. J. Manag. **35**(1), 158–188 (2009)
13. Staudinger, U.M., Bowen, C.E.: A systemic approach to aging in the work context. Zeitschrift für Arbeitsmarktforschung **44**(4), 295–306 (2011)
14. Kooij, D.T.: Successful aging at work: the active role of employees. Work Aging Retire. **1**(4), 309–319 (2015)
15. Zacher, H., Kooij, D., Beier, M.E.: Active aging at work: contributing factors and implications for organizations. Organ. Dyn. **47**, 37–45 (2018)
16. Hanington, B., Martin, B.: Universal Methods of Design: 100 Ways to Research Complex Problems, Develop Innovative Ideas, and Design Effective Solutions. Rockport Publishers, Beverly (2012)
17. Kuckartz, U.: Qualitative Text Analysis: A Guide to Methods, Practice and Using Software. Sage, London (2014)
18. Selting, M., Auer, P., et al.: A system for transcribing talk-in-interaction: Gat 2 translated and adapted for english by elizabeth couper-kuhlen and dagmar barthweingarten. Gesprächsforschung-Online-Zeitschrift zur verbalen Interaktion **12**, 1–51 (2011)
19. Elo, S., Kyngäs, H.: The qualitative content analysis process. J. Adv. Nurs. **62**(1), 107–115 (2008)
20. Van den Berg, A., Struwig, M.: Guidelines for researchers using an adapted consensual qualitative research approach in management research. Electron. J. Bus. Res. Methods **15**(2), 109–119 (2017)
21. Beier, G.: Kontrollüberzeugungen im Umgang mit Technik: ein Persönlichkeitsmerkmal mit Relevanz für die Gestaltung technischer Systeme. dissertation. de (2003)

Senior's Acceptance of Head-Mounted Display Using Consumer Based Virtual Reality Contents

Kenichiro Ito[1]([⊠]) [iD], Ryogo Ogino[1], Atsushi Hiyama[2], and Michitaka Hirose[3]

[1] Institute of Gerontology, The University of Tokyo,
7-3-1 Hongo, Bunkyo-ku, Tokyo 113-8656, Japan
k.ito@iog.u-tokyo.ac.jp
[2] Research Center for Advanced Science and Technology,
The University of Tokyo, 4-6-1 Komaba,
Meguro-ku, Tokyo 153-8904, Japan
[3] Graduate School of Information Science and Technology,
The University of Tokyo, 7-3-1 Hongo,
Bunkyo-ku, Tokyo 113-8656, Japan

Abstract. Head-mounted display has been commercialized and have made a considerable market in the virtual reality industry. While many seniors have interest to the consumer head-mounted display, the opportunity to experience the head-mounted display is still very limited. Hence this paper aims to resolve whether the current contents or products are acceptable and to clarify the challenges to discuss solutions. To investigate on this issue, an event to experience head-mounted display took place within a regional event for seniors at Kashiwa city in Japan. During the event, voluntary participants were asked to answer the questionnaires. The questionnaire was gathered from 5 seniors over age 60 and 10 young under the age 60. The seniors acceptance level was not so high in contrast to the young. However, positive results indicated seniors enjoyed experiencing the head-mounted display contents, willing to experience more opportunities, and also highly recommend to experience to others.

Keywords: Senior · Head-mounted display · Acceptance · Virtual reality

1 Introduction

Recently, head-mounted display (HMD) has been commercialized and have made a considerable market in the virtual reality industry. While it has become one of the successful virtual reality consumer products, it still requires technological knowledge to use as a home device. Meanwhile, many seniors are aware of consumer head-mounted display through broadcast on television. However, the opportunity to experience the HMD is still very limited.

© Springer Nature Switzerland AG 2019
J. Zhou and G. Salvendy (Eds.): HCII 2019, LNCS 11592, pp. 170–180, 2019.
https://doi.org/10.1007/978-3-030-22012-9_13

Supporting seniors are an important aspect within the aging society including to provide entertaining contents for their daily life. Therefore, providing the opportunity to experience a consumer type HMD to the senior is important. However, it is assumed that there are several challenges to resolve in order to provide a good experience to seniors using the HMD. Some of the challenges assumed or known, is about the aspects of physical depression due to age affecting virtual reality experience, and the complexity of the HMD use. To clarify the challenges, in this paper, a HMD experience event and questionnaire were prepared within a regional event for seniors.

2   Head-Mounted Display

Within the topic of this paper, we would first need to clarify the principles for virtual reality to understand the HMD's affections to the seniors. There are several well-known definitions or principles of virtual reality such as, the $I = 3$ [1] which is composed of *Immersion, Interaction, Imagination,* and AIP cube [2] which is composed of *Autonomy, Interaction, Presence.* While HMD has many possibilities in use such as an MR/AR device [3], recent low priced HMD's device are designed as a closed type HMD with a non see-through monitor placed in front of the field of view. Although they can be configured as a video see-through HMD for MR/AR, recent commercially available HMD contents are made as a VR content.

It has become very popular for consumer video games, with many contributions from Sony (PlayStation VR), Facebook (Oculus, Oculus GO), HTC (HTC Vive) for developing and releasing the HMD to the market. However, as reported in early studies [4] and recent studies [5] still report that game users experience motion sickness. Therefore, understanding the users' characteristics, and following early research literature and proposed guidelines [6–8] is important. However, not all of the released game always follows the suggested guidelines. There are no way the user can recognize whether the VR contents include some motion sickness aspects or not, which may lead to bad first time experience.

2.1   Consumer Market of Head-Mounted Display in Japan

Currently in Japan, there are several consumer HMD products that can be purchased. From a consumer point of view, the consumers' behaviour to purchase can be categorized into several points, such as the design, weight, performance and price. Firstly, it can be categorized into two types based on the difference in components, a smartphone-based type or a dedicated-device type.

A smartphone-based type HMD is fairly cheap and sometimes free, since it basically is just a smartphone mount kit sometimes made from cardboard. Some notable products are Google Cardboard [9], Hacosco [10], GearVR [11] and free companion HMD featured at CardboardClub [12]. Normally, the cardboard type HMD cost few hundred Yen to few thousand Yen according to cardboard quality (from about $1 to $20). When it is plastic manufactured like the GearVR the cost goes slightly up to around five thousand yen (about $50). Since it is fairly cheap has high portability, it provides many opportunities to people, and is expected and studied such as some serious game with pain management [13].

A dedicated-device type HMD are relatively expensive where the prices range from thirty thousand Yen to twenty hundred Yen ($500 to $2,000). Some notable products are PlayStation VR [14], Oculus CV [15], HTC Vive [16]. Since it is developed with a dedicated display and sensors, these HMD's provides one of the highest quality of virtual reality available for consumers in terms of I^3 or AIP cube. However, usage is still limited whereas the most popular use is within the entertainment field. Therefore, Oculus Go [17] has been released as a relatively cheaper model ($200) for consumers which may not want to pay for more than $500 for an entertaining device.

While the consumer market of HMD in Japan is rapidly increasing, the adoption rate is not that high yet. Using some classical theory of categorizing the consumers as adopters [18], in general, there is a well known diffusion curve to describe cumulative adoption of a new technological innovation [19–21]. The categories are named "innovators", "early adapter", "early majority", "late majority", and "laggard" as it differs in terms of the adoption rate. Innovators are the first adopters which has the positive attitudes to technology, and the laggards are who have extremely negative technology attitudes and therefore never adopt technology among the mainstream [22]. Seniors are relatively are considered to be close to laggards even though they gain some interest in the technologies since their attitudes in changing their life are not as high as the young. However, the attitude does depend on the individual so giving the opportunity and enhancing their interest still may convince seniors to purchase the HMD. In order to realize that situation, giving positive experience to the seniors will be the key, and also that experience shall consider further experience after they have purchased.

2.2   Head-Mounted Display for Seniors

Considerations of adapting the virtual reality technology to the seniors has been addressed in previous research [23]. While there is huge potential of new possible services, there has been many reports about the effect of spatial cognition ability declines due to increasing age. While there is individual difference, it suggests that at some point the individual becomes not capable to recognize the 3D environment as intended [24–26]. Although there are individual differences, some similar aspects can be observed such as motion sickness. There also has been some reports about sickness occurring even with a very simple virtual reality environment which is composed only from one CRT monitor [27,28]. Furthermore, some studies report some seniors may feel extreme sickness which can lead to some of the participants dropping out from the experiment [29,30]. Therefore, it needs cautions for the seniors not to feel too much sickness.

Early studies using high virtual reality environment CAVE [31] and HMD comparing the effect to the seniors showed better results for HMD [32,33]. While the CAVE is considered better in providing higher virtual reality aspects, reduction of some of the aspects such as texture or model of the 3D world may have some possibilities in reducing the sickness. Therefore, while some of the seniors are concerned about the *virtual reality*, interest about the HMD and providing the experience in HMD still has the capability of adoption to the new technology compared to the CAVE or much higher virtual reality device and experience.

3   Regional Community Event: Luncheon Meeting for Senior People Living Alone

Every year an event named "Luncheon meeting for senior people living alone" is organized at the Toyoshikidai area of Kashiwa City, Chiba Prefecture. Almost 200 local seniors attend this event, and some session within the event is organized by the Institute of Gerontology, the University of Tokyo. Although the event itself is organized by the local city government, the Institute of Gerontology has been significantly cooperating with the government to develop a successful community and social participation for seniors [34]. The 9th annual event was held 8th October 2018 at a facility within the Toyoshikidai area, which had the schedule shown in Table 1.

As showed in Table 1, the luncheon meeting starts at 11:30 with an opening speech for the event, and consists of 2 parts. Part 1 is composed from a 30 min activity time called *cognicise* (cognition + exercise), lunch time, and listen and sing time performed by the local senior electric band (Fig. 1). Part 2 is a session

Table 1. Event schedule of the luncheon meeting.

11:00	Open
11:30–11:50	Opening speech and greetings
Part 1	
11:50–12:20	Cognicise activity
12:20–12:50	Lunch time
12:50–13:20	Concert by the local senior electric band
Part 2	
13:30–15:00	Booth activity time(*)
15:00	Close

(*) The opportunity to experience HMD contents was provided in this session.

Fig. 1. Scenery picture of Part 1 of the luncheon meeting.

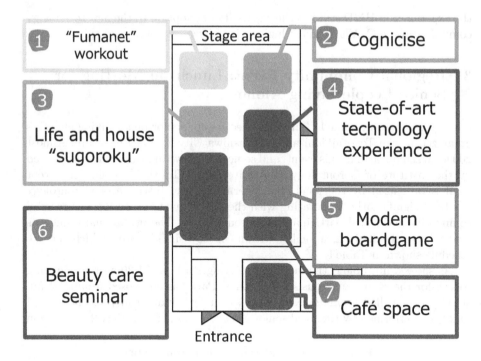

Fig. 2. Overview of the booth areas at the luncheon meeting Part 2. The opportunity to experience HMD contents was provided at the booth "State-of-art technology experience" area.

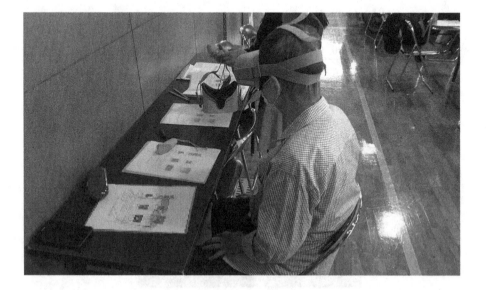

Fig. 3. Scenery of a senior experiencing a HMD content at the booth.

composed of six small parallel sessions (Fig. 2). Within the booth at *State-of-art technology experience*, an area was prepared for the senior to experience the HMD (Fig. 3). It is to be noted that within the area, a table to experience Internet of Things was also prepared for the seniors. Therefore, the booth was named *State-of-art technology experience* rather than using the words of virtual reality, such as VR or HMD.

Since the research aims to provide consumer level experience potentially leading the seniors to purchase an HMD, Oculus Go was chosen for the device to experience, and the applications were chosen from the application list downloadable at 1st October 2018. For the virtual reality contents, six contents were chosen which were named as *Art experience, Aquarium tour, CM experience, Pop star live event experience, Movie experience, Comic experience* listed on a simple instruction manual. Seniors chose the contents with their own will, after listening to precautions instructed from the instructor. The informed precautions are as follows (original sentences are written in Japanese).

- Experience time may be limited in case of crowded situation.
- We have carefully selected the VR contents from among the contents publically released by production companies, although, some people may feel VR sickness similar to car sickness by experiencing VR contents.
- The experience can be stoped at any time. Please do note hesitate to tell us if you are not feeling well.

The questionnaire consists of thirteen questions shown in Table 2. The questionnaire was designed based on the usability scale named System Usability Scale (SUS) [35]. Within this research we used Oculus GO for the HMD device to experience, therefore the function was very limited. Therefore, originally, SUS has a question *I found the various functions in this system were well integrated.* though it was skipped within the questionnaire list. However, to calculate the

Table 2. List of the 13 questionnaire to evaluate the seniors HMD experience.

List of questionnaire	
Q01	I enjoyed today's VR experience
Q02	I think that today's VR experience was easy to understand
Q03	I would like to take home the VR device I experienced today
Q04	I think that I would like to introduce VR device to my friends
Q05	I think that I would like to use this system frequently
Q06	I found the system unnecessarily complex
Q07	I thought the system was easy to use
Q08	I think that I would need the support of a technical person to be able to use this system
Q09	I thought there was too much inconsistency in this system
Q10	I would imagine that most people would learn to use this system very quickly
Q11	I found the system very cumbersome to use
Q12	I felt very confident using the system
Q13	I needed to learn a lot of things before I could get going with this system

SUS, respect to the original calculation, the question was calculated as a skipped question, considering it as a 3 within the five-level Likert scale. From Q05 to Q13 was taken from the SUS, and from Q01 to Q04 was prepared to evaluate the satisfaction of the booth experience and further possibilities whether the participants consider using the HMD at their home or not. For comparison, young staff at the event was also asked to voluntarily answer the same questionnaire after their experience of HMD.

4   Results and Discussion

The questionnaire was gathered from 5 seniors over age 60 and 10 youngs under 60. The means and standard deviations of the age of participants and the questionnaire results with SUS score is shown in Tables 3 and 4, for the young and senior, respectively. The young senior was labeled as *Group*, and a one-way analysis of variance was conducted for Q01 to Q04 and the SUS score (Tables 5, 6).

Table 3. Questionnaire results of young participants means and standard deviations on the age, Q01 to Q04, and SUS score.

Group: Young		
Statistic	Mean	SD
Age	29.800	8.176
Q01	4.900	0.316
Q02	4.900	0.316
Q03	3.700	1.636
Q04	4.400	0.843
SUS score	75.500	15.977

($n = 10$, Male $= 6$, Female $= 4$)

Table 4. Questionnaire results of senior participants means and standard deviations on the age, Q01 to Q04, and SUS score.

Group: Senior		
Statistic	Mean	SD
Age	71.600	7.436
Q01	4.800	0.447
Q02	4.400	0.548
Q03	3.000	1.871
Q04	4.000	0.707
SUS score	51.500	13.532

($n = 5$, Male $= 1$, Female $= 4$)

Table 5. One-way analysis of variance of *Q02* by *Group*.

	SS	df	F	p
Group	0.833	1	5.159	0.041 *
Residuals	2.100	13		

(* $p < .05$)

Table 6. One-way analysis of variance of *SUS score* by *Group*.

	SS	df	F	p
Group	1920	1	8.238	0.013 *
Residuals	3030	13		

(* $p < .05$)

From Q01 to Q04, only Q02 showed a significant difference (Table 5), implying that the seniors may have felt more difficulty compared to the youngs. However, the Q02 mean for senior is 4.4, which is rather high within the five-level Likert scale, indicating that seniors thought *that today's VR experience was easy to understand.* Although, results from SUS score for senior were 51.5, which is generally low score, considering there are suggestions that score less than 50 should be judged to be unacceptable [36]. According to Bangor [36], score of 50 indicates a serious usability failure rather than *being "half as good" as a product that scores 100.* Therefore, we can discuss that while the HMD experience was easy to understand there are still issues with usability.

For the young SUS score 75.5, according to Bangor's suggestion [36], the score indicates that the HMD experience is within the acceptable range, fairly good but not an excellent score. However, it is to be noted that it indicates that it shows that the HMD experience was not unacceptable, not that it is acceptable. As Lewis [37] points out, it is easier to show that a product is unacceptable than it is to show that it is acceptable. It also needs to consider the fact that to obtain reliable SUS results it is suggested it shall establish the "acceptability" within the number of participants in the hundreds [36].

Overall, consideration about "acceptance" can be argued within the objective point of view of the usability and whether if the usability is high from a subjective point of view. Even from the results of SUS score, the score is affected strongly from the subjective point of view, whereas the score rises if the participant thinks they are successful doing the tasks, even though if the participants were actually failing the tasks. To assess this problem, other scales and methods need to be combined for use [38]. However, if the product/system can be well popularized, if the basics are acceptable, it may be overall may not need to be strictly assessed. Recently, highly advanced products such as television and smartphones have already become popularized even within the seniors. There are many known issues such as the remote television controller becoming complex, or the smartphone becoming a very complex system, although, if there are needs or if there is high interest or desire, the product will well be purchased. Further research can be studied though it is still hard to distinguish if the product was really accepted, or if it is only a consumer behavior [39].

5   Conclusion

To provide a good experience to seniors using the Head-Mounted Display (HMD), this paper focused on the current acceptance level of consumer based HMD. While it is known that there are challenges for seniors using virtual reality devices, it is yet unclear how it may be accepted by the seniors which may not have much skill to use the device. To clarify the challenges, in this paper, a HMD experience event and questionnaire were prepared within a regional event for seniors. Based on statistical analysis, we obtained suggestive results that even while the current consumer based HMD'S SUS score is low, it may still satisfy their need or will. This may suggest that even products with usability difficulties to seniors may still provide high benefits to their life. However, it should be carefully argued with first impressions bias which shall be considered as topics which need to be featured in future research.

Finally, this paper suggests that consumer HMD products are nowadays in the phase to increase free and easily accessible contents to provide new opportunities to experience virtual reality. Especially, while many seniors gain knowledge about state-of-art consumer products through television programs, the opportunity to actually experience or consider buying the products are still low. The opportunities may be delivered through local events such as events held within local comprehensive care programs.

Acknowledgement. The authors are grateful to the elder citizens in Kashiwa city, to the voluntary students and voluntary staffs attending the regional event. The research was partially supported from the JSPS Program for Leading Graduate Schools (Graduate Program in Gerontology, Global Leadership Initiative for an Age Friendly Society, The University of Tokyo). Conflict of Interest: The authors confirm that there is no conflict of interest related to the content of this research.

References

1. Burdea, G.C., Coiffet, P.: Virtual Reality Technology. Wiley, London (1994)
2. Zeltzer, D.: Autonomy, interaction, and presence. Presence: Teleoperators Virtual Environ. **1**, 127–132 (1992)
3. Kiyokawa, K.: Trends and vision of head mounted display in augmented reality. In: 2012 International Symposium on Ubiquitous Virtual Reality, pp. 14–17 (2012)
4. Merhi, O., Faugloire, E., Flanagan, M., Stoffregen, T.A.: Motion sickness, console video games, and head-mounted displays. Hum. Factors **49**, 920–934 (2007)
5. Munafo, J., Diedrick, M., Stoffregen, T.A.: The virtual reality head-mounted display Oculus Rift induces motion sickness and is sexist in its effects. Exp. Brain Res. **235**, 889–901 (2017)
6. So, R.H., Lo, W., Ho, A.T.: Effects of navigation speed on motion sickness caused by an immersive virtual environment. Hum. Factors: J. Hum. Factors Ergon. Soc. **43**, 52–461 (2001)
7. Lin, J.J., Abi-Rached, H., Lahav, M.: Virtual guiding avatar: an effective procedure to reduce simulator sickness in virtual environments. In: Proceedings of the SIGCHI Conference on Human Factors in Computing Systems, pp. 719–726. ACM (2004)
8. Porcino, T.M., Clua, E., Trevisan, D., Vasconcelos, C.N., Valente, L.: Minimizing cyber sickness in head mounted display systems: design guidelines and applications. In: 2017 IEEE 5th International Conference on Serious Games and Applications for Health (SeGAH), pp. 1–6 (2017)
9. Google Cardboard - Google VR. https://vr.google.com/cardboard/. Accessed 01 Mar 2019
10. Hacosco website. https://hacosco.com/. Accessed 01 Mar 2019. (in Japanese)
11. Samsung Gear VR website. https://www.samsung.com/global/galaxy/gear-vr/. Accessed 01 Mar 2019
12. Cardboardclub website. http://cardboardclub.jp/get/giftkit/. Accessed 01 Mar 2019. (in Japanese)
13. Tong, X., Gromala, D., Amin, A., Choo, A.: The design of an immersive mobile virtual reality serious game in cardboard head-mounted display for pain management. In: 2015 International Symposium on Pervasive Computing Paradigms for Mental Health, pp. 284–293 (2015)

14. Playstation VR website. https://www.playstation.com/en-us/explore/playstation-vr/. Accessed 01 Mar 2019
15. Oculus Rift website. https://www.oculus.com/rift/. Accessed 01 Mar 2019
16. VIVE website. https://www.vive.com/us/product/vive-virtual-reality-system/. Accessed 01 Mar 2019
17. Oculus Go website. https://www.oculus.com/go/. Accessed 01 Mar 2019
18. Rogers, E.M.: Categorizing the adopters of agricultural practices. Rural Sociol. **23**, 346–354 (1958)
19. Robertson, T.: The process of innovation and the diffusion of innovation. J. Mark. **31**, 14–19 (1967)
20. Moore, C., Benbasat, I.: Development of an instrument to measure the perceptions of adopting an information technology innovation. Inf. Syst. Res. **2**, 192–222 (1991)
21. Plouffe, C., Vandenbosch, M., Hulland, J.: Why smart cards have failed: looking to consumer and merchant reactions to a new payment technology. Int. J. Bank Mark. **18**, 112–123 (2000)
22. Moore, G.: Crossing the Chasm: Marketing and Selling Technology Products to Mainstream Customers. Harper Business, New York (1991)
23. McGee, J.S., et al.: Issues for the assessment of visuospatial skills in older adults using virtual environment technology. CyberPsychol. Behav. **3**, 469–482 (2000)
24. Kline, D.W.: Optimizing the visability of displays for older observers. Exp. Aging Res. **20**, 11–23 (1994)
25. Cavanaugh, J.C.: Adult Development and Aging, 3rd edn. Brooks/Cole, Pacific Grove (1994)
26. Yetka, A.A., Pickwell, L.D., Jenkins, T.C.: Binocular vision: age and symptoms. Ophthalmic Physiol. Opt. **9**, 115–120 (1998)
27. Lee, H.C.: The validity of driving simulator to measure on-road driving performance of older drivers. In: 24th Conference of Australian Institutes of Transport Research, pp. 1 14 (2002)
28. Mouloua, M., Rinalducci, E., Smither, J., Brill, J.C.: Effect of aging on driving performance. In: Proceedings of the Human Factors and Ergonomics Society 48th Annual Meeting, vol. 48, pp. 253–257 (2004)
29. Park, G.D., Allen, R.W., Fiorentino, D., Rosenthal, T.J., Cook, M.L.: Simulator sickness scores according to symptom susceptibility, age, and gender for an older driver assessment study. In: Proceedings of the Human Factors and Ergonomics Society 50th Annual Meeting, vol. 50, pp. 2702–2706 (2006)
30. Allen, R.W., Park, G.D., Fiorentino, D., Rosenthal, T.J., Cook, L.M.: Analysis of simulator sickness as a function of age and gender. In: 9th Annual Driving Simulation Conference Europe (2006)
31. Cruz-Neira, C., Sandin, D.J., DeFanti, T.A., Kenyon, R.V., Hart, J.C.: The CAVE: audio visual experience automatic virtual environment. ACM Commun. **6**, 64–72 (1992)
32. García-Betances, R.I., Arredondo, W.M.T., Fico, G., Cabrera-Umpiérrez, M.F.: A succinct overview of virtual reality technology use in Alzheimer's disease. Front. Aging Neurosci. **7**, 80:1–80:8 (2015)
33. Bennett, C.R., Corey, R.R., Giudice, U., Giudice, N.A.: Immersive virtual reality simulation as a tool for aging and driving research. In: Zhou, J., Salvendy, G. (eds.) ITAP 2016. LNCS, vol. 9755, pp. 377–385. Springer, Cham (2016). https://doi.org/10.1007/978-3-319-39949-2_36

34. Ogino, R.: Role for higher education institutions in supporting lifelong learning and social participation (1) – Creation of learning site for seniors. Mombu Kagaku Kyoiku Tsushin (Commun. Educ. Cult. Sports Sci. Technol.) **370**, 20–22 (2015). (in Japanese)

35. Brooke, J.: SUS: a "quick and dirty" usability scale. In: Jordan, P.W., Thomas, B., Weerdmeester, B.A., McClelland, I.L. (Eds.), Usability Evaluation in Industry, pp. 189–194 (1996)

36. Bangor, A., Kortum, P.T., Miller, J.T.: An empirical evaluation of the system usability scale. J. Hum.-Comput. Interact. **6**, 574–594 (2008)

37. Lewis, J.: Binomial confidence intervals for small sample usability studies. In: Ozok, A.F., Salvendy, G. (Eds.) Advances in Applied Ergonomics: Proceedings of the 1st International Conference on Applied Ergonomics, pp. 732–737 (1996)

38. Stewart, T.: Ergonomics standards concerning human-system interaction: visual displays, controls and environmental requirements. Appl. Ergon. **26**, 271–274 (1995)

39. Seino, A.: Proposal for dissemination measures in new product for entertainment with image contents. Master Thesis, Keio Univeristy (2017). (in Japanese)

Older Adults' Perceptions About Commercially Available Xbox Kinect Exergames

Julija Jeremic[(✉)], Fan Zhang, and David Kaufman

Faculty of Education, Simon Fraser University, Burnaby, BC, Canada
jjeremic@sfu.ca

Abstract. Cognitive decline is one of the most feared aspects of growing older that may produce financial, personal, and societal burden and serious consequences on older adults' independence and quality of life. The findings of previous studies suggest that playing digital games can activate cognitive skills, while exergames can be beneficial both for physical activities and cognitive training. In this study, we used the Xbox 360 Kinect gaming console that employs advanced sensing technologies to allow players to interact with a game using body movements. The purpose of this research was to explore the gaming experience of older adults and to identify the benefits and obstacles they encounter while playing Xbox Kinect games. A total of ten older adults (an average age 82.8) were recruited from two senior centers in British Columbia, Canada. For five weeks, participants played mini exergames from collections: Kinect Sports, Dr. Kawashima Body and Brain Connection, Your Shape Fitness Evolved, Kinect Adventures, and Dance Central 3. Each session lasted for 30 to 60 min. Interviews were conducted after each session and at the end of the study. The findings show that older adults enjoyed most games they played, but preferred ones that are familiar to them. Also, they valued the exercise aspect of the games because they had to use their cognitive and physical abilities at the same time. However, they also report many obstacles while using the system.

Keywords: Exergames · Older adults · Xbox Kinect

1 Introduction

Modern society is aging. Statistical trends show an increase in the population of older adults aged 65 years and over [1]. If this trend continues by 2036 older adults "could constitute more than one-fourth of the population" [1, p. 59]. The problems of an aging population are seen in reduced mobility, raised the risk of falls and injuries [2], social isolation [3] and cognitive decline [4]. Accordingly, the number of older adults with mild cognitive impairment, Alzheimer disease, and dementia has been increasing in recent decades [5]. This increase in the aging population has as effects not only on the quality of life of these individuals and their families but on the world economy as well, mostly on the health care and pension systems [6]. To provide a better quality of life for older adults and their families and reduce burden on economy, researchers have been examining different types of cognitive training and "how technology and computing

© Springer Nature Switzerland AG 2019
J. Zhou and G. Salvendy (Eds.): HCII 2019, LNCS 11592, pp. 181–199, 2019.
https://doi.org/10.1007/978-3-030-22012-9_14

might reduce [the] deficit [of physical and cognitive abilities] and problem of old age" [6, p. 4]. Some researchers are developing hardware, devices or small appliances, and others are looking at the possibilities of how existent technology can be used to prevent a physical, cognitive and social decline in older adults. A special interest developed over the years in gerontology research has been on the use of digital games and gamified applications for improving many aspects of older adults' lives. On the contrary to traditional cognitive training, digital games present a fun and enjoying activities that can enrich a person's life, regardless if they are played in groups or individually. Results from some empirical studies show that digital games are known to reduce depression [7], loneliness [3], and improve self-confidence while enjoying social interactions and engaging in cognitive and physical activity [7, 8], but the results of many studies are not evidence-based (see for example the review by Loos and Kaufman [9]). All these aspects contribute to the overall quality of life which is defined not only as the absence of disease but as "...a state of complete physical, mental and social well-being" [10].

The purpose of this research was to investigate the gaming experience of Canadian older adults and identify the benefits and obstacles they report with commercially available off-the-shelf (COTS) Xbox Kinect games with the following research questions:

1. What types of Xbox Kinect games are suitable for older adults aged 65 and over? What are the features of these games?
2. Which challenges do older adults aged 65 and over encounter when playing Xbox Kinect games?
3. What are the opinions of older adults aged 65 and over on using Xbox Kinect games?

1.1 Cognitive Training

The effects of cognitive training have been a subject of many discussions in neuroscience, gerontology, education, and human-computer interactions, and there are many controversies around this issue. Review articles that have been investigating the benefits of any type of cognitive training, traditional, computer or game based, concluded: "that training improves immediate performance on related tasks, but there was no evidence for generalization effects to overall cognitive functioning" [11, p. 263]. Several review articles were investigating the cognitive benefits of both physical and cognitive training in older adults using digital games. Some of the findings suggest that there are short-term beneficial effects of playing digital games "on older adults' balance, mobility, executive function, and processing speed" [12, p. 14] regardless of the health and living conditions of this group. However, more research is needed to determine the effects of cognitive training to untrained tasks, activities of daily life, with the follow-up data on the far transfer of the training [11].

On the other hand, neuroscience research found "the relationship between serum BDNF [brain-derived neurotrophic factor], IGF-1 [insulin-like growth factor type 1], and VEGF [vascular endothelial growth factor], and functional connectivity in healthy elderly adults" [13, p. 90]. By measuring the presence of these factors in human blood, they determined "that aerobic exercise-related increases in circulating growth factors are related to temporal lobe functional brain connectivity in elderly humans" [13, p. 98]. This study provides evidence that exercise, even moderate, can influence changes in chemicals in our organism that are relevant for the age-related changes in the brain.

A new gaming technology that emerged in 2006, first used by Nintendo Wii, enabled a new form of physical activity using digital games called exergames [14]. As defined by Oh and Yang [15], an exergame is "a video game that promotes (either via using or requiring) players' physical movements (exertion) that is generally more than sedentary and includes strength, balance, and flexibility activities" [15, p. 9]. This new technology can detect movements of players body by either tracking of hand-held controllers [14] or by tracking the movements of player's body joints [16, 17]. The research shows that older adults are motivated to play exergames [18] and see them as fun and engaging physical activities that could be done indoors [19]. On the other hand, many older adults report issues with the use of new technologies which could be a consequence of the fact that digital games, including exergames, are usually created for a younger audience without the consideration of limitations that come with old age [18]. Exergames can range from light to vigorous physical intensity while at the same time being entertaining for users [14]. As neuroscience research indicates that physical activity is beneficial not only for physical health but also to age-related cognitive decline [13], these games could be valuable for improving both cognitive functioning and physical abilities in older adults. However, Loos and Kaufman [9] in their state-of-the-art paper about the impact of exergames on the mental and social well-being of older adults concluded that 6 out of 9 empirical studies they analyzed report some positive impact on the cognitive performance of older adults while others did not report any significant results, therefore, they advocate for more empirical research to be conducted.

1.2   Microsoft Xbox Kinect

In November 2010, Microsoft launched its new gaming technology named Kinect [16], which uses advanced sensing technologies [17]. To detect body movements, Kinect uses two cameras and one infrared projector that scan the environment to detect body joints and facial expressions [17, 20] with the ability to recognize different players. Also, Kinect uses voice recognition technologies that enable controlling a game with users' voice [17]. When tested, the Kinect sensor showed high sensitivity in both response time and accuracy [21], which is important when the game expects from a player to perform cognitive tasks and provides greater potential for adequate feedback on performance [22]. Besides Xbox Kinect, Nintendo Wii and PlayStation Move use motion tracking to control gameplay. However, Nintendo Wii uses Wiimote, a remote controller that requires users to push buttons on the remote during gameplay which can be challenging and frustrating for older adults. Features facilitated by Kinect present great improvement in the gaming experience especially for users with less experience in gameplay.

1.3   Usability of Xbox Kinect COTS Games

Research conducted using the Kinect system can be divided into two groups. One group that developed and tested their own applications/games, and the other that explored commercially available games. The development of new games is important for creating games that are suitable for older adults, especially concerning barriers of the user's interface [23], options for personalization and adaptation [24] and having dual-task activities included [25–27]. These applications are usually designed with the consultation of appropriate experts, but they still have to be tested for the usability of older adults and commercialized for broader use. On the other hand, there are numerous commercially available exergames developed for different gaming consoles [24].

To determine the usability of the Kinect system and COTS games for older adults, researchers have done several studies. Marinelli and Rogers [28] conducted a heuristic evaluation and hierarchical task analysis, using games from Body and Brain Connection and Your Shape Fitness Evolved, by decomposing large tasks into networks of nine sub-tasks and pre-requisites. Several studies explored the use of the Kinect games together with exergames for other platforms. Barenbrock, et al. [24] conducted a qualitative study with four participants aged from 71 to 86 years old "to investigate strengths and weaknesses of commercial exergames with regard to older people" [24, p. 1]. From nine games that were tested throughout three days in participants' homes only two were for Xbox Kinect, Dance Central games and one game from Kinect Adventures collection, 20,000 Leaks [24]. Harrington, Hartley, Mitzner and Rogers [23] conducted a qualitative study with 20 healthy older adults, aged 60–79, "to identify usability challenges of Kinect-based exergames for older adults" [23, p. 490] and provide recommendations for the design of the games for this population. They used Body and Brain Connections and Your Shape Fitness Evolved, recorded gameplay and conducted interviews after each session to analyze errors in starting and handling the system and to examine perceptions of the participants of the use of two game collections for older adults, especially in the personal home settings.

Difficulties in using gesture to control the game and navigate through the system were observed in all studies. When the system was placed in older adults' homes who were asked to play three games every day in for three weeks and to record their progress, participants expressed "difficulties adapting to the physical demands of Kinect play" [29, p. 18:16]. However, older adults did find ways to adapt to Kinect by developing strategies that will compensate their bodily limitations through anticipating required activities during gameplay, for example, starting required action few second in advance [29]. This finding suggests that for new technologies to be adopted by older users they should be present in everyday lives and practices so that the interactions can be modified based on personal abilities [29]. Also, it was noticed that initial errors were reduced when participants used another set of games due to the familiarity with the Kinect system [23].

Moreover, researchers proposed the recommendations for future game developers to follow: design less complex and dense environment, minimalize information presented on the screen, develop user-friendly interface, provide "on-screen instructional gestures … to serve as guidance and reinforcement" [23, p. 497], put the importance on progress in contrary to challenge, allow additional time for reactions, and create environments that support adaptability and realistic scenarios over fantasy settings [24]. While others concluded that "game redesign based on principles of universal accessibility would be ideal" [28, p. 1251] or the use of supplemental materials, complemented with guidelines or training, to accommodate knowledge and skill transfer from familiar games to the new ones.

We often speak about technology specifically designed for the use of a certain group. Similarly, researchers are developing special games or digital training targeted at older adults. While such an approach is innovative and creative, it takes time to produce, test and put into use these technologies. On the other hand, there are plenty of COTS games that are sporadically tested for the usability of older adults, often excluding participants with some physical or cognitive impairments. With that in mind, we conducted a study to explore older adults' perceptions about commercially available Xbox 360 Kinect games, especially in the context of physical and cognitive training.

2 Methods

2.1 Research Design

The research instruments for this study included a background questionnaire, post-session interview protocol, and post-intervention interview protocol. Also, about 40% of the gameplay was video-recorded. This paper will present only the results of the post-intervention interviews with some information taken from the background questionnaire, while the results of gameplay analysis and short post-session interviews will be the focus of another report.

2.2 Participants

We recruited ten older adults from two senior centers to participate in this research. Eight participants were female, and two were male. The average age of participants was 82.8 with the age span from 74 to 89. As we wanted to explore how COTS Xbox 360 Kinect games can be used in any situation where Xbox 360 with the Kinect sensor is available (independent living facilities, retirement communities, seniors' private homes, or the homes of their families), we decided not to exclude any participants with physical or cognitive limitations. Therefore, all participants that were willing to participate in two selected locations were included in the study. Both locations provided independent living arrangements, so most participants were able to take care of themselves independently. Nine participants lived alone, while one was living with his spouse and had an early stage of Alzheimer disease. However, their physical abilities did vary.

There were multiple physical challenges that participants were facing which interfered with their gameplay. Some of them reported having issues with balance and strength in lower extremities, or pain in legs, back and shoulders. A couple of participants had to use a walker, and one of them could not play any of the games that required extensive standing. One participant reported having heart conditions, and one was diagnosed with Alzheimer disease. Table 1. provides detailed information for each participant.

The level of education of participants also differed. Three of them had less than a high school, four finished high school, one was college and two university graduates. Experience with digital games was equally distributed. Five were non-gamers, and only one of them plays non-digital games (such as card games or puzzles) once a day.

Table 1. Characteristics of participants

Participant' code	Experience with digital games	Non-digital games or puzzles	Physical activities	Self-reported and observed physical limitations
AL87f	Never played	Never played	Light walking, stretching (a few times a week)	Severe back and legs pain, issues with balance.
RN87f	Plays once a week	Plays once a week	Other - bowling (a few times a week)	Generally, no issues, feels strong, sometimes may lose a balance. Considers herself active.
MP89f	Plays twice a week	Plays once a day	Light walking (once a day)	Uses walker, had to sit all the time, but was able to stand up to initiate the game with a help of a chair.
TD85mA	Never played	Never played	Stretching, fast walking/hiking, other - played soccer (once a day)	An early stage of Alzheimer disease, no physical limitations.
RT89m	Never played	Plays once a day	Light walking, stretching, fast walking/hiking (once a day)	Light shoulder pain. Considers himself active.
TA84f	Never played	Never played	Light walking, stretching, balance exercise, fast walking/hiking, gym exercise (once a day)	Low strength in lower extremities, had to sit frequently.
BD77f	Plays three times a day on her cell phone	Plays a few times a week	Light walking, other - shopping (once twice a month)	Back and shoulder injuries, heart diseases.
AM74f	Plays twice a week	Plays a few times a week	Light walking, yoga (a few times a week)	Some pain in legs, couldn't stand for too long.
AL82f	Never played	Never played	Other - yoga (once in two weeks)	Uses walker, wanted to sit down and play games, however, played them standing up. Did not report any physical limitations but said that she couldn't jump if needed.
RM74f	Plays once a day	Plays once a day	Light walking, square dancing (once a week)	No physical limitations reported or observed. Considers herself active.

Note: The first two letters in the participant's code represent their initials, the number represents the age of a participant, while "f" and "m" letters represent female or male gender, respectively. One participant is assigned with the letter "A" for Alzheimer disease.

For example: TD – initials, 85 – age, m – male, A – with Alzheimer disease.

The other five participants had some experience with digital games. Their involvement with digital games varied from a couple of times a day, once a day, once a week to a couple of times a week. Participants who played digital games, also engage in non-digital games activities from once a day to a couple of times a week. On the other hand, all participants practice light walking and stretching, while some engage in other physical activities such as yoga, hiking and fast walking, balance and gym exercises, and square dancing.

2.3 Games and Game Sessions

As the literature review showed a need for more research conducted on the evaluation of COTS games since only a small number of games were explored with older adults [23, 24, 28], this study aimed to expose older adults to a variety of games. It was also important to explore perceptions of participants about these games in the context of cognitive and physical training. Based on the previous research done on the usability of digital games with older adults [23, 24, 28] criteria for game design suitable for older adults were used. These criteria included: giving importance to the progress instead of a challenge, taking care of health risks during gameplay, the complexity of the game, and moderate visual and audio stimulations. After a thorough investigation of both gameplay and previous research, following game collections were selected: Kinect Sports, Body and Brain Connection, Your Shape: Fitness Evolved, Kinect Adventures, and Dance Central 3. These collections were also used in previous research. The most popular collection of games in the research with older adults is Body and Brain Connections that was used in at least three studies with older adults [24, 28, 30]. The reason for that popularity may be in the fact that games in this collection were developed under the supervision of a neuroscientist Dr. Ryuta Kawashima [31]. However, not all games of this collection were available to older adults to choose in these studies. For example, Chiang et al. [30] used only three games from this collection: Follow the arrow, Matchmaker and Mouse mayhem. Aside from this collection, Marinelli et al. [28] and Harrington et al. [23] explored the Kinect fitness games under the title Your Shape, while Barenbrock et al. [24] explored usability challenges of older adults while playing two Kinect games: Kinect Adventures and Dance Central 3. In this study, we decided to explore all these titles, but we also included the Kinect Sports games, as a collection with potentially familiar and fun activities for older adults.

Table 2 shows a schedule of games offered to older adults in the period of five weeks. Seniors were asked to play a specific list of games each week, but in later weeks, they were offered both games assigned for that week and games that were played in previous weeks. Also, participants were able to choose any game from available collections after they played required games to see if the motivation for play would help them overcome challenges they experienced with the system.

Each session lasted for 30 to 60 min. The reduced time of gameplay was noticeable for seniors who have less interest in gaming activities as seen in their background profile. For example, TA84f never played digital games, nor she engages in non-digital gaming activities, so her sessions were usually shorter as she reported not feeling motivated to play.

On most sessions, there were two research assistants present. One would observe gameplay, asking questions about games and video or audio record sessions, while the other one would assist older adults in their play.

Table 2. Game sessions

Session	Must play	Optional
Week 1: Sports	All mini sport games	Any other sports games under the Main Event Model
Week 2: Body and Brain Collection	Traffic control, What time is it?, Match Maker, Perfect 10, Math Jock, Balloon Buster	Other body and brain games, any sport games
Week 3: Your Shape	All body shape games	Any sport and body shape games
Week 4: Kinect Adventures	All adventure games with and without stories	Any sport, body/brain collection, and body shape games
Week 5: Dance Central 3	Any dance games participants choose	Any other game

2.4   Interviews

For this study, we collected data using two interview protocols. We interviewed participants after each session to collect participants perceptions about games right after gameplay. In addition, we conducted a final interview after participants completed the last session to understand their overall experience and opinions about games and the Kinect system. Questions for the final interview can be divided into three sections: opinions about games (most liked and least liked game and features of these games), experiences with the Kinect system (challenges in using the system, comparison to other consoles if applicable), and opinion about the usability of games and the system for cognitive and physical training of older adults (including observed changes in their abilities after the intervention).

2.5   Data Analysis

Data collected in this study were audio recorded and transcribed. Transcribed documents were uploaded to a qualitative data software, NVivo 12, to identify emergent themes using in-vivo coding method. These themes were then compared and organized using axial coding into higher categories [32].

3 Findings

In that sense, findings are organized in three sections: types of games and their features preferred by older adults; challenges experienced with games and the Kinect system; and opinions about games, the system and the potential of both for cognitive and physical training of older adults.

3.1 Game Preferences of Older Adults

Many participants highlighted that they *liked all games* "because they were different and gave a variety" (TA84f). However, the most popular games among older adults were games from *the Kinect Sports collection:* Bowling, Boxing and Soccer. Next in line were the Kinect Adventure games and Dance Central 3 games, while only two participants mentioned liking the best games from Body and Brain Connections and Your Shape, respectively.

The familiarity of games including the connection to previous experiences and *challenges* were reported equally as highly desirable features of games played. Participants felt a closer connection to the games which they played in real life and for some of them that brought up old memories:

"Bowling was good, yeah. I liked them all actually, because I have three sons that I brought up, so we did a lot of sports because their dad was... I was divorced so we always went with them... So, it was fun, three boys." - BD77f

For others, it was a matter of knowing the rules of the play and having personal interests in these activities:

"The boxing would be my favourite. [Why?] Possibly 'cos I did all that before: tennis, boxing, soccer." - RT89m

Even though seniors reported challenges that prevented them on playing and enjoying some games, like a game being too fast, most of them *like being challenged a bit.* They regard challenge as a motivation to engage with the game further and having fun in that process:

"I like to figure how things go, and I want to do the best I can so, yes, the challenge. No matter which one I do I'm going to try it and beat what I can...the astronaut games [Space Pop game from Kinect Adventures] where there's a bit of a challenge, but it's not overwhelming challenge. Like if you can laugh at yourself, that helps." - RM74f

Another important feature of games that emerged from the interviews was *enjoyment and fun:*

"It was a lot of laughs because I kept getting banged. [Kinect Adventure]" - BD77f
"Even if you don't make it. You know, if you don't... if you can't do it, it was still enjoyable... I had fun, yes." - MP89f

Reasons that made seniors dislike a game are usually *difficulties they experience playing,* such as a game being too complex or fast. Some participants disliked certain games as they perceived them "kind of childish" (AL87f).

When asked which games they would play again and potentially buy, opinions differed. Most participants still preferred sport games, while others liked adventure games and dances; some of them would like to play these games again and others would not. Reasons for that might be in personal preferences, the perceived difficulty of a game and even inabilities to play some games due to their physical limitations. One of the quotes describes the issue well:

> "If the dances were more in line with the age group, I'd probably go for the dances. I like the Macarena, and I like the YMCA one, the Hustle, and probably the other ones, I wouldn't have even attempted. I won't even attempt them with my grandson. Because these are all the young ones and I like the adventure ones myself. But I'm a go, go, go type of person." - RM74f

This quote also represents mixed perceptions about dance games. On the one hand, many older adults like dancing and would love to be able to play games from Dance Central collections. However, they find them too fast and challenging, or how seniors would put it "Not the dance. [You didn't like dance?] Because not that easy. Just the leg or the hand but both you... maybe the younger will be okay" (AL82f).

3.2   Challenges

Exergames that are available on the market are usually created for a younger audience, people who are physically able to complete moderately complex physical and dual-task activities. Also, previous research tended to exclude people with physical limitations [24], unless the goal was to develop a game or application targeting this population [25–27]. However, the availability of gaming consoles in senior centers and homes is increasing, so the accessibility of these games to older adults will be increasing as well. Having that in mind, we wanted to see what kind of challenges seniors experience when playing commercially available titles and what would be needed for them to enjoy gaming activities at their own home.

Fig. 1. Gameplay supported by objects from the environment

Since the background survey had shown the lack of experience of our participants with games and gaming consoles, we decided to set up the system each week ourselves. The first couple of sessions started with a research assistant navigating the interface and doing all necessary preparatory activities. After that, the game tutorial would be shown, and in some cases, the research assistant had to play the game before a participant would start playing. Some participants learned how to navigate the system easily, but for some others, we had to initiate the game each time. One participant especially had difficulties in navigating the system, as she had to sit all the time and was not able to use her body to control the system. As she had to stand up to initiate the game, we

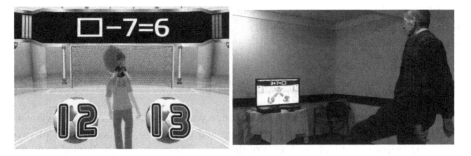

Fig. 2. Math Jock screenshot of gameplay [33] and a photo of the actual play

provided support in the form of additional chairs that she could hold on to be able to stand up (Fig. 1). We used the same adjustments in several cases. However, a chair on which a player would sit during gameplay presented an obstacle in some games. For example, in the game *Math Jock* from Body and Brain Connections, a mathematical equation is displayed at the top of the screen, and the player is supposed to kick the ball with the correct result of with their foot (Fig. 2). If the player had to sit and play, the system would detect a leg of the chair, which interfered with the ability of the Kinect sensor to respond to the player's actions correctly.

Challenges that participants reported as interfering with their gameplay can be grouped into several themes: their own physical limitations and injuries, the complexity of games or games being "fast and hard" (BD77f), inability to focus on dual-task activities, defined as "simultaneous locomotive and cognitive performance activity" [26, p. 348], issues with the Kinect sensor response, and learning new thing.

Physical abilities tend to decrease with age in some people [34]. Most participants in our study reported some *physical limitations* and *previous injuries* that prevented them from completing tasks in games:

> "The basic challenge was speed because I was having a hard time standing. I'm in pain all the time. You know, I shouldn't have signed up for this because I'm a disappointment to you." - AL87f
>
> "Just a sore back and bad shoulder, broken shoulder that's still not healing properly. So, it's just some injuries that can limit my activities or exercise." - BD77f

Although participants appreciated dual-task activities in games, they also found them *fast* and *challenging*. The fact that they had to process information cognitively and the same time thinks about physical movements made some activities too complex. Also, the time available to complete these activities was too short. Some participants suggested that time given in games (for example, 10 seconds to resolve an equation and kick the correct ball) is more suitable for younger people and felt that they needed either more time, less complex activities or activities involving only one section of the body in combination with cognitive activities. Here are some quotes from the participants:

> "Well, you're watching what is she [the virtual trainer] going to do next. I've done the Macarena before, but I have a hard time to follow. [Why?] Why, it's just so fast. Like you're standing there, there, there, this way and that way." - TA84f

While previous quotes illustrate participants highlighting physical challenges, some participants reported *an inability to focus on dual-task activities* regarding cognitive processing.

"Coordinating and focusing. Learning to really keep focused. In my mind it's like this is just a game so I had to learn to really concentrate and focus so I could do it properly and get the little bit of points that you can get." - BD77f

For some participants, the biggest challenge was *being recognized by the system.* The Kinect sensor was not able to recognize and connect to the body joints of two female participants that had to sit most of the time. This resulted in the limited scope of games they could play.

"What challenges? Just trying to be recognized on the TV, I guess." - AM74f

Another participant was upset that the system was responding late to his actions:

"I didn't really dislike any of it, but I was disappointed in some of them. The technology isn't quite there to respond to my responses. And I dislike them on account of that but not because... [Of the game.] It was quite good. Concept is excellent, but it could be quicker response to my actions. Like for instance when I was trying to kick the ball there if that was a real ball, I knew a real ball I know what to kick. And they were on the machine I was missing them." - RT89m

The last statement can be linked to another challenge seniors experienced *learning new things.* Some of them had to put a lot of energy into playing game and understanding its rules. It should be also noted that half of participants never played digital games before.

"Well, I really... let's put it this way. I had to put all my energy into it. I think this type of a game maybe 30 years ago then you're going to say, yeah, okay, this is a kiddie's game, right? But I won't say that now anymore. I really have to follow exactly what it says." - TD85mA

3.3   Opinions

Aside from exploring the experiences of older adults with the Kinect systems and selected game collections, we wanted to hear seniors' perceptions about the value of the system and games for older adults especially in the context of dual-task training and the perceived benefits of engaging in these activities. Several themes emerged in the analysis.

Value of the System and Games and Perceived Benefits
When asked if games and the system would be useful for seniors, participants see their *value as physical exercise and cognitive training, having fun while exercising, for learning new things,* and *making them feel better.* However, they believe that *some adjustments* should be made so older adults could play them.

Most participants believe that the system and games could be used in dual-task training:

"I think it's good if you can get people to take, use it, because when you're using it you're using your brain and what mobility you have. So, it's to keep everything working and because you use it, or you lose it." - RM74f

In addition, participants expressed belief in the high value of games played to make seniors *enjoy physical activities while having fun*. For some "time went very fast" (RT89m), while others appreciate exercising without knowing it:

"I enjoyed the games. It gave me exercise that didn't feel like exercise. I have never done exercise for the sake of doing exercise. And if you want people to do exercise without them knowing they're actually exercising, this is the way to get it... As far as I'm concerned, I never, I don't go for walks unless I've got to go somewhere. Okay. It's my own way, I've got a destination, I'll go. Am I going to walk around the corner just to say I walked? No... [So, you want to say that these are more fun activities than regular exercise.] Correct. These are fun activities that actually count as an exercise." - RM74f

Having fun while exercising made some of them *change attitude towards exercise*:

"Yeah, in general, I have a better attitude towards exercise... That's amazing because I don't want to do exercise, but this is showing me that it can be a lot of fun and very helpful." - BD77f

Some people think that these types of games would provide seniors ways to *learn something new*:

"Well, I was happy to try them all because it's something new and it gives... we're seniors. We don't do them. I go to the gym three times, but we do different ones and I do the step thing and then I practice standing a lot, you know, about 20 times. Then you can just get up. A lot of people can't get out of their chair if they don't have the strength in their legs." - TA84f

Or make them *feel better*:

"Usually when we all have sicknesses, when you get sick you start feeling miserable and get a headache or whatever. Here you don't notice nothing." - TD85mA

However, *some adjustments* are required:

"They could be very beneficial in like you're going to have to figure out which... how to moderate some of them a bit probably. [They would need some adjustments?] Some adjustments, I would say. Like the Hustle. I mean, there are some that are here that will try to learn something new but most of them it's not what they want to do. Have you seen that yourself? Yeah." - RM74f

The majority of older adults believe that their gaming skills improved during the five weeks of the study. They report learning how to play games and how to use the system, as illustrated in the following statement:

"Well, the gaming skills you got used to what was happening, so you get better at it." - AM74f

Some participants even reported seeing certain abilities improved during the study:

"I think it's improved my reaction. [We are interested in using these games to improve the physical and also the cognitive function of older adults. What's your opinion on this?] Oh, I think it helps." - AL87f

On the other hand, some of them think they would need more practicing time to improve their gaming skills:

"No, because I didn't do them that much, although they did improve while I was doing them. But if I had access to the machines all the time they would definitely go way up to what I did there for the first time. You just bring in the game and spend a... your real reaction to things." - RT89m

"That they're too short to indicate that with. I think if you play this game let's say four hours a day, every day, every single week you will do a lot better but that's not the idea." - TD85mA

Difference Between Digital Games and "the Real Thing"

Since only five participants played digital games before, they tend to compare games played during the study with activities like walking, playing sports, doing yoga, and dancing:

"[Well, do you think that these... you can replace your dancing courses with some of these games, dancing games?] Not even close. [Why? Just be honest.] Because I've always been extremely active and when I dance I love the fast... I don't know if you know what a polka is but that's one of the faster ones. And the jive, maybe you know that. And western dancing. And they're all very, very lively dances and they use every muscle in your body, your neck, your arms, your legs. 100% exercises. [And these are not like that?] They are trying to be, but they're still machine and..." - RT89m

Some participants even considered the Kinect games easier than real life activities:

"I did the hula hoop. That wasn't too bad. I didn't think I was going to do it because I haven't been able to do the hula hoop in like I can't remember. I think I got a daughter hula hooped and I tried it to show her, I couldn't do it anymore. But because it's animated it did work." - RM74f

Comparison to Wii Console

A couple of participants had some experience with the Nintendo Wii console and its remote controllers. We asked them whether they preferred using their body to control gameplay or controllers as used in the Wii system. Again, they had different opinions. Two female participants that had the biggest challenges with being detected by the Kinect sensor reported preferring Wii over the Kinect system:

"[And this system is... how different is this system from Wii?] It's quite a bit different. But yeah, it's quite a bit... well, it's similar. It's similar enough but you have to pick up the ball. And you're playing bowling and... [Which one would you choose?] I would still choose Wii bowling because it's less... you don't have to detect the person. [And it's not challenging for you to hold the remote?] No, no." - AM74f

On the contrary, some people feel more freedom without having to use the Wii controller:

"I like that. I like the bowling better than the Wii bowling because you don't have that... [remote]... on your wrist and because you go like this here, but that thing could turn a different way. So, this here it's your own hand that..." - RM74f

Lack of Interest in Digital Games

On the question whether they would use the system if it becomes available in their center, seniors had split opinions. Some see the opportunity to play these games as a new and exciting activity, or as a way to exercise and have fun at the same time. However, others are just *not interested in digital games*:

"I don't think I'll play. [Why?] Well, it just doesn't interest me. There's no real interest." - AL87f

Participants in this study lived in two senior communities in which there are many activities organized during a week. This means that they are usually surrounded by their peers with whom they can connect on a personal basis:

> "Will I use it? Probably not... For me if they're happening at a game night or something, then I might go and do something. But it's called a game night a fun night or something like that. And what machine is not going to generate a fun night, you know... Yeah. Like if you start all machines at the same time two players on each one or something then, okay, let's see who gets the best score, the best time or... [Actually, RT89m and TA84f danced together this morning, so that was fun.] Yeah. And that would make it more fun because you're not feeling like you're exercising." - RM74f

Personal Value for One Participant

Even though we had no aim in elaborating experiences of individual participants in this study, experiences with the system and games had a special significance to one participant. The biggest value of the system and games for the participant with Alzheimer disease was, in his perception, that these games could be a good assessment tool for tracking his decline. He emphasized this on several occasions:

> "I find all these games it's like a little challenge in itself. It's what I like about something like that, if you had these games you could test yourself and really do some of these things and really assess how far you go down." - TD85mA

One of the reasons for this belief may be in the description of the collection and an option for initial assessment present in Body and Brain Connections. Before selecting games, in this collection, there is an opportunity to be evaluated by playing sample games which will give an initial assessment of dual-task activities. Later on, games would provide an assessment based on the progress. TD85mA might have perceived that this option would be valuable for him.

> "I have nothing to hide or anything like that. Then the more I learned about myself that way, and I know better off I am. I know you're on a decreasing light, but it is always hard to find out exactly where you are on... So, I think even games like this remind me again, and I can assess a little bit where I am at." - TD85mA

However, he did indicate that in some games you can track your progress by tracking the amount of energy you put into gameplay, which could be seen as a self-evaluation:

> "Well, I think I like the idea of it. And I think also it's probably a good way, I don't know. I have so far on my journey I have never learned of a systematic way of assessing well, like noticing such... But games like this are actually very good because it shows in a practical way I think, how, where you are at on the whole thing... Well, I, for instance, assume I think he would know it by let's call it the energy you can produce in the...[game]...to set the same results." - TD85mA

3.4   Suggestions

While suggestions for designing the dual-task training will be derived from the analysis of the actual gameplay of participants and presented in a separate report, some valuable suggestions came from the interviews with participants. For example, since one of the challenges experienced by participants was speed and time allocated to complete game tasks, one of the suggestion was to make games easier or less complex:

"Comfortable would be easy game… Because, just as I said, if it's just hand or just leg will be easy. But if you want both leg and hand, move and match, they have the beat slowly." - AL82f

However, the certain degree of challenge should be present, enough to make it exciting and still be able to complete it successfully:

"I don't like being beat. I don't mind being not good at it, but I don't like not being able to get it." - RM74f

For some seniors having assistance in setting up the system and navigating the interface would be highly preferable:

"[Why is assistance from another person important?] Well, I didn't understand it [how to play those games] to begin with." - AL87f

In addition, providing more themes related to older adults' younger age and previous life experiences would provide more entertainment and motivation:

"Bring in some old-type dances. The hustle…There's the Bunny Hop. Just the fun… you know, just simple type moves that we can grasp and enjoy…So, if you're enjoying it and you're going to do it a little bit longer personally, I think that." - RM74f

4   Discussion, Conclusion and Limitations

While exploring the usability of commercially available titles, researchers suggested more empirical studies to determine the benefits of COTS games and to provide recommendations for the use of the Kinect system at homes. Additionally, they were discussing reasons for the small number of games designed for older adults and the lack of knowledge about gameplay preferences of this population, as well as challenges of game designers with age-related declines in sight, hearing, reduces motor and cognitive abilities [23, 35, 36]. Moreover, the research explored only several titles of COTS games [23, 24, 28], leaving the huge number of titles to be further explored [22]. After exploring five different Xbox COTS gaming collections with ten Canadian older adults, we can derive the following conclusions and provide answers to our research questions:

1. What types of Xbox Kinect games are suitable for older adults aged 65 and over? What are the features of these games?
   Older adults like games with familiar activities such as sports games, adventures and dances. They prefer games that can bring up old memories and provide a connection to previous life experiences and interests. Games that are fun and challenging are also valued more than games with simple activities that they regard as childish to some extent. They see the challenge as a motivation and a way for deeper engagement in gameplay.

2. Which challenges do older adults aged 65 and over encounter when playing Xbox Kinect games?

Older adults without physical limitations can use the Kinect system with some support, while people who have issues with their balance or extremities face challenges being properly detected by the Kinect sensor. In addition, seniors find most of the games too fast and complex. Although they appreciate dual-task activities in some games, they report having issues with focusing on both cognitive and physical activities at the same time and in a limited timeframe.

3. What are the opinions of older adults aged 65 and over on using Xbox Kinect games?
Doing physical activities while playing games and having fun participants saw as one of the strengths of exergames. Many report the lack of physical activities in their lives and believe that these games would motivate them in being more physically active. They also believe that games with dual-task activities could be useful for cognitive training.

The limitations of this study come from a small number of seniors who participated in the research, limited time for gameplay, and the broad scope of games tested. Even though we wanted to explore the usability of the wide variety of exergames, this broad scope also prevented us from gaining more precise knowledge of the features of games that are suitable for older adults. Exploring many games during one session could have also affected older adults' opinions on different games due to their similar content and activities. Lastly, exploring the experiences of a larger number of older adults could have provided deeper insights into seniors' perceptions and experiences in exergaming.

The potential of commercially available exergames exist, and while researchers should make more efforts in finding ways of using them in their current form, game developers and designers should be encouraged to create more fun and adventurous games that would include adjustments appropriate for older adults and other people with some physical limitations.

Acknowledgement. This work was supported by AGE-WELL NCE Inc., a national research network supporting research, networking, commercialization, knowledge mobilization and capacity building activities in technology and aging to improve the quality of life of Canadians and contribute to the economic impact of Canada. AGE-WELL is a member of the Networks of Centres of Excellence (NCE), a Government of Canada program that funds partnerships between universities, industry, government and not-for-profit organizations.

References

1. Lebel, A., Charbonneau, P., Landry, H., Dussault, J.: Annual Demographic Estimates: Canada, Provinces and Territories. Statistics Canada, Ottawa (2015). http://www.statcan.gc.ca/access_acces/alternative_alternatif.action?teng=91-215-x2015000-eng.pdf&tfra=91-215-x2015000-fra.pdf&l=eng&loc=91-215-x2015000-eng.pdf
2. Lai, C.H., Peng, C.W., Chen, Y.L., Huang, C.P., Hsiao, Y.L., Chen, S.C.: Effects of interactive video-game based system exercise on the balance of the elderly. Gait Posture **37**(4), 511–515 (2012)
3. Schell, R., Hausknecht, S., Zhang, F., Kaufman, D.: Social benefits of playing Wii Bowling for older adults. Games Culture **11**(1–2), 81–103 (2016)

4. Kayama, H., Okamoto, K., Nishiguchi, S., Yamada, M., Kuroda, T., Aoyama, T.: Effect of a Kinect-based exercise game on improving executive cognitive performance in community-dwelling elderly: case control study. J. Med. Internet Res. **16**(2), e61 (2014)

5. Prince, M.J.: World Alzheimer Report 2015: The Global Impact of Dementia: an Analysis of Prevalence, Incidence, Cost and Trends (2015)

6. Musselwhite, C., Marston, H.R., Freeman, S.: From needy and dependent to independent Homo Ludens exploring digital gaming and older people. Games Culture **11**(1–2), 3–6 (2016)

7. Astell, A.: Technology and fun for a happy old age. In: Sixsmith, A., Gutman, G. (eds.) Technologies for Active Aging, vol. 9, pp. 169–187. Springer, Boston (2013)

8. Kaufman, D., Sauve, L., Renaud, L., Duplaa, E.: Cognitive benefits of digital games for older adults. In: EdMedia: World Conference on Educational Media and Technology, vol. 2014, no. 1, pp. 289–297 (2014)

9. Loos, E., Kaufman, D.: Positive impact of exergaming on older adults' mental and social well-being: in search of evidence. In: Zhou, J., Salvendy, G. (eds.) ITAP 2018. LNCS, vol. 10927, pp. 101–112. Springer, Cham (2018). https://doi.org/10.1007/978-3-319-92037-5_9

10. World Health Organization: (1948). http://www.who.int/about/definition/en/print.html. Accessed 10 Aug 2016

11. Reijnders, J., van Heugten, C., van Boxtel, M.: Cognitive interventions in healthy older adults and people with mild cognitive impairment: a systematic review. Ageing Res. Rev. **12** (1), 263–275 (2013)

12. Zhang, F., Kaufman, D.: Physical and cognitive impacts of digital games on older adults a meta-analytic review. J. Appl. Gerontol. (2015). https://doi.org/10.1177/0733464814566678

13. Voss, M.W., et al.: Neurobiological markers of exercise-related brain plasticity in older adults. Brain Behav. Immun. **28**, 90–99 (2013)

14. Kooiman, B., Sheehan, D.D.: Exergaming theories: a literature review. Int. J. Game-Based Learn. (IJGBL) **5**(4), 1–14 (2015)

15. Oh, Y., Yang, S.: Defining exergames and exergaming. In: Proceedings of Meaningful Play, pp. 1–17 (2010)

16. Lowensohn, J.: Timeline: a look back at Kinect's history. CNET (2011). http://www.cnet.com/news/timeline-a-look-back-at-kinects-history/. Accessed 15 Mar 2016

17. Zhang, Z.: Microsoft kinect sensor and its effect. IEEE MultiMedia **19**(2), 4–10 (2012)

18. Loos, E.: Exergaming: meaningful play for older adults? In: Zhou, J., Salvendy, G. (eds.) ITAP 2017. LNCS, vol. 10298, pp. 254–265. Springer, Cham (2017). https://doi.org/10.1007/978-3-319-58536-9_21

19. Loos, E., Zonneveld, A.: Silver gaming: serious fun for seniors? In: Zhou, J., Salvendy, G. (eds.) ITAP 2016. LNCS, vol. 9755, pp. 330–341. Springer, Cham (2016). https://doi.org/10.1007/978-3-319-39949-2_32

20. Xbox 360 Kinect Teardown: IFIXIT (2010). https://www.ifixit.com/Teardown/Xbox+360+Kinect+Teardown/4066. Accessed 15 Mar 2016

21. Rolle, C.E., Voytek, B., Gazzaley, A.: Exploring the potential of the iPad and Xbox Kinect for cognitive science research. Games Health J. **4**(3), 221–224 (2015)

22. Kamel Boulos, M.N.: Xbox 360 Kinect exergames for health. Games Health: Res. Dev. Clin. Appl. **1**(5), 326–330 (2012)

23. Harrington, C.N., Hartley, J.Q., Mitzner, T.L., Rogers, W.A.: Assessing older adults' usability challenges using Kinect-based exergames. In: Zhou, J., Salvendy, G. (eds.) DUXU 2015. LNCS, vol. 9194, pp. 488–499. Springer, Cham (2015). https://doi.org/10.1007/978-3-319-20913-5_45

24. Barenbrock, A., Herrlich, M., Malaka, R.: Design lessons from mainstream motion-based games for exergames for older adults. In: 2014 IEEE Games Media Entertainment (GEM), pp. 1–8. IEEE (2014)
25. De Urturi Breton, Z.S., Zapirain, B.G., Zorrilla, A.M.: Kimentia: Kinect based tool to help cognitive stimulation for individuals with dementia. In: 2012 IEEE 14th International Conference on e-Health Networking, Applications and Services (Healthcom), pp. 325–328. IEEE (2012)
26. Kayama, H., Okamoto, K., Nishiguchi, S., Nagai, K., Yamada, M., Aoyama, T.: Concept software based on Kinect for assessing dual-task ability of elderly people. GAMES HEALTH: Res. Dev. Clin. Appl. 1(5), 348–352 (2012)
27. Pedraza-Hueso, M., Martín-Calzón, S., Díaz-Pernas, F.J., Martínez-Zarzuela, M.: Rehabilitation using Kinect-based games and virtual reality. Procedia Comput. Sci. 75, 161–168 (2015)
28. Marinelli, E.C., Rogers, W.A.: Identifying potential usability challenges for Xbox 360 Kinect exergames for older adults. In: Proceedings of the Human Factors and Ergonomics Society Annual Meeting, vol. 58, no. 1, pp. 1247–1251. SAGE Publications (2014)
29. Nansen, B., Vetere, F., Robertson, T., Downs, J., Brereton, M., Durick, J.: Reciprocal habituation: a study of older people and the Kinect. ACM Trans. Comput.-Hum. Interact. (TOCHI) 21(3), 18 (2014)
30. Chiang, I., Tsai, J.C., Chen, S.T.: Using Xbox 360 Kinect games on enhancing visual performance skills on institutionalized older adults with wheelchairs. In: 2012 IEEE Fourth International Conference on Digital Game and Intelligent Toy Enhanced Learning (DIGITEL), pp. 263–267. IEEE (2012)
31. Tohoku   University: https://www.tohoku.ac.jp/en/research/research_highlights/research_highlight_22.html. Accessed 10 Dec 2018
32. Merriam, S.B., Tisdell, E.J.: Qualitative Research: A Guide to Design and Implementation. Wiley, Hoboken (2015)
33. Math Jock: http://game.wakesidevision.com/wp content/uploads/2010/12/BODY_AND BRAIN_12.jpg. Accessed 10 Dec 2018
34. Glass, J.C.: Factors affecting learning in older adults. Educ. Gerontol. 22(4), 359–372 (1996)
35. De la Hera, T., Loos, E.F., Simons, M., Blom, J.: Benefits and factors influencing the design of intergenerational digital games: a systematic literature review. Societies 7, 18 (2017)
36. Loos, E.F.: Designing meaningful intergenerational digital games. In: Proceedings of the International Conference on Communication, Media, Technology and Design, Istanbul, 24–26 April, pp. 46 51 (2014

A Study of the Needs and Attitudes of Elderly People and Their Caregivers with Regards to Assistive Technologies

Rong Jiang[1], Zhinan Zhang[2(✉)], and Xiaoxuan Xi[3]

[1] School of Design, Shanghai Jiao Tong University, Shanghai, China
jiangrong1994@sjtu.edu.cn
[2] School of Mechanical Engineering, Shanghai Jiao Tong University,
Shanghai, China
zhinanz@sjtu.edu.cn
[3] ENSPM, Paris, France
vincentx_sjtu@foxmail.com

Abstract. Aging of population is now a serious and complex problem in many countries, including China. Due to the shortage of nursing resources for the elderly, the needs of their growing population are hard to satisfy. However, thanks to the development of assistive technologies, there is hope for the problem to be solved in the future. Discovering the needs and attitudes of senior citizens and the relevant caregivers, the main focus of this study is crucial for successfully applying new technologies to the elderly population. To do so, questionnaires and interviews were administered to 119 elderly people with different self-care abilities, who were residing in homes or nursing homes. Their caregivers were also included in the study. The data about their daily life, needs, abilities, and attitudes towards assistive products are analyzed and compared for different groups of participants. In addition, based on the analyses, key points for the design of assistive products and possible practical applications of assistive technologies in the future are discussed.

Keywords: Aging and technology acceptance · Assistive technology · Elderly people · Caregivers

1 Introduction

Nowadays, the problem of global aging is becoming more and more serious. It is projected that by 2030, 33% of the world's population will be over 65 [1]. The aging problem has become a social problem. In this context, the elderly will gradually transition from home care to social care and the attending of the elderly population becomes an urgent problem to be solved. Young people don't have enough time to look after old people so they have to ask for help. However, lack of nursing workers makes the demand for elderly care cannot be fully met and their lack of qualification and high intensity of work make care deficient.

To solve these problems, assistive technology could be a good way. Still, the concern with assistive technology is how to make the product really meet the needs of

© Springer Nature Switzerland AG 2019
J. Zhou and G. Salvendy (Eds.): HCII 2019, LNCS 11592, pp. 200–211, 2019.
https://doi.org/10.1007/978-3-030-22012-9_15

the elderly and make them accept it in their life. There are several papers that have done some research in this field. For example, a series of technology acceptance model has been proposed including Technology Acceptance Model (TAM) [2], Technology Acceptance Model 2 (TAM2) [3], the Unified Theory of Acceptance and Use of Technology (UTAUT) [4] and the Senior Technology Acceptance & Adoption model for Mobile technology (STAM) [5]. They are used to explain or predict the factors that influence or determine the attitude towards accepting new technologies. According to a survey [6], 53% of the elderly would like to be able to control a robot by voice or remote control. However, it is difficult to find such products on the market, and other methods to a certain extent increase the difficulty and cost of learning to operate for the elderly. Another study shows that, the older the user, the lower the technology acceptance [7] and the use of new technologies [8]. Similarly, needs and attitudes of elderly people towards assistive technologies change for different groups in physical [9–11], psychological [12, 13], social [10, 14] and cognitive aspects [9, 10].

The relative works remind us that, the needs and attitudes of elderly people towards assistive technologies cover many aspects and the apparent differences among older people need to be taken into account. Therefore, this paper further studies the needs and attitudes of the elderly and their caregivers towards assistive technologies, especially the differences among different groups of elderly people.

2   Methods

The results of this study were obtained by analyzing the data of a questionnaire and an interview. Considering the environments of the senior citizens in homes and nursing homes are different which may lead to diverse needs and attitudes with regards to assistive technologies. The two different groups with the relevant caregivers were included in the questionnaire. In addition, self-care abilities were also taken into consideration. The questionnaire included demographic questions, physiological and mental problems and attitudes to assistive technologies. To complement the study, the nursing workers in two old people's homes were interviewed.

2.1   Participants

The questionnaire included 119 elderly participants and their relevant caregivers including family members or nursing workers, and 58 of the elderly people were female. A number of 20 of the older adults lived in nursing houses. Ages of them were classified into 4 categories: between 60 and 69 (35%), between 70 and 79 (37%), between 80 and 89 (22%), and over 90 (6%). Forty-five percent of them reported fair self-care ability; 47% reported their self-care ability to be good or excellent; only 4% reported poor or very poor self-care ability. Three nursing workers in a welfare nursing house and two in a middle-to-high end nursing house were interviewed as a complement.

2.2   Procedure

The questionnaire started with a short introduction to the study. After that, a set of demographic questions were asked, which included age, gender, self-care abilities, and living situations. The second part is the old people's physical pain points which consisted of their athletic, optical, auditory, dental, memorial abilities and sickness status. Next, questions including the current situations and aspirations of group activities and interpersonal communications, and mental needs were asked. Finally, their knowledge and attitude toward assistive technologies were also examined. For the caregivers, the questions included the relationships between the older people they care for and themselves and the problems and needs they found while looking after the elderly. In addition, their levels of concern on the elderly people's physical health, mental health and personal safety were questioned in a five-point Likert Scale. As for the interviews, it was focused mainly on the assistants' working conditions.

SPSS was used in data analysis. Frequency analysis and histogram were used for the overall results. The reliability and validity of a Likert five-point scale were analyzed. Cross analysis of multiple variables was also carried out, including chi-square analysis, normality analysis, and non-parametric analysis. Finally, according to the interview results, the key points of comparison are summarized.

3   Results

3.1   Questionnaire Results of the Elderly

Table 1. The self-evaluation of the elderly participants' physical functions.

	Good	Not good but does not affect the quality of life	Not good and affect the quality of life
Mobility	62 (52.10%)	40 (33.61%)	17 (14.29%)
Vision	59 (49.58%)	56 (47.06%)	4 (3.36%)
Audition	62 (52.10%)	50 (42.02%)	7 (5.88%)
Dental function	49 (41.18%)	52 (43.70%)	18 (15.13%)
Memory	35 (29.41%)	44 (36.97%)	40 (33.61%)

For the self-evaluation of the physical functions of the elderly people, the results are shown in Table 1. From the table, we can see that poor memory (such as forgetting to take medicine or forgetting where they put something) is a common problem among the elderly people which affect the quality of life of one third of the elderly. Next come dental function and mobility (like get up, dress, walk, squat and bend). Only a few participants reported that their quality of life is affected by visual and auditory problems.

For the self-evaluation of the participants' attitudes towards collective activities, interpersonal communication, and assistive technologies, the results are shown in

Table 2. From the table, we can see that the number of participants who like collective activities is significantly greater than those who actually attend collective activities. It means that, due to certain restrictions or setbacks, some elderly people may have to give up collective activities which are against their will. The specific reasons are analyzed in the cross analysis. For communication, most participants often contact with others. The same amount of elderly people said that they like to communicate. It seems that the ability to communicate is less affected by degenerative body functions.

Check the attitudes towards assistive technologies, only 36.97% elderly people reported that they had smart devices. About half participants know of assistive technologies and also half accept the help from assistive technologies. This means that more people accept and understand assistive technology than use smart products.

Table 2. The self-evaluation of the elderly participants' attitudes towards collective activities, interpersonal communication, and assistive technologies.

	Yes	No
Attend collective activity	63 (63.03%)	44 (36.97%)
Like collective activity	87 (73.10%)	32 (26.89%)
Often contact with others	75 (63.03%)	44 (36.97%)
Like to communicate	78 (65.54%)	41 (34.45%)
Use intelligent electronic products	44 (36.97%)	75 (63.03%)
Know of assistive technologies	65 (54.62%)	54 (45.37%)
Accept help from assistive technologies	67 (56.30%)	52 (43.70%)

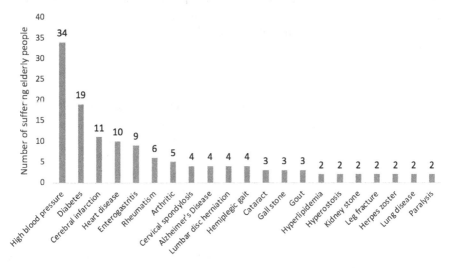

Fig. 1. The diseases the elderly participants once suffered from (only count the diseases of which the number of cases is greater than 1).

According to Fig. 1, the most common diseases among elderly participants are high blood pressure, diabetes and cerebral infarction. They are all chronic diseases which means long-term health cares are needed. In addition, from the raw data, we can realize that a lot of elderly people at least two of these three diseases at the same time. In addition, after classifying the diseases, we find out that circulatory system disease (45 person-times), endocrine metabolism disease (26 person-times), nervous system disease (21 person-times) and orthopedic disease (19 person-times) are four main types of diseases. Besides, fifty-three percent of the participants believe that illness has an impact on their quality of life. Finally, they reported that diseases mainly affect their mobility (37%), diet (36%), emotion (7%), communication (5%), medication compliance (5%), pain and physical discomfort (5%) and hypofunction (in addition to mobility) (4%).

3.2   Questionnaire Results of the Caregivers

For caregivers, firstly, their concern (attitude) about the physical health, mental health and personal safety of the elderly people are investigated and the results of it are shown in Table 3. This is a Likert five-point scale, and the options from 1 to 5 represent strongly disagree, disagree, neutral, agree and strongly agree respectively. The reliability of this question is analyzed by using the split reliability. It is found that the data is suitable for Spearman-Brown coefficient, and the value is 0.641 which is greater than 0.6, indicating that the data reliability is acceptable. The interpretation rate is 82.204% which is greater than 50%, indicating that the information of the study can be effectively extracted.

It can be seen from the results that, as caregivers, people have a high degree of concern for the three problems. However, people are more concerned about the safety (average = 3.97) and health (average = 3.86) of the elderly people, but less concerned about the psychological problems (average = 3.48).

Table 3. Caregivers' concern about physical health, mental health and personal safety of the elderly people.

Score	Physical health	Mental health	Personal safety
1 (Strongly disagree)	4 (3.36%)	10 (8.40%)	2 (1.68%)
2 (disagree)	8 (6.72%)	13 (10.92%)	7 (5.88%)
3 (neutral)	25 (21.00%)	32 (26.89%)	27 (22.69%)
4 (agree)	46 (38.66%)	37 (31.09%)	39 (32.77%)
5 (Strongly agree)	36 (30.23%)	27 (22.69%)	44 (36.97%)
Average	3.86	3.48	3.97

Next, according to the questionnaire, the most common tasks involved in the care of the elderly people are cooking (41%), housework (28%), chatting and psychological counseling (18%), auxiliary movement (7%), and medical assistance (7%). As for the pain points in the care process, unable to care for the elderly for a long time (63%), hard to take care of the elderly to go to the toilet or take a bath (13%), difficult in communicating with the elderly (8%), cannot meet the specific needs of the elderly (8%), cannot undertake heavy manual work (5%) and lack of specific knowledge about the health care for the elderly (5%) were reported.

Finally, for acceptable maximum spending on assistive technologies of the caregivers, the maximum is 100,000 RMB (approx. 14,800 USD); the minimum is 100 RMB (approx. 14.8 USD); the average is 8,384.82 RMB (approx. 1,200 USD); the median is 5,000 RMB (approx. 740 USD); the standard deviation is 14,361.98 RMB (approx. 2,100 USD).

3.3 Cross Analysis of Questionnaire Results

To analyze the different needs and attitudes of different group of elderly people and their caregivers, cross analysis including chi-square analyses and non-parametric tests are adopted.

Table 4. Chi-square analysis for elderly people of different age, gender, self-care abilities, and reside in homes or nursing homes.

	Age		Gender		Reside in homes or nursing homes		Self-care abilities	
	Chi-square	p	Chi-square	p	Chi-square	p	Chi-square	p
Mobility	26.271	0.000**	1.855	0.3	11.585	0.003**	57.475	0.000**
Vision	29.543	0.000**	2.836	0.242	2.118	0.347	31.120	0.000**
Audition	32.788	0.000**	0.973	0.615	4.522	0.104	21.958	0.000**
Dental function	15.450	0.017*	1.454	0.483	7.805	0.020*	20.024	0.000**
Memory	16.963	0.009**	5.296	0.071	14.704	0.001**	11.868	0.018*
Attend collective activity	10.880	0.012*	0.360	0.548	0.581	0.446	7.425	0.024*
Like collective activity	2.219	0.528	0.855	0.355	0.045	0.833	0.606	0.739
Often contact with others	7.339	0.062	0.588	0.443	16.690	0.000**	9.694	0.008*
Like to communicate	4.603	0.203	0.294	0.588	13.973	0.000**	5.735	0.057
Know of AT	13.330	0.004**	6.825	0.009**	19.461	0.000**	4.003	0.135

* $p < 0.05$, ** $p < 0.01$

Table 4 shows the results of chi-square analyses. For different ages, the body functions of elderly people are significantly different. Particularly, according to the raw data, body functions decline with age. At the same time, older people are less likely to participate in group activities while their desire to do so does not decrease. It can be understood that old people's physical function declines as they age, making it difficult for them to support their participation in collective activities. In addition, the older the participants are, the fewer of them have ever heard of assistive technology (hereinafter referred to as AT).

As for gender, the only factor which it significantly affects is the knowledge about AT. In detail, only 15.38% female participants have heard of AT while for males, the percentage is 59.26%.

For elderly people living at home or in nursing homes, the results show that mobility and memory are important factors. Dental function also has an effect on it. In addition, the frequency and willingness of the elderly people living in nursing homes to communicate with others are lower than those at home. At last, the number of elderly people living in homes who know of assistive technologies is significantly higher than those in nursing homes.

Finally, elderly people with bad physical condition (mobility, vision, audition, dental function and memory) are in bad self-care abilities which is reasonable. In addition, with worse self-care abilities, elderly people are less likely to engage in group activities and contact others. It is sustained by the fact that 50.00% of participants with bad self-care abilities reported that they usually don't take part in collective activities while only 21.05% of participants with good self-care abilities reported the same choice.

In the end, the nonparametric analysis is carried out for the caregivers' maximum spending on assistive technologies. First, the normality of the spending is analyzed which is shown in Table 5. Because the sample size is greater than 50, Kolmogorov-Smirnov test is used. The statistic is 0.329 with $p < 0.01$, which indicates that this item does not have the characteristic of a normal distribution. A nonparametric test can be considered to compare the data differences of different groups.

Table 5. Normality analysis results for acceptable maximum spending of caregivers on assistive technologies.

	Mean value (RMB)	Standard deviation (RMB)	Kolmogorov-Smirnov test	
			Statistic	p
Acceptable maximum spending on AT	8358.165 (approx. 1,200 USD)	14361.980 (approx. 2,100 USD)	0.329	0.000**

** $p < 0.01$

As shown in Table 6, using nonparametric analysis, we can see that with different level of mobilities of elderly people, the spending is significantly different ($p < 0.05$). For those who do not have good mobility, their caregivers are willing to spend more money on AT. More significantly ($p < 0.01$), those caregivers who concern more about the personal safety of the elderly would like to pay more on AT. The differences are evident in the median differences.

Table 6. Nonparametric analysis results for acceptable maximum spending of caregivers on assistive technologies.

	Median, Kruskal-Wallis test statistic and p	Acceptable maximum spending on AT (median, RMB)
Mobility	Good	3000
	Not good but does not affect the quality of life	5000
	Not good and affect the quality of life	5000
	Kruskal-Wallis test statistic	7.351
	p	0.025*
Concern about the personal safety of the elderly	1 (Strongly disagree)	1000
	2 (disagree)	2000
	3 (neutral)	2000
	4 (agree)	3000
	5 (Strongly agree)	5000
	Kruskal-Wallis test statistic	14.499
	p	0.006**

* $p < 0.05$, ** $p < 0.01$

3.4   Interview Results for Nursing Workers

The caregivers in the questionnaire are mainly the elderly people's relations which lead to a lack of data of the nursing homes and workers. As a result, interviews on nursing workers were done in two homes for seniors. One is Shanghai Gonghexin Rd. sub-district nursing home, a low-end and welfare institution. Another one is Kunming Changqing home for seniors, a state-run mid-to-high end institution. The comparisons are given in Table 7. From the table, we can see that most of the nursing workers are middle-aged and lack professional skills due to the simple pre-job training. Their work is intense, but their salary is not high. One said she was "*responsible for five elderly people who are partially disabled*" but actually they shouldn't take care of more than two people. This is caused by a shortage of nursing staff. Moreover, medical and psychological care for the elderly living in nursing homes is lacking, while recreational facilities and activities in low-end nursing homes are also lacking.

Table 7. Interview results for nursing workers.

Institution	Shanghai Gonghexin Rd. subdistrict gerocomium	Kunming Changqing home for seniors
Level	Low-end, welfare	State-run mid-to-high end
Interviewee	3 Nursing workers	2 Nursing workers
Current situation of nursing workers	local middle-aged women in Shanghai; after simple training on the post; high work intensity; lack of professional skills	Male: 30–60 years old, female: 30–50 years old; after simple training on the post; high work intensity; lack of professional skills
Salary of nursing workers	<3000RMB/month; underpaid	<3000RMB/month; underpaid
Medical care	Equipped with a doctor, 800 meters away from the nearest grade a hospital as the crow flies	Equipped with doctors and nurses; it is far away from large hospitals; there is a community hospital nearby, but its medical capacity cannot meet the requirements
Psychological care	Occasional care activities provided by volunteers	Lack of psychological care
Life and entertainment	Activity rooms are dilapidated and lack recreational facilities	Some recreational facilities

4 Discussion

From the above analysis, a series of key points can be found about the needs of the elderly and their attitudes towards assistive technologies. These points are discussed in this section as shown below.

First of all, at present, solving the physical problems of the elderly, especially the basic mobility problems, is the most helpful way to assist the elderly people and their caregivers. Firstly, mobility is affected by disease at a higher rate (37%). The number of elderly people whose mobility was affected was also higher (14.29%). In addition, housework, exercise assistance, assisted toilet use and assisted bathing are common tasks and pain points faced by caregivers on a daily basis, all of which are related to mobility. The weaker the elderly person's mobility is, the more the family is willing to spend money to buy assistive technology products. From this point, we can also see the importance of mobility in the needs of the elderly. Second, 33.61% of the elderly said their poor memory affected their quality of life, indicating that this is a common problem. For example, poor memory has led to increased compliance problems in elderly people. Third, many elderly people have dental problems, which lead to the need for special care in their diet. Caregivers also spend more time cooking soft food because of it. In addition, audition and vision problems also need to be concerned. Therefore, it is necessary to design and improve the products related to physical function assistance such as electric wheelchair, exoskeleton, medication management system and automatic cooking machine.

Secondly, long-term health management is an important direction for future design. Many elderly people are chronically ill and need long-term medication and care. As the elderly age increases, their physical function gradually weakens and their self-care ability also gradually declines. However, since home-based care cannot meet the needs of the elderly with insufficient self-care ability, such as diet, emotion and medication, more elderly people choose to live in nursing homes. However, nursing homes cannot fully meet the long-term health management needs of the elderly. In the future, intelligent health management, telemedicine, artificial intelligence-assisted diagnosis and treatment may be the hot topics in product design.

Third, safety is a high incidence of elderly problems, but also a need that the caregivers care about most. The more concerned the family is about the safety of the elderly, the more willing they are to spend money on assistive technologies. The most prominent pain point for the family is the inability to take care of the elderly for a long time, which is also the time when the elderly safety problems occur. As mentioned earlier, problems with mobility and memory are most pronounced in elderly people. On the one hand, limited mobility makes it more difficult for elderly people to save themselves in unexpected situations, such as falling. On the other hand, memory problems make older people more likely to get lost. As a result, safety functions should be taken into account when designing a product, such as fall detection, fall protection, electronic fence and behavior identification.

Fourth, psychological need is an important neglected need. According to our survey, as the elderly people age, their physical functions gradually decline, which leads to a decrease in the number of people taking part in group activities even though there is no obvious decline in their willingness. It is a pity that family members pay far less attention to the psychological needs of the elderly people than to safety and health. In addition, nursing homes lack facilities for psychological care and recreation. To improve it, games for the elderly, entertainment products and social products could be taken into consideration.

Fifth, elderly people have a general acceptance of assistive technologies, but more people are willing to try assistive technology than actually using smart products, showing significant gender and age differences. Therefore, the designers should pay attention to the different attitudes of different groups of older people towards assistive technologies, and pay attention to distinguish the target users. Voice interaction, eye movement input devices and intelligent products for elderly female users are all aspects that can be considered in the design.

Finally, common pain points for caregivers are lack of qualification, physical incapacity and inability to provide long-term care for the elderly. Therefore, the use of assistive technologies can make up for the deficiency of caregivers in these aspects, so as to assist the caregivers to take better care of the elderly. Care assistants, handling robots and service robots are practical examples.

5   Conclusion

In general, this paper investigated 119 older people with different self-care abilities, who were living at home or in nursing homes and their caregivers. In addition, 5 nursing workers were interviewed. Data about their pain points, needs, abilities, and attitudes towards assistive technologies are analyzed and compared for different groups of participants. The results show that the elderly people have obvious needs in physical function, health management, safety and psychological care. Among them, the mobility and safety of the elderly are the most urgent needs to be met. Psychological need, especially interpersonal need, is an important thing being ignored. In addition, the attitudes of the elderly towards assistive technologies show significant differences among different ages and genders. Finally, the professional, physical and time limitations of caregivers make it necessary to use assistive technologies to help caregivers better care for the elderly people. These are also the key points to pay attention to in design. In this study, the sample size of elderly people in nursing homes could be larger, and the questions involved in questionnaires and interviews are relatively limited. Therefore, more research should be carried out in the future. However, the design points presented in this paper can be used for relevant practical applications.

Acknowledgments. This research is partially supported by the Special Program for Humanistic and Sociological Research of Ministry of Education of China (Grant No. 17JDGC008), National Key R&D Program of China [Grant No. 2017YFB1401704], and Special Program for Innovation Methodology of the Ministry of Science and Technology of China [Grant No. 2016IM010100].

References

1. Vafa, K.: Census Bureau Releases Demographic Estimates and Projections for Countries of the World (2016). http://blogs.census.gov/2012/06/27/census-bureau-releases-demographic-estimates-and-projections-for-countries-of-the-world/
2. Davis, F.D.: Perceived usefulness, perceived ease of use, and user acceptance of information technology. MIS Q. Manag. Inf. Syst. **13**(3), 319–339 (1989)
3. Venkatesh, V., Davis, F.D.: Theoretical extension of the technology acceptance model: four longitudinal field studies. Manag. Sci. **46**(2), 186–204 (2000)
4. Venkatesh, V., Morris, M.G., Davis, G.B., Davis, F.D.: User acceptance of information technology: toward a unified view. MIS Q. Manag. Inf. Syst. **27**(3), 425–478 (2003)
5. Renaud, K., van Biljon, J.: Predicting technology acceptance and adoption by the elderly: a qualitative study. In: Proceedings of the 2008 Annual Research Conference of the South African Institute of Computer Scientists and Information Technologists on IT Research in Developing Countries: Riding the Wave of Technology, SAICSIT 2008, pp. 210–219. ACM, New York (2008). http://doi.acm.org/10.1145/1456659.1456684
6. Frennert, S., Eftring, H., Östlund, B.: What older people expect of robots: a mixed methods approach. In: Herrmann, G., Pearson, Martin J., Lenz, A., Bremner, P., Spiers, A., Leonards, U. (eds.) ICSR 2013. LNCS (LNAI), vol. 8239, pp. 19–29. Springer, Cham (2013). https://doi.org/10.1007/978-3-319-02675-6_3

7. Morris, M.G., Venkatesh, V.: Age differences in technology adoption decisions: implications for a changing work force. Pers. Psychol. **53**(2), 375–403 (2000). https://doi.org/10.1111/j.1744-6570,2000.tb00206.x

8. Peacock, S.E., Künemund, H.: Senior citizens and internet technology. Eur. J. Ageing **4**(4), 191–200 (2007). https://doi.org/10.1007/s10433-007-0067-z

9. Farage, M.A., Miller, K.W.: Design principles to accommodate older adults. Glob. J. Health Sci. **4**(2), 2–25 (2012)

10. Mallenius, S., Rossi, R., Tuunainen, V.K.: Factors affecting the adoption and use of mobile devices and services by elderly people-results from a pilot study. Ann. Glob. Mobil. Roundtable **31**, 12 (2007)

11. Tenneti, R., Johnson, D., Goldenberg, L., Parker, R.A., Huppert, F.A.: Towards a capabilities database to inform inclusive design: experimental investigation of effective survey-based predictors of human-product interaction. Appl. Ergon. **43**(4), 713–726 (2012). http://www.sciencedirect.com/science/article/pii/S0003687011001700

12. Ryu, M.H., Kim, S., Lee, E.: Understanding the factors affecting online elderly user's participation in video UCC services. Comput. Hum. Behav. **25**(3), 619–632 (2009). http://www.sciencedirect.com/science/article/pii/S0747563208001696

13. Werner, J.M., Carlson, M., Jordan-Marsh, M., Clark, F.: Predictors of computer use in community-dwelling, ethnically diverse older adults. Hum. Factors **53**(5), 431–447 (2011). https://doi.org/10.1177/0018720811420840. PMID: 22046718

14. Lee, Y.S.: Older adults' user experience with mobile phones: identification of user clusters and user requirements. Ph.D. thesis, Virginia Polytechnic Institute and State University (2007)

Improved Knowledge Changes the Mindset: Older Adults' Perceptions of Care Robots

Rose-Marie Johansson-Pajala[1], Kirsten Thommes[2], Julia A. Hoppe[2],
Outi Tuisku[3], Lea Hennala[3], Satu Pekkarinen[3], Helinä Melkas[3],
and Christine Gustafsson[1(✉)]

[1] Mälardalen University, Eskilstuna/Västerås, Sweden
christine.gustafsson@mdh.se
[2] Paderborn University, Paderborn, Germany
[3] Lappeenranta University of Technology, Lahti, Finland

Abstract. This paper explores Finnish, German and Swedish older adults' perceptions of a future welfare service with increased use of welfare technologies, specifically care robots. The issues are the rapid digitalization and development of health and welfare technology, which presently is mainly technology driven (not need or user driven), and the demographic challenge. The aim of the study was to explore older adults' perception of the future use of welfare technology or care robots. A qualitative approach with focus group discussions was employed, followed by thematic analysis. The results are presented in four overall themes: the impact on daily life for older adults and professional caregivers, codes of practice and terms of use, dissemination of information and knowledge, and conditions for successful implementation. There were significant differences in the informants' attitudes toward and knowledge about care robots. However, the informants' attitudes appeared to change during the focus groups and in general, became more positive. Authentic needs, which care robots could support, refer to independence, safety and security, and the ability to manage or ease daily life or working life. The results suggest that older adults, after receiving relevant information, were open to the idea of being supported by care robots in their daily lives.

Keywords: Care robots · Older adults · Implementation · Information · Perceptions · Welfare technology

1 Introduction

The number of older adults is growing rapidly throughout the world. These demographic changes will increase the need for health care services, but the number of people who can provide and finance these services is decreasing [1, 2]. Health technology, such as welfare technology, has been launched as a means of meeting these challenges [2, 3]. Different types of welfare technology are also changing the traditional health care organization. Welfare technology introduces technology in new spaces, such as private homes, and it provides new functions, such as offering social stimuli and entertainment [3]. This technology could make it possible for older adults to live

© Springer Nature Switzerland AG 2019
J. Zhou and G. Salvendy (Eds.): HCII 2019, LNCS 11592, pp. 212–227, 2019.
https://doi.org/10.1007/978-3-030-22012-9_16

longer in familiar surroundings, to have quick remote communication with professional caregivers if needed, and to have a (remote) physical examination in their homes [4]. The purpose of this paper was to provide a cross-country inventory (Finland, Sweden and Germany) of older adults' perceptions of a future welfare service with increased use of welfare technologies, in particular care robots, for support in daily life. The term care robots includes machines that operate partly or fully autonomously while performing care-related activities for people with disabilities, physical or mental, that are related to age or health restrictions [5]. In this paper, the term care robots refers to robotic technology that can be used to support older adults and care workers in providing physical, cognitive, or emotional support [6].

2 Elder Care and Welfare Technology

2.1 The Changing Landscape of Elder Care

Elder care, in particular, is facing a gigantic shift in technology and the demographic challenge of an aging population. In the near future, the relative population of older adults in Western Europe will increase because of aging and increased life expectancy [7]. By 2050, globally the number of people older than 60 years is expected to be higher than the number of people younger than 15 years [8]. We also live in a period of rapid digitalization and health and welfare development. Old technology such as the telefax machine required about 150 years from the time the patent was approved until the product was available on the market compared to the contemporary time to market of about 1 to 2 years [9]. Welfare technology is expected to help people live a healthy life with retained integrity. This technology is also expected to contribute to efficiency in elder care services and meet individuals' needs in living independently. The demographic challenge means that the older population is growing and the working population is decreasing [10, 11]. Thus, the elder care sector must evolve, and introducing welfare technology might be the most effective method.

2.2 Acceptance of Care Robots

In welfare technology, robots have acquired cognitive functions and possibilities for improved safety, which makes it possible to use them to provide new services for the primary users. Although care robots have great potential for health and welfare, the area is challenging due to ethical and social issues [12, 13] and the strong role of legislation. In addition, the public has a negative attitude toward the use of robots in elder care [14, 15]. To reap benefits, changes are needed at all levels of the individual–services–society axis and across them. Technological and in particular, service innovations that combine human and cognitive robotic skills might have high potential for easing care professionals' work and providing autonomy for older adults. These goals, however, can be achieved only if all stakeholders accept the new technology. Acceptance and the impact of digital technologies, such as care robots, on older adults who require elder care have implications for the possibilities of rooting technological innovations in care [5]. The way in which older adults are involved in the emerging area of care robots is essential for their health, well-being, and opportunities to learn and participate in society throughout the different stages of later life. Technology use is often a major change, but if planned carefully, technology may provide a welcome addition in services. In the area it is also recognized that the health of older adults can be promoted, sustained, and improved with technical aids [16, 17], but usable indicators of good welfare technology solutions for older adults are lacking [18]. The most significant factor related to the introduction of technology that motivates an individual is the benefit that he or she gets from using it.

The different types of impact of technology use are often indirect and difficult to identify. The skill levels of individuals differ, and a technical device is not born and used in a vacuum in care: Behind the technology, there is a user with his or her own values, living (or working) environment, and related service activities [19]. Technologies are still typically used in care services as separate 'islands' and a systemic view is missing. Moreover, the perspective of older adults is often neglected.

2.3 Meeting User Needs

Older adults as technology users are often viewed stereotypically or represented by assumptions or static identities, without cultural and historical constructions [20]. The benefits of robots and technology in elder care are often embedded in a specific set of claims, such as an aging population with rising care costs, a decreasing qualified workforce, and the desire of older adults to live independently as long as possible [21, 22]. Older adults are mostly positioned as having deteriorating health and needing costly care. In this narrow portrayal of older adults, old age is strongly related to illness, frailty, lost competences, and high costs. If these kinds of images underlie development processes, including the orientation phase, then the resulting technologies, for example, care robots, may implicitly or explicitly position older users as frail, ill, or in need of care [22]. If the design is based on stereotypical and homogenous sociocultural images of older adults, it may reinforce this imagery and translate into key design decisions [23]. If diversity in users is incorporated at all, it is most often only age and gender differences [24]. Moreover, today's older adults might differ from future generations of older adults, for instance, regarding acceptance of technology for social needs and the strong Western cultural value of being independent, which might be an incentive to use robots in daily life. There is often an imbalance between perceptions of older adults' technology needs and knowledge about their actual needs. The supposed user uses technology according to the manufacturer's idea of how the item should be used. However, this is distinct from the real user, who is actually using the technology and may, for instance, change its purpose [25]. According to Östlund et al. [20], the role of older adults in digital agendas may be simply to legitimize development for fictive users rather than real ones. Another aspect is that older adults are much more discerning than the manufacturers of robots for older adults believe. Frennert [26] found that older adults want to know what robots can do for them and are not interested in a service robot if it does not add anything useful. Many manufacturers have a view of older adults as passive recipients, and the stereotype of older adults governs robot development. Age-based assumptions that lie at the heart of technology design and implementation are maintained by ideologies that are resistant to change [27].

In Neven's [22] study that tested health care robots, participants' views did not influence the designers' overall view of elderly users. As designers and technology developers seem to rely on stereotypical views of gender and age, user diversity is neglected [23]. Old age is seen as a homogeneous stage in life, yet it covers tens of years and includes several phases. There is a need for a paradigm shift and proactive technology that meets the needs and demands of today's actual senior citizens [20], such as the robotic cat for people with dementia (JustoCat) [28, 29]. The changed view of older adults as heterogenic welfare technology users involves analysis of the explicit and implicit interactions among technology, designers, and users. A field study of the implementation process of the care robot Zora in Finland showed that robot use affects customers and their family members in many ways that are positive, negative, and neutral. For instance, the robot stimulated users to exercise and led to reminiscing because of its child-like character. The robot also created various new interactions with the customer or between customers and professional caregivers. This study also highlighted that customers should not be misled; the role of ethics is a key issue [30].

Rationale. The overarching aim of this paper was to explore older adults' perceptions of the use of welfare technologies, in particular care robots, for support in daily life. The issue is important because of the rapid digitalization and development of health and welfare technology, which is mainly technology driven (not needs or user driven), and the demographic challenge the global society is facing. The specific aims were to explore how older adults perceive care robots in elder care and how they discuss the introduction/implementation of care robots in elder care.

3 Method

3.1 Design

A qualitative approach with focus groups was employed. Focus group discussions are particularly suited to the study of attitudes, perceptions, and experiences. The interaction within the groups can help people explore and clarify their own attitudes in ways that would be less accessible in individual interviews [31, 32].

3.2 Setting and Recruitment

The present study is part of the ORIENT project under the Joint Programming Initiative 'More Years, Better Lives'. The ORIENT project focuses on orientation, introduction to technology use, and learning of different skills for effective use in the spirit of co-creation. Partners from three European countries (Finland, Germany, and Sweden) participate in the project. Various perspectives are considered within the project, such as the perspectives of older adults, older adults' family members, professional care-givers, and care service organizations. Societal and other stakeholders' (such as busi-ness, industry, public administration, and the nonprofit sector) perspectives are also included in the project.

The focus of this paper is the perspective of older adults who live at home. Pur-poseful sampling was used to recruit the informants. Recruitment was conducted through verbal and written requests to retirement organizations and through contacts. The inclusion criterion was that the informants should have an interest in the field, and variations in gender were also strived for.

3.3   Focus Groups

An interview guide was developed by the research team consisting of opening, introductory, and transition questions, followed by key questions [32]. One focus group was conducted in Sweden and Finland, and two focus groups were conducted in Germany, with four to seven informants in each group, for a total of four focus groups. In total, 24 older adults participated in the focus groups. The participants all lived in their own housing and did not receive help from home care services (Table 1).

Table 1. Informants' demographic data.

Characteristics	Finland	Germany	Sweden
Women/men	3/1	8/6	5/1
Age, mean (range)	75 (70–81)	68.6 (60–79)	72.5 (69–75)
Highest level of education			
University	0	4	6
Secondary school	3	0	0
Vocational education	1	9	0
Elementary school	0	1	0

Informed consent was obtained from all informants before the focus groups were held. Two to three researchers were present during the focus groups, one acting as a moderator and the others as assistant moderators. The focus groups were conducted in the informants' native language. Each focus group began with an introduction and description of the purpose of the discussion. Then, the moderator followed the inter-view guide, moving from general to more specific questions, and showed a short video and pictures that exemplified various types of care robots. The interview guide was used to ensure consistency between the different countries (Table 2). The focus groups lasted for 60–140 min and were audio recorded. The recordings were then transcribed verbatim and processed as texts.

Table 2. Interview guide.

Introduction question	Brainstorm about the use of and need for welfare technology in elder care
Transition question	Thoughts about the use/introduction of robotic technology in elder care. Should we use robots in elder care?
Key questions	Display of a short video (3 min) and pictures, exemplifying various types of care robots (used for service and support in daily life, such as social, physical, and mental stimulation and communication) - Reflections on the video and pictures; benefits and disadvantages from different perspectives Additional questions: - How would you feel about being cared for or assisted by a care robot when you get old and require help? - Do we, in general, need to know more about care robots? What? Why? How? By whom? - If you would like to learn more about care robots, what would you do? - How should the use of care robots be introduced in elder care, and what training is required?
Ending question	Reflection on what was said during the discussion; does anything need to be added? The assistant moderator is invited to reflect or ask additional questions

3.4   Analysis

The focus group discussions were analyzed using an inductive thematic analysis with a semantic approach [33]. The six phases consist of becoming familiar with the data, generating initial codes, searching for themes, defining and naming themes, and producing the report. Accordingly, the transcribed text was read and reread to capture the features associated with the research topic. The sentences and paragraphs, assessed as interesting or meaningful in relation to the phenomenon under study, were identified and marked, and initial codes were systematically generated across the entire data set. This first part of the analysis was performed in the original language and by the research team in each of the three countries. Then, all text (the codes) was translated into English, and the rest of the analysis was carried out by two researchers (RMJP and CG), though all authors reflected on the data during the process. The codes were grouped together into potential themes and sub-themes. The relevance of the themes was checked in relation to the codes and the entire data set. Finally, clear definitions and names for each theme were identified. The analysis resulted in four overall themes and 13 sub-themes (Table 3).

Table 3. Sub-themes and themes revealed in the analysis.

Sub-themes	Themes
Independence and safety Physical and mental assistance Communication and socialization Complement to human resources	**Impact on daily life for older adults and professional caregivers**
The individual's right to decide Expected functions	**Codes of practice and terms of use**
Introduction to technology earlier in life Tailored information Training on welfare technology and trust Multiple channels for information	**Dissemination of information and knowledge**
Convincing professional caregivers Multi-level collaboration Cost allocation	**Conditions for successful implementation**

4   Results

Four overall themes, including 13 sub-themes, illustrated older adults' perception of the future use of care robots. The term welfare technology is used alternately with care robots, because what kind of welfare technology the informants referred to was not always specified. The results are presented in themes and by underlying sub-themes. Quotes from the interviews, provided in the sub-themes, are marked with a letter (S, F or G) indicating the country of origin.

4.1   Impact on Everyday Lives of Older Adults and Professional Caregivers

This theme covers older adults' perceptions of different areas where welfare technology or care robots could have an impact in their daily lives or support and improve the delivery of care.

Independence and Safety. Welfare technology was perceived to provide conditions for prolonging the ability to live independently. The ability to manage by oneself implies maintained autonomy and integrity. *"I would like to have a robot that can help me pick up stuff, open the fridge...instead of somebody coming to help me, so I can decide for myself"* (S). Care service, perceived as threatening integrity, for example, in having support with hygiene, could preferably be provided by some kind of welfare technology. However, opposing views also appeared in the discussions, indicating rejection of the use of such technology and the claim that human attention is preferred. Welfare technology was also considered to ensure safety in different ways, for example, related to monitoring functions as sending health data (e.g., blood pressure and blood glucose levels), and distributing medication.

Physical and Mental Assistance. One common perception was that welfare technology could facilitate practical tasks at home, for example, doing household chores, picking up objects from the floor, and cleaning. Welfare technology that enables mobility was also discussed as useful. *"Yes, so if I had difficulties to move around at home and do household chores, I would probably accept it [a robot]"* (F). Supporting people with cognitive impairments was also mentioned as a possible area of use.

Communication and Socialization. Possibilities for communication with professional caregivers were perceived as beneficial. Welfare technology could then be useful for receiving information quickly. For example, a video connection in a robot could make it easier to get help from health care organizations. Professional caregivers, such as physicians, could be supported in detecting health incidents and in diagnosing patients. However, welfare technology with monitoring functions was viewed critically by some informants. Furthermore, technology could facilitate communication with family members, something that would be beneficial for both parties. Opportunities for a social life would also increase. *"...so it facilitate [for older adults] a social life, if I cannot get out, then society can come in"* (S). One perception was that welfare technology could enrich the daily lives of older adults, especially those in care homes, where it could be used for mental stimulation, entertainment, and different activities, such as reading and playing music.

Some informants would have conversations with robots while others would not. Similar disagreements existed in the case of social robots. Some perceived that a social robot could reduce feelings of loneliness, while others rejected the use of robots for social interaction. One concern was the risk that those who are not capable of handling the welfare technology could become even lonelier.

Complement or Replacement for Human Resources. Many informants perceived the technology as a complement to professional caregivers. By using this technology, professional caregivers would have more time for the older adults, and the human resources would be used where they were required. *"My spontaneous reaction is, welfare technology, yes, it gives staff more time, and they can spend that time with the older adult needing support"* (G). The informants suggested that robots could assist care professionals in different ways, for example, with personal hygiene, cleaning, and physically heavy work. Informants also suggested that technology could be helpful in the event of a shortage of professional caregivers. However, a major concern was whether professional caregivers would be replaced by technology. The informants felt that there was an imminent risk that this could occur, partly because in the end, technology is cheaper than human labor. However, some informants emphasized that there are situations where people cannot be replaced by technology. For example, a robot cannot provide human warmth, or act as a substitute for interpersonal relations, or provide psychological support. *"...the technology cannot replace interpersonal relations..."* (G).

4.2   Codes of Practice and Terms of Use

This theme describes regulations of practice needed when welfare technology or care robots are offered to older adults. Aspects of expected functions and usability are also addressed.

The Individual's Right to Decide. Regulations related to the implementation of welfare technology in care for the elderly were an important issue. A common perception among the informants was that each individual should be allowed to decide whether to use welfare technology or not. Some people wanted human hands, and some preferred welfare technology. Thus, welfare technology should not be forced upon older adults. There must be sensitivity in assessing when welfare technology is appropriate to use and when it is not. For instance, the use of welfare technology was discussed in relation to older adults with cognitive impairment, such as people suffering from dementia. Some perceived that welfare technology would work well for these persons, while others thought it was not appropriate. *"...but for people suffering from dementia, I find it shameful and inhuman to use robots" (G).* In contrast to the perception that welfare technology use should be optional, some informants thought that it should not always be possible to choose. Not everything can be optional, and sometimes, people just need to be told that this is the way of doing things. *"This is how nursing is done, this is the help we offer you, if it is cameras, help to turn off the stove... there are a lot of things like that"* (S). For health care services, an individual's actual needs are the basis for the assessment.

Expected Functions. This sub-theme mirrors different aspects of the expected functions and the usability of welfare technology artifacts. During the discussion, it was evident that some participants had high expectations for what care robots should be capable of doing (the expected functions). For example, the robots should recognize emotional situations and act accordingly. The robots should also be able to work autonomously, make suggestions, and have the function to have conversations. If the robot were dependent on additional instructions from professional caregivers, then the caregivers could perform the task themselves. *"I think, if an expensive nurse or trainee has to stand behind the robot and give instructions, it somehow seems pointless..."* (G). One informant expressed a fear of robots eventually making decisions independently. The question of safety was also a concern for some informants. In the case of malfunctions, there must be some kind of security system, to ensure that no human being comes to harm.

4.3   Dissemination of Information and Knowledge

This theme explores the general and societal needs for improving the introduction of welfare technology or care robots, as well as suggestions for orientation activities.

Introduction of Technology Earlier in Life. Welfare technology should be introduced earlier in life, before the actual need arises. When people become affected by old age and illnesses, it is difficult for them to make their own decisions. *"Inform as early as possible, before you develop dementia, it do not have to be dementia, it can also be physical and intellectual disabilities"* (S). Although an early introduction to welfare technology is preferred, older adults often do not perceive the information as interesting or necessary, until changes in their own life conditions occur. *"...since I do not think I need it [care robots] at the moment, I do not even know what to ask for and what kind of information I would need"* (F). However, with the gradually increasing use of welfare technology in society, it will eventually become more common and accepted. Some informants expressed that for future generations the use of welfare technology will likely constitute a natural part of life.

Tailored Information. Information about welfare technology must reach those concerned, older adults. To make decisions, one needs to know what kind of welfare technology is offered and what it can do or assist with. The acceptance of welfare technology depends on the level of information, and good examples need to be disseminated. For example, the term "robot" must be clarified as it has a negative connotation and is perceived as alienating and inhuman. The informants expressed that when welfare technology is offered to older adults, special attention should be paid to its introduction. Welfare technology should be taught in a way that suits older adults, and it should be ensured that they really grasp it. When young people give instructions, they often do it too fast, which makes older adults feel slow, and thus, they give up trying to understand the technology. *"...when it comes to technology, I can manage, but it goes too fast [instructions]...For us older adults, technology should be taught in such a way that people understand"* (F).

Different perceptions prevailed about who should provide information about available welfare technology. Some thought that information should be given by official sources or professional caregivers. Others thought sources for information could be friends, health insurance funds, the manufacturers of the technology, and consultants.

Training on Welfare Technology and Trust. Older adults need information and training that enable them to trust welfare technology. Concerning robots, this could involve practical training in how to use them, as well as how to approach and speak to a robot. Training could also involve environmental and security issues. *"They [robots] can also do something wrong or have a malfunction, just like humans do...you have to try to limit that so that no patient [older adult] will be injured"* (G). Some older adults were concerned about data security, how their data would be protected, and how they could have control over their data.

Multiple Channels for Information. Several suggestions were given regarding how to disseminate information about welfare technology. Welfare technology should be visible to create demand. Television was a common suggestion as practically every household has one. Other means for disseminating information could be social media, fairs, through senior citizens' associations, storytelling, shops, and similar places where many people pass by. Some informants pointed out that using welfare technology must be pleasurable and exciting. In addition, there should be opportunities to test it in real life, that is, learning by doing. Another suggested channel for disseminating information was through research and education; for instance, universities should offer education in robots. According to some informants, the prevailing attitude among today's professional caregivers is that there should be human hands, not welfare technology, an attitude that could change through education.

4.4   Conditions for Successful Implementation

This theme describes the conditions identified as important for the successful implementation of welfare technology and care robots in the elder care context.

Convincing Professional Caregivers. For the implementation to succeed, professional caregivers must be convinced and positive about the use of welfare technology. They should not perceive welfare technology as something separate; instead, it should be an integrated part of nursing care. *"Convince the professional caregivers, how we can do it, I do not know, but it has to be done"* (S). Some informants suggested that some caregivers could receive special training in welfare technology use. Then they could act as digital assistants and support other caregivers, as well as older adults.

Multi-level Collaboration. Successful implementation of welfare technology for older adults would require collaboration at multiple levels. The informants perceived that a whole chain of decisions and actions probably were required, ranging from legislation and public organizations to interest organizations and older adults themselves. Some informants pointed out that welfare technology should be developed in consultation with older adults. Their needs should form the basis for what technology is needed and produced; subsequently, they, relatives and professional caregivers, should be involved in the process. *"I think it [welfare technology] is the future. We cannot use the old system forever...but the older adults have to be taken into account when this is implemented, and their relatives as well"* (F).

Cost Allocation. The question of who should pay for welfare technology was a major concern among the informants. Should society bear the costs or older adults themselves, or perhaps should the costs be divided? *"It is the municipality's responsibility to pay, if the robot is absolutely necessary...those who have a high salary can pay for the robot by themselves"* (F). If so, how should the line be drawn between what is accessible to everyone and what is considered to add extra value? One fear was that the technology would cause further divisions in society, implying that only those with resources would have access to the technology. In contrast, some informants claimed that society cannot pay for everything, and people with the financial resources can pay for the welfare technology themselves.

5   Conclusions, Limitations and Implications

5.1   Increased Knowledge Changes Attitudes

The focus group discussions in the present study revealed significant differences in the informants' attitudes toward and knowledge about welfare technology and care robots: Some were negative and others positive. It is not that the attitudes in general were negative. However, the context of elder care seems to have an impact on their standpoints. This seems to make the use of care welfare technology or care robots questionable, which can be interpreted as whether the use of robots in elder care is not as accepted as in other areas of healthcare, as also shown by, for instance, Eurobarometer [34]. However, the attitudes appeared to change during the focus group discussion. Some informants even expressed that they had a negative attitude when they arrived, but it changed, mainly due to the increased knowledge and because they understood what care welfare technology and care robots are and how they can support daily life. As the results suggest that older adults are open to the idea of being supported by welfare technology or care robots in their daily lives when people have relevant information, we interpret the result as meaning that there is a general urgent need for an improved orientation within the field. This also applies to family members and professional caregivers, as they are the main users in the elder care context and are involved in the implementation processes.

However, all studies have several limitations. In the present study one limitation is that informant recruitment was conducted by purposeful sampling. Many of the informants were people interested in the subject welfare technology and care robots, given that we cannot state having informants representing the full population. Another aspect to highlight is that the informants in a majority were women. On the other hand, participating informants were interested and had something to discuss and say about the issue. This also refers to the present result showing that a negative attitude can change when having increased knowledge. Another weakness in the data, which were collected in three different countries all having different cultures and welfare systems, and importantly different languages. All these aspects have impact in the analysis, in the overall and contextual understanding. The final analysis were led by the Swedish team, this might had the consequence that culture and language specific nuances can be lost in that process, this were not further explored in the full research team.

5.2   Implementation of Care Robots in Elder Care

Examining the themes that appeared in the present study, it becomes clear that welfare technology and care robots, which are "knocking on the door" to be implemented in modern elder care, have important aspects that must be considered for successful implementation.

User Involvement to Meet Authentic Needs. One aspect is that welfare technology and care robots must have a considerable impact on users (older adults, family members, or professional caregivers) in improvements in daily life or daily working life. The authentic needs in which welfare technology or care robots could support improvements, according to the present results, are independence, safety and security, and the ability to manage or ease daily life or working life. Considering welfare technology in care for the elderly, authentic needs should play a more central role. Having the point of departure in authentic needs is described as crucial when developing health and welfare technology in this context [28]. End-user participation in developmental activities (co-creation) is one of the basic principles of user-centered methods [35]. Early and ongoing user involvement and participatory methods have been recognized [36] as one of the principles that are particularly important in health information technology [37, 38]. Robots have somewhat different characteristics compared to other technologies in elder care, such as embodied characters, which may provide emotional attachments. Studying the acceptance and use of robots may require consideration of other factors not included in the most frequently utilized technology acceptance models, such as social and hedonic factors [30, 39]. The structure of elder care is also different from other co-creation processes: Not only is the customer involved but also family members and professional caregivers.

We suggest closer collaboration and the integration of users' different perspectives to achieve a comprehensive view of authentic needs, user involvement, and technology possibilities when welfare technology and care robots are developed. All three perspectives should be emphasized equally for a successful development process. Regarding representative and collaboration obstacles, we understand the challenges, although they must be expressed and solved. Elder care representatives, must, for example, learn to identify and communicate authentic needs of elder care that can be solved by care robots and welfare technology. This refers to the overall aim to free up time in favor of care that really needs human affection, which is considered one solution for meeting the demands of the demographic challenge [7, 8].

Meeting the Needs of Information and Knowledge. There are expectations that the use of welfare technology and care robots should solve some of the problems of the demographic challenge. However, it is naïve to believe it is simple to implement care robots and welfare technology in elder care. Elder care is complex, and there are many aspects that must be respected. For example, there are conditions that must be clarified on different levels in the welfare system, for example, regulations that allow free choice to reject welfare technology or care robots. The question of financial responsibilities must also be clearly communicated, an aspect that was evident in the present results. Another important issue is the dissemination of information and knowledge about the possibilities and support that welfare technology and care robots use offer, an urgent aspect that must be resolved before the implementation can proceed successfully. Nilsen et al. [40] found that when welfare technology is implemented, resistance appears to play a productive role when the implementation is organized as a co-creation process. Implementation of welfare technology must be carefully planned and organized for successful results. For older adults and family members as users, storytelling is a powerful method that could complement the official authority practitioner's (care manager's) information [41]. Storytelling in different media, which have the target groups as readers, could be a strategy for meeting the information and knowledge aspects. Raappana, Rauma, and Melkas [42] found that most of the negative effects of welfare technology use could have been eliminated or relieved with a good orientation, based on previous information and assessment. Without an appropriate level of skills and knowledge, feelings of insufficiency and incapability arise, leading to decreased motivation and distress, and may mitigate the impacts on well-being that are pursued.

For innovators working in elder care, it is important to remember that the digital experiences and competences of today's and future generations of older adults most likely will differ [9]. This also refers to the rapid development of technology in general in modern society. Again, this points to the importance of involving the potential users and the right users in the development processes. When including potential users, the categorization of older adults might not be enough. More nuanced inclusion processes for users in the groups of today's and future users are recommended. In our understanding, the results indicate that today's older adults with sufficient and relevant information and knowledge of the possibilities of care robots and welfare technology, in general, have positive perceptions of being future users. However, we as representatives of welfare technology and care robots in elder care have an important and desired mission to develop the content for an effective orientation to welfare technology and care robots in elder care.

Acknowledgments. This study was supported by the ORIENT project under the JTC 2017 launched by JPI MYBL. The support of the JPI MYBL and the national funders within the JPI MYBL framework is gratefully acknowledged (award no. 2017-02300 by Forte, Sweden; award no. 16SV7954 by the Federal Ministry of Education and Research, Germany, and award no. 318837 by the Academy of Finland).

References

1. Scherer, J.M.: Technology adoption, acceptance, satisfaction and benefit: integrating various assistive technology outcomes. Disabil. Rehabil. Assist. Technol. **12**(1), 1–2 (2017). https://doi.org/10.1080/17483107.2016.1253939
2. Hoffman, B.: Ethical challenges with welfare technology; a review of literature. Sci Eng. Etics **19**(2), 389–406 (2013). https://doi.org/10.1007/s11948-011-9348-1
3. Nordic Centre for Welfare and Social issues. Focus on welfare technology (2010). https://nvc.brandfactory.se/Files/sv-SE/9047/RelatedFiles/Velferdsteknologi_eng.pdf
4. Harrefors, C., Sävenstedt, S., Axelsson, K.: Elderly people's perception of how they want to be cared for: an interview study with healthy elderly couples in Northern Sweden. Scand. J. Caring Sci. **23**(2), 353–360 (2009). http://doi.org/10.1111/j.1471-6712.2008.00629.x
5. Goeldner, M., Herstatt, C., Tietze, F.: The emergence of care robotics—a patent and publication analysis. Technol. Forecast. Soc. **92**, 115–131 (2015). https://doi.org/10.1016/j.techfore.2014.09.005
6. Glende, S., Conrad, I., Krezdorn, L., Klemcke, S., Krätzel, C.: Increasing the acceptance of assistive robots for older people through marketing strategies based on stakeholders needs. Int. J. Soc. Robot. **8**, 355–369 (2016)
7. United Nations Department of Economic and Social Affairs, Population Division. World population ageing 2015. (ST/ESA/SER.A/390). http://www.un.org/en/development/desa/population/publications/pdf/ageing/WPA2015_Report.pdf. Accessed 26 June 2018
8. United Nations. World Population prospects, January 2015. http://esa.un.org/unpd/wpp/Publications/Files/WPP2015_Volume-I_Comprehensive-Tables.pdf
9. Porras, J., et al.: User 2020 – A WWRF Vision. A white paper of the Wireless World Research Forum. 14/2014
10. Swedish Ministry of Health and Social Affairs. Den ljusnande framtid är vård. Delresultat från LEV-projektet Stockholm: Regeringskansliet (2010). https://www.regeringen.se/rapporter/2010/06/s2010.021/. Accessed 29 Nov 2018
11. ZEW, Monitoring-Report: Digital Economy 2012 - Added Value for Germany. https://www.zew.de/en/publikationen/monitoring-report-digital-economy-2012-added-value-for-germany/. Accessed 29 Nov 2018
12. Lin, P., Abney, K., Bekey, G.A. (eds.): Robot Ethics: The Ethical and Social Implications of Robotics. The MIT Press, Cambridge (2014)

13. Seibt, J., Hakli, R., Nørskov, M. (eds.): Sociable Robots and the Future of Social. Relations Frontiers in Artificial Intelligence and Applications, vol. 273. IOS Press, Amsterdam (2014)

14. Tuisku, O., Pekkarinen, S., Hennala, L., Melkas, H.: Robots do not replace a nurse with a beating heart - The publicity around a robotic innovation in elderly care. Inf. Tech. People (in Press)

15. Sharkey, A., Sharkey, N.: Granny and the robots: ethical issues in robot care for the elderly. Ethics Inf. Technol. 14(1), 27–40 (2012)

16. Herstatt, C., Kohlbacher, F., Bauer, P.: Silver product design – product development for older people. Working Paper No. 65. Institute for Technology and Innovation Management, Hamburg University of Technology, Hamburg, Germany (2011)

17. Kanoh, M., et al.: Examination of practicability of communication robot-assisted activity program for elderly people. Robot. Mechatron. 23(1), 3 (2011)

18. Taipale, V.T.: Global trends, policies and gerontechnology. Gerontechnology 12(4), 187–193 (2014). https://doi.org/10.4017/gt.2014.12.4.001.00

19. Melkas, H.: Effective gerontechnology use in elderly care work: from potholes to innovation opportunities. In: Kohlbacher, F., Herstatt, C. (eds.) The Silver Market Phenomenon: Marketing and Innovation in the Aging Society, pp. 435–449. Springer, Heidelberg (2011). https://doi.org/10.1007/978-3-642-14338-0_32

20. Östlund, B., Olander, E., Jonsson, O., Frennert, S.: STS-inspired design to meet the challenges of modern aging. Welfare technology as a tool to promote user driven innovations or another way to keep older users hostage? Technol. Forecast. Soc. Change 93, 82–90 (2015). https://doi.org/10.1016/j.techfore.2014.04.012

21. Sparrow, R., Sparrow, L.: In the hands of machines? The future of aged care. Minds Mach. 16(2), 141–161 (2006). https://doi.org/10.1007/s11023-006-9030-

22. Neven, L.: 'But obviously not for me': robots, laboratories and the defiant identity of elder test users. Soc. Health Illn. 32(2), 335–347 (2010). https://doi.org/10.1111/j.1467-9566. 2009.01218.x

23. Oudshoorn, N., Neven, L., Marcelle, S.: How diversity gets lost. Age and gender in design practices of information and communication technologies. J Women Aging 28(2), 170–185 (2016). https://doi.org/10.1080/08952841.2015.1013834

24. Flandorfer, P.: Population ageing and socially assistive robots for elderly persons: the importance of sociodemographic factors for user acceptance. Int. J. Popul. Res. (2012). https://doi.org/10.1155/2012/829835

25. Dekker, E.: 'Robot Zora: Friend or Foe? An Exploratory Study about the Emotional Attachment of Elderly to Robot Zora' (2015). http://arno.uva.nl/cgi/arno/show.cgi?fid= 606146

26. Frennert, S.: Older people meet robots: three case studies on the domestication of robots in everyday life. Doctoral dissertation. Department of Design Sciences, Faculty of Engineering, Lund University, Lund (2016)

27. Ginn, J., Arber, S.: 'Only connect': gender relations and ageing. In: Arber, S., Ginn, J. (eds.) Connecting Gender and Ageing: A sociological approach, pp. 1–14. Open University Press, Buckingham (1995)

28. Gustafsson, C.: Utveckling och implementering av välfärdsteknologi inom demensvård. Palliativ Omsorg 4(32), 26–30 (2015)

29. Gustafsson, C., Svanberg, C., Müllersdorf, M.: Using a robotic act in dementia care -a pilot study. J. Gerontol. Nurs. 41(10), 46–56 (2015)

30. Melkas, H., Hennala, L., Pekkarinen, S., Kyrki, V.: Human impact assessment of service robot implementation in Finnish elderly care. In: The 4th International Conference of Serviceology, ICServ2016, Tokyo, Japan, 6–8 September 2016

31. Kitzinger, J.: Qualitative research: introducing focus groups. BMJ **311**, 299 (1995). https://doi.org/10.1136/bmj.311.7000.299
32. Krueger, R.A., Casey, M.A.: Focus Group: A Practical Guide for Applied Research. Sage Publications, Thousand Oaks (2015)
33. Braun, V., Clarke, V.: Using thematic analysis in psychology. Qual. Res. Psychol. **3**(2), 77–101 (2006)
34. European Commission: Special Eurobarometer 427: autonomous systems. Technical report, European Commission (2015). http://ec.europa.eu/commfrontoffice/publicopinion/archives/ebs/ebs_427_en.pdf
35. Kristensson, P., Matthing, J., Johansson, N.: Key strategies for the successful involvement of customers in the co-creation of new technology-based services. Int. J. Serv. Ind. Manag. **19**(4), 474–491 (2008)
36. Elg, M., Engström, J., Witell, L., Poksinska, B.: Co-creation and learning in health-care service development. J. Serv. Manag. **23**(3), 328–343 (2012)
37. Nambisan, P.: Enabling consumer-driven service innovation in health care: the role of online Health Information Technologies (HIT). In: Nambisan, S. (ed.) Information Technology and Product Development. Annals of Information Systems, vol. 5, pp. 159–177. Springer, Boston (2010). https://doi.org/10.1007/978-1-4419-1081-3_8
38. Ghulam Sarwar Shah, S., Robinson, I.: User involvement in healthcare technology development and assessment: structured literature review. Int. J. Health Care Qual. Assur. **19**(6), 500–515 (2006)
39. Parviainen, J., van Aerschot, L., Särkikoski, T., Pekkarinen, S., Melkas, H., Hennala, L.: Motions with emotions? A double body perspective and human-robot interaction in elderly care. In: International Research Conference Robophilosophy 2016/TRANSOR 2016, Aarhus, Denmark, 17–21 October 2016
40. Nilsen, E., Dugstad, J., Eide, H., Gullslett, M.K., Eide, T.: Exploring resistance to implementation of welfare technology in municipal healthcare services – a longitudinal case study. BMC Health Serv. Res. BMC **16**(657) (2016). https://doi.org/10.1186/s12913-016-1913-5. Series – open, inclusive and trusted
41. Haigh, C., Hardy, P.: Tell me a story – a conceptual exploration of storytelling in healthcare education. Nurse Educ. Today **31**(4), 408–411 (2011). https://doi.org/10.1016/j.nedt.2010.08.001
42. Raappana, A., Rauma, M., Melkas, H.: Impact of safety alarm systems on care personnel. Gerontechnology **6**, 112–117 (2007). https://doi.org/10.4017/gt.2007.06.02.006.00

Investigating Users' Intention to Use Personal Health Management Services: An Empirical Study in Taiwan

Wen-Tsung Ku[1] and Pi-Jung Hsieh[2(✉)]

[1] Department of Physical Medicine and Rehabilitation,
St. Martin De Porres Hospital, Chia-Yi, Taiwan, R.O.C.
kib56265@gmail.com
[2] Department of Hospital and Health Care Administration,
Chia Nan University of Pharmacy & Science, Tainan, Taiwan, R.O.C.
beerun@seed.net.tw

Abstract. With the increasingly aged population and advances in health information technology (IT), personal health management services (PHMS) have become an important topic, since they enable people to input health-related data and to check preventive health records. Although several prior studies have focused on the factors that impact the adoption of personal health information management and electronic medical records, the literature directly related to people's self-management behaviors toward PHMS is scant. According to the technology acceptance and status quo bias perspectives, this study develops an integrated model to explain Taiwanese people's intention to use to a PHMS. A field survey was conducted in Taiwan to collect data from citizens over the age of 20. The results indicate that perceived ease of use (PEOU) and perceived usefulness (PU) have positive effects on usage intention, and PEOU has a positive effect on PU. The results also indicate a significant negative effect in the relationship between citizens' inertia and intention to use a PHMS. Furthermore, inertia was jointly predicted by behavioral-based inertia, cognitive-based inertia, and affective-based inertia. The study has implications for the development of strategies to improve personal health IT acceptance.

Keywords: Personal health management services · Self-management · Technology acceptance · Status quo bias

1 Introduction

The rapid evolution of mobile technologies and the increasing diffusion of smartphones have provided significant opportunities for health care organizations to create new healthcare solutions and to offer value-added services to their customers. With Taiwan now considered an aging society, Taiwan's Health Promotion Administration (HPA) must meet the growing demand for geriatric care and chronic illnesses care. By using information and communications services based on cloud technology, the Taiwan HPA established personal health management services (PHMS) in 2015. It provides the public with convenient, all-in one smart and multi-functional health

© Springer Nature Switzerland AG 2019
J. Zhou and G. Salvendy (Eds.): HCII 2019, LNCS 11592, pp. 228–237, 2019.
https://doi.org/10.1007/978-3-030-22012-9_17

management tools for the management of a healthy lifestyle, health examination records, health risk assessments, health alerts, and health education. It has become possible for people to use mobile channels to obtain accurate health information and preventive health services, leading to better health. Thus, the PHMS improves the transmission of personalized preventive health information to those most in need. Although some practitioners emphasize the opportunities that the PHMS offers to citizens, the overall adoption rate remains low; therefore, citizens' acceptance of, and support for, the PHMS is particularly critical in Taiwan.

It is a fact that some user resistance is unavoidable and may cause performance of the PHMS system to be lower than expected. Although prior studies have focused on the factors that impact the adoption or use of medical informatics [1–3], the literature directly related to citizens' self-management behaviors toward mobile health management services are scant. Empirically, self-management is not a simple activity, yet it is a lifesaving mechanism via the PHMS. Thus, the existing variables related to technology acceptance theories do not fully reflect the motives of health it uses. Previous research has suggested the need to incorporate additional inhibitors to improve the predictive capacity and explanatory power of these dimensions. A variety of behavior theories can be used to explain health IT adoption or use phenomena. Among them, two theoretical models that have been used extensively to predict user involvement in technology-related behaviors are the technology acceptance model (TAM; [4]) and status quo bias (SQB; [5]). In particular, the SQB theory aims to explain users' preferences for maintaining their current status. Thus, SQB theory provides a set of useful theoretical explanations for understanding the impact of inertia as an inhibitor of new health IT acceptance. Rooted in the TAM and SQB perspectives, this study proposes a theoretical model to explain citizens' intention to use mobile health management services.

2   Literature Review

2.1   The Technology Acceptance Model

The theory of reasoned action (TRA; [6]) has been tested across a variety of behaviors and contexts. It suggests that an individual's behavior is determined by his or her intention to perform the behavior, and that this intention is consequently a function of his or her attitude and subjective norms toward that behavior. Based on the TRA, Davis [4] introduced the TAM model to explain new technology use behaviors. The TAM assumes that there are two specified beliefs that determine system use: perceived usefulness (PU) and perceived ease of use (PEOU). PU refers to the extent to which users believe that system use will enhance their job performance, while PEOU is the extent to which users believe that their use will be relatively free of effort [4]. The TAM suggests that PU and PEOU are two salient, cognitive determinants of technology acceptance because users want to use new technology that benefits their tasks without costing them a lot of effort. Since its introduction, the TAM has become the most frequently cited and influential model for understanding the acceptance of new technology and has received extensive empirical support. Certain prior studies found that the TAM has good explanatory power for predicting health IT acceptance among individual professionals [7–12]. According to the technology perspective, TAM has focused on users' enabling perceptions related to IT use (e.g., its PU and PEOU) [13]. Thus, we propose that citizens' intent to use a new technology such as the PHMS is based on two enablers of system use: PU and PEOU.

2.2   The Status Quo Bias Theory

The SQB theory explains why individuals prefer to maintain their current status or situation, rather than to switch to a new action [5]. According to the SQB perspective, one may express the intent to continue using the incumbent course of action, since this is what they have always done, or in spite of being aware that better alternatives exist (i.e., due to inertia). Thus, inertia reflects a bias toward the status quo [5]. Polites and Karahanna [14] define inertia in a technology acceptance context as user attachment to, and persistence in using, an incumbent system even if there are better alternatives or incentives to change. Further, they conceptualize inertia as having behavioral, cognitive, and affective components. Behavior-based inertia implies that the use of an incumbent system continues simply because it is what a user has always done, and therefore it persists without them giving it much, if any, thought. Cognitive-based inertia implies that the user consciously continues to use an incumbent system, even though he or she is aware that it might not necessarily be the best, most efficient, or most effective way of doing things. Affective-based inertia occurs when a user continues using an incumbent system because it would be stressful to change, because they enjoy or feel comfortable using it, or because they have otherwise developed a strong emotional attachment to the current way of doing things. In the technology acceptance context, inertia occurs when expected learning tasks related to a new system are difficult. It could be reasonably argued that individual inertia inhibits users from accepting new technologies [15]. Inertia reduces the motivation to be and is a key predictor of the use of health technology services; this is well supported, from a theoretical perspective, in the literature [16]. Thus, the SQB view provides a set of useful theoretical explanations for understanding the impact of maintaining users current status as inhibitors (e.g., inertia).

3   Research Model

In keeping with the TAM and SQB perspectives, we propose that Taiwanese citizens' intention to use the PHMS is based on two opposing forces: enabling and inhibiting perceptions. In the case of enabling perceptions, we propose that users' intention to use the PHMS is based on two enablers of IS use: PU and PEOU. In the case of inhibiting perceptions, inertia is seen as a manifestation of the SQB. Further, this study conceptualizes inertia as a multidimensional construct comprising three components: behavioral-based inertia, cognitive-based inertia, and affective-based inertia. Figure 1 shows the proposed research model.

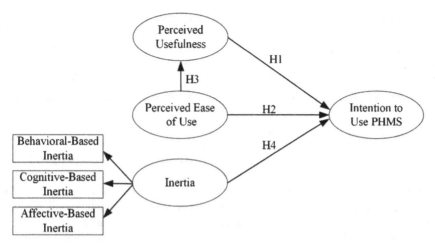

Fig. 1. Research framework.

According to the TAM perspective, PU and PEOU are two direct antecedents for determining behavioral intention to use, because users want to use new technologies that benefit their job tasks and that do not cost them a lot of effort [4]. Further, a new IT tool that requires less effort and is easier to use will be perceived as more useful than an older one. Since the PHMS is one specific instance of health IT, the salience and effects of PU and PEOU on system use should also apply to the healthcare context as enablers of system use. Tung et al. [17] and Yu et al. [18] provide empirical support for both associations within the healthcare context, leading us to hypothesize the following:

H1. The PU of PHMS use is positively related to the intention to use the PHMS.
H2. The PEOU of PHMS use is positively related to the intention to use the PHMS.
H3. The PEOU of PHMS is positively related to the PU of the PHMS.

According to the SQB perspective, users persist in using an incumbent system or work method either because this is what they have always done or because it may be too stressful or emotionally taxing to change [14]. For example, when an individual is confronted with a new technology and requested to develop a learning task for the new system, the new task's stress and (at least temporary) loss of control makes users produce negative emotions [15]. Thus, inertia will result in lowered use intentions. Hsieh and Lin [16] and Jaw [15] provided empirical support for both associations within the healthcare context. With this in mind, we suggest the following hypothesis:

H4. Inertia is negatively related to the intention to use the PHMS.

4   Research Method

4.1   Questionnaire Development

The construct measures shown in Fig. 1 were all adopted from previous studies and were rated using a 5-point Likert scale; the anchors ranged from "strongly agree" to "strongly disagree." Although previous studies have validated the questionnaire items, we conducted pretests by asking two health care professionals and an information management professor to evaluate each item. To ensure the questionnaire's validity and reliability, we conducted a pilot test with a sample that was representative of the actual respondents. We conducted structural equation modeling using partial least squares (PLS) estimations for the data analysis because the PLS method requires a minimal sample size and has few residual distribution requirements for model validation [19].

4.2   Sample and Data Collection

The target participants were Taiwanese citizens over the age of 20. This study employed an online survey for data collection, because online surveys provide researchers with various benefits, such as saving time and reducing expenses by overcoming geographic distance [20]. A total of 250 questionnaires were distributed through an online survey company, and 200 questionnaires were returned. We assessed nonresponse bias by comparing early and late respondents (i.e., those who replied during the first three days and the last three days). We found no significant difference between the two respondent groups based on the sample attributes (i.e., gender and age).

5   Research Results

The resulting 200 valid questionnaires constituted a response rate of 80%. Respondents' demographics are presented in Table 1. Most were female (51%) and between the ages of 20 and 49 (67.5%).

Table 1. Respondents' demographics.

Respondent characteristics		Frequency	Percent (%)
Gender	Male	98	49
	Female	102	51
Age	20–29	45	22.5
	30–39	45	22.5
	40–49	45	22.5
	50–59	41	20.5
	>60	24	12
Education	Secondary School or Less	37	18.5
	College	22	11
	University	99	49.5
	Master/PhD	42	21
Occupation	Industry	39	19.5
	Public service	28	14
	Service	44	22
	Students	8	4
	Farming	46	23
	Homemaker	16	8
	Others	19	9.5

We tested the reliability and validity of the proposed model. Reliability was assessed based on a construct reliability greater than 0.7 [21]. Convergent validity was assessed based on the following three criteria: (a) item loading greater than 0.7 and statistically significant, (b) composite construct reliability greater than 0.7, and (c) average variance extracted (AVE) greater than 0.5 [22]. The discriminant validity between the constructs was assessed based on the criterion that the square root of the AVE for each construct should be greater than the corresponding correlations with all other constructs [21]. In this study, the construct reliabilities are all greater than 0.9. For the convergent validity, the item loadings are all greater than 0.9, and the AVEs range from 0.86 to 0.97. For the discriminant validity, the square root of the AVE for a construct is greater than its corresponding correlations with other constructs. Table 2 shows the descriptive statistics of the principal constructs and the correlation matrix, respectively. These results indicate acceptable reliability, convergent validity, and discriminant validity.

Table 2. Reliability and validity of the scale

Construct	Item loading	CR	AVE	Correlation					
				PU	PEOU	BBI	CBI	ABI	IU
PU	.94–.96	.97	.91	**.95**					
PEOU	.90–.95	.97	.86	.28	**.93**				
BBI	.90–.96	.96	.88	−.04	−.32	**.94**			
CBI	.97–.98	.98	.97	−.03	−.27	.54	**.99**		
ABI	.92–.96	.97	.90	−.07	−.33	.57	.59	**.95**	
IU	.95–.96	.97	.92	.47	.57	−.53	−.52	−.51	**.96**

Note: Leading diagonal shows the square root of AVE of each construct Perceived Usefulness (PU), Perceived Ease of Use (PEOU), Behavioral-Based Inertia (BBI), Cognitive-Based Inertia (CBI), Affective-Based Inertia (ABI), and Intention to Use (IU)

The testing results in the structural model are indicated in Fig. 2. In general, the statistical testing conclusions all support this research model. In this study, intention to use was jointly predicted by PU ($\beta = 0.36$, standardized path coefficient, $p < 0.001$), PEOU ($\beta = 0.44$, $p < 0.001$), and inertia ($\beta = -0.40$, $p < 0.001$), and these variables together explained 68% of the variance of intention to use. As a result, hypotheses 1, 2, and 4 were all supported. In this study, PEOU ($\beta = 0.28$, $p < 0.001$) significantly influenced PU, explaining 10% of the total variance in PU. Accordingly, hypothesis 3 was supported.

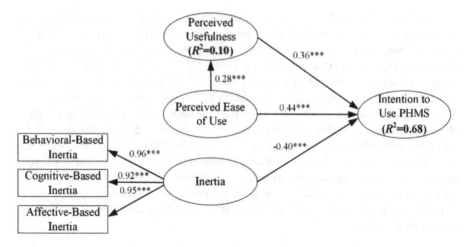

Fig. 2. Results of the structural model (Value on path: path coefficient; R^2, coefficient of determinant; ***p < 0.001)

6   Discussion

In this empirical study, we explored how variables affected citizens' intention to use the PHMS. Therefore, we extended the TAM by adding one belief construct (inertia) and its three major components (behavioral, cognitive, and affective) to understand whether our proposed extended model is a better model. The study results indicated that the TAM integrated with inertia provides a superior explanation of citizen intentions toward using PHMS, because the r-square of usage intention is 0.68. This implies that the TAM integrated with inertia might be a robust research model for predicting citizens' use intention toward health IT.

The results indicated that PU and PEOU are key determinants in citizens' use intentions. The PEOU also has a positive direct effect on PU. These findings are consistent with the results obtained by Tung et al. [17] and Yu et al. [18]. The effects of these usage intention variables were significant in explaining citizens' PHMS use behaviors by conforming to Davis [4], who maintained that the relative importance of PU and PEOU in predicting use intention varies across behaviors and situations. Inversely, inertia has a direct negative effect on citizens' use intentions, meaning that higher levels of inertia result in lower intention to use the PHMS. Inertia contains three major components: behavioral-based, cognitive-based, and affective-based elements. People persist in using the incumbent method either because it is what they have always done in the past (behavior-based inertia), because it may be too stressful or emotionally taxing to change (affective-based inertia), or despite their awareness that it might not necessarily be the best, most efficient, or most effective way of doing things (cognitive-based inertia). This result coincided with the findings of previous studies on IS adoption [14, 16]. In the absence of inertia, it is possible that a habitual user of an incumbent process or tool may readily recognize the advantages of switching to the

PHMS and may form genuine intentions to do so. These findings could interest and encourage researchers who are developing a health IT acceptance and resistance model.

This study has several implications for, and makes numerous contributions to, future research. A primary contribution is that technology acceptance and user resistance theories are combined to examine how individuals assess overall change related to a new health technology. By making use of the TAM to integrate and add to relevant concepts from SQB theory, the study contributes by operationalizing and testing the developed model through a survey methodology, which has little precedence in the user resistance literature. Hence, we provide theoretical insights that researchers may employ to encourage users to adopt a new health technology. Second, our study confirms that PU and PEOU are critical factors for facilitating the intention to use new health IT. While the role of inertia is important, the driving forces would have a negative effect on citizens' intent to use the PHMS. This finding could interest and encourage researchers who are developing a new health IT acceptance model. Future research should aim to identify additional incumbent action constructs and theorize on the interplay between incumbent action and new technology cognition and behaviors. As an extension of previous research, this study has demonstrated how inertia can be applied in health IT research to explain citizens' intention to make new health IT-related changes. Thus, this reliable and valid instrument provides an effective tool for researchers to measure users' behaviors and to explain, justify, and compare the differences in study results.

Our study findings provide useful recommendations for systems managers aiming to enhance citizens' usage intent regarding the PHMS. Because higher perceived levels of usefulness and ease of use encourage citizens to have more intentional behaviors, the PHMS should be designed in a more user-friendly manner that is consistent with current health needs. Those who can use the PHMS easily and who find that it enables them to access their health information efficiently will develop a better attitude toward it and increase their usage intentions. Systems managers should focus on creating an environment in which citizens have a positive attitude that encourages their use of the PHMS. Second, managers should be aware of the critical effect of inhibitors on users' intention behaviors. Managers can attempt to reduce inertia by enhancing citizens' favorable opinions toward new health IT-related changes. Furthermore, most health IT designs tend to focus on system considerations, such as new functionalities and connectivity, rather than on users' considerations, such as the system's impact on health behaviors. A better understanding of users' resistance to health IT may help facilitate the design of better systems that are both functionally good and acceptable to their targeted user populations.

The limitations of our findings should be acknowledged. The first limitation is our choice of constructs, which was based on prior literature and our own observation of the behaviors of users at our study site. There may be other inhibitors or enablers of health IT use that were not included in this study and which could be the subject of future research. There may be additional predictors of behavioral intention, beyond PU, PEOU, and inertia, that should be examined in future research. The identification and validation of such constructs will also help advance our preliminary model of health IT acceptance behavior. Second, the relevance of this study is confined to the health IT acceptance behaviors of the general public. The findings and implications drawn from this study cannot be readily generalized to other special groups, such as patients. A study targeting patients, who might have varying information needs and different levels of computing support and abilities, could yield different results. Future research should focus on accumulating further empirical evidence and data to overcome the limitations of this study.

References

1. Lai, J.Y., Wang, J.: Switching attitudes of Taiwanese middle-aged and elderly patients toward cloud healthcare services: an exploratory study. Technol. Forecast. Soc. Change **92**, 155–167 (2015)
2. Sun, Y., Wang, N., Guo, X., Peng, Z.: Understanding the acceptance of mobile health services: a comparison and integration of alternative models. J. Electron. Commer. Res. **14** (2), 183–200 (2013)
3. Kaur, P.D., Chana, I.: Cloud based intelligent system for delivering health care as a service. Int. J. Inf. Manag. **113**(1), 346–359 (2013)
4. Davis, F.D.: Perceived usefulness, perceived ease of use, and user acceptance of information technology. Manag. Inf. Syst. Qual. **13**(3), 319–340 (1989)
5. Samuelson, W., Zeckhauser, R.: Status Quo Bias in decision making. J. Risk Uncertain. **1**, 7–59 (1988)
6. Fishbein, M., Ajzen, I.: Belief, Attitude, Intention, and Behavior: An Introduction to Theory and Research. Addison-Wesley, Reading (1975)
7. Pai, F.Y., Huang, K.I.: Applying the technology acceptance model to the introduction of healthcare information systems. Technol. Forecast. Soc. Change **78**, 650–660 (2011)
8. Chau, P.Y.K., Hu, P.J.H.: Investigating healthcare professionals' decisions to accept telemedicine technology: an empirical test of competing theories. Inf. Manag. **39**, 297–311 (2002)
9. Holden, R.J., Karsh, B.T.: The technology acceptance model: its past and its future in health care. J. Biomed. Inf. **43**, 159–172 (2010)
10. Aldosari, B., Al-Mansour, S., Aldosari, H., Alanazi, A.: Assessment of factors influencing nurses acceptance of electronic medical record in a Saudi Arabia hospital. Inf. Med. Unlocked **10**, 82–88 (2018)
11. Özdemir-Güngör, D., Camgöz-Akdağ, H.: Examining the effects of technology anxiety and resistance to change on the acceptance of breast tumor registry system: evidence from Turkey. Technol. Soc. **54**, 66–73 (2018)
12. Nunes, A., Portela, F., Santos, M.F.: Improving pervasive decision support system in critical care by using technology acceptance model. Procedia Comput. Sci. **141**, 513–518 (2018)
13. Bhattacherjee, A., Hikmet, N.: Physicians' resistance toward healthcare information technology: a theoretical model and empirical test. Eur. J. Inf. Syst. **16**(6), 725–737 (2007)
14. Polites, G.L., Karahanna, E.: Shackled to the status Quo: the inhibiting effects of incumbent system habit, switching costs, and inertia on new system acceptance. MIS Q. **36**(1), 21–42 (2012)
15. Jaw, C.: The effects of consumer inertia and emotions on new technology acceptance. Int. J. Econ. Manag. Eng. **8**(8), 2014 (2014)
16. Hsieh, P.J., Lin, W.S.: Explaining resistance to system usage in the PharmaCloud: a view of the dual-factor model. Inf. Manag. **55**(1), 51–63 (2018)

17. Tung, F.C., Chang, S.C., Chou, C.M.: An extension of trust and TAM model with IDT in the adoption of the electronic logistics information system in HIS in the medical industry. Int. J. Med. Inf. **77**(5), 324–335 (2008)
18. Yu, P., Li, H., Gagnon, M.P.: Health IT acceptance factors in long-term care facilities: a cross-sectional survey. Int. J. Med. Inf. **78**(4), 219–229 (2009)
19. Chin, W.W., Marcolin, B.L., Newsted, P.R.: A partial least squares latent variable modeling approach for measuring interaction effects: results from a Monte Carlo simulation study and an electronic-mail emotion/adoption study. Inf. Syst. Res. **14**(2), 189–217 (2003)
20. Alharbi, S., Drew, S.: Using the technology acceptance model in understanding academics' behavioural intention to use learning management systems. Int. J. Adv. Comput. Sci. Appl. **5** (1), 143–155 (2014)
21. Chin, W.W.: Issues and opinion on structural equation modelling. MIS Q. **22**(1), 7–16 (1998)
22. Fornel, C., Larcker, D.: Structural equation models with unobservable variables and measurement error: algebra and statistics. J. Mark. Res. **18**(3), 382–388 (1981)

Understanding Long-Term Adoption and Usability of Wearable Activity Trackers Among Active Older Adults

Byung Cheol Lee[1(✉)], Toyin D. Ajisafe[2], Tri Van Thanh Vo[3],
and Junfei Xie[3]

[1] Department of Engineering, Texas A&M University – Corpus Christi,
Corpus Christi, TX 78412, USA
byungcheol.lee@tamucc.edu
[2] Department of Kinesiology, Texas A&M University – Corpus Christi,
Corpus Christi, TX 78412, USA
toyin.ajisafe@tamucc.edu
[3] Department of Computing Sciences, Texas A&M University – Corpus Christi,
Corpus Christi, TX 78412, USA
tvo5@islander.tamucc.edu, junfei.xie@tamucc.edu

Abstract. Many older adults do not sufficiently engage in physical activity and a sedentary lifestyle may pose a major health risk A recent survey showed that 71% of adults in the United States were overweight and obese between 2015 and 2016. To promote physical activities and reduce the risk of chronic diseases in older adults, an activity tracker is becoming a viable solution. However, adoption and long-term use of activity tracker are far less than a satisfactory level. This study conducted a 14-week longitudinal experiment to identify their adoption behaviors of activity trackers. We recruited 17 active senior adults who had no prior experience of the tracker use. Surveys about prior technology experience, affinity for technology interaction, and the attitude and usability of activity tracker adoption were given to the participants to identify perception on recent technology and to understand the adoption patterns and barriers to the acceptance of activity trackers. In addition, bi-weekly interviews were conducted to elicit older population-oriented usability and design issues. Results indicated that participants have a favorable view and interests of advanced smart technology, but they have not much recognized usefulness of activity data. Quantitative adoption scale also showed a flat or slightly decreasing pattern within two to three weeks before reaching to a satisfactory level. Participants reported major usability issues around activity tracker and interface designs, including data visualization and interpretation.

Keywords: Activity tracker · Adoption · Usability · Long-term use

1 Introduction

Exercise can be hard enough for healthy people, let alone older adults. According to the Behavioral Risk Factor Surveillance System (BRFSS), over 35% of older adults in the United States remain obese [1]. Obesity increases the risk for type 2 diabetes,

© Springer Nature Switzerland AG 2019
J. Zhou and G. Salvendy (Eds.): HCII 2019, LNCS 11592, pp. 238–249, 2019.
https://doi.org/10.1007/978-3-030-22012-9_18

cardiovascular disease, and some cancers [2]. It is recommended that adults engage in at least 2.5 h of moderate or vigorous physical activities per week and in muscle-strengthening workouts two days of a week [3]. However, these guidelines were suggested for both general adults and older population, and older adults are less likely to maintain the same levels of exercise as healthy young adults. Thus, older adult oriented guidelines need to be developed and the monitoring their regular physical activity is crucial to maintain or improve their health status and prevent obesity and other related chronic diseases.

The activity tracker is a valuable tool to assess whether older adults accumulate adequate physical activities [4]. Activity trackers have become pervasive following the miniaturization of sensors like accelerometers. These low-cost sensors are embedded in activity trackers, thereby allowing manufacturers to capture and analyze the wearer's movement data by deploying ad hoc algorithms. Consequently, activity trackers and the information they provide are thought to motivate the user to be more active and healthier [5]. Depending on the types of sensors that are integrated, activity trackers can monitor physical activity and other health indicators such as sleep quality and heart rate. They can also improve the user's awareness of their physical health behaviors by providing goal-relevant information [6]. Considering that only 14.7% of adults aged between 65 and 74 meet the physical activity recommendations for their age group, activity trackers have a huge potential to benefit older adults' physical and mental wellbeing [7].

However, empirical research supporting the long-term use and adoption of activity trackers is still emerging. More than half of activity tracker owners no longer use the device as a health management tool, and approximately one third abandon the devices after less than a year [8]. Ledger and McCaffrey [8] found that 50% of users who adopted an activity tracker stopped using it within the first two weeks, and 62% of users of an activity tracking mobile app abandoned it within six months after purchase. Similar adoption attitudes and patterns have been shown in older adults: previously, only half of 92 older adults intended to use the trackers to help achieve their physical wellbeing goals [9]. Three fourths of the participants stopped using their trackers after four weeks. A recent survey study reported that less than 2% of respondents aged 65 years and older took advantage of current activity logging or monitoring technology [10].

This study aimed to explore the adoption attitudes and usability issues among older adults who had not previously used activity trackers. This study provided free activity trackers to adults over 65 years old who indicated having a regular exercise regimen. Compared to peers who are sedentary, active older adults were presumed more likely to adopt activity trackers to help facilitate their goals related to physical wellbeing. They were also presumed more likely to elicit feedback regarding challenges and usability issues around activity tracker usage. Thus, we recognized informative patterns of the tracker adoption and active behavior changes.

Specifically, we focused on (1) investigating the impact of prior technology experience and affinity on active older adults' perceived acceptance of activity trackers by a longitudinal research approach, and (2) identifying the adoption patterns and usability of activity trackers from the perspective of active older adults. The results could inform design recommendations and yield strategies to educate and improve activity tracker adoption among older adults.

2 Method

A 3-month field study with 17 older adults was conducted to comparing their attitude and perception in pre and post adoption of activity tracker. Four different surveys and interview were given participants. Prior technology experience and the preference of activity tracker were examined at the beginning of the study. An activity tracker adoption survey and a quantitative usability scale were administered three times across the study period among novice active older adult users. Participants also completed bi-weekly interviews on issues around activity tracker usability and design.

2.1 Participants

Seventeen participants were recruited from a senior basic yoga class at a fitness facility in South Texas. The target participants of this study were active older adults who had a regular exercise regime or frequently attended exercise classes. We excluded partici-pants who had previously owned or used an activity tracker or other smart watches with activity tracking or monitoring function. This population was thought to be more likely to find activity trackers beneficial, adopt them, and be actively involved in identifying usability issues. Participants were asked to use the trackers for 14 weeks. The research team provided support for them to setup the device, including creating an account, familiarizing basic functions and features. The same information was also provided within the packaging of the device. The detailed demographic information is shown in Table 1.

Fig. 1. Activity tracker used in this study - Nokia Go

All participants in this study were aged more than 65 years, with an average age of 73.4 ± 4.0 years. Seventy five percent of the participants were female. Each participant received one activity tracker (Nokia Go, see Fig. 1) to wear. The tracker can monitor and measure various activities including walking, running, swimming and sleep quality and duration. It also provides distance data and calories burned. The selected device offers a simple basic function of tracking activity and maintains consistency between participants to avoid errors from device variation. The tracker also has a long battery life that does not require recharge or battery replacement during the experiment.

Table 1. Demographic information of experiment participants

Demographic factors		Number of participants (Percentage)
Gender	Female	13 (75%)
	Male	4 (25%)
Age	65–75	12
	76–85	4
	85 or older	1
Education	High school	2
	Bachelor	13
	Master	2
Race	Caucasian/White	6
	Hispanic	9
	Black	2

2.2   Experiment Procedure and Measures

Prior to use an activity tracker, a prior technology experience and perspective survey and the Affinity for technology interaction (ATI) scale [11] were given to the participants to assess their adoption attitudes and perception of activity trackers. The ATI survey is composed of nine unidimensional items using a 6-point Likert scale to understand why users differ in new technology adoption and provides insights to optimize the adoption process. This scale can quantify the assessment of users' personality in the context of technology interaction, and it provides a tool to discriminate how they engage in technology interaction.

The activity tracker adoption attitude survey was administered at three time points across the study: beginning (week 1), middle (week 7) and end (week 13). The survey was adapted from the survey scale developed for individual adoption of healthcare wearable devices [12]. Some of the language was modified to make the survey more pertinent to an activity tracker adoption context. In addition, a quantitative usability measure was also evaluated on a biweekly basis using System Usability Scale (SUS) [13]. A simple, 10 item scale provides an overview of usability and adoption patterns of activity trackers in an inexpensive and effective manner. This measure can be used by a broad range of population and any types of devices or user interfaces [14].

Interviews were conducted biweekly to identify usability and adoption issues. Each participant participated in an individual in-face interview designed to gather various opinions and user experience regarding the activity tracker usage. The interview lasted approximately twenty minutes per participant and the major questions were about their experiences of activity trackers and they were encouraged to answer in a flexible conversational manner. The entire proceeding was recorded, transcribed for thematic analysis, and reviewed by authors. The codes were independently developed through reviews of the interview transcripts and compared between authors to reach the agreement. Disagreements were resolved through consensus. Texas A&M University – Corpus Christi institutional review board approved the study.

3   Results

3.1   Background for Activity Tracker Adoption - Prior Technology Experience and Affinity Technology Interaction (ATI) Scale

As shown in Table 2, participants' prior experience with technology and their familiarity with various technology devices were assessed. All participants except one (94%) reported owning a smartphone. All participants (100%) reported using the internet or email. In addition, most (82%) participants reported frequently accessing social media. On average, participants were confident about using modern technology. They also showed neutral views of societal impacts of the technology.

Table 2. Technology experience and perspective

Experience questions	Number of participants	Percentage
Do you use the internet or email, at least occasionally?	17	100%
Do you have a smart phone?	16	94%
Do you access the internet on a cellphone, tablet or other mobile handheld device, at least occasionally?	17	100%
Do you ever use social media sites like Facebook, Twitter or LinkedIn?	14	82%
Please tell me if you happen to have each of the following items, or not. Do you have…		
- A desktop or laptop computer	17	100%
- A tablet computer like an iPad, Samsung Galaxy Tab, Microsoft Surface Pro, or Amazon Fire	11	65%
Perspective questions	Mean*	SD
How confident do you feel using computers, smartphones, or other electronic devices to do the things you need to do online?	5.7	0.46
Would you say technology has had a mostly positive effect on our society or a mostly negative effect on our society?	4.7	1.05

*Strongly positive 7, Positive 6, Somewhat positive 5, Neutral 4 Somewhat negative 3, Negative 2, Strongly negative 1

In this study, the term "technology" in the original ATI scale was displaced with "activity tracker." Responses to the three negative items need to be reversed, and mean score is calculated over all items per each participant. Table 3 shows the mean ATI scores and standard deviations for all participants. In addition, Cronbach's alpha was computed to assess internal consistency and the results are excellent ($\alpha = 0.93$). The outcomes of ATI scale support the notion that the dimensions of respondents' personality are associated with successful adoption of a technology in terms of problem solving and learning processes [15]. Based on the previous empirical results, the dimensionality, reliability and validity of the scale was confirmed [16].

Table 3. Technology experience and affinity for technology interaction

Affinity for technology interaction (ATI) scale	Mean	SD
1. I like to occupy myself in greater detail with activity trackers	4.3	1.22
2. I like testing the functions of new activity trackers	3.1	1.01
3. I predominantly deal with activity trackers because I have to	3.3	0.87
4. When I have a new activity tracker in front of me, I try it out intensively	3.5	1.33
5. I enjoy spending time becoming acquainted with a new activity tracker	4.3	0.91
6. It is enough for me that an activity tracker works; I don't care how or why	5.2	1.42
7. I try to understand how an activity tracker exactly works	4.9	1.01
8. It is enough for me to know the basic functions of an activity tracker	5.3	1.23
9. I try to make full use of the capabilities of an activity tracker	3.8	0.82
Average ATI score (all participants)	4.2	1.09

*6 Likert scale was used (6: Completely agree, 5: Largely agree, 4: Slightly agree, 3: Slightly disagree, 2: Largely disagree, 1: Completely disagree)

Mean and standard deviation (SD) of the ATI scores are shown in Table 3. The average ATI score in the sample is 4.2 which is higher than 3.5, the center of the response scale. This indicated that participants were moderately positive in learning and using an activity tracker. The average ATI score indicates that the participants moderately prefer the activity tracker. However, relatively high scores in item 6, 7, and 8 imply their interests in functional aspects of the activity trackers.

3.2   Attitudes and Perception Measures of Activity Tracker Adoption

Table 4 presents the results of the activity tracker adoption survey. We measured the constructs with 5-point Likert scale with anchors ranging from 1 'strongly disagree' to 5 'strongly agree'. Kruskal-Wallis test showed a difference of continuous dependent survey outcomes for each categorical construct (p = 0.0445).

Table 4. Integrated technology adoption survey results

Constructs	Beginning (1st week)	Middle (7th week)	Ending (13rd week)
Health information sensitivity	3.83	3.97	4.07
Personal innovativeness in IT	3.10	3.00	3.13
Legislative protection	4.30	4.27	4.30
Perceived prestige	3.97	3.93	4.00
Perceived informativeness	4.00	3.43	3.30
Functional congruence	3.83	3.53	3.53
Perceived privacy risk	4.07	4.07	4.10
Perceived benefit	3.97	3.77	3.60
Adoption intention	3.97	3.97	3.93
Actual adoption behavior	1.00	5.00	4.43

*5 Likert scale was used (5: Strongly agree, 4: Agree, 3: Neutral, 2: Disagree, 1: Strongly disagree)

There were moderate positive trends toward adopting and using activity trackers in the current sample. Most participants had favorable attitudes toward activity trackers on health information sensitivity, legislative protection, perceived prestige, perceived benefit and adoption intention, with scores well above the midpoint of 3 across all three time periods. However, the changes in perceived informativeness, functional congruence, and actual adoption behavior were notable. Average scores of perceived informativeness and functional congruence decreased by 22% (from 4.00 to 3.13) and 16% (from 3.83 to 3.23) respectively, in the first half period. Perceived informativeness and functional congruence decreased from week 7 to week 13 indicate that both scores remained relatively consistent over the second half of the study. Actual adoption behavior was lowest at the beginning, because participants had not received activity trackers.

3.3   Quantitative Usability Measure - System Usability Scale (SUS)

Figure 2 shows the results of System Usability Scale (SUS) analysis. To report results, a scoring template is adopted which turns the raw individual ratings across the participants into a single score based on Brooke's standard scoring method [13]. The results can be valid for both user interface designs or implementations [17].

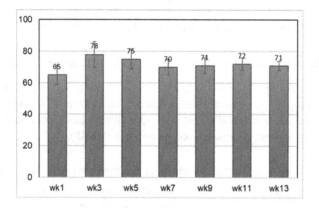

Fig. 2. System Usability Scale (SUS) scores for activity tracker

The SUS scores (mean 71.7) show that activity tracker usability did not reach the "Good" level, while 68 is widely considered as an average SUS score (Fig. 3). The SUS is not diagnostic and does not address specific problems, but it provides a measurable status of how users perceive usability of a system. Scores initially increased from week 1 to week 3, but were continuously maintained at "Marginal" levels thereafter.

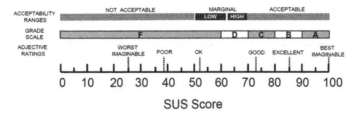

Fig. 3. SUS score evaluation criteria Image [18]

3.4   Usability Interviews

There were two major usability issues raised from the participants' interviews. Several participants reported that the number of steps provided by the activity tracker inaccurately represented their level of physical activity. Specifically, exercises such as cycling, swimming, and strength training, were either partially tracked, mis-tracked, or completely untracked. As one participant commented, *"The tracker was good at running and walking step count, but it wasn't for all exercises. For example, yesterday I rode a bike for an hour, and it didn't register anything for that entire time."* Conversely, all steps measured by an activity tracker are counted equally, yet they do not necessarily require equal effort. A participant denounced that, *"I can make many small steps to get to the same distance that can be reached by just taking a few big steps. This was not considered."* This lack of effort levels in activity actually discourages vigorous physical activity. Other participants mentioned that they often needed to supplement their activity measurements with additional information to appreciate the perceived exercise amounts and associated benefits. Sometimes, even when the measurement accurately displayed the daily step counts and activity levels, activity tracker data did not reflect participants' health conditions or specific exercise environments.

Another issue identified from the interviews was the lack of recognition and utilization of past activity history. Though exercise activity histories and trends are available in activity trackers or associated apps in a tablet or a smartphone, most older participants did not seem to be aware of how to integrate them for future exercise planning, including goal-setting. One participant mentioned that *"I like knowing what days I was getting what amount of activity, rather than just thinking. But, I don't know how my performance was and how I can use it."* Another participant explained how the previous exercise history impacted his goal setting, *"I had a really good work-out on Monday, but it's now Thursday and I haven't done any exercise. I don't know how much good exercise will be."* In addition, several participants suggested that although they could access their activity tracker data history, they hoped to find the patterns of success and failure that could help them plan for a more successful future.

Other usability issues around activity tracker device and mobile app interactions emerged from our interviews. Participants made various usability or user experience suggestions such as adopting large and easy to press buttons or icons at least on the main screen, adding options to allow users to start, pause, and terminate data recording and options to save the data to the cloud and send the data and/or feedback to the users.

4 Discussion

4.1 Active Older Adults' Willingness of Activity Tracker Adoption

This study focused on examining active older adults' activity tracker adoption attitudes and user experience for three months in free-living environment. We assumed that prior experience and affinity of technology facilitate activity tracker adoption and use. The results from the technology experience and perspective survey and ATI scale indicated that participating older adults have a favorable view of activity tracker. They were willing to adopt and use activity trackers.

The surveys indicated that despite demonstrating sufficient affinity (see Q. 6 and Q. 8 results in ATI), participants were more interested in utilizing basic functions of an activity tracker comparing to a tendency to engage in general interaction with activity tracker. Though the distinction between them is not clearly conspicuous, active seniors are more likely to be aware of those functions and not much attentive to operating activity trackers beyond basic functions. This suggests that the activity tracker design for active senior adults needs to be more concentrated on simple main function, tracking activities. In addition, designers or developers of a new technology device for older adults need to be aware the distinction between interests and understanding of technology. Simple design to basic functions rather than additional features are crucial to improve the device adoption and user experience.

4.2 Theoretical and Practical Implications for Long-Term Use

The integrated technology adoption survey found that participants have not much perceived usefulness of activity data, falling below 3 in their "Perceived informativeness" after usage and "Functional congruence." Additionally, no participants initially scored a 5 in "Adoption intention". However, after usage, four participants scored a 5. Therefore, most participants initially perceived activity trackers moderately favorably, but after using the trackers, participants became more polarized in their adoption of activity trackers. These outcomes point out that specific design factors that need to be considered and the importance of early training and detailed instructions when the tracker targets the elderly population. High scores which were initially at or above the midpoint of 3 on the 1 to 5 scales in "Health information sensitivity" and "Legislative protection" would represent their interests and concerns about the adoption of health information technology.

A quantitative SUS was administered to obtain a rapid and distinctive assessment of the adoption and/or usability of an activity tracker. Though the scale does not offer a full scale of diagnostic results and may not address what specific problems users face, it presents clear and simple criteria to know how much the usability needs to be improved. Though some measuring errors and individual differences by experts were reported, a commonly accepted average SUS score is estimated to be 68 [17, 19]. The average SUS score for the activity tracker across the study period is 71.7, which is slightly higher than the average score. It demonstrates that the participants' adoption and usability had not been reached enough to the satisfactory level, and the usability issues emerged in earlier periods had not been solved.

For a longitudinal score pattern, similar to adoption survey outcomes, the score was increased at early period and slightly decreased through the rest of study periods. This pattern implies that interests and expectation for the tracker positively affect the score, and some usability issues and lack of motivation for long-term use would be reflected in the decreasing score patterns. Considering the participants' positive perceptions on new technology and their regular exercise routine, the SUS scores were expected to be much higher and to show at least increasing patterns in the activity tracker adoption period. SUS scores indicated the direct experiences with the tracker usage and inform how usable the tracker actually is. Maintaining early expectation and motivation and user-oriented design are key aspects to encourage active older adults to maximize the benefits of activity trackers.

To investigate the reasons behind intention to use, and the roles of barriers and facilitators for long-term adoption, we examined the interview. Comfortability for continuous wearing, design comparability considering older population's mental and physical constraints, and utility of historical activity data were identified as major usability issues. Current activity trackers may need to be improved to accurately capture data during exercises like cycling and yoga, which are commonly adopted by older adults. The optimal tracker placement for data reliability and comfortability also need to be explored, especially during extended wear. In addition, historical data without any interpretation displayed in the tracker or associated apps may not be useful for older adults. The data needs to be more informative and deliver more meaningful and empowering directions for long-term use. For example, machine learning algorithm could be deployed to analyze historical data and determine more sustainable incremental physical activity goals for older adults. There is no appropriate and adaptive approach to set up individual target. Our results showed that more work is needed to further understand activity tracker usage patterns and the design issues that may constrain long term adoption among older adults who are already moderately active.

5   Limitation

A limitation of this study is the generalizability of the results due to small sample size. The number of participants in this study was limited to 17 older adults who were regularly exercising. Though they well understood the needs of activity trackers and were more apt to actively engage using it, their adoption attitudes and patterns would be biased and other older populations who have different life develop more conclusive and representative outcomes. Additionally, the outcomes of this study were mainly derived from subjective measures of surveys and interviews. Subjective measures are highly associated with the variables that are designed to capture but they are also damaged from many cognitive biases. Importantly, subjective measures are often complemented to objective measures. Thus, the attitudes and perception of activity tracker adoption can be more strengthened with quantified objective measures such as actual physical activity changes. Finally, three months would not be enough time to explore longitudinal implications of activity tracker adoption. Comparing other previous studies, three months is a quite lengthy period but may not enough time to draw conclusive adoption or usage patterns of suspended use.

6 Conclusion

This study investigated the adoption pattern and usability issues of activity trackers for active older adults. Active participants were recruited, because they were presumed more likely to adopt and use the activity tracker and provide feedback related to its usability. Longitudinal adoption surveys and interviews related to activity tracker adoption were administered. Survey and interview questions also addressed participants' backgrounds, prior technology experience, and perception and technology affinity. Contrary to conventional thought, older adults in the current sample reported being well exposed and familiar with modern and smart technological devices. It is concluded that active older adults appear to have favorable impressions of activity trackers. However, the adoption of activity trackers showed a flat or slightly decreasing pattern within two to three weeks before reaching to a satisfactory level. Participants identified major usability issues around activity tracker and interface designs, including data visualization and interpretation.

Future studies should recruit a more diverse and larger sample. Additionally, actual exercise data should be explored as they may provide practical insights on activity tracker adoption and long-term use in older adults.

References

1. Centers for Disease Control and Prevention: National Center for Chronic Disease Prevention and Health Promotion, Division of Population Health. BRFSS Prevalence & Trends Data. https://www.cdc.gov/brfss/brfssprevalence/
2. Flegal, K.M., Carroll, M.D., Ogden, C.L., Johnson, C.L.: Prevalence and trends in obesity among US adults, 1999–2000. JAMA **288**, 1723–1727 (2002)
3. US Department of Health and Human Service: Physical activity guidelines for Americans: be active, healthy, and happy! (2008). http://www.health.gov/paguidelines/guidelines/default.aspx
4. Walsh, M., Barton, J., O'Flynn, B., O'Mathuna, C., Hickey, A., Kellett, J.: On the relationship between cummulative movement, clinical scores and clinical outcomes. In: 2012 IEEE Sensors, pp. 1–4. IEEE (2012)
5. Walsh, M., O'Flynn, B., O'Mathuna, C., Hickey, A., Kellett, J.: Correlating average cumulative movement and Barthel Index in acute elderly care. In: O'Grady, M.J., et al. (eds.) AmI 2013. CCIS, vol. 413, pp. 54–63. Springer, Cham (2013). https://doi.org/10.1007/978-3-319-04406-4_7
6. Ananthanarayan, S., Siek, K.A.: Persuasive wearable technology design for health and wellness. In: 2012 6th International Conference on Pervasive Computing Technologies for Healthcare (PervasiveHealth), pp. 236–240. IEEE (2012)
7. Blackwell, D.L., Lucas, J.W., Clarke, T.C.: Summary health statistics for US adults: national health interview survey, 2012. Vital Health Stat. **10**, 1–161 (2014)
8. Ledger, D., McCaffrey, D.: Inside wearables: how the science of human behavior change offers the secret to long-term engagement. Endeavour Partners **200**, 1 (2014)
9. AARP: Building a Better Tracker: Older consumers weigh in on activity and sleep monitoring devices (2017). https://www.aarp.org/content/dam/aarp/home-and-family/personal-technology/2015-07/innovation-50-project-catalyst-tracker-study-AARP.pdf

10. Fox, S., Duggan, M.: Health Online 2013 (2013). https://www.pewinternet.org/2013/01/15/health-online-2013/
11. Attig, C., Wessel, D., Franke, T.: Assessing personality differences in human-technology interaction: an overview of key self-report scales to predict successful interaction. In: Stephanidis, C. (ed.) HCI 2017. CCIS, vol. 713, pp. 19–29. Springer, Cham (2017). https://doi.org/10.1007/978-3-319-58750-9_3
12. Li, H., Wu, J., Gao, Y., Shi, Y.: Examining individuals' adoption of healthcare wearable devices: an empirical study from privacy calculus perspective. Int. J. Med. Inf. **88**, 8–17 (2016)
13. Brooke, J., et al.: SUS-A quick and dirty usability scale. Usability Eval. Ind. **189**, 4–7 (1996)
14. Bangor, A., Kortum, P., Miller, J.: Determining what individual SUS scores mean: adding an adjective rating scale. J. Usability Stud. **4**, 114–123 (2009)
15. Nair, K.U., Ramnarayan, S.: Individual differences in need for cognition and complex problem solving. J. Res. Pers. **34**, 305–328 (2000)
16. Franke, T., Attig, C., Wessel, D.: A personal resource for technology interaction: development and validation of the Affinity for Technology Interaction (ATI) scale. Int. J. Hum.-Comput. Interact. **35**, 456–467 (2019)
17. McLellan, S., Muddimer, A., Peres, S.C.: The effect of experience on system usability scale ratings. J. Usability Stud. **7**, 56–67 (2012)
18. Brooke, J.: SUS: a retrospective. J. Usability Stud. **8**, 29–40 (2013)
19. Sauro, J.: Measuring usability with the system usability scale (SUS) (2011)

Influence of Age on Trade-Offs Between Benefits and Barriers of AAL Technology Usage

Julia Offermann-van Heek$^{(\boxtimes)}$, Susanne Gohr, Simon Himmel,
and Martina Ziefle

Human-Computer Interaction Center, RWTH Aachen University,
Campus-Boulevard 57, 52074 Aachen, Germany
{vanheek, gohr, himmel, ziefle}@comm.rwth-aachen.de

Abstract. An aging population due to demographic change along with rising care needs lead to higher efforts in concepts and developments of ambient assisted living (AAL) technologies aiming at a longer staying at home and more independency for older people. Although research on technology acceptance and user diversity gains in importance, real-life decisions with trade-offs between potential benefits and barriers of AAL technology usage have not been investigated so far. Therefore, the current study (n = 140) represents a conjoint analysis approach focusing on younger and older people's decisions between benefits (*safety and relief*) and barriers (*data handling and data access*) to use an assisting system in the home environment of a family member in need of care. The results revealed differences in the decision patterns of both groups indicating that data-relevant aspects were most relevant for the younger adults, while safety represented a more relevant criterion for the older participants. In addition, contradicting evaluations of both groups were found within the aspects data access and safety. The results contribute to a deeper understanding of real-life decisions regarding the use of assisting technologies focusing on age as relevant user factor.

Keywords: Ambient assisted living (AAL) · Technology acceptance ·
Benefit and barrier perception · Trade-off · Age

1 Introduction

An aging population and rising needs in care and support of older people characterize demographic change in western societies. This development represents tremendous challenges for health and social systems of nearly all countries as well as high burdens for care sectors and policy [1, 2]. In particular, care institutions suffer intensely from a persistent lack of care specialists in line with steadily rising numbers of older people and people in need of care [2–4].

Enabling most older people's wish of staying within the own home environment as long and as autonomously as possible requires new concepts and innovative technology development [5]. In the last decades, numerous single devices but also complex ambient assisted living (AAL) and smart home systems facilitate living at home,

© Springer Nature Switzerland AG 2019
J. Zhou and G. Salvendy (Eds.): HCII 2019, LNCS 11592, pp. 250–266, 2019.
https://doi.org/10.1007/978-3-030-22012-9_19

enhance safety by enabling monitoring of vital parameters or detecting falls, or act as reminders [6]. For user's acceptance and a sustainable adoption of devices and systems, a detailed understanding of diverse users' perspectives and perceptions of such technologies is necessary. Previous research has intensively investigated users' acceptance of specific technologies (e.g., [7–9]), their interaction with assisting technology (e.g., dementia patients [10]), and also their evaluations of specific benefits and barriers (e.g., [11–13]) regarding diverse technologies and systems.

In contrast, there has not been any research so far focusing on people's real-life decisions between benefits and barriers when thinking about using an AAL system in the own home environment or using an AAL system for a family member in need of care. Thus, the current conjoint analysis study was conceptualized aiming for an investigation of people's decisions between benefits and barriers of AAL technology usage. Using an online questionnaire, people (n = 140) of different ages were asked to think about an implementation of an AAL system in the home environment of a family member in need of care and to decide which aspects are most important for them (differing between relevant benefits and barriers of technology usage).

In the following, an overview of previous research in the field of AAL and user acceptance is provided. Subsequently, the applied approach is described including the selection of relevant attributes, the online questionnaire design, and the characteristics of the sample. Afterwards, the results are presented starting with (descriptive) results of acceptance as well as benefit and barrier evaluation, followed by the conjoint analysis differing between importance of attributes (benefits and barriers: safety, relief, data handling, data access) and the meaning of attribute levels (e.g., facets of safety). Finally, the results are discussed and research gaps for future work are highlighted.

2 AAL and User Acceptance

In the last decades, the number of new and innovative technologies, reaching from medical technologies or smart home technologies to supporting AAL technologies, has increased enormously. As research projects (e.g., [6, 14]) but also as commercial products (e.g., [15]), numerous single devices as well as more complex systems have been developed and are available on the market.

Concomitantly, the awareness and importance of (future) users' acceptance of innovative assisting technologies have increased as well. In this regard, a high number of studies have already focused on perception and acceptance of AAL and smart home technologies understanding the needs of user-centered technology development [7]. Most of the studies have focused on diverse stakeholders' acceptance or behavioral intention to use different types of assisting technology as well as on their perception of potential benefits and barriers of technology usage. This way, the perspectives of e.g., professional caregivers (e.g., [9, 11]), family caregivers (e.g., [8, 16]), older people suffering from dementia (e.g., [10]), or older predominantly healthy people (e.g., [13, 17]) have been investigated.

Most studies have in common that perceived benefits and barriers of using assisting technology were evaluated separately and isolated from each other. Independent from the investigated user group, enabling a longer staying at the own home, a feeling of increased safety, and enabling a more autonomous life for older people or people in need of care represent the most relevant benefits of using assisting technology (e.g., [7, 11, 13]). On the other side, the perception of barriers has been expressed differently with regard to diverse user groups. While family caregivers expressed in particular concerns about maintaining home security [8], professional caregivers mentioned especially concerns about data security, privacy, and perceived control in professional everyday [9, 11]. In addition, more detailed research found that – among professional caregivers – technology depends on the respective care area [12]. In contrast to the caregivers' perspective, concerns expressed by older people referred to dependency on technology and a lack of personal contact (e.g., [13, 17]).

Besides investigations of diverse user groups' perspectives, acceptance and perception of assisting technologies can also impact by individual factors of users, e.g., gender, previous experience, attitude towards technology, or education (user diversity). With regard to demographic change and an aging population, age-related factors such as the biological age, perceived age, or attitude towards aging (e.g., [18]) have been considered as relevant parameters for technology acceptance [19]. Some studies have already revealed significant influences of age and chronic illness on the acceptance of a vital signs monitoring system [20] and electronic safety devices [21]. With regard to evaluation of assisting health technologies, effects of age have not been found for the perception of benefits, while older adults showed higher ratings of barriers to use assisting technology compared to younger adults [22].

To sum up, previous studies have intensively investigated technology acceptance of diverse user groups, separate evaluations of benefits and barriers, and influences of age as relevant user factor. Hence, knowledge about real-life decisions, in which several advantageous and disadvantageous factors have to be weighed against each other, is missing regarding usage of AAL technologies in the own home environment. In addition, it is unclear if age – which has been proven to be a relevant factor for technology acceptance – has an impact on decisions between benefits and barriers of AAL technology usage. Therefore, the current study aims at an investigation of exactly these two research gaps applying a conjoint analysis differing between younger (<50 years) and older adults (50+).

3 Empirical Approach

The following section gives an overview of the study's empirical approach, starting with a description of the applied methodology "conjoint analysis". Then, the selection of attributes and attribute levels as well as the experimental questionnaire design are described. Further, information on the collection, processing, and analysis of data are provided, before the sample of the study is illustrated.

3.1 Applied Methodology

To examine the trade-off between perceived benefits and barriers of using AAL systems and technologies from the perspective of caring relatives, a conjoint analysis (CA) was carried out. The method of conjoint analysis emerged in the 1960s from the psychological measurement theory of the American mathematical psychologist Luce and the statistician Tukey [23]. The CA is used to measure preferences and allows a holistic examination of decision-making situations, in which selected attributes are weighed against each other [24]. Since its introduction to market research in 1971 by Green and Srinivasan [25], conjoint measurement is considered as one of the most frequently used methods for market segmentation, product planning, and pricing in marketing [26]. Nowadays, CA is also used in other disciplines such as social sciences and acceptance research (e.g., [21]), health and care research (e.g., [27]), or in environmental science (e.g., [28]).

In contrast to common methods in social science such as surveys, CA is based on a decompositional procedure. In CA, overall assessments of holistic concepts, referring to products or scenarios, are determined. For this purpose, different alternatives ("choice sets") are presented to the participants, which usually consist of three to five attributes and vary in specific characteristics of the attributes – called attribute levels. Participants are then asked to select the combination of attributes levels matching their preferences most closely. On the basis of these preferential decisions, information about an attribute's importance for the overall assessment can be gained in relation to all other investigated attributes. In addition, statements can be made about the relevance of individual attribute levels within the attributes. Nowadays, numerous variants of conjoint analysis exist. The form used in the present study is the choice-based-conjoint analysis (CBC), as is it a widely used approach and allows an investigation of complex decision processes in which various attributes influence the final decisions [24].

3.2   Relevant Attributes and Levels in the Field of AAL Acceptance

The most important step in the conception of a conjoint study is the definition of relevant attributes and levels that are evaluated in the choice tasks [29]. Relevant influencing factors for the acceptance of AAL technologies were selected on the basis of a literature analysis. Thereby, the following four attributes with each four different levels were identified and included in the consideration. For an overview, all attribute levels and their visualizations are depicted in Table 1.

As a first relevant aspect, the type of data access by third parties was identified to be an important barrier for AAL technology usage. Numerous studies have shown that concerns about limited individual privacy have a negative impact on the assessment of AAL (e.g., [30, 31]). An important role in dealing with health data refers to the question with whom data concerning AAL technology usage should be shared [32]. Therefore, data access was integrated in the current study as privacy-relevant potential barrier of using AAL technologies. Within the attribute levels, it was differentiated between *trusted persons* (selected by the person who is using AAL technology), a *circle of relatives* (consisting of several people), *medical experts*, and *emergency services*.

A second potential barrier of using AAL technology refers to the way the AAL technology or systems handles data. Thereby, the duration of data storage represents a frequently discussed data security-related aspect [11]. Hence, the duration of data handling was integrated as a potential barrier of using AAL technology. With regard to

Table 1. Attribute levels and their visualizations (red box marks an exemplary scenario).

Attribute	Attribute levels			
Data access	Trusted persons	Relatives	Medical experts	Emergency services
Data handling	Real time (no storage)	Short-term (1 week)	Middle-term (1 month)	Long-term (permanent)
Safety	Fast	Medical	Structuring	Felt
Relief of caring persons/family members	Temporal	Organizational	Financial	Emotional

the attribute levels, a distinction has been made between four storage periods: a *real time processing (no storage)* of data, a *short-term storage up to 1 week*, a *middle-term storage up to 1 month*, and *a long-term (permanent) storage* of data referring to the AAL system's usage. The various levels are accompanied by different ways of monitoring the state of health of the patient in need of care. While, for example, the real-time data acquisition only allows a situational analysis of the disease state, the long-term storage enables an analysis of acute and chronic disease progressions. These relationships were – of course – introduced and explained to the participants prior to the conjoint decision tasks.

Moving to benefits of using AAL technology, increased security represents one of the most mentioned aspects. Numerous studies proved a positive influence of the factor "gain in safety" on the acceptance of AAL technology (e.g., [7]). The high relevance of this aspect has been confirmed by a revealed higher willingness of participants to accept privacy restrictions if monitoring by AAL technology provides increased safety (e.g., [33]). Increase in safety was therefore also integrated as attribute in the current study. As diverse dimensions of safety were identified to play a role for AAL technology usage in preceding studies, the attribute levels referred to different types of safety: *fast safety* referring to fast assistance in emergencies, *medical safety* by checking and monitoring of medical parameters, *structuring safety* by reminding and organizational functions, and *felt safety* related to perceived safety and the feeling that the persons in need of care is not alone.

As an additional benefit of using AAL technology, the relief of caring persons and family members by means of using AAL technology has been identified. Relevant studies have indicated that participants show an increased willingness to adopt AAL technologies if technology usage has the potential to relieve the burden on caregivers (e.g., [34]). Similar to the safety attribute, diverse dimensions of relief were relevant and have therefore been integrated in the current study: *temporal relief* due to time savings (it is no longer necessary to visit the persons in need of care several times a day), *organizational relief* due to minor efforts in planning, organization, and infrastructure of everyday life, *financial relief* by saving costs of care services or costs of drives, and *emotional relief* by the knowledge that the system monitors the health state and contacts the caring relatives in emergencies.

3.3   Experimental and Questionnaire Design

The questionnaire consisted of different parts. The first section addressed demographic data (e.g., age, gender, educational level) as well as questions about the residential area and the proximity to close relatives and medical care centers. Afterwards, the participants' general attitude towards technology (five items) [35], privacy (three items), and data security (three items) (based on [36, 37]) were rated on a six-point Likert scale (min = 1: "I strongly disagree"; max = 6: "I strongly agree). In the third part, the participants' experiences in the field of health, care, and medicine were collected by using five statements which could be answered with "yes" or "no". Further, more detailed knowledge about the subjective state of health, e.g., with regard to chronic diseases or the need for regular medical check-ups, has been gained by six items (answer options: "yes", "no").

To enable that the participants emphasized with the situation of being a caregiver for a close family member in need of care, a fictitious scenario was presented in the next section of the questionnaire. The scenario focused on the integration of supporting technologies into the living environment of a person in need of care as well as on the everyday life of a family caregiver. Within a description of the daily routine, the functional scope of the technologies, prototypical usage situations, and the potential relief were described in more detail. After this, the participants were asked to evaluate possible benefits and barriers of AAL technology (each six items) as well as their acceptance (four items) and intention to use AAL (three items). Thereby, it was differentiated whether AAL technology was used for a) a relative in need of care and b) for the participants themselves. In line with the evaluations of attitudes, all statements were rated on six-point Likert scales (min = 1: "I strongly disagree"; max = 6: "I strongly agree).

In the subsequent section of the questionnaire, participants were introduced into the experimental CA study design by providing detailed information about the attributes, their levels, and visualizations. Subsequently, the participants were asked to put themselves in the perspective of a caring relative who decided, together with the person in need of care, to use supporting technologies. Then, the participants were instructed to choose in each decision task the scenario that meets their needs and wishes most closely. As described in Sect. 3.2, four attributes with each four levels were selected for the conjoint study (Table 1). The participants had to complete 10 decision tasks in which they had to choose their most preferred scenario constellation out of four different alternatives ("choice sets"). To avoid a loss of information, the CBC was executed in a forced choice format (no "none-option"). In order to increase the comprehensibility of the constructs, the levels in the selection tasks were displayed both verbally and visually in the form of pictograms. The uniqueness of the pictograms and semantic equivalence to the terms were positively evaluated within pretests. The number of decision tasks was limited to 10 randomized selection tasks, since the combination of all attribute levels would have led to 256 (4 × 4 × 4 × 4) possible alternatives. This reduction of decision tasks requires a test of the design's efficiency in order to ensure validity although the possible effect that probably some attribute levels might not appear together in a set of scenario decisions. For the present study, a median efficiency of 99% and a standard error below .05 confirmed that the current design (10 choice tasks) was comparable to the hypothetical orthogonal design [38].

3.4   Data Acquisition, Preparation, and Sample

Data was collected in Germany in summer 2018 by distributing a link to the online questionnaire. Due to the randomized design of the conjoint analysis, a paper-based survey could not be realized. Participants were acquired in social networks and in online forums with a focus on age-appropriate technologies, medical technology, and nursing care. The completion of the survey took approximately 20 min. The total number of participants gained was n = 228. For the analysis, dropouts as well as dubious answers (e.g., responses with a processing time under five minutes) were removed from the data set. After the data cleaning, the total sample contained n = 140 data sets.

A total of 140 (n) participants with an age range from 17 to 86 were included in the analysis. 56.4% (n = 79) of them were female and 42.9% (n = 60) male. One participant chose the answer option "no specification" for gender determination. The average age of the volunteers was 35.4 years, the standard deviation 16.8 years. Asked for their highest educational level, 45.7% (n = 64) indicated to have a university entrance degree (qualification), 38.6% (n = 54) a university degree, and 15.7% (n = 22) a secondary school degree. Thus, the sample turned out to be highly educated. Half of the participants (54.3%, n = 76) have not yet finished their education, 35.0% (n = 49) work in their professions, and - with a clear distance - 10.7% (n = 15) indicated to be retired.

Asked for experiences with health, medicine, and care, about one third of the participants had already gained professional experience either in a medical (17.9%, n = 25) or care area (14.3%, n = 19), while 44.3% indicated to have private experiences in the areas health, medicine, and care. Further, more than a third of the participants reported that a person in their environment is in need of care (36.4%, n = 51, "private passive care experience"). 18.2% (n = 25) indicated to have already been the caregiver for a family member in need of care ("private active care experience"). Asked for their health status, 21.4% of the sample (n = 30) indicated to suffer from a chronic disease, while only 2.9% (n = 4) indicated to depend on support and care.

4 Results

The conjoint data was analyzed using Sawtooth Software [39]. First, the relative importance of the attributes was calculated based on Hierarchical Bayesian analysis (HB). Thus, statements could be made about the relevance of an attribute for the selection of a scenario in relation to all other attributes. Secondly, part-worth utilities of the attribute levels were investigated also by using HB-analysis and provide information about the (positive or negative) meaning of each attribute level for the selection of a scenario. Besides conjoint data, also other relevant criteria of the online questionnaire were analyzed using descriptive as well as inference statistical procedures.

The results are presented in the following sections starting with a description of the investigated age groups. Further, participants' evaluation of benefits and barriers as well as their acceptance of AAL technology is analyzed. Finally, participants decisions and trade-offs between perceived benefits and barriers of AAL technology are investigated.

4.1 Age Groups and Their Characteristics

In order to understand potential age-related differences in AAL technology acceptance and the decision behavior regarding trade-offs between benefits and barriers of using AAL technology, two age groups were investigated: the sample was divided into a younger age group younger than 50 years of age (n = 102; M = 26.1; SD = 6.6; min = 17; max = 48) and an older age group being 50 years of age or older (n = 38; M = 60.4; SD = 8.3; min = 50; max = 86). As illustrated in Table 2, inference statistical analyses revealed that both age groups did neither differ regarding gender nor health status. However, they differed in terms of their living circumstances and their previous experiences with care. Concerning their living circumstances, both age groups differed with regard to the highest level of education, their current occupation, and their living area. In more detail, nearly all participants of the younger group hold a university degree or at least a university entrance qualification, while the majority of the older group reported to have a secondary school degree as highest educational level. In line with this, the three quarter of the younger group reported to have not finished their education yet. In contrast, the participants of the older group reported to have a professional activity or to be in pension. Concerning the living area, the majority of the younger group stated to live in the city center, while the older group indicated to live mainly in suburban or rural areas.

Regarding previous experiences, both groups differed significantly in terms of professional and private experiences with care. In tendency, higher proportions of participants belonging to the older group reported to have professional experiences with care, to have a person in their family circle depending on care (private passive experience), and to have already been the caregiver for a family member in need of care (private active experience). Overall, the younger group had comparably less experiences with care than the older group.

Table 2. Characteristics and inference statistical results regarding age groups.

Variables	Young (<50 years)	Old (50+ years)	P
Age (M (SD))	26.1 (6.6)	60.4 (8.3)	<.01
Gender	59.8% female (n = 61)	47.4% female (n = 18)	n.s.
	39.2% male (n = 40)	52.6% male (n = 20)	
Education	43.1% university degree (n = 44)	26.3% university degree (n = 10)	<.01
	53.9% university qualification (n = 55)	23.7% university qualification (n = 9)	
	2.9% secondary school degree (n = 3)	50.0% secondary school degree (n = 19)	
Occupation	74.5% ongoing education (n = 76)	0.0% ongoing education (n = 0)	<.01
	22.5% professional activity (n = 23)	65.8% professional activity (n = 25)	
	2.9% in pension (n = 3)	34.2% in pension (n = 13)	
Living area	54.9% city center (n = 56)	15.8% city center (n = 6)	<.01
	34.3% suburban area (n = 35)	42.1% suburban area (n = 16)	
	10.8% rural area (n = 11)	42.1% rural area (n = 16)	
Health status	19.6% chronic illness (n = 20)	26.3% chronic illness (n = 28)	n.s.
Prof. care experience	10.8% yes (n = 11)	23.7% yes (n = 9)	<.01
	89.2% no (n = 91)	76.3% no (n = 29)	
Private passive care experience	29.4% yes (n = 30)	55.3% yes (n = 21)	<.01
	70.6% no (n = 72)	44.7% no (n = 17)	
Private active care experience	11.8% yes (n = 12)	36.8% yes (n = 14)	<.01
	88.2% no (n = 90)	63.2% no (n = 24)	

4.2   AAL Acceptance

As a baseline, the participants assessed perceived benefits and barriers of the described AAL system's usage as well as their acceptance and intention to use the system. Starting with the benefits, MANOVA analyses revealed that the evaluation did not differ significantly for both age groups ($F(6,133) = 1.812$; $p = .101$; n.s.). Figure 1 shows the evaluation of all benefits for both age groups. All benefits were evaluated positively and were, thus, perceived to be real benefits of the AAL system's usage. Fast help in emergencies, increased feeling of safety, and relief of relatives represented important benefits for both groups.

Concerning potential barriers of the AAL system's usage, both age groups did also not differ significantly in their assessment ($F(6,133) = .879$; $p = .512$; n.s.). All barriers were only slightly confirmed, e.g., surveillance by technology ($M_{young} = 3.9$; $SD_{young} = 1.5$; $M_{old} = 3.5$; $SD_{old} = 1.3$), invasion of privacy ($M_{young} = 3.5$; $SD_{young} = 1.4$; $M_{old} = 3.4$; $SD_{old} = 1.3$), recording of data ($M_{young} = 3.8$; $SD_{young} = 1.4$; $M_{old} = 3.5$; $SD_{old} = 1.3$) or data sharing with third persons ($M_{young} = 3.7$; $SD_{young} = 1.4$; $M_{old} = 3.5$; $SD_{old} = 1.4$).

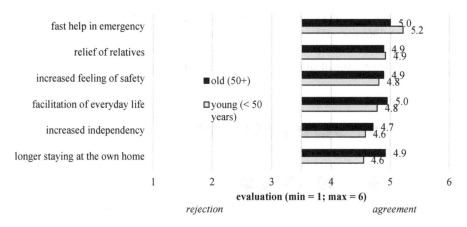

Fig. 1. Evaluation of single perceived benefits.

Asking for the participants' evaluation of acceptance and intention to use the AAL system, it was differed between using the system for a family member in need of care or for the participants themselves. Neither the acceptance of the system used for a family member $(F(4,135) = .455$; $p = .769$; n.s.) nor for the participants themselves $(F(4,135) = .170$; $p = .953$; n.s.) differed regarding the investigated age groups. Thereby, acceptance was confirmed indicated by rather high evaluations (family member: $M_{young} = 4.3$; $SD_{young} = 0.8$; $M_{old} = 4.2$; $SD_{old} = 0.7$; participants them-selves: $M_{young} = 4.2$; $SD_{young} = 0.9$; $M_{old} = 4.1$; $SD_{old} = 0.8$).

The same applied to the participants' intention to use the system. The evaluations were rather positive (family member: $M_{young} = 4.2$; $SD_{young} = 0.9$; $M_{old} = 4.2$, $SD_{old} = 0.8$; participants themselves: $M_{young} = 4.2$; $SD_{young} = 0.9$; $M_{old} = 4.1$; $SD_{old} = 0.8$) and did not differ for the age groups – neither for using the system for a family member $(F(3,136) = .946$; $p = .421$; n.s.) nor for themselves $(F(3,136) = .179$; $p = .910$; n.s.).

Although the results did not show significant evaluation differences for both age groups when assessing benefits, barriers, and acceptance of the AAL system, it is questionable whether decisions and trade-offs between benefits and barriers are influenced by age.

4.3 Decision Patterns

To analyze if age had an impact on the decision and trade-offs between perceived benefits and barriers of the AAL system's usage, the conjoint study's data is considered differentiating between both age groups. Figure 2 shows the relative importance of each attribute for the scenario decisions. For the young group, the privacy-related barrier attribute *data access* was most important (27.0%), followed by *data handling* (25.7%), *relief of relatives* (24.7%), and *safety* (23.6%). For the old group, *safety* (27.8%) and *data access* (27.7%) represented the most important attributes, while *relief of relatives* (22.9%) and *data handling* (21.7%) were comparably less important.

Inference statistical analyses revealed significant differences for the attributes *safety* (F(1,139) = 4.396; p < .05) and data handling (F(1,139) = 3.487; p < .1), while *data access* (F(1,139) = .103; p = .749; n.s.) and *relief of relatives* (F(1,139) = .079; p = .779; n.s.) were not of different importance for both age groups.

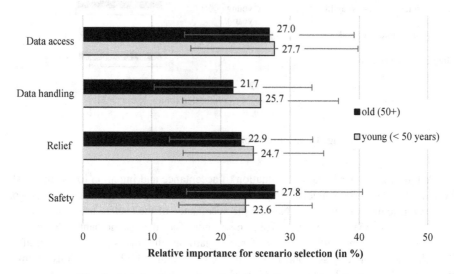

Fig. 2. Relative importance of attributes for scenario selection.

To understand differences in the attributes' importance, it is necessary to consider the evaluations of attribute levels. Figure 3 shows the part-worth utilities of all attribute levels indicating if an attribute level contributes – in tendency – negatively or positively to the scenario decisions.

Starting with the attribute data access, diverse decision patterns are striking for the age groups. For the young group, enabling data access for medical experts (+13.8) and a defined number of trusted persons (+11.7) contributed positively to the scenario decisions, while data access solely for emergency services (−3.1) contributes slightly negatively and for relatives (−22.4) strongly negatively to the scenario decisions. In contrast, for the older group, data access for defined trusted persons represented clearly the best (+22.3) and data access for emergency services (−27.2) definitely the worst option. Compared to that, data access for medical experts (+4.5) and relatives (+0.5) played only a marginal role for the scenario decisions.

Within the attribute *data handling*, short-term storage of data represented the best option (+14.9) for the young group, while long-term storage (−23.3) was clearly not desired. Real time processing (+5.8) and middle-term (+2.6) storage of data received slightly positive utility values. For the older group, short- (+7.9) and middle-term (+6.1) storage of data represented options contributing positively to the scenario decisions, while real time processing (−7.9) and long-term (−6.1) storage were comparably not desired.

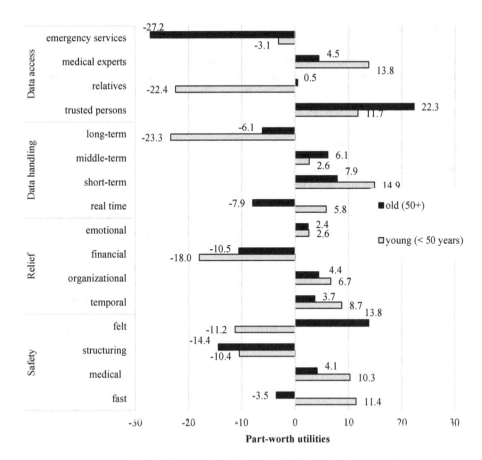

Fig. 3. Part-worth utilities of all attribute levels.

Moving to the benefits of AAL technology usage, rather similar decision patterns were found for the attribute relief of relatives. For both groups, temporal (young: +8.7; old: +3.7), organizational (young: +6.7; old: +4.4), and emotional relief (young: +2.6; old: +2.4) received positive utility values, while financial relief (young: −18.0; old: −10.5) contributed clearly negatively to the decisions. The evaluation pattern was overall stronger pronounced for the young group.

In contrast, the decision patterns referring to the beneficial attribute safety differed strongly for both groups: for the young group, fast (+11.4) and medical (+10.3) safety represented positive options and contributed positively to the scenario decisions, while it was vice versa for structuring (−10.2) and felt (−11.4) safety. Instead, felt safety (13.8) was the most relevant attribute level for the older group and structuring safety (−14.4) represented the comparably least desired option. Fast (−3.5) and medical (+4.1) safety were – in tendency – of less importance.

5 Discussion

The current study represented a first approach to analyze decision patterns with regard to trade-offs between benefits and barriers of AAL technology focusing on a potential impact of age. In the following, the results are discussed and limitations as well as suggestions for future work are given.

5.1 Meaning of Results

Within the results section, isolated evaluations of single benefits, barriers and acceptance of AAL technology were not significantly impacted by age as user factor. These results are contrary to previous research in the field, that identified significant impacts of age on technology acceptance [22] and on the perception of benefits and barriers [18].

In contrast to the evaluations of single benefits and barriers, the results showed influences of age on the decisions between benefits and barriers of technology usage. The results suggest that the investigated barriers data access and in particular data handling were the most decision-relevant factors for younger adults (aged under 50 years). In contrast, the interplay of the benefit safety and the barrier data access was most decision-relevant for the older participants (aged 50 and older).

In more detail, contradicting evaluation patterns of data access and safety were striking. Referred to data access, the younger participants preferred data to be accessible for medical experts and defined trusted persons, and clearly not for relatives. In contrast, the decision pattern of the older participants showed that data should only be accessible for trusted persons, while data should clearly not be accessible for emergency services. With regard to the benefit safety, the fast and medical facets of safety were perceived positively by the younger participants, while they tend to reject structuring and felt safety as decision criteria. In contrast, felt safety contributed clearly positively to the decisions of the older participants, who tend to reject structuring safety as decision-relevant facet of safety. Possible explanations for these differences lie in the age group themselves: the younger participants had different life experiences and circumstances than the older participants and were in particular less experienced in care. Presumably, experiences in care lead to higher needs for felt safety as the participants are – in tendency – more familiar with concerns about their family member in need of care and with the responsibility to care for a loved person in need of care. Future studies should in particular focus on care-relevant aspects (e.g., experience in care, handling of care, attitude towards aging and care) to investigate these potential and suggested relationships in more detail.

5.2 Limitations and Future Work

Besides new insights provided by the decisions and trade-offs between benefits and barriers of using AAL technology differing between younger and older people, there are some limitations of the current study that should be considered for future research.

With regard to the applied methodological procedure, it cannot be ensured that the scenario-based approach and the estimated preferences inevitably predict actual behavior of the participants: hence, the agreement or rejection might be higher or lower in real decisions [40]. Further, the participants were asked to empathize with the situation of having a close family member in need of care in the current study. Hence, they had to imagine to be the family caregiver and take the perspective of a caring relative. For future studies, it should be examined whether the decision profiles change for other perspectives, e.g., being the person in need of care or asking professional caregivers.

Another methodological limitation refers to the limited number of attributes that could be used within the choice-based conjoint analysis. For the current approach, the selection of attributes based on an extensive literature review and preceding studies. Nevertheless, integrating other benefit- or barrier-related aspects (e.g., independency/autonomy of people in need of care, type of recorded data) could provide interesting insights into people's decision behavior. However, extending the number of attributes would then lead to the necessity of applying different approaches such as an adaptive conjoint analysis design [41].

Discussing the sample, future research should aim for reaching a larger sample being more balanced with regard to the level of education as this study's sample was comparably high educated. Focusing on differences of user groups and the impact of user diversity, we assume that other factors besides the biological age – such as attitudes towards aging, attitudes towards care, and individual handling of care – are presumably even more relevant when it comes to concrete and "real" decisions affecting the own life as well as the life of a loved person in need of care. Future studies should therefore focus on more care-relevant individual factors referred to the investigation of real-time decisions. Further, it would be useful to investigate data-driven differences in decision patterns, e.g., by applying cluster analyses or latent class analysis [42]. As a last aspect for future work, the current study was conducted in Germany and represents a very country-specific perspective. Therefore, future research should focus on cross-national comparisons considering people's different cultures, their perspectives on aging and care, and their handling of aging within society.

Acknowledgements. The authors thank all participants for their openness to participate in the study and to share their opinions on relevant decisions regarding usage of AAL technologies. This work has been funded partly by the German Federal Ministry of Education and Research projects Whistle (16SV7530) and PAAL (6SV7955).

References

1. Pickard, L.: A growing care gap? The supply of unpaid care for older people by their adult children in England to 2032. Ageing Soc. **35**(1), 96–123 (2015)
2. WHO, World Health Organization: Aging and Health. https://www.who.int/news-room/fact-sheets/detail/ageing-and-health. Accessed 23 Jan 2018
3. Shaw, J.E., Sicree, R.A., Zimmet, P.Z.: Global estimates of the prevalence of diabetes for 2010 and 2030. Diab. Res. Clin. Pract. **87**(1), 4–14 (2010)

4. Roger, V.L., Go, A.S., Lloyd-Jones, D.M., Adams, R.J., Berry, J.D., Brown, T.M., et al., American Heart Association Statistics Committee and Stroke Statistics Subcommittee: Heart disease and stroke statistics–2011 update: a report from the American Heart Association. Circulation, **123**(4), e18–e209 (2011)
5. Blackman, S., et al.: Ambient assisted living technologies for aging well: a scoping review. J. Intell. Syst. (2015). https://doi.org/10.1515/jisys-2014-0136
6. Rashidi, P., Mihailidis, A.: A survey on ambient-assisted living tools for older adults. IEEE J. Biomed. Health Inform. **17**(3), 579–590 (2013)
7. Peek, S.T.M., Wouters, E.J.M., van Hoof, J., Luijkx, K.G., Boeije, H.R., Vrijhoef, H.J.M.: Factors influencing acceptance of technology for aging in place: a systematic review. Int. J. Med. Inform. **83**(4), 235–248 (2014)
8. Buckley, K., Tran, B., Prandoni, C.: Receptiveness, use and acceptance of telehealth by caregivers of stroke patients in the home. Online J. Issues Nurs. **9**(3), 9 (2004)
9. Larizza, M.F., et al.: In-home monitoring of older adults with vision impairment: exploring patients', caregivers' and professionals' views. J. Am. Med. Inform. Assoc. **21**(1), 56–63 (2014)
10. König, A., Francis, L.E., Joshi, J., Robillard, J.M., Hoey, J.: Qualitative study of affective identities in dementia patients for the design of cognitive assistive technologies. J. Rehab. Assistive Technol. Eng. **4**, 1–15 (2017)
11. van Heek, J., Himmel, S., Ziefle, M.: Caregivers' perspectives on ambient assisted living technologies in professional care contexts. In: Proceedings of the 4th International Conference on Information and Communication Technologies for Ageing Well and e-Health – Volume 1: ICT4AWE, pp. 37–48 (2018). https://doi.org/10.5220/0006691400370048
12. Offermann-van Heek, J., Ziefle, M.: They don't care about us! Care personnel's perspectives on ambient assisted living technology usage: scenario-based survey study. JMIR Rehab. Assistive Technol. **5**(2), e10424 (2018)
13. Beringer, R., Sixsmith, A., Campo, M., Brown, J., McCloskey, R.: The "acceptance" of ambient assisted living: developing an alternate methodology to this limited research lens. In: Abdulrazak, B., Giroux, S., Bouchard, B., Pigot, H., Mokhtari, M. (eds.) ICOST 2011. LNCS, vol. 6719, pp. 161–167. Springer, Heidelberg (2011). https://doi.org/10.1007/978-3-642-21535-3_21
14. Abtoy, A., Touhafi, A., Tahiri, A.: Ambient assisted living system's models and architectures: a survey of the state of the art. J. King Saud Univ.-Comput. Inf. Sci. (2018). https://doi.org/10.1016/j.jksuci.2018.04.009
15. Philips Lifeline: Senior Living Communities (2019). https://philipsseniorliving.com
16. Burstein, A.A., DaDalt, O., Kramer, B., D'Ambrosio, L.A., Coughlin, J.F.: Dementia caregivers and technology acceptance: interest outstrips awareness. Gerontechnology **14**, 45–56 (2015)
17. Demiris, G., et al.: Older adults' attitudes towards and perceptions of "smart home" technologies: a pilot study. Med. Inform. Internet **29**(2), 87–94 (2004)
18. Schomakers, E.-M., Offermann-van Heek, J., Ziefle, M.: Attitudes towards aging and the acceptance of ICT for aging in place. In: Zhou, J., Salvendy, G. (eds.) ITAP 2018. LNCS, vol. 10926, pp. 149–169. Springer, Cham (2018). https://doi.org/10.1007/978-3-319-92034-4_12
19. Himmel, S., Ziefle, M., Lidynia, C., Holzinger, A.: Older users' wish list for technology attributes - a comparison of household and medical technologies. In: Cuzzocrea, A., Kittl, C., Simos, D.E., Weippl, E., Xu, L. (eds.) CD-ARES 2013. LNCS, vol. 8127, pp. 16–27. Springer, Heidelberg (2013). https://doi.org/10.1007/978-3-642-40511-2_2

20. Lai, C.K., Chung, J.C., Leung, N.K., Wong, J.C., Mak, D.P.: A survey of older Hong Kong people's perceptions of telecommunication technologies and telecare devices. J. Telemed. Telecare **16**(8), 441–446 (2010)
21. Chappell, N.L., Zimmer, Z.: Receptivity to new technology among older adults. Disabil. Rehabil. **21**(5–6), 222–230 (1999)
22. Arning, K., Ziefle, M.: Different perspectives on technology acceptance: the role of technology type and age. In: Holzinger, A., Miesenberger, K. (eds.) USAB 2009. LNCS, vol. 5889, pp. 20–41. Springer, Heidelberg (2009). https://doi.org/10.1007/978-3-642-10308-7_2
23. Luce, R.D., Tukey, J.W.: Simultaneous conjoint measurement: a new type of fundamental measurement. J. Math. Psychol. **1**(1), 1–27 (1964)
24. Orme, B.: Interpreting the Results of Conjoint Analysis, Getting Started with Conjoint Analysis: Strategies for Product Design and Pricing Research, pp. 77–89. Research Publications LLC, Madison (2010)
25. Green, P.E., Srinivasan, V.: Conjoint analysis in consumer research: issues and outlook. J. Consum. Res. **5**(2), 103–123 (1978)
26. Baier, D., Brusch, M.: Erfassung von Kundenpräferenzen für Produkte und Dienstleistungen. [Collection of customer preferences for products and services]. In: Baier, D., Brusch, M. (eds.) Conjoint Analysis. Methods, Applications, practical examples, pp. 3–18. Springer, Berlin (2009). https://doi.org/10.1007/978-3-642-00754-5_1
27. Arning, K.: Conjoint measurement. In: Matthes, J., Davis, C.S., Potter, R.F. (eds.) International Encyclopedia of Communication Research Methods, pp. 1–10. Wiley, Hoboken (2017). https://doi.org/10.1002/9781118901731
28. Alriksson, S., Öberg, T.: Conjoint analysis for environmental evaluation. Environ. Sci. Pollut. Res. **15**(3), 244–257 (2008)
29. Phillips, K.A., Maddala, T., Johnson, F.R.: Measuring preferences for health care interventions using conjoint analysis: an application to HIV testing. Health Serv. Res. **37**(6), 1681–1705 (2002)
30. Orme, B.: Formulating attributes and levels in conjoint analysis. Sawtooth Software research paper, pp. 1–4 (2002)
31. Steggell, C.D., Hooker, K., Bowman, S., Choun, S., Kim, S.J.: The role of technology for healthy aging among Korean and Hispanic women in the United States: a pilot study. Gerontechnology **9**(4), 433–449 (2010)
32. Wilkowska, W., Ziefle, M., Himmel, S.: Perceptions of personal privacy in smart home technologies: do user assessments vary depending on the research method? In: Tryfonas, T., Askoxylakis, I. (eds.) HAS 2015. LNCS, vol. 9190, pp. 592–603. Springer, Cham (2015). https://doi.org/10.1007/978-3-319-20376-8_53
33. Joe, J., Chaudhuri, S., Chung, J., Thompson, H., Demiris, G.: Older adults' attitudes and preferences regarding a multifunctional wellness tool: a pilot study. Inform. Health Soc. Care **41**(2), 143–158 (2016)
34. Wild, K., Boise, L., Lundell, J., Foucek, A.: Unobtrusive in-home monitoring of cognitive and physical health: reactions and perceptions of older adults. J. Appl. Gerontol. **27**(2), 181–200 (2008)
35. Lorenzen-Huber, L., Boutain, M., Camp, L.J., Shankar, K., Connelly, K.H.: Privacy, technology, and aging: a proposed framework. Ageing Int. **36**(2), 232–252 (2011)
36. Himmel, S., Zaunbrecher, B.S., Wilkowska, W., Ziefle, M.: The youth of today designing the smart city of tomorrow. In: Kurosu, M. (ed.) HCI 2014. LNCS, vol. 8512, pp. 389–400. Springer, Cham (2014). https://doi.org/10.1007/978-3-319-07227-2_37
37. Xu, H., Dinev, T., Smith, H.J., Hart, P.: Examining the formation of individual's privacy concerns: toward an integrative view. In: ICIS 2008 Proceedings, p. 6 (2008)

38. Morton, A.: Measuring inherent privacy concern and desire for privacy - a pilot survey study of an instrument to measure dispositional privacy concern. In: International Conference on Social Computing (SocialCom), pp. 468–477. IEEE (2013)
39. Sawtooth Software: Testing the CBC Design. Technical Paper Series. Sawtooth Software (Version 9.6.1): [Software for the conceptual design and analysis of the online conjoint questionnaire]. Software Software Inc., Sequim (2018) http://www.sawtoothsoftware.com/help/lighthouse-studio/manual/index.html?hid_web_cbc_designs_6.html
40. Ajzen, I., Fishbein, M.: Understanding Attitudes and Predicting Social Behavior. Prentice-Hall, Englewood Cliffs (1980)
41. Green, P.E., Krieger, A.M., Agarwal, M.K.: Adaptive conjoint analysis: some caveats and suggestions. J. Mark. Res. **28**, 215–222 (1991)
42. DeSarbo, W.S., Wedel, M., Vriens, M., Ramaswamy, V.: Latent class metric conjoint analysis. Mark. Lett. **3**(3), 273–288 (1992)

Mapping the Future of Hearables: Lessons from Online and the "Oldest Old" Consumers

Taylor R. Patskanick[(⊠)], Julie Miller, Lisa A. D'Ambrosio,
Chaiwoo Lee, and Joseph F. Coughlin

Massachusetts Institute of Technology AgeLab, Cambridge, MA 02142, USA
trpats@mit.edu

Abstract. Living with hearing loss presents challenges for an aging population. Hearing loss without intervention is associated with a plethora of negative consequences for older adults including loneliness, cognitive decline and falls. In this study, members of the MIT AgeLab 85+ Lifestyle Leaders Panel were surveyed and interviewed to learn about their experiences with hearing loss and audio-assistive device adoption, and their hopes for the hearables of the future. Additionally, 583 written customer reviews were accumulated from Amazon.com and HearingTracker.com for analysis. Several themes emerged along with an imperative to industry to explore further the enduring challenges and future opportunities of human-hearable design.

Keywords: Hearing loss · Hearables · Online reviews · Older adults · Technology adoption

1 Introduction

As humans our sense of hearing is often considered vital to our ability to participate in and experience the world around us. Hearing engages our brains in continuous, complex information processing and is a powerful means of communication we often take for granted. In the United States, current epidemiological audiometry estimates suggest approximately one in three people between the ages of 65 and 74 has hearing loss, and nearly half of people 75 and older have difficulty hearing [1]. Unprecedented global longevity means that more people than ever before are living to an age where they will experience age-related hearing loss (or presbycusis) [2]. By 2050, the proportion of the world's population over age 60 will nearly double from 12% to 22% [3]. The World Health Organization (WHO) estimates that by 2025 over 500 million people over 60 years of age worldwide will suffer significant impairment from presbycusis [4]. In the United States, the number of people aged 85+ is projected to more than triple from 6 million to 20 million by 2060 [5]. Because hearing loss increases with age, particularly after age 65, these "oldest old" adults are more likely to have had some hearing loss and are in the position to offer a unique understanding of the motivations, challenges and opportunities of hearable adoption in the latest phase of life.

Hearing loss without intervention is associated with a plethora of biopsychosocial consequences for older adults. For example, in the United States, census survey estimates approximate that over 42.6 million older adults suffer from chronic loneliness

J. Zhou and G. Salvendy (Eds.): HCII 2019, LNCS 11592, pp. 267–280, 2019.
https://doi.org/10.1007/978-3-030-22012-9_20

[6]. Current research suggests there is a relationship between a sensory loss, such as hearing loss, and loneliness, particularly among older adults [7, 8]. Additionally, many studies have demonstrated strong associations between magnitude of hearing loss and accelerated cognitive decline, greater risk of dementia onset, and higher risk of falling [9–12]. Hearing loss negatively impacts the vestibular system and balance control, increases cognitive load, reducing people's ability to multi-task, and fundamentally changes how individuals evaluate, interact with and overcome obstacles within the environment [13]. As a result, research has continued to test the association between auditory interventions, such as hearing aid adoption, or modification of hearing impairment indicators (e.g., degree of hearing loss, hearing-related quality of life, etc.) and decreased loneliness, delayed cognitive decline, and reduced fall risk [14–18].

Hearing aids, direct-to-consumer devices and other audio-assistive devices referred to as *hearables* are technological solutions shown to promote positive outcomes among individuals with hearing loss. The development of hearables began with the early stethoscope, used by medical professionals to obtain biological information and eventually as a diagnostic instrument [19]. Medical grade hearing aids as well as audio headphones came with the boom of the radio and telecommunication industries in the early 1900s [19]. But it was not until the release of the Sony Walkman portable cassette player in 1979 that audio electronics offered beloved and customized experiences [20]. Today, though there is no universal definition of a hearable, they are best understood as a sub-category of wearables to be worn in or around the ear that use computing technology [21]. Current hearables include devices from smart hearing aids to wireless earbuds. They have evolved not only to improve individual hearing ability and communication, but to also collect biometric data, connect across devices, and offer more customization than ever before. Despite these advances, however, a gap persists between consumers who would benefit from hearable technologies and those who adopt these devices.

As hearable technologies proliferate and become accessible across diverse marketplaces, consumers face challenges around the choice of device that is best for them – what works best at the price points they can afford. Because many hearable technologies can be relatively expensive, consumers may seek expertise on which products are worth investing in. Traditionally organizations such as AARP or Consumer Reports served as clearinghouses for objective product advice. Yet other people one knows are often people's most trusted sources of advice. With the proliferation of platforms and websites that offer users the opportunity to review products and services, these public review systems provide people with an easy means to get advice from "other people like them."

Reviews offer rich insights into the narratives and nuances of the product purchase decision, real-world functionality, and normalization of user experience. Because such reviews can be accessed from anywhere, for older adults in particular they offer convenient opportunities to compare experiences, products and prices. For hearable technologies, which may not be widely used, online reviews provide potential users with reviews from a larger number and wider range of consumers with experience with a given product or device under varying conditions.

Traditionally the hearable industry has been medicalized: hearing aids were pre-scribed by doctors and fitted and adjusted by specialists. With the rise of a wider range of consumer audio-assistive devices, however, hearables have become much more accessible to all consumers. Given these shifts in the industry, little is known about what older consumers and online reviewers expect and desire from their hearable device(s). The objective of this study is to better understand hearable consumers' experiences with, expectations of, and aspirations for their devices. In an effort to understand the current state of human-hearable interactions, we draw on user reviews and survey data to explore consumers' current device use, overall experiences, and ideas for future device design.

2 Data Collection

Two unique sources of data were collected for the purposes of this study: online consumer reviews of the top 10 and bottom 10 hearable products by average user rating generated from HearingTracker.com and Amazon.com (see Tables 1 and 2); and in-depth interviews, discussion groups, and a survey with the Massachusetts Institute of Technology (MIT) AgeLab's 85+ Lifestyle Leaders panel. The online reviews provide snapshots of people's experiences with different devices and offer a picture of the nature of information available to consumers who are considering these different technologies. In contrast, the data from the Lifestyle Leaders offer in-depth portraits of people's experiences with different devices and insight into the decision-making pro-cess older adults rely on when choosing the hearable technology that is right for them.

Table 1. Top 10 and bottom 10 products from HearingTracker.com

Top 10 products	Bottom 10 products
1. Unitron N Moxi Fit Pro	1. Starkey Halo 2 RIC 13 i2400
2. Phonak Audeo V 312T V90	2. Oticon Agil Pro miniRITE
3. Widex BEYOND Fusion 2 440	3. Oticon Alta Pro CIC
4. Phonak Audeo B R B90	4. Oticon Chili SP9
5. Oticon Opn 1 BTE13 PP	5. Phonak Virto B Titanium IIC B90
6. Kirkland Signature (Costco) 8.0 Premium Hearing Aids	6. Starkey Muse micro RIC 312t i2400
7. Oticon Alta2 Pro miniRITE	7. Oticon Alta2 Pro BTE13 100
8. Kirkland Signature (Costco) 7.0 Premium Hearing Aids	8. Siemens Nitro x01 301
9. Unitron Moxi Kiss 20	9. Phonak Virto B Titanium CIC B90
10. Signia Pure Primax 13 BT 7px	10. Beltone Legend RIE 64 9

Table 2. Top 10 and bottom 10 products from Amazon.com

Top 10 products	Bottom 10 products
1. Toedler Ear Hearing Amplifier	1. HEARNA HAS338 Amplifier
2. Otofonix Apex Mini Hearing Amplifier	2. Flexzion Digital Hearing Amplifier Device
3. Otofonix Elite Mini Hearing Amplifier	3. NewEAR Digital Personal Sound Hearing Amplifier Aid
4. Empower Hearing Amplifier	4. Woodland Whisper II
5. Otofonix Encore Premium Hearing Amplifier	5. Soundlab Hearing Amplifier
6. Neosonic Digital Hearing Amplifier	6. Ultra Ear Hearing Enhancer Communication Aid (Walker Game Ear)
7. HA-302 from Hearing Assist	7. HEARNA HAS302 Amplifier
8. Ulaif Hearing Amplifier	8. Woodland Whisper
9. LumiHear Hearing Amplifier	9. AuriClear BTE Digital Bluetooth Amplifier
10. Wellness Tree Digital Personal Sound Amplifier	10. LifeEar Hearing Amplifier

2.1 Online Reviews

Online reviews were collected from HearingTracker.com and Amazon.com. The reviews on HearingTracker.com included a Hearing Tracker Rank based on a 10-question survey taken by users, as well as information about completeness and recency of the written review [22]. Some reviews also included audiograms and information about service providers. While Amazon.com does not sell medical grade hearing aids, the search term "hearing aid" was utilized to identify hearable devices designed to act most like a hearing aid. These products were then sorted by average customer review and compiled by the highest and lowest ranked products. The top reviews for each product, as determined by other site users' indication of "overall helpfulness," were included for analysis. Only products with more than three total reviews were included in analysis.

A total of 583 reviews were collected; 579 reviews were included in analysis. Four reviews were excluded from analysis as they were repeated reviews from the same user. Of the 579, 441 (76.2%) reviews were from HearingTracker.com and 138 (23.7%) reviews were from Amazon.com. The majority of products reviewed were audio amplifiers and receiver in the ear (RIC) hearing aids (HAs).

Across both platforms, there was wide variance in the date the review was completed, length of device use prior to review, reviewer relationship to device wearer, occupations of reviewers, and severity as well as onset of the device user's hearing loss. For example, the oldest review dates back approximately 5 years prior to this analysis, while the newest reviews were left less than 24 h prior to the time of this analysis. Several users had been wearing a device for over 40 years, while others had received a device a day prior to writing a review.

Three variables – person for whom hearable was bought, gender, and geographic location – were chosen to describe online review demographics because this information was publicly available and highlights potential considerations for different groups of consumers. Reviewers most often reported purchasing a device for themselves or their mothers. Gender of reviewers was determined by the username as displayed on the review posting. Gender was dichotomized into male and female. Usernames that were uncategorizable or listed as anonymous were grouped together in their own category. Across both platforms, the majority (65.1%) of reviewers were anonymous or uncategorizable. Relative to the percentage of anonymous or uncategorizable usernames, 34.9% of usernames were clearly male or female-sounding. Reviews that could be coded for gender had overwhelmingly male-sounding names (see Fig. 1).

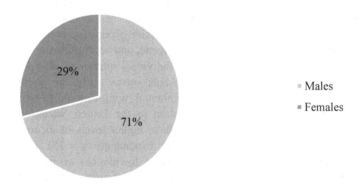

Fig. 1. Dichotomized gender demographic of reviewers, excluding anonymous users (n = 199).

When isolated by platform, 57% of Amazon.com reviewers were male compared to 43% female, while 80% of HearingTracker.com reviewers were male compared to just 20% female. For reviews where U.S. location was available, the majority of reviewers were concentrated in California and Florida. Texas, South Carolina, Pennsylvania, Oregon, and Michigan were closely behind. Among reviews for which an international location could be identified, reviewers were heavily geographically located in Canada.

Among Amazon.com reviews only, products listed in the bottom 10 product list were rated an average of 3.15 stars while products in the top 10 product list had an average of 4.59 stars. Similarly, more users were engaging with Amazon.com's top 10 product reviews versus the bottom 10 product reviews as measured by rated helpfulness. An average of 60 users per review found reviews among the top 10 products helpful compared to just 21 users per review for the bottom 10 reviews. Longer reviews were correlated with greater "helpfulness." Amazon.com product reviewers also more often indicated they had started with just one device for use in one ear as opposed to purchasing devices for two ears. Amazon.com reviewers were likely to state that they had tried other types of hearable products before. A smaller sub-population of Amazon.com reviewers noted they were using a device as a backup or alternative to a regular hearing aid due to cost barriers or practicalities of using hearing aids during events like travel or sporting. Amazon.com reviewers were more likely to provide an update to their review later on.

2.2 MIT AgeLab Lifestyle Leaders Panel

The Lifestyle Leaders are a panel of adults aged 85 and older who meet bimonthly at the MIT AgeLab in Cambridge, Massachusetts, to discuss a range of topics related to living longer. The MIT AgeLab hosted a Lifestyle Leaders workshop exploring hearing loss and hearables; data were collected via multiple methods. All participants were invited to complete a detailed questionnaire prior to the workshop either online or on paper. The questionnaire included questions on: (1) current hearing conditions and any changes in their hearing; (2) effects of hearing changes they have experienced; (3) experiences around adjusting to changes in hearing; and (4) attitudes and experiences regarding hearing technologies and devices. All participants were assigned to different small discussion groups according to their self-reported and previously-observed degree of hearing loss. The small discussion groups represented four degrees of hearing loss: no evident loss, and little, moderate, and severe hearing loss. A subset of panel members participated in additional individual interviews in order to capture breadth of device use (e.g., use of hearing aids versus use of an amplifier) and a spectrum of adaptive behaviors (e.g., environmental modifications) to hearing loss.

Compared with the overall 85+ population in the United States, the Lifestyle Leaders are overwhelmingly Caucasian and have higher levels of income, education and better overall health. Among questionnaire respondents (n = 25), 79.2% reported living independently in their own homes, condos, townhomes or apartments. A majority of the Lifestyle Leader respondents are widowed or married/living with a partner; thus most live alone or with a spouse/partner. Just under half receive help with daily tasks (e.g., shopping, making appointments) from adult children, spouses or friends. Just over half of the survey respondents identified as male (52.2%) and 47.8% identified as female. The average age was 89.96. Most respondents also participated in the Lifestyle Leaders workshop, meaning that the demographics of workshop participants closely mirrored that of survey respondents.

The vast majority (92%) of the Lifestyle Leaders reported that they have experienced or are currently experiencing hearing loss. Among all Lifestyle Leaders surveyed, 84% most frequently reported having either a little or a lot of trouble hearing (as opposed to no trouble hearing or no usable hearing) in both ears. Similar to online reviewers' descriptions, the Lifestyle Leaders also reported wide variance in age at hearing loss onset. Among those experiencing hearing loss, 43.5% stated they first noticed changes in their hearing only within the past 5 years. Unsurprisingly, the majority of the Lifestyle Leaders also report being relatively new hearable users – only having used their device(s) for 5 years or less. Overall, three-quarters of Lifestyle Leaders (75%) said they currently use a hearing aid or other audio-assistive device. Among Lifestyle Leaders wearing hearing aids, they most often reported wearing them in both ears every day for more than 8 h a day. Additionally, the Lifestyle Leaders used audio-enhancing headphones and Bluetooth streaming microphones both in place of and as augmentation to hearing aids.

3 Findings

3.1 Device Performance

Across both data sources, the theme of improving overall device performance was mentioned the most clearly and frequently. Online reviewers and Lifestyle Leaders expressed a desire for greater clarity, better reduction of background noise, and improved music quality. As one reviewer described their experience with background noise, "If there's loud background noise I can't hear at all. Overall it's like listening to a radio that's on the fritz." Many of the Lifestyle Leaders indicated that they will take off or stop using their hearables in response to background noise. "In a crowded restaurant, I typically remove the devices because they amplify the background noise, and this is an intolerable irritant," said one Lifestyle Leader. Focused efforts on improving the functional performance of hearables across everyday environments could contribute to increased device adoption in the future.

3.2 Physical Product Design

Hearables also leave much to be desired when it comes to physical product design. For online reviewers and Lifestyle Leaders, stigma related to device use came up less often compared to the desire for a larger physical device with improved access to a power button and volume knob and bigger batteries. One Lifestyle Leader with late onset hearing loss stated, "The craziest thing–here's what the problem is, everybody is vain, and they want to have hearing aids that nobody sees, but what the hell of a difference does it make if you're 70, 80 years old, if you have a hearing aid? Doesn't make a damn bit of difference, so you shouldn't care about it." Current device size was also associated with a host of concerns from poor fit in the ear to persistent loss of the device during daily tasks, forcing many users to use a personal sound amplifying product (PSAP) as a less expensive, more accessible alternative to hearing aids. Amazon.com alone sells over 300 different types of PSAPs – many of which are used by reviewers as alternatives to hearing aids in scenarios such as travel and sporting events. A male Lifestyle Leader and routine wearer of Bose Hearphones described his transition away from hearing aids: "I was asked to bring them [his Widex hearing aids] in today and I couldn't find them. Six thousand dollars and I don't know where it is. I have become somewhat of a prophet of these [his Bose Hearphones]. I proselytize actively."

3.3 Device Features

In addition to highlighting device functionality and design needs, when the Lifestyle Leaders were asked about what they hoped future hearable devices would do better than current iterations, many mentioned specific features that overlapped with those from online consumer reviewers. Seamless integration across devices (e.g. TV, phone), rechargeable batteries, waterproof properties, and ability to adjust volume or program settings for individual ears came up most frequently in both data sources. Both data sources also emphasized the relationship between their hearable and other technology devices; however, this connectivity was slightly more salient among online reviewers rather than Lifestyle Leaders, possibly due to age differences between the two data sources.

Bluetooth. Online reviewers in particular expressed either a deep satisfaction or outright disappointment with the quality of their device's Bluetooth. The reviewed PSAPs did not have Bluetooth capabilities, but among hearing aids reviewed, 50% had built in Bluetooth capabilities not requiring a secondary accessory or other device. Often described as "crackling," "popping" and "too much static," the quality of music, podcasts, phone calls or other audio material streamed through devices leaves much to be desired. One online reviewer stated about their Widex hearing aids, "I'm very disappointed in the sound quality of Bluetooth for conversation: it has some static and is somewhat distorted – as a psychologist who needs to talk to my patients on the phone, I must resort to my trusty Bang and Olufson headphones instead." On the other hand, others found customizable Bluetooth features highly desirable. According to a reviewer of Kirkland Signature (Costco) hearing aids, "I was blown away by my iTunes streaming music directly to my hearing aids directly from my iPhone 7+. The sound clarity and bass is hard to believe when you first hear it. You can even use iOS' sound equalizer to output sound tuned to your particular preference."

However, users also ran into trouble initially pairing or experiencing random unpairing of their hearables – particularly with cellular phones and vehicles. Two online reviewers illustrate these concerns best: "They [my hearing aids] continually disconnect from the Bluetooth and can't reconnect without me having to open and close the battery;" and "My Mercedes car Bluetooth allows me to dial out and speak directly, but I cannot receive incoming calls without having to find the phone. Driving whilst holding a phone is a penalty offence here [in the UK] so that is not possible and is driving me to distraction." As these reviewers noted, many found their own workarounds when their Bluetooth connectivity did not function, and despite Bluetooth dysfunction, user reviews generally highlighted their reliance on it and its significance for them. As one HearingTracker.com reviewer wrote, "The Bluetooth connection to phone is a feature that I would find hard to live without."

Mobile Applications. The state of current innovation in hearable-device interaction generally requires use of a third-party mobile application or "app." Online consumer reviewers overwhelmingly use an app with their hearable device if one is available. As one tech-savvy Lifestyle Leader mentioned, "Those who don't have an iPhone or a smartphone [connected to their device] aren't as happy." In fact, in reviews alone, the word "app" was mentioned at least 91 times. Mobile apps serve a variety of purposes for online reviewers and Lifestyle Leaders, including troubleshooting, controlling functionality, and preprogramming hearing environments. Many users noted the app associated with their hearable was either incompatible with or unavailable on their Android or iOS operating system, depending on the hearable model. However, when available, these applications still lack important practical capabilities. One online reviewer and new user of Kirkland Signature (Costco) hearing aids pointed out that the "app lacks a find-my-lost-hearing-aid feature, which ironically would have come in very handy on week two." Another reviewer mentioned, "I find the app lacking pretty much every feature I go looking for, starting with a basic equalizer. With everything being automatically adjusted constantly there are times when certain frequency ranges are amplified excessively. I would dearly love to just take control and tell it what to do at times. No can-do."

3.4   Trust in Customer Service and Audiology

In addition to hearable design and features, the future of human-hearable interaction will be built on the cornerstones of human relationships. For these samples, customer service can make or break the overall hearable fitting and acquisition experience and impacts short-term device adoption. Perceived competence of fitting specialists and/or company customer service representatives and timeliness of device delivery came up frequently among online reviewers. For example, for hearables acquired through Amazon.com, free shipping and rapid turnaround from order to delivery were salient among positive reviews. Comparably, for hearing aids acquired from Costco, quality of the in-store hearing specialist was varied. As one review commenter detailed, "Not to be mean, but I would suggest checking reviews about various Costcos in your area in regards to the Hearing Specialists. Or even just visiting another one. My original guy was wonderful and a great man but either didn't have the training or understood all the programming advantages."

Even when a device was not a good fit for a variety of reasons, positive customer service experiences could compensate for perceived device and company shortcomings. One reviewer explained, "This item was not comfortable for me, but I was quite impressed with the consideration afforded to me by the Otofonix staff. They made no attempt to convince me that I should not return them, and my payment was promptly refunded. I would recommend this product even though it was not comfortable for me personally." Nonmedical grade devices, such as those found on Amazon.com, accompanied by warranties, free and easy returns, and trial periods had reviews with more positive language and perceptions of company transparency. These reviewers were also more likely to suggest they would continue using the device. "Additionally, as icing on the cake, the company stands behind the product as a purchaser would hope; quickly, honestly, and with absolutely zero run-around. Customer support could not be better," explained one Amazon.com amplifier reviewer.

However, when an error or technical concern with their device arose, many online reviewers were apt to blame the hearable company. As one reviewer of a bottom 10 product stated, "I wish I could start all over again with another company." This was in contrast to the Lifestyle Leaders. When considering blame around the shortcomings of their devices or their failure to restore hearing capabilities completely, the Lifestyle Leaders often placed the locus of blame internally – on their own hearing difficulties – instead of on the company that made their device. Trust seemed to play a role in this exchange. As one Lifestyle Leader said, "I wholly trust Williams Sound [the manufacturer of her audio-assistive device]. I blame my hearing, not the Siemens company [manufacturer of her hearing aids] for my problems…" Of Lifestyle Leaders who responded, 64.7% of Lifestyle Leaders indicate they fully or somewhat trust the company who makes their hearable device (see Fig. 2).

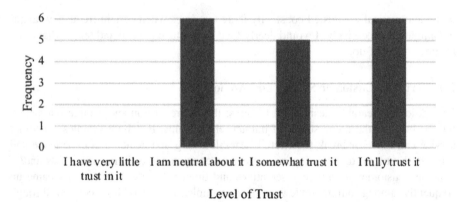

Fig. 2. Trust in companies that manufacture hearing aids and other audio-assistive devices among the Lifestyle Leaders (n = 17)

Additionally, the Lifestyle Leaders trusted the process of hearing aid acquisition. The most commonly trusted sources to help them decide on a brand of device include audiologists, doctors and organizations like AARP, Consumer Reports and the Better Business Bureau (see Fig. 3).

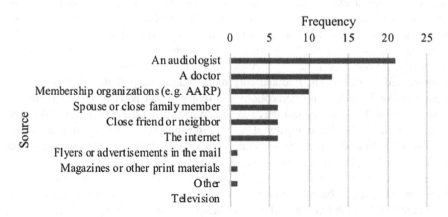

Fig. 3. Trusted sources of advice for hearing aids and other audio-assistive devices among the Lifestyle Leaders (n = 23)

The Lifestyle Leaders and online reviewers frequently mentioned the role and professional expertise of the audiologist in facilitating acquisition of a "good" hearing instrument. For online reviewers there was greater distrust in audiologists who only sell specific devices. One long-time member of HearingTracker.com advised others, "Try many brands - don't get railroaded into brands by audiologists whose business is limited to certain brands." The Lifestyle Leaders, however, had high trust in their hearing providers when it comes to their hearing health: they are most often receiving information from or talking with an audiologist, primary care physician or other doctor about hearables compared to other sources of potential advice. Furthermore, provider coordination could significantly ease or hinder access and continued use of hearables. One Lifestyle Leader stated, "I was actually going to another doctor who suggested this doctor to me because he knew he wasn't doing as good a job as he should be doing, and it made a world of difference, because once I got to this new doctor, I could actually hear much better." However, as many online reviewers expressed, repeated and long-wait times in between appointments created bottlenecks around device troubleshooting and fitting. This is perhaps best illustrated by one Lifestyle Leader and new user of hearing aids who said, "I got the hearing aid through my primary care doctor. But then he sent me to another specialist. That one sent me to another set of people, specialists." This Lifestyle Leader visited specialist doctors and an audiologist, yet her new hearing aids still fit her poorly and, as a result, she does not wear them.

3.5   Troubleshooting

Regardless of age, hearable adoption is often accompanied by learning a new technology and troubleshooting when things go wrong. The Lifestyle Leaders described some of the difficulties in learning how to use a new device. One self-described "tech-savvy" Lifestyle Leader said, "You open up the box, and there are 14 different wires and connectors there. And the book is about this thick. And I just haven't had the gumption or the unction to go through the whole thing." Many Lifestyle Leaders used a variety of resources when they needed help with their devices, but when asked about the most effective methods to teach them new skills about their device(s), they repeatedly mentioned the value of a mentoring-based or classroom-style teaching model. A Lifestyle Leader and new user of hearing aids exclaimed, "[I have] a strict income and I have to question money-wise things. But I have time, and I would love to have somebody to assist me until I feel comfortable I'm okay."

A feature of online reviews is that consumers can access them not only when making purchase decisions but also when troubleshooting. Hearable users took to reviews to detail an exact problem they were having with their device, to share sources of information for problem solving, and to caution others of defects or poor aspects of devices. A new hearing aid user from HearingTracker.com warned, "Within 5 days [my hearing aids] were sent back to repair but came back with the same problem." Several reviewers frequently included the quality of the device instruction manual as a contributor to their overall satisfaction with a hearable product. A verified purchaser of an Amazon.com amplifier mentioned, "The instructions: The text, although it contained a few errors, was pretty easy to see and comprehend. The pictures are so tiny they are basically worthless."

4   Conclusion

Historically, the hearable industry has been medicalized – specialists address the challenge of fitting an advanced piece of intricate technology within the ear and adjusting it to meet the user's needs as best as they are able. Meanwhile, however, the competitive development of new audio-assistive devices and market demand requires all hearables to be better, leaner and more connected. The growth of artificial intelligence and the Internet of Things means that consumers will increasingly demand more and demand better of their devices.

Older adults and online consumers alike are inundated with choices and must negotiate quality, brand recognition, price, and style when they decide to purchase a hearable. A mixed methods approach with the MIT AgeLab's Lifestyle Leaders and online consumer reviews was used to explore engagement with and decision making about hearable technologies.

The experiences and observations of these consumers reviewers offer unique insights. The first is that generational differences in expectations around aging, hearing devices and the companies that make them may change over time. As Baby Boomers, for example, age into hearing loss, their expectations are likely to shift around phenomena like device functionality and connectivity compared with previous generations of users in the oldest old market segment. How will these expectations of hearing devices evolve for later "digital native" generations as they grow older? Even now there are rapid changes around norms of wearing something in the ear – as long as it is not the "big, beige and boring" of hearing aids of old: witness the rise in popularity of products like Apple AirPods or Bose SoundSport in-ear headphones [23]. Similarly, increased access to information and social media have forced companies to embrace a new reality of transparency – a transparency that can shape long-term brand loyalty, recognition and trust over time. Generational cohorts from Millennials to Baby Boomers perceive access to and interact with their favorite companies in different ways. How will they hold manufacturers responsible for their hearing experiences with a certain device, and how might this change as these groups grow older?

Another implication is the capacity of the hearing care industry to anticipate and adapt to the development of technologies such as amplifiers, microphones, conversation-enhancing headphones and other direct to consumer products that consumers like the Lifestyle Leaders have found to be as functional (if not more functional) and less expensive than hearing aids. Devices are increasingly linked and integrated around the user experience. How might products from the hearing care industry, for example, fit into a bigger picture of a connected smart home? Future investment into new hearing technologies will have to strike a balance between delivering on sophistication and integration – while still being easy for wearers to use – and offering accessible value.

Without intervention, hearing loss has major negative effects on loneliness, cognitive functioning, and fall risk [7–13]. Further research is needed to assess the relationship between online review use, hearable purchase decision-making, and subsequent adoption rates. Additional research should also investigate cross-cultural similarities and differences in experiences with hearing loss and hearable adoption across age cohorts, gender and geography. Emerging hearable technologies for an aging population will require industry to stay up-to-date and engaged with an older end-user. As one reviewer wrote, "If Starkey wants to succeed in this market space they cannot ignore the poor quality of this current offering. The Baby Boomers that are just reaching retirement age are technologically sophisticated." Both Lifestyle Leaders and online consumer reviewers are an active and engaged marketplace - ready not only for the promise of the future hearable, but to also hold hearable technologies and the companies that make them to a high standard. The hearing care industry will always face the challenge of forging imperfect solutions at an imperfect cost. But as the demand for hearing support increases, the industry has an opportunity to leverage emerging science and technologies to deliver increased ease in access and value from using hearing aids and audio-assistive devices that can yield life-changing outcomes.

This is a cross-sectional study that leverages multiple data sources collected at a single point in time. Findings were integrated across data sources; however, certain themes emerged more saliently among online reviewers versus the Lifestyle Leaders and vice versa. Results from these data sources may not be generalizable. User reviews are written by self-selected individuals who may have particularly good or bad experiences with a product. Reviewers may be more likely to be male. Findings from the Lifestyle Leaders are not generalizable to all individuals aged 85 and up or to all older adults. However, a mixed methods approach adds value to the reliability and validity of results and hedges against the limitations and biases of a single methodological approach.

In addition to directly surveying the Lifestyle Leaders, online reviews represent a popular source older adults may use to help make a purchase decision about a hearable. Hearable reviews, in particular, differ from reviews written about other technology products because they are heavily impacted by degree of hearing loss and device fitting. Two individuals with the same device and hearing provider may have very different experiences and levels of satisfaction. Findings from online consumer reviews and the MIT AgeLab's 85+ Lifestyle Leaders Panel create an imperative for further research, development and adoption of best products and practices for the hearables market.

Acknowledgements. This study was completed with support from Sonova Holding AG and an unrestricted grant from AARP.

References

1. National Institute on Deafness and Other Communication Disorders (NIDCD), NIH Pub. No. 97-4235, March 2016. https://www.nidcd.nih.gov/health/age-related-hearing-loss. Accessed 29 Jan 2019
2. Coughlin, J.: The Longevity Economy: Unlocking the World's Fastest-Growing, Most Misunderstood Market. PublicAffairs, New York (2017)
3. Steverson, M.: Ageing and health. World Health Organization (WHO), February 2018. https://www.who.int/news-room/fact-sheets/detail/ageing-and-health. Accessed 29 Jan 2019
4. Blevins, N., Deschler, D., Kunins, L.: Presbycusis- UpToDate. Wolters Kluwer. https://www.uptodate.com/contents/presbycusis. Accessed 29 Jan 2019
5. Mather, M., Jacobsen, J., Pollard, K.: Aging in the United States. Population Bulletin, Population Reference Bureau, December 2015. https://www.prb.org/wp-content/uploads/2016/01/aging-us-population-bulletin-1.pdf. Accessed 29 Jan 2019
6. AARP Research, Loneliness Among Older Adults: A National Survey of Adults 45+ (2010). https://www.aarp.org/content/dam/aarp/research/surveys_statistics/general/2012/loneliness-fact-sheet.doi.10.26419%252Fres.00064.002.pdf. Accessed 29 Jan 2019

7. Sung, Y., Li, L., Blake, C., Betz, J., Lin, F.: Association of hearing loss and loneliness in older adults. J. Aging Health **28**(6), 979–994 (2016). https://doi.org/10.1177/0898264315614570

8. Mick, P., Parfyonov, M., Wittich, W., Phillips, N., Pichora-Fuller, M.: Associations between sensory loss and social networks, participation, support, and loneliness. Can. Fam. Physician **64**, e33–e41 (2018)

9. Lin, F., et al.: Hearing loss and cognitive decline in older adults. JAMA Intern. Med. **173**(4), 293–299 (2013). https://doi.org/10.1001/jamainternmed.2013.1868

10. Deal, J., et al.: Hearing impairment and incident dementia and cognitive decline in older adults: the health ABC study. J. Gerontol.: Med. Sci. **72**(5), 703–709 (2017). https://doi.org/10.1093/gerona/glw069

11. Su, P., et al.: Age-related hearing loss and dementia: a 10-year national population-based study. Eur. Arch. Oto-Rhino-Laryngol. **274**, 2327–2334 (2017). https://doi.org/10.1007/s00405-017-4471-5

12. Lin, F., Ferrucci, L.: Hearing loss and falls among older adults in the United States. Arch. Intern. Med. **172**(4), 369–371 (2012). https://doi.org/10.1001/archinternmed.2011.728

13. Gopinath, B., McMahon, C., Burlutsky, G., Mitchell, P.: Hearing and vision impairment and the 5-year incidence of falls in older adults. Age Ageing **45**, 409–414 (2016). https://doi.org/10.1093/ageing/afw022

14. Contrera, K., Sung, Y., Betz, J., Li, L., Lin, F.: Change in loneliness after intervention with cochlear implants or hearing aids. The Laryngoscope **127**, 1885–1889 (2017)

15. Amieva, H., Ouvrard, C., Giulioli, C., Meillon, C., Rullier, L., Dartigues, J.: Self-reported hearing loss, hearing aids, and cognitive decline in elderly adults: a 25-year study. J. Am. Geriatr. Soc. **63**, 2099–2104 (2015)

16. Maharani, A., Dawes, P., Nazroo, J., Tampubolon, G., Pendleton, N.: Longitudinal relationship between hearing aid use and cognitive function in older Americans. Am. Geriatr. Soc. **66**, 1130–1135 (2018). https://doi.org/10.1111/jgs.15363

17. Rumalla, K., Karim, A.M., Hullar, T.E.: The effect of hearing aids on postural stability. The Laryngoscope **125**, 720–723 (2015)

18. Lacerda, C., Silva, L., de Tavares Canto, R., Cheik, N.: Effects of hearing aids in the balance, quality of life and fear to fall in elderly people with sensorineural hearing loss. Int. Arch. Otorhinolaryngol. **16**(2), 156–162 (2012)

19. Plazak, J., Kersten-Oertel, M.: A survey on the affordances of "hearables". Inventions **3**(3), 48 (2018). https://doi.org/10.3390/inventions3030048

20. Haire, M.: The Walkman. Time, 1 July 2019. http://content.time.com/time/nation/article/0,8599,1907884,00.html. Accessed 29 Jan 2019

21. HEARnet Online.: Hearables. HEARing CRC, The University of Melbourne. https://hearnet.org.au/hearing-technology/hearables. Accessed 29 Jan 2019

22. HearingTracker.com. https://www.hearingtracker.com/hearing-aids. Accessed 14 Sept 2018

23. Coughlin, J., Yoquinto, L.: Technology for older people doesn't have to be ugly. The Wall Street Journal, 14 October 2018. https://www.wsj.com/articles/technology-for-older-people-doesnt-have-to-be-ugly-1539546423. Accessed 29 Jan 2019

Study on Usefulness of Smartphone Applications for the People with Parkinson's

Mujahid Rafiq[1(✉)] ⓘ, Ibrar Hussain[1] ⓘ, C. M. Nadeem Faisal[2] ⓘ,
and Hamid Turab Mirza[3] ⓘ

[1] The University of Lahore, 1 KM Defense Road Campus, Lahore, Pakistan
mujahid.rafiq@se.uol.edu.pk
[2] National Textile University, Faisalabad 37610, Pakistan
[3] COMSATS University Islamabad, Lahore Campus, Islamabad, Pakistan

Abstract. The population of developed countries is becoming older and likely more chances of elderly people to face problems due to Parkinson. Mobile applications play a vital role in the lives of people having Parkinson. They use mobile applications for communication, social media network, surfing websites, medication, online shopping, and for many other purposes. However, the developers normally consider the youngster while designing the mobile Apps, consequently, the people with Parkinson (PwP) face numerous usability related issues while interacting with applications. This study elaborates the detailed limitations of PwP regarding the use of mobile applications and also determined the impact of related factors such as ease of use, information quality, and aesthetic quality on the usefulness of mobile applications. The objective is to purpose a theoretical model or framework for the usefulness of mobile applications in case of PwP. An empirical study is conducted on 25 PwP to test this model. A Structure equation modeling with other reliability tests are applied to verify and validate the proposed model. The results illustrate that ease of use and information quality strongly influence the usefulness whereas, aesthetic quality has a weak but indirect effect on usefulness. This study will provide the guidelines to the developers of the mobile application to understand the limitations of PwP and also to improve the usefulness of mobile applications by employing the appropriate design features.

Keywords: Usefulness · User experience · Structure equation modelling · Ease of Use · Information Quality · Aesthetic Quality · Parkinson Disease · People with Parkinson

1 Introduction

Traditionally the "elderly" word considered for those people who have aged more the 65 years. The rate of growth in this segment of the population is growing rapidly especially in developed countries like in the US and European countries due to birth control and other related factors. According to data by National Center for Health Statistics (NCHS), between 1987 and 2030 the total US population is projected to increase by 26% but older is expected to increase by 100 percent that is estimated around 67 million [1]. It is likely more chances of elder people to affect with Parkinson

© Springer Nature Switzerland AG 2019
J. Zhou and G. Salvendy (Eds.): HCII 2019, LNCS 11592, pp. 281–299, 2019.
https://doi.org/10.1007/978-3-030-22012-9_21

Disease (PD), Study estimates that the number of an individual over the age of 50 affected with PD was between 4.1 and 4.6 million and projected this figure will double in 2030 to between 8.7 and 9.3 million [2]. Parkinson's is a non-reversible chronological disorder, that affects the nervous system, slowness of movement, poor balance, gait freezing, impairment related to cognition and other age-related limitations [3]. These symptoms are likely to reduce the autonomy and mobility of an Individual that may force to change lifestyle [4]. Symptoms of PD also affect the interaction of smartphones [5].

According to [6], most of the elderly people in developed countries use the internet as a regular part of their lives. Most of them use smartphones with touch screen enabled to use the internet. In a study by [7], argue that 69% of elderly people have their own mobile phones. In the elegant literature, various researches emphasized on the development of smartphone application for the People with Parkinson (PwP) e.g. [8, 9]. However, limited research presented related to interface design or user experience (UX) factors that affect the PwP. The mobile application plays a vital role in the improvements in the lives of PwP. They use mobile application for exercising, medicine recommender systems, watching movies, social media usage and other purposes. Due to the lack of guidance or limited literature on PD patient's mobile/smartphone usage, the usefulness of mobile applications is still considered an important problem for PwP. In a recent survey, titled "Parkinson's IT challenges" on the usage of computers by PwP [10]. The statistics show that 80% of users with PD reported severe or highly severe difficulties by using computers. A similar study conducted on the usefulness of computer peripherals for PwP reported core limitations of PD regarding computer usage and suggested a projector based technology for PwP to use computers easily [11].

The aim of this study is to examine what are the core factors may affect the use of a smartphone by PD patients. Furthermore, also to determine the impact of some UX attributes i.e. ease of use (EOU), information quality (IQ), and aesthetic quality (AEQ) on the overall usefulness (UF) of mobile applications in the context of PwP. An empirical study is performed on 25 PwP to test this model. Structure Equation Modeling (SEM) with some other reliability tests are applied to verify and validate the model. The overall results show that EOU and IQ have a direct and high impact on the UF while AEQ indirectly influences the UF. The current study will provide the guidelines to designers and developer to adopt appropriate design strategy to design mobile or smartphone applications for PwP.

This study is organized as follows: Sect. 2 provides a detailed literature review on Parkinson's disease, its symptoms, interaction with smartphones/touchscreens and related factors employed in the current study. Section 3 purposes the research model and hypotheses; Sect. 4 describes the research method; and Sect. 5 provides the results of empirical tests and discussions. Section 6 presents conclusions, limitations and Future work.

2   Literature Review

2.1   Parkinson's Disease

The first step in this research is to understand the basic characteristics of PD and the basic symptoms of PD. This will minimize our effort to make the interaction of smartphone-related to people with Parkinson [12]. This portion of the research reviews PD symptoms from medical literature, some publications from patient associations and other health-related websites. Some areas are covered like motor and non-motor symptoms of PD. The On/Off phenomenon is also a specific characteristic of PD. These symptoms are discussed below.

Motor Symptoms
Some common types of symptoms of Parkinson's are bradykinesia, rigidity, rest tremor and gait impairment [13]. There is another issue which is that every patient of Parkinson's experiences different symptom. According to an estimate, around 70% of Parkinson patients are affected with Tremor [14], and around 47%, must affect with gait impairment [15]. Movement of hands and body in PD patients is very much affected due to Bradykinesia. Main issues involve the slowness of amplitude and speed while performing simultaneous and sequential tasks [16]. Changes in voice, facial expressions and handwriting are also documented [13]. These things directly affect mobile phone use by the patients of Parkinson's.

Rest tremor is basically an involuntary movement that occurs when usually muscles are relaxed and are supported by some kind of surface [17]. Sometimes this tremor is looking quite normal but sometimes it became vigorous. They may shake the whole body of a patient with hands. So, in this state, mobile phone usage is a very difficult task.

Rigidity is another type of motor symptom that increases the resistance to passive movement of a limb [15]. Rigidity has direct effects on fine motor tasks such as getting up from the chair, turning around and sometimes even on facial expressions [18]. It also makes general movement difficult and is also responsible for pain [15].

Gait impairment and Postural instability are also very common in Parkinson's patients, It usually occurs during the advance phase of diseases [15]. As disease more increases the gait became more unstable and slower [13]. And ultimately it also effects on smartphone usage.

Non-motor Symptoms
Non-motor symptoms tend to be under-recognized because complaints are very rare by the patients during medical appointments [19]. These symptoms may include sexual dysfunction, cognitive or sensory abnormalities and neurobehavioral disorders [19]. Sensory symptoms like akathisia, genital pain, oral pain, olfactory etc. are much common in patients with Parkinson's but these are not recognized or considered as Parkinsonian's symptoms [20].

Cognitive disorders are also very common in PD. Neuropsychological investigations have shown impairments in early stage/part of disease [21], which are usually shortfall of behavioral regulation in planning, regulation in sorting and low use of memory stores [22]. Cognition has a direct and indirect relationship with the usage of the smartphone can be easily found in HCI literature [23].

2.2 Parkinson's Patient Interaction with the Smartphone

The researchers found in their study that PD directly affect the usage of input devices while using computers [24]. As mentioned in the previous studies related to the usage of the smartphone in PD patients and limitations. Recent research is also conducted on 39 people with Parkinson. The authors provide detailed guidelines related to interface design [25]. Similarly [12] also conducted interviews with the patients of Parkinson's, Neurologists and Physiotherapists because they have directly or indirectly related to PD patients. The major goals of these interviews were to understand how the major and minor symptoms of that disease related to daily activity like smartphone usage. The interview was focusing on the four main areas that are

- How PD changes and affects the lives of patients with Parkinson?
- How cognitive skills and motor affect Parkinson's disease?
- How a mobile phone is used by the people of Parkinson's? and
- What are the basic symptoms that directly affect the usage of the smartphone?

The detailed questions were asked in the interview and lasted between 30 min to an hour and were recorded using a recording device. The audio-recorded were then analyzed by grounded theory [26]. The analysis was also supported by [12], using qualitative data. Similar attributes were also observed in a medical study but the results analyze from this study are quite different from the available literature. The results of the interview mainly divided into three categories i.e. motor characteristics, cognitive characteristics, and general characteristics. These characteristics have direct effects on smartphone usage. The details of these characteristics are given below. These characteristics must be under-considered while designing an application for people with Parkinson's.

Bradykinesia, Rigidity, Dyskinesia's, visual disabilities are some common motor problems found in patients with Parkinson's disease. These disabilities make the movement very slow and difficult. Some different uncontrolled movements also occur that directly related to the use of a smartphone. Parkinson's does not directly link up with visual disabilities but incoordination and weakness in muscles caused blurred and double vision, discrimination in color and contrast also occurs which also affects the use of mobile phone [12]. There are some other issues that are faced by Parkinson's patients related to the use of smartphones like short-term memory loss, slowness of thoughts, depression, and dementia.

2.3 Parkinson Disease and Touch Screen

Parkinson's is a disease which is found mostly in elderly people. PD is based on a disorder that affects the human being's nervous system. According to the study an estimated two million people are affected with PD only in Europe [27]. PD symptoms vary from patient to patient and the conditions of disease are also different from the initial level to high severity levels. The conditions of Parkinson's patients are often characterized by the symptom of motors, which includes slowness of movement or tremor [14]. Sometimes it is also due to Non-motor Problem [13]. These symptoms reduce the mobility of the patient and thus change its lifestyle [18].

In a study [5], the authors argue that motor symptom affects the interaction of the patient with a smartphone. The authors also determined how PWP performs some gestures with touch screen and also purposes some set of guidelines for the designing of applications for PwP. Summary of previous studies regarding interaction with small screen devices by PwP is discussed below.

Some studies are available regarding the development of an application that is especially for the people that are affected by Parkinson's disease, such as [8]. Some research/studies are also available regarding the use of the stylus in the application of PWP. These studies are not so much mature nor provide guideline related to the interface of the application and their usability [12]. Neither these studies evaluated the systematical interaction of PWP with applications. The findings from these studies are mostly based on the researchers self-assumptions. [5] and documented only to the interaction of PWP with a smartphone. Tremors, as well as fine motor skills, are also the major cause that affects the interaction of PWP with a smartphone. Similarly, in another study, the researchers observed an estimated 15% error rate while selecting a target on touch screen [28] and review became broaden from smartphone to some other touch screen interfaces. In the study [29], the researchers also designed a platform that was tablet interface, and this was specially designed for PD patients, also underline the importance of large screen or targets that overcame potential issues in fine motor skills or issues in visions. This contributes a lot to this field and research of this dimension but the study of [29] is not complete to design an interface of smartphones for PD patients.

2.4   Existing Interface Design Guidelines for Parkinson's Patients

It is the reality that Parkinson's disease is very complex and demonstrates different symptoms in the patients, that's why we cannot generalized its pattern, neither the guidelines can be applied to all type of patients having this disease. However, few usability related heuristics are suggested by [12] based on interviews from the Parkinson's patients. The authors argue that it is very complex to apply these guidelines on all type of patients that's why the developers must need more dynamic and proactive in this regard. The guidelines are as follows i.e. targets using tap must of 14 mm or more in both of sides, always prefer multi-tap over the drag, always use high colored contrast elements, always must avoid time controlled information, consider the design guidelines presented by other authors for elderly people [30–33] and present clear information if needed.

By considering these limitations of PD, the usefulness of mobile is still a problem. How we design a mobile phone useable for the PWP and what are the basic parameters that affect the usefulness? There are different factors that may influence the UF but in the current study, the authors attempt to determine the impact of IQ, EOU, and AEQ on UF.

2.5 Usefulness

According to [34], UF is the degree or comfort-ability of a user while performing certain activities. It also refers to "persons believe that using a system would enhance his or her performance" [35]. A recent study conducted on the usefulness of computers peripherals for PD people [11]. In this study, the researcher conducted a usability test using a standard peripheral on the people with Parkinson (PwP). They studied the individuals' limitations while using these peripherals and claimed that how projector-based technology may improve computer interaction without risking strain injuries. As the literature on Parkinson disease, clearly shows the limitations regarding mobile usage. Most of the studies were conducted using the technology acceptance model (TAM) in different contexts and observed UF is the core variable in TAM [36]. In another study, the researchers adopted the TAM to determine the mobile usage acceptance and they observed UF as a key determinant of acceptance [37]. In the current study, we consider UF as a key attribute in the PD usage context. In several studies [34, 38–54], TAM was adopted to measure the UF or related factors. The common variables used in the above studies such as EOU, IQ, and AEQ were assessed previously through questionnaire strategy [35, 55–58].

2.6 Information Quality

Information Quality is the term used frequently in various domains of human-computer-interaction and information visualization, several researchers defined IQ from a different perspective. In the current research, the authors adopted the IQ in terms of information arrangement and design to develop the interfaces of the mobile application. According to [59], the IQ is the quality of important contents of the website, it is also considered as the suitability of the information i.e. format, accuracy, and relevancy. There are some other information related aspects discussed in the prior studies such as information must be accurate, believable, timely presentable, the level of details included in information and the presentation of information in an appropriate format. Martin [60] in his studies categories the IQ into the following factors that are consistency, accessibility, conciseness, clarity, accuracy, traceability, interactivity, speed, and comprehensiveness. We can also consider these factors while designing the interfaces for a smartphone because better IQ leads us to better usability [61]. The smartphone has small size screen as compared to desktop computers and has the equal or large amount of information to be presented to users due to this developers and designers of the smartphone have to pay much attention to IQ. It is also very complex to manage all aspects of IQ on a small screen of smartphones. It was observed in the previous studies that the better the IQ the better the user satisfaction [62]. According to [63], IQ influence the user, information system (IS), service quality, and system quality. In another study [64], the researchers proposed that there are 14 major directions or dimensions of IQ i.e. accuracy, accessibility, completeness, believability, appropriate amount, consistency, complexity, understandability, timeliness, security, reputation, relevance, objectivity and ease of operation. Accessibility is usually known as the ease and ability of information that is to be accessed on and displayed by the user on a specific type of media like a smartphone or screen of a laptop or personal computers.

Accuracy is defined as the amount of data that is accurate enough or contains enough or accurate information for the user. Appropriate amount term is defined as the appropriate amount of data or information displayed at a certain time on screen. Believability is the ability and credibility of the information that can be trusted by the user. Complexity involves the structure of information i.e. the information displayed on the screen is far enough to present to the user. Thus, it has been proved that less the complexity in information higher the quality of information. Ease of operation is known as the ability of the user to process information like to find the required content from complete displaying information. Objectivity belongs to the relevancy of information i.e. the information displaying on screen is only relevant content that user wanted to show on the screen. Security of information belongs to the unauthorized or fake use of information for example information on the other website you are using in your information or any other person will not use your information. Timeliness is the regular update of information like a regular update in the information of date or some other contents related to the information you want to present. Understandability is the way to understand information by the user can easily understand the required information. A similar study conducted by [65], to check the effect of information quantity and user thoughts on the satisfaction level. In the study [66], the researcher combines the product quality with IQ and observed that we can achieve more usefulness through this, they conducted this experiment on 3 different firms and achieve positive results. [67] Used 8 items of IQ to evaluate the usefulness of an MIS system. The study related to mobile word of mouth [68] researchers proved that there is a significant impact of IQ on the usefulness of information. Another study on the impact of Information System Quality on the intention to use IPTV [69], and observed that IQ has a positive effect on usefulness. There are several other studies also showing the positive impact of IQ on EOU and UF [38–49, 69, 70].

2.7 Ease of Use

Ease of Use is the most common adopted term in HCI related studies. Like IQ, EOU also discussed in different perceptivities but in the current study, we employed this in terms of cognitive complexity to assess the mobile applications for Parkinson Disease patients. According to [34], EOU is basically the degree of simplicity associated with the user while using mobile interface or technology. If you are deeply involved with the software or certain type of application then it definitely affects the EOU [71]. EOU is the degree the person believe or think to use the system without effort [35]. Computer anxiety is known as the fear to face the computer and it is mostly found in elderly people related studies [72]. Computer anxiety is another important factor that directly influences the EOU of computer or smartphone usage [73]. In another study [50], it was observed that EOU has a significant positive impact on UF in the context of internet usage. The authors argue that if the internet is easy to use the more favorable chances of a person to use the internet more. A study conducted by [51], argue that EOU influences the UF for older people. Another model proposed by [74], adopted the EOU, system quality, IQ to observe the comparative effect on user satisfaction. Similarly, various other researchers [34, 50–53] also observed the positive impact of EOU on UF in the related contexts.

2.8   Aesthetic Quality

The aesthetic word simply associated with the beauty, attractiveness, or the appreciation of beauty. According to [75], the aesthetics used to design the engaging environment by incorporating the colors, visual elements, sounds, and multimedia artifacts
to increase the level of individuals level of involvement. According to [76], aesthetic is
known as heuristics for attractiveness. It mainly focuses on the use of color, typography, designs, flash, and animations. Sometimes, we employed it to improve the
legibility via size of text displayed on mobile screens, layout, expressions, style, and
pattern. It is mainly used to improve the website and mobile usability. Guidelines form
researchers and scientists are available for making better AEQ. It also supports the
contents understandability and increases functionality. The aesthetic effect also related
to age, gender and shows strong implication from the cultural perspective. Different age
group peoples prefer different colors scheme and both male or female have also different opinion on the usage of aesthetics aspects. Aesthetic involves the target audience
for better results. A study conducted related to the aesthetic design by [77], suggest that
aesthetic design is an important aspect while assessing usability. Different studies
observed the relationship between the usability and AEQ of an interface and also
between AEQ and satisfaction [76]. Several researchers also observed the impact of
AEQ on EOU and UF [49, 54, 78–80] that's why we include this in our study to check
the impact in our scenario.

3   Conceptual Model and Hypothesis Development

Figure 1 illustrates the hypothetical/conceptual research model proposed in our study.
It is actually a modified model derived from previous studies. It asserts that the UF of
mobile applications is determined by IQ, EOU, and AEQ. Further, EOU used as a
mediator between the relationship of IQ and UF and also between AEQ and UF.

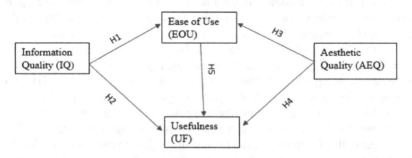

Fig. 1. Purposed hypothetic research model for usefulness

Definition of constructs, the network of relationship illustrated in the above model
and the rationale for the proposed links are explained in the literature review section.
According to [59], IQ is the quality of informational contents of a website, it is also
considered in term of the suitability of the information such as format, accuracy, and

relevancy. various studies in different contexts observed the positive impact of IQ on EOU and UF [43–48, 69]. Accordingly, we hypothesize:

Hypothesis 1: IQ positively influences the EOU.
Hypothesis 2: IQ positively influences the UF.

According to [76], Aesthetics is known as heuristics for attractiveness. It mainly focuses on colors, typography, designs, flash, and animations. Previous studies discussed the relationship between AEQ and EOU and also between AEQ and UF [49, 54, 78–80]. Accordingly, we hypothesize:

Hypothesis 3: AEQ positively influences the EOU.
Hypothesis 4: AEQ positively influences the UF.

According to [34], EOU is the degree of simplicity associated with the user while using mobile interface or technology. Based on the prior studies, the researchers believe that EOU significantly influences the UF of the smartphone. The relationship between EOU and UF was also observed in prior studies [34, 50–53]. Accordingly, we hypothesize:

Hypothesis 5: EOU positively influences the UF.

4 Methodology

4.1 Participants/Sample

The questionnaire was filled by 25 Patients of Parkinson's. In order to increase better or concise results, the researchers used an enormous method [81] to help the patients in the understanding of the context of questions that were asked in the questionnaire. All employed patients were above the age of 65 therefore, written as elderly patients in the most part of the paper. Out of 25 respondents, 18 (72%) were male and 7 (28%) were female. Moreover, 56% of the respondents had 1–3 years of experience in using the smartphones and the remaining 24% of respondents had more than 3 years of experience. (The purpose of the usage of smartphone/mobile applications is discussed in the section of results i.e. Table 5). 29% of respondents had up to primary level education, 12% up to middle and 59% had a higher level of education respectively.

4.2 Measurement Development

The questionnaire was developed from the elegant literature and the list of items are presented in Appendix A. In recent years similar studies were conducted and published in which various researchers used these similar items [56]. Hence most of the items were derived from the existing literature and modified slightly to suit the context of mobile applications. Furthermore, the think-aloud technique [82] is also used on 5–10 patients regarding the use of the mobile application to correct or modify items of various constructs.

Apart from the demographic factors, additional question explained in result section See Table 5. Each item/question employed in this study were measured using a five-point Likert scale, ranging from strongly disagree (1) to strongly agree (5). Before conducting the main survey, we performed a pilot and pre-test to validate the instrument. Pre-test involved 10 respondents (PwP) that had higher education and wide experience of smartphones and mobile applications. The respondents were asked to comment on employed items that corresponded to the constructs, including scale wording, length, and format of the questionnaire. Furthermore, the instrument was also discussed with more than 7 Neurologists from different hospitals in Pakistan to verify the exact requirements regarding the usefulness of mobile applications in Parkinson' Patients.

5   Results

5.1   Descriptive Statistics

Table 1 describes the means and standard deviations (SD) of different constructs. It is found that the average mean of respondents in case of EOU is 4.2 explaining the fact that out of total respondents' majority of the individuals have provided their outcomes in a range of agree and strongly agree. The response against IQ proxies is slightly less with 2.7 that means it is in between disagree and neutral. Respondents do not agree with the presentation of IQ in applications. The AEQ mean value is 3.3 explaining the fact that users quite agree with the proxies of AEQ.

Table 1. Descriptive statistics (Means and SD)

Constructs	Mean	SD
Ease of Use (EOU)	4.2	0.6
Aesthetic Quality (AEQ)	3.3	0.8
Information Quality (IQ)	2.7	0.9

5.2   Analytical Strategy for Assessing the Model

The purposed research model has tested through the structural equation modeling (SEM) technique. SEM is a second-generation most popular and powerful multivariate technique. It is mostly used to analyze casual models that involve two or more components of a causal model. The structure model is also used to investigate the direction and strength of relationship among the theoretical constructs. It specifies how the latent variable will be measured through observed variables. In recent years this technique is mostly used by HCI (mobile application) researchers [83–87]. In this study, the AMOS an additional SPSS module was used in order to access the structure model and measurement [88].

5.3   Measurement Model

The results of the Measurement Model test are written in Table 2. The values/data show that the reliability of different items is ranging from 0.62 to 0.89 that exceeds the acceptable value which is 0.5. Composite Reliability is computed to access the internal consistency of the measurement model. According to the benchmark presented by [89], composite reliability must be above 0.6. In our model, the value of the composite reliability of all the constructs is greater than 0.6. The [90], recommended that the value of average variance extracted (AVE) must exceed the threshold of 0.5 since in our case the values of all the constructs are greater than the threshold limits. Due to this, we have confidence regarding the reliability of our all constructs.

Table 2. Reliability

Construct	Item	Item reliability	Composite reliability	Average variance extracted
Ease of Use	EOU1	0.651	0.68	0.66
	EOU2	0.743		
	EOU3	0.682		
	EOU4	0.676		
	EOU5	0.753		
	EOU6	0.669		
	EOU7	0.605		
Aesthetic Quality	AEQ1	0.649	0.69	0.67
	AEQ2	0.671		
	AEQ3	0.764		
Information Quality	IQ1	0.897	0.75	0.69
	IQ2	0.654		
	IQ3	0.623		
	IQ4	0.738		
	IQ5	0.867		

Different fitness measures were applied to the data and model, the result is presented in Tables 3 and 4. All the measures of fitness are acceptable. Measures taken in this work consequently showing that the model is a good fit to the data.

Table 3. Extended reliability

Construct	Cronbach's alpha coefficients	Full collinearity VIFs
Ease of Use	0.72	1.184
Aesthetic Quality	0.62	1.052
Information Quality	0.82	1.886
Recommended criteria by authors	[91]	[92]

Table 4. Fitness indicators for the measurement

	X2/df	GFI	AGFI	CFI	NFI	NNFI
Results	2.12	0.96	0.92	0.98	0.96	0.98
Recommended criteria	<3.0	>0.9	>0.8	>0.9	0.9	0.9
Suggested by authors	[93]	[94]	[94]	[95]	[91]	[91]

5.4   Structure Model

Structure Equation Model (SEM) is also used to test the hypothetical relationship between constructs. Figure 2 is showing the complete details of the relationship among employed constructs and their effect on each other and overall on UF. The results show the positive influence of IQ on EOU (β = 0.25, p = 0.01), supporting H1. The results also support H3, β = 0.26, p < 0.01). The effect of IQ on UF is significant with (0.61, P < 0.01) and supporting the H2. Contrary to expectations, the effect of AEQ on UF is not much significant with β = 0.04, however, it has an indirect effect on UF due to its significant impact on EOU. Lastly, the results also support the H5 with β = 0.33, P < 0.01.

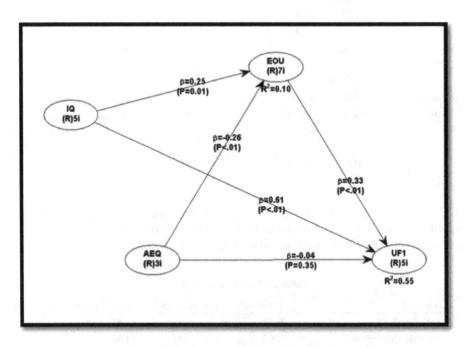

Fig. 2. Results of structural modeling analysis

5.5 Purpose and Problems of Mobile Applications for Parkinson's Patients

To gain further insights into information about the usefulness of mobile applications in case of Parkinson's Patients, the two questions (close-ended) were also added to obtain the following information:

Table 5. Purpose of using mobile applications by Parkinson's patients

Items	Number of respondents	Percent
Communication	25	82
Kill time	25	77
Watching movies and songs	25	25
Playing games	25	62
Other use	25	25

Purpose: To find out the purpose of using mobile applications by Parkinson's Patients, Users were asked why they use mobile applications.

6 Conclusion, Future Work and Limitation of Study

The results show that EOU significantly influences the UF, similarly, the positive relationship is also observed between IQ and EOU and also between IQ and UF. On the other side, AEQ observed as a strong determinant of EOU but indirectly influence the UF. The finding indicates that both IQ and EOU are important aspects to determine usefulness. Thus, both aspects are important while designing the interface of the mobile application for PwP. In our case participants are less satisfied with the employed constructs related to AEQ that why the AEQ has a weak impact on UF. Overall the findings from the current study may contribute to the future development of mobile apps for PwP. The proposed model also provides a conceptual depiction of key factors that heighten the PwP involvement in the design of mobile Apps. In the future, the researcher may extend the proposed model by incorporating the other aspects to provide the additional design related guidelines for PwP. The current study also suffers several limitations; this study involves a few numbers of participants due to the non-availability of PD patients in local hospitals. This is because people do not consider it as a disease or disorder except an aging factor. Second, the Parkinson's disease, includes 4–5 stages from less severe to high severity, in the current we employed all type of people and did not categorize participants that is why may have different results (Table 6).

Table 6. Appendix A: list of items by construct

Construct	Items
Ease of Use	I often get confused when I use the Cell/Mobile phone [35]
	Existing applications are easy to use [96]
	Using the existing Mobile Application, I became more productive [35]
	Whenever I make a mistake using application, I am unable to recover easily and quickly [96]
	I can use the existing mobile applications with confidence [96]
	The existing applications make me frustrated [35, 96]
	It is very complicated to operate the existing systems [96]
Aesthetic Quality	Icon and colors used by applications are very good and appealing [97]
	Reading character on the screen is very hard to read in existing applications [98]
	Shortcuts/Gestures are clearly identified and can be used [99, 100]
Information Quality	All menu and functionality are clearly visible and readable in current applications [66]
	Messages displaying on the screen are clearly visible and understandable [66]
	The organization of information on the application screens is clear [101]
	The information provided for the existing applications are easy to understand [101]
	Organization of information is very confusing [66, 101]

References

1. A Strategy for Quality Assurance'. National Academies Press (1980)
2. Dorsey, E., et al.: Projected number of people with Parkinson disease in the most populous nations, 2005 through 2030. Neurology **68**(5), 384–386 (2007)
3. Canning, C.G., et al.: Exercise therapy for prevention of falls in people with Parkinson's disease: a protocol for a randomised controlled trial and economic evaluation. BMC Neurol. **9**(1), 4 (2009)
4. Bloem, B., Stocchi, F.: Move for change part I: a European survey evaluating the impact of the EPDA charter for people with Parkinson's disease. Eur. J. Neurol. **19**(3), 402–410 (2012)
5. McNaney, R., et al.: Exploring the acceptability of Google glass as an everyday assistive device for people with parkinson's. In: Exploring the Acceptability of Google Glass as an Everyday Assistive Device for People with Parkinson's, pp. 2551–2554. ACM (2014)
6. Zickuhr, K., Madden, M.: Older adults and internet use. Pew Internet & American Life Project, p. 6 (2012)
7. https://www.researchgate.net/publication/220671508_Parkinson%27s_disease_A_motor_control_study_using_a_wrist_robot
8. de Barros, A.C., Cevada, J., Bayés, À., Alcaine, S., Mestre, B.: User-centred design of a mobile self-management solution for Parkinson's disease. In: User-Centred Design of a Mobile Self-management Solution for Parkinson's Disease, p. 23. ACM (2013)

9. Sharma, V., et al.: SPARK: personalized parkinson disease interventions through synergy between a smartphone and a smartwatch. In: Marcus, A. (ed.) DUXU 2014. LNCS, vol. 8519, pp. 103–114. Springer, Cham (2014). https://doi.org/10.1007/978-3-319-07635-5_11
10. Nes Begnum, M.E.: Challenges for Norwegian PC-users with Parkinson's disease – a survey. In: Miesenberger, K., Klaus, J., Zagler, W., Karshmer, A. (eds.) ICCHP 2010. LNCS, vol. 6179, pp. 292–299. Springer, Heidelberg (2010). https://doi.org/10.1007/978-3-642-14097-6_47
11. Begnum, M.E.N., Begnum, K.M.: On the usefulness of off-the-shelf computer peripherals for people with Parkinson's Disease. Univ. Access Inf. Soc. 11(4), 347–357 (2012)
12. Nunes, F., Silva, P.A., Cevada, J., Barros, A.C., Teixeira, L.: User interface design guidelines for smartphone applications for people with Parkinson's disease. Univ. Access Inf. Soc., 1–21 (2015)
13. Massano, J., Bhatia, K.P.: Clinical approach to Parkinson's disease: features, diagnosis, and principles of management. Cold Spring Harbor Perspect. Med. 2(6), a008870 (2012)
14. Hoffmann, N.C.: Using art therapy to address cognitive symptoms of Parkinson's disease. Int. J. User-Driven Healthc. (IJUDH) 3(3), 74–95 (2013)
15. Jankovic, J.: Parkinson's disease: clinical features and diagnosis. J. Neurol. Neurosurg. Psychiatry 79(4), 368–376 (2008)
16. Berardelli, A., Rothwell, J., Thompson, P., Hallett, M.: Pathophysiology of bradykinesia in Parkinson's disease. Brain 124(11), 2131–2146 (2001)
17. Reynard, J., Turner, K., Mark, S., Feneley, M., Armenakas, N., Sullivan, M.: Urological surgery. Oxford University Press, Oxford (2008)
18. Fernandez, H., Odin, P.: Levodopa–carbidopa intestinal gel for treatment of advanced Parkinson's disease. Curr. Med. Res. Opin. 27(5), 907–919 (2011)
19. Bonnet, A.M., Jutras, M.F., Czernecki, V., Corvol, J.C., Vidailhet, M.: Nonmotor symptoms in Parkinson's disease in 2012: relevant clinical aspects. Parkinson's disease (2012)
20. Djaldetti, R., Shifrin, A., Rogowski, Z., Sprecher, E., Melamed, E., Yarnitsky, D.: Quantitative measurement of pain sensation in patients with Parkinson disease. Neurology 62(12), 2171–2175 (2004)
21. Foltynie, T., Brayne, C.E., Robbins, T.W., Barker, R.A.: The cognitive ability of an incident cohort of Parkinson's patients in the UK. The CamPaIGN study. Brain 127(3), 550–560 (2004)
22. Dubois, B., Pillon, B.: Cognitive deficits in Parkinson's disease. J. Neurol. 244(1), 2–8 (1996)
23. Norman, D.A.: Cognitive artifacts. In: Designing Interaction: Psychology at the Human-Computer Interface, vol. 1, pp. 17–38 (1991)
24. Hartikainen, M., Ovaska, S.: People with Parkinson's Disease Using Computers. In: People with Parkinson's Disease Using Computers, pp. 407–408. ACM (2015)
25. Nunes, F., Silva, P.A., Cevada, J., Barros, A.C., Teixeira, L.: User interface design guidelines for smartphone applications for people with Parkinson's disease. Univ. Access Inf. Soc. 15(4), 659–679 (2016)
26. Charmaz, K.: Constructing Grounded Theory: A Practical Guide through Qualitative Analysis. Introducing Qualitative Methods Series (2006)
27. Zhan, W., et al.: Regional alterations of brain microstructure in Parkinson's disease using diffusion tensor imaging. Mov. Disord. 27(1), 90–97 (2012)
28. Montague, K., Nicolau, H., Hanson, V.L.: Motor-impaired touchscreen interactions in the wild. In: Motor-Impaired Touchscreen Interactions in the Wild, pp. 123–130. ACM (2014)

29. Maziewski, P., Suchomski, P., Kostek, B., Czyzewski, A.: An intuitive graphical user interface for the Parkinson's disease patients. In: An Intuitive Graphical User Interface for the Parkinson's Disease Patients, pp. 14–17. IEEE (2009)

30. Gregor, P., Newell, A.F., Zajicek, M.: Designing for dynamic diversity: interfaces for older people. In: Designing for Dynamic Diversity: Interfaces for Older People, pp. 151–156, ACM (2002)

31. Marcus, A., Gould, E.W.: Crosscurrents: cultural dimensions and global web user-interface design. Interactions 7(4), 32–46 (2000)

32. Hawthorn, D.: Interface design and engagement with older people. Behav. Inf. Technol. 26 (4), 333–341 (2007)

33. Hawthorn, D.: Possible implications of aging for interface designers. Interact. Comput. 12 (5), 507–528 (2000)

34. Ramírez-Correa, P.E., Arenas-Gaitán, J., Rondán-Cataluña, F.J.: Gender and acceptance of e-learning: a multi-group analysis based on a structural equation model among college students in Chile and Spain. PLoS ONE 10(10), e0140460 (2015)

35. Davis, F.D.: Perceived usefulness, perceived ease of use, and user acceptance of information technology. MIS Q. 13, 319–340 (1989)

36. Malhotra, Y., Galletta, D.F.: Extending the technology acceptance model to account for social influence: theoretical bases and empirical validation. In: Extending the Technology Acceptance Model to Account for Social Influence: Theoretical Bases and Empirical Validation, p. 14. IEEE (1999)

37. Van Biljon, J., Kotzé, P.: Modelling the factors that influence mobile phone adoption. In: Modelling the Factors that Influence Mobile Phone Adoption, pp. 152–161. ACM (2007)

38. Al-Mamary, Y.H., Shamsuddin, A., Abdul Hamid, N.A.: Factors affecting successful adoption of management information systems in organizations towards enhancing organizational performance. Am. J. Syst. Softw. 2(5), 121–126 (2014)

39. DeLone, W.H., McLean, E.R.: Information systems success: the quest for the dependent variable. Inf. Syst. Res. 3(1), 60–95 (1992)

40. Lee, H.-M., Chen, T.: Perceived quality as a key antecedent in continuance intention on mobile commerce. Int. J. Electron. Commer. Stud. 5(2), 123–142 (2014)

41. Almaiah, M.A., Man, M.: Empirical investigation to explore factors that achieve high quality of mobile learning system based on students' perspectives. Eng. Sci. Technol. Int. J. 19(3), 1314–1320 (2016)

42. Al-Debei, M.M.: The quality and acceptance of websites: an empirical investigation in the context of higher education. Int. J. Bus. Inf. Syst. 15(2), 170–188 (2014)

43. Landrum, H.T., Prybutok, V.R., Strutton, D., Zhang, X.: Examining the merits of usefulness versus use in an information service quality and information system success web-based model. Inf. Resour. Manag. J. (IRMJ) 21(2), 1–17 (2008)

44. Wang, Y.S.: Assessing e-commerce systems success: a respecification and validation of the DeLone and McLean model of IS success. Inf. Syst. J. 18(5), 529–557 (2008)

45. Demoulin, N.T., Coussement, K.: Acceptance of text-mining systems: the signaling role of information quality. Inf. Manag. (2018)

46. Ali, B.M., Younes, B.: The impact of information systems on user performance: an exploratory study. J. Knowl. Manag. Econ. Inf. Technol. 3(2), 128–154 (2013)

47. Lan, P., Ruan, A.-Q., Zhang, W.: User adoption intention of the tourism APP based on experimental method. In: DEStech Transactions on Environment, Energy and Earth Sciences, EESD (2017)

48. Hassn, H.A.H., Ismail, A., Borhan, M.N., Syamsunur, D.: The impact of intelligent transport system quality: drivers' acceptance perspective. Int. J. Technol. 4, 553–561 (2016)

49. Pantano, E., Rese, A., Baier, D.: Enhancing the online decision-making process by using augmented reality: a two country comparison of youth markets. J. Retail. Consum. Serv. **38**, 81–95 (2017)
50. Porter, C.E., Donthu, N.: Using the technology acceptance model to explain how attitudes determine Internet usage: the role of perceived access barriers and demographics. J. Bus. Res. **59**(9), 999–1007 (2006)
51. McCloskey, D.W.: The importance of ease of use, usefulness, and trust to online consumers: an examination of the technology acceptance model with older consumers. J. Org. End User Comput. **18**(3), 47 (2006)
52. Amin, M., Rezaei, S., Abolghasemi, M.: User satisfaction with mobile websites: the impact of perceived usefulness (PU), perceived ease of use (PEOU) and trust. Nankai Bus. Rev. Int. **5**(3), 258–274 (2014)
53. Karahanna, E., Straub, D.W.: The psychological origins of perceived usefulness and ease-of-use. Inf. Manag. **35**(4), 237–250 (1999)
54. Nwokah, N.G., Ntah, S.W.: Website quality and online shopping of e-tail stores in Nigeria. J. Serv. Sci. Manag. **10**(06), 497 (2017)
55. Lund, A.M.: Measuring usability with the use questionnaire12. Usability Interface **8**(2), 3–6 (2001)
56. Assila, A., Ezzedine, H.: Standardized usability questionnaires: features and quality focus. Electron. J. Comput. Sci. Inf. Technol. eJCIST **6**(1) (2016)
57. Erdinç, O., Lewis, J.R.: Psychometric evaluation of the T-CSUQ: the Turkish version of the computer system usability questionnaire. Int. J. Hum.-Comput. Interact. **29**(5), 319–326 (2013)
58. Lewis, J.R.: Psychometric evaluation of the post-study system usability questionnaire: the PSSUQ. In: Psychometric Evaluation of the Post-Study System Usability Questionnaire: The PSSUQ, pp. 1259–1260. Sage Publications, Los Angeles (1992)
59. Barnes, S.J., Vidgen, R.: Measuring web site quality improvements: a case study of the forum on strategic management knowledge exchange. Ind. Manag. Data Syst. **103**(5), 297–309 (2003)
60. Eppler, M.J., Muenzenmayer, P.: Measuring information quality in the web context: a survey of state-of-the-art instruments and an application methodology. In: Measuring Information Quality in the Web Context: A Survey of State-of-the-Art Instruments and an Application Methodology, pp. 187–196. Citeseer (2002)
61. Chiu, C.-M., Hsu, M.-H., Sun, S.-Y., Lin, T.-C., Sun, P.-C.: Usability, quality, value and e-learning continuance decisions. Comput. Educ. **45**(4), 399–416 (2005)
62. Chae, M., Kim, J., Kim, H., Ryu, H.: Information quality for mobile internet services: A theoretical model with empirical validation. Electron. Markets **12**(1), 38–46 (2002)
63. Tandi Lwoga, E.: Measuring the success of library 2.0 technologies in the African context: the suitability of the DeLone and McLean's model. Campus-Wide Inf. Syst. **30**(4), 288–307 (2013)
64. Gandhi, A., Shihab, M.R., Yudhoatmojo, S.B., Hidayanto, A.N.: Information quality assessment for user perception on Indonesia Kreatif web portal. In: Information Quality Assessment for User Perception on Indonesia Kreatif Web Portal, pp. 171–176. IEEE (2015)
65. Gao, J., Zhang, C., Wang, K., Ba, S.: Understanding online purchase decision making: The effects of unconscious thought, information quality, and information quantity. Decis. Support Syst. **53**(4), 772–781 (2012)
66. Kahn, B.K., Strong, D.M., Wang, R.Y.: Information quality benchmarks: product and service performance. Commun. ACM **45**(4), 184–192 (2002)

67. Swanson, E.B.: Management information systems: appreciation and involvement. Manag. Sci. **21**(2), 178–188 (1974)
68. Erkan, İ., Rahman, M., Sap, S.: Mobile word of mouth (MWOM) in messaging applications: an integrative framework of the impact of MWOM communication
69. Lee, D.-M., Chae, Y.-S., Lee, Y.-K., Choi, M.-J., Jang, S.-H.: The impact of information system quality and media quality on the intention to use IPTV. J. Inf. Commun. Convergence Eng. **10**(1), 71–77 (2012)
70. Ujakpa, M.M., Heukelman, D.: Extended Technological Acceptance Model for Evaluating E-Learning: The African Context (ETAM-4EEA)
71. Saadé, R., Bahli, B.: The impact of cognitive absorption on perceived usefulness and perceived ease of use in on-line learning: an extension of the technology acceptance model. Inf. Manag. **42**(2), 317–327 (2005)
72. Laguna, K., Babcock, R.L.: Computer anxiety in young and older adults: Implications for human-computer interactions in older populations. Comput. Hum. Behav. **13**(3), 317–326 (1997)
73. Van Raaij, E.M., Schepers, J.J.: The acceptance and use of a virtual learning environment in China. Comput. Educ. **50**(3), 838–852 (2008)
74. Kassim, E.S., Jailani, S.F.A.K., Hairuddin, H., Zamzuri, N.H.: Information system acceptance and user satisfaction: The mediating role of trust. Procedia-Soc. Behav. Sci. **57**, 412–418 (2012)
75. Thorlacius, L.: The role of aesthetics in web design. Nordicom Rev. **28**(1), 63–76 (2007)
76. Lindgaard, G., Dudek, C.: What is this evasive beast we call user satisfaction? Interact. Comput. **15**(3), 429–452 (2003)
77. Norman, D.A.: Emotional Design: Why We Love (or Hate) Everyday Things. Basic Books, New York (2005)
78. Deng, S., Fang, Y., Liu, Y., Li, H.: Understanding the factors influencing user experience of social question and answer services. Inf. Res.: Int. Electron. J. **20**(4), 4 (2015)
79. Sohn, S.: A contextual perspective on consumers' perceived usefulness: The case of mobile online shopping. J. Retail. Consum. Serv. **38**, 22–33 (2017)
80. Peng, X., Peak, D., Prybutok, V., Xu, C.: The effect of product aesthetics information on website appeal in online shopping. Nankai Bus. Rev. Int. **8**(2), 190–209 (2017)
81. Kjeldskov, J., Paay, J.: A longitudinal review of mobile HCI research methods. In: A Longitudinal Review of Mobile HCI Research Methods, pp. 69–78. ACM (2012)
82. Dickinson, A., Arnott, J., Prior, S.: Methods for human–computer interaction research with older people. Behav. Inf. Technol. **26**(4), 343–352 (2007)
83. Wu, J.-H., Wang, S.-C., Lin, L.-M.: Mobile computing acceptance factors in the healthcare industry: a structural equation model. Int. J. Med. Inform. **76**(1), 66–77 (2007)
84. Xu, D.J., Liao, S.S., Li, Q.: Combining empirical experimentation and modeling techniques: a design research approach for personalized mobile advertising applications. Decis. Support Syst. **44**(3), 710–724 (2008)
85. Matemba, E.D., Li, G., Maiseli, B.J.: Consumers' stickiness to mobile payment applications: an empirical study of WeChat wallet. J. Database Manag. (JDM) **29**(3), 43–66 (2018)
86. Wright, S.R.: Mobile technology adoption: assessing faculty acceptance using the technology acceptance model. ProQuest LLC (2018)
87. Al Amri, S.Q., Sadka, A.H.: The moderating role of personality traits on the relationship between behavioral intention and actual use of mobile government. In: The Moderating Role of Personality Traits on the Relationship Between Behavioral Intention and Actual use of Mobile Government, p. 279. Academic Conferences and Publishing Limited (2018)

88. Byrne, B.M.: Structural Equation Modeling with AMOS: Basic Concepts, Applications, and Programming. Routledge, Abingdon (2016)
89. Fornell, C., et al.: A second generation of multivariate analysis: classification of methods and implications for marketing research. Solstice: Electron. J. Geogr. Math. **5**(2)
90. Fornell, C., Larcker, D.F.: Structural equation models with unobservable variables and measurement error: algebra and statistics. J. Mark. Res. **18**, 382–388 (1981)
91. Bentler, P.M., Bonett, D.G.: Significance tests and goodness of fit in the analysis of covariance structures. Psychol. Bull. **88**(3), 588 (1980)
92. Kock, N.: Common method bias in PLS-SEM: a full collinearity assessment approach. Int. J. e-Collab. (IJeC) **11**(4), 1–10 (2015)
93. Burr, R., Hayduk, L.A.: Structural Equations Modeling with Lisrel, p. 396. Johns Hopkins University Press, Baltimore (1987). $37.50 (hard cover). Res. Nurs. Health **11**(5), 352–353 (1988)
94. Scott, J.E.: The measurement of information systems effectiveness: evaluating a measuring instrument. ACM SIGMIS Database: Database Adv. Inf. Syst. **26**(1), 43–61 (1995)
95. Bagozzi, R.P., Yi, Y.: On the evaluation of structural equation models. J. Acad. Mark. Sci. **16**(1), 74–94 (1988)
96. Lewis, J.R., Utesch, B.S., Maher, D.E.: UMUX-LITE: When There's No Time for the SUS, pp. 2099–2102. ACM (2013)
97. Sutcliffe, A.: Assessing the reliability of heuristic evaluation for web site attractiveness and usability. In: Assessing the Reliability of Heuristic Evaluation for Web Site Attractiveness and Usability, pp. 1838–1847. IEEE (2002)
98. Nielsen, J.: Designing Web Usability: The Practice of Simplicity. New Riders Publishing, Indianapolis (1999)
99. Kim, J., Lee, J., Choi, D.: Designing emotionally evocative homepages: an empirical study of the quantitative relations between design factors and emotional dimensions. Int. J. Hum Comput Stud. **59**(6), 899–940 (2003)
100. Lavie, T., Tractinsky, N.: Assessing dimensions of perceived visual aesthetics of web sites. Int. J. Hum Comput Stud. **60**(3), 269–298 (2004)
101. Lewis, J.R.: IBM computer usability satisfaction questionnaires: psychometric evaluation and instructions for use. Int. J. Hum.-Comput. Interact. **7**(1), 57–78 (1995)

Reappraising the Intellectual Debate on Ageing in a Digital Environment

Lilia Raycheva[(✉)] and Nelly Velinova

The St. Kliment Ohridsky Sofia University, Sofia, Bulgaria
lraycheva@yahoo.com, nelikdkd@gmail.com

Abstract. Ageing is expected to raise significant challenges to the European community in the coming decades. These challenges are connected not only with the problems related to the labor market employment, the provision of healthcare, and the welfare programming for older people, but also with the quality of their social life, and in particular, with their communication activities. In this regard, the article presents a brief overview of the population ageing tendencies and the deficits in the institutional attention towards age discrimination. It also presents the analysis of a survey, conducted by the authors of the article, among senior citizens (61 of age and older, N = 30), which aims to answer the basic research question: how the digital communication technologies impact some aspects in their everyday life, namely: healthcare, professional life and communication. Also, the article seeks to find whether the Bulgarian media perform their basic task to inform the publics for the activities related to the improvement of the life of the older people over 61 years of age.

Although many detailed expert studies and public discussions have focused on the problem of overcoming prejudices and negative stereotypes related to the working capacity, health status and communication habits of older people in Bulgaria, there is a telling need to reappraise the intellectual debate on ageing in digital environment and the degree of capacity of elderly people to take part in, and contribute to social developments.

Developed in the framework of the COST Actions IS 1402, CA 16211, and CA 16226 of the European Commission, the article concentrates on the need to boost the debates on finding solutions for the better well-being of the older persons in Bulgaria – a country with disturbing tendencies of population ageing.

Keywords: Ageing population · Digital technologies · Healthcare ·
Professional realization · Communication

1 Introduction

The structure of the article includes a brief overview of the population ageing tendencies, the deficits of institutional attention towards age discrimination, and the research efforts on the topic of three COST Actions IS 1402, CA 16211, and CA 16226 of the European Commission. It also presents the analysis of a survey, conducted by the authors of the article on the summer of 2018, among senior citizens (61 of age and older, N = 30), which aims to answer the basic research question: how the digital communication technologies impact some aspects in their everyday life, namely:

J. Zhou and G. Salvendy (Eds.): HCII 2019, LNCS 11592, pp. 300–312, 2019.
https://doi.org/10.1007/978-3-030-22012-9_22

healthcare, professional life and communication (see also [1, 2]). In parallel, a research was carried out on the information reported in the first half of 2018 in Bulgarian media related to the subject of the well-being of the elderly people over 61 years and the societal attempts to improve their living environment.

In 2015, humankind commemorated two significant anniversaries – the tenth year since May 17 was first celebrated as *World Information Society Day* and 25 years since October 1 was named *International Day of Older Persons*. The rise of the proportion of retired and older people over the next few decades is considered to be one of the greatest challenges to the economic and social system of the EU [3]. Perhaps this is why 2012 was proclaimed, unprecedented for the second time (the first was 1993), to be the *European Year for Active Ageing and Solidarity between Generations*. The aim of these and other initiatives is to enhance public awareness of the many-sided contribution of older people to society, and to promote measures that create better opportunities for their active life [4].

The population trends display the growing percentage of the aged population. In global terms, the expectations are that, after the year 2050, the number of people over 60 years of age will exceed the number of those under 60. Although it is expected that the overall population of the European Union will grow to 532 millions by 2060, the population in nearly half of the member states (Bulgaria, Croatia, Germany, Greece, Estonia, Hungary, Latvia, Poland, Portugal, Rumania, Slovakia, Slovenia, and Spain) will decrease. The forecasts show also that the ratio between persons of working age and those in retirement age will decrease from 4:1 to 2:1, if retirement age remains stable [3]. According to World Bank data Bulgaria ranks among the countries with highest tendency of population ageing with 20.8% (Japan has the highest percentage – 27.5%, followed by Italy – 23.02, Portugal – 21.50, Germany – 21.45, and Finland 21.23) [5].

Despite these forecasts, the amount of attention devoted to older people is still not proportionate to the challenges they face in the modern world. For instance, in the United Nations *Universal Declaration of Human Rights (UDHR)*, adopted in 1948, in the *International Covenant on Economic, Social and Cultural Rights* (1966) as well as in the *International Covenant on Civil and Political Rights* (1966), which lay the basis of the *International Bill of Human Rights* (adopted in 1976), age discrimination is not explicitly referred to.

The active efforts to promote the adoption of a special *Convention on the Rights of Older Persons* by the UN have not been successful so far. Although many UN and EU institutional documents related to technology, business models and the editorial responsibility of the media have been adopted, the multi-faceted attitude at older people as objects of coverage and as subjects of the communication process have still not been treated effectively.

The Active Ageing Index (AAI), jointly developed in 2012 by the United Nations Economic Commission for Europe and the European Commission is a key monitoring tool for policy makers to enable them to devise evidence-informed strategies in dealing with the challenges of population ageing and its impacts on society. The Index is built on four domains: employment; participation in society; independent healthy and secure living; capacity and enabling environment for active ageing. Among the six factors of the fourth domain are use of ICT, social contacts and educational attainment. Two

Nordic countries, namely Sweden and Denmark, come at the top of the overall ranking across EU Member States. In contrast, the majority of the Central and Eastern European countries, as well as Greece, is at the bottom of the ranking and needs further improvements [6].

It is perfectly obvious that the rights of the ageing population cannot be thoroughly defined and protected without taking into consideration the modern information and communication environment. The trend is that older adults will be not only passive users of the traditional media (press, radio, and television); they may also become prosumers, i.e. active participants and creators of content in online space.

Providing high speed access to advanced public services and diverse multimedia content for work, training and entertainment has become the mainstay of the knowledge based society. Contemporary broadband connections have a great impact on improving life quality, as well as on intensifying social cohesion, especially for older adults. Therefore, intensive improvement of ICT skills and digital literacy are critical to the effectiveness of any media strategy and to the further advancement of 'user-centered' to 'user-driven' developments for achieving the universality of the digital services. This will help to overcome the negatives of the digital divide, i.e. the economic, educational, and social inequalities between those who have computers and online access and those who do not [7].

2   Recent COST Actions of the European Commission on Population Ageing

The European Commission has identified active and healthy ageing as a major societal challenge common to all European countries. It created a special platform for European Innovation Partnership on Active and Healthy ageing [8]. This platform serves as a communication and information hub for all actors involved in active and healthy ageing throughout Europe. It provides a space to encourage partner engagements, to promote news and events, to meet and exchange ideas with peers, and to look for potential partners on innovative projects.

Three COST Actions of the European Commission for cooperation in science and technology dealt lately relevantly and timely with different aspects of the population ageing:

Ageism (i.e., the complex and often negative social construction of old age) as highly prevalent in contemporary European societies, which has negative consequences at the individual, familial, and societal levels was a subject of comprehensive analysis by the COST Action IS 1402: *Ageism - A Multi-National, Interdisciplinary Perspective* (2014–2018). The goal of this Action was to challenge the negative practices of ageism and to allow older people to realize their full potential. This has been done in four strands: healthcare system, judicial/legal system; media; work force [9].

COST Action CA 16226: *Indoor Living Space Improvement: Smart Habitat for the Elderly (Sheld-On)* (2017–2021) addresses Article 25 of the EU Charter of Fundamental Rights, which recognises and respects the rights of the elderly to lead a life of dignity and independence and to participate in social and cultural life. It is also in tune with the EU Employment Equality Directive (2000/78/EC)5, which besides prohibiting age discrimination in employment and occupation, encourages reducing the impact of physical and cognitive barriers at the workplace for staying active and productive for longer time. The aim of this Action is to establish a multidisciplinary network to support the development of solutions that allow the elderly to live safely, comfortably, and healthily at home through integrating design, ICT, ergonomics and health knowledge into furniture and building design [10].

Drawn on a transnational, interdisciplinary cooperative network, COST Action CA 16211: *Reappraising Intellectual Debates on Civic Rights and Democracy in Europe* (2017–2021) contributes to bridge the gap that separates politics and policy actions from humanities and social science research focused on the intricate relations between civic rights and the practices of democracy in Europe. This COST Action aims at recasting the interface between intellectual debates, public debates, politics, and policy action with the contributions of more argumentatively- and historically-oriented social science accounts and better institutionally-, politically- and legally-informed humanities research, which also includes a variety of aspects of population ageing [11].

The demographic shifts may have a dramatic impact on consumers' expectations from media and communication industries, as well for their ICT literacy and skills while navigating the digital world. Thus, the habits of the millennials (the generation born between 1981 and 1997) differ from those of the senior citizens. The demand for technology services that offer convenience, memorable experiences and instant access to content anywhere and anytime by the younger population is often juxtaposed to the preferences of the older people for health and wellness, entertainment and education services designed especially for them. Contemporary media ecosystem, developed in the digital environment, requires not only e-reading and e-writing practices but also e-producing talents and e-disseminating skills [12].

3   Qualitative Survey on the Shortcomings of the Well-Being of the 61 and Older Population in Bulgaria

In order to find out what are the shortcomings regarding the well-being of the 61 of age and older population in Bulgaria a survey of ten questions was carried out in the summer of 2018 among 30 respondents of the age between 61 years and 93 years. Respondents were selected on the principle of being over the age of 61 (the lowest most common retirement age in the country) without having an upper age limit. Object of the study were the elderly people of 61 years and older in the context of the contemporary reality in Bulgaria. Subject of the study was the way these people live and/or work and in particular, whether they use specific technologies that facilitate their everyday life. The purpose of the undertaken survey was to answer the basic research question: how the digital communication technologies impact some aspects in their everyday life, namely: healthcare, professional life and communication.

Geographically the respondents were divided equally into three groups: residents of the capital city – Sofia, residents of a smaller place – town of Varna and residents of the home for elderly people *Rezidentsia Karamel* located in the village of Dobrevtsi, Yablanitsa Municipality. Altogether N = 30 - 10 respondents form Sofia, 10 - from Varna and 10 - from the village of Dobrevtsi answered the questionnaires.

The health and socio-economic division of respondents led to a greater aggregation of results, as there were more serious differences in the respondents' lifestyle than in the place of residence indicator. Even the age gap and the education level were not as important as the general health and financial stability.

An interesting result that can be summed up by the participants' in the survey answers is that the majority (75% of the respondents with health problems - those with health problems constitute 37% of the total number of the respondents), also face financial difficulties, which aggravate their general condition. It is a problem for them that every month they have to buy a lot of medicines and only a minimum percentage of their cost is borne by the National Health Insurance Fund. They need alleviations in this aspect but almost do not receive any such. These people use simpler medical devices (or none at all), like ordinary blood pressure monitors, for example. They are compelled to use dysfunctional hearing aids that often damage their hearing abilities.

In fact this group of respondents needs a cardinal solution to their health problems – carrying out extensive medical examinations followed by surgical or medicinal approach to curing them. The lack of resources to adequately care for their health makes them physically and mentally unfit to work and this condemns them to poor financial standing and inability to keep themselves in good shape and be of benefit to the society and to their relatives – the so-called doomed circle is constructed, out of which there is no way out.

Most of these respondents (63% – Fig. 2) do not have a computer with internet or a smartphone. They cannot handle these technologies and they do not understand how these technologies could facilitate their everyday life. These people are not aware of the innovative technologies that would be useful in their everyday life and would make their being easier and more valuable. However, even if they were technologically informed, they could not afford financially any technological acquisition. Part of this group uses television mostly as entertainment and therefore prefers to watch more movies, music and shows and less - news. They do not use the functions of some digital TV sets, namely to return the broadcasts and news back in time, so they watch only what is being offered to them at the particular moment.

The results from the answers point also to the contrary conclusion – adults of 61 years and older who are still mobile and working (70%), are more likely to use computers, smart phones, tablets, and Internet for both professional and personal needs. They are informed about what is happening around them namely through technologies. The more active in respect of intellectual terms the respondents are, the higher is the percentage of their use of communication technologies (internet applications, social networks, cloud space, smartphone applications, etc.). Accordingly, the higher is also the percentage of a certain kind of "addiction", which they have developed towards technologies. Nearly 60% of the active people of 61 years and older claims that they cannot live without the technologies they use on a daily basis. They are better informed and more aware of how to find sources for certain technological innovations that would be useful to them in everyday life.

The results of the answers to the questionnaire show that the social and health status of the people residing in the nursing home for the elderly in the village of Dobrevtsi, Yablanitsa Municipality is the worst one. Besides having almost no funds, deprived of a normal environment where to communicate with relatives and family members, they often cease to be interested in what is happening around them. The most popular type of technology these people use (90%) is the TV. What is characteristic for them is that they do not even choose what to watch – predominantly they watch movies and news. They do not have a device to play programs back and watch only what is being offered at the moment. 100% of the respondents from the nursing home for elderly people are retired and do not perform any activities. They are former teachers, accountants, engineers, electricians, etc., and over 50% of them suffer from dementia. Apart from the survey, the healthcare staff shared the opinion that these people are not interested in anything but watching TV programs and use only telephone with buttons. They can hardly set up the channels of a TV set themselves and cannot handle other technologies at all. Their disease has advanced to such an extent that they often forget the water to flow and lights to be switched on.

When asked for what do they use communication over the Internet more often, 63% of the respondents answered that they never use the Internet because they do not have a computer or do not know how to handle it. 6% claimed that they do not use the Internet themselves, but with the help of relatives and friends they use social networks (Facebook) or applications such as Skype and Veiber to communicate with their relatives living abroad. 13% answered that they use the communication possibilities that the Internet offers for personal needs (conversations with relatives who are far away) and for professional needs (sending business emails, using social networks at work, etc.). Likewise – 13% said that the time they spend on the Internet is dedicated to issues related to their professional activity. For the remaining 11% the Internet usage is for personal purposes only (Fig. 1).

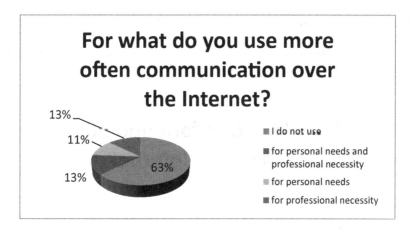

Fig. 1. Most often reasons for communication over the Internet

63% of the respondents do not use the Internet to inform themselves, for the simple reason that they do not have a computer and internet connection. 7% use it rarely, 10% – once a day, and only one fifth, i.e. – 20% – several times a day. Those, communicating on the Internet, need to be informed in most cases about a medicine, a hearing aid or some innovative technology in the field, as well as about cultural events. Some of them ask their relatives or friends with Internet connections to do that instead. Those with vision problems also use the help of their relatives to receive information on issues related to their work, as well as to specific news and current affairs (Fig. 2).

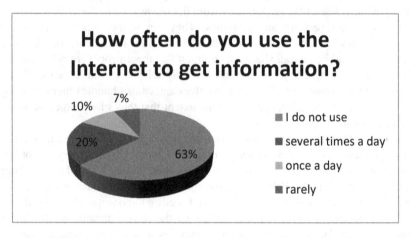

Fig. 2. Most often usage of the Internet for acquiring information

Answering the question of what information they are looking for over the Internet, 56% of the respondents noted that they are not using the Internet at all. Many of them added that they still find the information they need in newspapers and television. 24% of the respondents claimed that they are basically looking for news over the Internet. 6% answered that they are interested in curiosities. Equally, for 3% of the respondents Internet is important for: information related to their work; watching films; reading e-books; and getting references from the world wide web. At least – 2% answer that they check the Internet for the weather forecast (Fig. 3).

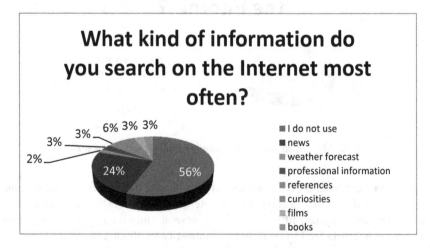

Fig. 3. Information most often searched over the Internet

Half of the respondents answered that they do not use Internet for communication purposes. 17% claimed that they use the net once a day to send and check e-mail messages, to use different social media applications or to access social networks. The most dedicated 7% of the respondents use the Internet for communication purposes several times a day. Also 7% use the network for these purposes once a week. However, 17% of the respondents answered that they rarely use the Internet for communication purposes, and 2% – that they are entering the Internet once a month to communicate (Fig. 4). This means that the regularity of Internet usage among the participants in the survey is not a common habit.

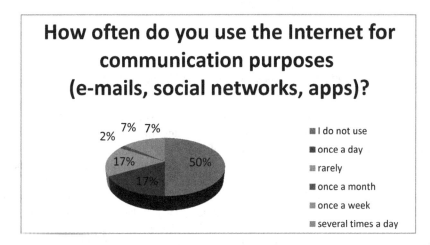

Fig. 4. Regularity of Internet usage

When asked about what health benefits are the respondents applying in terms of improvement of their health conditions, the largest percentage of them answered that they use the ordinary blood pressure monitor (75%), followed by 13% who use an electronic blood pressure monitor, 6% - a blood glucose meter, 3% wear a hearing aid and another 3% possess an electronic bracelet that shows different parameters of the human body such as pulse rate, blood pressure, worked out kilocalories, traveled paces, etc. Less than half of the respondents appreciate the importance of using these devices and believe they improve their quality of life (Fig. 5).

Those 60% of the active people of 61 years and older who claimed that they cannot live without the technologies on a daily basis are better informed and more aware of how to find sources for certain technological innovations that would be useful to them in everyday life. This part of the respondents is in a better financial condition due to the fact that they work. On a healthy basis, they use electronic blood pressure monitors, blood glucose monitors, electronic bracelets, showing a number of parameters of the person's physical condition such as pulse, strides passed, spent kilocalories, etc. In this way they maintain their health status at a better level. However, this part of the respondents believes that they do not have benefits and privileges and that these

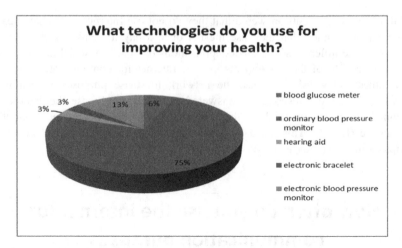

Fig. 5. Technologies used for health improvement

technologies at their disposal are obtained with hard work and funds of their own. Representatives of this group of respondents are categorical in their opinion that they have to fight individually for a better way of life.

Merit deserves the fact that 100% of the respondents answered that they have neither received any social or other kind of benefits, nor are they familiar with programs offering any alleviations for elderly or sick people. In fact, there are a number of initiatives and projects in different municipalities related to helping elderly people. An Action Plan (2018–2021) for the implementation of the National Strategy for Long-Term Care has been approved. It is published on the website of the Ministry of Labor and Social Policy [13]. It aims to develop long-term care for elderly people and to improve their quality of life in line with the National Strategy for Long-Term Care adopted in the beginning of 2014 [14].

The National Strategy envisages establishment of accessible and quality services in the community and at home that will ensure the possibility of social inclusion of people with disabilities and elderly people and, at the same time, and thus, will have a preventive role regarding the institutionalization of these people. Strong emphasis in the Strategy is placed on the de-institutionalization of the care for the disabled people and elderly people, on the development of the services including technological services in the domestic environment and on the support of families with increased responsibility for the care of family members in need of special care.

Among the priorities of the Strategy is also the promotion of synergy between social and health services, including the development of innovative cross-sectoral services, as well as the implementation of an integrated approach. Also, among the main priorities of the Strategy is the creation of a more efficient mechanism for financing the long-term care and the achievement of sustainable growth of the financial resources for services in the community and in the domestic environment.

However, there a mismatch between good intentions and real actions are observed, among them - the failure to pass a special law for the elderly in the Parliament. The good practices of some municipalities and non-governmental organizations that are successfully implemented (mostly through European programs and projects) are targeted at specific small segments of society and are extremely insufficient to cover all the needy Bulgarian population of 61 years and older.

Media also do not give a sufficiently broad coverage of these initiatives, which is why information about them is hardly reaching the end recipients – people with special needs. Few are the mass media that reflect the topic about elderly people and the various initiatives to improve their lifestyle. Thus, for example, in a publication dated 02.05.2018 entitled "Special Law for the Elderly: Yes, but No", it is stated that the idea of the socialists to adopt a special law for the elderly people has failed. The rejected texts provided for the creation of a special fund to the Social Minister that will be filled out each year by the state treasury in order to finance various activities for the elderly people. Another idea of the socialists, according to the media, was to have a "foster care" service for elderly people who have no relatives or when these do not want or cannot take care for them – similarly to the foster families for children. One of the authorities' obligations, according to the failed draft law, was, for example, for every 25 000 people to build and operate "resident-type social services" for at least 100 people. Municipalities should have the imperative obligation to open and maintain "clubs for elderly people" – one in each settlement with over 100 people 61 years or older and one in every 15 000 people of population [15].

An article in the newspaper "24 chasa" (24 h) dated 02.03.2018 entitled "Experts: The Elderly Labor Force is the Fuel of the Bulgarian Economy", reflects the holding of a forum on the topic "For an Active and Fulfilling Life of the Elderly People in Bulgaria" with lecturers Assoc. Prof. Dr. Georgi Bardarov from the Sofia University "St. Kliment Ohridski" and Ivan Neikov – Director of the Balkan Institute of Labor and Social Policy. The article draws attention to the demographic crisis and to the fact that Bulgaria is among the ten countries in the world with the highest share of ageing population. In this regard the author of the article draws attention to the competences, professionalism and experience that the working people of 61 years and older possess. The idea of the article is to encourage elderly people to continue to work for the benefit of the society and for their own benefit [16].

In another article of 13.10.2017 entitled "Creating a Virtual Assistant (Coach) for Elderly" it is stated that a high-tech modular system would help lonely elderly people to live actively and independently in their home, despite the severity of their years and illnesses. The article refers to Yordan Dimitrov from the Balkan Institute for Labor and Social Policy (BILSP), who has presented an innovative project for creating a virtual assistant in support of the active ageing. The SAAM (Supporting Active Ageing through Multimodal Coaching) project is funded with nearly € 4 million from the EU Framework program for research and innovation "Horizon 2020". Its ultimate goal is to maximize the active and independent life of people 61 years and older in their own homes while maintaining good physical, emotional and mental well-being, as well as the social contacts of its users for as long as possible [17]. The article explains that the virtual assistant will help elderly people to feel well in their usual environment by collecting data about their health and emotional status by using sensors, smart measuring devices, video and audio receivers. The system will also monitor the vital functions and taking of medication, will detect and alert for negative changes in the mood and behavior of its users. The future autonomous modular system has had the idea of collecting information through unobtrusive sensors suitable for permanent wear or installation in the house (at home). The idea has been to make discreet monitoring of the living environment and the personal activity under a privacy guarantee. Direct communication with end-users is foreseen by developing clear user interfaces – visual and audio, adapted to the needs and habits of the elderly people. The purpose of the system is to analyze the collected personal information and to make independent decisions, to remind or encourage its users for certain actions in the interests of their physical and mental health (e.g. to take their medication, to cook, to call a friend or to go for a walk). For this purpose special strategies and technologies should be developed to influence by persuasion.

4   Conclusions and Limitations

The process of digitization is among the main milestones tracing the dimensions of humankind's transformations in the 21st century. Today these transformations are catalyzed by the intense development of the communication technologies. As positive as their impact might be on progress in all areas of life, it is no less true that they pose challenges for the social stratification of society. The trend of population ageing determines the need for urgent prevention of elderly people's social exclusion from the modern digital environment.

Although a National Strategy for Long-Term Care and an Action plan for its implementation have been adopted in Bulgaria the results of the conducted survey showed that the digital communication technologies do not facilitate sufficiently the everyday life of the participating older adults. Almost two thirds of the respondents do not or use very rarely computers and Internet. The rest one third uses Internet for personal and professional needs. 24% of the respondents are basically looking for news over the Internet. A small amount of the interviewees are interested in curiosities, followed by information related to their work; watching films; reading e-books; getting references from the world wide web, and checking the weather forecast. The answers displayed a scarce usage of digital technologies for healthcare. While two thirds of the respondents use ordinary blood pressure monitor, less than one fifth use electronic devices for their health needs. Also, there was not enough evidence that the improvement of the life of the older people over 61 years of age through digital technologies is an important point of interest to the Bulgarian media. Thus, answering the research question of how the digital communication technologies impact some aspects in the everyday life of the senior citizens it may be concluded that their impact is not sufficient.

Based on the results of the conducted survey and the analyzed Bulgarian media, reflecting the topic, it can be concluded that many of the ideas, disseminated in the public domain, related to improving the living environment of the elderly remain unrealized. Thus, none of the respondents has received any form of assistance or information about the existence of an approved Action Plan for the period 2018–2021 for implementation of the national long-term care strategy of the Republic of Bulgaria. A comprehensive awareness campaign to inform citizens about the existing opportunities for better living conditions and to urge them to be more active in their search for such opportunities could be a productive communication step.

The number of media, which reflect issues related to the lifestyle, professional engagement and communication of people over the age of 61 and older, is too small. Besides, the media present reality too fragmentarily and inconsistently without the necessary commitment and responsibility [18]. More real action is needed to enable modern Bulgarian senior citizens for receiving adequate technological support to improve their living, professional and social status. Thus, through various technological means of treatment, professional realization and communication, the elderly in contemporary society could have a more meaningful, active and fulfilling life.

The demographic trends determine the need for urgent prevention of the digital generation divide, i.e. of the vulnerability and the social exclusion of older people from the ICT world. In order to deal with the challenges to population ageing, it is important to find solutions that allow the elderly to live safely, comfortably, and healthily at home by integrating design, ICT, ergonomics and health knowledge.

Acknowledgements. The text has been developed within the framework of two COST Actions of the European Commission: CA 16226: Indoor Living Space Improvement: Smart Habitat for the Elderly and CA 16211: Reappraising Intellectual Debates on Civic Rights and Democracy in Europe supported by the projects of the National Scientific Fund of Bulgaria: DCOST-01.25-20.12.2017, and the Program "Young scientists and post-doctoral students" of the Ministry of Education and Science.

References

1. Loos, E., Mante-Meijer, E., Haddon, L.: The Social Dynamics of Information and Communication Technology. Ashgate, Aldershot (2008)
2. Loos, E., Haddon, L., Mante-Meijer, E.: Generational Use of New Media. Ashgate, Farnham (2012)
3. European Commission: The 2015 Ageing Report. Economic and Budgetary Projections for the 28 EU Member States (2013–2060) (2015). http://ec.europa.eu/economy_finance/publications/european_economy/2015/pdf/ee3_en.pdf
4. Peicheva, D., Raycheva, L.: The transformation of reading among the ageing population in the digital age. In: Zhou, J., Salvendy, G. (eds.) ITAP 2016. LNCS, vol. 9754, pp. 216–225. Springer, Cham (2016). https://doi.org/10.1007/978-3-319-39943-0_21
5. World Bank: Population ages 65 and above (% of total) (2017). https://data.worldbank.org/indicator/SP.POP.65UP.TO.ZS?view=map
6. Active Ageing Index (AAI). https://www.euro.centre.org/downloads/detail/1542
7. Merriam-Webster: Digital Divide (2018). https://www.merriam-webster.com/dictionary/digital%20divide
8. European Commission: European Innovation Partnership on Active and Healthy ageing European Innovation Partnership on Active and Healthy Ageing (2018). https://ec.europa.eu/eip/ageing/home_en
9. COST Action IS 1402 Ageism - A Multi-National, Interdisciplinary Perspective (2014–2018) (2018). www.notoageism.com
10. COST Action CA 16226: Indoor Living Space Improvement: Smart Habitat for the Elderly (Sheld-On) (2017–2021) (2017). www.sheld-on.eu

11. COST Action CA 16211: Reappraising Intellectual Debates on Civic Rights and Democracy in Europe (2017–2021) (2017). www.uma.es/costactionrecast
12. Miteva, N., Raycheva, L.: Consuming the media and ICT environment: challenges to vulnerability of older adults. In: sén, E.E., Olle, F. (eds.) Consuming the Environment 2017 – Multidisciplinary Approaches to Urbanization and Vulnerability. Proceedings. University of Gävle, Sweden, pp. 99–113 (2017) https://www.hig.se/download/18.1a5c0163b4c29a901e 4af/1529907576487/180622_HIG_Consuming_the_Environment_Proceedings.pdf
13. Ministry of Labor and Social Policy. Action Plan for the Period 2018–2021 for Implementation of the National Long-Term Care Strategy of the Republic of Bulgaria (2018). https://www.mlsp.government.bg/ckfinder/userfiles/files/politiki/socialni%20uslugi/ deinstitucionalizaciq%20na%20grijata%20za%20vuzrastni%20hora%20i%20hora%20s% 20uvrejdaniq/Plan_LTC.pdf
14. Ministry of Labor and Social Policy. National Strategy for Long-Term Care (2014). http:// www.strategy.bg/StrategicDocuments/View.aspx?lang=bg-BG&Id=882
15. Dnes Tsvetanova, K.: Special Law for the Elderly? Yes, but No (2018). https://www.dnes. bg/politika/2018/05/02/specialen-zakon-za-vyzrastnite-hora-da-ama-ne.375274
16. Chassa: Experts: The Elderly Labor Force Is the Fuel of the Bulgarian Economy (2018). https://www.24chasa.bg/novini/article/6744042
17. Technews.bg: A Virtual Adult Assistant Is Being Created (2017). https://technews.bg/ article-102766.html
18. Raycheva, L., Tomov, M., Amaral, I., Petrovćić, I., Vukelić, M., Čizmić, S.: Ageing women in the media mirror maze. In: Angova, S., et al. (eds.) Media Environment, Public and Strategic Communication, pp. 39–47. UNWE Publishing House, Sofia (2018)

Privacy Concerns and the Acceptance of Technologies for Aging in Place

Eva-Maria Schomakers$^{(\boxtimes)}$ ⓘ and Martina Ziefle ⓘ

Human-Computer Interaction Center, RWTH Aachen University,
Campus-Boulevard 57, 52074 Aachen, Germany
{schomakers,ziefle}@comm.rwth-aachen.de

Abstract. Technologies to support older adults in Aging in Place have the potential to address the challenges that aging populations pose on healthcare systems. Technology acceptance and the way individuals' privacy concerns are met are decisive determinants for their success. To understand the nature and impact of privacy concerns, two empirical studies were conducted. In focus groups, privacy concerns and conditions are identified. Participants worry especially about illicit information abuse, but also about feelings of surveillance and loss of control. In a subsequent questionnaire study, privacy concerns and their impact on acceptance are quantified (n = 97). Privacy concerns are not as pronounced as are benefits of technology use and show less impact on acceptance. Differences between a fall detection system and remote monitoring of vital parameters are detected. Older adults are less positive towards care-assistive technologies than younger adults. Findings contribute to an understanding on how technologies should be designed to match the desires of potential users.

Keywords: Technology acceptance · Privacy concerns · Aging ·
Technologies for Aging in Place · Ambient Assisted Living

1 Introduction

The proportion of senior citizens in Europe will increase from 19% (2015) to approximately 28% in 2050 (Eurostat 2015). The baby boom generation born in the 1960s will soon reach retirement age. Life expectancy is still increasing. 11% of the European population will be older than 80 years in 2050.

These demographic developments have already become reality in many regions of the world and are even more advanced in some countries, for example in Germany (Eurostat 2015). The aging populations constitute an enormous challenge for the welfare state, society, and healthcare systems. Other societal trends amplify these problems: almost every third senior citizen lives alone, only 8% live under one roof with younger generations, and more women are working. Correspondingly, informal care by family caregivers becomes more complex or inapplicable. Still, most senior citizens prefer to live in their own home as long

© Springer Nature Switzerland AG 2019
J. Zhou and G. Salvendy (Eds.): HCII 2019, LNCS 11592, pp. 313–331, 2019.
https://doi.org/10.1007/978-3-030-22012-9_23

as possible, even when everyday chores become harder to cope with (Benefield and Holtzclaw 2014). *Aging in Place* can contribute to a sense of independence, autonomy, and social connectedness, providing both, psychological and emotional benefits (Wiles et al. 2012). Aging in Place is not only favored by many older adults but also by policy makers and health providers as healthcare costs and resources can be reduced (Graybill et al. 2014). Technologies can support and assist older adults in Aging in Place and support their formal and informal caregivers. With improving independence, safety, social contacts, and quality of care, *Technologies for Aging in Place* can contribute to a high quality of life in older age and prolong the stay of older adults in dignity in their own four walls (Siegel and Dorner 2017).

In the last decades, much research effort has been put into the development of technologies for Aging in Place (Van Grootven and van Achterberg 2016). But these technologies will only then be successful and exploit their full potential, when they suit the needs of the potential users and the respective contexts, in which technology is used. Technology acceptance is decisive, but is a great challenge for technologies for Aging in Place which is torn between multiple obstacles. First, the target group of older adults is heterogeneous regarding the use of novel technologies (Czaja et al. 2006). Secondly, the home has an emotional meaning for us and also for older adults who spent much time and activities in their own four walls. Altering this place of life may cause resentments (Mortenson et al. 2016). Finally, most technologies for Aging in Place are based on the collection of sensitive and intimate information from the body or the home of the users. Accordingly, privacy concerns are a crucial barrier for acceptance (Yusif et al. 2016).

The focus in this study is put on privacy concerns as a key barrier to acceptance within the context of the home and older adults as potential users.

2   Related Work

2.1   Aging in Place and Technology Support

The concept Aging in Place can be described as the provision of appropriate services and assistance for older adults to remain living in their current home or community in relative independence (Vanleerberghe et al. 2017). Various terms for similar technologies are used: for example, smart homes for the elderly, Ambient Intelligence, Ambient Assisted Living or assistive ICT. In Europe, the terms *Ambient Assisted Living*, and *Active and Assisted Living* are popular based on the Ambient Assisted Living (AAL) Joint Programme that was established by the European Union to develop appropriate technology solutions (Ambient Assisted Living Joint Programme 2012). In this publication, the wider term of *technologies for Aging in Place* is used as umbrella term to include all technologies designed to support older adults in Aging in Place in the areas of safety and security, therapy support and remote monitoring, home automation, support of daily chores as well as telemedicine and social communication. These include stand-alone devices, interconnected systems, robots, and applications for ICT devices. Popular examples for such technologies are, e.g., fall detection systems, vital parameter monitoring, medication reminders, video-mediated communication, and automated door and window openers (Blackman et al. 2016).

The goal of Aging in Place is to prevent or delay moves to dependent facilities and thereby meet the desire of most older adults to stay home. Aging in Place can also counteract the financial challenges of the aging population, as the costs are much lower than the costs of institutionalization (Graybill et al. 2014). Aging in Place can thus contribute to a high quality of life, giving a sense of independence and autonomy as well as emotional and social connection to the community and spaces (Biermann et al. 2018; Wiles et al. 2012). For older adults, the home is the major place not only for retreat and privacy but also for many activities and social relationships. Home is an extension of the self and connects to self-identity (Himmel and Ziefle 2016; Oswal and Wahl 2005).

2.2   Technology Acceptance

Still, the adoption of technologies for Aging in Place in the population is slower than anticipated (Hallewell Haslwanter and Fitzpatrick 2016). One key aspect for the diffusion of such technologies is the technology acceptance (Lee and Coughlin 2014). The research stream of technology acceptance explains why users use technologies and models the determinants of acceptance. The wide range of factors and determinants on acceptance can be structured into three levels: (1) the technology itself, (2) the users and their characteristics, and (3) environmental and contextual aspects. Popular models of technology acceptance, for example TAM (Technology Acceptance Model, Davis (1989)) and UTAUT (Unified Theory of Acceptance and Use of Technology, Venkatesh et al. (2003)), include attitudes and beliefs, social influence and demographic user factors to predict acceptance. Acceptance is operationalized as the intention or willingness to use a technology, which is modelled as the predictor of use behavior.

Regarding older adults and technologies for Aging in Place, these models are not sufficient to explain the diversity of aspects that shape the intention to adopt these technologies. Age, specifics of the context, as well as privacy concerns need to be additionally considered.

Age: The group of older adults is everything but homogeneous. Physical and cognitive changes in aging are highly individual and influence the capabilities to interact with technologies as well as the willingness to use them, creating a large diversity (Arning and Ziefle 2009). Additionally, the experiences with technologies during upbringing and working life influence familiarity and expectations towards technologies (Sackmann and Winkler 2013). The technology generations of today's older adults learned strategies of use and interactions with technologies that do not fit modern technologies. Additionally, the perspective of women needs to be considered in these age groups due to the still existing differences with regard to (professional) experiences with technologies and the simultaneously higher proportion of older women. Contrary to many prejudices, many older adults are willing to try new technologies, but these need to match their specific needs and capabilities (Czaja et al. 2006). Still, on average, technology adoption by today's older adults is limited, which is intensified with poor health status, education, and older age (Heart and Kalderon 2013).

Context: Most technology acceptance models were developed for the organizational or consumer electronics context. They have been adapted to other contexts, but the transferability has rarely been validated (Arning and Ziefle 2009). Technologies for Aging in Place act within the intersection of home and health. The home is not just a physical space to live but a meaningful place that is the major focus of older adults, especially when frailty increases (Mortenson et al. 2016). The home means a refuge for privacy and intimacy, social connectedness as well as identity and emotion (Oswal and Wahl 2005). Technologies for aging in place may intrude, altering perceptions of home and changing routines (Mortenson et al. 2016). At the same time, many operate in a health context which is very intimate. The perception of need for technological support is a decisive determinant for the acceptance, especially by older adults (Czaja et al. 2013). Many older adults do not see themselves in need of this assistance. The availability of alternatives, e.g., support by family members, and habits of compensating or just accepting problems, diminish the perception of need for oneself (Schomakers et al. 2018).

Privacy: Technologies for Aging in Place, especially monitoring technologies, utilize many sensors and collect, analyze and transmit intimate data from the home, behavior, and health of the user. Correspondingly, privacy concerns are a major barrier to their acceptance and use (Yusif et al. 2016). Users trade off perceived barriers, particularly privacy concerns, against benefits of the technology use for them to decide on the overall acceptance (van Heek et al. 2017). This *privacy calculus* has been studied in various contexts including health and assistive technologies (Ermakova et al. 2014; Halbach et al. 2018).

2.3   Privacy Concerns

The perceived essence of privacy is the sense of being in control. Privacy can be categorized into the control over access to the physical self (*physical privacy*), social interaction and communication (*social privacy*), thoughts and feelings (*psychological privacy*), as well as control over personal information (*informational privacy*) (Burgoon 1982). With the advent of digital technologies and data collection in almost every area of life, informational privacy becomes an integral part of the other dimension of privacy (Koops et al. 2017). Technologies for Aging in Place collect, store and transmit very intimate data about the social, physical, and psychological self from areas of life which formerly used to be 'offline'. Correspondingly, people feel that they lose control over their privacy and privacy concerns arise.

Privacy concerns have been extensively studied in Information Systems (IS) research (Smith et al. 2011). Privacy concerns in IS regard the collection, unauthorized secondary use and abuse, improper access, and errors in personal information as well as specific concerns over e.g., profiling and de-anonymization, targeted advertisement, identity theft, and credit card fraud (Schomakers et al. 2018; Smith et al. 1996). Solove (2006) categorizes privacy violations from a legal perspective into violations of information collection, information processing, information dissemination, and invasion.

In the context of technologies for Aging in Place which affect health, aging, and home, additional concerns are prevalent: e.g., feelings of permanent surveillance, invasions of personal space, obtrusiveness of the technology, and stigmatization (Boise et al. 2013; Kirchbuchner et al. 2015; van Heek et al. 2017). As medical information, information about mental illnesses is perceived as particularly sensitive (Valdez and Ziefle 2018), privacy concerns are again intensified. Moreover, older adults seem to be generally more concerned about privacy (e.g., Van den Broeck et al. 2015).

Privacy concerns and the acceptance of technologies for Aging in Place are also influenced by technology characteristics, e.g., the what, where, how, and to whom of data collection and transmission as well as the obtrusiveness of the design (Hensel et al. 2006; Rashid et al. 2007). Here, further research is needed to identify and understand specific privacy concerns and how the characteristics of the technology and application context shape these concerns. With the wide range of available technologies, the additional question arises whether privacy concerns and their impact on technology acceptance vary between technologies for Aging in Place.

3   Questions Addressed and Empirical Approach

The aim of the study is to examine, firstly, the specific nature of privacy concerns by potential users of technologies for Aging in Place and, secondly, the impact of these privacy concerns on the acceptance in comparison between two technology examples. A two step empirical approach was chosen which is depicted in Fig. 1. In study one, focus group interviews were conducted to collect the opinions of potential users towards technologies for Aging in Place with focus on their privacy perceptions and concerns. The outcomes from the focus group study were taken as empirical base for the development of the subsequent quantitative data collection in study 2. In a subsequent survey, the influence of privacy concerns on technology acceptance is quantified with a larger sample and differences between the two technology examples within the domain of technologies for Aging in Place are examined.

For both studies, a sample was targeted consisting, on the one hand, of a group of adults older than 50 years, with varying background regarding their demographic characteristics, health status, and experience with technologies. These adults belong to the technology generations of *technology spread* and *household revolution* (Sackmann and Winkler 2013). On the other hand, adults

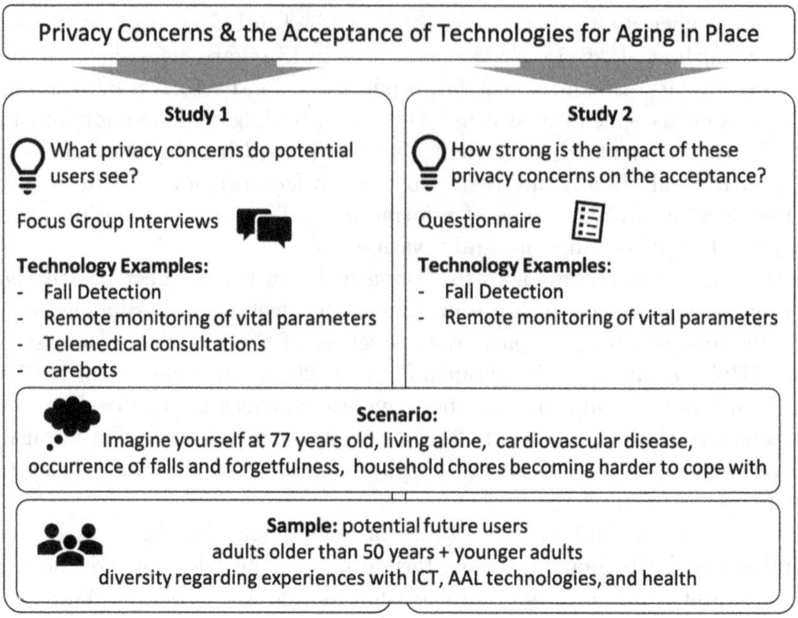

Fig. 1. .

aged 50 years or younger were surveyed to compare opinions and examine age-related effects regarding attitudes towards Aging in Place. These younger adults are from the *computer* or *internet generation* and have been experiencing ICT since their upbringing. All participants were asked to empathize with a scenario of being older and need for support (cf. Fig. 1).

In the following sections, first the methodology and results of the focus group study are reported, before the subsequent questionnaire study is focused.

4   Focus Group Study

In focus group interviews, the interaction between the participants sparks the discussion as they can share, oppose, and argue ideas. Especially when participants are new to the topic and may need some elaboration time to make up their minds, a discussion approach can trigger thoughts that may not come up in in-depth interviews. Thus, a focus group approach was most suited for the first research question regarding the nature of privacy concerns of potential users of technologies for Aging in Place.

4.1   Method

Three focus group sessions were conducted based on a semi-structured guideline. The participants discussed their opinions of technologies for Aging in Place based on technology examples explained by the moderator. Focus lay on the identification of potential privacy perceptions and concerns. The interviews and focus groups were audio-taped and transcribed verbatim. The study was carried out in German. For the publication, selected quotes were translated to English.

The Procedure: After an introduction to the topic and the focus group, the participants were first asked to brainstorm which technologies they already use in their home to help them at everyday chores and medical tasks. Next, understandings of privacy and examples for privacy within the home environment should be given. With a short explanation of technologies for Aging in Place and the introduction of the first example, the main part of the interview started. The participants were asked to state their general opinion to the technologies and whether they would be willing to use it. They should further elaborate on privacy perceptions as well as conditions that they would pose. After the focus groups, the participants were asked to complete a post-questionnaire, which assessed demographic data, health status, experiences with general ICT and technologies for Aging in Place.

The Technology Examples: The technology examples were chosen to include a wide range of technologies and were introduced with pictures for a better understanding and memorizing. A fall detection system using wearable sensors and one using infrared sensors, remote monitoring (weight, blood pressure, heart rate), telemedical consultations, and carebots were included.

The Sample: Three focus groups interviews were conducted with the aim to cover on one hand, the opinions of adults older than 50 years of both genders with diverse background (e.g., different education levels, health status, and experience with ICT) as well as a group of younger adults. Four women between 53 and 73 years of age participated in the first focus group. The second one included five men aged between 56 and 72 years, and the third one included six students aged between 22 and 30 years (50% women). Overall, the level of education was rather high, with 46.7% holding a university degree, 40% a university entrance diploma, and 13.3% having completed an apprenticeship.

All participants were experienced with general ICT, as they all used a smartphone, tablet, or computer regularly. Regarding their experience with medical equipment, ten participants possessed a blood pressure device, two a blood sugar monitor, and one a hearing aid. No participant had used specific technologies for Aging in Place yet, but five had already heart about such.

Regarding their health status, eight participants were chronically ill, and nine needed to go to a physician regularly. One participant needed to use medical devices regularly and none was in need for care.

4.2   Results

A content analysis was conducted to derive categories from the data with a focus on privacy concerns. These concerns are summarized in the next section.

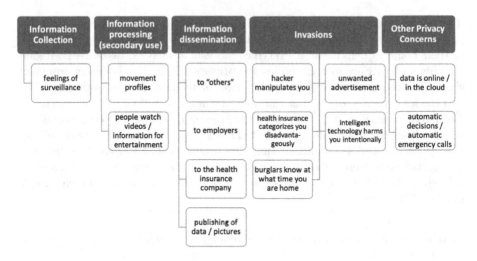

Fig. 2. Privacy concerns of participants regarding technologies for Aging in Place.

Privacy Concerns. The participants expressed various privacy concerns regarding the use of AAL technologies. In Fig. 2, these concerns are categorized into the privacy taxonomy by Solove (2006) which differentiates between privacy violations regarding information collection, information processing, information dissemination, and invasions. Additionally, other concerns were voiced by the participants that could not be allocated to these categories.

The participants expressed that **information collection** itself, e.g., by cameras, microphones, creates feelings of surveillance. Even if a camera would uses additional privacy filters (e.g., Cardinaux et al. 2011), would not send picture material to anyone, or would be switched on only in emergency cases, the mere presence of a camera is felt as a privacy violation.

> "With cameras, I have to think about George Orwell all the time: 'Big brother is watching you'. It's a disconcerting thought for me."
> "I still have a problem with the camera staying in my apartment."

In the **information processing** stage, unauthorized secondary use of the information is cause for concern. The participants were concerned about movement profiles that could be made based on the data as well as about people who access data, especially videos, for their own entertainment.

"We still have the unknown third person sitting in the same boat. Maybe there are people who get turned on when someone has fallen."

The participants also worried about unwanted **information dissemination** to employers, health insurance companies, as well as undefined others. Moreover, the publishing of information, especially pictures, was discussed.

"Every time that someone gets it [personal data] who I don't want to get it, it's a violation of my privacy."
"Where else does the data go to?' is the important question."
"It is a risk that your health insurance listens, or a pharmaceutical company."
"You fall, break your hip, and two days lay you see yourself in the newspaper."

Various concerns regarded **invasions** of the users life (cf. Fig. 2). The participants especially feared illicit information abuse in forms of hackers, burglars using information to discover at what time the apartment is vacant, or even that the technology itself intends to harm the user.

"But the thought that a hacker might interfere and then somehow manipulates you and harms you."
"We live in a world where there is a lot of mischief. Maybe someone is able to hack the connection. He just takes a look at the camera to see what's going on in the apartment and if it's worth it to break in."
"A terminator that kills you in your sleep or something." "Or it puts your cocktail of tablets together the wrong way."

Moreover, the participants discussed two **other concerns** that did not fit the privacy taxonomy by Solove (2006). They are anxious about personal data being online or 'in the cloud' in general with out naming specific risks or consequences. Also, automatic decisions, like automatic emergency calls, are felt as privacy violation by some participants.

"I think that once you do not have a face-to-face conversation anymore and its mediated by technology than your privacy is at risk."
"As soon as the decision is taken away from me whether I press a button for an emergency or not. I think than it is a violation of my privacy."

An interesting finding is that in some cases the participants evaluate their privacy to be better respected when tasks are handled by technology than when it is done by humans.

"It's a machine, it doesn't judge you. [...] A human would see all the embarrassing things in your apartment and under your bed. Technology doesn't judge you."
"I can decide at what time it is switched on. With a nurse [out-patient treatment], usually a time is allocated to you whether you like it or not."

Imposing of Conditions and the Privacy Calculus. Two additional important themes regarding users' privacy emerged: the participants discussed conditions under which technologies for Aging in Place are acceptable which result from the privacy concerns they perceive. Additionally, they emphasized that privacy concerns need to be weighed against the utility of the technology to make a decision about acceptance as suggested by the theory of the Privacy Calculus.

As **conditions for the acceptance** of technologies for Aging in Place, especially the controlability by the user was empathized. Users shall be able to switch off the technology or single functions at any time, determine what sensors are used, what data is collected, where sensors are installed, and who has access to the data. Also, the granularity with which data is transmitted, e.g, the frequency of data transmission and resolution of the data, and whether the technology may make automatic transmission of data and place automatic emergency calls are important conditions that users want to control individually.

> "I think it depends on who is in control and how much control you yourself have over the technology. [...] Can I restrict what it can do? If for example I don't want it to capture my mood, can I tell it not to do that?"

> "I think a camera system would be okay, for example if someone from my family saw the picture. If my daughter saw this transmission, it would be okay."

> "If he [her grandfather] sends data himself maybe, he is retired and has the time. But if it is sent automatically all the time, I think that would be too much loss of privacy."

> "If it only switches on when I have fallen."

> "If it would be calculated at home in my system, and then only the information gets out of my network that someone has fallen. Then for me that's okay."

Several participants indicated that they perform **trade-off decisions between privacy and utility**. The perceived risks for the user's privacy is weighed against the possible utility and benefit. This 'Privacy Calculus' is not only performed to form a general opinion on acceptance of the technology, but also to decide the detailed privacy settings, e.g., where sensors may be installed or who has access to data.

> "I think that this weighing is important. Are there more benefits, or more risks? What happens with my personal data? Will there be mischief? Who uses it, the health insurance mafia? What is more relevant? I think that most people see more dangers than benefits. Because you just do not fall that often."

> "Most people have no interest in my data anyway and if it's analyzed anonymously or in some other way, then you have more benefits than the abstract dangers."

> "It makes a differences whether only the neighbor comes by and has a look if everything is in order, or whether the ambulance comes directly. But on the other hand, you would lose important seconds, for example, for a heart attack."

"Especially in those rooms where it would make sense I wouldn't want to have it: bathroom, bedrooms."

5 Questionnaire Study

In the focus group interviews, focus was laid on privacy concerns and perceptions. This resulted in an emphasis of privacy concerns as influence on the acceptance of technologies for Aging in Place. In the subsequent quantitative study, this influence of privacy concerns on the acceptance shall be validated and quantified with a larger sample, thereby comparing two technology examples. Therefore, the acceptance and attitudes towards the two exemplary technologies – a fall detection system and remote monitoring of vital parameters – were assessed.

5.1 Hypotheses

Based on the qualitative results and previous empirical research, the following hypotheses are formulated for both exemplary AAL technologies:

H1. With older *age* the *use intention* decreases.
H2. *Perception of benefits* increase *use intention.*
H3. *Privacy concerns* decrease *use intention.*
H4. *Perception of other barriers* decrease *use intention*
H5. *Privacy concerns* moderate the relationship between *perception of benefits* and *use intention.*

Hypothesis H5 is based on the findings of trade-offs between utility and privacy. This trade-off as it is described by the participant would lead to a stronger relationship between perception of benefits and use intention when privacy concerns are low. In the case that privacy concerns are high enough to outweigh the benefits, the relationship between benefits and use intention would be weaker.

5.2 The Questionnaire

The items of the questionnaire were developed based on the literature study and supplemented with findings from the focus group interviews. The evaluation of two exemplary AAL technologies was assessed in a repeated measures design, a fall detection system (FD) and vital parameter monitoring (VPM). Both technologies were motivated within a scenario, which included the occurrence of falls and the need for daily measurement and diary keeping of vital parameters, respectively.

The questionnaire was structured as follows: First, demographic data (age, gender, education level), health status, experiences with ICT (e.g., smartphone, computers, tablets) and technical self-efficacy (Beier 1999) was assessed. Then, the two technologies were introduced and subsequently evaluated. The order of the technology evaluation was randomized to prevent sequence effects.

The participants evaluated benefits, barriers (including privacy concerns), and use intention for the presented technology. The items were measured on 6-point Likert scales from 0 (*'I do not agree at all'*) to 5 (*'I fully agree'*). Cronbach's Alpha was calculated to confirm the reliability of the scales. In Table 1, exemplary items and the reliability are depicted.

Completing the questionnaire took approximately 20 min. The participants were incentivized with a small donation to a charity organization made for each completed questionnaire. After finishing the questionnaire, the participants could chose to which charity organization the donation should be made.

Table 1. Variables with item examples and Cronbach's α for the fall detection system (FD) and the vital parameter monitoring (VPM), n = 97.

	FD: α	VPM: α
Technical Self-Efficacy, 4 items (Beier, 1999)		.827
I can solve most technical problems on my own.		
Perception of Benefits, 12 items	.961	.965
I would use the technology, because I would feel safer		
... because I would be able to live independently at home.		
Privacy Concerns, 7 items	.923	.913
*I would **not** use the technology, because I would feel monitored.*		
... because I worry about abuse of my personal data.		
Perception of Other Barriers, 9 items	.874	.877
*I would **not** use the technology, because I worry about its reliability.*		
...because I am concerned that the interaction with the system is difficult.		
Use Intention, 4 items	.892	.863
I would like to use the technology.		

5.3   The Sample

The questionnaire was distributed online as well as in paper-and-pencil form. The participants were recruited from the social network of the author as well as online discussion forums. The sample covered a majority of adults older than 50 years as well as younger participants with diverse demographic characteristics, health status, and experiences with technology. 97 participants completed the questionnaire aged between 19 and 85 years ($M = 43.58, SD = 20.58$) including 56.8% older than 50 years and 59% women. The education level of the sample was, on average, quite high, with 55.7% holding a university degree, 7.2% having completed an apprenticeship, and 25.8% holding a university entrance diploma.

Usage of ICT: All participants used either a smartphone, tablet, or computer at least weekly and were, thus, experienced with ICT. The sample reported on average to have a moderately high technical self-efficacy ($M = 3.14, SD = 0.58$, measured from min = 0 to max = 5).

Health Status: 32% of the participants reported to be chronically ill, 32% needed to visit a physician regularly, and 27% needed to use medical technology aids regularly. No participant was in need for professional care.

5.4 Results

Two equivalent regression analyses were calculated to determine the impact of privacy concerns and other influencing factors on the acceptance of the two exemplary technologies for Aging in Place. As assumptions of linearity were partly violated, bootstrapping was used for robust regression. All variables were zero-centered before the regression analysis. Additionally, analyses of variance (ANOVAS) were used to examine differences between the two technology examples. For all analyses, the level of significant was set to 5%.

Vital Parameter Monitoring: The regression model of the prediction of *intention to use vital parameter monitoring* is summarized in Table 2. The model can explain 77.3% of variance in use intention ($R^2_{adj} = .773$). Perception of Benefits shows a large impact on use intention ($\beta = .865, p < .001$). Correspondingly, whether one sees utility in the technology predicts the willingness to use it. Additionally, with increasing age the intention to use vital parameter decreases significantly ($\beta = -.12, p = .029$), thus older adults - the target group of Aging in Place Technologies - are less willing to use vital parameter monitoring in comparison to younger adults. Other variables cannot significantly predict use intention nor is there a moderation effect of privacy concerns on the relationship between perception of benefits and use intention.

Table 2. Linear regression model. Predictors of intention to use vital parameter monitoring, with 95% bias corrected and accelerated confidence intervals of the regression coefficient reported in parentheses (based on 1000 bootstrap samples).

	b	SE B	β	p
Constant	0.224 (−0.928, 0.95)	0.506		.659
Age	−0.007 (−0.012, −0.001)	0.003	−.117	.029
Perception of benefits	0.925 (0.472, 1.151)	0.159	.865	<.001
Privacy concerns	0.058 (−0.332, 0.274)	0.157	.056	.714
Perception of other barriers	−0.157 (−0.384, 0.023)	0.093	−.107	.094
Privacy concerns x Perception of benefits	−0.017 (−0.098, 0.102)	0.037	−.066	.651

$R^2_{adj} = .773$

Table 3. Linear regression model. Predictors of intention to use a fall detection system, with 95% bias corrected and accelerated confidence intervals of the regression coefficient reported in parentheses (based on 1000 bootstrap samples).

	b	SE B	β	p
Constant	0.004 (−0.193, 0.25)	0.076		.956
Age	−0.01 (−0.018, −0.003)	0.004	−.172	.008
Perception of benefits	0.671 (0.445, 0.793)	0.07	.634	<.001
Privacy concerns	−0.191 (−0.392, −0.043)	0.078	−.193	.017
Perception of other barriers	−0.224 (−0.441, −0.058)	0.112	−.156	.048
Privacy concerns x Perception of benefits	0.012 (−0.11, 0.181)	0.038	.019	.76

$R^2_{adj} = .665$

Fall Detection. The predictors of the intention to use a fall detection system is depicted in Table 3. Again, the perception of benefits shows a strong influence on use intention ($\beta = 0.634, p < .001$). Privacy concerns show a significant negative impact ($\beta = -.193, p = .017$) as does the perception of other barriers ($\beta = -.156, p < .048$). As in the case of vital parameter monitoring, age has a weak impact on use intention of fall detection ($\beta = -0.172, p < .008$). There is no significant interaction effect of privacy concerns and perception of benefits. The included variables can explain 66.5% of variance in the intention to use a fall detection system ($R^2 = .665$).

Differences Between Remote Monitoring and Fall Detection. Now, the results of the regression analyses are compared. Privacy concerns and the perception of other barriers only show a significant impact on the acceptance in the case of fall detection, but not in the case of vital parameter monitoring. This goes in line with the differences in agreement to privacy concerns, use intention, perception of benefits, and perception of other barriers (depicted in Fig. 3). Privacy concerns regarding fall detection seem to be more pronounced than regarding vital parameter monitoring, especially in the younger group of adults. But these differences between technologies and the interaction of technology and age are not statistically significant ($F(1, 96) = 3.26, p = .073$ and $F(1, 96) = 1.36, p = .247$). Also, no difference between the age groups can be detected ($F(1, 96) = 0.43, p = .514$).

But, privacy concerns are not rejected in contrast to the perception of other barriers for both technologies. Benefits, on the other hand, are agreed to for both technologies as is the intention to use the technology. For three variables, differences between the age groups seem present, with older adults perceiving more barriers and agreeing less to benefits and use intention than do younger adults. These effects are not statistically significant, with one exception: younger adults show a significantly higher use intention for both technologies than older adults ($F(1, 96) = 6.92, p = .010$).

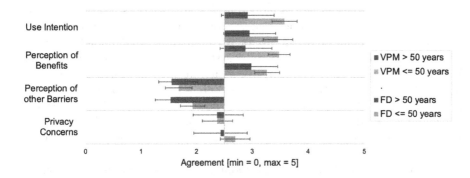

Fig. 3. Differences of the agreement to use intention, perception of benefits, perception of other barriers, and privacy concerns between the fall detection (FD) and vital parameter monitoring (VPM) dependent on age group with 95% confidence intervals (n = 97).

6   Discussion and Conclusion

To unfold their full potential, technologies for Aging in Place need to be accepted by the potential users. But privacy concerns represent a decisive barriers to technology acceptance (Yusif et al. 2016). In order to contribute to the understanding of reasons for privacy concerns, we conducted two studies. In a focus group study, these privacy concerns were identified and conditions for acceptance summarized. Using a questionnaire approach, the influence of privacy concerns on the acceptance was quantified and compared between two typical technologies for Aging in Place - a fall detection system and a vital parameter remote monitoring.

Privacy concerns regard illicit privacy invasions (particularly hackers) and the dissemination of information to unwanted others (e.g., the health insurance company). The major source for concerns is that data is *online* as devices are connected to the internet. Another stream of privacy concerns especially regard feelings and the feeling of loss of control. A camera that does not send any video information to others or automatic emergency calls are also perceived as privacy intrusions, because of a feeling of surveillance and loss of control. Here we see, that privacy concerns in technologies for Aging in Place do not only concern information privacy and data security, but all dimensions of privacy are touched as intimate and private aspects of life are digitized and the physical, psychological, and social self is made more available to others than desired. Therefore, encountering privacy concerns in the context of technologies for Aging in Place only with data security does not fully cover the worries.

Control is the key condition for privacy preservation. Users want to decide what, how, at what time, where, and to whom data is collected and transmitted. Acceptance is formed based on a trade-off decision between privacy concerns and utility - the privacy calculus. Correspondingly, users only accept those technology and functions whose perceived usefulness surpasses the perceived privacy risks. For the development of technologies for Aging in Place, it is thus very important to provide a clear benefit for the individual and to give users choice and control over the specific system characteristics: which sensors are installed where, at what time is data collected, what data is collected, in what granularity is the data transmitted and to whom? Modular systems – in which users can start with just a few functions that they perceive as useful but can switch on additional functions when the health status declines – are a good solution to consider the privacy utility trade-off as well as changing needs. At the same time, we see that perceptions of privacy risk and benefits vary strongly between individuals. Such modular system would prove a good starting point to account for user diversity as well.

The regression analysis of the questionnaire data shows that the perception of benefits is the best predictor of use intention for both technologies. Privacy concerns, on the other hand, influence use intention only significantly regarding fall detection. Here, privacy concerns are also slightly more pronounced. These results indicate that differences between technologies for Aging in Place need to be considered. Privacy concerns are not similarly high for all technologies and utilized sensor types.

As the focus group discussions focused on privacy, strong privacy concerns were expressed. In the questionnaire, privacy concerns are seen rather ambivalent, not agreed to and not rejected on average. With the triangulation approach using both methods, the advantages and strengths of both methods could be combined, showing which privacy concerns are prevalent plus their influence on use intention and quantification.

Moreover, age and generation effects could be examined in the quantitative approach. Significantly, it is exactly the group which is the main target, the older adults, which shows the most cautious and self-determined attitude towards being monitored. It is therefore of utmost importance to find solutions which do meet both, the wish to stay independently at home on the one hand and the fragile attitudes towards privacy concerns on the other hand. One hypothesis is that the familiarity and identification of ICT is lower in the group of older adults. Today's older adults have not grown up with ICT in their early years resulting in different experiences, expectations, and attitudes towards technology. Age constitutes a carrier variable that is confounded with other variables, e.g., technology generation, experiences, health status. If this hypothesis is true then future older adults will be more positive towards home care data collection. On the other hand it is equally possible that older adults – independently of their generation – might be more sensitive towards any "being cared" heteronomy, even by impersonal technology. Here, longitudinal studies, repeating measurement years later, should be conducted to shed light onto the effects that technology generations have independent from age. The results are needed to plan ahead for the generations of older adults yet to come.

This study could contribute to an understanding of the nature of privacy concerns regarding technologies for Aging in Place and its impact on acceptance. But some methodological limitations need to be considered.

First of all, both methods comprised of scenario approaches and *reported* attitudes. Most participants needed to empathize with a situation that they have not yet experienced. Also, opinions were based on brief explanations of the technologies, not on detailed information or hands-on experiences. The quantitative results are based on a rather small sample of more than averagely educated participants. Future studies should include more participants, particularly more participants with experiences with technologies for Aging in Place and more participants who are not as experienced with general ICT. Also, privacy perceptions are highly culturally influenced (Krasnova and Veltri 2010). With contrasting privacy perception of different cultures, a better understanding of privacy may be reached.

References

Ambient Assisted Living Joint Programme: Ambient assisted living joint programme - ICT for ageing well (2012). http://www.aaleurope.eu/

Arning, K., Ziefle, M.: Different perspectives on technology acceptance: the role of technology type and age. In: Holzinger, A., Miesenberger, K. (eds.) USAB 2009. LNCS, vol. 5889, pp. 20–41. Springer, Heidelberg (2009). https://doi.org/10.1007/978-3-642-10308-7_2

Beier, G.: Kontrollüberzeugungen im Umgang mit Technik [Technical self-efficacy]. Rep. Psychologie (9), 684–693 (1999)

Benefield, L.E., Holtzclaw, B.J.: Aging in place: merging desire with reality. Nurs. Clin. North Am. **49**(2), 123–131 (2014)

Biermann, H., Himmel, S., Offermann-van Heek, J., Ziefle, M.: User-specific concepts of aging – a qualitative approach on AAL-acceptance regarding ultrasonic whistles. In: Zhou, J., Salvendy, G. (eds.) ITAP 2018. LNCS, vol. 10927, pp. 231–249. Springer, Cham (2018). https://doi.org/10.1007/978-3-319-92037-5_18

Blackman, S., et al.: Ambient assisted living technologies for aging well: a scoping review. J. Intell. Syst. **25**(1), 55–69 (2016)

Boise, L., Wild, K., Mattek, N., Ruhl, M., Dodge, H.H., Kaye, J.: Willingness of older adults to share data and privacy concerns after exposure to unobtrusive home monitoring. Gerontechnology **11**(3), 428–435 (2013)

Burgoon, J.K.: Privacy and communication. Ann. Int. Commun. Assoc. **6**(1), 206–249 (1982)

Cardinaux, F., et al.: Video based technology for ambient assisted living: a review of the literature. J. Ambient Intelli. Smart Environ. (JAISE) **1364**(3), 253–269 (2011)

Czaja, S., Beach, S., Charness, N., Schulz, R.: Older adults and the adoption of healthcare technology: opportunities and challenges. In: Sixsmith, A., Gutman, G. (eds.) Technologies for Active Aging. International Perspectives on Aging, vol. 9, pp. 1–228. Springer, Boston (2013). https://doi.org/10.1007/978-1-4419-8348-0_3

Czaja, S., et al.: Factors predicting the use of technology: findings from the center for research and education on aging and technology enhancement (CREATE). Psyhol. Aging **21**(2), 333–352 (2006)

Davis, F.D.: Perceived usefulness, perceived ease of use, and user acceptance of information technology. MIS Q. **13**(3), 319–340 (1989)

Ermakova, T., Fabian, B., Zarnekow, R.: Acceptance of health clouds a privacy calculus perspective. In: European Conference on Information Systems, pp. 0–13 (2014)

Eurostat: People in the EU: who are we and how do we live? (2015)

Graybill, E.M., McMeekin, P., Wildman, J.: Can aging in place be cost effective? A systematic review. PLoS ONE **9**(7), e102705 (2014)

Halbach, P., Himmel, S., Offermann-van Heek, J., Ziefle, M.: A change is gonna come. In: Zhou, J., Salvendy, G. (eds.) ITAP 2018. LNCS, vol. 10926, pp. 52–69. Springer, Cham (2018). https://doi.org/10.1007/978-3-319-92034-4_5

Hallewell Haslwanter, J.D., Fitzpatrick, G.: Why do few assistive technology systems make it to market? The case of the HandyHelper project. Univers. Access Inf. Soc. **16**(3), 1–19 (2016)

Heart, T., Kalderon, E.: Older adults: are they ready to adopt healthrelated ICT? Int. J. Med. Inform. **82**(11), e209–e231 (2013)

Hensel, B.K., Demiris, G., Courtney, K.L.: Defining obtrusiveness in home telehealth technologies: a conceptual framework. J. Am. Med. Inform. Assoc. **13**, 428–431 (2006)

Himmel, S., Ziefle, M.: Smart home medical technologies: users' requirements for conditional acceptance. I-Com. J. Interact. Media **15**(1), 39–50 (2016)

Kirchbuchner, F., Grosse-Puppendahl, T., Hastall, M.R., Distler, M., Kuijper, A.: Ambient intelligence from senior citizens' perspectives: understanding privacy concerns, technology acceptance, and expectations. In: De Ruyter, B., Kameas, A., Chatzimisios, P., Mavrommati, I. (eds.) AmI 2015. LNCS, vol. 9425, pp. 48–59. Springer, Cham (2015). https://doi.org/10.1007/978-3-319-26005-1_4

Koops, B.-J., Newell, B.C., Timan, T., Skorvanek, I., Chokrevski, T., Galic, M.: A typology of privacy. Univ. Pennsylvanica J. Int. Law **38**(2), 1–93 (2017)

Krasnova, H., Veltri, N.F.: Privacy calculus on social networking sites: explorative evidence from Germany and USA. In: Proceedings of the Annual Hawaii International Conference on System Sciences, pp. 1–10 (2010)

Lee, C., Coughlin, J.F.: Older adults' adoption of technology: an integrated approach to identifying determinants and barriers. J. Prod. Innov. Manag. **32**(5), 747–759 (2014)

Mortenson, W.B., Sixsmith, A., Beringer, R.: No place like home? Surveillance and what home means in old age. Can. J. Aging **35**(1), 103–114 (2016)

Oswal, F., Wahl, H.-W.: Dimensions of the meaning of home in later life. In: Home and Identity in Late Life: International Perspectives, pp. 21–45 (2005)

Rashid, U., Schmidtke, H., Woo, W.: Managing disclosure of personal health information in smart home healthcare. In: Stephanidis, C. (ed.) UAHCI 2007. LNCS, vol. 4555, pp. 188–197. Springer, Heidelberg (2007). https://doi.org/10.1007/978-3-540-73281-5_20

Sackmann, R., Winkler, O.: Technology generations revisited: the internet generation. Gerontechnology **11**(4), 493–503 (2013)

Schomakers, E.-M., Lidynia, C., Ziefle, M.: Hidden within a group of people mental models of privacy protection. In: 3rd International Conference on Internet of Things, Big Data and Security, pp. 85–94. SCITEPRESS - Science and and Technology Publications (2018)

Schomakers, E.-M., van Heek, J., Ziefle, M.: A Game of wants and needs. The playful, user-centered assessment of AAL technology acceptance. In: Proceedings of the 4th International Conference on In-formation and Communication Technologies for Ageing Well and e-Health (ICT4AgeingWell 2018), pp. 126–133 (2018)

Siegel, C., Dorner, T.E.: Information technologies for active and assisted living— inuences to the quality of life of an ageing society. Int. J. Med. Inform. **100**, 32–45 (2017)

Smith, H.J., Dinev, T., Xu, H.: Information privacy research: an interdisciplinary review. MIS Q. **35**(4), 989–1015 (2011)

Smith, H.J., Milberg, S.J., Burke, S.J.: Information privacy: measuring individuals' concerns about organizational practices. Manag. Inf. Syst. Q. **20**(2), 167–196 (1996)

Solove, D.J.: A taxonomy of privacy. GW Law Fac. Publ. Other Works **154**(3), 477–560 (2006)

Valdez, A.C., Ziefle, M.: The users' perspective on the privacy-utility trade-offs in health recommender systems. Int. J. Hum.-Comput. Stud. **121**, 108–121 (2018)

Van den Broeck, E., Poels, K., Walrave, M.: Older and wiser? Facebook use, privacy concern, and privacy protection in the life stages of emerging, young, and middle adulthood. Soc. Media+ Soc. **1**(2) (2015)

Van Grootven, B., van Achterberg, T.: The European Union's ambient and assisted living joint programme: an evaluation of its impact on population health and well-being. Health Inform. J. **25**, 27–40 (2016)

van Heek, J., Himmel, S., Ziefle, M.:Helpful but spooky? Acceptance of AAL-systems contrasting user groups with focus on disabilities and care needs. In: Proceedings of the 3rd International Conference on Information and Communication Technologies for Ageing Well and e-Health (ICT4AWE 2017), pp. 78–90 (2017)

Vanleerberghe, P., De Witte, N., Claes, C., Schalock, R.L., Verté, D.: The quality of life of older people aging in place: a literature review. Qual. Life Res. **26**(11), 2899–2907 (2017)

Venkatesh, V., Morris, M.G., Davis, G.B., Davis, F.D.: User acceptance of information technology: toward a unified view. MIS Q. **27**(3), 425–478 (2003)

Wiles, J.L., Leibing, A., Guberman, N., Reeve, J., Allen, R.E.: The meaning of "aging in place" to older people. Gerontologist **52**(3), 357–366 (2012)

Yusif, S., Soar, J., Hafeez-Baig, A.: Older people, assistive technologies, and the barriers to adoption: a systematic review. Int. J. Med. Inform. **94**, 112–116 (2016)

Factors Influencing Proxy Internet Health Information Seeking Among the Elderly in Rural China: A Grounded Theory Study

Xiaokang Song[1(✉)] , Shijie Song[1] , Si Chen[1] ,
Yuxiang (Chris) Zhao[2] , and Qinghua Zhu[1]

[1] Nanjing University, Nanjing 210023, Jiangsu, China
sxksxk666@163.com
[2] Nanjing University of Science and Technology,
Nanjing 210094, Jiangsu, China

Abstract. Online health information seeking is becoming increasingly important for self-health management. As a special group, the elderly are at a disadvantage in online health information search. Recent studies have found a large number of proxy searchers who help old people search for health information online. The purpose of this paper is to explore the factors that influence the old people to adopt proxy internet health information seeking (PIHIS). We chose 20 old people in rural China as the research object, and used grounded theory to analyze the interview data, so as to understand old people's attitudes and concerns towards PIHIS. The results of this study provide both theoretical contributions and practical implications on how the Internet benefits the old people.

Keywords: Proxy Internet use · Health information seeking · The elderly · Grounded theory

1 Introduction

The elderly group is growing both in proportion and in size of the total population in China from the year 2000. Especially, the speed of the ageing population has exceeded the world average level [1]. By the end of 2017, the number of people aged over 65 years in China had reached more than 158 million, which accounts for 11.4% of the total population [2]. The accelerated growth of the elderly population leads to the increasing demand for health care and community services, which has become a major challenge for China. At the same time, the aging of the population contributes to the emergence of the "silver-hair market" and provides a huge potential market for the development of gerontechnology [3].

In addition, there is another growing tendency towards widespread dissemination of health information on the Internet from the year 2000 [4]. The Internet plays an increasingly important role as the source of health information for people, including the elderly group. Compared with off-line community hospitals, it is more convenient for

© Springer Nature Switzerland AG 2019
J. Zhou and G. Salvendy (Eds.): HCII 2019, LNCS 11592, pp. 332–343, 2019.
https://doi.org/10.1007/978-3-030-22012-9_24

the elderly to obtain health information on the Internet. Health information is particularly useful to help the elderly maintain physical and psychological health, and strengthen self-education on personal care and disease prevention [5, 6]. Prior studies show that seeking health information is one of the main reasons that older people use the Internet in America [7, 8].

Despite rapid development of Internet technology, digital inequalities always exist, especially for the elderly in rural areas. According to the report (2018) issued by China Internet Network Information Center (CNNIC) [9], the Internet penetration rate in rural areas of China is only 36.5%, and rural population is the main component of non-netizens. Although the benefits of using the Internet to obtain health information are obvious, there are some obstacles for the older people, such as lack of access to the Internet, lack of knowledge and skills, and concerns with the security and privacy [10].

Proxy Internet use is considered as one of the effective ways to bridge digital inequalities [11]. Proxy Internet use refers to the indirect access to Internet resources and services through others [12]. Selwyn *et al.* [13] pointed out that the most frequent proxy Internet use focused on seeking online health-related information while family members, especially children or grand-children, and friends acted as the proxies in most cases. Recent studies have found that 61% of online health information searchers seek for health information on behalf of others [14]. However, little research refers to the factors that affect proxy Internet use. This paper aims at filling this research gap by carrying out an in-depth interview with 20 older people in rural China. The results provide a basis for the research on intervention of proxy health information seeking, and further contribute to the reduction of health information acquisition inequalities among the elderly in rural areas.

2   Related Work

2.1   Old People's Internet Use for Health Information

Internet has become a new source of health information for the elderly. Older people are more likely to suffer from chronic diseases than the younger generation, which leads to a great level of health information need [15]. Previous studies have found that Internet users with chronic diseases are more likely to get health information online and share it with others regardless of age and education [16]. Health information helps older people reduce health risks, enrich health literacy and establish a more positive relationship with doctors. Seeking and utilizing health information will be beneficial to their physical and mental health [17]. Since there are a limited number of doctors in China and the inquiry time is short, the Internet is very important for patients to obtain health information, especially for the elderly [18].

Although Internet use may bring great benefits to the elderly, there are still many problems for them to use the Internet. For examples, their lack of experience in Internet use has a negative impact on online health information seeking, which is associated with greater anxiety and lower confidence [19]. Wong et al. [17] found that perceived ease of use and attitudes had significant predictive effects on online health information seeking behavior of the elderly. There are also some physical and psychological factors that affect the Internet use of the elderly, such as lack of access to the Internet, lack of use skills, memory and information processing capabilities, and concerns about the security and privacy [10]. It is necessary to help the elderly improve the Internet use and identify reliable online health information source, so as to improve their ability and satisfaction in searching and using online health information.

2.2 Proxy Internet Use

Proxy Internet use could bring the benefits of the Internet to more people. Recent studies on the digital divide have questioned the dichotomy between Internet users and non-users. Some studies have found that the forms of indirect Internet use are less explored in the traditional Internet use research [20, 21]. In particular, among the elderly population, a considerable number of proxy Internet users have been identified. They do not surf the web themselves, but do things online by others. They mainly rely on their children and/or grandchildren, who act as enthusiastic experts [22]. This form of proxy Internet use provides cognitive, mental and socio-material support for the elderly who do not use the Internet by themselves, and helps them with the practice of accessing online information resources [13].

The conceptual model of proxy health information seeking includes three main components: health information demander, proxy searcher and online health information resources (shown in Fig. 1). Dolničar et al. [11] studied the proxy Internet use from the perspective of social support network. Some studies focused on the proxy searchers. Proxy searchers, also called "surrogate seekers" [21] or "lay information mediary searchers" [23], are considered as non-medical professionals who search health information for others [14]. Surrogate seekers are more likely to be married middle-aged people with good physical condition [24]. Moreover, they are more likely to live with others, visiting social networking sites to read and share information on medical topics frequently, and participate in online health group activities [21].

In summary, the review suggests that, although there are many studies on online health search and proxy Internet use for the elderly, little is known about the influencing factors of using proxy health information seeking among the elderly. This study intends to fill this research gap.

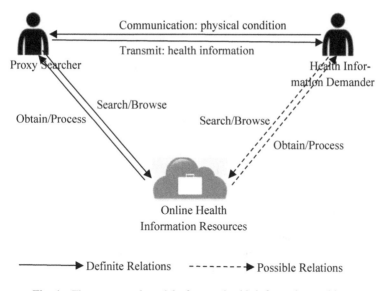

Fig. 1. The conceptual model of proxy health information seeking.

3   Research Design

3.1   Methods

This paper explores and analyses the factors that affect the old people's proxy health information seeking behavior. Since this problem is unfolded in the absence of a solid theoretical basis, this paper adopts grounded theory as the research method. Grounded theory rises original data to systematic theory through systematic analysis [25]. Specifically, there are two reasons for choosing this method. (a) Firstly, the research on the proxy Internet use is still in the preliminary exploratory stage. There are many problems that need further analysis. It is suitable to use qualitative research methods for exploratory research; (b) Secondly, this study aims to analyze the elderly's proxy health information seeking. However, there are few relevant references. This paper uses three stages of data analysis in grounded theory to analyze data, including open coding, axial coding and selective coding [26].

3.2   Participants

This study chooses 20 old people in rural areas of Xuzhou City, Jiangsu Province as the research objects, as shown in Table 1. They are 60–79 years old and have experience in proxy health information seeking. Under the guidance of the interview outline, we interviewed each of the participants for 30–50 min. The interview outline focuses on the following issues: (a) In what circumstances have you experienced proxy health information seeking, and what are your attitudes and views towards this model? (b) Do you think this model is suitable for the old people in rural areas? And why? (c) Could you briefly describe your feelings about the proxy health information seeking and the main problems encountered in the process? (d) Under what circumstances would you voluntarily ask someone to search for health information on the Internet on behalf of you? And why?

Table 1. Characteristics of the participants.

Variables	Number	Proportion
Gender		
Female	9	45%
Male	11	55%
Children		
1–2	4	20%
3–4	11	55%
5–6	5	25%
Live with children		
Yes	7	35%
No	13	65%
Education		
Unlettered	6	30%
Primary school	9	45%
Junior middle school	3	15%
High school and above	2	10%
Chronic		
Yes	14	70%
No	6	30%
Smartphone		
Yes	5	25%
No	15	75%
Computer experience		
No	16	80%
Less than 1 year	3	15%
1-2 years	1	5%
Note: n = 20		

4   Data Analysis

4.1   Open Coding

Open coding is used to decompose and refine data on the basis of collation and induction [27]. In open coding process, the concepts that describe various phenomena are abstracted from the initial data and then these concepts are further generalized to various categories. In this study, a total of 32583 words (including punctuation) were recorded in 20 interviews. Since there are three researcher conducting open coding processes, the number of initial concepts generated is large and some of the concepts are repetitive. Therefore, in the process of categorization, we review the initial concepts again and combines the repetitive concepts. Finally, 18 initial concepts are identified, as shown in Table 2.

Table 2. The results of open coding.

Concepts	Connotation	Original data
Health status	Physical condition of the elderly	"When I'm not feeling well for a long time and I don't know what's going on, I'll talk to my family and ask them to help me see what's going on"
Need care	Old people need care and help from their families	"My daughter often searches some information on the Internet and tells me how to pay attention to my body and what food I can't eat. I'm glad to see that my children care so much about me"
Own experience	Ways for the old people to keep themselves healthy	"Apart from going to the hospital. Usually there are some commonly used medicines at home. If I am not feeling well, I will take some medicines based on experience. Then go out for more walks and exercise"
Security concerns	Old people consider Internet information may be unsafe	"The health information on the Internet is too messy. There are various opinions. A lot of information is false and deceptive"
Privacy concerns	Older people are unwilling to give publicity to their health conditions	"I know my own health. I don't want to talk to others"
Independent life	Old people are able to take care of themselves	"I think I'm in good health. I am fully capable of taking care of myself"
Medical difficulties	It's troublesome for the old people to go to the hospital	"It's really troublesome to go to the hospital. I need to queue up many times. I don't usually go to the hospital if it's not necessary"
Peer influence	Peer influence affects the attitudes of old people	"My friends often get health knowledge from the Internet. They consult some questions online with the help of their children. I think that's a good thing"
Knowledge level	Lack of knowledge among the old people	"I am lack of the knowledge and skills to use computers and smartphones. If I need to search health information online, I can only ask my children to help me"
Thirst for health	Old people want to keep healthy condition	"I'm old now. I think health is more important than anything. When I'm not feeling well, I want to know the reason and treatment plan as soon as possible"
Trouble others	Proxy health information seeking will get others into trouble	"Children are usually busy. I don't want to bother them. And I don't want them to worry about me"

(*continued*)

Table 2. (*continued*)

Concepts	Connotation	Original data
Connection with children	Degree of communications among the elderly and their children	"The children don't live with me and have few contacts. I don't often talk to them about my own health"
Attitudes towards layman	The trust of old people on non-medical professionals	"I believe in the expertise of doctors. Others don't know medical knowledge"
Economic factors	Searching for health information on the Internet save money	"Visiting a doctor in a hospital requires registration and various examinations. It costs a lot of money. If you can find useful information on the Internet, I can save some money"
Relevance	Is the health information on the Internet relevant to my own situation	"There are many health information on the Internet. I'm not sure if this information is suitable for my situation"
Advertisement	Television advertising could influence the willingness of the old people	"I often see app advertisements on TV about online medical treatment, such as "Hao dai fu". I think it's convenient. I'd like to try it"
Accessibility of Internet	Old people have no access to the Internet	"I don't have a computer or a smartphone. My son has a smartphone"
Trust family members	Old people trust their families	"I will talk to my family if I feel sick. I am reassured that the children can help me search for health information online. They will certainly not deceive me or hurt me"

4.2 Axial Coding

Axial coding aims to discover and establish relationships among concepts and categories. Researchers constantly compared the relationship among concepts through micro-analysis, and gradually merged concepts to form an axis [27]. In this study, since the participants are old people in rural areas, their statements are not professional. Therefore, in the process of axial coding, researchers focused on the re-analysis and summary of the original concepts.

According to the initial concepts of open coding, we further summarized and classified them. Nine categories have been formed, including personal features, social situation, external motivation, affection needs, perceived benefits, distrust of the Internet, self-confidence, self-care, and family environment. In addition, these nine categories were further analyzed and summarized, and finally three fundamental categories were concluded. The correspondence of fundamental categories, categories and initial concepts are shown in Table 3.

Table 3. The results of axial coding.

Fundamental categories	Categories	Concepts
The objective motivation of adopting PIHIS	Personal features	Health status
		Knowledge level
	Social situation	Medical difficulties
		Accessibility of Internet
	External motivation	Peer influence
		Advertisement
The subjective motivation of adopting PIHIS	Affection needs	Need care
		Trust family members
	Perceived benefits	Thirst for health
		Economic factors
Obstacles to PIHIS	Distrust of the Internet	Security concerns
		Relevance
	Self-confidence	Own experience
		Attitudes towards layman
	Self-care	Privacy concerns
		Independent life
	Family environment	Connection with children
		Trouble others

4.3   Selective Coding

Selective coding is designed to integrate and refine the classification, and then present findings in the form of theoretical framework [26]. The three main categories formed in the axial coding stage were analyzed concretely. Then, we revealed the typical relationship among the main categories and the behavioral phenomenon. The purpose of this paper is to explore the factors that influence the use of proxy Internet health information for older people. Therefore, the core issue is the adoption of PIHIS among the elderly. The typical relationship structure of the fundamental categories in this stage is shown in Table 4.

The results of the coding processes show that the factors that affect the adoption of PIHIS of old people include objective motivation, subjective motivation and obstacles. In addition, objective conditions are able to adjust subjective psychology to influence the intensity of adopting PIHIS. Based on the story line sorted out from the grounded analysis stages, the preliminary theoretical model of influencing factors of PIHIS adoption by old people is summarized, as shown in Fig. 2. It is worthwhile noting that this paper summarizes the influencing factors model of PIHIS adoption from the first-hand interview data, which has strong theoretical value. However, this model could not be directly applied to empirical analysis, and need to be combined with other theoretical foundations to build specific empirical models and frameworks.

Table 4. The structure of the typical relationships.

Typical relationships	Relationship structures	The connotation of the relationship structure
Objective motivation → adopt PIHIS	Causality	Personal features, social situation, and external motivation objectively motivate old people to adopt PIHIS
Subjective motivation → adopt PIHIS	Causality	Old people need the care and help of their families, and think that the Internet can bring benefits to them. Therefore, they have psychological motivation to adopt PIHIS
Obstacles → adopt PIHIS	Causality	There are some obstacles affecting the adoption of PIHIS by the elderly. For example, they want to live independently, they don't want to trouble your children, and they don't trust the Internet et al.
Objective motivation ↓ Subjective motivation → adopt PIHIS	Moderated	Some objective conditions faced by the elderly, such as personal features, social situation, and external motivation, can adjust subjective psychology to influence the intensity of adopting PIHIS

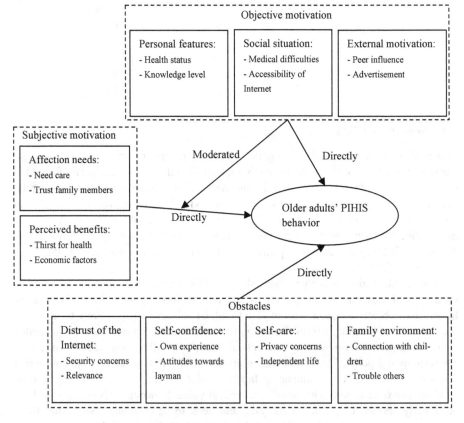

Fig. 2. Theoretical model.

5   Discussion

5.1   The Objective Motivation of Adopting PIHIS

According to the results of grounded theory, this paper argues that the objective motivation that affects PIHIS behavior of old people includes three aspects: personal features, social situation, and external motivation. There are some common characteristics of old people in rural areas. In this study, 70% of participants reported that they had chronic diseases, and 75% of them had a primary school education or below. In China, medical resources are limited and it is difficult for old people to see a doctor. Old people also report that they do not have computers or smartphones, have no access to the Internet. However, with the development of Internet application in China, all aspects of people's lives are impacted, even for old people in rural areas. In the process of communicating with peers and watching TV, old people are exposed to the idea that the Internet is beneficial to personal health management. Accordingly, on the one hand, old people have the motivation to obtain health information on the Internet due to health status, medical difficulties, peer influence and advertising. On the other hand, there are some objective obstacles to their use of the Internet, such as lack of access to the Internet and their lack of knowledge of using the Internet.

5.2   The Subjective Motivation of Adopting PIHIS

The research findings show that the subjective motivation that affect PIHIS behavior of old people includes two aspects: affection needs and perceived benefits. Firstly, 65% of the elderly reported they are not living with their children. Psychologically, old people in rural areas may be alone for a long time. They need emotional care from their children, especially when they are ill. Older people generally trust their families, and they believe their family numbers would do something beneficial to them. Secondly, 80% of the elderly reported that they considered the most important thing was to keep healthy. Five participants (25%) reported that they considered it would be useful and saves money to get health information on the Internet. Based on the analysis above, we proposed that old people in rural areas have subjective motivation to adopt PIHIS, regardless of their care needs from psychological level and perceived benefits from cognitive level.

5.3   Obstacles to PIHIS

Although there are some objective and subjective motivation to promote old people's willingness to adopt PIHIS, there are also some obstacles for the adoption. The elderly are also known as "digital immigrants" [28]. They have some difficulties in accepting the Internet. Nine participants (45%) reported that they believed that health information resources on the Internet could be deceptive and could have a negative impact on their security. Ten participants (50%) feared that online health information might not be appropriate for their conditions. Half of the elderly said they trusted doctors, followed by their own experience. After a long period of treatment, they know how to take medicines and exercises. In the group of laypersons, old people trust their college-educated children rather than their spouse. Four participants (20%) said they were not willing to tell others about their illness, and they considered they had the abilities to take care of themselves. The most important obstacle is lack of communication among old people and their children, and they are worried they would influence their children's normal life. The analysis above shows that we still need a lot of work to make PIHIS truly benefit the old people.

6   Conclusion

Since the research of proxy internet health information seeking is still in the initial stage, there is no mature theory or framework for empirical analysis. This paper explores the factors that affect the adoption of PIHIS for the elderly in rural areas. The grounded theory was used to analyze the interview data from 20 participants. Eighteen concepts were extracted from open coding analysis, and the classification system of influencing factors of PIHIS among old people was summarized from axial coding and selective coding. The research results not only show the views of PIHIS adoption that the elderly in rural areas take, but also provide implications on how to improve the abilities of old people in rural areas for obtaining health information and maintaining healthy life in the future. However, only interview data is used for qualitative analysis, which is the limitation of the study. In the follow-up study, the authors will combine the relevant theoretical frameworks to model the elements extracted from the grounded analysis. We will use empirical methods to test our findings.

References

1. Chen, K., Chan, A.H.: Predictors of gerontechnology acceptance by older Hong Kong Chinese. Technovation 34(2), 126–135 (2014)
2. National Bureau of Statistics of the People's Republic of China. The China Statistical Yearbook 2018. http://www.stats.gov.cn/tjsj/ndsj/2018/indexch.htm. Accessed 4 Jan 2019
3. Kohlbacher, F., Herstatt, C., Tim, S.: Product development for the silver market, 2nd edn. Springer, Heidelberg (2011). https://doi.org/10.1007/978-3-642-14338-0_1
4. VanBiervliet, A., Edwards-Schafer, P.: Consumer health information on the web: trends, issues, and strategies. Dermatol. Nurs. 16(6), 519–524 (2004)
5. Leung, A., Ko, P., Chan, K.S., Chi, I., Chow, N.: Searching health information via the web: Hong Kong Chinese older adults' experience. Public Health Nurs. 24(2), 169–175 (2007)
6. Chang, S.J., Im, E.O.: A path analysis of Internet health information seeking behaviors among older adults. Geriatr. Nurs. 35(2), 137–141 (2014)
7. Macias, W., McMillan, S.: The return of the house call: the role of Internet-based interactivity in bringing health information home to older adults. Health Commun. 23(1), 34–44 (2008)
8. Crabb, R.M., Rafie, S., Weingardt, K.R.: Health-related internet use in older primary care patients. Gerontology 58(2), 164–170 (2012)
9. China Internet Network Information Center: Thirty-ninth China Internet development statistics report 2018. http://202.119.32.195/cache/7/03/www.cnnic.net.cn/55cc22fe4ce4a6970d696905e9a5f28e/P020180820630889299840.pdf. Accessed 10 Jan 2019

10. Pan, S., Jordan-Marsh, M.: Internet use intention and adoption among Chinese older adults: from the expanded technology acceptance model perspective. Comput. Hum. Behav. **26**(5), 1111–1119 (2010)

11. Dolničar, V., Grošelj, D., Hrast, M.F., Vehovar, V., Petrovčič, A.: The role of social support networks in proxy Internet use from the intergenerational solidarity perspective. Telematics Inform. **35**(2), 305–317 (2018)

12. Grošelj, D., Reisdorf, B.C., Petrovčič, A.: Obtaining indirect internet access: an examination how reasons for internet non-use relate to proxy internet use. Telecommun. Policy (2018). https://doi.org/10.1016/j.telpol.2018.07.004. Accessed 10 Jan 2019

13. Selwyn, N., Johnson, N., Nemorin, S., Knight, E.: Going online on behalf of others: an investigation of 'proxy' internet consumers (2016). http://eprints.lse.ac.uk/83436/1/Nemorin_Going%20online_2017.pdf. Accessed 10 Jan 2019

14. Reifegerste, D., Bachl, M., Baumann, E.: Surrogate health information seeking in Europe: influence of source type and social network variables. Int. J. Med. Inform. **103**, 7–14 (2017)

15. Kovner, C.T., Mezey, M., Harrington, C.: Who cares for older adults? Workforce implications of an aging society. Health Aff. **21**(5), 78–89 (2002)

16. Stellefson, M., et al.: Web 2.0 chronic disease self-management for older adults: a systematic review. J. Med. Internet Res. **15**(2), e35 (2013). https://doi.org/10.2196/jmir.2439

17. Wong, C.K., Yeung, D.Y., Ho, H.C., Tse, K.P., Lam, C.Y.: Chinese older adults' Internet use for health information. J. Appl. Gerontol. **33**(3), 316–335 (2014)

18. Hao, H.: The development of online doctor reviews in China: an analysis of the largest online doctor review website in China. J. Med. Internet Res. **17**(6), e134 (2015). https://doi.org/10.2196/jmir.4365

19. Wagner, N., Hassanein, K., Head, M.: Computer use by older adults: a multi-disciplinary review. Comput. Hum. Behav. **26**(5), 870–882 (2010)

20. Dutton, W.H., Blank, G.: Next generation users: the internet in Britain. Oxford Internet Institute, University of Oxford, Oxford (2011). http://dx.doi.org/10.2139/ssrn.1960655. Accessed 8 Feb 2019

21. Cutrona, S.L., Mazor, K.M., Vieux, S.N., Luger, T.M., Volkman, J.E., Rutten, L.J.F.: Health information-seeking on behalf of others: characteristics of "surrogate seekers". J. Cancer Educ. **30**(1), 12–19 (2015)

22. Dolničar, V., Hrast, M.F., Vehovar, V., Petrovčič, A.: Digital inequality and intergenerational solidarity: the role of social support in proxy internet use. AoIR Sel. Pap. Internet Res. **3**, 1–4 (2013)

23. Abrahamson, J.A., Fisher, K.E., Turner, A.G., Durrance, J.C., Turner, T.C.: Lay information mediary behavior uncovered: exploring how nonprofessionals seek health information for themselves and others online. J. Med. Libr. Assoc.: JMLA **96**(4), 310–323 (2008)

24. Sadasivam, R.S., Kinney, R.L., Lemon, S.C., Shimada, S.L., Allison, J.J., Houston, T.K.: Internet health information seeking is a team sport: analysis of the Pew Internet Survey. Int. J. Med. Inform. **82**(3), 193–200 (2013)

25. Strauss, A.L.: The Discovery of Grounded Theory: Strategies for Qualitative Research. Aldine. Aldine de Gruyter, Chicago (1967)

26. Heath, H., Cowley, S.: Developing a grounded theory approach: a comparison of Glaser and Strauss. Int. J. Nurs. Stud. **41**(2), 141–150 (2004)

27. Strauss, A., Corbin, J.M.: Basics of qualitative research: grounded theory procedures and techniques. Mod. Lang. J. **77**(2), 129 (1990)

28. Prensky, M.: Digital natives, digital immigrants part 1. Horizon **9**(5), 1–6 (2001)

Usage of a Technical Communication and Documentation System by Older Adults and Professionals in Multidisciplinary Home Rehabilitation

A. Steinert[1(✉)], J. Kiselev[1], R. Klebbe[1], M. Schröder[2], A. Russ[3],
K. Schumacher[3], N. Reithinger[3], and U. Müller-Werdan[1]

[1] Geriatrics Research Group, Charité – Universitätsmedizin Berlin,
Berlin, Germany
Anika.Steinert@charite.de
[2] Serrala Solutions GmbH, Berlin, Germany
[3] German Research Center for Artificial Intelligence, Berlin, Germany

Abstract. Mobile Home Rehabilitation (MHR) is a concept of outpatient health care in Germany. A multidisciplinary team consisting of medical doctors, therapists, social workers, psychologists and nursing staff is responsible for the treatment of patients with severe health conditions. Challenges for communication, organization and documentation occur due to a multidisciplinary team, highly variable and dynamic home settings and the vulnerable target group. For this reason, the Morecare project, funded by the Federal Ministry of Education and Research (2016–2018), merged various technologies into a comprehensive concept in order to work on the identified problems and to enable a more effective and sustainable working method for all actors. In a pilot study with 10 Older Adults (OA) (aged ≥ 65 years) and a multidisciplinary Mobile Rehabilitation Team (MRT, N = 10), we evaluated the Morecare system with the main focus on the usage and usability of the tablet application and its acceptance by older adults and the MRT towards a complex communication, documentation and notification system. Both the MRT and the OA did not use all functions to the full extent, only those functions which offered an individual added value for the users. The usability of the system was evaluated as only moderate. Technical assistance systems can support mobile rehabilitation, but must be clearly adapted to the needs and circumstances of this particular user group.

Keywords: Mobile rehabilitation · Usability · Older Adults · Mobile devices

1 Introduction

Together with curative medicine and prevention, rehabilitation is the most important pillar of the German health system [1]. However, regardless of the form of care, it is important to adapt it to the needs and abilities of the respective target group. This applies in particular to the field of geriatrics, in which older patients are characterized

© Springer Nature Switzerland AG 2019
J. Zhou and G. Salvendy (Eds.): HCII 2019, LNCS 11592, pp. 344–354, 2019.
https://doi.org/10.1007/978-3-030-22012-9_25

on the one hand by the presence of several chronic diseases, some of which are interdependent and influential, and on the other hand by the "normal" aging process to be expected in their performance with limitations in functional and cognitive capacity as well as mobility and perceptive faculty [2].

2 Background and Objectives

Mobile Home Rehabilitation (MHR) is a concept of outpatient health care in Germany. A multidisciplinary team consisting of medical doctors, therapists, social workers, psychologists and nursing staff is responsible for the treatment process of patients with severe conditions. The rehabilitation takes place in the patient's home environment with a duration of six to eight weeks and approximately 40 therapeutic sessions. In MHR, the decentralized working methods of the various occupational groups involved mean that there is a high level of coordination and communication effort both for these groups themselves and for the patients and their relatives. For therapists working in rehabilitation, documentation of the therapy content is often difficult due to a lack of infrastructure (e.g., documentation must be completed in the car or at home) and leads to a correspondingly high documentation effort. In addition, agreements between colleagues are just as difficult as passing on relevant information. On the organizational level, both the planning of the daily routines themselves and their necessary adaptation due to current events is associated with a high level of effort.

For this reason, the Morecare project, funded by the Federal Ministry of Education and Research (2016–2018), merged various technologies into a comprehensive concept in order to work on the identified problems and to enable a more effective and sustainable working method for all actors. At the beginning of the project, the addressed barriers were specified within a requirements analysis and technical solutions were accordingly designed [3]. The aim of the applied technologies was to simplify the rehabilitation process and make it more comprehensible for patients, thus strengthening patient autonomy and the ability for successful self-management. Within an evaluation of the developed Morecare system, the following research question should be answered:

- How is a technical assistance system used and accepted by patients and therapists in mobile rehabilitation?
- How are skills in handling mobile devices changing?

3 Methods

To answer these questions, a study was conducted with two different groups of participants:

(1) Mobile Rehabilitation Team: 10 employees of a MRT tested the Morecare system for seven months.
(2) Older Adults (OA): 10 older adults aged $\geq$ 65 years evaluated the Morecare patient system for two weeks.

The methodology and results described below are presented for each of these two groups.

3.1 Developed System

Within the project, a system was created from various components:

(1) Tablet application, which supports the MRT in organizing appointments and communicating with each other as well as with patients and enables digital documentation.
(2) Patient System consisting of a tablet application for the coordination of appointments or communication with the MRT and with the possibility of conducting training sessions independently at home. The patient system was supplemented by a modular notification and operating system, which consists of Flic buttons for simplified operation of the tablet, Hue lamps for visual display of new notifications and a sensor wristband, which raises the number of steps of the patient and vibrates upon receipt of a notification (Fig. 1).
(3) Web interface for the coordinator of the Mobile Rehabilitation, which enables the setting of appointments for the therapy sessions and communication with the MRT and patients.
(4) Vital data sensor for recording oxygen saturation, pulse and number of steps during therapy units.

Fig. 1. Constituent parts of the modular notification and operating system: Hue lamps, sensor wristband, flic buttons

3.2   Procedure

Mobile Rehabilitation Team.
The evaluation of the Morecare system by the MRT was undertaken over a period of seven months divided into two phases (Figs. 2, 3).

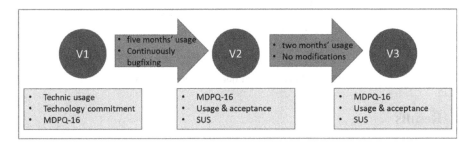

Fig. 2. Procedure and questionnaires for the MRT

On the first study visit (V1), the MRTs' technical experience and technology commitment as well as their knowledge of the handling of mobile devices (Mobile Device Proficiency Scale, MDPQ-16, [4]) were assessed. In addition, there was extensive training on the system, in which all areas of the application were explained by the study staff. Therapists, caregivers, social workers, doctors and the coordinator then used the system for a total of seven months. In the first five months there were still fundamental changes to the application, which resulted from the requirements of the MRT. A total of 27 new versions of the application were released during these five months, in which several changes were made. After five months of testing, an interim study visit (V2) was carried out again to assess the knowledge of how to use mobile devices and the previous use and evaluation of the application using a questionnaire. Subsequently, the MRT used the Morecare system for another two months, during which no more changes were made to the application. After this period, the third study visit (V3) took place, in which the users were asked about their mobile devices proficiency as well as about the use, acceptance and usability (System Usability Scale, SUS, [5]) of the Morecare system.

Older Adults (OA).
The OA tested the Morecare system for two weeks. The two study visits were carried out by study staff in the participants' homes. At the first study visit (V1), participants' sociodemographic data, use of technology and the technology commitment as well as their knowledge in handling mobile end devices (MDPQ-16) were assessed. Subsequently, the Morecare system was set up in the homes of the study participants who were trained in the different components and functions. After two weeks' system usage, the participants were again asked about their knowledge of mobile devices. In addition, a questionnaire was issued to subjectively assess the usability of the technical system and various questions were asked about the acceptance, use and user-friendliness of specific system functions and components (Fig. 3).

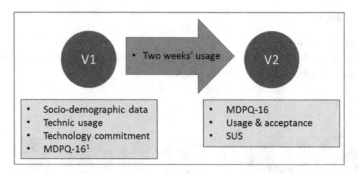

Fig. 3. Procedure and questionnaires for OA

4 Results

4.1 Sample

Mobile Rehabilitation Team (MRT).
A total of 10 members of the team took part in the three survey stages (V1, V2, V3). Physiotherapists formed the largest group in the MRT. Most of the respondents were female (Table 1).

Table 1. Basic data of the MRT (n = 9)

	Characteristic	Number (n)
Professional category	Physiotherapists	3
	Occupational therapists	1
	Speech therapists	1
	Nursing staff	1
	Physicians	2
	Social worker	1
	Coordination	1
Sex	Male	3
	Female	7
Technology usage (frequently, occasionally, rarely, never)	Computer	7 / 2 / 0 / 0
	Internet	9 / 0 / 0 / 0
	Tablet	3 / 3 / 1 / 2
	Smartphone	8 / 1 / 0 / 0
	Phone	7 / 1 / 1 / 0

All respondents of the MRT indicated they use the Internet frequently. Computers, smartphones and telephones were frequently used by the majority of respondents. A tablet had not previously been used by two people at the beginning of the study. On the scale ranging from one to five for technical commitment (one = low TC, five = high TC) the respondents of the MRT achieved a mean value of 3.7. This corresponds to the norm values of the validation study by Neyer et al. [6] in which 825 subjects aged 18–80 years were included (M = 3.73).

Older Adults (OA).
A total of 10 participants were included in the evaluation of the Morecare patient system. The mean age of the participants was 72.5 years (range: 66–76 years). During the recruitment process, attention was taken to ensure that an equal proportion of men and women were included in the study (Table 2).

Table 2. Basic data of the OA (N = 10)

	Characteristic	Number (n)
Age (yrs)		M = 72.2
Sex	Male	3
	Female	7
Technology usage (frequently, occasionally, rarely, never)	Computer	9 / 1 / 0 / 0
	Internet	9 / 0 / 1 / 0
	Tablet	3 / 2 / 1 / 4
	Smartphone	6 / 3 / 0 / 1
	Phone	4 / 5 / 1 / 0

The study group of OA was also examined with regard to their technical commitment. On average, the group achieved a value of M = 3.9, which, in accordance with the standard values mentioned, indicates a high level of technical commitment.

4.2 Mobile Device Proficiency

Mobile Rehabilitation Team (MRT). The mobile device proficiency was assessed at the three study visits with the help of the Mobile Device Proficiency Questionnaire (MDPQ-16). On average, the skills of the respondents increased during the course of the study. Overall, the score increased from 31.0 (16.5–38.5) to 33.3 (27.0–40.0) points with the duration of tablet use. The score increased by 0.2–0.85 points especially in the subscales basics, internet, entertainment, privacy and troubleshooting (Table 3).

Table 3. Results of the MDPQ in the MRT (N = 10)

	V1 M (Min–Max)	V2 M (Min–Max)	V3 M (Min–Max)
MDPQ score	31.00 (16.5–38.5)	31.80 (14.0–40.0)	33.30 (27.0–40.0)
Basics	4.65	4.70	4.85
Communication	4.35	3.90	3.95
Data/file storage	3.70	3.50	3.80
Internet	4.55	4.60	4.90
Calendar	3.40	3.20	3.65
Entertainment	3.60	3.90	4.10
Privacy	3.45	4.30	4.30
Troubleshooting	3.30	3.65	3.75

Older Adults (OA).
Knowledge on the handling of mobile devices was collected both at the beginning and at the end of the study of the OA by completion of the MDPQ. Overall, the skills of the respondents increased slightly on average during the course of the study. The total value increased from 27.7 (11.0–39.5) to 28.6 (15.0–40.0) points. Particularly in the subscales for *basics* and *internet*, the scale averages increased by 0.6–0.65 points. At the same time, the scale averages in the subscales *communication* and *calendar* fell by 0.2–0.4 points at the end of the study (Table 4).

Table 4. Results of the MDPQ in OA (N = 10)

	V1 M (Min–Max)	V2 M (Min–Max)
MDPQ score	27.65 (11.0–39.5)	28.60 (15.0–40.0)
Basics	3.90	4.50
Communication	4.10	3.70
Data/file storage	3.15	3.25
Internet	3.70	4.35
Calendar	3.40	3.20
Entertainment	2.75	2.80
Privacy	3.40	3.55
Troubleshooting	3.25	3.25

4.3   Usage of the System

Mobile Rehabilitation Team (MRT).
For the sake of clarity, only the frequency of use at the end of the study is presented here, but not the results of V2. Almost all respondents stated that they used the Morecare system frequently. Therapy documentation was cited as the most frequently

used function. In addition, at least half of the participants used the patient file, the daily overview and the possibility to view appointments. Three functions were not used by any of the participants (Fig. 4).

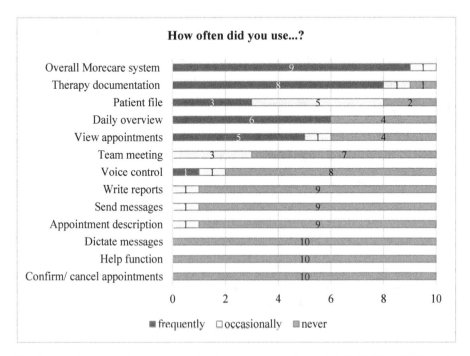

Fig. 4. Use of the individual functions of the Morecare system by the MRT, V3 (N = 10). Note: The five points of the questionnaire answer scale were grouped into three categories to improve clarity: "daily" and "several times a week" = frequently; "once a week" and "<once a week" = occasionally; "never" = never.

Older Adults (OA).

With regard to the frequency of use, four of the 10 study participants stated that they used the Morecare application (almost) daily. The remaining six participants used it several times a week. When considering the frequency of use of the individual functions of the Morecare application, the ability to review the activity data was used most frequently. Participants also frequently used the areas of self-exercise and appointment overview as well as the control of the system via flic buttons. Two study participants occasionally used the help function (Fig. 5).

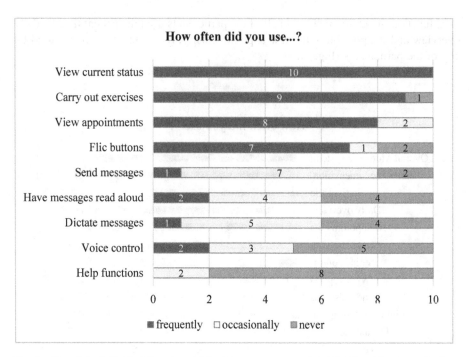

Fig. 5. Use of the individual functions of the Morecare system, OA, V2 (N = 10). Note: The five points of the questionnaire answer scale were grouped into three categories to improve clarity: "daily" and "several times a week" = frequently; "once a week" and "<once a week" = occasionally; "never" = never.

4.4   Evaluation of the Morecare System

Mobile Rehabilitation Team (MRT).
The MRT was asked how they value the various functions in the app. Of the functions used, the therapy documentation was rated as best. Six out of eight users rated the patient file as "good" or "very good". In addition, six participants rated the daily overview "good" or "very good" (Fig. 6).
With regard to the evaluation of user-friendliness using the system usability scale, the rating were very divergent. On average, the app was given 53.25 (25.0–82.5 points) rating points, which corresponds to a low level of user friendliness.

Older Adults (OA).
Within the evaluation of the individual functions of the Morecare system, it can be stated that these were predominantly rated "very good" or "good" by the OA. The participants liked the ability to view activity data and appointments the most. In contrast, more than half of the participants did not use the help function available within the tablet application (Fig. 7).

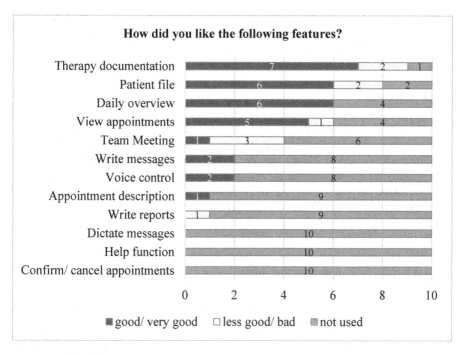

Fig. 6. Rating of the different features by the MRT (N = 10)

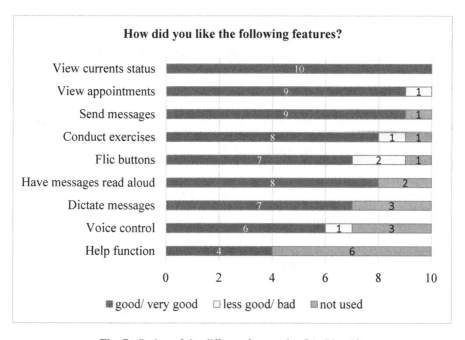

Fig. 7. Rating of the different features by OA (N = 10)

Compared to the team, the seniors rated the usability of the system slightly better. On average, the app was given 63.0 (45.0–85.0 points) rating points, which corresponds to a moderate level of user friendliness.

5 Conclusion

The present study examined the use and acceptance of a technical assistance system in mobile rehabilitation. For this purpose, the system was tested by employees of a mobile rehabilitation team and by elderly people. It was shown that although the system was used regularly by the majority of the respondents, not all functions were used by both MRT and OA. In particular, the help function was hardly used by either user group. One reason for this could be the poorly rated usability of the system. In order to improve usability and acceptance as well as to increase the use of the system, it must be geared even more strongly to the needs of the target group. For example, not all previously integrated functions are necessary for the MRT, but the employees would like to integrate other functions that would make everyday work easier.

The results of this study provide valuable insights into the ability of older and functionally limited people to use and accept modern technologies. This is particularly important because the technical progress currently being observed in care and therapy can lead in the medium term to a selection based on individual knowledge and acceptance of these technologies. This is to be judged negatively in so far as a lack of acceptance on the part of the patients leads to a new group of affected persons who cannot be adequately rehabilitated and thus the dependence on care and everyday life is increased. On the other hand, on the part of care and therapy professionals, a negative attitude towards new technologies can contribute to making the profession less attractive and thus increase the existing shortage of available labor. Both these possible developments must be counteracted as far as possible during the development of such technologies.

References

1. Steiner, M., Zwingmann, P.D.C., Riedel, W., Schüssler, R., Zweers, U.: Die medizinische Rehabilitation Erwerbstätiger–Sicherung von Produktivität und Wachstum, p. 88 (2009)
2. Schulz, R.-J., Kurtal, H., Steinhagen-Thiessen, E.: Rehabilitative Versorgung alter Menschen. In: Kuhlmey, A., Schaeffer, D. (eds.) Alter, Gesundheit und Krankheit, pp. 334–351. Huber, Bern (2008)
3. Steinert, A., Kiselev, J.: Chancen & Barrieren in der Mobilen Rehabilitation – eine qualitative Erhebung mit medizinischem Personal, Koordinatoren, Patienten & Angehörigen. Sozialer Fortschritt. **67**, 99–112 (2018). https://doi.org/10.3790/sfo.67.2.99
4. Roque, N.A., Boot, W.R.: A new tool for assessing mobile device proficiency in older adults: the mobile device proficiency questionnaire. J. Appl. Gerontol. **37**, 131–156 (2018). https://doi.org/10.1177/0733464816642582
5. Bangor, A., Kortum, P.T., Miller, J.T.: An empirical evaluation of the system usability scale. Int. J. Hum.-Comput. Interact. **24**, 574–594 (2008)
6. Neyer, F.J., Felber, J., Gebhardt, C.: Entwicklung und Validierung einer Kurzskala zur Erfassung von Technikbereitschaft. Diagnostica **58**, 87–99 (2012). https://doi.org/10.1026/0012-1924/a000067

Aging and the User Experience

Are Mobile Apps Usable and Accessible for Senior Citizens in Smart Cities?

Elenia Carrasco Almao[(⊠)] and Fatemeh Golpayegani

School of Computer Science and Statistics, Trinity College Dublin, Dublin, Ireland
{carrasce,fgolpaye}@tcd.ie

Abstract. The population in cities is expected to exponentially grow by 2050, and so is the world population aged 65 and over. This has increased the efforts to improve citizens' quality of life in urban areas by offering smarter and more efficient IT-based services in different domains such as health-care and transportation. Smart phones are key devices that provide a way for people to interact with the smart city services through their mobile applications (Apps). As the population is ageing and many services are now offered through mobile Apps, it is necessary to design accessible mobile interfaces that consider senior citizens' needs. These needs are related to cognitive, perceptual, and psycho-motor changes that occur while ageing, which affect the way older people interact with a smart phone. Although a comprehensive set of design guidelines are suggested, there is no evaluation on how and to what extent they are considered during the mobile App design process. This paper evaluates the implementation of these guidelines in several industry-built Apps, which are either targeted at older people or critical city services Apps that may benefit older people, but are targeted at a broader audience.

Keywords: Ageing population · Accessible App design · Smart cities

1 Introduction

Cities and the services offered in them are going towards being smarter in different domains such as mobility, health-care, and economy. Figures show that in 2007 half of the world population lived in cities and urban areas and this is expected to grow up to 70% by 2050 [1–3]. This is why major efforts have been put towards improving the citizen's life quality in urban areas, by offering smarter and more efficient IT-based services. Additionally, the growth rate of population aged 65 and over is likely to double by 2050 [4], and as cities expand, more older people will live in urban areas. This is why, it is essentially important for smart cities to offer services that are age-friendly to include more age demographic of cities.

Smart phones are key components that provide a way for people to interact with the smart city services through their mobile Apps. Smart phones have become indispensable devices in people's everyday life, facilitating many activities such as health-care, banking, transportation, or accessing information. The

© Springer Nature Switzerland AG 2019
J. Zhou and G. Salvendy (Eds.): HCII 2019, LNCS 11592, pp. 357–375, 2019.
https://doi.org/10.1007/978-3-030-22012-9_26

use of such technologies is rapidly increasing around the world. As reported in [5], in 2017 approximately 2.4 billion people were smart phone users. By 2020 it is forecast that there will be 2.9 million people using smart phones, a 20% growth. This figures include the increased number of older people who are using a smart phone [6,7], not only for communication purposes, but also for its help as assistive technology through mobile Apps. This assistive technology allows an ageing person to feel more secure and carry out a more autonomous life. However, many older adults still find interacting with a smart phone difficult. In [8,9], it is suggested that older people expect smart phones to be reliable means of communication, which can improve their safety and quality of life.

As the global population is rapidly ageing, and many services are now offered online through mobile Apps, it is necessary to design accessible mobile user interfaces (UI) that consider senior citizens' needs. These needs are related to cognitive, perceptual, and psycho-motor changes that occur in the ageing process, which affect the way older people interact with a mobile device. As a result, they often need support in carrying out tasks and activities [8]. For example, due to visual degrading, to be able to perceive a mobile interface they require larger UI elements than the average user. Also, due to cognitive loss, which causes a decline in memory and the speed at which older people process information, they prefer simplified menus. These are some of the reasons why accessibility should be part of the UI design process, putting a special emphasis on making an interface usable for older people. The issue is that there are still not as many accessible websites and Apps for them as there should be. Which is even more concerning in the context of smart phones, as they are rapidly growing and constantly changing, making it harder to properly address accessibility.

Smart phones can open new opportunities for people with different levels of impairment through the assistive technology in the phone's Apps. However, if interfaces are still not accessible for people with impairments, then they cannot take advantage of the technology in smart cities. By addressing accessibility during the mobile App design process, it is possible to improve older population's life quality in these cities. Several design standards and guidelines are suggested by both industry and research communities, to decrease the impact of older adults limited motor, cognitive, and visual skills when interacting with smart phones [8,10–12]. Guidelines solve the issue of recruiting, retaining, and working with older people during heuristic evaluation [12]. The inclusion of these guidelines also help to facilitate the interaction between older people and smart phones.

The work of Petrovčič et al. is a review of different published research-based guidelines and checklists for designing age-friendly mobile interfaces [12]. This work suggests a set of 38 age-friendly guidelines, that include aspects such as having big buttons with clear feedback to address visibility issue among older people. In addition to the research-based guidelines, the World Wide Web Consortium (W3C) is also putting a major effort into developing guidelines for designing usable and accessible mobile interfaces [10]. The W3C, based on [13], divides the guidelines into four principles related to barriers experienced by people with impairments.

Although a comprehensive set of design guidelines have been suggested, there is no evaluation on how and to what extent they are implemented during the mobile App design process. The aim of this paper is to evaluate the usability and accessibility of two groups of mobile Apps based on research-based and standards guidelines. These groups include Apps that are designed for older people, and Apps that are designed for critical city services that may benefit older people, but are targeted at a broader audience. The Apps are selected based on their popularity in the main domains of interest: health, mobility, socialising, entertainment, emergency, assistance, customization, finance and location.

The following section is a literature review of the available guidelines for designing age-friendly mobile interfaces. Sect. 3 describes the evaluation design. Section 4 presents the results, and finally, Sect. 5 provides the final discussion and conclusion of the results.

2   Literature Review

Smart phones through the Apps installed in them, allow citizens to interact with provided smart city services that improve people's life quality. An important group of citizens that may benefit from these smart services are the older population. Smart services face certain issues, especially in understanding the real needs of the people living in the city [14]. Older people's needs are associated to the age related changes they face. The main issue is that services targeted at older people do not seem to address these needs in the visual presentation of information. This represents a universal barrier to communicate with older people, which prevents an active ageing [1]. Major operative systems include built-in accessibility functionalities, such as Voice Over in iOS or TalkBack in Android. Both functionalities allow to turn the interface into text to speech for people with visual disabilities. Not only that, to address older people age-related needs, the industry and the academia has proposed age-specific design guidelines for mobile devices. Guidelines, enable the designers to create accessible interfaces without the need to hire older people for heuristic evaluation. This is why in this study the available guidelines are used as parameters to evaluate the Apps

This section presents an overview of the available research, from both industry and academia, regarding accessible mobile UI design for older people.

2.1   Research-Based Guidelines

Research-based guidelines are the ones developed in the academic context, which are published in indexed conferences and journals. Based on eight different age-friendly mobile design guidelines and checklist [15–21], Petrovčič et al. suggested a set of 38 senior friendly usability guidelines [12]. Table 1 summarizes the list of 38 guidelines, grouped within seven different dimensions associated with various interaction elements of smart phones. These dimensions are: screen, touchscreen, keypad, text, menu, exterior, and content.

Table 1. Usability dimensions and categories for designing age-friendly mobile interfaces.

Dimension	Guideline	Source
Screen	Display size	[19]
	High contrast	[19]
	Colors	
	High resolution	[22, 23]
	Slower dimming	[24]
	Zooming and magnification	[25–27]
Touchscreen	Touchscreen gestures	[28–30]
	Feedback	[31]
	Target/Icon properties	[32]
	Content layout	[12]
	Animation	[25]
Keypad	Button type	[12]
	Button shape	[25]
	Button size	[24, 25, 33]
	Button feedback	[34]
	Button responsiveness	[33]
	Labelled buttons	[35]
	Button positioning	[12, 31, 36]
	Number of buttons	[12]
Text	Ease of text entry	
	Font size	[29–31]
	Font type	
Menu	Simple menu	[30]
	Consistent menu	
	Minimized nesting	
	Ease of navigation	
	Current location in the menu	
Exterior	Device size	[25, 26, 32]
	Shape	
	Material	
	Battery charging	
	External volume buttons	
	Hearing aid compatible	
Content	Terminology	[12]
	Function labels	
	Additional languages	
	User help and/or manual	
	Error messages	

Screen. Older people favour a big display size, with a high resolution screen, and options to magnify the content. Colors in the screen should have a high contrast between the foreground and the background, and should be conservative. Since there is no agreed definition of conservative colors in the provided guidelines, the following definitions are considered: "marked by moderation or caution" [19], and "sober and conventional" [37]. Conservative colors are: black, white, grey, blue, beige, and various shades, tones, or tints of these colors. As well as, any color palette with a mix of neutral and highlight colors, where the neutral color appears in the biggest amount.

Touchscreen. The touch technology in mobile device creates difficulties for older people. They are not familiarized with tapping on the screen, so they need more time to comprehend and learn gestures [28–30]. Therefore, it is highly recommended to keep gestures simple. It is also suggested to include auditory and tactile signals that give distinctive feedback to the user [31].

Keypad. Buttons play an important role in age-specific UI design. Older people prefer large buttons with clear and immediate feedback (visual, tactile, and/or auditory) that helps them avoid mistakes when pressing a button [24,33,34]. It is suggested that older adult's pointing performance is better with: large buttons; a wider spacing between buttons; a target size between 14 and 17.5 mm; and by placing the buttons in the upper right direction from the centre point [31,36]. Buttons should not be too sensitive, and they should be visually differentiated from other actionable elements [25].

Text. Older people prefer a bigger font size that allows the to better perceive the screen. Also, it is recommended to provide easier ways for them to input data [29–31].

Menu. The increased number of features and services offered on a smart phone has resulted in more complex menus that are harder to understand by older people. That is why, a menu should be simple, consistent, have minimised nesting, and Show the current location in the menu [30].

Exterior. Several studies have revealed that phones for older people should: be big, facilitate an ergonomic grip, be lightweight, and have the shape of a bar [25,26,32]. Additionally, it is advisable to include audio adjustment, preferably from an external button, with a wide number of volume levels.

Content. Function labels have a fundamental role in UI design for older people who do not know what to do while navigating a menu [12]. Therefore, terminology used in a function label should be simple, consistent, self-explanatory, non-ambiguous, and should avoid foreign expressions, abbreviations, and technical terms. Instructions and error messages should be easy to understand and be always available.

2.2   Design Standards

Design standards are guidelines developed in standards organizations like ISO or W3C. The W3C is the main standard's organization for the web. They have published "Web Content Accessibility Guidelines" (WCAG) [13], where they categorize guidelines into four principles: perceivable, operable, understandable, and robust [38]. These principles are the required foundation to develop any accessible web and mobile content [38]. Table 2 shows the W3C's suggested guidelines for designing accessible mobile devices.

Table 2. W3C's mobile accessibility guidelines.

Principle	Category	Guideline
Perceivable	Small screen size	Minimize the amount of information displayed
		Provide a reasonable default size for text and touch controls
		Adapt the length of link text to the view-port width
		Position form fields below their labels.
	Magnification	Allow customization of default text size, preferably on page controls
		Allow for magnification of entire screen
		Allow for magnifying lens view under user's finger
	Contrast	Provide high contrast text
Operable	Keyboard control for touchscreen devices	Allow interfaces to be operated by external keyboards
	Touch target size and spacing	Touch targets should be at least 9 mm high by 9 mm wide and be surrounded by a small amount of inactive space
		Allow a reasonable spacing between buttons
	Touchscreen gestures	Gestures should be as easy
		Allow activating elements via the mouse up or touch end event
		To manipulate a device always provide touch and keyboard operability
	Buttons	Provide button positioning alternatives based on different scenarios
Understandable	Screen orientation	Support both portrait and landscape
	Layout	Repeated interaction elements should be displayed consistently across different pages, screen sizes and orientations
		Position important page elements before having to scroll
	Operable elements	Group operable elements that perform the same action
		Provide clear indication that elements are actionable
	Instructions	Provide instructions for custom touchscreen and device manipulation gestures
		Instructions should be easily discoverable and accessible at anytime
Robust	Data input	Set the virtual keyboard to the type of data entry required
		Provide easy methods for data entry
		Support the characteristic properties of the platform

Perceivable. Some of the W3C's recommendations to create perceivable UI components are:

- Reduce the amount of information displayed in a phone's viewport, through hierarchizing the information and only including what is necessary.
- Position form fields below their labels to increase the size of input elements, and improve visibility.
- Allow to customize the text size and magnification, through on page controls that are visible and recognizable.

Operable. An operable mobile device is when all UI elements and navigation can be easily controlled by the user without requesting to perform an unknown interaction. Some of the suggested guidelines to design operable UI are:

- Set the touch target to at least 9 mm high by 9 mm wide. If the elements are close to the minimum value then they should have an inactive space around them. This makes the touch target bigger and makes it easier to interact with the elements.
- Provide a prudent separation between the interaction elements.
- Avoid complex gestures like pinch and spread, which is a standard gesture for zooming in and out [27].

Understandable. An interface is understandable when everyone is able to comprehend all the information and operations in it. Some suggestions to turn a mobile interface understandable are:

- Support both screen orientations, landscape and portrait, and not to force the user to change their orientation if they do not want.
- Display repetitive elements across the interface consistently, even in different screen sizes and orientations.
- Provide visual hints that differentiate actionable from non-actionable elements through colour, shape, iconography, positioning, and text label.

Robust. An interface is robust if it remains accessible through the changes and adaptation of an App. Some recommendations for a robust interface are:

- Automatically trigger the type of keyboard that matches the kind of data entry required in a form. So for example, if only numbers are required, then enable only the numeric keyboard.
- Provide easy methods for data entry. A convenient way to do so is to include select menus, radio buttons, check boxes, and even auto-complete acquainted information.
- Support the characteristic properties of the platform, such as the accessibility feature in Android or iOS smart phones.

3 Evaluation Design

The aim of this research is to assess how and to what extent industry takes into account the usability and accessibility needs of the ageing population in the design of mobile Apps in smart cities. Two sets of mobile Apps are selected and evaluated based on the research-based guidelines and design standards. These sets include age-specific Apps and Apps that are critical city services that may benefit older people, but are targeted at a broader audience. This section describes the procedure and method applied to evaluate the Apps, including the Apps and checkpoint selection criteria.

3.1 Checkpoint Selection

In this section, the selected guidelines are grouped into two lists of checkpoints (Tables 3 and 4), which serve as metrics to evaluate the Apps. To facilitate the evaluation process, a code name is assigned to each checkpoint. RBG for research-based guidelines and DS for design standards.

Research-Based Checkpoints From Table 1, all the guidelines listed under exterior dimension, along with three out of six guidelines from the screen dimension are excluded. These guidelines are not in the scope of this study, as they address more physical characteristics of a mobile device, than the UI components. Also, content layout, number of buttons, font type, animation and additional languages are not considered in this study, as there is not clear explanation in the corresponding literature into what they mean. Finally, high contrast is also excluded, because there are not enough resources available to evaluate it. Therefore, from the original set of 38 guidelines in Table 1, only 23 are selected as the first set of checkpoints to evaluate the selected Apps (Table 3).

Design Standards Checkpoints. From the design standards on Table 2, contrast, touch target size and spacing are not considered in this study due to tools limitations. Additionally, keyboard control for touchscreen devices, device manipulation gestures, allowing for magnifying lens under user's finger, and adapting link text width to the view-port width are excluded as there is not enough clarification on their importance to older people. Hence, from the original 26 guidelines on Table 2, 20 of them are considered for the final evaluation (Table 4).

Table 3. Selected list of checkpoints from the research-based guidelines.

Dimension	Checkpoint	Code
Screen	Colors' conservativeness	RBG-01
	Zooming and magnification	RBG-02
Touchscreen	Touchscreen gestures	RBG-03
	Feedback	RBG-04
	Target/Icon properties	RBG-05
Keypad	Button type	RBG-06
	Button shape	RBG-07
	Button size	RBG-08
	Button feedback	RBG-09
	Button responsiveness	RBG-10
	Labelled buttons	RBG-11
	Button positioning	RBG-12
Text	Ease of text entry	RBG-13
	Font size	RBG-14
Menu	Simple menu	RBG-15
	Consistent menu	RBG-16
	Minimized nesting	RBG-17
	Ease of navigation	RBG-18
	Current location in the menu	RBG-19
Content	Terminology	RBG-20
	Function labels	RBG-21
	User help and/or manual	RBG-22
	Error messages	RBG-23

Table 4. Selected list of checkpoints from the design standards.

Principle	Dimension	Checkpoint	Code
Perceivable	Small screen size	Reduce information	SG-01
		Font size	SG-02
		Form field below label	SG-03
	Magnification	Text resizing	SG-04
		On-screen control to change text size	SG-05
		Zoom	SG-06
Operable	Touchscreen gestures	Easy	SG-07
		Touch-end event	SG-08
	Buttons	Accessible	SG-09

(*continued*)

Table 4. (*continued*)

Principle	Dimension	Checkpoint	Code
Understandable	Screen orientation	Support both	SG-10
	Consistent layout	Multiple pages	SG-11
		Screen orientations	
	Page elements	Important page elements before page scroll	SG-12
	Operable elements	Group operable elements performing same action	SG-13
		Visually differentiate actionable elements	SG-14
	Instructions	Available	SG-15
		Easily discoverable and accessible	SG-16
		Available anytime	SG-17
Robust	Data input	set virtual keyboard to the type of data entry required	SG-18
		Reduce amount of text entry required	SG-19
	Support characteristic properties of platform	Zoom	SG-20
		Font size	
		Captions	

3.2   App Selection and Evaluation Process

To find a set of suitable mobile Apps for the evaluation, a systematic review of the market was performed. The review was carried out using Google's browser, Apple App Store, and Google Play Store. Throughout the review, certain keywords were used to ensure that all the relevant Apps for the ageing population were detected: best, older, App, senior, elder, older people. Every hit was reviewed in terms of its relevance and based on the following selection criteria:

- The App must be targeted at older people and/or be an App designed for critical city services that may benefit older people, but targeted at a broader audience.
- The App should be up to date, meaning that it is still in use and developers still support it.
- The App should be for iOS and/or Android.
- The App should be free or at least should have a demo version.

Based on these criteria 22 Apps are selected and grouped by functionality to facilitate the evaluation process (see Table 6).

To assess the usability and accessibility of the selected Apps for older people, an expert-based usability evaluation has been performed. This method involved an expert review of the Apps in terms of usability and accessibility on the basis of the defined list of checkpoints. Throughout the evaluation, each individual checkpoint was tested manually for every App.

To grade each checkpoint, a scale system that goes from 0 to 2, in which 0 is given where the checkpoint is not addressed, 1 is given to a partially addressed checkpoint, and 2 is given to checkpoint fully addressed. To evaluate the Apps level of accessibility, a 5 level score system was designed (see Table 5). The 5 levels are high, high-moderate, moderate, low-moderate, and low, which are calculated based on the number of checkpoints each of the Apps have covered in each of the guidelines or standards. Each list of checkpoints obtained an individual preliminary score (Table 6). The final score was obtained by calculating the average between these preliminary scores. The final App score (Table 6) presents the most and least accessible Apps which shows how the industry is complying with older people's accessibility requirements in the design of mobile interfaces.

The Apps' evaluation was performed using two different devices: an iPhone 5s with iOS 11.3, and a Moto G 2014 with Android 7.1.1. In both cases, the platforms' built-in accessibility settings were disabled, unless necessary.

Table 5. Guideline/standard coverage scoring systems.

	High	High-mod.	Moderate	Low-mod	Low
RBG Score	37-46	33-36	28-32	23-27	0-22
DS Score	32-40	28-31	24-27	20-23	0-19
Total Score	34.9 - 43	30.6 - 34.8	26.3 - 30.5	21.6 - 26.2	0 - 21.5

4 Results

4.1 Apps Results per Set of Checkpoints

Research-Based Checkpoints. The results show that there is a high level of inclusion of the research-based checkpoints in more than half of the Apps. Figure 1 (left) shows that 17 out of 23 checkpoints are fully addressed in more than half of the Apps. While, Table 6 shows that 54% of the Apps (11 out of 22) reached high and high-moderate level of accessibility. However, Two checkpoints from this set of guidelines, Zooming and Magnification (RBG-02) and Feedback (RBG-04), are not included in more than 75% of the Apps (see Fig. 1 Left). These checkpoints impact how older people interact with a mobile interface, and have been recurrently mentioned in several guidelines since 2014 [12,16,25–27,31,33,61–66].

Design Standards Checkpoints. Unlike the results from the research-based guidelines, the evaluation of the Apps based on the design standards show a low level of addressing of the checkpoints. As reflected on Fig. 1 Right, only 9 out of 20 checkpoints were fully addressed in more than 50% of the Apps. While 8 out of the 20 checkpoints were not addressed in at least 50% of them. Among these checkpoints were aspects that allow to make an interface perceivable, understandable and robust for older people. The checkpoints with low level of inclusion are: Form field below label (DS-03), Text resizing (DS-04), On-screen control to change text size (DS-05), Zoom (DS-06), Support both Screen Orientations (DS-10), Instructions easily discoverable and accessible (DS-16), Instructions available anytime (DS-17), and Set virtual keyboard to the type of data entry required (DS-18). From these checkpoints DS-05 is not even part of any of the sample Apps. Furthermore, the design standards scores on Table 6 show that none of the Apps obtained a high level of accessibility, only 2 obtained a high-moderate level, 6 a moderate level, and 14 out of 22 Apps reached between low-moderate and low levels of accessibility.

In the evaluation it was observed that almost all the Apps support the zoom from the accessibility menu in the device, which means that even though an App does not include a zoom feature, the platform will allow to do so if activated from the phone's menu. However, asking an older person to interact with a complex menu like that represents a difficulty [12].

4.2   Apps Total Score

From the results on Table 6, it is clear that mobile Apps are still not accessible enough for older people. Out of the 22 evaluated Apps, none of them reached a high level of accessibility, and only 5 had a high-moderate level of accessibility. While the remaining 17 Apps are still not accessible enough for older people. Particularly, in most of the evaluated Apps, including the age-specific and non-age-specific Apps, there are problems with aspects that address visual degrading for older people such as zooming, text resizing and on-screen controllers to modify text. Additionally, most of the Apps lacked proper instructions and options to ease the data input process for users. These features decrease the impact of older adults' degrading cognitive skills when interacting with an interface. Thus, there are different guidelines that could be better addressed by the industry to design mobile Apps for older people. By making sure that these guidelines are applied during the design process of a mobile App, it is possible to contribute to senior citizens' inclusion and engagement in smart cities.

Table 6. Apps evaluation results

Domain	App	Score (RBG)	Score (DS)	Total Score
Emergency	Red Panic Button [39]	33	23	28
	Fade: fall detector [40]	29	17	23
Assistance	Magnifying Glass With Light [41]	26	21	23.5
	Magnifying Glass Flashlight [42]	32	22	27
	Usound (Hearing Assistant)[43]	42	26	34
	MyEarDroid - Sound Recognition [44]	22	18	20
	Live Caption [45]	36	29	32.5
Personalisation	Wiser – Simple Senior Launcher [46]	40	19	29.5
	Nova Launcher [47]	28	20	24
Health	MindMate - Healthy Aging [48]	32	23	27.5
	WebMD [49]	28	22	25
	Pocket Physio [50]	37	23	30
	Blood Pressure Monitor [51]	23	20	21.5
	Pill Reminder by Medisafe [52]	35	23	29
Enterteinment	Lumosity - Brain Training [53]	40	29	34.5
Social	Skype *1 [54]	26	26	26
	Stitch Companionship [55]	34	24	29
Location	Find My Family, Friends, Phone Safe365 [56]	38	24	31
Finance	Bank of Ireland * [57]	31	19	25
	RevApp * [58]	36	26	31
Mobility	Dublin Bus * [59]	33	24	28.5
	Mytaxi * [60]	37	21	29

* Apps that are designed for critical city services that may benefit older people, but are targeted at a broad audience

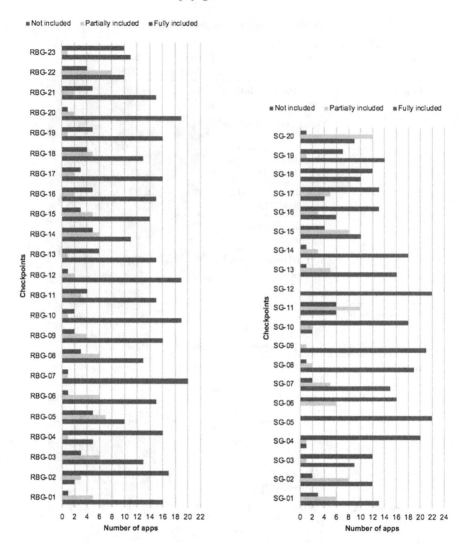

Fig. 1. Checkpoints level of inclusion in Apps. Left: research-based. Right: design standards

5   Conclusion

The aim of this study was to assess how and to what extent is the industry taking into consideration the existing usability and accessibility guidelines to design suitable mobile interfaces for older people. To assess the industry, 22 industry-built mobile Apps were selected. These Apps included sample Apps specifically targeted at older people and sample Apps designed for critical city services that may benefit older people, but targeting a broader audience. These

Apps were then evaluated on the basis of two sets of checkpoints, retrieved from available age-specific academic and industry design guidelines.

It was observed that overall the Apps had a weakness in all the accessibility principles that make an interface perceivable, operable, understandable and robust for the older people [10,13]. The most concerning checkpoints were the lack of text resizing and zooming in more than 70% of the Apps. Although, it was also observed that most of the Apps (95%) supported the platform's accessibility settings, which allowed to zoom and adjust the font size. However, a major issue with this, as pointed in [12], is that older people are being forced to find such settings in the platform's menu, which generally represents a complexity for them. For operability and understandability the most surprising finding was the lack of adequate instructions, without which the interface turns incomprehensible and inoperable for older people. Finally, regarding robustness 55% of the Apps were found to not set the virtual keyboard to the type of data entry required, which facilitates older people inputting data through a smart phone.

An interesting finding from the study was the relevant difference between the results from the research-based guidelines and design standards. In Fig. 1 (Left), it was observed that at least half of the Apps fully included 82% of the checkpoints. While in Fig. 1 (Right), only 45% of the checkpoints were fully included in at least half of the Apps. As shown in Table 6, the Apps obtained a higher level of accessibility when evaluated on the basis of the research-based checkpoints. In this case, 54% of the Apps scored between high and high moderate. While in the case of the design standards set, only 9% of the Apps obtained a high-moderate level of accessibility, and no Apps reached a high level of accessibility. This difference in scores can be explained because at least half of the checkpoints from each set measured different usability and accessibility aspects. This reveals that the industry is considering more accessibility aspects related to the research-based guidelines than the design standards.

On the Apps total score on Table 6, none of the Apps achieved a high level of accessibility and only 23% achieved a high-moderate level of accessibility. From the remaining Apps, 41% moderately includes age-specific aspects, but not enough to be regarded as fully accessible Apps. Meaning that only 23% of the sample Apps can be considered accessible enough for older people. This clearly shows the low efforts from the industry to implement age-friendly guidelines in the design of mobile Apps for older people. Thus, there is still a lot of work to be done to reach an inclusive smart city that benefits older people as much as any other citizen. As the results of this study show, a good starting point to do so are smart phones, which are key component that provides a way for older people to interact with the smart city through their mobile Apps. Thus, mobile Apps in the context of smart cities should be designed in such a way that they are accessible by all citizens.

5.1   Limitations and Future Work

Even though this study presents some insights into how accessible are mobile Apps for older people in smart cities, its findings are subject to some limitations.

First, the Apps evaluations was not performed by old users. However, a set of guidelines previously tested by older and impaired people, was employed in this study. This type of guidelines, have been suggested as an effective heuristic-tool when the end-user is not available. Second, the study was performed using free Apps only and this might have limited the sample set. Thus, in the future it is interesting to evaluate paid Apps and compare them to the results obtained in this study. Third, not all guidelines could be evaluated, and these could have an impact on the final results. So, as future work, the evaluation can be performed including all the guidelines from the research-based guidelines and design standards. Despite of the limitations, the study provided useful information to use available usability and accessibility guidelines for the evaluation of age-specific mobile Apps. This study shows weaknesses of mobile Apps today, to avoid them in future age-friendly mobile App design. Thus, it can be used as a framework by designers in the industry when developing mobile Apps targeted at older people.

References

1. World Health Organization: Global Age-Friendly Cities: A Guide. World Health Organization, Geneva (2007)
2. Albino, V., Berardi, U., Dangelico, R.M.: Smart cities: definitions, dimensions, performance, and initiatives. J. Urban Technol. **22**(1), 3–21 (2015)
3. Caragliu, A., Del Bo, C., Nijkamp, P.: Smart cities in Europe. J. Urban Technol. **18**(2), 65–82 (2011)
4. World Health Organization: World Report on Ageing and Health. World Health Organization, Geneva (2015)
5. Statista: Number of smartphone users worldwide from 2014 to 2020 (in billions), June 2016. https://www.statista.com/statistics/330695/number-of-smartphone-users-worldwide/. Accessed 15 Dec 2018
6. Pew Research Center: Tech adoption climbs among older adults (2017)
7. Berenguer, A., et al.: Are smartphones ubiquitous?: an in-depth survey of smartphone adoption by seniors. IEEE Consum. Electron. Mag. **6**(1), 104–110 (2017)
8. Díaz-Bossini, J.-M., Moreno, L.: Accessibility to mobile interfaces for older people. Procedia Comput. Sci. **27**, 57–66 (2014)
9. Abascal, J., Civit, A.: Mobile communication for older people: new opportunities for autonomous life. In: Proceedings of EC/NSF Workshop on Universal Accessibility of Ubiquitous Computing: Providing for the Elderly, vol. 487 (2001)
10. W3C: How WCAG 2.0 and Other W3C/WAI Guidelines Apply to Mobile (2015). Dosegljivo: https://www.w3.org/TR/mobileaccessibility-mapping
11. Husain, W., Shahiri, A.M., Ibrahim, A.W.: User interface design for elderly mobile assistive systems. In: ISICO 2015 2015 (2015)
12. Petrovčič, A., et al.: Design of mobile phones for older adults: an empirical analysis of design guidelines and checklists for feature phones and smartphones. Int. J. Hum.-Comput. Interact. **34**(3), 251–264 (2018)
13. W3C: Introduction to Understanding WCAG 2.0, 7 October 2016. https://www.w3.org/TR/UNDERSTANDING-WCAG20/intro.html. Accessed 20 Mar 2018
14. Alam, M., Porras, J.: Architecting and designing sustainable smart city services in a living lab environment. Technologies **6**(4), 99 (2018)

15. Pattison, M., Stedmon, A.W.: Inclusive design and human factors: designing mobile phones for older users. PsychNol. J. **4**(3), 267–284 (2006)
16. Massimi, M.: Participatory design of mobile phone software for seniors. University of Toronto, Toronto, Ontario (2007)
17. Al-Razgan, M.S., Al-Khalifa, H.S., Al-Shahrani, M.D., AlAjmi, H.H.: Touch-based mobile phone interface guidelines and design recommendations for elderly people: a survey of the literature. In: Huang, T., Zeng, Z., Li, C., Leung, C.S. (eds.) ICONIP 2012. LNCS, vol. 7666, pp. 568–574. Springer, Heidelberg (2012). https://doi.org/10.1007/978-3-642-34478-7_69
18. van Dyk, T., et al.: Mobile phones for the elderly: a design framework In Steyn. Public and private access to ICTs in developing regions. In: Proceedings of the 7th International Development Informatics Conference (IDIA 2013), Bangkok, Thailand (2013)
19. Calak, P.: Smartphone evaluation heuristics for older adults. Dissertation (2013)
20. Silva, P.A., Jordan, P., Holden, K.: Something old, something new, something borrowed: gathering experts' feedback while performing heuristic evaluation with a list of heuristics targeted at older adults. In: Proceedings of the 2014 Workshops on Advances in Computer Entertainment Conference. ACM (2014)
21. Mi, N., et al.: A heuristic checklist for an accessible smartphone interface design. Univers. Access Inf. Soc. **13**(4), 351–365 (2014)
22. Cambridge Dictionary: High-resolution. Cambridge Dictionary. https://dictionary.cambridge.org/dictionary/english/high-resolution
23. PC Encyclopedia: Definition of: high resolution. PC Encyclopedia. https://www.pcmag.com/encyclopedia/term/44255/high-resolution
24. Hassan, H., Md Nasir, M.H.N.: The use of mobile phones by older adults: a Malaysian study. ACM SIGACCESS Accessibility Comput. **92**, 11–16 (2008)
25. Caprani, N., O'Connor, N.E., Gurrin, C.: Touch screens for the older user. Assistive technologies. InTech (2012)
26. Wang, Q.: The effects of interface design about mobile phones on older adults' usage. In: 4th International Conference on Wireless Communications, Networking and Mobile Computing, WiCOM 2008. IEEE (2008)
27. Olwal, A., Lachanas, D., Zacharouli, E.: OldGen: mobile phone customization for older adults. In: Proceedings of the SIGCHI Conference on Human Factors in Computing Systems. ACM (2011)
28. Furuki, K., Kikuchi, Y.: Approach to commercialization of Raku-Raku smartphone. Fujitsu Sci. Tech. J. **49**(2), 196–201 (2013)
29. Motti, L.G., Vigouroux, N., Gorce, P.: Interaction techniques for older adults using touchscreen devices: a literature review. In: Proceedings of the 25th Conference on l'Interaction Homme-Machine. ACM (2013)
30. Zhou, J., Rau, P.-L.P., Salvendy, G.: Use and design of handheld computers for older adults: a review and appraisal. Int. J. Hum.-Comput. Interact. **28**(12), 799–826 (2012)
31. Hwangbo, H., et al.: A study of pointing performance of elderly users on smartphones. Int. J. Hum.-Comput. Interact. **29**(9), 604–618 (2013)
32. Boustani, S.: Designing touch-based interfaces for the elderly, p. 93. University of Sydney (2010)
33. Kim, H., Heo, J., Shim, J., Kim, M., Park, S., Park, S.: Contextual research on elderly users' needs for developing universal design mobile phone. In: Stephanidis, C. (ed.) UAHCI 2007. LNCS, vol. 4554, pp. 950–959. Springer, Heidelberg (2007). https://doi.org/10.1007/978-3-540-73279-2_106

34. Harada, S., Sato, D., Takagi, H., Asakawa, C.: Characteristics of elderly user behavior on mobile multi-touch devices. In: Kotzé, P., Marsden, G., Lindgaard, G., Wesson, J., Winckler, M. (eds.) INTERACT 2013. LNCS, vol. 8120, pp. 323–341. Springer, Heidelberg (2013). https://doi.org/10.1007/978-3-642-40498-6_25

35. Razak, A., Hanis, F., et al.: How simple is simple: our experience with older adult users. In: Proceedings of the 11th Asia Pacific Conference on Computer Human Interaction. ACM (2013)

36. Leitão, R., Silva, P.A.: Target and spacing sizes for smartphone user interfaces for older adults: design patterns based on an evaluation with users. In: Proceedings of the 19th Conference on Pattern Languages of Programs. The Hillside Group (2012)

37. Oxford: English Oxford: Living Dictionaries. https://en.oxforddictionaries.com/definition/conservative. Accessed 15 Apr 2018

38. Stößel, C., Wandke, H., Blessing, L.: Gestural interfaces for elderly users: help or hindrance? In: Kopp, S., Wachsmuth, I. (eds.) GW 2009. LNCS (LNAI), vol. 5934, pp. 269–280. Springer, Heidelberg (2010). https://doi.org/10.1007/978-3-642-12553-9_24

39. Red Panic Button. Ultimate Communication Software LTD. http://redpanicbutton.com/. Accessed 14 Nov 2017

40. Fade: fall detector. ITER S.A. https://play.google.com/store/apps/details?id=com.iter.falldetector&hl=es. Accessed 14 Nov 2017

41. Magnifying Glass With Light. Falcon In Motion LLC. https://itunes.apple.com/us/app/magnifying-glass-light-digital/id406048120?mt=8. Accessed 14 Nov 2017

42. Magnifying Glass Flashlight. Bzing. https://play.google.com/store/apps/details?id=com.IdanS.magnifyingglassflashlight&hl=en. Accessed 2014 Nov 2017

43. Usound (Hearing Assistant). Newbrick S.A.. https://www.usound.co/. Accessed 14 Nov 2017

44. MyEarDroid - Sound Recognition. Tecnalia - Salud. https://www.tecnalia.com/en/myeardroid/what-is-myeardroid.htm. Accessed 14 Nov 2017

45. Live Caption, Wiser - Simple Senior Launcher. RyFly. http://www.livecaptionapp.com/. Accessed 14 Nov 2017

46. Wiser Launcher. UIU LTD. http://www.wiser.site/. Accessed 2014 Nov 2017

47. Nova Launcher. TeslaCoil Software. http://novalauncher.com/. Accessed 14 Nov 2017

48. MindMate - Healthy Aging. MindMate LTD. https://www.mindmate-app.com/. Accessed 14 Nov 2017

49. WebMD. WebMD Health Corporation. https://www.webmd.com/mobile. Accessed 14 Nov 2017

50. Pocket Physio. Care UK. http://www.careukhealthcare.com/pocketphysio. Accessed 14 Nov 2017

51. Blood Pressure Monitor. Taconic System LLC. http://www.taconicsys.com/. Accessed 14 Nov 2017

52. Pill Reminder by Medisafe. MediSafe Inc. https://medisafe.com/. Accessed 14 Nov 2017

53. Lumosity - Brain Training. Lumos Labs Inc. https://www.lumosity.com/. Accessed 14 Nov 2017

54. Skype. Skype Communications S.a.r.l. https://www.skype.com/en/. Accessed 14 Nov 2017

55. Stitch Companionship. Stitch Holdings Pty Ltd. https://www.stitch.net/. Accessed 14 Nov 2017

56. Find My Family, Friends, Phone Safe365. Alpify. http://www.safe365.com/. Accessed 14 Nov 2017
57. Bank of Ireland Mobile Banking. Bank of Ireland. https://itunes.apple.com/ie/app/bank-of-ireland-mobile-banking/id520821023?mt=8. Accessed 14 Nov 2018
58. RevApp. Office of the Revenue Commissioners (Ireland). https://itunes.apple.com/il/app/revapp/id1165437420?mt=8. Accessed 14 Nov 2018
59. Dublin Bus 4. Biznet IIS Ltd. https://itunes.apple.com/ie/app/dublin-bus/id450455266?mt=8. Accessed 14 Nov 2018
60. mytaxi: Tap & Move Freely. Intelligent Apps GmbH. https://itunes.apple.com/us/app/mytaxi-tap-move-freely/id357852748?mt=8. Accessed 14 Nov 2018
61. Lee, Y.S.: A survey of mobile phone use in older adults. In: Proceedings of the Human Factors and Ergonomics Society Annual Meeting, vol. 51, no. 1. Sage Publications, Los Angeles (2007)
62. Bruder, C., Blessing, L., Wandke, H.: Training the elderly in the use of electronic devices. In: Stephanidis, C. (ed.) UAHCI 2007. LNCS, vol. 4554, pp. 637–646. Springer, Heidelberg (2007). https://doi.org/10.1007/978-3-540-73279-2_71
63. Hasegawa, S., et al.: Aging effects on the visibility of graphic text on mobile phones. Gerontechnology 4(4), 200–208 (2006)
64. Matsunaga, V.T.I.V.K., Nagano, V.Y.: Universal design activities for mobile phone: Raku Raku phone. Fujitsu Sci. Tech. J. 41(1), 78–85 (2005)
65. Kurniawan, S.: Older people and mobile phones: a multi-method investigation. Int. J. Hum.-Comput. Stud. 66(12), 889–901 (2008)
66. Mann, W.C., et al.: Use of cell phones by elders with impairments: overall appraisal, satisfaction, and suggestions. Technol. Disabil. 16(1), 49–57 (2004)

Older Adults in ICT Contexts: Recommendations for Developing Tutorials

Sónia Ferreira[1(✉)] and Ana Isabel Veloso[2]

[1] CSETH Center for the Study of Education, Technologies and Health,
School of Education, Polytechnic Institute of Viseu,
R. Maximiano Aragão, 3504-501 Viseu, Portugal
sonia.ferreira@esev.ipv.pt

[2] DigiMedia Research Centre, Department of Communication and Art,
University of Aveiro, Campus Universitário de Santiago,
3810-193 Aveiro, Portugal
aiv@ua.pt

Abstract. In the context of Information and Communication Technologies (ICT), there is clearly a great difficulty in persuading older people to use them, particularly those with low digital literacy. This reality is mainly due to their lack of access opportunities, physical and psycho-sociological individual characteristics, and by the functionality of technology. Even though many older people are still digitally-excluded, the number of who are willing to use ICT is increasing. Older people aren't afraid to try new technology when they see a clear benefit. This study focuses on the analysis of empirical projects, solutions and/or experiences, national and international, guided to the applicability of tools to support the use of technological tools and services by older adults. The main goal is to draw up some guidelines for designing tools that can facilitate the older adults' use of the miOne community. MiOne is an online community created under the project *SEDUCE 2.0 - Use of Communication and Information in the miOne online community by senior citizen*. Relevant electronic databases were searched using the following keywords, in Portuguese and English language: help tutorial, video tutorial, multimedia tutorial, older adults, and help tools. Findings suggest some recommendations for the adequate development of solutions that can help older users to use different ICT contexts.

Keywords: Tutorials · Information and Communication Technologies · Older adults · miOne

1 Introduction

Once retired and dedicated the rest of their lives to the grandchildren and to relive memories, older adults present today a greater vitality to carry out new projects, in the short term, and contribute and take part of socially, culturally and politically decisions [1]. By being determined of their own wishes [2], they are not afraid to use the new technologies when they see a clear benefit.

It is consensual that we are facing an increasingly aging society [3–5] and doubly excluded. Beyond the biological, physical and psychological changes resulting from

© Springer Nature Switzerland AG 2019
J. Zhou and G. Salvendy (Eds.): HCII 2019, LNCS 11592, pp. 376–387, 2019.
https://doi.org/10.1007/978-3-030-22012-9_27

the natural aging process, there is a lack of access opportunities - consequence of economic, cultural and educational variables – [2, 6, 7], and the functionality of technology [6–8].

No less true is the fact that we are facing an increasingly technological society and various studies demonstrate that ICT use brings real benefits to older adults, including general enhancement of their mental status; strengthening of their self-concept, self-esteem and self-realization [9]; increase in their quality of life [10–13] and sense of independence [14, 15], decrease in feelings of loneliness [8, 16]; reduction in stress perception and the level of social support [17–19]; increase in feelings of connected-ness [20], and a positive connection to health [21, 22].

However, integrating Information and Communication Technologies (ICT) into your everyday life is not a simple task.

In fact, a report that studied the way the Portuguese population interacts with the Internet seems to remain updated. It reveals that there is clearly a gap between this target group and other generations in terms of ICT usage [23]. Specifically, the info-exclusion groups include the people retired, with lower education level and income, and/or lack of access to digital platforms and Internet. From now to 20 years later, it is estimated that the individuals that participate in this research will continue to be digital and info excluded [23]. The age group that will be mostly affected is the one aged between 45 to 64, with a level of education up to the second cycle of basic education and the solely use of Internet will be done by relatives or other household members.

All this context justifies the promotion of strategies that improve the use of ICT by older adults, specifically the development of audiovisual or multimedia tutorials.

Thus, the research question of this paper is: *What recommendations should be followed in the development of tutorials that help the ICT use by older adults?*

The objective is to analyze various national and international examples that cover the development of tutorials for older adults in different ICT contexts.

2 Aging and Technology Interaction

To exam the development of tutorials, the first step would be to understand the interference of aging characteristics in ICT use.

In the visual system, changes are significant – e.g. changes in the cornea and lens added to the loss of ciliary muscle tonicity; reduced pupil size; and a decrease in the number of retinal cells [24]. These transformations lead to difficulties in reading, night vision and perception of rapid changes in the environments with different luminosity, difficulties in differentiating details, tired sight, in which the quality of the near vision is reduced, cataracts and physiological degenerative processes in the retina [25, 26]. Color discrimination also changes, in particular, decreases the blue discrimination capacity and increases the distinction between red and green. These losses can reduce an individual's ability to use non-verbal information in communication [25].

The aging process is also responsible for several motor changes [26], namely, the response time to actions is slower. There is also a decrease in the ability to maintain continuous movement; disturbances in coordination and variability of movements and loss of flexibility. In fact, older adults are 1.5 to 2 times slower than younger adults.

The presence of chronic conditions, such as arthritis, also affects movements and these changes in the motor skills have a direct relevance to computer use. In specific, [26] report that for older adults to master the use of the mouse can be a greater challenge than learning how to use software.

Auditory changes, such as its gradual decline, the s buzz, the difficulty about the attention to cases of environmental noise or group conversations, a low tolerance for high volume and high intensity sounds [25, 26], can be also limitations and interfere with the experience of using technological systems, especially when the sounds made available by the software and/or digital information environments are not presented in a clear way or not available to increase/reduce the sound volume.

Cognitively, the aging process is responsible for many changes [26–28]: increased difficulty in understanding long and/or complex messages to recall specific terms and to develop reasoning activities that involve the analysis of logical and organized abstract or unfamiliar material; repetitive discourse; through the difficulty in selecting information; by reducing the ability to perform new tasks and fast psychomotor skills; memory impairment, especially the memory related to the acquisition of new information and the sharing of attention in multiple tasks and, finally, difficulties in inductive behavior, spatial orientation, numerical and verbal skills and in perceiving speed.

As for intelligence, it also changes. Intelligence can be classified as crystallized and fluid. Crystallized refers to the source of general information, vocabulary or acquired knowledge, whereas fluid intelligence refers to the ability to understand the relationships between things and the manipulation of information. According to [27], until the age of 70 people maintain their level of intelligence crystallized. From that moment, a decline begins. In turn, fluid intelligence peaks at the age of 20 and follows a progressive decline. In this sense, with aging, the functions that require the manipulation of new information are more problematic than those that only require the use of the acquired knowledge.

The clear understanding of these changes contribute to the identification of specific elements that can be implemented in technological development services, especially interface and support-related. The adequate design of an intuitive interface can contribute to the inclusion of a greater number of users, for reasons of ease of access and use [29].

3   Method

To respond to the question that guides this study, *What recommendations should be followed in the development of tutorials that help the ICT use by older adults?*, we opted for the systematic review of literature based on the concepts: help tutorial, video tutorial, multimedia tutorial, older adults, and help tools. The databases searched were SciELO Portugal, ISI Web of Knowledge, and Google Scholar, with publications since 2010. In this phase, 24 publications potentially eligible for this study were identified. We proceeded by identifying articles that met the following criteria: (i) the sample should include elderly people, even if they integrate other ages as well; (ii) use of ICT; (iii) and original studies involving older users at some stage of help tools development.

After the process of analyzing the studies, which involved reading the title, keywords, abstracts and full texts, only 4 seemed to fulfill all requirements. Analyzing the articles references, we identified another publication, totaling 5 examples.

Most of the studies about help tutorials relates to education and e-learning systems and not integrate older users.

In the analysis of the publications, the following aspects were observed, when available: (i) size and sample selection; (ii) instruments used; (iii) results; (iv) and limitations.

4   Findings and Discussion

As this is a theme that attracts the interest of scientific and governmental communities, Table 1 shows the five initiatives that were found: OpenISA project; SEDUCE project, which unfolds in two investigations; Help Center; and the case of MedlinePlus.

Table 1. Projects and initiatives examples that use help tutorials to support the use of technological systems

Projects/Initiatives	Goals
OpenISA – Open Innovation Platform for Health-related Services during Old Age 2009–2012	Study the development, implementation and evaluation of an open online platform geared towards the health of older adults. This integrates video that support effective learning
Active aging: audiovisual in the promotion of physical exercise 2014	Integrated within the scope of the SEDUCE project - Senior Citizen Use of computer mediated communication and information in web Ecologies, this study [30] aimed to develop audiovisual tutorials to support the practice of physical exercise, integrated in the health area of the miOne community
Audiovisual tutorials for ICT use by senior citizens: planning, development and evaluation 2015	Integrated study within the scope of the SEDUCE project, in which a set of video tutorials teach senior citizens how to use the registration and communication areas of the miOne social community
Help Center - Design of Interactive Tutorials on Mobile Applications 2017	Design an interactive tutorial, which can adapt to mobile applications
MedlinePlus - Trusted Health Information for You 2018	Belonging to the US National Institute of Health, United States of America, the website provides updated health information by the National Library of Medicine. Taking special consideration of the older population, it includes a set of explanatory videos about the functioning of the website and health information

Developed from European Union incentives, since 2009 to 2012, the OpenISA project - Open Innovation Platform for Health, related Services during Old Age, focused on creating an innovative platform for providing health information and services to older adults. OpenISA, in which the main research focus is the OICs (Online Innovation Contests), aimed at integrating the target audience aged 50 years old and over in the development and evaluation of the interdisciplinary platform, in order to eliminate barriers and encourage it use.

Innovation Contests (ICs) are popular tools that enhance the integration of the general public in the development of innovative technologies often used to solve problems that affect society as a whole. That is, companies, organizations or individuals use ICs to encourage specific groups to submit their contributions related to tasks (general or specific) during a given period (hours, days or months) in exchange for incentives (monetary, non- monetary or both). The target audience of older adults are a group considered to be interesting for this type of dynamics, not only because they recognize the vast life experience [31], but also because of the challenging market for products that are now expanding. As part of the project, Digmayer and Jakobs have qualitatively studied the integration of video tutorials in support of the learning of key Innovation Online Contests (IOCs) functions by older adults in the development of mobile phone design for older adults [31].

After surveying about the difficulties when using the IOCs, video tutorials were created as a help resource and their usability was tested. The results of the study show that the tutorials are an appropriate tool to provide an overview of the IOCs and its main functions. Digmayer and Jakobs suggest that, in more complex tasks, video tutorials help to reduce error rates however, task execution times tend to increase [31]. Also, beginning users are interested in targeted tutorials and step-by-step instructions, while more experienced users prefer help tools that do not interrupt the workflow.

Regarding interface design and the tutorial content, the same study presents some important recommendations:

- Learning occurs when users are involved in solving real-world problems. This principle focuses on the presentation of the problem, its deconstruction in tasks in order to solve it, followed by its operationalization and consequent action of making them feasible;
- The video tutorial should appear where the user expects it to be made available, i.e. on the first page. If the help tool is not recognized, the user will not use it;
- Ensure that the video can be viewed in full screen mode and in the best possible resolution;
- It is important to clarify that it is only an aid and not part of the website. To do this, you can add along the video, for example, the reference *Tutorial*;
- Provide the preview progress bar and interactive elements of the video player;
- Display a logical order following the presentation of the menu options;
- Provide incentives that motivate users to use or remain in the tutorial, such as including humor or a joyful experience;
- Provide visual and audio support options. A hearing impaired user should be able to choose a textual version, for example;
- Maintain consistency of the element names presented throughout the video;

- The purpose of each function should be presented at the beginning, as well as the benefits of its use;
- The transition to the next step should be the user's choice, progressing only when they are prepared;
- The operations must be explained in detail and the technical terms duly explained;
- It is important to clarify what the user should do at the end of each part of the tutorial. This can be achieved by offering interactive elements.

The *SEDUCE* project, developed from 2010 to 2014, is another example of the use of tutorials in supporting the online social community miOne (see Fig. 1).

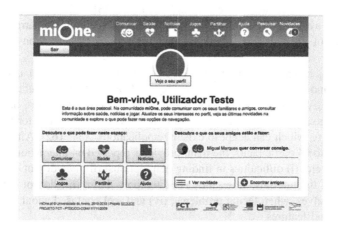

Fig. 1. miOne community homepage Source: www.mione.pt

This was conceptualized with the active participation of senior citizens from four Aveiro Private Institutions of Social Solidarity. *MiOne* distinguishes from other online communities because it integrates five areas of interest confirmed by the older adults: (i) communication through email and instant messaging; (ii) health information; (iii) news information; (iv) games; (v) and access and sharing of experiences among members [32].

The project enabled the development of two studies specifically aimed at the use of video tutorials to support the use of the *miOne* community by older adults and to practice physical exercise [30]. The study of Caldas, Veloso and Antunes included the planning, development and evaluation of a set of four video tutorials dedicated to registration, general presentation of the community, use of the electronic mail service and use of the conversation system [33]. This process had the participation of two distinct groups, the specialists who participated in the focus group sessions and the older adults who participated in the tutorial evaluation [33]. Studies of Czaja and Sharit and Caldas, Veloso and Antunes suggest that tutorials should incorporate the following characteristics [26, 33]:

- Non-use of technical terms, but an informal language and quiet narration, preferably with a masculine voice;

- Avoid noise and echoes. When background music is used, it must be audible only when the narrator does not intervene;
- Textually avoid decorative typefaces;
- As mentioned in the study by Digmayer and Jakobs, use segmented tutorials [31]; and
- Use 50:1 contrasts, that is, black background, white letter and vice versa.

Nunes in turn, and also using two groups of different participants, specialists and older adults, presented a set of three videos: the first is an introduction and incentive to practice physical exercise, the second is a Yoga tutorial and the third is a Tai-Chi tutorial [30].

To the results of Caldas, Veloso and Antunes [33] and Nunes [30] adds the importance of avoiding the scrolling in the texts and of adapting the narration voice to the character of the video. If a female character is used, the narration must also be female.

The fourth example is the *Help Center* (see Fig. 2), developed under Beijing Humanities and Social Sciences fund Project Construction of Public Education Rehabilitation Aids and Beijing Key Laboratory of Network System and Network Culture. The goal of this research "is to design an interactive tutorial for middle-aged and older adults, which can adapt to existing applications" [34: 162]. After applying a questionnaire to 64 participants, the main problems reported on interaction with mobile applications were: (i) difficulties in finding help options; (ii) they do not remember the instructions of the tutorials, when they need to apply them; (iii) do not know how to express themselves, when facing problems; (iv) and feel confused about the meanings of the icons and features.

In light of these results, the *Help Center* was designed to implement: (i) a fixed Floating Action Button (FAB) to access the help resource, whenever any doubts appear (ii) a PIP (Picture in picture) tutorial that allows the user to continue to do the operations while watching the instructions; (iii) a learning center (that help users learn to use the mobile applications, including *Discovery, Tasks and Collections*); (iv) and in the "meaning icons and features" mode users can tap an icon or feature to learn what it used for. From related work and findings from the survey study applied, Chen et al. summarized the following design principles [34]:

- improve the accessibility, as reported by Digmayer and Jakobs [31];
- help tools need to be accessible at any time to help the users, when they forget about the instructions;
- the searching for troubleshooting need to be improve with well-organized and related information;
- tutorials may include a feature introduction, meanings of icons and features, features access;
- allow applications with the interactive, step-by-step, self-based and visual instructions (see Fig. 3) on the same interface;
- alert for interfaces' changes;
- improve appropriate feedback;
- and motivate users to relieve from anxiety while learning.

Fig. 2. *Help Center* interface Source: [34: 174]

Fig. 3. Feedback in *Icon and Features* feature Source: [34: 178]

The fifth example is the *MedlinePlus* website. As mentioned in Table 1, the website is owned by *US National Institute of Health* that financially supports studies that aimed the development of tutorials, such as the project coordinated by Bo Xie, *Developing an e-health tutorial for older adults to use online health*, started in September 2017.

In *MedlinePlus*, video tutorials are used in the website support (see Fig. 4) and in the explanation of health information [35].

Fig. 4. Video tutorial to support website navigation Source: https://medlineplus.gov/aboutmedlineplus.html

The navigation video support for the MedlinePlus page is located on *About MedlinePlus* tab. Although it is not possible to specify the date of publication, it presents characteristics that corroborate some of the recommendations [30–33]:

- narrative paused;
- background music audible, or lower, only when the narrator does not intervene;
- the video progress bar and interactive elements of the player are visible;
- presents a logical sequence of page navigation options; and
- enables the video to be viewed in full-screen mode and in good resolution. In addition, the areas referred to in the audio are highlighted through visual magnification and color strategies (see Fig. 5).

Fig. 5. Highlighted areas in MedlinePlus tutorial Source: https://medlineplus.gov/aboutmedlineplus.html

When used for health information explanation, the tutorials are presented in the form of animations (see Fig. 6), in addition to the particularity of offering the audio description options or without audio description.

Fig. 6. Example of health information tutorial Source: https://medlineplus.gov/ency/anatomyvideos/000002.htm

5   Conclusions and Limitations

This paper intended to provide a relevant input to the development of tutorials for older adults in the context of Information and Communication Technologies.

The information collected enabled us to answer to our research question and propose some recommendations for the adequate solutions development: improve the accessibility tools. The help should appear where and when the user expects it to be made available, i.e. on the first page and be accessible at any time; it is important to clarify that it is only an aid and not part of the website; provide the preview progress bar and interactive elements of the player; provide visual and audio support options paused but when background music is used it must be audible only when the narrator is not talking; to allow feature help in full-screen mode and with good resolution; the areas referred in the audio should be highlighted through visual and color strategies; tutorial may include a feature introduction, meanings of icons and features, and the purpose of each function; avoid decorative typefaces and use 50:1 contrasts; the transition to the next step should be a user's choice; provide incentives that motivate users to use or remain in the tutorial; and clarify what the user can do at the end of the tutorial.

Limitations of the work include the paucity of studies that directly involve help tools in ICT contexts and older users. However, all the examples analyzed respond to the selection criteria and shows a relevant theoretical framework and a coherent empirical research.

Acknowledgements. We thank to Centre for the Study in Education, Technologies and Health (Polytechnic Institute of Viseu) and DigiMedia (University of Aveiro). This work was supported by Fundação para a Ciência e Tecnologia and C3I under Community Support Framework III the project SEDUCE 2.0 nr. POCI-01-0145-FEDER-031696.

References

1. Kachar, V.: Inclusão digital e terceira idade. In: Atuar - Educação e Cultura. Secretaria Estadual de Assistência e Desenvolvimento Social: Fundação Padre Anchieta, Brasil (2009)
2. Vaportzis, E., Glausen, M., Gow, A.: Older adults perceptions of technology and barriers to interacting with tablet computers: a focus group study. Front. Psychol. **8**, 1687 (2017)
3. Instituto Nacional de Estatística: Mantém-se o agravamento do envelhecimento demográfico, em Portugal, que só tenderá a estabilizar daqui a cerca de 40 anos. Instituto Nacional de Estatística, Lisboa (2017)
4. UN News: População mundial atingiu 7, 6 bilhões de habitantes UN News page. https://news.un.org/pt/story/2017/06/1589091-populacao-mundial-atingiu-76-bilhoes-de-habitantes. Accessed 22 Jan 2019
5. Pordata: Indicadores de envelhecimento in Pordata (2018). https://www.pordata.pt/DB/Portugal/Ambiente+de+Consulta/Tabela
6. Czaja, S., Lee, C.: The impact of aging on access to technology. Univers. Access Inf. Soc. **4**(5), 341–349 (2007)

7. Pfeil, U., Zaphiris, P., Wilson, S.: Online social support for older people: characteristics and dynamics of social support. In: Workshop Enhancing Interaction Spaces by Social Media for the Elderly, Vienna (2009)
8. Hill, R., Betts, L., Gardner, S.: Older adults' experiences and perceptions of digital technology: (Dis)empowerment, wellbeing, and inclusion. Comput. Hum. Behav. **48**, 415–423 (2015)
9. Whitbourne, S., Sneed, J.: The paradox of well-being, identity processes, and stereotype threat: ageism and its potential relationships to the self in later life. In: Nelson, T. (ed.) Ageism: Stereotyping and Prejudice Against Older Persons, pp. 247–273. MIT Press, Cambridge (2002)
10. Blusi, M., Asplund, K., Jong, M.: Older family careers in rural areas: experiences from using caregiver support services based on Information and Communication Technology. Eur. J. Ageing **10**(3), 191–199 (2013)
11. Kiel, J.M.: The digital divide: internet and e-mail use by the elderly. Med. Inform. Internet Med. **30**(1), 19–23 (2005)
12. Leung, L., Lee, P.: Multiple determinants of life quality: the roles of internet activities, use of new media, social support, and leisure activities. Telemat. Inf. **22**(3), 161–180 (2005)
13. Zheng, R., Hill, R., Gardner, M.: Engaging Older Adults with Modern Technology: Internet Use and Information Access Needs. Idea Group Global, Harrisburg (2012)
14. Plaza, I., Matin, L., Martin, S., Medrano, C.: Mobile applications in an aging society: status and trends. J. Syst. Softw. **84**, 1977–1988 (2011)
15. Leung, K., et al.: Developing and evaluating the social axioms survey in eleven countries: its relationship with the five-factor model of personality. J. Cross-Cult. Psychol. **43**(5), 833–857 (2012)
16. White, H., et al.: A randomized controlled trial of the psychosocial impact of providing internet training and access to older adults. Aging Mental Health **6**(3), 213–221 (2002)
17. Bradley, N., Poppen, W.: Assistive technology, computers, and internet may decrease sense of isolation for homebound elderly and disabled persons. Technol. Disabil. **15**, 19–25 (2003)
18. Bruck, L.: Connecting: residents meet computers. Nurs. Homes Long Term Care Manag. **51**(3), 31–34 (2002)
19. Clark, D.: Older adults living through and with their computer. Comput. Inform. Nurs. **20**(3), 117–124 (2002)
20. Gatto, S., Tak, S.H.: Computer, internet, and e-mail use among older adults: benefits and barriers. Educ. Gerontol. **34**(9), 800–811 (2008)
21. Choi, N.: Relationship between health service use and health information technology use among older adults: analysis of the US National Health Interview Survey. J. Med. Internet Res. **13**(2), e33 (2011)
22. Werner, J.M., Carlson, M., Jordan-Marsh, M., Clark, F.: Predictors of computer use in community-dwelling, ethnically diverse older adults. Hum. Factors **53**(5), 431–447 (2011)
23. Espanha, R.: A Relação entre TIC, Utentes, Profissionais e Redes Tecnológicas de Gestão de Informação em Saúde. Centro de Investigação e Estudos em Sociologia, Instituto Universitário de Lisboa (2011)
24. Marta, B.: A legibilidade gráfica face a uma sociedade envelhecida. Um estudo de caso: folheto informativo medicamentoso da Aspirina. Dissertação de mestrado, Universidade de Aveiro (2008)
25. Sales, M., Cybis, W.: Development of a checklist for the evaluation of the web accessibility for the aged users. In: Latin American Conference on Human-Computer Interaction, Rio de Janeiro, Brasil (2003)
26. Czaja, S., Sharit, J.: Designing training and instructional programs for older adults. In: Human Factors & Aging Series. CRC Press, Taylor & Francis Group, New York (2013)

27. Vaz-Serra, A.: O que significa envelhecer? In: Firmino, H., Leuchner, A., Barreto, J. (eds.) Psicogeriatria, pp. 21–33. Psiquiatria Clínica, Coimbra (2006)
28. Pak, R., McLaughlin, A.: Designing Displays for Older Adults. CRC Press, Boca Raton (2010)
29. Ferreira, S.: Tecnologias de Informação e Comunicação e o Cidadão Sénior. Universidade de Aveiro e Universidade do Porto, Tese de doutoramento (2013)
30. Nunes, M.: Envelhecimento ativo: o audiovisual na promoção do exercício físico. Dissertação de mestrado, Universidade de Aveiro (2015)
31. Digmayer, C., Jakobs, E.: Interactive video tutorials as a tool to remove barriers for senior experts in online innovation contests. In: INTED 2012 Proceedings, Valência, Espanha (2012)
32. Veloso, A.: SEDUCE - utilização da comunicação e da informação em ecologias web pelo cidadão sénior, Edições Afrontamento/CETAC.MEDIA, Porto (2014)
33. Caldas, A., Veloso, A., Antunes, M.: Construção de tutoriais audiovisuais para o uso da comunidade miOne pelo idoso. Augusto Guzzo Revista Acadêmica **14**, 53–76 (2014)
34. Chen, X.O., Wang, F., You, Z.W., Wang, X.C., Tao, C.J., Liu, J.: Design of interactive tutorials on mobile applications for chinese middle-aged and older adults. Art Des. Rev. **5**, 162–180 (2017)
35. Xie, B.: Developing an eHealth Tutorial for Older Adults to Use Online Health Resources. National Institutes of Health. http://grantome.com/grant/NIH/R21-AG052761–02. Accessed 26 Jan 2019

Motivational Affordances for Older Adults' Physical Activity Technology: An Expert Evaluation

Dennis L. Kappen[1(✉)], Pejman Mirza-Babaei[2],
and Lennart E. Nacke[3]

[1] Humber College Institute of Technology & Advanced Learning,
Toronto, ON, Canada
dennis.kappen@humber.ca
[2] University of Ontario Institute of Technology, Oshawa, ON, Canada
pejman.m@acm.org
[3] University of Waterloo, Waterloo, ON, Canada
Lennart.Nacke@acm.org

Abstract. Gamification has become popular as a behavior change strategy to increase the motivation and engagement of clients in health and wellness applications. Motivational affordances or gamification elements can help to foster intrinsic or extrinsic motivation for an activity as mundane as achieving fitness and wellness goals. Research indicates that there are many motivations among older adults for playing digital games and exergames to encourage physical activity (PA). Although studies investigate the influence of game elements in exergames on older adults PA, our study focuses on the usage of gamification elements for gamified PA technology. We designed Spirit50, a gamified PA technology app and conducted an expert evaluation using long form questionnaires and the Heuristics Evaluation for Gameful Design instrument. Content analysis and comparisons of expert ratings of the heuristics provided specific insights into motivational affordances for older adults' PA technology.

Keywords: Gamification · Older adults · Motivational affordances ·
Expert evaluation · Physical activity · Intrinsic motivation ·
Extrinsic motivation · Behavior change

1 Introduction

Older adults struggle to develop adequate exercise habits to maintain their health [1] and face the challenges of decreasing strength [2], potential diminished mental capacity [3], and social isolation [4]. Encouraging older adults to participate in physical activity (PA) through persuasive technology interventions provides the additional benefit of being able to track user activity. One study showed that overcoming sedentary lifestyles can be achieved through systems like UbiFit Garden where rewards and tracking functions were used to encourage older adults to participate in physical activity [5]. Embodied gaming or full-body interaction games improved the feeling of capability

© Springer Nature Switzerland AG 2019
J. Zhou and G. Salvendy (Eds.): HCII 2019, LNCS 11592, pp. 388–406, 2019.
https://doi.org/10.1007/978-3-030-22012-9_28

and encouraged older adults to play together for fun [6]. Interactive computer games [7] or exergames (technology combining exercises with digital gaming) have helped to overcome loneliness and encourage PA [8, 9] and improved physical functioning and cognition health outcomes [10–12]. Exergames have also served as a therapeutic instrument for improving physical function, cognition and social wellbeing [13, 14], provided a user-friendly medium for social interaction, diversion, wellness and rehabilitation [15–17].

While digital games and exergames exist to facilitate PA, gamification is a form of persuasive strategy which incorporates game design elements such as rewards and tracking functions to make mundane actions more playful and serves as a behavior change agent [18–20]. Such applications of a reward mechanism or gamification elements [21–23] or motivational affordances [24, 25] for PA facilitation are elements which help facilitate intrinsic or extrinsic motives. Persuasive technologies using gamification as a strategy indicated emergent themes such as feedback and monitoring, reward and threat, and goals and planning [26].

Prior research on the motivations and preferences to participate in PA indicated that health pressures and ill-health avoidance were significant motives for older adults to maintain an active lifestyle [27]. Understanding older adults' and their intrinsic and extrinsic motivation for PA is an essential primary strategy for the design and development of technology solutions facilitating PA [22, 28–31]. Therefore, we designed a PA motivation gamified technology that was goal-based (vague goals and specific goals) [32] with specific gamification elements and carried out an expert evaluation of this app.

The key findings of this expert evaluation showed that goal-based PA motivation technology designed for older adults' ability to do exercises based on their physical health conditions can be leveraged to foster intrinsic motivation to improve their health and wellness objectives. The contributions of this work can be used by PA technology designers and user-interaction researchers to customize and tailor gamified PA technology for older adults.

2 Theoretical Development

A comparison of existing gamification apps for PA technology revealed that the challenges of aging related to physical ability were not taken into consideration in the design of these apps [32]. These apps and gamified technology were not designed with older adults' needs and wants, and physical challenges due to aging. Based on preliminary studies [22, 27], these needs and wants were further categorized into vague-goals, specific-goals, barriers and current health conditions [32]. This taxonomy of goal-based differentiation of older adults' PA was developed into the Exercise Motivation Technology Framework (EMTF) (Fig. 1) [32]. Therefore, our research group designed Spirit50, a gamified PA technology specifically tailored for older adults' PA needs and challenges.

Spirit50 was a gamification application that was designed to provide customized and personalized exercise routines for older adults to help them participate in PA through daily and weekly exercise routines. This technology used the Self Determination Theory

(SDT) [33, 34] and the Kaleidoscope of Effective Gamification (KEG) for its design and development. While considering the physical challenges faced by older adults, this artifact was tailored to adapt to the short-term and long-term motivations for PA (Fig. 1) that was based on the SDT [35, 36]. This theory posits that individuals participate in activities due to the inherent satisfaction from the activity (intrinsic motivation) or doing something for an external reward (extrinsic motivation) [20, 29, 35–37] or a combination of both.

In the specific context of this paper, an expert evaluation was sought for reviewing the motivational affordances emerging from a prior study [38] and the technology facilitation of PA using Spirit50. Motivational affordances emergent from the participant interviews helped with creating the mapping of motivational affordances for PA technology [38]. However, based on user experience research, it was important to review the technology mapping with experts to evaluate these motivational affordances in the context of older adults PA motivation. This paper illustrates the expert evaluation of a gamification application (Spirit50) using heuristics and questionnaires to review the technology facilitation of PA, its applicability, usefulness and ease of use of the Spirit50 application in the context of the guidelines of motivational affordances for PA by older adults [38].

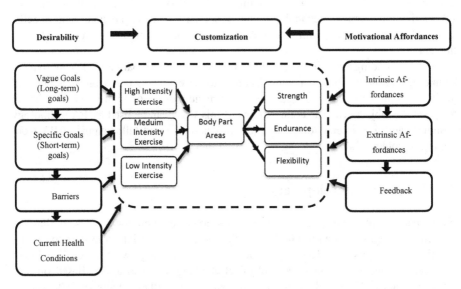

Fig. 1. Exercise Motivation Technology Framework (EMTF) [32]

3 Method

In this section, we explain the expert review method and instruments used to evaluate the motivational affordances in Spirit50 for older adults' motivationfor PA.

3.1 Expert Evaluation

Expert evaluations are normally conducted to inspect an application or a tool from the vantage point of applicability and usability [39, 40]. An expert heuristic evaluation, or expert review, is a method of assessing a product or service for its usefulness, applicability and ease of use [41–43]. A panel of experts from multidisciplinary domains spanning HCI, computer science, game design and gamification were identified and sent requests for participation in the expert evaluation process.

3.2 Objectives of the Expert Evaluation

Motivational affordances [24, 25] for PA facilitation are elements which help facilitate intrinsic or extrinsic motives to participate in PA. Gamification is essentially applying strategies from game design (e.g., mechanics, dynamics, and aesthetics) to daily activities to make people's actions more engaging. In this expert evaluation "Motivational Affordances" and "Gamification Elements" terms were used interchangeably. Experts were recruited to evaluate the technology artifact (Spirit50.com) for the following objectives:

1. Evaluating motivational affordances for technology facilitated PA
2. Evaluating the usefulness of the Spirit50 application
3. Evaluating the ease of use of the Spirit50 application.

3.3 Materials

While user testing of the Spirit50 design helped to resolve usability and interaction issues, the prior eight-week experimental study provided motivational affordances guidelines for technology facilitated PA [38]. Spirit50, to the best of our knowledge, was the only gamified technology designed specifically for older adults and tailored to their age-related abilities. A backup Spirit50 site was set up on a separate server so that it would not conflict with the commercial version of the site. Spirit50 is a web application designed with gamification elements for older adults over 50 years of age. Spirit50 incorporated the following gamification elements (motivational affordances): goal definition (quests: short-term and long-term goals), daily challenges, weekly challenges, goal progression meter, points and badges (stars), roadmaps and accolades for completing activities.

The survey questionnaire posed questions for motivational affordances from the Heuristics Evaluation for Gameful Design (HEGD), a heuristic toolkit, designed for gamification applications [44] and also consisted of long-form (LF) questions pertinent to applicability of the Spirit50 for the older adult demographic and its usefulness. The LF questionnaire section comprised of the following questions:

1. Do you think any specific gamification elements/motivational affordances/game elements should be given higher importance than others?
2. In your expert opinion, what other gamification elements/motivational affordances/game elements would be more impactful in the context of the Spirit50?
3. Do you think that the application provided adequate feedback to the participants?

4. If feedback provided in the Spirit50 application was not adequate, can you suggest any pointers to improve the feedback to potential users?
5. From an expert evaluation perspective, please list a few limitations of the Spirit50 application, if any?
6. From the perspective of older adults, can you suggest ways to improve this application?
7. Do you see any major hindrances in implementing Spirit50 application for older adults (over 50 years of age) in the context of Physical Activity and challenges caused due to aging?
8. Do you see any usability challenges with this application in context of older adults (over 50 years of age) physical activity and challenges caused due to aging?
9. From an older adult's perspective, do you think that the Spirit50 application could provide the opportunity of challenges and achievement in the form of exercise variations and/or levels of exercise intensities?

The combined survey questionnaire was set up using *LimeSurvey*[1], an open source survey platform on a secure password protected site.

3.4 Participants

As part of the recruitment process, seventeen experts in the domain of gamification and HCI were invited to participate in the expert evaluation. Twelve agreed to participate in the expert evaluation study. Three experts were unable to complete the expert evaluation process due to which reason only data collected from nine experts (F = 1, M = 8) was used in the final analysis. Experts represented gamification (n = 5), games user research (n = 2), and human computer interaction (n = 2) specializations. Seven of them had Masters Degrees and two held Doctorates. Five experts averaged four years and six months of expertise in gamification or gameful design [45]. While the most experienced expert had more than seven years' experience, the least experienced had two years of research expertise. The experts were invited to evaluate the motivational affordances, usefulness and ease of use of Spirit50.

3.5 Procedure

The expert evaluation was conducted in two stages.

Stage1: The Spirit50 site was cloned and given a login and password for remote access. Step-by-step instructions to access the site and to select the eight-week testing option was provided in a PowerPoint. While the commercial site had a payment plan, a discount code had to be set up so that experts would not have to pay for the site during evaluation. They were encouraged to use the web application as a user and evaluate the process of setting up their goals to exercise, input current health challenges, and select known barriers to exercising. All experts were asked to evaluate the setting up of their eight-week fitness roadmap for the specific goal of

---

[1] https://www.limesurvey.org/.

"Getting up and down off the floor with ease". This specific goal was chosen because it was the same specific goal used by participants in the experimental study described in a prior study [38]. Experts were required to perform all the fitness activities as indicated on the site and step through the task provided on a daily basis. They were allotted a time of one hour to evaluate the site and continue with the activities indicated in the app if they felt the need to do so.

Stage 2: Once the evaluation phase as completed, experts conducted an online assessment of the application using the survey questionnaire.

4 Results

The data from the expert evaluation stored through *LimeSurvey* and exported to SPSS for analysis. Comparisons of the ratings for the HEGD questionnaire and content analysis was carried out for answers to long form questions.

4.1 Comparison of HEGD and Content Analysis of LF

While the number of participants were low, the selections of experts from all 17 dimensions of the HEGD [44] were compared for correlations which are shown in Table 1. Results from detailed qualitative content analysis (QCA) [46, 47] of long-form questions are posted in Table 2.

Table 1. Scale correlations for the HEGD [44]

Intrinsic motivation	Extrinsic Motivation	Context-dependent
Autonomy - Creativity and Challenge - Competence	Ownership and Completeness - Mastery	Feedback and Completeness - Mastery
Autonomy - Creativity and Completeness - Mastery	Rewards and Completeness - Mastery	Feedback and Autonomy-Creativity
Relatedness and Completeness - Mastery	Rewards and Autonomy - Creativity	Feedback and Rewards
Immersion and Completeness - Mastery	Rewards and Relatedness	Actionable Feedback and Immersion
	Rewards and Immersion	Graspable Progress and Autonomy - Creativity
	Rewards and Ownership	Graspable Progress and Feedback
	Virtual Economy and Relatedness	Graspable Progress and Actionable Feedback
		Unpredictability and Relatedness
		Unpredictability and Scarcity
		Unpredictability and Graspable Progress
		Disruption Control and Ownership
		Innovation and Loss Avoidance

Table 2. Content analysis of LF questionnaire

LF1   *Do you think any specific gamification elements/motivational affordances/game elements should be given higher importance than others?*

LF1	EX01	EX03	EX04	EX05	EX07	EX08	EX11	EX12	EX20	n	%age
Goals	goals	goals	goals	goals			goals		goals	6	19%
		points	points		points				points	4	13%
Achievement							achievement		achievement	3	10%
						ability	ability	ability		3	10%
Competence						competence				2	6%
Mastery								mastery		2	6%
progress bar	progress bar	progress bar							progress bar	2	6%
			improved perfor-mance					improved performance		2	6%
feedback		feedback	feedback		feedback					2	6%
					stars				stars	2	6%
				competition						1	3%
				collaboration						1	3%
					commenting					1	3%
									Total	31	100%

LF2   *What other gamification elements/motivational affordances/game elements would be more impactful in the context of the Spirit50 application?*

LF2	EX01	EX03	EX04	EX05	EX07	EX08	EX11	EX12	EX20	n	%age
EX01	challenges	challenges	challenges	challenges	challenges		challenges	challenges		6	12%
	goals	goals		goals		goals	goals		goals	5	10%
Choice				choice		choice		choice	choice	5	10%
					ability	ability	ability	ability		4	8%
	stars	stars			stars		stars		stars	4	8%
Socialization					socialization	socialization	socialization			4	8%
					points		points		points	3	6%
				achievement			achievement		achievement	3	6%
Mastery			mastery					mastery		3	6%
	progress bar	progress bar						progress bar	progress bar	3	6%
Comparison					comparison				comparison	3	6%

(Continued)

Competence										Total	n	%age
	feedback					competence leaderboard commenting	leaderboard				2	4%
					feedback commenting						2	4%
								leaderboard			2	4%
			collaboration								2	4%
Freedom								collaboration	freedom		2	4%
			competition								2	4%
		onboarding									1	2%
				content creation							1	2%
Randomness										avatars	1	2%
											1	2%
										Total	51	100%

LF3   *Do you think that the application provided adequate feedback to the participants?*

	EX01	EX03	EX04	EX05	EX07	EX08	EX11	EX12	EX20	Total	n	%age
Progress bar	progress bar	progress bar	progress bar	progress bar	progress bar		progress bar	progress bar	progress bar		8	21%
Points	points	points		points	points		points		points		6	15%
Completion status	stars	stars		stars	stars		stars		stars		5	13%
				completion status	completion status		completion status		completion status		5	13%
Timer			timer		timer	timer			timer		5	13%
More feedback required		more feedback required		more feedback required		more feedback required	more feedback required				5	13%
More progress details			more progress details					more progress details			3	8%
			onboarding required					onboarding required			2	5%
										Total	39	100%

LF4   *If feedback provided in the Spirit50 application was not adequate, can you suggest any pointers to improve the feedback to potential users?*

(Continued)

EX01	EX03	EX04	EX05	EX07	EX08	EX11	EX12	EX20	n	%age
Correctness			correctness	correctness	correctness	correctness	correctness		6	16%
	challenges		challenges			challenges	challenges	challenges	5	14%
Value of exercises			value of exercises			value of exercises		value of exercises	4	11%
Performance			performance		performance	performance			4	11%
		onboarding		onboarding			onboarding	onboarding	4	11%
Exercise to goal contribution				exercise to goal contribution				exercise to goal contribution	3	8%
About rewards	about rewards			about rewards					3	8%
Importance of exercises				importance of exercises			importance of exercises		3	8%
	intensity of exercises					intensity of exercises			2	5%
	points usage						points usage		2	5%
		reason for timer							1	3%
								Total	37	100%

LF5   *Limitations of the Spirit50 application, if any?*

EX01	EX03	EX04	EX05	EX07	EX08	EX11	EX12	EX20	n	%age
	show graphs		show graphs			show graphs		show graphs	4	12%
Limited onboarding				limited onboarding			limited onboarding	limited onboarding	4	12%
Single health issue		single health issue				single health issue			3	9%
	show use of points				show use of points			show use of points	3	9%
Feedback on value of exercises			feedback on value of exercises				feedback on value of exercises		3	9%
Limited to single goal				limited to single goal					2	6%

(Continued)

	EX03	EX04	EX05	EX07	EX08	EX11	EX12	EX20	n	%age
Weekly achievements							weekly achievements		2	6%
Lacking socialization						lacking socialization			2	6%
Add randomness		add randomness		add randomness					2	6%
	not responsive						not responsive		2	6%
	add more quests					add quests			2	6%
			more health details				more health details		2	6%
			add collaboration				add collaboration		2	6%
Add unpredictability									1	3%
Total									34	100%

From the perspective of older adults, can you suggest ways to improve the Spirit50 application?

LF6

	EX01	EX03	EX04	EX05	EX07	EX08	EX11	EX12	EX20	n	%age
Simplify app		more onboarding	more onboarding	simplify app	more onboarding		simplify app	more onboarding	more onboarding	5	17%
		improve interface design		improve interface design				improve interface design	simplify app	4	13%
				add usefulness of exercises	add usefulness of exercises		add usefulness of exercises		improve interface design	4	13%
Add more choices						add more choices		add more choices		3	10%
			add responsiveness			add responsiveness	add responsiveness			3	10%
Add benefits of routines				add benefits of routines						2	7%

(Continued)

	add value of rewards	add overall workout plan	add feedback on form/gait	add value of rewards	add overall workout plan	add feedback on form/gait	n	%age
							2	7%
							2	7%
		add overall workout plan			add overall workout plan		2	7%
Total							30	100%

LF7 *Any major hindrances in implementing Spirit50 application for older adults in the context of PA and challenges caused due to aging?*

							older people and technology	n	%age
Older people and technology	older people and technology			older people and technology	older people and technology		older people and technology	4	19%
	interface design		interface design		interface design	interface design	interface design	4	19%
Safety issues	safety issues	usability issues				safety issues	safety issues	4	19%
	usability issues			usability issues		usability issues	usability issues	3	14%
Awareness of benefits	awareness of benefits		awareness of benefits			awareness of benefits	awareness of benefits	3	14%
	limitations of unsupervised activity			limitations of unsupervised activity			limitations of unsupervised activity	2	10%
				less patience				1	5%
Total								21	100%

LF8 *Do you see any usability challenges with this application in context of older adults' physical activity and challenges caused due to aging?*

	EX01	EX03	EX04	EX05	EX07	EX08	EX11	EX12	EX20	n	%age
Interface design	interface design	interface design		interface design	interface design		interface design	interface design	interface design	6	23%
			simplicity of interaction steps		simplicity of interaction steps	simplicity of interaction steps	simplicity of interaction steps	simplicity of interaction steps		5	19%
		onboarding			onboarding	onboarding				3	12%

(Continued)

LF8 (continued)

	EX03	EX04	EX05	EX07	EX08	EX11	EX12	EX20	n	%age
explanation of the value of the app	explanation of the value of the app					explanation of the value of the app		explanation of the value of the app	3	12%
feedback loop						feedback loop			3	12%
Explanations of icons							explanations of icons		2	8%
explanation of rewards			explanation of rewards						2	8%
simplicity of app			simplicity of app		simplicity of app				2	8%
Total									**26**	**100%**

LF9

From an older adult's perspective, do you think that the Spirit50 application could provide the opportunity of challenges and achievement in the form of exercise variations and/or levels of exercise intensities?

	EX03	EX04	EX05	EX07	EX08	EX11	EX12	EX20	n	%age
EX01 meaningfulness to users	meaningfulness to users		meaningfulness to users		meaningfulness to users	meaningfulness to users			**4**	14%
mindful of health issues	mindful of health issues		mindful of health issues			mindful of health issues		mindful of health issues	4	14%
onboarding	onboarding			onboarding	onboarding				3	11%
Increased choice					increased choice			increased choice	3	11%
Opportunity for competence						opportunity for competence		opportunity for competence	3	11%
increased difficulty levels	increased difficulty levels			increased difficulty levels					3	11%
Enable mastery			enable mastery				enable mastery		2	7%
Increased options			increased options						2	7%
increased challenges incorporate safety		increased challenges incorporate safety					increased challenges incorporate safety		2	7%
Total									**28**	**100%**

Within the **intrinsic motivation** dimensions from the HEGD [44] correlation between *Autonomy - Creativity and Challenge – Competence* imply that the app facilitated the freedom of choice of vague goals (long-term goals) and specific goals (short-term goals) with respect to their health conditions. The increase in difficulty level of the exercise routines afforded the correlation between *Autonomy - Creativity and Completeness – Mastery*. The potential of comparing their performance and their progression on a daily and weekly basis and sharing with others facilitated the *Relatedness and Completeness - Mastery* dimension. Engagement while doing the exercise routines with increasing difficulty levels afforded the corelation between the *Immersion and Completeness - Mastery* dimensions.

With the **extrinsic motivation** heuristics [44], achievement of virtual goods (points and stars) based on the completion of specific tasks of increasing difficulty facilitated positive correlations between the dimensions *Ownership and Completeness – Mastery*. Additionally, freedom of selection of tasks based on the individual's ability and health conditions afforded the *Rewards and Autonomy – Creativity dimension*. Fair acquisition of rewards [44] within the Spirit50 app and meaningful interaction with the narrative of the app afforded the dimensions *Rewards and Relatedness,* and *Rewards and Immersion.* Furthermore, the app facilitated the collection of rewards (points and stars) for task completion and daily and weekly progression helped with correlations between the dimensions *Virtual Economy and Relatedness.*

Within the **context dependent** heuristics [44], positive correlation *between Feedback and Completeness - Mastery, Feedback and Autonomy-Creativity, Feedback and Rewards* indicated that the system communicated the completion of tasks and achievements. Expert evaluation also affirmed the dimensions *Actionable Feedback and Immersion, Graspable Progress and Autonomy – Creativity, Graspable Progress and Actionable Feedback,* and *Graspable Progress and Feedback* due to the presence of progression feedback, daily and weekly roadmap, and comparison of their current standing in the roadmap. Furthermore, intermittent tasks, randomness of tasks contributed to ratings between *Unpredictability and Relatedness, Unpredictability and Scarcity,* and *Unpredictability and Graspable Progress.* Protection against cheating, and allowing ideas to be added for exercise routines, specific goals and health challenges helped with ratings between the dimensions *Disruption Control and Ownership,* and *Innovation and Loss Avoidance.*

5 Discussion

We conducted the expert evaluation of Spirit50, to determine the efficacy of the motivational affordances used in the gamification technology, its usefulness and ease of use for the older adult demographic.

5.1 Motivational Affordances and Older Adults' PA

Experts indicated that *autonomy* can be fostered by empowering older adults' the opportunity to do manageable and achievable PA within the app. Helping them take ownership of their PA activities can help to achieve specific goals [32] such as improving mobility in arms, legs and further leading to full-body mobility. Furthermore, selection of the type of exercise (strength, endurance and flexibility) and the intensity of exercises (high, medium and low) will help with self-regulation and taking ownership of their PA decisions.

The opportunity to level up, competing on levels of exercise which increase in difficulty level and exercise intensity fosters *competence*. Creating achievement levels based on exercise intensity will enable mastery of specific-goals leading to a feeling of accomplishment. While incremental success at exercise routines in the app is a positive reinforcement for the PA, simplicity of routines can also lead to boredom. Therefore, randomness in the occurrence of difficult challenges could add to the element of curiosity and spontaneity in the gamified app.

Sharing of individual successes and task completion status with others fosters relatedness. The aspect of coaching others based on their own experiences at the activity could help with the concept of sharing. Portability of the app on a smartphone or a mobile device helped with the ease of access to the routines. Furthermore, being able to review the correctness of one's body-form in an exercise routine repeatedly adds value to the gamified PA technology.

Rewarding effort over task completion is an extrinsic motivator. This could be facilitated by interjecting praise for effort done throughout the app which would, in turn, reassure older adults about being on the right track. The app would serve as a virtual assistant or a virtual coach in the PA program. Such rewards would also provide validation of efforts and serve as achievement markers.

5.2   Spirit50 and Motivational Affordances

Intrinsic motivation: Content analysis showed that Spirit50 was one way to facilitate PA amongst older adults. Gamification elements like goals (quests), challenges, and routine activity can help to foster intrinsic motivation among older adults who are focused on improving their health and wellbeing. It could provide a platform for habit formation leading to the continued usage of the app over prolonged periods of time. The exercise routines were simple and could afford the possibility of easily remembering routines for quick repetition. The freedom of selection of vague-goals (long-term goals) and specific goals (short-term goals) [32] afforded *autonomy* among users. *Competence* at being able to do the exercise routines, completing the tasks on a daily basis, performing challenges which were laid out at higher exercise intensities in progressive weeks was also seen in the Spirit50 app. This was also seen in the comparisons of the answers to the HEGD [44] questionnaire, namely the *autonomy-creativity*, and the *challenge-competence, and completeness-mastery* dimensions. Furthermore, this showed that the challenges presented in the Spirit50 app were adapted to user's ability, health challenges and achievement of goals.

Extrinsic Motivation: Experts valued the presence of virtual rewards' (points and stars) as a means to validate the effort of achieving the goal-based activity. The presence of progression on daily challenges and weekly increments indicated in the road map provided the assurance of task achievement and accomplishment of set activities within the app. This in turn, served as virtual praise for task completion. Therefore, the presence of a simple reward mechanism for task completion would be meaningful to the user engaged in performing PA as specified by the app.

Feedback Options: Experts noted that the presence of goal selection, number of steps and reps completed, the daily fitness roadmap and the visual representation of PA progression was essential feedback for older adults. Experts considered the simplicity of daily activities to be similar to achieving small achievable goals that could be scaled to more complex PA tasks. The presence of new exercise routines that were interjected spontaneously contributed to the surprise, curiosity and unpredictability dimensions of the HEGD [44].

5.3   Limitations of Spirit50 and Future Work

While the Spirit50 app used specific gamification elements', experts indicated that social interaction and community formation [1, 22, 28], two very important aspects for the continuance of PA were missing. Presence of this attribute would help older adults' with overcoming the feeling of loneliness in the aspect of doing PA [48–50]. Additionally, providing a performance rating (correctness vs effort) similar to the feedback provided by a fitness trainer could help with modulation of PA posture, stance, gait and feeling of improvement [27, 51, 52]. An eight-week study using Spirit50 also indicated the need for greater feedback on posture correction and stance improvement within the gamified system [38]. Such features within the system would help to improve older adults confidence in the system and foster competence [22, 53, 54]. While Spirit50 engendered a select collection of fitness routines, the closed system did not allow for the addition of new activities quickly because of depth of programming needed to make such additions. Providing options to change the exercise intensity and difficulty level on a real-time basis was not possible, which would have helped to foster greater *autonomy*.

Expert evaluation also indicated that the sizing of the points, stars and progression icons were small. Additionally, the interface design did not showcase the accomplishments of the users well on the page, leading to a lack of hierarchy of gamification elements on the interface. Furthermore, presenting a time to completion and current levels with reference to future levels in a graphical format would enhance the understanding of the PA quests within the gamified system.

Expert evaluation also showed that real-time feedback regarding correctness of posture could help older adults in improving their form while performing PA routines. This missing feature would need real-time scanning of body positions and overlaying with the computer-generated sequence of PA activities. Spirit50 also lacked showcasing the importance or value of doing a specific set of exercise routines. Additional pop-out screen with this information could help to reassure the value of doing specific PA routines in relation to the selected vague goals and specific goals [32]. Limited dexterity of their hand could also be a deterrent to older adults using a computer mouse when playing the gamified app. Concerns about the perception/misconception of older adults about games and gamification elements were also raised by experts indicating the need for onboarding opportunities within the gamified PA system.

6 Conclusion

Spirit50 was a gamified PA technology designed to improve motivation of older adults to participating in PA while considering their physical limitations and ability to do PA. We conducted an expert evaluation of this app which showed that the purposeful usage of motivational affordances (gamification elements) in PA technology can help with older adults' PA motivation. The expert evaluation used long-form questionnaires and the HEGD [44], a gamification toolkit to evaluate Spirit50. Experts indicated that Spirit50, with select gamification elements can foster intrinsic and extrinsic motivation for PA. Intrinsic motivation among older adults for PA can be achieved through the use of gamification elements like goals (quests), challenges, achievements, and task completion of specific exercise routines on a daily basis leading to an eight-week fitness program [38]. Reward mechanisms in the form of points, stars and progression metrics for task completion serves as a validation of effort and could foster extrinsic motivation for PA. Experts also indicated that Spirit50 could be improved by the addition of sub-goals, graphical progression meters, collaborative community building and deployment of the design on mobile devices such as smartphones and tablets. This expert evaluation helps to show that motivational affordances can help with PA motivation of older adults and identified how this app could be improved. Results of this expert evaluation can be used by PA technology designers and user-interaction researchers to customize and tailor gamified PA technology for older adults.

Acknowledgements. This paper is partially based on one chapter of the first author's PhD dissertation, Adaptive Engagement of Older Adult's Physical Activity through Gamification [32]. The authors would like to thank the experts who participated in this research study. Furthermore, the First Author would like to thank the Faculty of Applied Sciences and Technology, Humber College of Technology and Advanced Learning and the Humber Employees Scholarship Fund for their support of this research.

References

1. Bethancourt, H.J., Rosenberg, D.E., Beatty, T., Arterburn, D.E.: Barriers to and facilitators of physical activity program use among older adults. Clin. Med. Res. **12**, 10–20 (2014)
2. Gerling, K.M., Schulte, F.P., Smeddinck, J., Masuch, M.: Game design for older adults: effects of age-related changes on structural elements of digital games. In: Herrlich, M., Malaka, R., Masuch, M. (eds.) ICEC 2012. LNCS, vol. 7522, pp. 235–242. Springer, Heidelberg (2012). https://doi.org/10.1007/978-3-642-33542-6_20
3. Evenson, K.R., Buchner, D.M., Morland, K.B.: Objective measurement of physical activity and sedentary behavior among us adults aged 60 years or older. CDC - Prev. Chronic Dis. **9**, 2–11 (2012)
4. Porter, K.N., Fischer, J.G., Johnson, M.A.: Improved physical function and physical activity in older adults following a community-based intervention: relationships with a history of depression. Maturitas **70**, 290–294 (2011)
5. Consolvo, S., et al.: Activity sensing in the wild: a field trial of UbiFit garden. In: Proceedings of CHI 2008, pp. 1797–1806 (2008)

6. Aarhus, R., Grönvall, E., Larsen, S.B., Wollsen, S.: Turning training into play: embodied gaming, seniors, physical training and motivation. Gerontechnology **10**, 110–120 (2011)
7. Bleakley, C.M., Charles, D., Porter-Armstrong, A., McNeill, M.D.J., McDonough, S.M., McCormack, B.: Gaming for health: a systematic review of the physical and cognitive effects of interactive computer games in older adults. J. Appl. Gerontol. **34**, NP166–NP189 (2015)
8. Brox, E., Fernandez-Luque, L., Evertsen, G., González-Hernández, J.: Exergames for elderly: social exergames to persuade seniors to increase physical activity. In: Proceedings of the 5th International ICST Conference on Pervasive Computing Technologies for Healthcare, pp. 546–549. IEEE (2011)
9. Cota, T.T., Ishitani, L.: Motivation and benefits of digital games for the elderly: a systematic literature review. Rev. Bras. Comput. Appl. **7**, 2–16 (2015)
10. Hall, A., Chavarria, E., Maneeratana, V., Chaney, B., Bernhardt, J.: Health benefits of digital videogames for older adults: a systematic review of the literature. Games Health J. **1**, 402–410 (2012)
11. Villani, D., Serino, S., Triberti, S., Riva, G.: Ageing positively with digital games. In: Giokas, K., Bokor, L., Hopfgartner, F. (eds.) eHealth 360°. LNICST, vol. 181, pp. 148–155. Springer, Cham (2017). https://doi.org/10.1007/978-3-319-49655-9_20
12. Zhang, F., Kaufman, D.: Physical and cognitive impacts of digital games on older adults: a meta-analytic review. J. Appl. Gerontol. **35**, 1189–1210 (2015)
13. Loos, E., Zonneveld, A.: Silver gaming: serious fun for seniors? In: Zhou, J., Salvendy, G. (eds.) ITAP 2016. LNCS, vol. 9755, pp. 330–341. Springer, Cham (2016). https://doi.org/10.1007/978-3-319-39949-2_32
14. Chao, Y.-Y., Scherer, Y.K., Montgomery, C.A.: Effects of using Nintendo Wii™ Exergames in older adults: a review of the literature. J. Aging Health (2014)
15. Larsen, L.H., Schou, L., Lund, H.H., Langberg, H.: The physical effect of exergames in healthy elderly—a systematic review. Games Health J. **2**, 205–212 (2013)
16. Kappen, D.L., Mirza-Babaei, P., Nacke, L.E.: Older adults' physical activity and exergames: a systematic review. Int. J. Hum.-Comput. Interact. **00**, 1–28 (2018)
17. Loos, E.: Exergaming: meaningful play for older adults? In: Zhou, J., Salvendy, G. (eds.) ITAP 2017. LNCS, vol. 10298, pp. 254–265. Springer, Cham (2017). https://doi.org/10.1007/978-3-319-58536-9_21
18. Deterding, S., Dixon, D., Khaled, R., Nacke, L.E.: From game design elements to gamefulness: defining "gamification". In: MindTrek 2011, Tampere, Finland, 28–30 September 2011, pp. 9–15 (2011)
19. Kappen, B.D.L., Orji, R.: Gamified and persuasive systems as behaviour change agents for health and wellness (2017)
20. Kappen, D.L., Nacke, L.E.: The kaleidoscope of effective gamification: deconstructing gamification in business applications. In: Proceedings of the First International Conference on Gameful Design, Research, and Applications – Gamification 2013, pp. 119–122 (2013)
21. Brauner, P., Calero Valdez, A., Schroeder, U., Ziefle, M.: Increase physical fitness and create health awareness through exergames and gamification. In: Holzinger, A., Ziefle, M., Hitz, M., Debevc, M. (eds.) SouthCHI 2013. LNCS, vol. 7946, pp. 349–362. Springer, Heidelberg (2013). https://doi.org/10.1007/978-3-642-39062-3_22
22. Kappen, D.L., Nacke, L.E., Gerling, K.M., Tsotsos, L.E.: Design strategies for gamified physical activity applications for older adults. In: Proceedings of the Annual Hawaii International Conference on System Sciences, vol. 49, pp. 1309–1318. IEEE Computer Society (2016)
23. Hamari, J., Koivisto, J.: "Working out for likes": an empirical study on social influence in exercise gamification. Comput. Hum. Behav. **50**, 333–347 (2015)

24. Hamari, J., Koivisto, J., Sarsa, H.: Does gamification work? - a literature review of empirical studies on gamification. In: Proceedings of Annual Hawaii International Conference on System Sciences, pp. 3025–3034 (2014)
25. Lister, C., West, J.H., Cannon, B., Sax, T., Brodegard, D.: Just a fad? Gamification in health and fitness apps. JMIR Serious Games 2, 1–12 (2014)
26. Edwards, E.A., et al.: Gamification for health promotion: systematic review of behaviour change techniques in smartphone apps. BMJ Open 6, e012447 (2016)
27. Kappen, D.L., Mirza-Babaei, P., Nacke, L.E.: Gamification through the application of motivational affordances for physical activity technology. In: Proceedings of CHIPLAY 2017, pp. 5–18 (2017)
28. Schutzer, K.A., Graves, B.S.: Barriers and motivations to exercise in older adults. Prev. Med. (Baltim) 39, 1056–1061 (2004)
29. Dacey, M., Baltzell, A., Zaichkowsky, L.: Older adults' intrinsic and extrinsic motivation toward physical activity. Am. J. Health Behav. 32, 570–582 (2008)
30. Kuroda, Y., Sato, Y., Ishizaka, Y., Yamakado, M., Yamaguchi, N.: Exercise motivation, self-efficacy, and enjoyment as indicators of adult exercise behavior among the transtheoretical model stages. Glob. Health Promot. 19, 14–22 (2012)
31. Motalebi, S.A., Iranagh, J.A., Abdollahi, A., Lim, K.: Applying of theory of planned behavior to promote physical activity and exercise behavior among older adults. J. Phys. Educ. Sport. 14, 562–568 (2014)
32. Kappen, D.L.: Adaptive engagement of older adults' fitness through gamification (2017). http://hdl.handle.net/10155/881
33. Boulos, M.N.K., Yang, S.P.: Exergames for health and fitness: the roles of GPS and geosocial apps. Int. J. Health Geogr. 12, 18 (2013)
34. Zuckerman, O., Gal-Oz, A.: Deconstructing gamification: evaluating the effectiveness of continuous measurement, virtual rewards, and social comparison for promoting physical activity. Pers. Ubiquitous Comput. 18, 1705–1719 (2014)
35. Ryan, R.M., Deci, E.L.: Intrinsic and extrinsic motivations: classic definitions and new directions. Contemp. Educ. Psychol. 25, 54–67 (2000)
36. Deci, E.L.: Self-determination theory: a macro-theory of human motivation, development and health. Can. Psychol. 49, 182–185 (2008)
37. Ryan, R.M., Frederick, C.M., Lepes, D., Rubio, N., Sheldon, K.M.: Intrinsic motivation and exercise adherence. Int. J. Sport Psychol. 28, 335–354 (1997)
38. Kappen, D.L., Mirza-Babaei, P., Nacke, L.E.: Gamification of older adults' physical activity : an eight-week study. In: Proceedings of the Annual Hawaii International Conference on System Sciences, vol. 51, pp. 1–12 (2018)
39. Nielsen, J.: Finding usability problems through heuristic evaluation. In: Proceedings of the SIGCHI conference on Human, pp. 373–380 (1992)
40. Nielsen, J.: Heuristic evaluation. In: Usability Inspection Methods, pp. 25–62. Wiley, New York (1994)
41. Desurvire, H., Desurvire, H., Blvd, W., Rey, M., Caplan, M.: Using heuristics to evaluate the playability of games. In: Proceedings of CHI '04 (2016)
42. Nacke, L.E., Drachen, A., Kuikkaniemi, K., De Kort, Y.A.W.: Playability and player experience research. In: Proceedings of DIGRA (2009)
43. Paavilainen, J.: Critical review on video game evaluation heuristics : social games perspective. In: ACM FuturePlay 2010, pp. 56–65 (2010)
44. Evaluation for Gameful Design. In: Proceedings of 2016 Annual Symposium on Computer-Human Interaction in Play Companion Extended Abstracts - CHI Play Companion 2016, 315–323 (2016)

45. Landers, R.N., Tondello, G.F., Kappen, D.L., Collmus, A.B., Mekler, E.D., Nacke, L.E.: Defining gameful experience as a psychological state caused by gameplay: replacing the term 'Gamefulness' with three distinct constructs. Int. J. Hum.-Comput. Stud. (2018)
46. Krippendorff, K.: Content Analysis An Introduction to Its Methodology. SAGE Publications Inc., Thousand Oaks (2013)
47. Schreier, M.: Qualitative Content Analysis in Practice. SAGE Publications Ltd., London (2012)
48. Fife, D.L.: Reasons for physical activity and exercise participation in senior athletes (2008)
49. Marston, H.R.: Digital gaming perspectives of older adults: content vs. interaction. Educ. Gerontol. **39**, 194–208 (2013)
50. Enouraging social interaction for older adults. Int. J. Hum. Comput. Interact. **7318** (2016)
51. Pruitt, L.A., et al.: Use of accelerometry to measure physical activity in older adults at risk for mobility disability. J. Aging Phys. Act. **16**, 416–434 (2008)
52. Bamidis, P.D., et al.: A review of physical and cognitive interventions in aging. Neurosci. Biobehav. Rev. **44**, 206–220 (2014)
53. Irvine, A.B., Gelatt, V.A., Seeley, J.R., Macfarlane, P., Gau, J.M.: Web-based intervention to promote physical activity by sedentary older adults: randomized controlled trial. J. Med. Internet Res. **15**, e19 (2013)
54. Franco, M.R., et al.: Older people's perspectives on participation in physical activity: a systematic review and thematic synthesis of qualitative literature. Br. J. Sports Med. **49**, 1268–1276 (2015)

Durkheim's Legacy in the Digital Age: The "Elementary Forms" of Digital Communication of Portuguese Senior Users of Social Network Sites

Tiago Lapa[(⊠)]

Department of Sociology, ISCTE – University Institute of Lisbon,
Av. das Forças Armadas, 1649-026 Lisbon, Portugal
tjflsl@iscte-iul.pt

Abstract. The present paper investigates the usefulness of the cultural theory of Durkheim to analyze modes of utilization and functions of digital communication, especially through social network sites (SNS), by surveying their capability for normative and social integration. It explores to what extent can the analytical tools of Durkheim's study concerning the elementary forms of religious life be used to describe, comprehend and explain social media domestication by seniors? It is contented that this approach is especially useful in the analysis of the mediated rites of exchange of digital content, which is itself infused with social meaning. Distinctive uses of symbolic forms on digital communication can be a routine method of peer-sharing and support, a means of reaching out, reinforcing an emotional attachment and the cohesion of a social group that shares an identical cultural code and type of domestication of digital devices. For instance, the content exchanged on SNS and on the Internet can be understood, since their popularization, to form a cultural code that constitutes, simultaneously, an element of group cohesion between peers and of segmentation between generations and social groups. Albeit acknowledged analytical problems in functionalist perspectives, it is also argued that their utility lies in the capacity to associate cultural features with tangible forms of social media domestication and motivational aspects concerning that domestication.

Keywords: Seniors · Social network sites · Durkheim

1 Introduction

This paper examines the usefulness of Durkheim's cultural theory to study and interpret data regarding the uses, functions and gratifications of digital communication among seniors, in social network sites and mobile devices, in particular, by surveying their capability for normative and social integration. Therefore, the main goal of this article is to examine to what extent can the analytical tools of Durkheim's study regarding the elementary forms of religious life [1] be employed to describe, interpret and explain digital media domestication by seniors. According to this approach, the shared (mediated) symbolic forms and the rites of exchange of such forms can be considered

© Springer Nature Switzerland AG 2019
J. Zhou and G. Salvendy (Eds.): HCII 2019, LNCS 11592, pp. 407–420, 2019.
https://doi.org/10.1007/978-3-030-22012-9_29

as fundamental units of analysis which endow the message of social meaning beyond explicit or manifest content. Consequently, the mediated rite of symbolic exchange is a key element of analysis since it is permeated with social meanings. Following Lessig [2] these meanings can be understood as the semiotic content attached to various actions (such as send messages, click like, post, etc.), inactions, or statuses (through online disclosure), within a particular (digital) context. Moreover, for seniors and younger individuals alike, distinctive uses of symbolic forms on digital communication can be a routine method of peer-sharing and social support, a means of reaching out, reinforcing an emotional attachment among peers.

Many research evidence points out older adults barriers to social media use such as cognitive debilities [3], privacy concerns [4, 5], income and trust [5]. But other studies focus on the engagement in Social Media Relationship Maintenance Behaviors by seniors and indicate that older adults experience such behaviors in social network sites (SNS) as actively as younger counterparts [6]. Past studies also show that SNS senior usage is associated with increased feelings of connectedness with friends [7] and that older adults often cultivate new connections to counterbalance the loss of ties in later-life situations, such as retirement and widowhood [8]. Thus, there is evidence that social media contributes to the social cohesion of older adults that might share an identical cultural code and certain types of domestication of digital devices.

The messages exchanged on digital platforms such as SNS and on mobile phones can be understood, since their vulgarization, as communication modalities that form cultural codes constituting, simultaneously, elements of group cohesion and of segmentation between generations and social groups. Therefore, digital rites can also be studied in terms of their segregation potential to jeopardize intergenerational normative and social integration and as a factor of individuation.

Albeit acknowledged analytical problems in functionalist perspectives [9, 10], Alexander [11] argues that the attractiveness of functionalist approaches lies in their ability to interconnect cultural aspects with concrete social action. Thus, following Alexander, it is argued that their utility lies in the capacity to associate cultural features with tangible forms of media domestication and motivational aspects concerning that domestication. In fact, it is an approach that fits very well with the research interests of Blumler and Katz [12] concerning individuals' *uses and gratifications* and the intervening variables between the media and their audiences [13]. In this approach there is less concern for the transmission of ideas or points of view than other studies, since the focus is "on the social and psychological "needs" of audiences which they argued actively shaped media consumption and the ways that audiences understood media content" [13].

The Durkheimian model is highly operable in media studies and helps the understanding of a series of empirical results concerning the domestication of digital devices and platforms among Portuguese users, including seniors. The model contributes to identify the elementary forms of the digital life of older people and see if the separation between the sacred and the profane is still played in the division between real or virtual or between lived and mediated experience, setting them apart from younger people, or if they are becoming closer to younger generations that sacralize digital connectivity.

The use of the social network sites and mobile phones might be illustrative of this proposition. For instance, most Portuguese children surveyed online in a past study report they receive calls, often or always in social situations where communication from outside could be considered as disruptive [14]. And in a networked logic of social action, embodied in a practical rationality, if a communication link is broken another link will be sought (either by changing the medium or ties). Concerning seniors, it is also the aim of this paper to find clues to see if the profane world of seniors is becoming also one of disconnection. It is likewise argued that the Durkheim's cultural model is consistent with the role of media devices in the maintenance of ontological security [15] of seniors, and with the domestication approach in new media studies.

2 Theoretical Framework

In an influential text, Carey [16] pointed out two main conceptualizations of communication: as transmission and as ritual. Communication as transmission refers to its traditional meaning, that is, as an instrumental form of information dissemination and as the process through which messages are transmitted and distributed through space [16, p. 15]. This sort of notion addresses a functionalist idea of communication as an influence, capable of producing effects, thus a power, and emphasizes the transport of information and distance. However, it can be a challenge to clarify what can be regarded as media effects and to what extent can we consider media technologies as independent factors. In fact, early work on the influence of media technologies on audiences focused on "behavioral effects" and assumed an unsuspecting and largely passive audience [13], instead of considering the active selection, uses, intentions and involvement of audiences [17]. For Bryant and Zillmann [18], media effects can be understood as the social, cultural, and psychological impacts of communicating via media. But while is useful to have a broad perspective on media effects in order to comprehend the extraordinarily extensive variety of influences the media exert, it also contributes to the dispersion of the effects research and to the successive reconceptualizations and destabilization of what is meant by effects. This situation still demonstrates an insufficient systematization on its conceptual beaconing. For these reconceptualizations has also contributed the change from a context dominated by mass media to a contemporary context where the pervasiveness of new media (internet, mobile phones, etc.) in everyday life, of younger adults and seniors alike, has been increasingly evident [19].

Moreover, when many individuals in their everyday lives think about media effects, they might bound their thinking to negative outcomes that happen to other people after being exposed to "bad" content [20] such as nowadays "fake news". In addition, academic literature regarding new media effects has been considering not just the effective negative outcomes (damage) but also potential negative outcomes (risks) to vulnerable individuals [21]. Therefore, the literature has identified risks encompassing new media effects considered to be harmful, such as the risks of social disintegration (between individuals, generations or social groups) or social isolation [22], of addiction or the risk of info-exclusion [23, 24]. This risk-centering analytical focus often leaves out the analysis of other effects (that can be understood as opportunities or positive externalities) as, in a neo-Durkheimian approach, the media's contribution to the social cohesion of a given group through ritual sharing of meanings. This builds on Durkheim's idea that society needs "upholding and reaffirming at regular intervals the collective sentiments and the collective ideas which make its unity and its personality" [1, p. 474-5]. It is suggested here that, to some extent, media technologies coupled with civic rituals provide a functional equivalent to religious rituals in modern secularized societies. Besides, we can articulate this approach with a praxeological perspective, that is the contribution of the media to the structuring of daily routines with impacts on the ontological security of individuals [15], among others. In this way, a reflection on the social construction around what constitutes positive or negative effects of the media is considered important, and how this construction mediates the way individuals carry on the daily consumption of digital media.

It is also important to consider the latent meaning within digital media content, regarding what digital content means to senior audiences rather than a mere view of how new media affects them. According to Carey [16], if we consider the conception of communication as ritual, we can link this concept to the notions of community, communion, sharing, participation and association, thus assuming transmission as the basis of social existence, occurring at all levels, in space and time, and promoting exchange and relationship. To this extent communication is a symbolic process through which reality is both (re)produced and transformed [16, p. 23]. This more Durkheimian perspective invokes simultaneity, emphasizes the maintenance of society over time through shared modes of thinking and sees communication as a form of cultural reproduction, promoter of order and shared experiences. In this way, communication does not appear merely as a neutral transmission of information, denoting a factual function. It never occurs in a cultural and social vacuum, being then contingent on the cultural and social maps in which it takes place and, in a dialectical process, will help in the production of those same matrices of perception of reality where it is inscribed. That is, it is in and through communication that the visions of the world are constructed and destroyed, confirmed and refuted. Communication is both a producer and a product of culture and society, and these are not separate entities. This extended conception of communication not only as a mere process of information flow, but also as secular ritual and mediating element of social (re)production is updated by Couldry with his notion of media rituals [25]. These "ritual communication approaches", although intending to move away from an over-functionalist view, refer to the norm and to the stable forms of integration [26], and have been investigated in numerous ways where media technologies are seen as vehicles to reproduce notions of community and solidarity [13].

3   Methods

The data employed here comes from two face-to-face surveys representative of Portuguese individuals living in mainland Portugal aged 15 or more. One is the 2015 questionnaire survey "ERC—Públicos e Consumos de Média" (ERC — Media Audiences and Consumption) ($n = 1018$) lead by the Portuguese Media Regulatory Authority (ERC—Entidade Reguladora para a Comunicação Social). The other is the survey "Sociedade em Rede" (Network Society) ($n = 1542$) employed by the Centre for Research and Studies in Sociology - CIES-IUL (Centro de Investigação e Estudos de Sociologia). The analysis combined the use of univariate and bivariate descriptive statistics carried out with the SPSS program. Data was analysed and interpreted according to the insights presented in the theoretical framework. Using the Portuguese survey Network Society, for the purposes of the analysis we considered older adults aged 65 years old or more ($n = 344$).

4 Portuguese Seniors and Social Network Sites: Some Results

The emergence of innovations at the software level, namely, the emergence of applications that have been labeled by Web 2.0 applications, has built up the social media ecology [27, 28]. Web 2.0 has opened doors for innovation in the use and appropriation of applications by Internet users, making it easier to produce and disseminate user generated content. With social media it has become feasible for ordinary users to create online networks around newly created content and exchange comments on such content, thus recreating the communicative role of networks. Web 2.0 provides a way to consolidate social networks by expanding existing online communication opportunities, whether through instant interaction or the sharing and networking of online content. The same technologies facilitate the production of audiovisual materials for private use, as well as the articulation of content storage and broadcasting with mass audiences [27]. In fact, one of the great changes in the way people have been using the internet since 2005 has been the increasing popularity of social network sites [29], which has reverted in the expansion of the possibilities for individuals to communicate and interact with one another, such as e-mail, chats and blogs.

As shown by the representative survey conducted by the Portuguese Regulatory Authority for the Media (Entidade Reguladora para a Comunicação Social – ERC, 2015), Portugal is still marked by acute generational differences as we can see in Table 1 and by the digital exclusion of most the senior population. These data are in line with data from 2013, when the representative Portuguese survey Network Society registered 11,8% of internet users older than 65 years old, of which 10,8% are direct users of the internet and 1% can be considered proxy users since they access the internet via another person. To put it in other perspective, among seniors who are internet users, 92% is a direct user while 8% uses through another person.

Table 1. Are you an Internet user (at least once per week)? Source: ERC2015 - The new dynamics of audio-visual consumption in Portugal

Age group	Yes (%)	No (%)
15 to 24 years	96,3	3,7
25 to 34 years	93,1	6,9
35 to 44 years	81,4	18,6
45 to 54 years	63,4	36,6
55 to 64 years	36,1	63,9
65 or more years	11,5	88,5

The ERC survey (2015) also indicates that the majority (60%) of senior internet users use social network sites (SNS), while the previous Network Society Survey indicated 51,3% of SNS users among senior internet users, and all of them have an account on Facebook. This shows, according to Cardoso and Araújo [30], a contribution to increasing the central role of communication in networks. It is therefore important to look at how seniors use SNS, supported by the data collected from the Portuguese Network Society survey (2013). There were no senior Twitter users in 2013 and Google+ appeared far behind in terms of its usage rate, around 14.3%. The most common device for accessing social network sites (SNS) was the computer (for 89.6% of senior respondents), and a much lower percentage (16.0%) used the mobile phone to access SNS.

Table 2. On average, how many hours per week you spend in contact with: (Senior SNS users) Source: Portuguese survey Network Society, 2013

	Family			Friends (outside work/school)		
Mean	Face-to-face	Mobile phone	Social network sites	Face-to-face	Mobile phone	Social network sites
	2,65	1,29	1,38	2,3	1,22	1,59

Regarding the perceived time spent by senior SNS users in social interactions, Table 2 gives us an image of the weekly hours spent on social network sites vis-à-vis the hours spent on the mobile phone and in face-to-face interactions with family and friends. It shows that seniors perceive they spend more hours per week in SNS than in mobile phones, although some methodological caution is required in reading the data since we cannot know how the question was interpreted by the respondents, that is, if it refers only to sending or receiving calls or to other activities such as sending messages, or even accessing SNS. The mobile phone is also an instrument for accessing social network sites, which complicates, methodologically, the measurement of what is to use one thing or another. This refers to the more general difficulty of measuring media usages in a networked communication model.

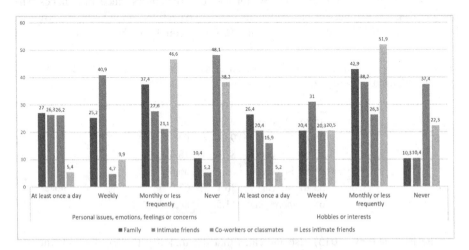

Fig. 1. Frequency of speaking or sharing ideas on your social network site ... (Senior SNS users) Source: Portuguese survey Network Society, 2013

As Fig. 1 above shows, it is with the closest friends' network that more than half of the senior SNS users share, at least once a week, personal issues or concerns and interests or hobbies. In addition, for some respondents, the people they deal with daily (family, co-workers or classmates) are also everyday targets for matters relating to personal issues, feelings and concerns, as well as for other less or non-intimate interests.

The data do not seem to be in line with the study by McPherson, Smith-Lovin, and Brashears [31], which indicates that internet users, specially the most intensive ones, have fewer people to discuss important issues, and that these discussions occur less frequently compared to the relatively recent past. Here we do not possess diachronic data to make a comparison with the past, but as it turns out, intimate affairs, along with less intimate interests, are the subject of daily or weekly conversation in the SNS with the nearest circles for appreciable percentages of senior Portuguese users. Also, contrary to what Bauman and Lyon [32] suggest, the data reveal a strong relationship with the inner circle, where SNS appear as a bridge between offline and online social spaces. The 'virtual' social networks add to and multiply the connections with peers in the 'real' world. Because seniors use online social networks to facilitate pre-established relationships, they interact primarily with the people they trust. There is also no indication that online social spaces have widespread negative impacts on what we can understand as the social capital of seniors, in the sense attributed by Putnam [33][1].

Table 3. On social network sites where you have a profile created, what kind of features do you use? (Senior SNS users) Source: Portuguese survey Network Society, 2013

Features	%
Chat service	59,2
Send messages	84,4
Play (Farmville, Mafia Wars, etc.)	20,9
Join/support Causes	25,0
Create photo albums	41,1
Send virtual gifts	9,9
Comment posts	56,0
Like the posts of others	67,3
Create/join groups	15,1
Disclose events	20,9
Search, make and suggest friends	42,1
Post music or video	10,4
Write comments on wall	20,2
Birthday alerts	47,6

---

[1] The concept refers to elements of social organization such as networks, norms and social trust that facilitate coordination and cooperation with mutual benefits [34].

According to the data of Table 3, relational uses and communicative practices are prominent in terms of SNS practices. Features that stand out for many are: send messages, like the posts of others, chat service usage and comment posts. The use of the like feature, for instance, can have some readings. It can be understood as a gesture of recognition, a phatic form of communion in relation to a certain content (a photo, a video or commentary), a form of communion facilitation or even a measure of symbolic capital and social interaction. The data shows that many activities on SNS are sparse since most of them are not carried out daily. Still, curiously, the most frequent daily activity among, for 10,5% of respondents aged 65 years or older, is to play. According to 5.2% of the seniors surveyed, the communicative and phatic usage of sharing a novelty is performed at least once a day, and a similar percentage of senior users reports to support causes on daily basis. In general, this is the most common activity on SNS since most of the Portuguese senior users (51,2%) state doing it at least from time to time. Sharing a novelty and lurk the profiles of acquittances are activity performed at least once in while by around 46% of the respondents.

It is in this sense that Bauman and Lyon [32] speak of a liquid surveillance where, in addition to business, SNS users engage in mutual social voyeurism. However, our data do not reveal that this is a widespread or at least very common or frequent practice among senior users. Another concern, which has emerged with the popularization of SNS, is the devotion it requires to track updates and manage a broad network of "friends" or contacts. However, there is a limited limit on the number of people in whom one is personally and emotionally investing and one who is committed to "quality" relationships, which has repercussions on online interactions [35].

Table 4. Reasons you signed up in social network sites. (Senior SNS users) Source: Portuguese survey network society, 2013

	%
Strengthen social ties that already exist offline	56,8
Meet new people	26,4
Professional reasons	15,3
Because most of the people I know are on such sites	84,2
To keep in touch with people who are far away	89,7
To meet and keep in touch with people I have not seen in a long time	79,0
So as not to feel left out	21,2
To be able to share thoughts/comments/videos/photos	41,5
Because I was invited	46,6
Initiate/foster a loving relationship	5,4
To promote my work	10,0
To promote events	10,6
To promote causes or political positions	15,3

According to our data, only small minorities of the senior SNS users felt, at least once, uncomfortable because they could not keep up with updates from all their friends on social network sites (12%) or had difficulty managing their online social relationships (5,2%). For 19% of Portuguese seniors (not just internet users) the main feeling of being "left out" comes from the technological change itself, since they felt, at least once, out of touch because of the pace of that change. Looking at Table 4, one finds that among the main motivations for enrollment in the networks are the desires to keep in touch with people who are far away (in 89,7% of the cases) or that respondents haven't seen in a long time (in 84,2% of the cases) and because respondents feel that most people they know are on such sites (in 79% of the cases). This last indicator seems a bit contradictory with the much lower percentage (21,2%) of senior SNS users that point out as a reason as not to feel left out, since both reasons suggest a Durkheimian normative pressure. Also, a majority points out as motivation the strengthening of pre-existent social ties, which may be indicative of a set of phenomena: the extension in space and time of interactions in the social space of SNS; the use SNS features for phatic communication, where shared content is a form of strengthening ties; sharing of interests. SNS can still be understood as social spaces in the sense given by Giddens [9], that is, spaces built by social relations, where spaces of consumption, social connection or entertainment and communication intersect. Boyd [36] also suggests that social media has contributed to the constitution of a public space in a network, which shakes up constructed definitions of public and private life and refers to a social structure whose contours we begin to know gradually, We can also call into question, as Bauman, Lyon [32] and Putnam [33] do, the "quality" of internet and SNS relationships, that is, the strength or intensity of forms of social cohesion based on online mediated communication. But if we look at social networks in the light of the Durkheimian cultural model, we can assume that social organization in social network sites is symbolic, where individuals look for a set of meanings that can be shared with others to form social bonds. The symbolic forms shared in SNS profiles, comments and messages play a role in the intensity of the links that communication between peers reveals. In this approach there is no fundamental differentiation between mediated and unmediated communication and interaction.

This dynamic is close to what Malinowski dubbed "phatic communion," in which the social value of symbolic exchange is not in the content itself (information, ideas or values) but in the ritualistic form that brings the gratification of speaking with others, that is, to use speech to establish a social link between the sender and receiver [37]. Such a notion inspired the field of sociolinguistics, applicable in the understanding of communication in everyday life and, consequently, in social contexts such as SNS where the phatic language refers to the trivial and symbolic exchanges that are obvious and expected in everyday life, composed of catchphrases and predictable statements. In short, small talk (or its many digital variants) is an important lubricant of social bonds [38, 39]. In this way, we can differentiate, within a given social network, phatic content (guided by relations of friendship/personal) from non-phatic content (guided by interests) but also distinguish SNS practices according to the phatic inclination of the motives that behind them.

Looking at Table 5, it turns out that substantial majorities of senior respondents agree or fully agree that online social networks allow for greater rapprochement and a deeper understanding of friends' tastes, opinions, and activities. That is, there are indicators that the phatic uses of SNS are privileged over the relational uses guided by specific interests or support for political or social causes.

Table 5. Since signing up in social network sites, agree or totally agree with the following statements: (Senior SNS users) Source: Portuguese survey Network Society, 2013

	%
Feel closer to your friends	63,4
Greater knowledge of friends' tastes	68,6
Greater knowledge of friends' opinions	72,5
Greater knowledge of friends' activities	88,2
Feel closer to people with whom you share interests	57,3
Feel more involved in political or social causes	35,5
Feel more inclined to express your opinion or support causes	36,3

The social affirmation of social network sites is linked to individual and group strategies, with the aim of reinforcing pre-existing social networks linked to belonging groups such as family, group of friends or work, reference groups as socializing agents, the sports club, the geographic and/or linguistic community, etc., or the insertion in communities of geographically dispersed interests, which find in social network sites a facilitated form of connection between individuals.

5   Discussion: The "Elementary Forms" of Social Media Communication

Adopting a Durkheimian cultural model, we will look at the function of social media applications by their capacity for social and normative integration or, on the contrary, by the ways in which they can jeopardize integration itself, constituting a factor within society itself of anomie, individualization, isolation and breaking of traditions. Social media communication forms a ritual system of reciprocal exchanges, which means commitment in a network of relationships. In this sense, Portuguese senior SNS users point out that they spend on average more hours on social network sites in contact with family and friends than on mobile phones. In addition, around two thirds of the respondents report that they speak or share personal issues, emotions, feelings or concerns with intimate friends weekly or at least once a day, and more than half share them with family with the same frequency. The sharing of hobbies or interests through SNS is overall less frequent. This is coherent with the notion that individuals primarily seek a set of meanings that can be shared with others to form social bonds. Thus, the Durkheimian interpretation of SNS use seems adequate to identify forms of social and emotional regulation through networks of relations and of "phatic communion," in which the social value of communication is to be found in the ritualistic form of maintaining social links between the transmitters and receivers. Similarly, regarding mobile phones, Ling and Yttri [40] affirm that beyond the content there is a meta-content: as the receiver is in the thought of the emitter and messages serve for the development of a common history and a narrative.

Relational uses and communicative practices are prominent in senior SNS practices. Sending messages is the most widely used feature on social network sites by the senior respondents, reported by 84,4%, clicking "Like" in the posts of others is the second most used feature, reported by 67,3% of respondents, followed by chat service usage (59,2%) and commenting posts (reported by 56% of respondents). These practices do have a phatic interpretation where digital content and performances can gain special affective meanings. It is associated with the sender and at a certain moment, it might represent a connection among people, being part of a heritage of memories, which constitutes both an internal and external memory, present and ready to be re-read in the timeline or logs of digital devices. Like other individuals, a growing number of seniors are starting to manage a portfolio of different tools and communication modalities (which in Durkheimian language can be seen as digital totems) to support their social and family relationships: such as chat service for fast and intimate conversations, messages, and status updates, as a ritualistic way of being present (and regulating social emotional connections) with a larger group. In fact, most senior respondents state that they signed up in SNS to keep in touch with people who are far away (89,7%), because most people they know are on such sites (84,2%) and to meet and keep in touch with people they have not seen in a long time (79%). Curiously, much less (56,8%) state as a reason to sign up "strengthen social ties that already existed offline", and only a minority (26,4%) points out as a reason to meet new people.

The domestication of digital media for relational routines and social and emotional regulation of ties may follow two perspectives on their motivations, which we can link or retrofit to the data analysis. The first has its roots in Durkheim, but also in Goffman, on the phatic features or "communion" of mediated and unmediated interactions. This is tantamount to focusing the analysis on ritualized and routinized communicative practices rather than communicated content which helps to frame the response. Moreover, in this perspective there is no fundamental differentiation between face-to-face communication and mediated communication. However, senior users might reflexively differentiate between the "quality" of face-to-face communication and mediated communication, but perhaps not in practice. Also, considering the data presented above, for many older users, communication through SNS might be regarded as a substitute or less than optimal medium that is particularly useful to reach those who are far away or to re-enact contacts not seen in a long time. This is something that only further research can clarify. Still, the great majority of respondents point out that since signing up in SNS, they agree or totally agree that they have a greater knowledge of friends' activities (88,2%), opinions (72,5%) and tastes (68,6%). The majority also agrees or totally agrees with the statement that they feel closer to their friends (63,4%) and to people with whom they share interests (57,3%).

The second perspective on the motivations of social media usage is based on the Giddenian distinction [9, 41] between ontological security and anxiety. In this sense, we can understand the domestication and appropriation of social network sites as forms of regulating ontological security through the routinization of (mediated) social relationships. New media appropriation can likewise be understood as a way of creating and accessing social spaces that extend beyond the domestic place. This points to another Giddenian distinction between the place (the physical context of social activity) and social space, constructed in terms of social relations. As for seniors, the strategic use of social media to "keep in touch" allows the hyper-coordination - which involves social and emotional interaction and the construction of common narratives between social agents [40] - of family life and friendship at a distance. We can understand, following Giddens, the communicative routines provided by social network sites as accustomed modes of behavior that support and are supported by agents' sense of ontological security [9, p. 60-4]. Therefore, the routinization of mediated uses and interactions refers to the prevalence of forms of conduct that support and are supported by the ontological sense of security.

6 Conclusion

It is contended that the Durkheimian model is highly operable in media studies and helps the understanding of a series of empirical results concerning the domestication of social network sites among Portuguese senior users. It might not be much adequate to analyze, for example, overt content or to employ in an abductive approach that tries to capture agents' rationale on why they use SNS and its features in their own terms. But Durkheim's cultural model is consistent with the role of digital platforms in the maintenance of ontological security of seniors, regarded as a powerful motivator of social action, and with the domestication approach in communication studies. When Collins suggests that emotions appertain in "situational ways of acting in conversational encounters" [43, p. 1010], he is referring to the social and emotional effects of Durkheimian rituals, that have been lately transposed to digital platforms.

This framework is also useful since a whole research program can be derived from it. In this sense, we can raise a series of questions and hypothesis for future research. First, we can put forward the hypothesis that the increasing presence of digital devices in seniors' lives is also creating among them a moral order and expectations around permanent digital connectivity, integrating them, with more or less resistance, in an always-on culture [19]. Following this, a concurrent hypothesis is that the breakdown of the moral order and expectations around permanent connectivity and message exchange can produce disorientation when connection to digital networks or the digital ability to "keep in touch" is broken. According to Sum et al. "using the Internet for communication and information seeking were more likely to have positive effects on participants' social capital, loneliness and wellbeing" [44, p. 216]. Durkheim's contributions to the study of relational or associational effects at different levels of analysis [42] also suggest the development of a line of research that focus on the links between new media usage by seniors, wellbeing and active aging [45]. For instance, the elementary forms of digital life might play an important role in the expression of seniors' identities, self-esteem and social recognition. Although, it might also raise concerns about the tensions and emotional load of managing different modes of communication and complex social hierarchies with relatively simple digital tools. SNS and digital communication can also enhance family ties bridging generations and raising the awareness of family members' activities, opinions and tastes. When applied to the study of digital communication of seniors, the Durkheimian perspective coupled with more recent approaches in media studies might, thus, help us understand and produce hypothesis regarding the emotional importance and consequences of digital devices in seniors' mediated daily lives.

References

1. Durkheim, E.: The Elementary Forms of the Religious Life. Free Press, New York (1912, 1965). Translated by Joseph Ward Swain
2. Lessig, L.: The regulation of social meaning. Univ. Chicago Law Rev. **62**(3), 943–1045 (1995)
3. Czaja, S.J., Sharit, J., Hernandez, M.A., Nair, S.N., Loewenstein, D.: Variability among older adults in Internet health information-seeking performance. Gerontechnology **9**(1), 46–55 (2010)
4. Xie, B., Watkins, I., Golbeck, J., Huang, M.: Understanding and changing older adults' perceptions and learning of social media. Educ. Gerontol. **38**(4), 282–296 (2012)
5. Momeni, M., Hariri, N., Nobahar, M., Noshinfard, F.: Barriers and challenges experienced by seniors in using online social networks: a phenomenological study. Middle East J. Rehabil. Health **5**(1), 1–6 (2018)
6. Yu, R.P., Ellison, N.B., Lampe, C.: Facebook use and its role in shaping access to social benefits among older adults. J. Broadcast. Electron. Media **62**(1), 71–90 (2018)
7. Yu, R.P., McCammon, R.J., Ellison, N.B., Langa, K.M.: The relationships that matter: social network site use and social well-being among older adults in the United States. Ageing Soc. **36**(9), 1826–1852 (2016)
8. Cornwell, B., Laumann, E.O.: The health benefits of network growth: new evidence from a national survey of older adults. Soc. Sci. Med. **125**, 94–106 (2015)
9. Giddens, A.: The Constitution of Society – Outline of the Theory of Structuration. Polity Press, Cambridge (1984)
10. Alexander, J.: The form of substance: the senate Watergate hearings as ritual. In: Ball-Rokeach, S., Cantor, M.G. (eds.) Media, Audience and Social Structure. Sage, London (1986)
11. Alexander, J.: Analytic debates: understanding the relative autonomy of culture. In: Alexander, J., Seidman, S. (eds.) Culture and Society. Contemporary Debates. Cambridge University Press, Cambridge (1990)
12. Blumler, J.G., Katz, E.: The Uses of Mass Communications: Current Perspectives on Gratifications Research. Sage Annual Reviews of Communication Research Volume III. Sage Publications Inc., Beverly Hills (1974)
13. Matthews, J.: The Sociology of mass media. In: Korgen, K.O. (ed.) The Cambridge Handbook of Sociology. Core Areas in Sociology and the Development of the Discipline, vol. 1, pp. 197–204. Cambridge University Press, Cambridge (2017)
14. Cardoso, G., Espanha, R., Lapa, T.: Do Quarto de Dormir para o Mundo: Jovens e Media em Portugal. Âncora Editora, Lisboa (2009)
15. Silverstone, R.: Television and Everyday Life. Routledge, London (1994)
16. Carey, J.W.: Communication as Culture. Essays on Media and Society. Routledge, London (1992)
17. Biocca, F.A.: The pursuit of sound: radio, perception and utopia in the early twentieth century. Media Cult. Soc. **10**(1), 61–79 (1988)
18. Bryant, J., Zillmann, M.B.: Media Effects: Advances in Theory and Research. Lawrence Erlbaum Associates, Hillsdale (1994)
19. Lüders, M., Gjevjon, E.R.: Being old in an always-on culture: older people's perceptions and experiences of online communication. Inf. Soc. **33**(2), 64–75 (2017)
20. Potter, W.J.: Media Effects. Sage, Thousand Oaks (2012)

21. Nash, V.: The politics of children's internet use. In: Graham, M., Dutton, W.H. (eds.) Society and the Internet: How Networks of Information and Communication are Changing our Lives, pp. 67–80. OUP, Oxford (2014)

22. Turkle, S.: Alone Together: Why We Expect More from Technology and Less from Each Other. Basic Books, New York (2010)

23. Schiller, H.: Information Inequality. Routledge, New York (1996)

24. Livingstone, S., Bovill, M.: Children and Their Changing Media Environment. A European Comparative Study, pp. 3–30. Lawrence Erlbaum Associates, Mahwah (2001)

25. Couldry, N.: Media Rituals: A Critical Approach. Routledge, London (2003)

26. Lievrouw, L.A.: New media, mediation, and communication study. Inf. Commun. Soc. **12** (3), 303–325 (2009)

27. Dutton, W.H., Helsper, E.J.: Oxford internet survey 2007 report: the internet in Britain (2007)

28. Ellison, N.B., Boyd, D.M.: Sociality through social network sites. In: The Oxford Handbook of Internet Studies. Oxford University Press, Oxford (2013)

29. Lenhart, A., Purcell, K., Smith, A.: Social Media and Mobile Internet Use Among Teens and Young Adults. Pew Research Centre, Washington (2010)

30. Cardoso, G., Araújo, V.: Out of information and into communication. Networked communication and internet usage. In: Cardoso, G., Cheong, A., Cole, J. (eds.) World Wide internet. Changing Societies, Cultures and Economies, vol. 1, pp. 197–204. University of Macao Press/PRC, Macao (2009)

31. McPherson, M., Smith-Lovin, L., Brashears, M.E.: Social isolation in America: changes in core discussion networks over two decades. Am. Sociol. Rev. **71**(3), 353–375 (2006)

32. Bauman, Z., Lyon, D.: Liquid Surveillance. Polity Press, Cambridge (2012)

33. Putnam, R.D.: Bowling alone: America's declining social capital. In: Culture and politics, pp. 223–234. Palgrave Macmillan, New York (2000)

34. Putnam, R.: Bowling alone: America's declining social capital. J. Democr. **6**(1), 1–11 (1995)

35. Amichai-Hamburger, Y., Hayat, Z.: The impact of the Internet on the social lives of users: a representative sample from 13 countries. Comput. Hum. Behav. **27**(1), 585–589 (2011)

36. Boyd, D.: Why Youth (Heart) Social Network Sites: The Role of Networked Publics in Teenage Social Life. MacArthur Foundation Series on Digital Learning – Youth, Identity, and Digital Media Volume. MIT Press, Cambridge (2007). Buckingham, D. (ed.)

37. Burke, K.: A Rhetoric of Motives. University of California Press, Berkeley (1950)

38. Boxer, D.: Applying Sociolinguistics: Domains and Face-to-Face Interaction, vol. 15. John Benjamins, Amsterdam (2002)

39. Casalegno, F., McWilliam, I.M.: Communication dynamics in technological mediated learning environments. Int. J. Instr. Technol. Distance Learn. **1**(11), 15–33 (2004)

40. Ling, R., Yttri, B.: Hyper-coordination via mobile phones in Norway. In: Katz, J., Aakhus, M. (eds.) Perpetual Contact, Mobile Communication, Private Talk, Public Performance. Cambridge University Press, Cambridge (2002)

41. Giddens, A.: Modernity and Self-Identity. Polity Press, Cambridge (1991)

42. Emirbayer, M.: Useful Durkheim. Sociol. Theory **14**(2), 109–130 (1996)

43. Collins, R.: On the micro-foundations of macro-sociology. Am. J. Sociol. **86**, 984–1014 (1981)

44. Sum, S., Mathews, M.R., Pourghasem, M., Hughes, I.: Internet technology and social capital: how the internet affects seniors' social capital and wellbeing. J. Comput.-Mediat. Commun. **14**(1), 202–220 (2008)

45. WHO Active Ageing: A Policy Framework. World Health Organization, Geneve (2002)

Usability Study of Electronic Sphygmomanometers Based on Perceived Ease of Use and Affordance

Chao Li[✉], Mei-yu Zhou, Xiang-yu Liu, and Tian-xiong Wang

School of Art Design and Media,
East China University of Science and Technology, No. 130, Meilong Road,
Xuhui District, Shanghai 200237, China
dreamingjiangnan@163.com, Zhoutc_2003@163.com

Abstract. Aging is becoming an urgent issue in China, the curve of aging growth rate is rising. Home-based medical care for the elderly is important to their quality of life, especially for those who live independently in countryside. An electronic sphygmomanometer (ES) can measure blood pressure to detect physical condition and greatly assists the elderly. However, studies have shown that age has a certain hindrance to people's ability to deal with information. Due to the use of products that have various functions and complex operations, the ergonomic problems of elderly people are increasingly prominent today. Many existing products are not well adapted to their needs. In the face of new products and new technologies, they often show up as retreat. This paper studies the factors that affect the intention to use new products for the elderly (60–70 years old) based on Perceived Ease of Use (PEU) and Affordance, taking ES as an example. There are two experiments in the study. The first experimental task, 10 experts and 10 elderly rated the 10 representative ES based on PEU (1–7 points). Appearance (affordance) characteristics was found out based on score ordering. The second experimental task, another 10 elderly used these ES in the last score order and rated the 10 representative ES. The Studies showed that the elderly was more willing to use the products with affordance features. Features such as text affordance, color affordance, and form affordance have a good guiding effect on the use of new products by elderly.

Keywords: Elderly · Perceived ease of use · Affordance ·
Electronic sphygmomanometers

1 Introduction

1.1 The Problem of Using New Products for the Elderly

The aging of the population has become an extremely serious social problem in China, and its population aging is accelerating. Because the incidence of chronic diseases such as cardiovascular and cerebrovascular diseases is significantly increased, the use of medical auxiliary products can greatly prevent the diseases of the elderly, such as electronic sphygmomanometers (ES) and other medical devices that can measure physical and physiological indicators. As McCann et al. pointed out, medical devices

© Springer Nature Switzerland AG 2019
J. Zhou and G. Salvendy (Eds.): HCII 2019, LNCS 11592, pp. 421–430, 2019.
https://doi.org/10.1007/978-3-030-22012-9_30

that measure the physical indicators of the elderly are used at home to provide continuous health care for the elderly, reducing the cost of physical examination and the risk of life [1]. Because there are a large number of elderly people in the country of China, it is very expensive to go to the hospital frequently. As such, elderly people can significantly promote their health services by using home medical equipment. The elderly can quickly understand the physical condition. The equipment even can transmit information to the medical staff through the network to achieve the telemedicine guidance. Health assessment and decision support was conducted, which plays an important role in the early prevention and timely medical treatment of the elderly.

Since home medical testing equipment has such an important role, the elderly should use the equipment frequently. However, due to the gradual decline of the physiology of the elderly and their ability to process information is also declining, their learning and memory skills are also significantly less than young people's [2]. Therefore, the elderly often shy away in the face of new products and new technologies. Previous studies have also found that elderly people have low acceptance of home medical equipment [3–6]. There is reported to be greater fear and anxiety associated with using computers, and in addition, their assessment of their own skills and abilities, with both using and learning to use them, is generally lower than for other age groups. New productions' interfaces and interaction styles are continually evolving. There are many reasons for being digitally excluded including those related to financial constraints, lack of training and prior experience.

Through a survey of Chinese elderly, it has been found that one key obstacle is always difficult for them to learn to operate new equipment [7]. They are concerned about the negative consequences of erroneous operations, avoiding the use of new devices, and the perceived ease of use (PEU) of medical devices has an important role in promoting the intended use of older people. They avoid the use of new devices because of the negative consequences of erroneous operations. Thereby, the PEU of medical devices has an important role in promoting the intended use of older people.

1.2 Purpose of the Study

PEU requires designers to promote the use of new technology products from the perspective of mental models and visual guidance. PEU is important for the use and acceptance of the product, and affordance has a strong positive correlation with PEU [8]. Elderly people often afraid to use the product for the first time because of the obstruction caused by visual perception. Previous studies indicate that usability is one of the important determinants of technology used by older people [9], and the research models commonly used in this field are Technology Acceptance Model (TAM) and UTAUT Model [10, 11], which provide a solution to the problem of perceived usability. Norman's affordance to extended HCI is also well applied in the user perception of usability [12].

Affordance and PEU have many applications in product and technology, but few studies have focused on the PEU of home medical devices by older people. This study provides guidance for older people to more easily use medical products, combining the above models to discuss the main influencing factors of the perceived availability of ES design from the perspective of affordance.

2 Literature Review

2.1 Previous Frameworks and Models

TAM was early framework that effectively explain adoption of technology innovations [10, 13]. The susceptibility or difficulty of understanding and use has been identified as a key determinant of TAM adoption. TAM identified two factors that determine the user's decision to use the new technology: perceived usability and ease of use. In the past, safety and functional factors were watched for older products. However the usability of products was neglected. The actual expectations and needs of older.

The Diffusion of Innovations Model has also confirmed the importance of usability for older products [14]. While it is important to meet older adults' needs by providing practical benefits, it is critical to make technology easy to use so that such benefits are realized. The combined effects of these age-related changes may affect older people, making it easy to use technology to achieve these benefits [15].

Pan studied the factors affecting the adoption of the Internet by Chinese elderly by applying the Extended Technology Acceptance Model (TAM) [16]. The results show that perceived use richness (PU) and perceived ease of use (PEU) Subjective norms (SN) and facilitate conditions (FC) are four key predictors, while gender and age play an important role in two key TAM components (PU and PEU).

Lee et al. through a literature review of the Technology Acceptance Model (TAM) research field, concludes with 10 final and most important influencing factors, namely value, usability, affordability, accessibility, Technical support, social support, emotion, independence, experience and confidence, among which availability is identified as an important determinant of the adoption of technology by older people [9]. The study demonstrates two important characteristics of older users' anxiety about technology and resistance to change. Cao integrates context-aware and unified theory of acceptance and use of technology (UTAUT) models to explain the use of Alipay users from both the perspective of technology perception and context awareness. Researchers believe that users' behavior depends not only on their perceptions and attitudes toward technology, but also on good contextual perception [17].

Affordance theory is based on user contextual awareness and has been successfully applied in the field of perceived usability. Hsiao et al. used an online availability assessment model to measure the degree of availability to evaluate products. Availability [12]. Designers can gain PEU and easily identify the look and feel of products that need to be modified and optimized by using this model.

2.2 Summary

The above studies as shown in Table 1 show that, the PEU of medical products is critical for older people are willing and able to use them such as ES. This study will obtain the key influencing factors of the PEU of ES through Affordance theory, based on the research models such as TAM and UTAUT. The design of an ES that is more attractive, practical and usable for the elderly, to interact safely, healthily, independently, with mobility and happiness between the elderly and technical products.

Table 1. Summary of technology acceptance and use models.

Theoretical model	Object	Conclusion	Author (time)
Technology Acceptance Model (TAM)	Explaining the adoption of technology innovations effectively	PEU may actually be a causal antecedent to perceived usefulness, as opposed to a parallel, direct determinant of system usage.	Davis (1989); Venkatesh (2000)
Diffusion of Innovations Model (DIM)	Explaining the main elements in the diffusion of innovations model, and to apply them to the special case of the diffusion of new telecommunications technologies	Usability plays an important role for elderly	Rogers (1995)
Unified theory of acceptance and use of technology (UTAUT)	A unified model provides a useful tool for managers needing to assess the likelihood of success for new technology introductions and helps them understand the drivers of acceptance in order to proactively design interventions targeted at populations of users that may be less inclined to adopt and use new systems	PEU and context awareness are very important for elderly	Venkatesh et al. (2003); Cao (2019)

3   Method

3.1   Experimental Sample

An Electronic Sphygmomanometer (ES) is a medical device that uses modern electronic technology and indirect measurement of blood pressure to measure blood pressure. The ES is divided into an arm type, a wrist type, and a watch type. Older people choose the upper arm type ES because the pulse is weaker and the wrist ES is not suitable for patients with blood circulation disorder. Therefore, we mainly chose the upper arm type ES in this study.

Samples of Electronic Sphygmomanometer. First of all, 56 types of ES were found out from the mall and e-commerce website. In this study, considering the factors affecting the use of new products by the elderly (60-70 years) and feedback of markets, combining with experts' opinions and the purpose of this experiment, 10 samples were selected. The final choice is shown in Table 2. Ten types of upper arm ES are shown.

Table 2. 10 samples

1	2	3	4	5
Xiaomi iHealth	Happy i2 upgrade	Happy i5 upgrade	OMRON U32K	OMRON U31

6	7	8	9	10
Xiaomi Bluetooth Connection Edition	OMRON U30	OMRON HEM-1020	YUWELL YE670D	YUWELL 690C

Perceptual Usability Evaluation Questionnaire. According to the relevant research methods of the literature [10, 18], choose 9 dimensions of the Use of Comfortable, Function Clear, First Step Operation Clear, Reading Clear, the Role of Each Button Clear, Operation Ideas Clear, Easy to Get Started, Operation No Risk, Willing to Use and 1 overall evaluation of Feel Easy to Use, select the above 10 kinds of upper arm ES pictures. In order to avoid the influence of factors such as brand and view, use Photoshop cc to delete all the logo information on the image, and modify all the images to 577 * 577 pixels, all of which use the view that reflects the product information as much as possible, except 8 uses 3D view. All of them use the front view, and finally t a perceptual usability evaluation questionnaire (Fig. 1 shows one sample) is generated through WJX.cn (a website for making a questionnaire).

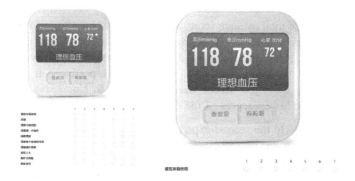

Fig. 1. Expert's questionnaire and elderly's

3.2   Participants

20 elderly participants aged between 58 and 72 are selected from Wuxi, China. The 10 experts have experience of design more than 10 years. 1 expert works in the enterprise. The other 9 are lecturers and associate professors of university.

3.3   Experimental Procedure

First experiment. The first experiment was conducted to allow 10 experts to score the PEU (1–7 points) of the above 10 ES from the perspective of affordance. The total average score of the different dimensions and was calculated. The scores of experts are shown in Table 3.

Table 3. Expert score.

Serial number	1	2	3	4	5	6	7	8	9	10
The average score of PEU	6.37	5.57	5.43	5.14	5.43	4.53	5.83	5.37	5.79	4.8
Total average score	6.43	5.06	5.07	5.29	5.36	4.71	5.86	5.57	6.14	5.43

In addition, 10 elderly people were found (mean = 64, SD = 3.5) to subjects. The above 10 types of ES were scored (1–7 points) from the perspective of PEU. Because the elderly did not understand the survey questionnaire clearly, the experimenter guided elderly when they scored the sample. The average score of PEU of each ES was obtained. The elderly scores are shown in Table 4.

Table 4. Elderly score.

Serial number	1	2	3	4	5	6	7	8	9	10
Total average score	6.09	4.63	4.67	4.06	4.25	3.56	5.12	4.39	5.32	3.65

Experts scored the total average score, and the elderly chose to feel easy to use the average score, sorted by comprehensive evaluation. The top 5 experts' evaluations are No. 1, No. 9, No. 7, No. 8 and No. 10, and the top five results of the evaluation of the elderly group are No. 1, No. 9, No. 7, No. 3 and No. 8, respectively. It was found that the four products in the top 5 scores were No. 1, No. 9, No. 7, No. 3 and No. 8, respectively, and the lowest scores of the experts and the elderly group was No. 6.

Second Experiment. In the second experiment, the test group was elderly. The order was sorted according to the overall evaluation of the elderly scores, sorted as 1, 9, 7, 3, 2, 8, 5, 4, 10, and 6. The other 10 elderly people (mean = 64, SD = 3.3) as subjects were found, and divided into 2 groups. Each group was randomly selected, and each of them used these ES in turn. The first group (mean = 63.6, SD = 3.6) was used for the forward exercise in the order obtained in the first experiment, and the other group (mean = 64.4, SD = 3.6) was used in the reverse exercise (see Fig. 2). The perceptual usability ranking of the test product was not told before the experiment. After the task was completed, the two groups of participants evaluated the usability of 10 products separately. Finally, the two sets of data were analyzed.

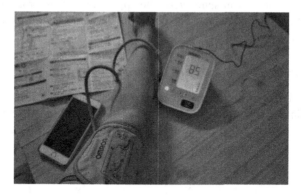

Fig. 2. Using ES of OMRON U30

4   Result and Discussions

4.1   Relationship Between Appearance Characteristics and PEU

From the first experiment, it can be found that the products with the top 5 scores in the top 5 are No. 1, No. 9, No. 7, No. 8. By summarizing the appearance characteristics of the four products, we can find that the above-mentioned products have important effects on the PEU in terms of text affordance, color affordance, and form affordance (See Fig. 3).

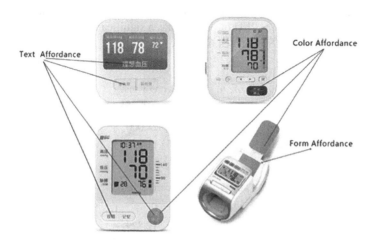

Fig. 3. Key Feature Affordance.

Key Feature Affordance. In addition, we will revisit the appearance of the product based on the previous score. From the perspective of product complexity, the top four products do not have many function buttons, and not seem complicated. However, No. 6 with the lowest score needs to rely on the mobile APP to connect and use, which may be an important reason for the perception that the score of product's PEU is low. From this experiment we can summarize, the appearance of the product has a certain impact on the PEU of the product. Therefore, the design of ES for the elderly should focus on Key Feature Affordance.

4.2   Relationship Between Accepted to Use (AU) and PEU

From the second experiment, it was found that the average total score of the forward exercise used in the first group was 47.80, and the average total score used in the reverse exercise of the second group was 44.08, as shown in Table 5.

Table 5. Forward and reverse score.

Group	1	2	3	4	5	6	7	8	9	10
Forward	6.2	5.2	4.8	4.6	4.8	4.8	4.6	4.6	4.4	3.8
Reverse	6.4	5.4	5.0	4.8	4.6	4.4	4.0	3.6	3.4	3.2

The total score for forward order use is greater than the total score for reverse order use indicating that perceived usability can also help the performance of older people. Due to the learning effect, the products used later have higher scores than the previous products. The scores of the forward order group No. 1 ES and the reverse group No. 1 ES may not be objective. Therefore, we chose to compare the scores of the 5 (experimental NO. 2) and 6 (experimental NO. 8) products in the middle of the sequence. Data obtained in the second experiment were input to SPSS 19.0, and the data of samples 2 and 8 were subjected to mean T test. We found that the forward order use group scores of the samples 2 and 8 were significantly higher than the reverse group scores. As can be seen, PEU of product has a significant effect on the use of new products by older people. See Tables 6 and 7.

Table 6. NO. 2 score T test

Group	N	Mean	SD	t	Df	Sig.
Forward	5	4.8000	0.44721	24.000	4	.000
Reverse	5	4.6000	0.89443	11.500	4	.000

Table 7. NO. 8 score T test

Group	N	Mean	SD	t	Df	Sig.
Forward	5	4.8000	0.83666	12.829	4	.000
Reverse	5	4.4000	0.54772	17.963	4	.000

5   Conclusions and Shortages

Conclusions. This study shows that older people are more willing to use an ES with good PEU. The ES showed affordance characteristics through features such as text affordance, color affordance, and form affordance, making it easy for the elderly to perceive the product use to ease, which in turn makes older people more willing to use ES products and learn to use them faster. The products designed for the elderly should not seem too complicated. The buttons and colors of the product interface should not be too much, and the function of the product should be practical and easy to operate.

Shortages. The main Shortages of this study are that the number of samples is small, and it is not possible to comprehensively and objectively respond to the scores of the samples in the experiment. In addition, the Affordance characteristics of the product itself may be related to many factors, which cannot be completely attributed to the points mentioned in the conclusion.

Future study. The next step the Affordance characteristics of the product will be further refined, and the perceived ease of use of the product from the product characteristics will be analyzed. And it is hoped to improve the medical level and quality of life of the elderly through increasing the usability of home-based medical care products.

Acknowledgements. We would like to thank all participants and experts for this research. We thank the editor for reviewing and editing this paper.

References

1. McCann, M., Donnelly, M., O'Reilly, D.: Living arrangements, relationship to people in the household and admission to care homes for older people. Age Ageing **40**(3), 358–363 (2011)
2. John, D.R., Cole, C.A.: Age differences in information processing: understanding deficits in young and elderly consumers. J. Consum. Res. **13**(3), 297–315 (1986)
3. Alaiad, A., Zhou, L.: The determinants of home healthcare robots adoption: an empirical investigation. Int. J. Med. Inform. **83**(11), 825–840 (2014)
4. Postema, T.R.F., Peeters, J.M., Friele, R.D.: Key factors influencing the implementation success of a home telecare application. Int. J. Med. Inform. **81**(6), 415–423 (2012)
5. Liddy, C., Dusseault, J.J., Dahrouge, S., Hogg, W., Lemelin, J., Humber, J.: Telehomecare for patients with multiple chronic illnesses. Can. Fam. Phys. Médecin De Famille Canadien **54**(1), 58–65 (2008)
6. Spagnolli, A., Guardigli, E., Orso, V., Varotto, A., Gamberini, L.: Measuring user acceptance of wearable symbiotic devices: validation study across application scenarios. In: Jacucci, G., Gamberini, L., Freeman, J., Spagnolli, A. (eds.) Symbiotic 2014. LNCS, vol. 8820, pp. 87–98. Springer, Cham (2014). https://doi.org/10.1007/978-3-319-13500-7_7
7. Guo, X., Sun, Y., Wang, N., Peng, Z., Yan, Z.: The dark side of elderly acceptance of preventive mobile health services in china. Electron. Mark. **23**(1), 49–61 (2013)
8. Norman, D.A.: Affordance, conventions, and design. Interactions **6**(3), 38–42 (1999)

9. Lee, C., Coughlin, J.F.: PERSPECTIVE: older adults' adoption of technology: an integrated approach to identifying determinants and barriers. J. Prod. Innov. Manag. **32**(5), 747–759 (2015)

10. Davis, F.D.: Perceived usefulness, perceived ease, and user acceptance of information technology. MIS Q. **13**(3), 319–340 (1989)

11. Bahli, B.: The impact of cognitive absorption on perceived usefulness and perceived ease of use in on-line learning: an extension of the technology acceptance model. Inf. Manag. **42**(2), 317–327 (2005)

12. Hsiao, S.W., Hsu, C.F., Lee, Y.T.: An online affordance evaluation model for product design. Des. Stud. **33**(2), 126–159 (2012)

13. Venkatesh, V.: Determinants of perceived ease of use: integrating control, intrinsic motivation, and emotion into the technology acceptance model. Inf. Syst. Res. **11**(4), 342–365 (2000)

14. Rogers, E.M.: Lessons for guidelines from the diffusion of innovations. Jt Comm. J. Qual. Improv. **21**(7), 324–328 (1995)

15. Wang, A., Redington, L., Steinmetz, V., Lindeman, D.: The adopt model: accelerating diffusion of proven technologies for older adults. Ageing Int. **36**(1), 29–45 (2011)

16. Pan, S., Jordan-Marsh, M.: Internet use intention and adoption among Chinese older adults: from the expanded technology acceptance model perspective. Comput. Hum. Behav. **26**(5), 1111–1119 (2010)

17. Cao, Q., Niu, X.: Integrating context-awareness and UTAUT to explain Alipay user adoption. Int. J. Ind. Ergon. **69**, 9–13 (2019)

18. Maier, J.A., Fadel, G.M.: Affordance-based methods for design. In: International Design Engineering Technical Conferences and Computers and Information in Engineering Conference, 15th International Conference on Design Theory and Methodology, pp. 785–794. ASME, Chicago (2003)

From "Cane" to "Sugar": Empowering Taisugar History of Digital Design with "Interactive Visual Storytelling"

Yang-Chin Lin[1]([✉]), Jui-Yang Kao[2], and Wang-Chin Tsai[3]

[1] Department of Digital Content Design, Chang Jung Christian University,
No. 1, Changda Road, Gueiren District, Tainan City 71101, Taiwan (R.O.C.)
yangchih@mail.cjcu.edu.tw
[2] Department of Product Innovation and Entrepreneurship,
National Taipei University of Business, No. 321, Section 1, Jinan Road,
Zhongzheng District, Taipei City 100, Taiwan (R.O.C.)
[3] Department of Creative Design,
National Yunlin University of Science and Technology,
123 University Road, Section 3, Douliou 64002, Yunlin, Taiwan (R.O.C.)

Abstract. Taisugar have developed over 300 years since 17th century in Taiwan, it has been committed even more to research and development of sugarcane varieties than to control of sugarcane pests and diseases prevention. This study aims to discover this Eco-museum by empowering sugarcane pests and diseases as a start point and convert these elements into a task-based treasure-gathering mechanism, then integrate into "Service engineering and knowledge management" within a LBS-AR (Local-Base Service Augments Reality) system. This study hopes that it can help more and more people via experiencing this LBS-AR game to learn more knowledge from sugarcane history and culture of Taisugar. Beside the biodiversity, the process from "cane" to "sugar" is rich in humanity and culture, which is a very important element in the process of digital design. The players will be deepened and improved after the gameplay and experience the local sugar industry. Another cultural key point is Taiwanese "Sugar Mill", whose role played in the past is similar to foundry manufacturing today. In the field, it can be explored a series of production of modernization from original "Sugar Mill", modified "Sugar Mill" to mechanized "Sugar Mill". So that, this study integrated task-level and multiple catching treasures mechanism to improve the player's adhesion of the game.

Keywords: Taisugar history · Local-Base Service Augments Reality (LBS-AR) ·
IP (Intellectual property) character design · Interactive Visual Storytelling ·
Pokémon GO

1 Introduction

More than 300-year-history in Taiwan, Taisugar Corporation delivered both ecology and industry data as a "Digital Museum". Due to the biodiversity, from "cane" to "sugar" will be inevitably entangled with humanity and culture in the process of digital

© Springer Nature Switzerland AG 2019
J. Zhou and G. Salvendy (Eds.): HCII 2019, LNCS 11592, pp. 431–440, 2019.
https://doi.org/10.1007/978-3-030-22012-9_31

design. For example, there are more than 10 species pests of planting sugar cane divided into: leaf worms, stem pests, underground pests and vector pests, etc. They are not only related to the soil, but also seasonal change, therefore, multidimensional corresponding elements should be complex to the game. This paper aims to discover its Eco-museum by empowering sugarcane pests and diseases within LBS-AR "Interactive Visual Storytelling" game.

2 Literature Review

During 1895 to 1945, Taiwan was colonized by the Japanese. For of the suitable terroir conditions and the policies advocacy of the Colonial Government, 44 sugar factories had been erected between central and southern Taiwan. The sugar industry had become an important economic development of the Colonial Government. After the World War II, most of these sugar mills has been closed after 1986 but only 2 factories remain operating. Because of the highly maintaining cost and the replacement from the highway systems, the transportation using of the sugar industry railway systems has declined since 1982, and all of the lines have been shouted down, even though two factories functioning. Some of the buildings of the sugar factories were designated as "monuments" under the Cultural Heritage Preservation Act before its amendment in 2005. Due to the restrictions of this Act of "no changes to building appearance" led to a fossil conservation, the owners of those buildings against to be registration or designation. After amendment to the Cultural Heritage Preservation Act, the category of Cultural Landscapes was added to the Act, which includes the spaces and related environment of myths, legends, circumstances, historical events, community life, and/or ceremonies. The Operational Guidelines of the Act indicate detailed categories as the location of myths and legends, the routes of historical or cultural facts, religious landscapes, historical gardens, the locations of events, agricultural landscapes, industrial landscapes, transportation landscapes, irrigation facilities, military facilities, and the landscapes interaction between humankind and the natural environment. In this sense, the sugar factories could be industrial landscapes, one of the sub-categories of cultural landscapes. Up to 2010, the Qiaotou and Hualien sugar factories left only had been registered as cultural landscapes finally. However, most of the cultural heritages had been designated as monuments in the past, while only the buildings and the territory of the factories were included in the registration of cultural landscapes of the sugar industry. However, the farms and railway systems related to the production of sugar were both excluded [1]. In a near future, AR glasses contact lenses in public place surrounded by a number of bystanders could be uncomfortable with the user recording them. Moreover, the user could cheat bystanders without consensus similar to an advanced spy cam [2]. For this sake, another combination of advanced technologies as mobile wireless, AR, multimedia and game that have all been brought together in a cultural context to provide meaningful engagement. The mobile-AR application to cultural organizations added value to visitors' experience by investing in developing applications for hardware owned by their visitors [3]. Under the game refinement theory, it is effectively used worldwide in domains of games as board games, video games, Somatosensory sports and Pokémon GO included. After a reasonable information game model establishment which could be used as a helpful tool to measure the game attractiveness and enable game designers to make a target game more sophisticated [4]. In this program, the same situation by solving puzzles through collecting cards, swapping cards, personalizing items, linking consoles together to share items, powers and characters, playful technological platforms scaffold imaginative enquiry, exploration, and the collection and sharing of virtual creatures and knowledge. Universal transmedia of Pokémon is a techno-aesthetic platform that facilitates particular kinds of imaginative engagement, from the rule-bound and intentional, to more unpredictable and expansive semiotic and performativity play. Thus there are an infinite number of ways in which reality is augmented in play albeit their material and technical realities will be particularly vivid and technically complicated [5].

3 Methodology and Procedure

3.1 Research Design

Based on the biodiversity from "cane" to "sugar", richness of cultural humanity of sugar mills' landscapes has been indicated transform by following process (see next page Fig. 1) as below:

1. Intellectual Property character design: It focused on translating pictogram consists of signifier and signified into significance by means of identification, parallelization, deduction and inference. Moreover, encoding and decoding communication with pictogram in shapes, colors, materials, media, and receiver, where cultural background is a pivotal key successfully for IP character design;
2. Scenes and mobile device selection: Recognition with the feature of pictograms, transfer to the visual cortex by optic nerve for feature and structure matching, and comprehension. "Trend" as a central design concern when time goes by, and then applying universal design concepts to make pictogram design more tolerant [6];
3. LBS-AR game design: Firstly, experience design through consider constituent elements of sugar mill and diversity insects in sugarcane growth life. And then, integrated the IP characters, UI pattern, special effects etc. into a game engine software named "Unity" and a plugin software named "Vuforia", finally through program debugging to accomplish game experience mechanism.

3.2   Intellectual Property Character Design

Based on the organisms that endanger the growth of sugar cane, the design elements of this study are mainly representative biometrics like the common insects such as Cerambycidae, Mogannia hebes, Arvicolinae, and Locust etc. (see Table 1). Taking Cerambycidae as an example, its characteristics of the beetle are the rigid appearance and the outer shell and the luster of the texture. The jacquard and the foot with the jagged section are used as the reference for the designer.

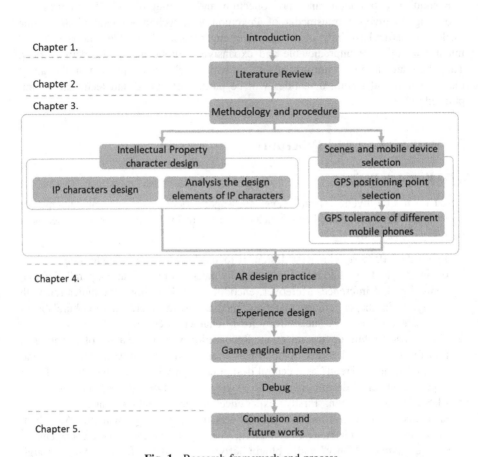

Fig. 1. Research framework and process

Table 1. Instructions of character design extraction

Names	Original images	Description	Intellectual property pictograms
Ceram-bycidae		1. Six feet. 2. Black or brown body. 3. A pair of strong tentacles on its forehead 4. A pair of long joggled tentacles on both sides of froehead. 5. Bright and straight textured of hard back. 6. Bigger ass than head.	
Mogan-nia hebes		1. Six feet. 2. Transparent geometric pattern of wings. 3. Watery blue eyes. 4. Green and brown body 5. A paire of tentacles on its head 6. Approximated triangle head.	
Arvicol-inae		1. Round body. 2. Four feet and a long tail. 3. A pair of round big ears. 4. Brown back and white abdomen. 5. A pair of big watery black eyes 6. White beards on both sides of red nose.	

(Continued to the next page.)

Locust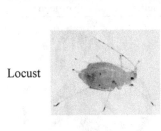

1. Crystal clear green gradient body.
2. Rugby-like body.
3. Six feet.
4. A pair of long tentacles upon its forehead.
5. A pair of abdominal tubes are located on both sides of body.

Table 2. GPS tolerance of different mobile phones

Brands	Model	Tolerance
Sony	Xperia XA1	1–2 m
Apple	IPhone 7	1–2 m
Samsung	J7	4–6 m

3.3 Scenes and Mobile Device Selection

This study selected five locations in one idle grass of Chang Jung Christian University as a demonstration field where is designed to be a "Sugar Mill" exhibition place also. Furthermore, the five locations selected the GPS was used as the trigger point of the game. Because of the positioning accuracy of various brands of mobile phones may be different, so the commonly used mobile phones of selected Sony, Apple and Samsung, etc. (see Table 2). The demonstration scene is the location of the "Sugar Mill" with five GPS sensing points (see Fig. 2).

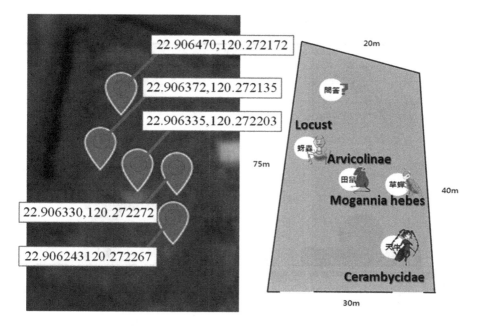

Fig. 2. Game site and the field of sensor points

4 LBS AR Game Design

The content of this AR game will be divided into "fixed point for catching treasure" and "question and answer" two major part. The "fixed point for catching treasure" is mainly to bring the pest character designed into AR game, which also helps to deepen the player's awareness of the pest. The "question and answer" game mechanism allows the player to deepen the knowledge of sugarcane pests through answer questions. The process of experiencing the game including: 1. while opening the APP the introduction of the glycoside will appear; 2. click the play symbol to enter the game screen. The bottom left corner of the screen is the game, and the magnifying glass in the lower right corner is the reminder for the device to open. Click on the blue button. The game map will appear when the icon is placed; 3. after entering the game map, the green dot indicates that the level has been unlocked, and the player must complete the capture of the green unlocked level object, and the blue blocked level will be unlocked. Then click on one of the mission points to experience; 4. when entering the experience, the satellite map will guide the player to the actual location and display the distance between the player and the level event; 5. before reaching each level object for treasure capture, Triggering the task point will play the pest and the task description. When the blue play button is pressed, the treasure can be captured (there are 4 task points for the treasure grab); 6. while entering the treasure screen, there will be a baby ball below. Players can use the finger to slide the baby ball to lose the ball to the randomly moving treasure. When the player throws the treasure before the limited number of balls is used, the screen will appear radial, and the player will catch the ball. Treasures, on the

Table 3. Experience process of LBS-AR

Step 1	Step 2
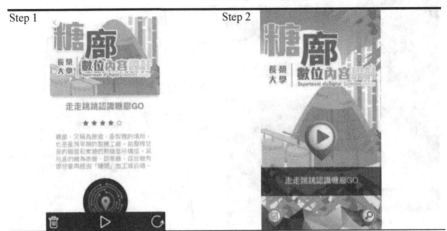	
Starting screen as introduction to the sugar mills.	Tap the blue button to enter the game.
Step 3	Step 4
	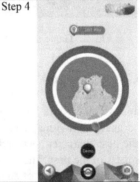
The green button unlocked task until it completed and blue button activate.	Map will guide you location and distance between the mission points after clicking.
Step 5	

While reaching the anchor point, pests will be showed in a icongraph before catching the treasure, so that players have to leaen their habits and harms deeply to pick up the treasure after clicking the play pictograms.	

(Continued to next page)

Step 6	

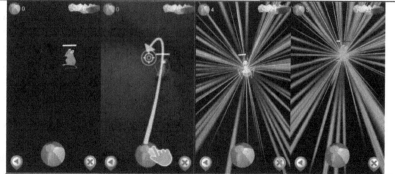

The players will drop the ball on the sliding screen whlie entering the treasure collection section, it will record the number of balls and score as long as the pests are successfully conquered but the energy bar above is exhausted.

Step 7	

There is only one item in the question and answer mode, after answering the question the player can get the treasure directly.

contrary, fail; 7. when entering the anchor point of the question and answer item, the screen will display the title and options. When the player answers correctly, they can directly obtain the treasure reward (see Table 3).

5 Conclusion and Future Works

Based on the development of LBS-AR, this study developed a new SDK AR that combines the cultural history of sugar, commercial marketing and online community functions. Its interactive AR game design integrate sightseeing tours, cultural creative industry in the digital business model. It designed 4 original IP characters to help develop specialty products in the future. The treasure hunt production of experience game proposed in this study, the capture mode is different from that of Pokémon, which only provides the player with a static capture mode. In addition to moving in the video screen with the dynamic treasure character, the player is caught. In addition to the difficulty of taking the character of the treasure, the entertainment experience is combined with the design of the subject of the knowledge, so that the player can also obtain the history of the development of sugar mills, the history of modern sugar production and the basic knowledge of sugarcane planting in China during the entertainment experience. This mode helps to improve the player's deep experience in the field, thus enhances the player's adhesion to local cultural tourism.

Acknowledgements. The authors hereby sincere thanks to Ministry of Science and Technology (MOST) of the Republic of China (R.O.C) for financial support, whose project code is MOST 106-2420-H-309-007-MY2. It extends to thank the generous patronage of MOST that this study performed smoothly and also appreciate all the participants. And, thanks for Taiwan Go gave us LBS-AR technology support.

References

1. Wang, C.H., Fu, C.C.: The conservation of disappearing sugar industry cultural landscapes in Taiwan. J. Asian Arch. Build. Eng. J. Asian Arch. Build. Eng. **10**(1), 1–6 (2011)
2. Manuri, F., Sanna, A.: A survey on applications of augmented reality. Adv. Comput. Sci. Int. J. **5**, **1** (19), 18–27 (2016)
3. Angelopoulou, A., et al.: Mobile augmented reality for cultural heritage. In: Venkatasubramanian, N., Getov, V., Steglich, S. (eds.) MOBILWARE 2011. LNICST, vol. 93, pp. 15–22. Springer, Heidelberg (2012). https://doi.org/10.1007/978-3-642-30607-5_2
4. Panumate, C., Xiong, S., Iida, H., Kondo, T.: Evolutionary changes of Pokemon game: a case study with focus on catching Pokemon. In: International Conference on Entertainment Computing 2015: Entertainment Computing, pp. 182–194 (2015)
5. Giddings, S.: Pokémon GO as distributed imagination. Mob. Media Commun. **5**(1), 59–62 (2017)
6. Lin, P.C., Chang, C.L.: Theoretical foundation for pictogram communication systematization. J. Des. Sci. **12**(2), 45–68 (2009)

A Study of Performance on Multi-touch Gesture for Multi-haptic Feedback

Shuo-Fang Liu, Yu-Shan Chueh$^{(\boxtimes)}$, Ching-Fen Chang, Po-Yen Lin,
and Hsiang-Sheng Cheng

Department of Industrial Design, National Cheng-Kung University,
No. 1, University Road, Tainan City 701, Taiwan, ROC
susan70434@gmail.com

Abstract. With the popularization of mobile devices and the trends in population aging, it becomes important to consider aging issues on the development of mobile devices. Many studies have shown that mobile devices with haptic feedback provide users with the better user experience. This study combines pinch open/close and clockwise/counter-clockwise rotation gesture with four different types of vibration modes, and compares the task completion time and idle ratio of each. The aim is to increase the haptic feedback variety and explore haptic feedback technology applicability in the future. The result shows that the vibration mode can shorten the average operation time compared to the non-vibration mode, wherein the lasted-vibration mode has a significant shortening of the operation time. While the ratio of the idle time, there has a significant different between both non-vibration lasted vibration (p-value = 0.04) and non-vibration versus reminded-vibration (p-value = 0.039) in pinch open gesture.

Keywords: Elderly · Multi-haptic · Tactile · Haptic feedback · Gesture

1 Introduction

According to United Nations statistics, the number of people aged over 60 in the world was 962 million in 2017, more than twice the number of 382 million the elderly in 1980. It is expected that by 2050, the number of elderly people will double again to reach nearly 2.1 billion [7]. The problems and needs of the elderly who are declining in their physical function are one of the focuses of many studies today. The use of mobile devices by the elderly has gradually spread. Although most users are between the ages of 20 and 50, there is an increasing number among older users who are older than 50 or even 60 [6]. Mobile services can enhance social ability and entertainment of the elderly, thereby promoting their quality of life, and the elderly have the ability to learn about information and communication technology. Because the elder are accustomed to the use of traditional mobile phones, it is an important factor for researchers to consider how the elderly adapt to use smart mobile devices [18].

© Springer Nature Switzerland AG 2019
J. Zhou and G. Salvendy (Eds.): HCII 2019, LNCS 11592, pp. 441–449, 2019.
https://doi.org/10.1007/978-3-030-22012-9_32

In terms of using mobile devices, it is more difficult for an elderly to touch a button or to operate complicated gesture with a small interface. On the other hand, due to the decline in visual and auditory acuity, inconvenient mobility, and memory loss in the elderly, it often makes them feel anxious and unacceptable to use mobile devices. Although many studies have been solved these problems, there is still room for improvement [3].

A review of the literature on tactile perception indicates that devices that communicate messages to the body through physical contact or physical touch are called tactile sensor, and tactile perception techniques have been developed by researchers and companies in the past forty years, and also indicated that the tactile perception technology in the future will be the trends [17]. To further understand the problems faced by the elderly in operating mobile devices, the following will review the literature on the tactile degeneration, multi-touch gestures and feedback of the elderly.

1.1   The Impact of Hand Degeneration in the Elderly

Due to the physiological deterioration of the elderly, the sensitivity and stability of their hands are declined, which makes them more difficult to do complicated movements. In terms of using mobile devices, miniaturized design makes it difficult to use and read, and the range of hand wrist activity is reduced, which may cause hand function, muscle and bone damage [4]. In addition, as the age increases, the body muscle fibers gradually decrease and shorten, and it makes the elderly operate mobile devices more difficult. Moreover, slower neural responses may affect the brain's ability to receive and process information, affecting its coordination and stability [12].

Some studies have conducted experiments on the exertion and coordination of the fingers of the elderly and young people, and measured the ability of the fingers to generate force and moment. The results show that the elderly need higher forces and showed less accurate when performing the tasks. The study inferred that ageing can affect the coordination of fingertips [13]. In the study of finger tactile acuity, it was found that the fingers tactile recognition ability of the older subjects was lower than young subjects [14]. In view of the above, the physiological decline may increase the fatigue and burden of the elderly using the mobile device, and may reduce the willingness of the elderly to operate the mobile device.

1.2   Elderly and Multi-touch Gesture

Touch gesture is a common method of operation on mobile devices. Although elderly people have lower touch accuracy and sensitivity than younger people, touch operation is more efficient than mouse or other assisting devices [8]. For the elderly, direct operation of the mobile device is better than operation through the assisting device, and the gesture operation can promote the interaction of the elderly and effectively reduce the error rate [5].

Nowadays, more and more software and hardware support the operation of multi-touch technology. Some studies have pointed out that the elderly are acceptable for touch gestures and clearly indicate that it is helpful for the initial software or hardware learning [11]. However, for operating mobile devices, the elderly prefer single-touch gestures and they are less willing to perform multi-touch gestures. These results show that multi-touch gestures increase the difficulty and complexity of the elderly to operate the mobile devices [15].

Therefore, the physiological changes increase the limitation of the elderly in operating multi-touch gestures, and it is an important issue to find out how to effectively help the elderly to operate gestures to improve the coordination and stability of the mobile devices.

1.3   Multi-haptic Feedback

Tactile feedback is a physical response when touched the devices. Studied have shown that for visually impaired users, increasing tactile feedback in the graphical user interface can improve operational efficiency [16]. The use of gestures to operate the mobile device with tactile feedback enhances usability and provides a better user experience [10]. In addition, tactile feedback can create richer interactions than visual and auditory feedback [1]. Tactile feedback is used as an aid when using mobile devices, and operations can be performed more accurately [9], and another research suggest that adding visual feedback when operating software can help the elderly understand the operation of multi-touch gestures [11]. In the study of using keyboard input, it is pointed out that adding a keyboard with tactile feedback will allow the user to input more words and fewer errors. On the other hand, in the moving environment, the benefits of tactile feedback are slightly reduced, but it can still effectively reduce errors [2].

According to above literature, the elderly are more difficult to perform multi-touch gestures due to tactile degeneration, so additional tactile feedback may be able to improve operational performance. Therefore, the purpose of this study is to investigate whether tactile vibration feedback can help the use of multi-touch gestures in the elderly, and further compare the task performance of different vibration samples.

2   Method

The purpose of the experiment is to investigate whether haptic feedback can increase the performance of multi-touch gestures in the elderly. There are 29 subjects including 4 males and 25 females who are over 50 years old with experience in using smart phones. The experiment device is Xiaomi - Mi 6, equipped with a linear motor and Android system. And the experiment tasks and the data recording are setting by Unity program. And there are four types of vibration mode for tasks, which are pinch open, pinch close, clockwise rotation and counter-clockwise rotation.

The experiment analyzes the completion time and the idle ratio. The completion time is the time when the subject completes the task and the idle ratio is the ratio of the time when the subject's finger away from the screen and the total time. If the idle ratio is higher, it means that the subject is less aware of whether he or she has reached the task goal.

2.1   Subjects

According to the literature, humans sense began to degenerate at the age of 50. Therefore, the community recruited a total of 29 elderly (male 4; female 25). And all subjects have the experience of using smart phones.

2.2   Vibration Samples

This experiment sets four tactile vibration samples. Shown as Table 1, non-vibration (general operation), touch vibration (when the user starts zooming), lasted-vibration (keep vibrating during operation) and reminded-vibration (to alert the user when the task is not completed), respectively. In touch vibration is given to subjects vibration feedback as if they touch the screen. The lasted-vibration provides vibration feedback during the whole task, and reminded-vibration is a reminder when the subject finishes the operation without completing the task.

Table 1. Vibration sample

Vibration mode	Touch	During	Error
Non-vibration	×	×	×
Touch vibration	O	×	×
Lasted-vibration	O	O	×
Reminded-vibration	×	×	O

2.3   Procedure

This experiment uses basic multi-touch gestures (pinch open/close and clockwise/counter-clockwise rotation gestures) with four different vibration modes to allow subjects to perform task. To understand whether the different vibration mode can assist the subjects to complete the task, and compare the task completion time and the idle ratio in different vibration modes.

Task description: (1) enlarge the photo to the specified size; (2) reduce the photo to the specified size; (3) rotate the photo clockwise to the specified size; (4) rotate the photo counterclockwise to the specified size, as shown in Table 2.

Table 2. Experiment task diagram

Experiment task / Gesture	Start screen	Completion screen
Pinch Open		
Pinch Closed		
Clockwise Rotation		
Counter-clockwise Rotation		

3 Result

3.1 Average Completion Time

This study explores performance of the basic multi-touch gestures and four types of vibration mode. The pinch open (PO), pinch close (PC), clockwise rotation (CR) and counter-clockwise rotation (CCR) are respectively compared with average completion time of non-vibration, touch vibration, lasted-vibration and reminded-vibration. If the average completion time of the vibration mode is shorter than non-vibration mode, it means that the vibration mode can improve the performance of the elderly. The results are shown in Table 3.

Table 3. Average completion time between gestures and vibration modes

Vibration mode	Gestures			
	PO	PC	CR	CCR
Non-vibration	5.806 (s)	6.191 (s)	3.765 (s)	4.201 (s)
Touch vibration	5.296 (s)	4.099 (s)	3.659 (s)	3.284 (s)
Lasted-vibration	3.757 (s)	4.960 (s)	3.524 (s)	3.208 (s)
Reminded-vibration	4.539 (s)	6.152 (s)	3.165 (s)	3.168 (s)

The results of comparing average completion time of each vibration mode show that the completion time of lasted-vibration mode is shorter than the non-vibration mode by nearly 1 s, as shown in Table 4.

Table 4. Average completion time in different mode

Vibration mode	Average completion time
Non-vibration	4.990 (s)
Touch vibration	4.085 (s)
Lasted-vibration	3.862 (s)
Reminded-vibration	4.256 (s)

In order to investigate whether the various vibration samples are different from the current non-vibration mode, we perform paired sample t-test with non-vibration, touch vibration, lasted vibration and reminded-vibration. The results show that there has significant difference (p-value = 0.011) between non-vibration and lasted-vibration, as shown in Table 5.

Table 5. Completion time verification result

Comparison (Vibration)	p-value
Non vs Touch	0.063 (s)
Non vs Lasted	0.011 (s) *
Non vs Reminded	0.182 (s)

*Significant at p < 0.05.

3.2   Idle Ratio

Comparing the idle ratio of four vibration modes by four multi-touch gestures respectively. The results show that non-vibration mode has the highest idle ratio with pinch open gesture; the touch vibration mode has the lowest idle ratio with clockwise rotation gesture, as shown in Table 6.

Table 6. Idle ratio

Vibration mode	Gestures			
	PO	PC	CR	CCR
Non-vibration	44%	37%	14%	14%
Touch vibration	28%	31%	13%	14%
Lasted-vibration	27%	35%	18%	14%
Reminded-vibration	27%	36%	15%	19%

Furthermore, using t-test to analyze four gesture to find out whether there has any different between them. And the results show that in pinch open gesture has a significant different between both non-vibration versus lasted vibration (p-value = 0.04) and non-vibration versus reminded-vibration (p-value = 0.039), as shown in Table 7.

Table 7. Idle ratio verification result

Comparison	Gestures			
	PO	PC	CR	CCR
Non vs Touch	0.097 (s)	0.221 (s)	0.459 (s)	0.438 (s)
Non vs Lasted	0.004 (s) *	0.341 (s)	0.159 (s)	0.471 (s)
Non vs Reminded	0.039 (s) *	0.278 (s)	0.387 (s)	0.135 (s)

*Significant at p < 0.05.

4   Discussion

The study explores four basic multi-touch gestures including pinch open and close, clockwise and counter-clockwise rotation. According to the experimental results, in terms of the average completion time of different gestures, the average completion time of clockwise rotation gesture in non-vibration mode is the shortest, and the pinch close gesture is the longest, indicating that the elderly are easier to operate the clockwise rotation gesture. The differences could result from the characteristic of rotation gesture. Through observation, subjects were able to use one of their fingers as supporting point to assist performing the task. In terms of average completion time of different vibration modes, the vibration mode with gestures is shorter than the non-vibration mode. If we further analyze each vibration mode with the non-vibration mode, we can find that the lasted-vibration mode is significantly shortened than the non-vibration mode. In addition, in terms of idle ratio, pinch close gesture is the highest, and the touch vibration mode has the lowest idle ratio with the clockwise rotation gesture. Further analysis shows that the idle ratio is significantly reduced when performing the task of pinch open on the photo with vibration mode.

To sum up, the elderly encounter more difficulties in operating pinch gestures than rotation gestures, but with vibration feedback can significantly shorten the completion time of the pinch gestures, and the effect of lasted-vibration mode is most obvious due to the feedback and reminder that provided by haptic feedback. On the other hand, the vibration feedback is less obvious for rotating tasks that are easier to perform. However, as for the average, subjects still have better performance when conduct tasks that combined with haptic feedback. In conclusion, adding haptic feedback is helpful for the elderly to perform multi-touch gestures.

Further research could improve this study in three directions. First, explore more on the feedback mode by considering the subjective feelings of the elderly. Second, explore more on the auxiliary level by examination the vibration duration period and intensity. Last but not least, this study using paired t-test as statistical method to reduce the difference between subjects which inevitably face the effect of repeat tests. Further research could recruit different groups of subjects for each vibration sample to further verification the effect of haptic feedback.

Acknowledgements. We are thankful for the financial support from The Ministry of Science and Technology (MOST), Taiwan. The grant MOST 106-2221-E-006-156.

References

1. Banter, B.: Touch screens and touch surfaces are enriched by haptic force-feedback. Inf. Disp. **26**(3), 26–30 (2010)
2. Brewster, S., Chohan, F., Brown, L.: Tactile feedback for mobile interactions. In: Proceedings of the SIGCHI Conference on Human Factors in Computing Systems, pp. 159–162. ACM, New York (2007)
3. Caprani, N., O'Connor, N.E., Gurrin, C.: Touch screens for the older user. In: Assistive technologies, InTech (2012)
4. Carmeli, E., Patish, H., Coleman, R.: The aging hand. J. Gerontol. Ser. A: Biol. Sci. Med. Sci. **58**(2), M146–M152 (2003)
5. Chaparro, A., Rogers, M., Fernandez, J., Bohan, M., Choi, S.D., Stumpfhauser, L.: Range of motion of the wrist: implications for designing computer input devices for the elderly. Disabil. Rehabil. **22**(13), 633–637 (2000)

6. Cozza, M., De Angeli, A., Tonolli, L.: Ubiquitous technologies for older people. Pers. Ubiquit. Comput. **21**(3), 607–619 (2017)
7. Department of Economic and Social Affairs: World Population Ageing 2017 Highlights. United Nations (2017). http://www.un.org/en/development/desa/population/publications/pdf/ageing/WPA2017_Highlights.pdf. Accessed 27 Dec 2018
8. Findlater, L., Froehlich, J.E., Fattal, K., Wobbrock, J.O., Dastyar, T.: Age-related differences in performance with touchscreens compared to traditional mouse input. In: Proceedings of SIGCHI Conference on Human Factors in Computing Systems, pp. 343–346. ACM, New York (2013)
9. Hoggan, E., Brewster, S.A., Johnston, J.: Investigating the effectiveness of tactile feedback for mobile touchscreens. In: Proceedings of the SIGCHI Conference on Human Factors in Computing Systems, pp. 1573–1582. ACM, New York (2008)
10. Koskinen, E., Kaaresoja, T., Laitinen, P.: Feel-good touch: finding the most pleasant tactile feedback for a mobile touch screen button. In: Proceedings of the 10th International Conference on Multimodal Interfaces, pp. 297–304. ACM, New York (2008)
11. Piper, A.M., Campbell, R., Hollan, J.D.: Exploring the accessibility and appeal of surface computing for older adult health care support. In: Proceedings of the SIGCHI Conference on Human Factors in Computing Systems, pp. 907–916. ACM, New York (2010)
12. Seidler, R., Stelmach, G.: Motor Control, Encyclopedia of Gerontology: Age, Aging and the Aged. Academic Press, San Diego (1996)
13. Shim, J.K., Lay, B.S., Zatsiorsky, V.M., Latash, M.L.: Age-related changes in finger coordination in static prehension tasks. J. Appl. Physiol. **97**(1), 213–224 (2004)
14. Skedung, L., et al.: Mechanisms of tactile sensory deterioration amongst the elderly. Sci. Rep. **8**(5303), 1–12 (2018)
15. Stößel, C., Blessing, L.: Mobile device interaction gestures for older users. In: Proceedings of the 6th Nordic Conference on Human-Computer Interaction: Extending Boundaries, pp. 793–796. ACM, New York (2010)
16. Tekli, J., Issa, Y.B., Chbeir, R.: Evaluating touch-screen vibration modality for blind users to access simple shapes and graphics. Int. J. Hum Comput Stud. **110**, 115–133 (2018)
17. Tiwana, M.I., Redmond, S.J., Lovell, N.H.: A review of tactile sensing technologies with applications in biomedical engineering. Sens. Actuators, A: Phys. **179**, 17–31 (2012)
18. Yang, H.L., Lin, S.L.: The reasons why elderly mobile users adopt ubiquitous mobile social service. Comput. Hum. Behav. **93**, 62–75 (2019)

Sustainable Development and ICT Use Among Elderly: A Comparison Between the Netherlands and Italy

Paola Monachesi[✉]

Utrecht University, Trans 10, 3512 JK Utrecht, The Netherlands
P.Monachesi@uu.nl

Abstract. The paper analyzes the participation of the elderly in the digital society by comparing the situation in the Netherland and in Italy. While the Netherlands are at the forefront in internet and social media use with 80% of the seniors in the age group 65–75 being online in 2016, the situation is different in Italy with only 28,8% of the population in this age group using Internet. We have carried out two surveys in Italy to highlight the reasons for this difference which seems to be due to lack of digital competences. We suggest that the widespread use of ICT in The Netherlands can have a positive impact on urban sustainability and on healthy ageing through caring and volunteering activities of the elderly in the natural environment promoted through social media.

Keywords: Social media · Internet · Elderly · Urban sustainability · Italy · The Netherlands

1 Introduction

The elderly are usually considered a problem for sustainable development since the exponential growth of the ageing population threatens the resources that are globally available [1]. In the context of the European project Grage [2], we have carried out an interdisciplinary research on the challenges of ageing and sustainable development in urban areas. The study has evolved around the idea of citizenship, healthy environment and suitable urban solutions for an ageing society. The themes addressed in the project are elderly legal rights, green urbanization, food sustainability and analysis of elderly urban behavior. In this context, we have investigated the role that information and language technology can have in transforming cities into environments that support green and healthy lifestyles.

The elderly can be a resource for sustainable development if we stimulate their involvement in reducing the environmental footprint as well as their volunteering activities in a natural environment, an important aspect of healthy ageing [3]. Internet and social media can play an important role in supporting these best practices: they are affecting the way we live in urban areas since many activities such as social interactions, production, consumption and exchange of services, are now also occurring in online spaces. More specifically, information and language technology can play an important role in the promotion of sustainable development based on a behavioral

J. Zhou and G. Salvendy (Eds.): HCII 2019, LNCS 11592, pp. 450–462, 2019.
https://doi.org/10.1007/978-3-030-22012-9_33

analysis of the data produced by old adults. Therefore, we adopt the view that cities are characterized by the connectivity of the people and the digital devices that make them important data producers, especially through social media, allowing thus an analysis of the content and of the interactions of the users. These data can provide useful insights to deal with current issues in green economy, healthy lifestyles and healthy ageing and more generally they can help redefine urban spaces. In this context, the participation of the elderly in the digital society is essential, however, there are still crucial differences at European level in this respect.

In this paper, we analyze the situation with respect to ICT use by focusing on a comparison between the Netherlands and Italy, two countries with quite different behavior. It is based on data available from the respective national statistical institutes (i.e. CBS and ISTAT, respectively) and from two surveys we have carried out in Italy within the Grage project. We show that the Netherlands are at the forefront in Internet and social media use even among the elderly, while this is not the case in Italy where Internet and social media adoption are lagging behind and we investigate the reasons for this difference.

2   ICT Use Among Elderly in the Netherlands

The knowledge economy is a growing sector in the Netherlands: companies use social media extensively to communicate with their clients that are quite often online. Eight out of ten Dutch citizens use mobile internet on a daily basis: while Internet use is pervasive in the youngest age groups, we notice a considerable growth also among old adults and the elderly, in the last years [4].

Mobile technologies contribute to the 'datafication' of the (urban) space since social actions are transformed in online data that allow for predictive analysis of people's behavior [5, 6]. The (big) data produced trigger new forms of entrepreneurship that are at the basis of the knowledge economy that is driven by innovation and creativity, giving rise to smart cities [7, 8]. In the Netherlands, one out of five companies carries out analysis in this area, creating new jobs and business opportunities, positioning thus the Netherlands at the forefront in Europe, in this sector [4].

If we look more specifically at ICT use in the Netherlands and we focus on the elderly, statistics [4] reveal that in the age group between 65 and 75 years old, 80% of the Dutch population made use of Internet in 2016, while the seniors above 75 years old were 50%, as can be seen in Fig. 1. Furthermore, an investigation of the percentage of households with internet access in Fig. 2, shows that The Netherlands, in 2016, were at the forefront within Europe, with 97% of households being online. Similarly, for the Scandinavian countries, Luxembourg, Great Britain and Germany where 9 of the 10 households have an internet account. The percentage is lower in Southern Europe that is lagging behind, in particular, Italy is quite below the EU average with less than 80% of the households with Internet.

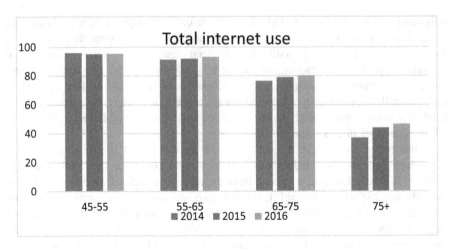

Fig. 1. Internet use in the Netherlands per age group (Source: CBS)

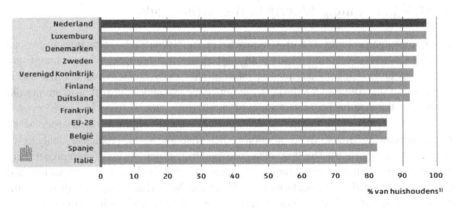

Fig. 2. Households with internet in EU countries 2016 (Source: Eurostat)

It is interesting to analyze, per age group, the type of technology that is being used in order to be online. As can be seen in Fig. 3, the smartphone is the device most used by the youngest age group; in the age group 65 until 75 years old, it is the laptop that is the most used while in the age group of 75+, the use of the various devices is rather equivalent except for the smartphone that is used less than the others.

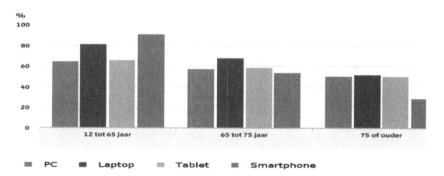

Fig. 3. Devices used to access internet in the Netherlands in 2016 (Source: CBS)

As for the types of activities carried out online among the elderly, Fig. 4 shows that in 2016, the 75+ group uses internet mainly for email (light blue), while almost 70% of the respondents use it for finding information about goods and services (dark blue) and for banking (light green), around 60% use it for buying online (dark green) and for finding information about health (orange), more than 50% use it to read the newspaper (purple). Percentages are higher in the group of 65–75 years old.

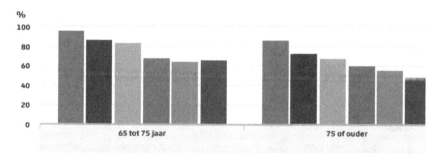

Fig. 4. Internet activities in the Netherlands in 2016 (Source: CBS) (Color figure online)

We can thus conclude that Internet is pervasive in the Netherlands with a high percentage of old adults and the elderly gaining access to it.

If we consider the social media use of the Dutch population, which includes online chatting, writing or reading weblogs, e-mailing and use of social and professional platforms, in 2016, we notice an extended use in all age groups (cf. Fig. 5). Almost 60% of adults between 65 and 75 years old are active on social media while those above 75 years old are 20%. If we focus on social networks, in Fig. 6 it is possible to visualize the development in use, in the last years, per age group. Even though young people made more use of social networks than the elderly, the difference has become smaller since 2014. The use in the age group 45–65 years old has registered an increase from 70% to 83%. In the age group above 65 years old, the increase has been from 26% to 39%.

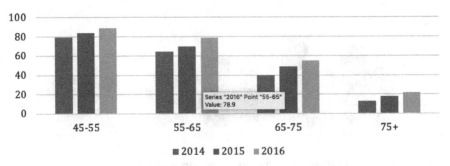

Fig. 5. Social media use in the Netherlands (Source: CBS)

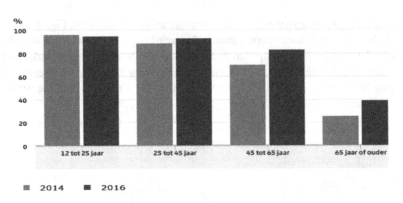

Fig. 6. Social networks use in the Netherlands (Source: CBS)

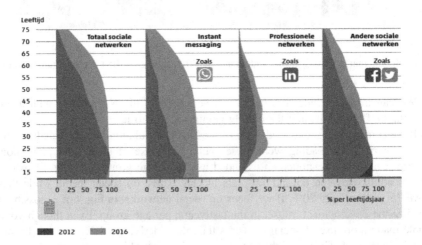

Fig. 7. Use of various social networks in The Netherlands (Source: CBS) (Color figure online)

Figure 7 shows the development in the use of the various social networks in the years 2012 and 2016. These two years are represented over each other and they partially overlap, in this case the color is grey-blue. It is possible to see that young people use platforms such as Facebook and Twitter less while the elderly are using social networks more, this is especially the case for instant messaging. Furthermore, the use of professional social networks has increased in the age group 22–35 years old.

3 ICT Use Among Elderly in Italy

In the previous section, we have shown that the elderly are at the forefront in ICT use in the Netherlands while in this section we analyze the situation in Italy, where we notice striking differences with respect to the analysis previously presented.

The Digital Economy and Society Index tracks the evolution of the European member states in digital competitiveness and it shows the differences attested among its member states. The analysis in [9] shows that the Nordic European countries, among which The Netherlands, are in the first positions while Italy has one of the lowest scores. It occupies the 25th position among the 28 members states with a digitalization index of 44,3 that is calculated on the basis of connectivity, basic digital competencies, internet use and digitalization of private and public companies. It is almost 30 points behind The Netherlands which is in the fourth position (cf. Fig. 8).

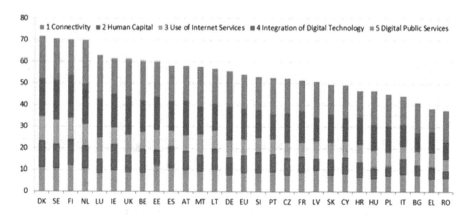

Fig. 8. Digital Economy and Society Index (DESI) 2018 ranking

More specifically, if we consider statistics in internet use [10], there has been a constant growth in Italy, as can be seen in Fig. 9 and a considerable increase in the age group 15–24 years, whose use is above 90%, furthermore, the users between 55–59 years old have also notably increased. We notice a similar tendency also among the elderly even though the percentages in usage are still rather low with only 28.8% of the population between 65 and 74 years old using internet in 2016 and only 7.7% of those aged 75+. This is quite a big difference if compared to The Netherlands. A gender gap in internet use is also attested in Italy: in 2016, 67,6% of the males were online, against 59% of the females. Regional differences still play a role and this is the case especially between those regions in Northern Italy (67,6%) compared to Southern Italy (55,9%) and the islands (55,7%), while the Central regions score similarly to the North. Social differences are also attested: while 91,6% of people with a university degree are online and 93,8 of managers and professionals, the percentage goes down to 63,9% among those with a middle school diploma and to 77,6% among factory workers.

SESSO, CLASSI DI ETÀ, RIPARTIZIONI GEOGRAFICHE E CONDIZIONE OCCUPAZIONALE	2011	2012	2013	2014	2015	2016	2017
Maschi	56,7	58,3	60,3	62,4	65,0	67,6	69,5
Femmine	46,7	47,1	49,8	52,8	55,8	59,0	61,3
Totale	51,5	52,5	54,9	57,5	60,2	63,2	65,3
6-10	38,3	40,8	45,1	44,6	43,8	48,2	53,7
11-14	78,1	76,5	80,8	80,9	80,4	82,9	86,1
15-17	89,1	88,5	89,7	91,2	92,0	91,6	93,9
18-19	88,8	88,8	90,0	93,9	92,0	93,0	92,7
20-24	85,8	86,0	85,7	89,3	90,7	91,3	92,4
25-34	77,5	79,2	80,3	83,9	85,1	87,1	89,8
35-44	69,7	69,1	73,5	76,1	80,1	84,3	85,7
45-54	56,2	58,7	61,7	66,1	70,0	75,1	77,6
55-59	42,2	45,3	48,5	52,0	60,4	62,7	68,2
60-64	28,6	31,0	36,0	41,1	45,9	52,2	56,0
65-74	13,8	16,4	19,0	21,2	25,6	28,8	30,8
75 e più	2,7	3,3	3,5	4,4	6,7	7,7	8,8
Totale	51,5	52,5	54,9	57,5	60,2	63,2	65,3
Nord-ovest	56,4	57,3	58,3	61,5	64,6	67,6	69,1
Nord-est	55,9	57,7	60,1	61,5	65,2	66,9	68,0
Centro	54,5	55,1	57,8	60,4	61,6	66,4	67,8
Sud	43,6	43,3	46,6	49,2	53,1	55,9	59,1
Isole	43,9	47,3	49,8	53,0	53,8	55,7	59,6
Italia	51,5	52,5	54,9	57,5	60,2	63,2	65,3

Fig. 9. Internet use in Italy (Source: Istat)

As for social networks, in 2015, in the age group 65–80 years old, only 14.3% of the users were on Facebook while only 6.6% used YouTube [11], as can be seen in Fig. 10.

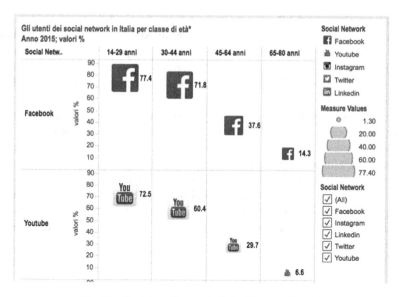

Fig. 10. Social media use in Italy (Source: Censis)

To conclude, while we have seen that in the Netherlands the extended use of Internet and social media triggers the production of big data and a flourishing knowledge economy, the situation is different in Italy where even the digital competence within companies is limited. Only 16,2% of those companies with 10 people has personnel specialized in ICT and only 12,9% of them organizes informative sessions on digitalization [10].

4   ICT Analysis of Italian Elderly in the Grage Project

The differences with respect to ICT use in The Netherlands and in Italy are quite striking and in the context of the Grage project, we have carried out an exploratory cross-sectional survey in the city of Macerata to gain insights into the reasons for this different behavior and the low penetration of ICT in Italy among the elderly. Macerata is located in the Marche region, which is in central Italy.

We created a tailor-made questionnaire on the basis of a checklist of the essential features of age-friendly cities developed by the WHO [12] to measure the perception of age-friendliness of the urban context the elderly live in. The original WHO checklist, which includes several domains covering physical, social and service environments, has been adapted to the Italian context and we have added additional questions related to ICT and technology, which are of relevance in this paper. The survey comprises 58 items, in addition to 16 demographic questions aiming at assessing the status of the respondents with respect to their personal situation.

The respondents are individuals belonging to two age groups, that is between 55 and 64 (pre-retirement) and older than 64 (retired). We have asked 166 residents, aged on average 64.57, that have provided an answer based on their personal experience and their subjective perception. Responses are based on a 6-point Likert scale, ranging from 1 ('strongly disagree') to 6 ('strongly agree'). The questionnaire has been carried out in elderly centers, community halls, summer vacation camps for the elderly, churches, university offices and public offices. Data were collected by means of face-to-face interviews while younger (i.e. between 55 and 67) and literate respondents administered their own questionnaire.

One of the items in the survey asks whether computers and internet are available for free (or for a reasonable price) in public places such as libraries, municipality offices and elderly centers. The majority of the respondents disagree with this statement (i.e. 48%), while 20% didn't answer, responses are visualized in Fig. 11. In Fig. 12, we can see the results of the item that assesses whether there are courses being offered to learn how to use Internet and the various digital services based on it, such as internet-banking, reading news, buying products online or sending emails. In this case, the disagreement is even higher with the statement (65%) while 21% of the respondents didn't answer.

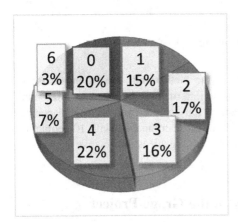

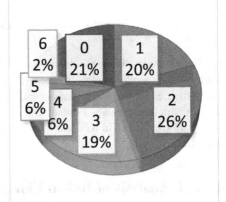

Fig. 11. Availability of computers in public places

Fig. 12. Internet support

Similar disagreement is attested with respect to the item whether the elderly are aware of social media platforms, such as Facebook and whether they use them to be in touch with family and friends and to receive information. In this case, 67% disagree while 14% didn't answer, as can be seen in Fig. 13. However, the majority of the respondents agree that Internet and social media would be very useful for the elderly because they support social inclusion and allow for information to be gained as well as for relations to be maintained with family and friends. As can be seen in Fig. 14, the majority agrees with this statement (59%) while 10% didn't answer.

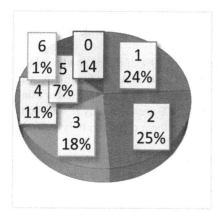

Fig. 13. Elderly and social media use

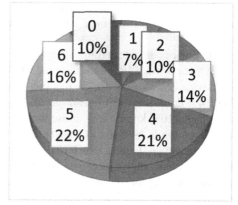

Fig. 14. Usefulness of social media for the elderly

From these responses, we can conclude that the elderly are interested in Internet and social media and they are aware of their potential, but they are limited in their use due to lack of digital competences and limited support through courses to become more acquainted with them.

This conclusion seems to be also supported by an additional survey that we have carried out at regional level to assess the attitude of elderly with respect to ICT, that is whether elderly own devices and whether they are familiar with them. The survey has been filled by 203 respondents from the Marche region, including not only inhabitants of Macerata and its province but also seniors from the other 4 provinces living in small (i.e. less than 30.000 inhabitants) and medium size municipalities (more than 30.000 inhabitants). The average age of the respondents is 73 years old, including both men (52%) and women (48%), with medium-low level of education, of which 76% were retired.

In the context of this study, four questions are relevant, that is whether the respondents own a computer, an internet connection, a smartphone or a tablet and what is their level of familiarity with them. With respect to the possession of computers, 63% of the respondents answer that they have one at home, while 32% don't and 5% haven't answered. Results are similar with respect to internet connection indicating that people that buy a computer do so to be online. The responses are the same also with respect to familiarity with these devices, that is 11% of users declare that they don't use them and are not interested in using them, 8% don't use them but would like to use them, 7% use them only if somebody helps them, 9% knows how to use them, but don't use them regularly, only 21% use them often while 43% didn't answer.

As for smartphones, the results are the same as for the other two devices with respect to possession, however, regarding familiarity, there are some differences indicating that the elderly are more acquainted with this device. Results indicate that 4% of users don't use them and are not interested in using them, 4% don't use them but would like to use them, 5% use them only if somebody helps them, 14% knows how to use them, but don't use them regularly, only 30% use them often while 42% didn't answer.

Differences are attested in ownership of tablets, since 39% of the respondents have one at home while 54% don't have one while 6% didn't answer. As for familiarity with this device, 5% of users declare that they don't use them and are not interested in using them, 4% don't use them but would like to use them, 4% use them only if somebody helps them, 10% knows how to use them, but don't use them regularly, only 12% use them often while 64% didn't answer.

These results indicate that ICT devices are present at home but people tend not to use them often: the percentages of internet and computer use are in line with the national statistics for this age group, discussed in the previous section. Tablets are used less than computers, while smartphones are used the most, but in this case one wonders whether they are used as simple phone or whether all their functionalities are known, including internet use. Interviews with some of the elderly have revealed that the use of apps makes access to services through the smartphone easier for them, especially the use of instant messaging apps such as WhatsApp, that is becoming popular among this population also in Italy. However, the fact that a high percentage of seniors didn't respond might indicate that even though these devices are at home, possibly because they are owned by a younger member of the family, seniors are not much concerned about their use or the possibility to use them or to learn how to use them (cf. low percentages for this option in the survey).

To conclude, it seems that the Italian respondents being asked are aware of the advantages of ICT devices, they have one at home, but they lack information and knowledge on how to use them. The survey has indicated that the reason might be that not enough courses and education tailored for the elderly are available to support them in acquiring ICT skills. This conclusion is in line with a recent report from ISTAT that concludes that while two thirds of Italian family have access to broad band at home, the majority of families without access indicate lack of digital competences as main reason for not being online (55,5%) while 25,3% of the respondents doesn't consider Internet an interesting and useful tool. Economic reasons seem to play a more marginal role and are mentioned only by 16,2% of the respondents while privacy concerns are mentioned only by 2,4% of the people being asked [10].

5   Conclusions

We have shown, on the basis of detailed statistics [4], that the Netherlands are at the forefront in Internet and Social media use, their adoption includes not only the young generation but also a growing number of old adults as well as the elderly population. The situation is different in Italy that still lags behind in ICT use, which is the case not only for the elderly but also for small enterprises that score low in digital competitiveness [10, 11]. The reasons, that emerged from the two surveys we have carried out, seem related to lack of digital competences as well as shortage of education opportunities being offered to the elderly to contrast the digital divide.

In the Netherlands, where the ICT use is widespread, the online activities support the production of data that are at the basis of a flourishing knowledge economy, which relies on big data and behavioral analyses. A problematic side effect of this development is that citizens and social media users, including the elderly, are considered merely as data providers [13]. It is only recently that a debate has emerged in which questions of data ownership are being raised and whether these data benefit the needs of the citizens or instead the interests of the big tech companies [14].

In [15], we have shown that a behavioral analysis of the Dutch elderly based on Twitter data, can be useful to assess their attitude and interests and can have a potential positive impact on urban sustainability and healthy ageing. The analysis of hashtag use reveals that while the younger age groups have an interest in nature and sustainability, this doesn't seem to be the case for the seniors that exhibit, however an interest in locations. We hypothesize that this apparently negative result might reveal that the debate on sustainable development in Twitter revolves around economic and work-related aspects and it is thus less relevant for the elderly that are not part of the work force since they are usually retired. It is, however, interesting for the younger age groups that use Twitter for work related activities. While initial insights seem to confirm this hypothesis, further research is necessary to validate it and to investigate, on the basis of geo-location information, whether the location hashtags used by the elderly are employed to promote the city they live in. If this is the case, we could conclude that they are more apt to relate to the environment they live in, rather than to abstract concepts such as sustainable development. This interest could be exploited to promote an alternative discourse on sustainable development with social media being employed by the elderly to develop actions in support of the local environment, including environmental policies and volunteering. Activities in the natural environment are restorative experiences and can benefit human beings [16, 17] they tend to involve physical movement and thus promote health, consequently reducing expenditure for health care systems and the connected risks of social marginalization. The Dutch are quite active in this respect given that 49% of the population, in the period 2012–2016, was involved in volunteering activities and this percentage is even higher among older adults aged 65–75, raising to 52% and then decreasing to 34% for those aged 75 and above [18].

In this view, the elderly would act as innovators and could play an important role in restoring the bond between individuals and the environment which constitutes an essential component of sustainable development [3].

Acknowledgements. This paper is based on results of a project that has received funding from the European Union's Horizon 2020 research and innovation program under the Marie Skło-dowska-Curie grant agreement No 645706. This article reflects only the author's view and the REA is not responsible for any use that may be made of the information it contains. I would like to thank Ninfa Contigiani and Giovanna Fanci from the University of Macerata for their support in carrying out the WHO survey. I am also grateful to Daryna Petlina and Olena Motuzenko from Taras Shevchenko National University of Kiev for sharing the results of the regional survey on technology with me.

References

1. Wright, S.D., Lund, D.A.: Gray and green? Stewardship and sustainability in an aging society. J. Aging Stud. **14**, 229–249 (2000)
2. Grage. https://www.grageproject.eu/
3. Carella, V., Monachesi, P.: Greener through grey? Boosting sustainable development through a philosophical and social media analysis of ageing. Sustainability **10**(2), 499 (2018)
4. CBS2017: ICT, kennis en economie 2017. Centraal Bureau voor de Statistiek, Den Haag (2017)
5. Cukier, K., Mayer-Schoenberger, V.: The rise of big data: how it's changing the way we think about the world. Foreign Aff. **92**, 28–40 (2013)
6. van Dijk, J.: Datafication, dataism and dataveillance: big data between scientific paradigm and ideology. Surveill. Soc. **12**, 197–208 (2014)
7. Kitchin, R.: The real-time city? Big data and smart urbanism. GeoJournal **79**(1), 1–14 (2014)
8. Allen, A., Lampis, A., Swilling, M.: Untamed Urbanism. Routledge Advances in Regional Economics, Science and Policy. Routledge, New York (2016)
9. DESI 2018: Digital Economy and Society Index 2018 Report. Digital Single Market, DG Connect (2018)
10. ISTAT2017: Cittadini, Imprese e ICT. ISTAT (2017)
11. Prato, M.: Social network: gli anziani sempre più 'social'. Facebook il piu' popolare tra giovani e anziani. Il sole 24 ore (2016)
12. WHO: Checklist of Essential Features of Age-Friendly Cities. World Health Organization, Geneva, Switzerland (2007)
13. Calzada, I.: (Smart) citizens from data providers to decision-makers? The case study of Barcelona. Sustainability **10**(9), 1–25 (2018)
14. Morozov, E.: There is a leftwing way to challenge big tech for our data. Here it is. The Guardian (2018)
15. Monachesi, P., de Leeuw, T.: Analyzing elderly behavior in social media through language use. In: Stephanidis, C. (ed.) HCI 2018. CCIS, vol. 851, pp. 188–195. Springer, Cham (2018). https://doi.org/10.1007/978-3-319-92279-9_26
16. Kaplan, S.: The restorative benefits of nature. Toward an integrative framework. J. Environ. Psychol. **15**, 169–182 (1995)
17. Ulrich, R., Simons, R., Losito, B., Fiorito, B., Miles, M., Zelson, M.: Stress recovery during exposure to natural and urban environments. J. Environ. Psychol. **11**, 201–230 (1991)
18. CBS Statline. https://statline.cbs.nl/Statweb/

Optimal Designs of Text Input Fields in Mobile Web Surveys for Older Adults

Elizabeth Nichols[⊠], Erica Olmsted-Hawala, and Lin Wang

U.S. Census Bureau, Washington, D.C., USA
elizabeth.may.nichols@census.gov

Abstract. Online forms and surveys often include text input fields to gather information such as name, address, comments, or other information that is not in a small set of pre-defined answers. This paper shares results of three different experiments investigating how older adults using smartphones interact with different user-interface designs of text input fields in online surveys. Experiment 1 compares different ways of labeling the text input field. Experiment 2 investigates the impact of using a character countdown on the field. Experiment 3 investigates whether predictive text in such fields helps with data entry. Results confirm that label placement does not affect time to complete the task, but users prefer either labels above the field or inline labels that move above the field when focus is placed in the field. Most participants were not aware of the character countdown feature and there was not a strong preference for it. Although it did significantly reduce deleting characters, it did not increase the number of characters typed or decrease time on task. Predictive text was preferred and when used, there is some indication that it might make the task quicker without increasing incorrect answers.

Keywords: Mobile survey design · Mobile guidelines · Older adults · Predictive text · Field label placement · Character countdown features

1 Introduction

While most respondents answer an online survey on a computer, increasingly survey respondents are using a smartphone to complete online surveys. This smaller device poses particular challenges for developers and survey designers as the display area on a smartphone is much less than that on a computer screen. This smaller amount of screen "real estate" affects many areas of the survey, including the response option designs for questions. In this paper, we explore one particular type of response option design on mobile devices: the text input field. Text input fields allow users to enter characters or numbers using the keyboard or keypad. Typically, they are used for questions with too many possible answers for a radio button or drop down design. Common examples of questions that use a text input field are name and address questions, ethnicities or ancestry questions, or food or medicine questions. Text input fields are used to collect open-ended comments or a personal note for a gift purchased online. The field is also used in forms for business purposes, such as collecting credit card numbers [1].

This is a U.S. government work and not under copyright protection in the United States; foreign copyright protection may apply 2019
J. Zhou and G. Salvendy (Eds.): HCII 2019, LNCS 11592, pp. 463–481, 2019.
https://doi.org/10.1007/978-3-030-22012-9_34

To analyze the data entered into these fields, often the open-ended responses are coded, either by a machine or an analyst, into categories or groups for further analysis. Coding answers that do not have enough context or content is challenging. Spelling and grammatical errors can interfere with correct coding as well. These limitations can lead to measurement error or more labor intensive, and therefore more expensive, manual coding. When there are several text input fields on a web page, survey respondents need to understand what to enter and where to enter the data so the correct answer is in the correct field. They also need to understand how detailed an answer to give without exceeding the space limitation of the field. To investigate these issues, we conducted experiments to examine field label placements; character countdown features; and predictive text (sometimes known as auto-correction, or type-ahead). We describe these three elements in detail below.

When considering the design of text input fields, it is essential to label each field so that users know what to enter. Nielsen and Norman (2010) recommend placing a label close to the correct field (either above or to the left) so that there is no confusion about which label goes with which field [2]. Labeling form fields has been researched using PC monitors [3, 4] with somewhat consistent results. For example, neither group found that the label position affects the time spent on a web page. However, field labels either above the field or to the left of the field (either aligned left or aligned right) are more preferred and generate fewer eye fixations on a PC than other label designs [5]. That same research found that the flow design where the label is left aligned and the field immediately follows the label such that a web page with multiple fields has a jagged design, is not preferred by users. Inline labels, or placeholder text, where the label disappears when focus is put into the field (by either clicking into, tabbing into, or touching the field) is sometimes used to save space on forms. However, this design has several problems. Inline labels tax short-term memory because the user must remember what the field was for and research has shown that users do not prefer this design [5, 6]. More recent advancements with inline labels allow the label to jump to the top of the field (either right outside or inside the field but small and above the text entered) once focus is placed in the field. Google calls these designs *outlined text fields* or *filled text fields*, but we refer to them as *inline labels that move* [7]. To our knowledge, research on these type of labels has not been conducted on mobile phones. It is possible that *inline labels that move* may be more advantageous for surveys on mobile phones where space is limited as it could reduce the length of the page without relying on short term memory. Given the prior research on PCs, we do not expect time to complete the task (i.e., efficiency) to differ because of label placement, but we do expect user preference for labels to differ. We hypothesize that *inline labels that move* would be preferred and over labels above or to the left of the field.

Another important decision for open text fields concerns how to communicate the amount of text input that is expected. On well-designed forms, the input field is the size of the expected entry [8, 9]. One design feature that is sometimes used to communicate the field size is a character countdown. With a character countdown, the maximum number of characters allowed in the field is placed near the open-text field, usually below the field. This number reduces directly in relation to the number of characters typed, letting users know how many characters remain to be used. When the maximum number of characters is reached, sometimes users can no longer type and the character countdown remains zero, but other designs let the countdown go negative and the number turns color, typically red. This feature is often used in open-text fields with a limited number of characters, such as a note to the receiver of an online purchase. However, this feature is not used in a field asking for name or address. While there is research that suggests respondents can share as rich and meaningful information with a known 160-character text limit as with larger fields in an email [10], little to no research has been conducted on character countdown features in web surveys. We hypothesize that character countdowns lead to a more efficient survey experience because respondents would know how much text is expected and they would not exceed the limit.

Finally, predictive text is a technology that uses the context of the existing text and the first letters typed into a field to suggest a complete word to insert. The words typically appear below the field and update on the fly depending on what additional letter is added to the word being typed. Instead of continuing to type, the user can touch the word and it will appear in the field. The feature is frequently used when texting on a mobile phone, yet it is not often used in open-ended input fields in a survey. Early research used tactile vibrations in combination with predictive text to increase accuracy and speed with typing on mobile devices [11]. One set of guidelines for forms suggest that predictive text should be used for fields with a lot of predefined options [12]. Questions with a large number of possible, but predictable answers such as car models, vacation destinations, ethnicities, or medicine, could be candidates for an open-text field response option with predictive text. Early research on mobile phones indicates that suggesting words could reduce the amount of time and key presses needed to compose messages [13]. When using predictive text, spelling errors are eliminated and thus answers might be more likely to be machine coded. If the predictive text was limited to a list of finite words to "suggest" to the user, it also might make coding more efficient as researchers would not have to spend time attempting to code a word that was meaningless or that did not precisely "fit." Couper and Zhang conducted an experiment with a predictive text prototype with a finite word list, conducted primarily on PCs [14]. They found more codable answers using drop boxes and the predictive text dictionary, but response time was longer than entering data in a plain open text-field – the opposite finding of the research on mobile [13]. Given the conflicting findings, we hypothesize that predictive text with a finite word list would lead to more codable answers, but we have no hypothesis about whether it would take longer than plain text.

The purpose of the present study was to conduct a series of systematic assessments on a mobile phone to determine how older adults use different user-interface designs to answer online survey questions and to identify preferred designs based on performance. The results of these assessments could be used as guidelines for developing mobile online surveys. We focused on older adults because they have reduced vision, mobility, and memory compared to younger adults [15–17]. Our rationale was that if we develop guidelines for a mobile web survey interface that older adults can successfully complete, then younger adults would do at least as well because of their superior perceptual and motor capabilities. In addition to conducting the field label experiment with older adults, we also conducted it with younger participants to help assess the assumption. This study is a continuation of the research on other mobile survey elements [18]. For more information on this entire research project please see [19].

2 Methods

Below are highlights of methods relevant to the three experiments described in this paper. In the analysis, we consider significance to be at $p = 0.05$ or less.

2.1 Participants

We aimed to recruit a sample of persons aged 60–75. We prescreened to include only participants who had at least 12 months of experience using a smartphone under the assumption that these participants were more typical of respondents who choose to use mobile devices to complete online surveys than those with less experience using smartphones. Additionally, we prescreened participants to include only individuals who had an education of 8th grade or more, who were fluent in English, and who had normal or corrected to normal vision. The participants were a convenience sample recruited from senior and/or community centers in and around the Washington DC metropolitan area between late 2016 and the summer of 2018.

The participant characteristics are provided in Table 1. Experiment 1 was conducted with a pool of 64 older adult participants, Experiment 2 was conducted with a pool of 40 participants; and Experiment 3 was conducted with 37 participants. With regards to familiarity with using a smartphone, on a 5-point scale where 1 was "Not at all familiar" and 5 was "Extremely familiar," participants in each pool reported an average of 3. Experiment 1 was also conducted on 58 younger adults from community colleges.

Table 1. Participant demographics for 3 experiments

Experiment	Average age (standard error (SE))	Gender (male/female/missing)	Smartphone usage* (SE)
Experiment 1 Field labels older adults (n = 64)	68.5 (0.6)	14/50	3.8 (0.1)
Young adults (n = 58)	26.4 (1.6)	35/23	4.5 (0.1)
Experiment 2 Character countdown (n = 40)	69.7 (0.6)	8/31/1	3.7 (0.1)
Experiment 3 Predictive text (n = 37)	66.9 (0.9)	6/31	3.8 (0.2)

*1 – Not Familiar to 5 – Extremely familiar

2.2 Data Collection Methods

One-on-one sessions were conducted at senior centers and community centers. Participants were walk-ups that day or were scheduled by the center. At the appointment time, they were screened by Census Bureau staff and signed a consent form. Then, each participant worked with a test administrator (TA) and completed between 4 to 6 experiments, only some of which are the subject of this paper. The experiments were designed into apps and loaded on a Census-owned iPhone 5S or 6S. TAs provided participants with one of these devices for purposes of the test, and gave instructions to the participants. This included instructing participants *not* to talk aloud during the session, and to complete the survey to the best of their ability as though they were answering the survey at home without anyone's assistance. The participants performed the task independently, taking 10–20 min for each experiment, depending upon the experimental design. At the end of the session, each participant was given $40 honorarium.

3 Experiment 1: Text Input Field Labels

3.1 Designs Tested in the Experiment

In this experiment, we tested five different label locations for text input fields using a between-subjects experimental design with five conditions. Sixty-two older adults participated in this study. They were randomly assigned to a condition. Condition 1 included the label above the text box, left justified (Fig. 1). Condition 2 included the inline labels, where labels were initially inside the box as shown in (Fig. 2), and when focus was placed in the field (by touching it), the label moved above the text box, and thus appeared similar to condition 1. In condition 3, the label was to the left of the text box and left aligned (Fig. 3). Condition 4 was similar to condition 3, in that the label was to the left of the text box, but it was right aligned so that it was near the field (Fig. 4). The label was to the right of the text box in condition 5 (Fig. 5). Our hypothesis was that questions with inline labels that move or labels above the text boxes would be most preferred, but there would be no difference between conditions in the time needed to complete each question.

Fig. 1. Label above box

Fig. 2. Inline labels that move

Fig. 3. Label to left of box and left align

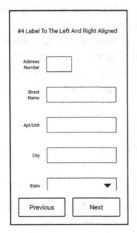 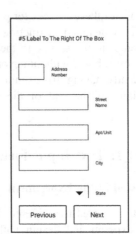

Fig. 4. Label to left and right align

Fig. 5. Label to right of box

Each condition had the same 14 open-ended questions on a range of topics. Each question, aside from Question 14[1] which was one long scroll, was presented in full display on one screen. Some questions requested basic information like name and street address, that required little thought; while other questions were more complex, collecting information that might require more thought, such as the hours spent reading a book in the past week.

After the survey questions, satisfaction data were collected. The participant was asked to rate how easy or difficult it was to complete the task on a 5-point scale with the endpoints labeled 1 = Very Easy and 5 = Very Difficult. Then, the participant was shown the address question in all five labels locations and asked which one(s) he or she preferred.

3.2 Analysis Methods

The app collected behavioral measures including time on screen. For each condition, we measured respondent burden, operationalized as time to complete a screen (our efficiency measure), self-reported satisfaction and self-reported label location preference. We then compared these measures between conditions.

We modeled the log of time to complete a screen at the question level using a mixed model because the residuals of the model with time untransformed were slightly skewed. Modeling at the question level increases the number of observations and allows us to account for different question characteristics. See Table 2 for the question characteristics. In the model, we controlled for the condition, the type of data requested

---

[1] Question 14 was added mid-way through the data collection sessions because we thought it was possible that a long scroll could have an impact on the optimal location of the field label. This meant that some participants answered 13 questions and some answered 14 questions.

Table 2. Text input field label experiment: question characteristics

Question number	Topic	Answer was basic information or more complex
1	Name	Basic
2	Date of birth	Basic
3	Address	Basic
4	Email	Basic
5	Security question and answer	Complex
6	Number of rooms and bedrooms in home	Complex
7	Cost of electricity	Complex
8	Hours spent outside in the past week	Complex
9	Opinion question about what is the essential characteristics of democracy	Complex
10	Sources they use to find out what is happening in the country	Complex
11	Hours spent in the past week reading a book, magazine, or website	Complex
12	Number of days in past week that they ate the evening meal alone	Complex
13	Type of work	Complex
14	Rating question on a number of different topics such as the courts, labor unions, universities, banks, etc.	Complex

(basic or complex), and any interaction between condition and those characteristics. To control for any participant effect because each participant would contribute up to 13 or 14 times (one time for each question), we included a random effect for the participant. As a check we also modeled time controlling for the question number instead of the question characteristics.

We tabulated satisfaction scores for each of the five conditions. For these analyses, we conducted a Chi-square test of independence. And, finally we tabulated the preference data.

In this experiment we also collected data from 58 participants younger than 60 years old. We compared whether the younger adults performed similar to the older adults or if their performance differed by adding a cohort variable to the model to indicate whether the data was from a young individual or an older individual. We also included an interaction between the condition and the cohort indicator.

3.3   Results

Table 3 contains the results of the experiment for older adults, including how many participants were in each condition, the number of observations in each condition (this is the number of questions/screens); the average time to answer a question by condition, and the average satisfaction rating for each condition.

Table 3. Experiment 1 metrics by condition

Condition and description	No. of older participants	No. of observations	Average time per screen in seconds (SE)	Average satisfaction rating (SE)
1–Label above the box	15	206	36 (1.8)	1.7 (0.2)
2–Inline labels	11	151	34 (2.0)	1.8 (0.3)
3–Label to the left and left-aligned	12	165	39 (2.0)	1.3 (0.1)
4– Label to the left and right-aligned	12	165	42 (3.3)	1.6 (0.2)
5– Label to the right of the box	14	192	39 (2.6)	1.9 (0.3)

Burden as Measured By Time to Complete (Efficiency). Controlling for the type of data requested (whether it was basic information like name or address, or whether it was a complex question that required more thought), and using a mixed model predicting the log of time with a random effect for the participant, there was no difference in the amount of time spent on a screen by condition ($F = 0.24$; $p = 0.9$) for the older adults. When modeling with the question number instead of the type of data requested, the pattern of results was unchanged. When including the younger adults in the model, the pattern of results was unchanged and there was no interaction between the age cohort and the condition. Using a t-test, we found that the older adults took on average 12 seconds longer ($p < 0.001$) to complete each screen in the survey than the younger adults.

Satisfaction Scores By Condition. Satisfaction was measured on a 5-point scale where 1 was very easy and 5 was very difficult. We found no differences in satisfaction scores by condition ($\chi^2(16) = 11.4$, $p = 0.8$) when combining the older and younger adults and there was no difference by condition for older adults ($\chi^2(12) = 5.8$, $p = 0.9$) or younger adults ($\chi^2(16) = 20.1$, $p = 0.2$).

Label Position Preference. At the end of the experiment, participants were shown each of the designs, and we asked them which one(s) they preferred. Participants could choose one or more designs so the percentages below do not sum to 100. Results for older adults were:

- 43% preferred the inline labels that move;
- 42% preferred the label above the box;
- 14% preferred the label left aligned and left justified;
- 11% preferred the label left aligned and right justified; and
- 6% preferred the label to the right of the field.

4   Experiment 2: Use of Character Countdowns

4.1   Designs Tested in the Experiment

In this experiment, we tested a character countdown feature where the character countdown shows 0 characters left and stops accepting characters into the box when the field is at the maximum number of characters. The survey contained six open-text field questions with different character limits asked in this order: Ancestry (20 characters); Kind of work (200 characters); Employer's main business (35 characters); Main reason left job (15 characters); How you search for work (30 characters) and What you did yesterday (250 characters). Each question was on its own screen and the field size matched the number of characters allowed. Predictive text was offered for all questions in all conditions.

We used a between-subjects experimental design with three conditions and 40 participants. Condition 1 did not include a character countdown feature on the screens (Fig. 6); condition 2 included a character countdown feature left-justified below the field (Fig. 7); and condition 3 included a character countdown feature left-justified above the field (Fig. 8). Our hypothesis was that more information would be typed with the character countdown features because the number gives a sense of how much text is wanted; the use of a character countdown would reduce the number of people who tried to type more than was allowed in the field; and the presence of a character countdown would minimize the amount of changes within the text field.

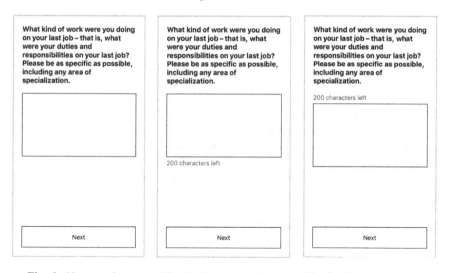

Fig. 6. No countdown   **Fig. 7.** Countdown below   **Fig. 8.** Countdown above field

After the six survey questions, satisfaction data were collected. The participant was asked to rate how easy or difficult it was to complete the survey and, to enter the answer. Both questions were on a 5-point scale with the endpoints labeled 1 = Very Easy and 5 = Very Difficult. The final tasks were for the participant to select the type of input field design he or she had used (all three conditions were shown) and which one he or she preferred. We refer to the second to last task, where the participant had to select which input field design he or she used, as the memory task. This task was included as another measure of whether participants were aware of the feature.

4.2   Analysis Methods

The app collected behavioral measures, including time on screen, the number of characters submitted for each question, whether the user tried to type when out of room in the field, how many times the user selected a predictive text word for the question, and the number of characters deleted while typing in a question. We used two criteria to measure respondent burden which address efficiency as a whole. First, burden was operationalized as time to complete (both the amount of time on the screen and the amount of time typing in the field). Secondly, we considered erasing characters in the text input field (whether by backspacing or by selecting and deleting) to be an indicator of burden. To measure accuracy, we counted the final number of characters entered into the field and submitted. We tabulated satisfaction scores and preference data for each of the three conditions. We measured awareness of the character countdown feature by capturing whether the participant ran out of room in the field and kept trying to type and by calculating how many participants selected the correct input field design they had seen during the session in the memory task.

We modeled the log of the two time variables at the question level using a mixed model. Modeling at the question level increases the number of observations from 40 to 40×6 or 240 and allows us to account for the different maximum field lengths. We modeled the log of time because the residuals of the model with the untransformed time variables were slightly skewed. In the model, we controlled for the condition, the question number, and the number of characters submitted (because more characters might mean more time). To control for any participant effect because each participant would contribute up to 6 times (one time for each question), we included a random effect for the participant. We tried several other models including question number as an ordinal variable, and models with interactions and the results did not change.

We modeled the number of characters typed at the question level using the same type of mixed model, but we removed the last question's data because an error in the programming allowed users to type more than what was allowed. Because we dropped a question, there were only 200 observations to use in that model. We controlled for the condition, the number of predictive text words used, and the question number and added a random effect for the participant.

We used a Chi-Square statistic for the remaining analysis: (1) did backspacing and/or deleting characters differ by condition; (2) did typing more than allowed in a field differ by condition; (3) was there a difference in memory task by condition; and (4) was there a difference in satisfaction by condition. We then investigated the significant Chi-squares by performing logistic regressions to determine the direction of the significance. Finally, we tallied preference of design.

4.3   Results

Table 4 includes the results of the experiment, including how many participants received each condition, the average time to answer a question by condition, the percent of questions where at least one character was deleted while typing; and the average satisfaction rating for each condition.

Table 4. Experiment 2 metrics by condition

Condition and description	No. of participants	Average time per screen in seconds (SE)	Percent of questions where at least one character was deleted	Average satisfaction rating (SE)
1–No countdown	14	110 (17)	55%	1.6 (0.3)
2–Countdown below the field	13	90 (13)	37%	1.5 (0.1)
3–Countdown above the field	13	83 (10)	37%	1.5 (0.2)

Burden as Measured By Time to Complete (Efficiency). Modeling log of time to complete and the log of time to type at the question level, we did not find a difference by condition for either time variable (log of screen completion time: $F = .32$, $p = .73$; log of typing time: $F = .54$, $p = .58$) with question number and the number of characters submitted as covariates and with a random effect for the participant.

Burden as Measured By Deleting Characters (Efficiency). Participants in condition 1 deleted at least one character while they typed in 55% of the questions, while in both character countdown conditions, participants deleted at least one character in 37% of the questions. Deleting characters was dependent on the condition using the Chi-Square statistic ($\chi^2(2) = 6.9$, $p = .03$). Using a logistic regression model, we found that participants were more likely to delete a character when typing in the condition without the character countdown than in either of the other two conditions with a character countdown ($p < .01$) when the question number was added as a covariate.

Accuracy (Effectiveness). There was no difference ($F = .39$, $p = 0.68$) in the number of characters typed by condition using a mixed model controlling for question number, the number of predictive words used, and adding a random effect for the participant.

Satisfaction. Chi-square results reveal no difference in satisfaction ratings between conditions ($\chi^2(6) = 6.0$, $p = 0.5$).

Preference for Character Countdowns: At the end of the experiment, participants were shown each of the designs, and we asked them about preference. Results were:

- 25% preferred the condition with no character countdown;
- 25% preferred the condition with the character countdown below the field;
- 20% preferred the condition with the character countdown above the field; and
- 30% had no preference.

However, several participants who selected the countdown above the box commented that when it was below the box they were/would not be able to see it when the keyboard appeared because the keyboard might cover up the lower half of the screen, including the character countdown.

Awareness of Character Limits. Based on how few participants selected the correct design used and how many tried to enter more information than the field would hold, we conclude that not everyone was aware of the countdown feature.

Identifying the Design Used: Only 8% of the participants who received the character countdown above the field correctly recalled their condition when presented with a picture of each of the designs. Forty-six percent of participants who received the character countdown below the field correctly selected that picture when asked which design they used. Fifty percent of the participants who did not receive a character countdown, reported that they did, when asked to select the design they used.

Trying to Type More than Allowed: There was no significant difference between the conditions in the number of times participants tried to type more than allowed ($\chi^2(2) = 1.5$, $p = .47$). Without a character countdown, participants attempted to type more than allowed in 24% of the questions; when the countdown was below the field, they attempted to type more than allowed in 21% of the questions and when it was above the field, they attempted to type more than allowed in 16% of the questions.

5 Experiment 3: Use of Predictive Text

5.1 Designs Tested in the Experiment

Experiment 3 focused on predictive text. The research question was whether predictive text within an open-ended question on a survey improved the respondent experience and led to higher data quality than without predictive text.

We used a within-subjects experimental design to investigate the topic. The survey had two questions: the person's race and the medicine the person uses. Since the population was older individuals, we expected most individuals to be on at least one prescription. One question would have predictive text and the other question would not.

Participants were randomly assigned to one of four question presentations to counter balance order effects. Thirty-seven participants completed the survey with two questions: 6 with predictive text on the first question of race; 8 with predictive text on the first question of medicine; 14 with predictive text on the second question of race; and 9 with predictive text on the second question of medicine. In total there were 74 data points. See Figs. 9, 10, 11 and 12.

Fig. 9. Race with predictive text   **Fig. 10.** Race without predictive text

Fig. 11. Prescription with predictive text   **Fig. 12.** Prescription without predictive text

After the two survey questions, we measured satisfaction by asking the participant to rate how easy or difficult it was to complete the survey on a 5-point scale with the endpoints labeled 1 = Very Easy and 5 = Very Difficult. The final task was for the participant to select whether he or she preferred predictive text or not. The participants were shown a paper with a screen shot of the race survey question with predictive text showing and without predictive text and asked which they preferred. Then, the participant was directed to the same preference question on the phone and asked to touch the option they preferred. We used this two-step approach because we found that on preference questions it was easier for participants to understand the preference when they could see both choices at the same time and you could not on the phone (which was not possible on the phone because of scrolling).

5.2 Analysis Methods

The app collected behavioral measures, including time on screen, number of touches per screen, and use of the backspace key. A touch was captured on any part of the screen except the QWERTY keyboard. The minimum number of touches for a question without the predictive text was two, one to enter the field, and one for the next button. The minimum number of touches if the participant used the predictive text was three: one to enter the field, one to touch the predictive text and one for the next button. The app also captured the race and medicine answers that had been entered and the participant's satisfaction score and design preference.

Burden was operationalized as time to complete the task (the amount of time on the screen) and the number of touches per screen. We calculated whether there were too many touches by taking the minimum number of touches by factor (predictive or not predictive) and then created a variable for each factor whether the number of touches was the minimum number or more than the minimum of touches.

We used two criteria to measure accuracy. Accuracy was measured by whether the entered data matched to a real word or not. The race and medicine answers were coded by a reviewer into two categories - matched and not matched, which we assumed meant accurate and not accurate. Accuracy was also measured by the use of backspace, with more backspacing suggesting more error.

Satisfaction scores were not particularly meaningful because it was a within-subjects design and each participant saw each of the two factors, but even still, there were no differences in those scores by the randomization order ($p > 0.8$).

We modeled log of time at the question level using a mixed model. The model with the untransformed time variable produced slightly skewed residuals. A total of 72 observations, instead of 74, was used in the model. Two observations were dropped from analysis because they were three standard deviations away from the mean time. In the model, we controlled for the factor of predictive text presence or absence and question content of race or medicine.

We used a Chi-Square statistic for the remaining analysis: (1) did the number of additional touches differ by the factor and (2) did backspacing differ by factor. We tallied preference of design.

We measured awareness of the predictive text feature by examining how many participants used the feature both in this experiment and in Experiment 2, where the feature was present on all questions.

5.3   Results

Table 5 includes the results of the experiment, including how many participants received each condition, the average time to answer a question by condition, the percent of questions where at least one character was deleted while typing; and the average satisfaction rating for each condition.

Table 5. Experiment 3 metrics by factor

Factor description	No. of observations	Average time per screen in seconds (SE)	Response matched a real word	Percent of too many touches	Preference (n = 37)
No predictive text	37	21 (4)	81%	15%	24%
Predictive text	35	16 (3)	91%	3%	76%

Burden Operationalized as Time to Complete (Efficiency). Modeling log of time to complete at the question level, we did not find a difference by factor (predictive text or not) with the question content as a covariate ($F = 1.5$, $p = 0.2$). It took significantly longer to answer the medicine question than the race question ($F = 13.2$, $p < .001$). A previous model demonstrated that there was no interaction between the question content and the availability of the predictive test ($F = .09$, $p = 0.8$).

Burden Operationalized as Number of Touches on Screen (Efficiency). The number of extra touches on the screen was not significantly different by factor ($\chi^2(1) - 1.0$, $p - 0.3$).

Accuracy Operationalized as Codable/Uncodable Answers (Effectiveness). Responses to the race and medicine questions were able to be matched to real words (e.g., coded) most of the time. Ninety-one percent of the answers to the questions where the predictive text was available matched a real word. Eighty-one percent of the answers to the questions without predictive text availability matched a real word. Overall, 14% of the responses did not match a real word, but this did not differ by factor (predictive text available or not available) ($\chi^2(1) = 1.6$, $p = 0.2$).

Accuracy Operationalized as Use of Backspace. Backspace was used in 24 out of 72 questions, or 33% of the time. Use of the backspace key also did not differ by whether the question had predictive text available or not ($\chi^2(1) = .03$, $p = 0.9$).

Overall Preference. Almost 76% of the 37 participants preferred the predictive text compared with just over 24% that preferred the text input fields without the predictive text option.

Knowledge of Predictive Text Options. Examining Experiment 2 data we conclude that most older adults were familiar with predictive text. While Experiment 2 did not evaluate predictive text, that feature was offered at all questions. In that experiment, only 3 of the 40 participants never used predictive text. But, predictive text was used in only 56% of the questions, so even when participants knew it was there, they did not necessarily use it.

In Experiment 3, not all participants who could have used the predictive text feature, did so. The feature was used in only 22 of the 35 questions or (63%). Use of the feature did not differ by question content ($\chi^2(1) = .09$, $p = 0.8$) nor by whether the predictive feature was available on the first question or second question ($\chi^2(1) = 0.36$, $p = 0.5$). When modeling time for only the questions with the predictive text available, time differs greatly by whether the predictive text was used or not. Those questions where it was used took only 11 s ($SE = 2$) (n = 22), while those questions where it was not used took 26 s ($SE = 7$) (n = 13) (t-statistic = 2.06, $p < .05$). However, it could be that the difference was due to participant characteristics that we could not measure. Based on Experiment 2 data, we believe participants knew about the predictive text.

6   Discussion

The purpose of this research was to learn more about how to design text input fields on mobile web surveys for older adults. Results from the first experiment confirmed our hypothesis that label placement does not affect time on the screen and that there was a preference for labels to be located above the field (Fig. 1) and the newer inline labels that move (Fig. 2). Other researchers have also found that label placement does not affect time on task for PCs but that labels above the field are preferable and lead to fewer eye movements [4, 5]. While we did not use eye tracking in these experiments and our participants were older adults, we nonetheless draw the same conclusion for field labels on mobile phones. Because we also gathered additional data from younger participants, we can conclude that the time-on-task finding does not differ by age of the user, but that older adults are slower than younger adults during survey completion with text input fields regardless of label placement. These results contribute to the literature in two ways. We found respondent interaction with field labels to be the same on smartphones as they were on PCs, suggesting that device size does not matter for optimal label placement. We also found a preference for the inline labels that move. Inline labels that move have the benefit of saving space and not relying on short term memory.

To our knowledge, results from Experiment 2 is the first to show that while character countdowns are not explicitly noticed by older adults, they do appear to reduce the action of users erasing letters (or words) which is in keeping with our hypothesis. Surprisingly however, character countdowns did not lead to a reduction in the amount of time spent within the field nor did they increase the amount of information shared. While fewer participants were aware of the feature when it was above the field then when it was below the field, we did hear a few participants comment while selecting the design they preferred. Comments included that they would not be able to see the feature when it was below the field when the keyboard appeared because the keyboard would cover the countdown. This suggests that for smartphones, it might be a good idea to keep the countdown feature above the field.

Our results from the third experiment show that there were no real time differences for questions with predictive text offered compared to those where it was not offered. This is in contrast to the work done on PCs, by [14] where the predictive text feature took longer than the plain text. This difference may be due in part to the mechanism for using predictive text on a PC. Using a keyboard and mouse may make the task of selecting a choice more difficult than the single touch needed on a mobile phone virtual keyboard. Our timing finding is also in contrast to the prediction by [13] that predictive text would save time on mobile. It is possible that this too was due to the mechanism used in the early 2000s where at that time, the type of mobile keypad had at least three letters and one number associated with one button. Those researchers did not use a full virtual keyboard as was used in this research. Virtual keyboards on mobile devices are now the norm and so our timing data did not follow the expectations of [13].

However, when predictive text was offered, we found participants spending less time per question when they used the predicted words compared to those who simply typed all their response, which perhaps is what [13] was suggesting. This finding combined with the overwhelming number of users that preferred the predictive text option suggest survey designers should offer predictive text on questions that would benefit from it (e.g., open-ended questions with a finite list of response options, such as a list of prescription drugs).

Contrary to our hypothesis, there were no differences in the number of errors in made with or without the predictive text offered nor the number of codable terms. This may be due to a ceiling effect as the percent of codable answers were high across the board. Future research should test additional open-ended questions with long finite lists of items to see if those coding results still hold.

7 Conclusions

This research set out to examine three features of open-text fields in surveys accessed by mobile phones and whether they lead to more efficient and accurate data entry by older adults and more satisfaction by older adults. We found that placing field labels above or using inline labels that move was preferred by older and younger adults; not all older adults were aware of a character countdown feature but having that feature reduced erasing characters; and including a predictive text option does not necessarily affect overall time or accuracy for questions when offered, but it is a preferred option.

8 Limitations

Our research used a convenience sample of older adults who traveled to community centers, owned smartphones for a year or more, and lived in the Washington, D.C. metropolitan area. While we are unaware of any regional differences in smartphone use, it could be that older adults who cannot travel outside of their homes would behave differently.

Disclaimer. This report is released to inform interested parties of research and to encourage discussion. The views expressed are those of the authors and not necessarily those of the U.S. Census Bureau.

Acknowledgements. We thank Russell Sanders, Brian Falcone, Ivonne Figueroa, Chris Antoun for their help in study plan discussions and data collection; Rebecca Keegan, Jonathan Katz, Alda Rivas, Shelley Feuer and Sabin Lakhe for data collection help; Eugene Loos, Paul Beatty, and Joanne Pascale for reviews of the paper; Luke Larsen for the statistical review; Kevin Younes for coordinating the recruiting, and staff at Metrostar for developing the apps used in this research.

References

1. Jarrett, C., Ganey, G.: Forms that Work: Designing Web Forms for Usability. Morgan Kaufmann, New York (2008)
2. Nielsen Norman Group: Form design quick fix: group form elements effectively using white space. NN/g Nielsen Norman Group Articles (2013). https://www.nngroup.com/articles/form-design-white-space/. Accessed 3 Dec 2018
3. Bojko, A., Schumacher, R.: Eye tracking and usability testing in form layout evaluation. In 38th International Symposium of Business Forms Management Association, Las Vegas (2008). https://www.researchgate.net/publication/264878180_Eye_Tracking_and_Usability_Testing_in_Form_Layout_Evaluation. Accessed 3 Dec 2018
4. Penzo, M.: Label placement in forms. UXmatters, issue, July 2006. https://www.uxmatters.com/mt/archives/2006/07/label-placement-in-forms.php. Accessed 3 Dec 2018
5. Seckler, M., Heinz, S., Bargas-Avila, J., Opwis, K., Tuch, A.: Designing usable web forms – empirical evaluation of web form improvement guidelines web. In: Conference on Human Factors in Computing Systems - Proceedings (2014). https://doi.org/10.1145/2556288. 2557265. https://www.researchgate.net/publication/263350416_Designing_Usable_Web_Forms_-_Empirical_Evaluation_of_Web_Form_Improvement_Guidelines_Web. Accessed 3 Dec 2018
6. Sherwin, K.: Placeholders in form fields are harmful. NN/g Nielsen Norman Group Articles (2018). https://www.nngroup.com/articles/form-design-placeholders/. Accessed 15 Jan 2019
7. Google material design – forms (2018). https://material.io/design/components/text-fields.html
8. Babich, N.: Designing perfect text field: clarity, accessibility and user effort (2016). https://uxplanet.org/designing-perfect-text-field-clarity-accessibility-and-user-effort-d03c1e26004b. Accessed 3 Dec 2018
9. Whitenton, K.: Website forms usability: top 10 recommendations. Nielsen Norman Group (2016). https://www.nngroup.com/articles/web-form-design/. Accessed 16 Nov 2018

10. Walsh, E., Brinker, J.: Short and sweet? Length and informative content of open-ended responses using SMS as a research mode. J. Comput.-Mediat. Commun. **21**(1), 87–100 (2016). https://doi.org/10.1111/jcc4.12146
11. Dunlop, M., Taylor, F.: Tactile feedback for predictive text entry. In: Proceedings of SIGCHI Conference on Human Factors in Computing Systems, pp. 2257–2260. ACM Press, Boston (2009)
12. Taylor, M.: 58 form design best practices & form UX examples. Blogpost from Venture Harbour (2008). https://www.ventureharbour.com/form-design-best-practices/. Accessed 15 Jan 2019
13. Dunlop, M., Crossan, A.: Predictive text entry methods for mobile phones. Pers. Technol. **4** (2–3), 134–143 (2000). https://doi.org/10.1007/BF01324120
14. Couper, M., Zhang, C.: Helping respondents provide good answers in web surveys. Surv. Res. Methods **10**(1), 49–64 (2016). https://doi.org/10.18148/srm/2016.v10i1.6273
15. Craik, F.I.M., Salthouse, T.A.: The Handbook of Aging and Cognition, 3rd edn. Psychology Press, New York (2008)
16. Fisk, A., Rogers, W.: Handbook of Human Factors and the Older Adult. Academic Press, San Diego (1997)
17. Salthouse, T.: When does age-related cognitive decline begin? Neurobiol. Aging **30**(4), 507–514 (2009)
18. Olmsted-Hawala, E., Nichols, E., Falcone, B., Figueroa, I.J., Antoun, C., Wang, L.: Optimal data entry designs in mobile web surveys for older adults. In: Zhou, J., Salvendy, G. (eds.) ITAP 2018. LNCS, vol. 10926, pp. 335–354. Springer, Cham (2018). https://doi.org/10. 1007/978-3-319-92034-4_26
19. Wang, L., et al.: Experimentation for developing evidence-based UI standards of mobile survey questionnaires. In: Proceedings of the 2017 CHI Conference Extended Abstracts on Human Factors in Computing Systems, pp. 2998–3004. ACM Press, Colorado (2017)

Atmosphere Sharing with TV Chat Agents for Increase of User's Motivation for Conversation

Shogo Nishimura[1,2], Masayuki Kanbara[1,2(✉)], and Norihiro Hagita[1,2]

[1] Nara Institute of Science and Technology, 8916-5 Takayama, Ikoma, Nara, Japan
{nishimura.shogo.nj0,kanbara}@is.naist.jp
[2] Advanced Telecommunications Research Institute International,
2-2 Hikari-dai, Seika, Kyoto 619-0237, Japan
hagita@atr.jp

Abstract. This paper proposes atmosphere sharing method with chatting agent during TV watching in order to improve user's motivation for conversation with the agent. Dialogue agents like interactive robots which include physical and virtual robots are expected to be companion to talk with the elderly or social isolated people to monitor or support them. Although the technologies of interactive robots, which are speech recognition and synthesis or auto chatting engine etc., have been developed, the agents are not continuously utilized for daily-life yet. We have developed TV chat agent which have light conversation with user during TV watching. To increase user's motivation of conversation with the agent, the agent gives interesting and funny talk by using SNS comments that are provided by users who are watching the TV program. This study attempts to share atmosphere, such as scene with exciting or of bursting into laughter, by using the TV chat agent.

Keywords: Human robot interaction · TV chat agent ·
Atmosphere sharing · Behavior modification

1 Introduction

This paper proposes atmosphere sharing method with chatting agent during TV watching in order to improve user's motivation for conversation with physical or virtual agents. Since people who live alone increase due to aging society or changing of life-style, they tend to lose the opportunity of conversation with other people. If people lack opportunity of daily-life, there is possibility that function of brain or health changes for the worse. It is important to increase the opportunity of conversation in daily-life for healthcare of the elderly people.

In order to overcome the problem, some studies attempted to give users opportunities of the daily conversation by using communication agents, such as interactive robots which have physical body or virtual agent in smart phone or tablet. Kanda et al. proposed that it is important to built trust relationship

© Springer Nature Switzerland AG 2019
J. Zhou and G. Salvendy (Eds.): HCII 2019, LNCS 11592, pp. 482–492, 2019.
https://doi.org/10.1007/978-3-030-22012-9_35

between people and interactive agents to accept the communication agents as social partner of in daily life [1].

Minami et al. [2] developed a TV chat robot that enables to reply quickly enough to seem spontaneous by making comments on social media. This robot was developed with the aim of promoting continuous dialog with a user. It chats while watching TV with the user. It allows to respond to what the user says as quickly as a human. Its dialog function allows it to compose comments derived texts from social media on what is being broadcast on the TV. This system embodies "sociality" and "favorite information" and so, it was proposed, would be able to motivate the user to communicate with a chat robot continuously. However, a mismatch occurs due to the time delay of the topic content of the TV program and the utterance contents of the robot, due to the time-lag between the robot's acquisition of texts from social media that relates to content of the TV show and the verbal output of the chatting robot. Also, the user allows to find it difficult to hear the sound of the TV and the robot when they are both "speaking" at the same time.

This paper develops atmosphere sharing methods with TV chat agents by using SNS comments which are submitted by user who is watching TV. This study also carries out evaluation experiments to investigate effectiveness of agents behavior in exciting and laughing scenes. This research compares effects of users in different conditions which are with/-out atmosphere sharing by using physical robots or virtual agents.

2   Related Work

In order for the chat robot to increase the opportunities of speech of the elderly and young people, they need provide suitable opportunities for dialog with the robot. Miyazawa et al. [3] identified the factors that promote the motivation of a user to engage in daily-use communication with robots. Two factors are required for effective interaction. One is "sociality," which means social nature or tendencies created by a user interacting with SNS communities via a chatting robot. To promote sociality, it is important to give the user a sense that the robot enables to listen to him or her. The other is "favorite information," which means providing unexpected or new information. Miyazawa et al. established that it is important that two factors should be incorporated into a robot whose function it is to communicate. We classify and summarize under two headings on-going research based on this point of view with regard to communication robots.

Minami et al. [2] aims to improve the sociality and favorite information of robots to encourage daily dialog in the long term. In order to realize this, they developed a TV chat robot by combining the method of Kobayashi et al. [6] which produced a dialog system that is smooth, and another method of Takahashi et al. [7] which generated one that is interesting. This robot has four dialog functions: backchannel [4], repetition [6], machine answering [5] and social media comments [7]. It is found out that the motivation of users to continuously use the robot is enhanced more when all the functions are combined than when it embodies each function alone or a combination of some functions. The problems with this system are indicated Fig. 2. One of the dialog functions, the "social media comments" function takes time to implement. The system needs to process comments written in social media on the web to arrive at the corresponding utterance of the chatting robot. Due to this time delay, there is a mismatch between the topic contents of the TV program (which might, by the time the utterance is ready, may have moved on to another topic) and what the robot says. Also, the television and chat robot may end up speaking simultaneously, making it difficult for the user to attend to both. There is a fear that these problems will reduce the motivation of the user to interact with the robot.

This paper develops atmosphere sharing methods with TV chat agents by using SNS comments which are submitted by user who is watching TV. Section 2 reviews related work of interaction technology with agents for continuous conversation. The overview of our proposed method is mentioned in Sect. 3. The experiment results of interactive agents with atmosphere sharing is shown in Sect. 4 and concluded in Sect. 5 (Fig. 1).

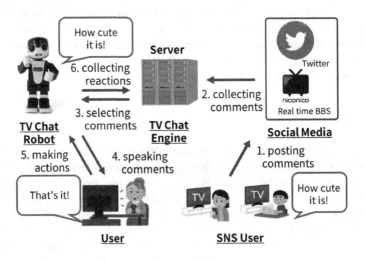

Fig. 1. TV chat agent system.

3   Development of Atmosphere Sharing with Agents

3.1   Atmosphere Sharing with TV Chat Agents

This research develops atmosphere share method with user and agents which are interactive robots as physical agent and CG agent as virtual agent during TV watching. Kinds of atmosphere generally include anger, sadness, fear, or exciting etc. This study focuses on exciting and laughing scenes because we assume that these situations can affect user's motivation for conversation. We handle the sport and comedy show programs for atmosphere sharing with TV chat agents. In order to determine agent's behavior for the atmosphere sharing, system has to estimate timing and level of the exciting or laughing situation in TV program. In general, There are two approaches to estimate the timing and level of them in TV program. First way is to detect atmosphere status of TV program by analyzing SNS comments which were submitted by TV viewers. General atmosphere status of TV program can be estimated by using reactions of TV viewers through SNS. Another way is to determine them by directly sensing the reaction of each TV viewer. This approach can estimate status of atmosphere individually because atmosphere is analyzed by a reaction of each TV viewer. In other words, the approach can personalize for atmosphere estimation. However, it is difficult to precisely estimate user's reaction from appearance of TV viewers. As above reason, This study employs the first approach which determines the atmosphere of TV program. In this paper, the effects of users are evaluated when they are watching TV with agents of which behaviors are decided by using estimated atmosphere.

3.2   Atmosphere Estimation of TV Program

This study handles excite and laughing scene as atmosphere in TV program for TV chat agents. This section describes estimation method of timing of atmosphere status changing and level of atmosphere status.

Timing Estimation of Atmosphere Status Changing. We assume that the atmosphere in TV program is decided by emotion of TV viewers. Therefore, in order to determine the atmosphere, the emotion of TV viewers is estimated by analyzing SNS comments submitted by them in real-time. Exciting scene can be estimated by detecting periods which SNS comments suddenly increase because the magnitude of exciting scene in TV program generally depends on the number of SNS comments. Related work proposed the detection method of important scene by using the number of comment in Twitter. In this study, exciting scenes are detected by Eqs. (1) and (2).

$$Threshold_C = \mu + 2\rho \tag{1}$$
$$C_i < Threshold_C \; : exciting \; scene \tag{2}$$

where C_i is the number of comments every 5 s. μ and ρ are average and standard deviation in a period which is not laughing scene for past 15 min, respectively.

The laughing scenes are detected by Eqs. (3) and (4).

$$Threshold_{L1} = \mu + \rho \tag{3}$$
$$L_i < Threshold_{L1} \; : laughing \; scene \tag{4}$$

where L_i is the number of comments which express laugh meaning every 5 s. μ and ρ are average and standard deviation in a period which is not exciting scene for past 15 min, respectively.

Level Estimation of Atmosphere Status. We also assume that there is level of the exciting and laughing scenes. This section describes definition of the levels of the exciting and laughing scenes and estimation methods of them. In this study, we define there are four levels of the exciting and laughing scenes The level of exciting scenes are estimated by form Eqs. (5) to (8).

$$C_i < Threshold_C : level0 \tag{5}$$
$$Threshold_C < C_i < 1.3 \times Threshold_C : level1 \tag{6}$$
$$1.3 \times Threshold_C < C_i < 1.6 \times Threshold_C : level2 \tag{7}$$
$$1.6 \times Threshold_C < C_i : level3 \tag{8}$$

where C_i is the number of comments every 5 s and $Threshold_C$ is estimated in previous section.

$$L_i < Threshold_L : level0 \tag{9}$$
$$Threshold_L < L_i < 1.3 \times Threshold_L : level1 \tag{10}$$
$$1.3 \times Threshold_L < L_i < 1.6 \times Threshold_L : level2 \tag{11}$$
$$1.6 \times Threshold_L < L_i : level3 \tag{12}$$

where L_i is the number of comments which express laugh meaning every 5 s and $Threshold_L$ is estimated in previous section.

3.3 Behavior Determination

This section explain control method of agent behavior in exciting and laughing scene for atmosphere sharing. There are two types of interactive agents; physical and virtual agents. Virtual agent is drawn by computer graphics in smart phone or tablet. Physical agent is real interactive robot which has physical body. Appearance of both agents are human-like. Smart phone application "Davelive" (amirbo tech Inc.) is used as virtual agents as shown in Fig. 2. Outside body of interactive robot "Kabo-chan" (PIP Inc.) is used as physical robots. Two servo motors are installed at both solder joints of the physical robots to wave robot's arm.

TV chat engine which gathers SNS comments in real-time provided by [2] is utilized for deciding utterance contents. A server of the engine sends utterance contents and atmosphere information estimated in previous section every seven seconds. Clients, such as smart phone which provides virtual robot or small computer which controls physical robots, talk based-on information received from the chat engine server.

In exciting scene, atmosphere is expressed by speaking with multiple agents at same time. Behavior of multiple agents are controlled based-on levels as follows.

level 0 one agent utters one comment.
level 1 two agents utter one comment.
level 2 three agents utter one comment.
level 3 five agents utter one comment.

Fig. 2. Agent behavior in exciting scene.

In case of virtual agents, some virtual robots appear based on the levels as shown in Fig. 2. On the other hand, by using physical agents, five physical robots are prepared.

In laughing scene, atmosphere is expressed by speaking with multiple agents at same time. In addition, three levels (small, medium, and loud) of laughing voices set up in advance Behavior of multiple agents are controlled based-on levels as follows.

level 0 one agent utters one comment.
level 1 one agent utters one comment and other one agent gives small laugh.
level 2 one agent utters one comment and other two give medium laugh.
level 3 one agent utters one comment and other four give loud laugh.

In case of virtual agents, some virtual robots appear based on the levels as shown in Fig. 3.

4   Evaluation Experiments of Atmosphere Sharing

This section describes experiments of atmosphere sharing during TV watching with virtual and physical hat agents and effects of users against the agents.

Fig. 3. Agent behavior in laughing scene.

4.1 Experimental Environment

For exciting scene, football game is selected as TV program because timing of exciting periods can be detected easily and there is small differences among individuals. In this experiments, sportscasting of football game between Japan and Uruguay on October 16th 2018 is used for exciting scene. On the other hand, Japanese comedy show is selected as TV program contents for laughing scene as shown in Fig. 4. TV program contents for experiments are made by collecting SNS comments about these TV programs. As physical agents, customized physical robots are used, and each robot takes clothes of different color to recognize robot easily. Voice of the each robot is synthesized by using VioceText Web API. Behaviors of the agents are decided in advance due to repeatability.

As shown in Fig. 5, we ask the 11 subjects to use the chat robot as they watch four types of TV programs each in the case of conditions as follows.

- **without** atmosphere sharing, **virtual** agents
- **with** atmosphere sharing, **virtual** agents
- **without** atmosphere sharing, **physical** agents
- **with** atmosphere sharing, **physical** agents.

Subjects answer a questionnaire after each of TV watching sections. The contents of the questionnaire is as follows. The questionnaire takes the form of 7-point Likert scales.

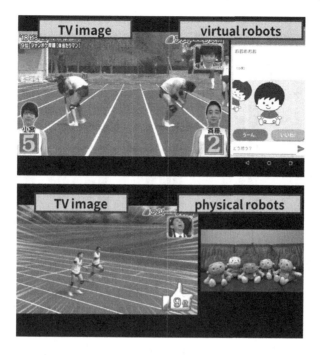

Fig. 4. Movie contents in laughing scene with physical and virtual agents.

Fig. 5. Experimental environment with physical and virtual agents.

In exciting scene:

- Do you feel exciting between robots?
- Do you feel friendliness?
- Do not you feel strange?
- Do you feel motivation to use?
- Do you feel empathy?

In laughing scene:

- Do you feel fun between robots?

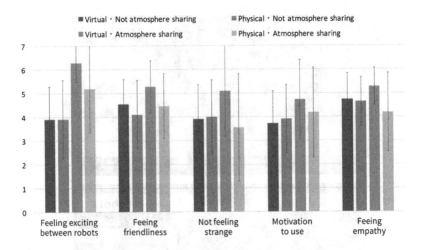

Fig. 6. Results of subjective evaluation in exciting scene.

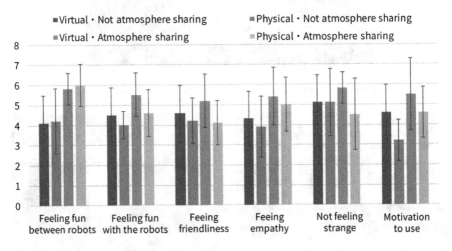

Fig. 7. Results of subjective evaluation in laughing scene.

- Do you feel fun with the robots?
- Do you feel friendliness?
- Do you feel empathy?
- Do not you feel strange?
- Do you feel motivation to use?

4.2 Results and Discussion

Figure 6 shows results of subjective evaluation in atmosphere sharing of exciting scene. In case of using virtual agents, score under condition with atmosphere sharing is compared with that under condition without sharing, and the significant value difference ($p < 0.05$) is shown. When atmosphere sharing is provided, score under condition using virtual agents is compared with that under condition using physical agents, and the significant value difference ($p < 0.05$) is shown. From the results, effects of atmosphere sharing in exciting scene is better than one without it regardless of appearance of agents.

Figure 7 shows results of subjective evaluation in atmosphere sharing of laughing scene. In case of using virtual and physical agents, score under condition with atmosphere sharing is compared with that under condition without sharing, and the significant value difference ($p < 0.05$) is shown. When atmosphere sharing is provided, score under condition using virtual agents is compared with that under condition using physical agents, and the significant value difference ($p < 0.05$) is shown. From the results, condition with virtual agents get higher score than one with physical agents. As a reason for that, we think there are some functions which only system of virtual agents have. For examples, only virtual agents have face expression and utterance sentences is displayed on smart phone.

5   Conclusion

This paper has proposed atmosphere sharing method with chatting agent during TV watching in order to improve user's motivation for conversation with the agent. We have developed TV hat agent which have light conversation with user during TV watching. To increase user's motivation of conversation with the agent, the agent gives interesting and funny talk by using SNS comments that are provided by users who are watching the TV program. This study attempts to share atmosphere, such as scene with enthusiasm or of bursting into laughter, by using the TV chat agent. A behavior of the chat agents is decided by estimating the atmosphere of TV audience by analyzing SNS comments about TV program. It is possible to dynamically change the amount of utterance of the robot according to the excitement and laughing section and the level, and it is considered that more natural excitement can be realized. By comparing the excitement of people with one of SNS during TV watching, features of them are extract and characterize. In addition, by analyzing the feature promoting excitement impression, appropriate SNS comments for TV chat agents can be selected. As a result of subjective evaluation of the user by the robot utterance reflecting each feature, it was confirmed that the utterance of a human who contains a lot of sensuous verbs gives the impression of excitement to the user with a significant difference recognized.

Acknowledgments. A part of this research was supported by the JSPS Foundation 18H03274 and Research Complex Promotion Program.

References

1. Kanda, T., Sato, R., Saiwaki, N., Ishiguro, H.: A longitudinal field trial for human-robot interaction in an elementary school. J. Hum. Interface Soc. **7**(1), 27–37 (2005)
2. Minami, H., Kawanami, H., Kanbara, M., Hagita, N.: Chat robot coupling machine responses and social media comments for communication conversation. In: MUSTEH (2016)
3. Miyazawa, K., Tokoyo, T., Masui, Y., Matsuo, N., Kikuchi, H.: Factors of interaction in the spoken dialogue system with high desire of sustainability. Trans. IE-ICE (A) **95**(1), 27–36 (2012)
4. Matsubara, D., Ueda, H.: A robot listening to users grumble. IEICE Techn. Rep. MVE **111**(38), 45–50 (2011)
5. NTT DOCOMO: DOCOMO to Launch Shabette Concier Voice-agent Application
6. Kobayashi, Y., Yamamoto, D., Yokoyama, S.: De-sign targeting voice interface robot capable of active listening. In: Proceedings of the HRI 2010, pp. 161–162 (2010)
7. Takahashi, T., Kanbara, M., Hagita, N.: A social media mediation robot to increase an opportunity of conversation for elderly: mediation experiments using single or multiple robots. IEICE Techn. Rep. CNR **113**(84), 31–36 (2013). (in Japanese)
8. Huang, H., Shibusawa, S., Hayashi, Y., Kawagoe, K.: Proposal of a numeric model of mutual evaluation between the participants in dyadic active listening conversation for developing listener agents. J. Hum. Interface Soc. **18**(4), 65–76 (2016)
9. Pollack, M.: Intelligent technology for an aging population: the use of AI to assist elders with cognitive impairments. AI Mag. **26**(2), 9–24 (2005)
10. Gockley, R., et al.: Designing robots for long-term social interaction. In: International Conference on IEEE/RSJ, pp. 1338–1343. IEEE (2005)
11. Ritter, A., Cherry, C., Dolan, B.: Data-driven response generation in social media. In: Proceedings of the 2011 Conference on Empiricial Methods in Natural Language Processing (EMNLP), pp. 583–593 (2011)

Interfaces of Medication Reminder Applications: An Analysis Aimed at the Elder Age

Jaqueline Donin Noleto$^{(\boxtimes)}$, Vítor José Costa Rodrigues ,
Rhenan Castelo Branco Cirilo Carvalho ,
and Francisco Ribeiro dos Santos Júnior

Federal University of Paraíba, João Pessoa, Paraíba, Brazil
jdonin@eng.ci.ufpb.br

Abstract. Despite how technologies are, nowadays, becoming integrated to several branches of society, there are still many groups with trouble to follow these technological advancements. Among them, the group that most likely suffers from this difficulty are the elders. An area strongly benefited by technology is health, currently counting with multiple mobile applications for smartphones, designed to upkeep the users' health. In this context, the current paper proposes an analysis of interfaces from medication reminder apps focused on the elderly. The following techniques were implemented: An Usability Test through Exploration (UTE) to evaluate easiness in learning by exploration, the System Usability Scale (SUS) method to ascertain the usability level of said applications and the Heuristic Evaluation of their Interfaces. With those techniques, it was possible to build a solid benchmark to evaluate the level of elder-friendliness of an app in the given context. Results from the case study have shown that the apps lack a design focused on the elder public, which might have led to troubles during the tests performed with volunteers. The expert-based results have also found general interface issues on these apps that may need to be improved.

Keywords: Technology · Elderly · Interface analysis · Applications

1 Introduction

In Brazil, as stated by the Brazilian Institute for Geography and Statistics (*Instituto Brasileiro de Geografia e Estatística*, IBGE), the number of people over 60 years old has surpassed the milestone of 30.2 million in 2017, presenting a 18% growth in the group over the last five years [1], which means that, in a growing motion, this group contains more than 14% of the country's total population.

A distressing characteristic related to the advanced age is the considerable loss in cognitive skills, specially those related to memory [3]. On top of this populational ageing, and all that comes with it, the number of people with

© Springer Nature Switzerland AG 2019
J. Zhou and G. Salvendy (Eds.): HCII 2019, LNCS 11592, pp. 493–512, 2019.
https://doi.org/10.1007/978-3-030-22012-9_36

chronic diseases is also increasing and, therefore, the consumption of drugs and the use polypharmacotherapy among said people [2].

Associated with the consumption of drugs, there is a problem that has become a matter of concern. According to reports by the World Health Organization (WHO), it's estimated that around half the patients with chronic diseases don't actually take their medication as prescribed [4].

In this context, the adoption of technology may be an alternative solution to the correct usage of medication and also a useful tool for health professionals to follow their patients along their treatment. In contrast to that, barriers of cognitive, motion and, in some cases, financial origins may be limiting factors to the access of new technology by the elderly [5].

Facing what has been exposed, and considering the special needs of the elderly, as well as the increase in smartphone usage by them, the current paper aims to perform a mapping of market solutions for mobile apps, regarding medication reminders. By using the SUS method, UTE and Nielsen's heuristics, evaluations were performed in terms of interface usability and easiness of learning from the users.

The remainder of this paper is organized as follows: In Sect. 2, we discuss weaknesses found in related works on the field as some justification for the proposed methodology; In Sect. 3, we present the apps evaluated in this paper and the techniques used on said evaluations; Followed by Sect. 4, which describes, in detail, the actual procedure of evaluation; Afterwards, in Sect. 5, we present the results obtained through the process and how they are interpreted; Finally, in Sect. 6, we give our final thoughts on the matter approached, on the methods applied and on the results obtained.

2   Related Works

By researching the state-of-art, some deficiencies were verified along related works dealing with evaluation of medication reminder apps regarding the elderly. Among those deficiencies, the most proeminent were the small number of apps evaluated per work and the lack of details on some of the methods used and results found.

To give context, there were chosen three papers related to the approached theme, that were used as basis to develop the methodology of this article.

The first paper, entitled *Medication Management Apps: Usable by Older Adults?* [6], performed its analysis solely on the *Medisafe* app, with two usability experts applying Nielsen's heuristics. Results obtained show that the app present a couple of usability problems related to layout and interface design, as well as difficulties found by the experts in relation to certain features of the app, like the *Medfriend* feature, that allows the register of trusted contacts to aid the users in their treatments.

The second work, entitled *Acceptance Factors of Mobile Apps for Diabetes by Patients Aged 50 or Older: A Qualitative Study* [7], is a study focused on the acceptance of elder people in relation to the usage of mobile apps for aiding in diabetes control. The evaluation had 32 participants with an average age of 68.8 years. In total, two apps were evaluated, *OnTrack Diabetes version 2.8.8* and *Glucose Monitor Version 2.7*. Difficulty on interacting with the applications was among one of the main reports of the evaluation group, which resulting in resistance by them on using solution proposed by the researchers, as well as complaints about the lack of additional benefits and resources on the presented apps.

The third article, with the title *Design and Evaluation of a Medication Adherence Application with Communication for Seniors in Independent Living Communities* [8], proposes the development of a tablet-based app focused on the elderly with the purpose of reminding them of medications that must be consumed. In addition to that, a web platform was also developed, with the purpose of helping caretakers and guardians in keeping up with the ingestion of medication by the elders. During the tests with the app, sixteen participants were recruited with an average age of 66 years. During three months, those participants used tablets provided by the developers with the app installed on them. In this period, users were instructed to answer all medication reminders and report changes in medication. Resulting from this work's feedback, a series of recommendations were defined that can be used when developing apps focused on the elderly.

3 Materials and Methods

Apps that promise to help in the control of medication are pretty common, with many available solutions in Apps Stores. Among the better reviewed, there are apps who stand out with functionalities such as stock control, posology and reminder notifications. However, as it is common in commercial products, its development is not design for a niche, meaning that it doesn't seek to attend to the needs of a specific group, but instead to reach the largest number possible of people.

In that case, to select the scope of evaluated apps, it was considered only those developed for smartphones with Android as their running operational system, available to download at the Google Play service, from which only three were selected. These three apps, *Medisafe*, *My Therapy* and *Cuco Health* were chosen according to their number of downloads and number of positive reviews by users.

The *Medisafe* app has, until the writing of this paper, more than 1 million downloads and over 167 thousand reviews. It allows its users to add medication, receive reminders and learn how to correctly use this resource. According to the developers, their goal is to offer tools and support so that users may correctly take their medication.

MyTherapy, until now downloaded by more than 500 thousand users, having over 13 thousand reviews, has the unique feature of Drug Stock Control, where users may register their medications in use.

Cuco Health, a Brazilian app that counts with more than 50 thousand downloads and over 3.2 thousand reviews. It offers the feature of Health History, which logs all data of previous treatments done with the app, besides also allowing the

496   J. D. Noleto et al.

creation of a team of "caretakers", with messages and tips about treatments and diseases.

Of all three apps evaluated, none possess in their description or in their advertising any explicit usability features aimed at the elder public. All three propose mildly similar solutions for medication reminding, however they show no engagement in attending a specific demographic.

3.1   Selecting the Evaluation Techniques

In order to evaluate usability, three techniques were used. The first was the SUS method, proposed in *SUS - A quick and dirty usability scale* [9]. On this paper, the author states that, in many cases, when in need of evaluating the general usability of a system, it is desirable to have measurements that aren't too complex or extense and also don't demand too much effort to apply, but also present a certain level of reliability. Thus, in his work, a simple system its proposed, containing ten items that offer a global view in subjective evaluations of usability based on a Likert scale [10], that is, using a scale built on that model, the evaluator may indicate his degree of agreement or disagreement to certain statements about the subject evaluated, with values ranging from 1 (strongly disagree) to 5 or 7 (strongly agree) (Fig. 1).

Fig. 1. An example of likert scale application

In order to calculate the SUS score of a system, the evaluator must use the following equation:

$$S = [\sum_{o=1}^{5}(Q_o - 1) + \sum_{e=1}^{5}(5 - Q_e)] \cdot 2.5 \tag{1}$$

Where S is the normalized SUS score obtained on a single evaluation, Q_o is the individual value of an odd answer and Q_e is the individual value of an even answer.

It's highly suggested to perform multiple evaluations for each systems, to obtain a more realistic average score, where:

$$S_{avg} = \sum_{i=1}^{k}(\frac{S_i}{k}) \tag{2}$$

Where S_{avg} is the average SUS score, S_i is the value of a single score and k is the total number of evaluations performed on that system. This average normalized score may range from 0 to 100 [9].

Through the use adjective ratings, based on statistical results, a survey score may be considered above average (over 50% of statistical results), if bigger than 70.5 and it may be considered good it if bigger than 71.4 [11].

According to Research Collective [12], there are a couple of advantages in using the SUS method, which are:

- It has a Cronbach's Alpha rating of 0.92. This coefficient is rated from 0 to 1 and measures the level of reliability in a research-oriented survey;
- It might be used for a plethora of different systems and products to aid and evaluate the users' experiences;
- It can be used even with small sample sizes;
- It's cost less and it's questions may be easily found on internet researches, being heavily mentioned and/or utilized by works focused on usability scale.

The core objectives of a system with good usability include, a raise in productivity, a shortage in training costs, reduction of user errors, a precision increase during use and interpretation of data and the decrease in technical support necessity. With that in mind, the second technique approached was the User Based UTE.

The goal of this evaluation was to analyse the easiness in learning through exploration in mobile apps and to observe which main difficulties the volunteers may face. This technique was implemented by following a set of four basic steps [14,15]:

1. **Preparation:** Where the tasks that will integrate the evaluation are defined;
2. **Gathering and Interpretation of Data:** Part where the execution of tasks is observed;
3. **Consolidation of Results:** Where the data produces conclusive information;
4. **Result Reporting:** When information is formally registered and submitted as feedback or guidelines.

The employment of this technique facilitates the identification of day-by-day issues faced by the average user. An user based evaluation is also more prone to produce unbiased results, as the lack of expertise offers a less subjective and more practical view of the system. And although sometimes it isn't possible to find willing volunteers to perform evaluations for free, this is a method without any cost of elaboration, requiring only the planning of which activities are going to be performed.

The third app evaluation technique was performed through the use of the ten Nielsen's heuristics. The heuristic evaluation is made by observing an interface and trying to obtain an opinion about what is good and bad on it [16]. Ideally, evaluations are conducted under certain rules, such as those listed in typical guideline documents. In this case, the heuristic evaluation follows the guidelines proposed below [17]:

- **Visibility of the system status:** the user is informed about system status, whether they are the current status or generated only after performing an action;
- **Compatibility of the system with the real world:** the system must be simple and use a vocabulary which is the closest possible from colloquial language;
- **Control and freedom for the user:** the system must provide ways so that the user may easily undo an action that he considers wrong;
- **Consistency and standardization:** the system must be consistent over the use of interface elements in a way that avoids causing confusion or influencing the user to commit mistakes, e.g., standardization of buttons, menus and etc;
- **Prevention of Errors:** the system must be designed in a way to minimize errors that users may commit;
- **Recognition instead of Memorization:** the system must be simple and intuitive, in a way that the user shouldn't need to remember steps to perform a task;
- **Providing shortcuts:** the system must provide ways that allow the user to have experience with the system in order to execute tasks more rapidly;
- **Minimalist design and aesthetics:** the system must be as simple as possible, avoid irrelevant functionalities and data;
- **Helping the user to recognize, diagnose and correct errors:** the system must provide clear error messages, that indicate to the user that something wrong has happened and also how to proceed to correct such errors;
- **Help and documentation:** the system must provide a help functionality for the user, be it in the form of system documentation or some sort of communication channel for questions and doubts.

To qualify the severity level of disagreement with the heuristics, a scale from 1 to 4 was used, on which:

1. It's not faced as a problem of usability.
2. Aesthetic problem, no need to be corrected, unless there is available time and resources.
3. Serious Problem, needs to be corrected and may cause problems on system usage.
4. Extremely Serious Problem, must be corrected at once, creates serious troubles in usage and might drive users to abandon the system.

The heuristics are largely consolidated when it comes to interface evaluation. It requires at least one professional familiarized with its guidelines and can be done with a small group of people. In a short window of time it's possible to obtain feedback about what works and what doesn't on an interface. The original guidelines proposed by Nielsen can easily be found online, facilitating the access. There are also variations on the heuristics focused to specific systems and products.

4   Performing the Evaluations

In order to proceed with the evaluations, thirteen elders from the city of João Pessoa, Brazil, were approached to join the research as *users* (also interchangeably referred as *volunteers* on the remainder of this paper). Their were all locals with ages ranging from 60 to 78 years old. Also, three of the authors also performed as *usability experts*.

The chosen research site was the Informatics Laboratory, at the Center of Exact and Nature Sciences of the Federal University of Paraíba (UFPB). While performing the tests, all volunteer evaluators used their own personal smartphones.

The participation of the selected *users* was part of a practical activity realized under the project of University Extension denominated "Basic Informatics for Elders", hosted at the UFPB in the period between March and December of the year 2018. Because of that, the evaluations that made use of results provided by volunteer evaluation followed the ethics guidelines present on the Official Submission Notice of the Institution's program of University Extension, called PROBEX/2018.

In a beforehand interview, several *users* reported to be using, at least, one type of medication, varying from two to ten pills a day and occasionally had difficulties reminding dosages of their medications. After being informed about the subject of the research, they presented themselves as interested, curious and surprised about the existence of applications focused on aiding with that kind of problem.

4.1   Usability Evaluation Through the SUS Method

The usability evaluations of the chosen apps (Medisafe, MyTherapy and CUCO Health) through the SUS method, were realized by all the thirteen selected *users*.

Each *volunteer* was guided in to the process of installing all three apps in their own devices. Prior to the beginning of the tests, they were deprived of any instructions on how to use the applications and were advised not to solve any questions they had during the whole process.

The *users* had the opportunity to choose one of their day-to-day therapy or to choose one fictitious therapy suggested by the researchers. After all of them had registered their selected medication prescription, they were instructed to answer a survey containing ten Likert-based questions in relation to the experience they had using the current app. This process was repeated with every *volunteer* for all the three apps evaluated.

The survey presented to the *users* contained the statements listed below. Odd-numbered statements take a positive view about the app while Even-numbered statements take a negative view:

1. I think I would like to use this app frequently;
2. I think it's unnecessarily complex;
3. I think it's easy to use;

4. I think I would need help from a person with technical knowledge to use it;
5. I think that many functions of the app are very well integrated;
6. I think that the app presents a lot of inconsistency;
7. I imagine that people will learn to use the app quickly;
8. I though the app was clumsy to use;
9. I felt confident while using the app;
10. I had to learn new things before I could use the app.

4.2   Easiness of Learning via Usability Testing Through Exploration

For the exploration usability text, three of the thirteen *users* were randomly selected. The objective of this evaluation was to determine the difficulty that users with zero to minimal background of mobile apps might face when learning how to navigate them.

Two tasks were selected as goals for the *users*. They had limited time to figure out the process on how to do them on each app. These tasks were:

- Finish the User Registration;
- Add a Medication Reminder.

Since these evaluators had the apps already installed on their smartphones and had a small knowledge on how to use them since they previously performed a SUS application, the test consisted on the usability experts following each *users'* walk-through during (x minutes) and observing the issues they faced to complete the proposed tasks.

4.3   Interface Evaluation Through Nielsen's Heuristics

The heuristic analysis of the apps' interfaces were performed by three usability experts, each evaluating all three apps. The application of Nielsen's heuristics occurred through expert-based usability walkthrough of pre-selected system features, from which the evaluators deemed which elements were out of usability standards.

The evaluated features on the apps were User Registration and Medication Adding/Insertion. In order to evaluate these, a worksheet was created, itemizing the Ten Heuristics. Screens on which no problems were found, according to the experts, received an "OK" pass and weren't included in the results described below.

After the expert usability test of the mentioned features, all three evaluations were confronted against each other, with the purpose of overlapping the issues found by each expert in order to obtain more fine results.

With these early results in hand, in order to apply the Heuristics, a fictitious *persona* was used, prescribed with a fictitious treatment, in order to create a standard for all evaluations to follow.

Persona: Maria Silva, 66 years old.

Maria has asthma and an early stage of pneumonia. In a checkup at her local Community Health Center (*Posto de Saúde da Família*, PSF), in the *bairro* where she lives, Mangabeira, in João Pessoa. Her doctor prescribed the following drugs and dosages:

- **Ventolin/Salbutamol:** One inhalation every six hours;
- **Amoxicillin:** One pill every twelve hours;
- **Budesonide:** One inhalation every eight hours.

5   Results and Discussions

The following results are presented and discussed separately for each method implemented in order to verify their degree of credibility and, afterwards, are crossed and combined in order to create a definitive diagnose for each evaluated app.

5.1   Results Given by SUS Method

Here, the obtained results from the evaluation of each app are represented. They are disposed in a table format, containing the individual grades from each *user* to each question, raw mean scores for each question (the mean of each raw score given to that question through all 13 evaluations), SUS score for each evaluation and, finally, the average SUS score (S_{avg}) for the app.

Table 1 contains data related to Medisafe app.

Table 1. Results from SUS evaluation on Medisafe.

User	Q_1	Q_2	Q_3	Q_4	Q_5	Q_6	Q_7	Q_8	Q_9	Q_{10}	SUS score
1	3	4	5	2	4	3	2	1	5	3	65
2	5	1	5	1	5	1	5	1	5	1	100
3	3	1	5	1	5	1	5	1	5	1	95
4	5	2	4	2	4	2	5	5	2	5	60
5	5	1	5	1	5	1	5	1	5	1	100
6	5	1	5	1	5	1	5	1	5	1	100
7	4	2	4	1	2	2	3	1	3	2	70
8	2	2	5	1	4	1	4	1	5	1	85
9	5	5	5	5	5	1	4	4	5	5	60
10	5	1	1	5	5	5	5	5	5	5	50
11	5	1	5	1	5	1	5	1	5	1	100
12	5	1	5	1	5	1	5	1	5	1	100
13	5	1	5	1	5	1	5	1	5	1	100
Mean	4.38	1.77	4.54	1.77	4.54	1.62	4.46	1.85	4.62	2.15	83.46

According to the results shown above, the Medisafe app obtained very good raw mean scores on questions that evaluated easiness, functionality integration and confidence in use (questions 3, 5 and 9). Besides, on questions 2, 4 and 6, who deals with negative usability aspects, it obtained the lowest scores.

Table 2 contains data related to MyTherapy app.

Table 2. Table captions should be placed above the tables.

User	Q_1	Q_2	Q_3	Q_4	Q_5	Q_6	Q_7	Q_8	Q_9	Q_{10}	SUS Score
1	5	4	5	3	3	1	4	2	5	1	77.5
2	5	5	5	4	5	1	5	1	3	1	77.5
3	5	2	2	3	2	2	5	4	5	2	65
4	2	3	5	2	2	5	5	5	5	1	57.5
5	5	5	5	5	5	5	5	5	5	5	50
6	5	5	5	5	5	5	5	5	5	5	50
7	4	2	5	2	3	2	4	5	4	2	67.5
8	2	5	5	5	2	5	2	5	5	5	27.5
9	5	5	2	1	5	5	4	3	5	1	65
10	5	5	5	1	5	5	5	5	5	5	60
11	5	5	5	2	5	1	5	1	5	1	87.5
12	5	5	5	5	5	5	5	5	5	5	50
13	5	5	5	5	5	5	5	5	5	3	55
Mean	4.46	4.31	4.54	3.31	4	3.62	4.54	3.92	4.77	2.85	60.77

On the evaluation of MyTherapy, the raw mean scores with highest values were from questions who deal with easiness, learning and confidence during use (3, 7 and 9). Questions who dealt with negative aspects, however, also received high scores, resulting in a negative feedback when it comes to using this app and, by consequence, a significant decrease in its SUS average score.

Table 3 contains data related to CUCO Health app.

In the CUCO Health evaluation, questions about easiness, learning and confidence during use obtained low scores in relation to the other two apps and, in addition to that, similar to what happened in MyTherapy, it also received high scores in questions about negative aspects, leading to the worst SUS average score among the evaluated apps.

According to the adopted SUS average score standard (70.5 for an overall positive result and 71.4 for an "Good" classification), only Medisafe obtained enough points to be ranked as "Good", presenting a remarkable level of usability.

The other two apps didn't obtained a satisfactory rank, altough, by Brooke's adjective ranking [9], they were defined as the "OK" neutral rank, meaning that, with minor improvements, they would be eligible to a positive classification.

Also regarding the reproved apps, both obtained similar point contribution on the even-numbered questions, since the sum of all even raw mean scores of those apps only differs by a value of 0.1, which means that both have presented resembling results in relation to their negative aspects of usability. This leads to the conclusion that, what made MyTherapy as the second place was it's good

Table 3. Table captions should be placed above the tables.

User	Q_1	Q_2	Q_3	Q_4	Q_5	Q_6	Q_7	Q_8	Q_9	Q_{10}	SUS Score
1	5	3	5	3	4	2	5	2	5	2	80
2	5	4	5	5	2	5	5	5	5	2	52.5
3	3	5	5	1	3	5	2	5	2	2	42.5
4	5	2	5	4	4	5	3	2	4	4	60
5	5	5	5	2	5	5	5	5	5	5	57.5
6	5	5	5	5	5	5	5	5	5	5	50
7	1	2	2	4	3	2	3	2	3	1	52.5
8	1	4	1	4	2	4	1	1	1	4	22.5
9	5	1	5	3	5	1	2	2	5	1	85
10	5	5	1	1	5	5	5	1	5	1	70
11	5	5	5	4	5	5	5	5	5	1	62.5
12	5		2	1	5	5	5	5	5	5	52.5
13	5	5	5	5	5	5	5	5	5	5	50
Mean	4.23	3.92	3.92	3.23	4.08	4.15	3.92	3.46	4.23	2.92	56.73

scoring in positive aspects of usability, showing that positive aspects have a slightly larger impact on the *user*'s experience.

5.2   Results Given by UTE Method

The first app evaluated through this method was CUCO Health. The first steps on the app induced volunteers to commit several, otherwise avoidable, mistakes, as they had trouble in finding the starting screen of the app, since it has three initial screens showing a little of how the app works, but only actually giving options for the *user* in the last one, with the button "Let's begin", which leads the user to a user registration screen. In said screen, two *volunteers* were able to find a smaller button to "Enter without Social Media" and the other one managed to register using the button to login using a *Google* account.

After performing the registration, the *users* were guided by an animated assistant called *CUCO*, which gave them instructions on how to access the main screen. None of the *users* reported trouble in this step, as well as in the next step of finding the Medication Register screen, due to a strong symbolic representation for that feature (a red button with an addition sign). Guided by the assistant CUCO, all three managed to perform both tasks easily.

The second app evaluated was Medisafe, which presented a smaller amount of steps to Medication Register in relation to CUCO Health and, due to that, was perceived as more intuitive, according to *users*. Their main issue was to write the name of the medication being added, since the smartphone touch keyboard didn't activated along with the screen. Two *users* tried to activate the keyboard by randomly touching the screen, while the third tapped directly over the text box, activating the keyboard. To finish the therapy registration, the app presented the finishing button "DONE" in multiple locations of the screen, which facilitated the completion of the task, according to the users.

At last, MyTherapy was evaluated. And so as the one prior to it, MyTherapy conducted it's *users* very well to the medication register screen. However, there were issues with the lack of information when the *volunteers* tried to finish the insertion, as all three reported an error message appearing. The larger number of data required during registration led to certain confusion. The location of the "Save" button, which finishes the registration, localized on the top part of the screen, also caused trouble to the *users*, which took a notable amount of time to find it.

While performing the medication register, it was solicited that the reminder notification was set for 30 min after the evaluation, so that it's main core feature, the medication reminding, could also be evaluated. Due to time constraints, however, each *user* only evaluated the notification on a single app.

On the CUCO Health reminder, the *user* identified that the two buttons who appeared were to either confirm or not the ingestion. He stated to have found interesting that, when the "Don't Confirm" button was pressed in a therapy notification, the app visually represented that fact by decreasing the number on the Health meter.

On MyTherapy, the ingestion notification was selected by the *user* through the push of a button. A screen with a medication list was opened, but the *user* was unable to take any further actions, as the app didn't clearly specified that he should have informed about the ingestion.

On Medisafe, the notification appears with the name and color registered for the medication along with three buttons with texts "Ignore", "Take" and "Postpone". By clicking in "Ignore", the *user* faced a box on which he would choose one of few pre-defined reasons for the non-ingestion, of which he chose a random one and, afterwards, ender the app.

Although the amount of people selected to apply this method was quite limited, the election of which application was the easiest to use was unanimous, being Medisafe the favorite of all three evaluators. It showed the easiest interface to validate medication ingestion, with three very visible and intuitive buttons and identification by name associated with customizable color tags.

5.3   Results Given by Nielsen's Heuristics

From the results given from the SUS and UTE methods, an alarming issue with the sizing of screen elements, specially buttons, shows up. With that in mind, an eleventh heuristic was proposed, denominated *Screen Dimensioning Adaptation*, focused on evaluating the behavior of apps' screens based on an existing functionality in the *Android* Operational System (OS) 7.0 or newer.

In the Settings menu of *Android* smartphone devices there is an submenu of Accessibility Resources, where it's possible to find the option *Exhibition Size* (as shown in Fig. 2). The purpose of this feature is to increase the size of the screen's elements in order to allow better visualization to people with varying degrees of visual capacity.

Fig. 2. Exhibition size adjustment feature on Android 7.0+ systems

The results from the evaluations of each app was subdivided as follows: (1) Expert-based Usability Walkthrough; (2) Presenting unattended heuristics and justification; (3) Screen Captures; (4) Severity of Issue; (5) Proposal of Solution.

MyTherapy. Both walkthroughs were troubled, on which five problems were found.

Walkthrough: User Registration Screen.

IV - Consistency and Standardization: When the user clicks the *Start* button, he's directed to the next screen (Fig. 3b), but from there he is unable to return to the previous one. In case the user tries to use the *Return* button, he's is directed to a third screen (Fig. 3c), related to Medication Registration.

Severity of Issue: 4 - Considered an Extremely Serious Problem.

Solution: Provide return path to the first screen in a way that the user might choose another entry option to the app, e.g., from the small "Enter" button shown in Fig. 3a, used only in case the user already has an account for the app and wishes to recover previous data.

V - Prevention of Errors: The *Enter* button is small in size and badly polished, which might lead to difficulties to the user at the moment of clicking or confusion under the functionality of the button itself (Fig. 3a).

Severity of Issue: 4 - Considered an Extremely Serious Problem.

Solution: Provide better sizing and signalization for the button, as well as placing Privacy Policies terms on a lower portion of the app screen.

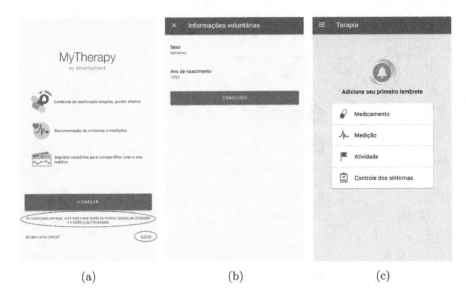

(a)   (b)   (c)

Fig. 3. MyTherapy app issues with navigation. (a) MyTherapy main screen. The blue button reads "Start"; and the circled small button on the bottom right reads "Enter"; (b) screen after the "Enter" button is pressed, requesting basic info from the user; (c) "Therapy" menu screen that pops-up if the user tries to return to the main screen, showing it's four main features (Color figure online)

Walkthrough: Screen to Register Medication.

IV - Consistency and Standardization: The screens of *Today* (Fig. 4a) and *Therapy* (Fig. 4b) menus both have similar sections with the exactly same name (*Add Medication*). However, on the *Therapy* menu, this feature is focused on medication taken regularly, where as in the *Today* menu, this functionality is focused on medication which the user must take only once. This ambiguous usage of terms and menus without further clarification may lead to severe confusion and induce the user to commit mistakes.

Severity of Issue: 3 - Considered a Serious Problem.

Solution: Standardize two different section types to insertion of medication, one for each screen, in order to minimize possible confusions from the user's part.

X - Help and Documentation: The *Help* menu (Fig. 5a) is found inside the *Settings* menu (Fig. 5b) and is, ironically, of little help, since the user is only provided with a single channel of communication through e-mail, also lacking any sort of documentation about the app.

Severity of Issue: 4 - Considered an Extremely Serious Problem.

Solution: Detach the *Help* menu from the *Settings* menu, with a direct button for it on the lateral quick menu, facilitating it's acess by the user. Also providing documentation with at least basic usage information or a How-to-Use tutorial.

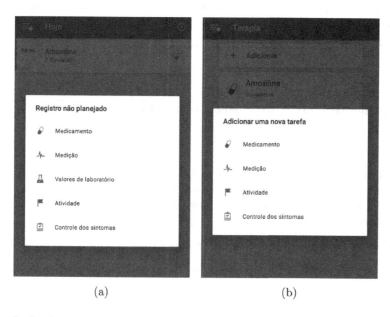

Fig. 4. Redundant screens on MyTherapy app. (a) "Add Medication" screen on the "Today" menu; (b) "Add Medication" screen on the "Therapy" menu

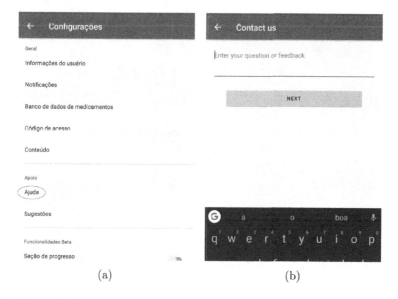

Fig. 5. Channel of communication on MyTherapy app. (a) "Configuration" menu screen, where the "Help" submenu is shown; (b) "Help" submenu screen

IV - Consistency and Standardization: The *Help* menu (Fig. 5b) has texts in english, but all other screens are in brazilian portuguese.

Severity of Issue: 3 - Considered a Serious Problem.

Solution: Provide consistent use of a single language in all screens.

CUCO Health. Both walkthroughs were troubled, on which two problems were found.

Walkthrough: User Registration Screen.

IV - Consistency and Standardization: The placing of buttons to *Register* and *Login* on the application are disproportionate (Fig. 6a). The entry option of login without a social network becomes totally shadowed by all the other network-based entry options.

Severity of Issue: 4 - Considered a Serious Problem.

Solution: Provide better sizing to a non social network register option to facilitate access.

(a)   (b)

Fig. 6. CUCO health app. (a) user login/register screen; (b) main user screen, showing "Health Meter" and registered therapies

Walkthrough: Screen to Register Medication.

XI - Screen Dimensioning Adaptation: The medication adding button (+) prevents the visualization of the Therapy Timeline when it's full (Fig. 6b).

Severity of Issue: 4 - Considered a Serious Problem.

Solution: Provide automated adequation to screen size in order to prevent information loss and so that the user is not impaired when the screen sizing is altered.

Medisafe. Only one walkthrough was troubled, on which two problems were found.

Walkthrough: Screen to Register Medication.

V - Prevention of Errors: Using purely icon-based representations may induce users to error, leading them to dubious interpretations, like the case with the "pencil" icon to represent "Edit" but without any proper text caption (Fig. 7a).

Severity of Issue: 3 - Considered a Serious Problem.

Solution: It's important that icons, even those considered intuitive by a certain group of users, have clear and simple captions, in order to avoid any errors.

(a)   (b)

Fig. 7. Medisafe app. (a) warning screen of a scheduled therapy, containing time and dosage of medication; (b) warning settings screens, containing storage for dosage and resupply of medication

XI - Screen Dimensioning Adaptation: The Add *Medication/Posology Edit* screen (Fig. 7b), whenever the screen sizing is enlarged, suppresses some titles and important information, e.g., the resupplying medication feature.

Severity of Issue: 4 - Considered a Extremely Serious Problem.

Solution: The disposition of elements in a screen must follow a certain spacing standard, considering all elements, so that the user don't suffer information loss on the resizing.

6   Conclusion

The UTE with the *users* allowed for the diagnose of some deficiencies appointed during the text, such as trouble with finding the "Enter" button on the apps' main screens, a large amount of information required to be inserted during medication register and the issue of touch keyboards not appearing by default on screens which demanded text typing.

The application of the SUS survey made possible to identify the degrees of usability of the apps. Some positive points were listed, such as easiness of use, which was scored positively for all the apps, as well as, learning and confidence of the *users* during the time of evaluation. However, even though all three reached reasonable scores on positive aspects of usability, only Medisafe was able to overcome the adopted standard, thus, being the only one already owning enough usability features to be considered Elder-friendly.

Results shown on the methods above created the need of a new Heuristic of number 11, denominated "Screen Dimensioning Adaptation" and adopted during the heuristic evaluation along with the ten traditional heuristics, having the purpose of making applications more accessible to people with varying degrees of visual capacity.

From the implementation of Nielsen's Heuristics, it was possible to enumerate a couple of issues found in the apps' interfaces. The most serious, located on CUCO Health and MyTherapy, were a few disproportionate screen elements, which also caused issues on the usability tests performed by the *users*, as well as others such as screens with similar design but different functionalities or an disadvantaged location of the Help menu, both presented on MyTherapy app.

The addition of the new heuristic also brought its own results. The apps Medisafe and CUCO Health had screens rated as problematic for showing responsiveness flaws when utilized on larger Screen Sizes options, through accessibility resources from the Android OS.

In a general sense, the response of the methods employed was very satisfactory. The employment of three distinct methods revealed results that, sometimes overlapped and sometimes contrasted, in a way that the final result was more complete and, thus, more closer to reality.

From the research presented in this paper, further studies must be made, with a larger pool of users and with a broader set of applications in order to precisely quantify the level of certainty that this method presents while evaluating how elder friendly an medication reminder app can be.

Also, in continuity of this work, a set of guidelines of good practices for app development in medication reminding apps will be made, based on the results presented, which may improve programmers and software engineers in creating services that also take in to consideration the elder public and its limitations.

Thus, it's believed that this developed methodology is capable of determining the level focus on the elder public, based on subjective, qualitative and technical parameters.

The employment of such methodology on the evaluation of other medication reminder apps is totally feasible, as well as its application in a general way to any kind of mobile application involving registrable reminders and/or other populations with cognitive skills similarly reduced to the elders.

It's also believed in the potential of this methodology to be implemented in the accessibility evaluation of any type of application, in a broad sense. However, it's important to emphasize the need pf adapting the methodology accordingly to the specific characteristics and needs of the target audience and of the evaluated service.

References

1. Instituto Brasileiro de Geografia e Estatística: Número de idosos cresce 18% em 5 anos e ultrapassa 30 milhões em 2017 (2018). https://agenciadenoticias.ibge.gov. br/agencia-noticias/2012-agencia-de-noticias/noticias/20980-numero-de-idosos-cr esce-18-em-5-anos-e-ultrapassa-30-milhoes-em-2017
2. Duarte, L.R., et al.: Hábitos de consumo de medicamentos entre idosos usuários do SUS e de plano de saúde (2012). http://www.cadernos.iesc.ufrj.br/cadernos/ images/csc/2012_1/artigos/CSC_v20n1_64-71.pdf
3. Logue, R.M.: Self-medication and the elderly: how technology can help. AJN Am. J. Nurs. **102**(7), 51–55 (2002)
4. World Health Organization: Adhere to long-term therapies: evidence for action, p. 48 (2003). https://www.who.int/chp/knowledge/publications/adherence_full_report.pdf
5. Tavares, M.M.K., de Souza, S.T.C.: Os idosos e as barreiras de acesso às novas tecnologias da informação e comunicação (2012). https://seer.ufrgs.br/renote/article/viewFile/30915/19244
6. Stuck, R.E., et al.: Medication management apps: usable by older adults? In: Proceedings of the Human Factors and Ergonomics Society Annual Meeting, pp. 1141–1144. SAGE Publications, Los Angeles (2017)
7. Scheibe, M., et al.: Acceptance factors of mobile apps for diabetes by patients aged 50 or older: a qualitative study (2015). https://www.ncbi.nlm.nih.gov/pmc/articles/PMC4376102/
8. Dasgupta, D., et al.: Design and evaluation of a medication adherence application with communication for seniors in independent living communities. In: AMIA Annual Symposium Proceedings, p. 480. American Medical Informatics Association (2016)
9. Brooke, J.: SUS: a "quick and dirty" usability scale. In: Usability Evaluation in Industry, vol. 194, pp. 189–194. Taylor and Francis, London (1996). https://hell.meiert.org/core/pdf/sus.pdf

10. Likert, R.: A technique for the measurement of attitudes. In: Archives of Psychology, vol. 140, pp. 44–52 (1932). https://legacy.voteview.com/pdf/Likert_1932.pdf
11. Bangor, A., Kortum, P., Miller, J.: Determining what individual SUS scores mean: adding an adjective rating scale. J. Usability Stud. **4**, 114–123 (2009). http://uxpajournal.org/wp-content/uploads/pdf/JUS_Bangor_May2009.pdf
12. Research Collective: The pros and cons of the system usability scale (SUS) (2017). https://research-collective.com/blog/sus/
13. Veiga, V.S.O., et al.: Repositórios Institucionais: Avaliação da Usabilidade na Fundação Oswaldo Cruz (2013). http://enancib.ibict.br/index.php/enancib/xivenancib/paper/viewFile/4636/3759
14. Rocha, H.V., Baranauskas, M.C.C.: Design e Avaliação de Interfaces Humano-Computador. Unicamp, Campinas (2003)
15. Silva, B.S., Barbosa, S.D.J.: Interação Humano-Computador: Projetando a Experiência Perfeita. Campus, Rio de Janeiro (2010)
16. Nielsen, J., Molich, R.: Heuristic evaluation of user interfaces. In: Proceedings of ACM CHI 1990 Conference, Seattle, WA, pp. 249–256 (1990)
17. Nielsen, J.: Heuristic Evaluation. In: Mack, R., Nielsen, J. (eds.) Usability Inspection Methods, pp. 25–62. Wiley, New York, NY (1994)

Design and Deploying Tools to *'Actively Engaging Nature'*

The My Naturewatch Project as an Agent for Engagement

Robert Phillips[1(✉)], Amina Abbas-Nazari[1], James Tooze[1],
Bill Gaver[2], Andy Boucher[2], Liliana Ovalle[2], Andy Sheen[2],
Dean Brown[2], Naho Matsuda[2], and Mike Vanis[2]

[1] Design Products, Royal College of Art, Kensington SW72EU, UK
robert.phillips@rca.ac.uk
[2] Interaction Research Studio, Goldsmiths, London, UK

Abstract. 'Shifting Baseline Syndrome' is highly apparent in the context of generational shifts in work and life patterns that reduce interaction with and knowledge of the natural world, and therefore expectations of it. This is exacerbated by changes in the natural world itself due to climate change, biodiversity decline and a range of anthropogenic factors. Distributed and accessible technologies, and grass roots approaches provide fresh opportunities for interactions, which enable active engagement in ecological scenarios. The *My NatureWatch* project uses digital devices to collect visual content about UK wildlife, promoting 'active engagements with nature'. The project embodies *Inclusive Design in the Digital Age,* as the activity; engages a wide demographic community, can be used by all, provided user led agency and produced methodological design lessons.

The article frames *My Naturewatch* as an agent for active designed engagements with nature. The research objective is to comprehend 'how to design tools for positive nature engagement' holding value for; (1) academic communities as validated methodologies (2) the public through access to enabling technologies, content and knowledge (3) industry in the form of new; experiences, engagements and commerce. The approach is specifically designed to yield insights from a multitude of engagements, through the deployment of accessible, low-cost products. Project reporting documents the benefits, pitfalls and opportunities in the aforementioned engagement uncovered through design-led approaches. Insights are gathered from public/community facing workshops, wildlife experts, ecologists, economists, educators and wildlife NGO's. The engagement methodologies are compared highlighting which initiative yielded *'Active Engagement with Nature'*.

Keywords: User centred design · Nature · Engagement · DIY

J. Zhou and G. Salvendy (Eds.): HCII 2019, LNCS 11592, pp. 513–531, 2019.
https://doi.org/10.1007/978-3-030-22012-9_37

1 Introduction

1.1 What is a Nature Engagement?

Governments are implementing policies to "increase people's engagement with and connection to nature" [1] owing to the widespread decline of the world's biodiversity [2] and the benefits that connection brings to pro-environmental behaviours [3] and human health [4]. The National Trust commissioned the Natural Childhood report [5]. Moss (founding producer of BBC Springwatch) highlights;

"Nature Deficit Disorder: focuses on the lives of Britain's children, particularly with regard to their lack of engagement with nature. [Impacting on] physical health including obesity, mental health problems, and children's growing inability to assess risk. Imagine a world where our children are physically and mentally healthier, communities more cohesive and connected, and everyone enjoys a closer relationship with the natural world. Reduced costs to the NHS, higher educational attainment in schools, and happier families" [5].

Engagements with the natural world presents positive impacts (for all ages) including; cognition and development [6], tourism [7], mental health [8], fitness [9], risk taking [10], child development [11] and protecting the ecosystem that supports human life [12]. The 2018 *Living Planet Report* concludes a "60% fall in [wildlife and biodiversity] in just over 40 years – is a reminder and ultimate indicator of the pressure we exert on the planet" [12]. City design (in developed worlds) comprises of infrastructures, concrete, built to move cars and people including buildings sustaining human comfort. Developments "largely ignore the natural processes through which humans are sustained" (food, energy, and water), thereby perpetuating a human disconnection from nature [13]. In *How does engaging with nature relate to life satisfaction* identifies nuances between rural and urban participants, in approaches and engagements in nature. The "rural residents responded more positively to the questions over residents from urban and suburban areas" due to their differences in perspective [14].

This design space provides 'mechanisms' for laypeople to engage in their natural surroundings with examples including; the Wildlife Trusts '30 days wild' [15], the British Beekeeping Association's adopt a beehive [16], Wild Cities [17], Chris Packham's walk for wildlife [18], photography exhibitions [19], twitching apps [20] etc. Existing 'nature engaged' audiences have intrinsic motivation e.g. in *From Poachers to Protectors* it contextualizes the motivations for saving local wildlife through community engagement to "understand how community-level approaches can effectively help combat the Illegal Wildlife Trade" [21]. The World Health Organisation is deeming air pollution the new tobacco as "the act of breathing is killing 7 million people a year and harming billions more" [22]. Our human relationship with the natural world is intertwined, to reach resilience for a sustainable bio-diverse future, change needs to be embedded. The Natural England *Access to Nature Report*, Highlights nature engagements can "increase communities' sense of ownership of local natural places, by establishing strong partnerships between communities, voluntary organisations, local authorities and others" [23].

1.2   What is the Importance of Making?

The act of 'making' provides; agency [24], economy [25], craft [26] and control over our material environment [27]. Open Design, digital manufacture and accessible technologies have transformed the access to manipulate/create 'personal products' [28]. Professor of surgical education R. Kneebone, stated, "young people have so little experience of craft skills that they struggle with anything practical", stressing 'making' inexperience is impacting dexterity in operating theatres [29]. The *Make or Break: UK's Digital Future* presents "the role of technology must create a sustainable society for global development" [30]. House of Commons report *Digital Skills Crisis* comments to "equip the next generation with industry [aptitude] but also with skills they require for a future not yet imagined" [31]. Traditional making tools extend to digital tools like 'Raspberry Pi', a low cost, "credit-card sized computer that plugs into a computer monitor or TV, and uses a standard keyboard and mouse. The Raspberry Pi has been used in an array of digital maker projects, from music machines and parent detectors to weather stations" [32]. The *People Fixing the World* establishes "the public desire to fix and repair goods, for sentimental or economic reasons", leading to "res-killing and sharing knowledge" [33].

Designer Enzo Mari wanted to produce furniture described as cheap, high quality and long lasting. Mari believed that "if someone tried to build something, they would learn something"... resulting in 'Autoprogettazione' [34], that translates as 'self-design'. He believed in the pedagogical element of design and his instructions for self-made furniture served as a tool for learning and were instructions for self-fabrication and Open Design. Open Design is the "free distribution, documentation and permission of modifications and derivations" of an object, product, service or designed intervention [35]. Open Design "empowers people to make and understand products and processes, with more transparency", leading to more independent user led design [35]. *DIY Citizenship, Critical Making and Social Media*, identifies that we are moving past people just making for themselves and using "DIY construction to provide new modes and possibilities for political and social engagement" [36]. These cases align to the unknown importance of making, that it is not just about the artefact but includes; wellbeing, accomplishment, knowledge, satisfaction, skill development, economic values and most importantly... agency.

1.3   Combining Making and Nature Engagement

The 2017 *Woodland Wise report, Nature Inspires Education,* comments the "need to maximise the education and development of everyone by using the outdoors as a tool for learning about nature, to acquire life skills, and as a platform for standard curricular subjects" [37]. In the UK, an "estimated 87% of households have access to a private garden, varying from a few square metres to several hectares" [38]. Nature facing organisations lack knowledge of people's gardens. The rationale is that "resources are usually placed in visible locations, thereby increasing the reliability of sightings, particularly of rarer species" [39]. The combination of 'making, nature engagement and private space' offer the opportunity for enhanced design experiences. The challenge is balancing i.e., informed public understanding and the contextual requirements without consequences. For example bird feeders can transmit, *Trichomonas gallinae,* a common parasite to pigeons. 2012 studies documented a "30% reduction in green finch numbers" due to the transmission of parasites to other species, via unclean bird feeders [40]. The Dorset Wildlife trust reports smart "phone apps imitating bird song have been used negatively to lure species for amateur photography" [41]. Tony Whitehead, RSPB public affairs officer states, "repeatedly playing a recording of birdsong to encourage a bird to respond, in order to see it or photograph it, can divert a territorial bird from important duties, such as feeding its young" [41]. This space results in the requirement of non-invasive design proposals to explore the natural world. The work frames a process beyond participatory design, co-design and public engagement and enacts 'Design for Active Engagement' in the surrounding world. The *My naturewatch* project follows "Human-centred design, develop[ing proposals] based on direct interactions with individuals" [42].

Traditionally, participatory design has involved users in "evaluative research: testing existing products or prototypes of developed concepts" [43]. Participatory design has more "open-ended outputs to look for [design] opportunities" [44]. The often non-linear process of participatory design involves the client, user, designer(s) and alternate stakeholders [45]. Participatory design processes explore users' either "existing or possible contexts of use, aiding the design team to have a more empathetic approach" [44]. Including users in design processes should include "looking at people in context, actively involving [them to] try things" [46]. The design of the *My naturewatch* camera embodies some of Chapman's *Emotionally Durable Design* as "The product is developing a tangible character through time and use and some-times misuse" [47]. *My Naturewatch* uses digital devices to collect visual and audio content about UK wildlife around the British Isles to promote positive engagements with nature. Project objectives include, people investigating nature outside of their back door in all its forms, giving its users agency. The value in wildlife outside of your back door is not often explored in urban and suburban areas.

The *My Naturewatch* project makes the opportunity for interaction accessible to all. The *My Naturewatch* Camera is designed to capture pictures of wildlife when it detects movement designed to be inexpensive, and aligned to the interests of the BBC's Natural History Unit. The cameras are available as DIY designs for people to make themselves. Constructed entirely from commercially available components, using instructions and software from project website *(mynaturewatch.net)*, designed to be as easy to make, and require no direct contact with the project team for success.

1.4   Research Objective

The *My Naturewatch* project is a design led exploration engaging the public in surrounding wildlife with the intention of evolving their knowledge of design, technology and nature, and or informs their actions over time. This article is framing the project as an agent for change.

2 Collective Method

The following workshops had a similar methodology and only changed by context, demographic or the business type; amends are highlighted in each section, as they were design workshops that had contextual input, influences and agendas. Design workshops help researchers include participants in questioning problems, situations or defining design territories. In 'Developments in Practice', Suri identifies that the "design profession's major strengths [are] the ability to create tangible expressions of ideas and to invent and exploit new tools" i.e. translating insights into tangible design outputs [46]. The 'new tools' Suri describes range from technologies to services, from construction to execution. Design workshops are tools for incubating design outcomes and translating insights as they "establish user needs, test product designs and evaluate final concepts" providing grounded tangible outputs [48].

Workshop participants were recruited by the host communities or by an open call through the Internet and the host's social media channels. The *My naturewatch* camera trap was designed specifically using off the shelf parts that were accessible by a third party and could be assembled without tools on a kitchen table with pre-approved CE certified components. The cameras are; repairable, reusable and utilise components found in schools, homes or technology enthusiasts place of work. All of the parts are publically accessible and purchasable. The cameras were used as an agent to encourage engagement with the natural world and surrounding nature.

Urban Birder David Lindo believes you should "see your urban environment as a bird would: the buildings are cliffs and any green areas are an oasis for nesting, resting and feeding" [49], as we are surrounded by wildlife, it does not solely exist in rural areas. The workshops approach embodied "contact, meaning, emotion, compassion and beauty indicators of, pathways towards nature connectedness" as five strong indicators for positive nature engagement [50]. The workshops included a 30–45 min camera assembly and check, with follow-ups, or tech support offered by email, website or forum. Factors informing workshop locations were; type of organization, motivation, locality, communities and prior technology or nature knowledge (Fig. 1).

Fig. 1. A *My naturewatch* camera deployed before a workshop at Wakehurst Place.

In parallel research Hecker *et al.* state "research in citizen science takes a diverse approach where the balance between scientific, educational, societal and policy goals varies across projects" [51]. The authors noted, "a major obstacle [in] preventing the adoption of technologies is the presence of those entrenched in traditional solutions" the *My naturewatch* advantages do not compete with traditional methods, but advance them [52]. Participants early images where evocative, but they often deleted them feeling unworthy, personally comparing to project partner BBC Earth pictures.

2.1   Sussex Wildlife Trust, Beta Development (Study 1)

Sussex Wildlife Trust is "a conservation charity for everyone caring for nature in Sussex. [They] focus on protecting the rich natural life that is found across our towns, countryside and coast" [52]. SWT are uniquely placed with local; expertise, networks, outreach, passion for surrounding environment(s), the negatives of potential use cases and have experience in engagement campaigns e.g. 30 days Wild. SWT are linked to the Sussex Biodiversity Record Centre, actively contribute to local wildlife media, Wildlife Festival and run a public facing troubleshooting hotline called 'Wild Call' [53]. Contextual methods included; using a local site (Woods mill) that regularly engages diverse audiences, schools and welcomes volunteers. The organisation was in prime position to help future awareness and use the tool for their own benefit. The workshop was run with 9 rangers and volunteers. The delivery involved a build workshop, example camera placement, with a review of captured content after 1 month.

2.2   Sussex Wildlife Trust/Results

The rangers highlighted scaling 'baiting' to attract different wildlife and its challenges. Baiting of "wildlife involves the purposeful placement of natural or artificial food resources in the environment to manipulate the behaviour of wild species so as to attract and/or retain them in an area" [53]. Large "concentrations of wildlife activity centred around feeding or baiting sites have been widely implicated as a mechanism influencing transmission of infectious diseases" [54]. This highlighted the need for endorsement by wildlife expertise and the delicate balance that is required. Repeatable placing and providing more knowledge of how and when to attract different species, whilst not over attracting vermin and spreading disease, was raised as a concern. Researchers found that 'permission giving' was imperative e.g. if participants broke them, through usage it was ok as they could repair or rebuild them. The participants sought external validation from social media 'as a goal', to share content.

2.3   Schumacher College, Beta Development (Study 2)

Schumacher College embodies EF Schumacher's "small is beautiful", providing a combination of ecology, design and economy teaching [55]. Their Ecological Design course "believe[s] in a future where the things we design no longer need to be detrimental to the wellbeing of our planet, in a future that pioneers ecological possibilities that redress social, environmental and economic imbalance" [56]. Contextual methods; founded by bringing design, ecology, economics together and understanding environments. It was a captive non-tech audience, interested in documenting local wildlife. They were selected as a design orientated audience providing honest feedback, as they had no pre-bias to the project.

2.4 Schumacher College/Results

The participants found the technology magical in its connectivity and simplicity in its connection to a mobile device. In contrast frustrations occurred, as they did not "catch" what they wanted, however 'wildlife is not an on demand performance' nor should be made to be so. The "product language" [57] of off-the-shelf technologies and the physical interaction they bring was challenging, as the Raspberry Pi offers countless adjustment rather than restricting the users and lead to confusion. Participants thought the camera kits would instantly catch new species… in this case it did not, highlighting the need to frame the technology appropriately within events.

2.5 Wakehurst National Trust (Study 3)

This was the first workshop after BBC SpringWatch launch, so was out of Beta testing phase. Wakehurst is a "Kew [owned] Wild Botanic Garden in Sussex, situated on the High Weald, [with] more than 500 acres of ornamental gardens, woodlands and a nature reserve. Wakehurst also home[s] the Millennium Seed Bank [58] the largest wild seed conservation project in the world" [59]. Visitor numbers to Wakehurst in 2017 were "2,124,138" [60]. Wakehurst was selected as the National Trust has "5.2 million members of which families [their] (biggest growing group), accounts for over 23% of memberships" [61]. It built on the National Trusts network for further engagement. *My naturewatch* cameras were placed throughout the Wakehurst site a month before the workshop gathering material and familiarising the keepers with the equipment. Participant recruitment included an open call, through Wakehurst's social media, with 40% of places offered to participants invited through local schools for people estranged to National Trust properties. Local head teachers sent supervised school pupils, rewarding good behaviour. The format, introduced the technology, featured a live demonstration outside, 30–45 min build with a local ranger offering advice on camera positioning, practicalities and experience.

2.6 Wakehurst National Trust/Results

Families were assembling the kits together and crossed generations. Participants fed off the group dynamic and actively helped each other. Participants actively discussed camera placement and helped each other. The venue acted as validation for the venture. Visitors highly engaged with the *My naturewatch* project online (that researchers had never met) turned up to show us their own builds & specific hedgehog camera rigs. Participants sharing material post workshop was very challenging over a digital medium, as it required the simple effort of them putting on to social media. Participant's definition of a good photo or good output was critical, as they did not need to be a professional. The outputs of 'drop-in sessions' were harder to measure as participants had less time invested.

Comments from an attending Wakehurst ranger (Fig. 2);

"The beauty of the project is that technology usually makes kids stay indoors and not explore the outside world, the combination is powerful" *(host comment)*.

Fig. 2. *My naturewatch* Wakehurst Place workshops *(Image credit, James McCauley).*

2.7   Depot Cinema (Study 4)

Lewes is situated in the South Downs National Park and is a "Transition Town', where people offer knowledge forming a sustainable community" [62]. Depot is an "independent community cinema and cafe-restaurant with education facilities, created and operated by the charity Lewes Community Screen. *Lewes Community Screen* aspires to create a venue that serves as a focal point for the local community, not only in the area of film but through a wider range of art forms" [63]. The location was selected, as the researchers had not yet focused on the usage of the material but predominantly on the inputs. As Manzini comments "the convergence of social and technical innovation interacts with the way people are and think, in this way new values emerge, impacting what we count as well-being" [63]. Mazini states:

"Collaborative organisations are social groups emerging in highly connected environments. Their members choose to collaborate with the aim of achieving specific results, and, in doing so, they also create social, economic, and environmental benefits" [64].

The authors empowered social groups in every case study, but the Depot was specific as the result was a film, with the intention on wider benefits. Cinema's can be "social levelling, social hubs" that cross generations and unite audiences [65]. The organisation hosted an open call for filmmakers of all ages, with the incentive of a trailer to be played in the cinema over the coming months. The age ranges (advertised) were from 8–15, 55–80. Locals who could not attend were also invited to digitally submit imagery. The follow up workshop focused on community film making techniques.

2.8   Depot Cinema/Results

Researchers were surprised that the participation incentive was not inclusion in a trailer, but people exploring their gardens, rooftops and local space. The process highlighted the importance of repeat visits, also solving early tech support issues were vital as if people got frustrated, they would not seek the information on the forum or ask friends. A number of participants to this day are still sending images that they feel are important to them and the trailer still remains to be of interest.

> "The camera is doing its job well, I regularly look in the garden from the window or when I am working in the garden. 24 species in the garden (so far) and another 6 "from" the garden like Swift and Peregrine" *(Participant email).*

2.9   Victoria & Albert Museum, Digital Design Weekend (Study 5)

Digital Design Weekend "presents installations, workshops, talks and performances from over 40 artists, designers, scientists and engineers", it is a "weekend of free events exploring human-machine interaction and potential future worlds" [66]. The researchers ran open workshops hoping to invite a multicultural art and design facing audience. This time researchers relied on passing traffic and timed workshop sessions rather than pre-sign ups. The Victoria and Albert museum, was also selected as; it has great experience in running engagement events, is of international significance and has a mixed visitor demographic with 3,789,748 [67] visitors in 2018, that is free and accessible. The workshop was run during the 2018 London Design Festival.

2.10   Victoria & Albert Museum/Results

Venue's significance offered trust and contextualisation as in discussion people thought they were creating 'works of art' rather than just taking photos. Adhoc participants commented they 'wanted to see what they would get' from a 45 min assembly workshop before they committed their time. The negative of running a workshop in such a prestigious location, was the re-enforcement that we were a research project and not just an extension of the museum was sometimes confusing to participants. One shared result was a participant using the technology to form a link with their next-door neighbour as they did not have a garden. Whilst the interaction between the participant and neighbour lasted a month, it did bridge an age divide of 45 years between two people that had not interacted before or created a technology intervention. The participant responded by email with:

> "A fruitful collaboration with a neighbour (an old lady) who has a birdbath, we got some pretty amazing shots of the (quite busy!) bird ecosystem in both of our backyards. It was a really nice thing to collaborate on" *(participant email).*

2.11   The Design Museum (Study 6)

The Design Museum "champions design and [it's] impact on the world. Design is about innovation, technology, creativity and craftsmanship and influences our lives. The museum is an independent charity and relies upon its loyal members to continue this valuable work" [68]. Since opening the museum has attracted "672,000 visitors, in 10 months" [69]. Authors initiated a 'sixties + nature tech group' meeting weekly for a month. Participants were local to the Design Museum and Holland Park (collaborating as local wildlife experts) opening their Ecology Centre [70] and staff. The process utilised repeat visits over 4 weeks for support. Session (1) camera assembly and troubleshooting session (2) deployment in Holland Park, advising camera placement after a week living with the cameras, to ensure debugging. Session (3) participants collected the cameras for image review, taking the cameras home with them. Session (4) group discussion, followed by a pop-up exhibition providing the participants the opportunity to share data with family members. The approach borrowed lessons from citizen science and community practices. In *The Knowledge Gain and Behavioral Change in Citizen Science Programs* Jordan *et al.* comment that trial participants claimed that the largest motivating factor for participation is "content knowledge" [71]. Content knowledge is the education that participants experience from exploring the world, it also offers training opportunities where volunteers can increase their skills, expertise and 'content knowledge'. In *The Rise of The Expert Amateur: DIY Projects, Communities, and Cultures,* Kuznetsov describes the main motivation of users contributing to DIY projects as the "learning of new skills and communal sharing" [77] (Fig. 3).

Fig. 3. Assembly and deployment of *My naturewatch* cameras, over 60's tech group.

2.12   The Design Museum/Results

The number of sessions meant that participants did not loose faith due to technical difficulties, as each session could troubleshoot, building confidence. The places participants deployed their cameras included participants; window boxes, allotments, gardens and small green spaces. The feedback opened up the conversation to include how the *My naturewatch* project could be used as a health tool, against sedentary lifestyle and contribute towards a good physical and mental wellbeing. The sessions empowered them to use different tools that they had not used before. There was great power in making a group of 60–80 year olds, know more about a technology over their grandchildren, as they commented on numerous occasions. The sessions re-enforced a social impact, due to participation they subsequently met externally (to the organised events) creating; friends, made bread together, learnt a language together, as a social group, which previously did not know each other before.

"It's a fantastic project and it's shown us how the museum can support older people to get engaged in nature and technology" *(Host institution email).*

The Design Museum study was the most successful of all of the workshops, as it established a small community that led to a wider impact. The participants also felt the value in sharing their 'captures' as it was straight forward and they could learn of each other quickly. The participants commented that re-skilling [72], was an important skill of the workshops, they understood things they had not done before. Researchers witnessed a change in ownership once the participants 'I made that to take that photo'. The feedback highlighted a number of themes unknown in other prior workshops with following statements from participants (Fig. 4):

"The process has made me feel re-skilled and I am keen to learn more" (workshop participant).
"I know more about this technology than my grandchildren, which is empowering" (workshop participant).

Fig. 4. Captured images from, *My naturewatch* over 60's tech group.

3   Discussion

3.1   Project Support

The authors found that physical repeat visits to the locations were important, not from a debugging perspective but from a social side unifying workshop participants to share their stories and insights that might not have happened through an online presence as we focused on attracting participants that had not previously engaged in creating technologies. The groups over-reviewed their imagery and deleting very valuable images that might not have "captured" a species, but had taken a great photograph. The concept of "group making" re-enforces the social sustainability and exploration provided by others and not just undertaking a solo activity [73]. The workshops also uncovered the value of peer-to-peer knowledge, especially in elderly participants sharing their knowledge with grand children [74]. The authors believe that this support can also build project sustainability over time supporting Hess's theories of Community Technology that combines a community with empowerment.

"To light that candle which is so much better than cursing the darkness. To be as much as the human condition can sustain, rather than being only what a system can allow... To be... To do... That is Community Technology" [75].

3.2   Motivation

Clary describes that the "protection of one's self-interest is key to motivation" [76]. Motivation to participate remains a challenge, however communities 'self-interest' can be designed in to it appropriately. Borrowing from Citizen science, to "engage a public it should be innovative and imaginative combining the collation of data while appealing to the volunteer community" [77]. Hieman also agrees with the importance of 'appealing CS activities to participants' and comments that "democratize[d] science should not fall solely to those formally trained in the natural sciences" [78]. When participants were asked they often responded with "I want to see the garden when I am not there" or "I have never made a piece of technology before". The motivations were surprising as the 'big sell' of trailers or 'recognised on TV' were not the incentive, but learning the tech and the feeling of constructing it yourself.

3.3   Barriers

Where possible we encouraged serendipity, so participants could use cameras to explore. The work followed a "research through design" process responding to engagement and participants [79]. The barriers to entry highlighted through the workshops were the type of people that felt they could attend or were able. The researchers made the workshops as accessible, in times appropriate to 'childcare', school access and on weekends. A 3rd party, Pimioroni, who packaged componentry for easy purchase, removed one large barrier for the project. The final barrier was giving 'permission' to participants. When they attended workshops there was a different approach to the object after they had 'made it' as they had invested their time and skill into its assembly. Researchers had to give them permission to edit, repair and even break them through use, rather than not use them. The last barrier was limited to participants "fieldsense" in how they engaged or scared wildlife, in urban settings this was less of a challenge; in rural settings had quite elaborate positioning [80].

3.4   Trust and Ethics

The authors are aware, that everything is open to abuse, its how you design out the detrimental abuse to engage people in the natural world... to aid positive interactions is the challenge. As highlighted by [81] the simple act of "tourism and footfall in areas of natural beauty" require careful consideration, however the authors are highlighting that documenting our back garden and surrounding parks in urban and suburban environments could not only provide interesting design material or content but in turn effect our relationship with the natural world. The work was conducted using institutional ethics procedures and IDEO's mandate of "Respect, Responsibility and Honesty", as the work continually "acted to protect people's current and future interests" of the information they were gathering [82]. Ethics of capturing and wider scale, safeguarding was an issue in certain schools if there was a child with a "fear that a vulnerable child might be identified", even though that was virtually impossible [83]. The work also identified the possible ethical situations of 'do no harm' and "empathy with wildlife challenges of conservation" [84]. Some participants often got frustrated they did not 'catch anything', researchers had to re-enforce that "Wildlife is not performative" [85] "managing peoples expectations" [86] that things are not "on demand" in this space, nor should they be [85]. Baiting en-mass if all the public participated at the same time could be catastrophic, "attracting vermin and disease" [87].

3.5   Health and Wellbeing

The health benefits of 'engaging with nature' are documented earlier in this paper. Hartig *et al.* discuss the health benefits of 'nature experiences' including; physiological impacts, restorative aspects, learning and personal development supporting "views about nature and health, are using methods and theories now viewed as scientifically credible" [88]. The NHS is now using "Social prescribing involves helping patients to improve their health, wellbeing and social welfare by connecting them to community services which might be run by the council or a local charity. For example, signposting people who have been diagnosed with dementia to local dementia support groups" [89]. This is further grounded as the "government says about 200,000 older people have not had a conversation with a friend or relative in over a month" [90]. In *Active Ageing, Pensions and Retirement in the UK,* "Active ageing has the potential to provide a framework for strategies relating to population ageing, ultimately it can assist with the process of optimising opportunities for health, participation" [91]. Prescribing 'nature as healthcare' could be a valid direction for *'Actively Engaging in Nature'*. Gaming platform Pokémon GO, surprised health experts as a "Real World Gaming Platform us [ing] real locations to encourage players to search far and wide in the real world to discover Pokémon. Pokémon GO helps you find and catch Pokémon by exploring your surroundings" [92]. This platform created for profit and exploration; never considered the health implications of getting people to explore their world. In studies Igmar *et al.*, [93] documented 32,000 users "added a total of 144 billion steps to the US physical activity". Pokémon players were going to locations previously unvisited [94] and helped people with social withdrawal [95].

3.6   Meaningful Engagement

The World Wide Fund for Nature (WWF) highlight issues with smart phone apps recording sightings, specifically in Yellowstone, national park. Not only does it remove the 'wild nature of discovering wildlife' with "grizzly bear sightings at such spots are especially challenging for park rangers, who have to both direct traffic and keep people a safe distance away" [96]. This extreme example of 'logging wildlife', does raise the issue of health and safety and drawing people to locations, that do not have the knowledge to cope with that environment. Public Engagement is defined as "the involvement of specialists listening to, developing their understanding of, and inter-acting with, non-specialists" [97]. The authors see 'Design for Active Engagement' differently as it is not passive; it presents design to actively engage through physical, system or digital interactions. Authors see active engagement as an opportunity for potential behaviour change over time. Workshop activities established a deep level of engagement with participants; investigating there surroundings, public environments, presenting findings at camera clubs, sharing it with friends both personally and via social media.

4 Conclusion

The repeat visits gave permission; yield data, establishing a community was important to the success of the work for the demographics we engaged with. The design language of off the shelf parts, was intimidating to some participants and can be confusing to the public, so the overall design was imperative. The researchers had to frame the work appropriately as it often came across during feedback as a 'doing good tool' rather than just people exploring their outdoor space with a designed product. The project appeal to the volunteer community was paramount, as people often became champions of the project telling their friends and families. Giving permission was essential especially when given kits as somewhere to scared to break them. The issue of giving things for free did present bias's that would require further investigation over time. The notion of 'public press' or 'getting their name in the paper' was not of interest to the majority of the participants. Finally as Clary describes that the "protection of one's self-interest is key to motivation" [76], is of the upmost importance and remains a challenge, however communities 'self-interest' can be designed in to it appropriately. An intrinsic motivation/bias was noted as participants were given kits for free.

Acknowledgements. Lewes Railway Land Trust, The Depot Cinema, The Sussex Wildlife Trust, Wakehurst Place, Schumacher College, The Victoria and Albert Museum, Holland Park Ecological Centre & The Design Museum, for hosting workshops. The participants both attendees and armchair photographers have been patient with updates and kind at sharing images. We thank the Goldsmiths, Interaction Research Studio for collaborating and the Royal College of Art, Design Products + Futures Programme. The project was made possible through EPSRC funding Grant EP/P006353/1.

References

1. HM Government: The Natural Choice: Securing the value of nature, Stationery Office (2011)
2. Barnosky, A.D., et al.: Has the earth's sixth mass extinction already arrived? Nature **471** (7336), 51 (2011)
3. Frantz, C.M., Mayer, F.S.: The importance of connection to nature in assessing environmental education programs. Stud. Educ. Eval. **41**, 85–89 (2014)
4. Nisbet, K., Zelenski, J.M., Murphy, S.A.: The nature relatedness scale: linking individuals' connection with nature to environmental concern and behavior. Environ. Behav. **41**(5), 715–740 (2009)
5. Moss, S.M.: Natural Childhood, 1st edn. National Trust London, London (2012)
6. Berman, M.G., Jonides, J., Kaplan, S.: The cognitive benefits of interacting with nature. Psychol. Sci. **19**(12), 1207–1212 (2008)

7. Penteriani, V., et al.: Consequences of brown bear viewing tourism: a review. Biol. Conserv. **206**, 169–180 (2017)
8. Kuo, F.E., Taylor, A.F.: A potential natural treatment for attention-deficit/hyperactivity disorder: evidence from a national study. Am. J. Publ. Health **94**(9), 1580–1586 (2004). www.treesintrouble.com/wp-content/uploads/2016/03/0941580.pdf [pii]
9. Milligan, C., Bingley, A.: Restorative places or scary spaces? The impact of woodland on the mental well-being of young adults. Health Place **13**(4), 799–811 (2007)
10. Joye, Y., Pals, R., Steg, L., Evans, B.L.: New methods for assessing the fascinating nature of nature experiences. PloS ONE **8**(7), e65332 (2013)
11. Chawla, L.: Growing up green: becoming an agent of care for the natural world. J. Dev. Process. **4**(1), 6–23 (2009)
12. Grooten, M., Almond, R.E.A. (eds.): Living Planet Report – 2018. Aiming Higher, Blackpool (2018)
13. Church, S.P.: From street trees to natural areas: retrofitting cities for human connectedness to nature. J. Environ. Plan. Manag. **61**(5–6), 878–903 (2018)
14. Biedenweg, K., Scott, R.P., Scott, T.A.: How does engaging with nature relate to life satisfaction? Demonstrating the link between environment-specific social experiences and life satisfaction. J. Environ. Psychol. **50**, 112–124 (2017)
15. The Wildlife Trusts: From 30 days wild, to everyday wild (2018). https://www.wildlifetrusts.org/30DaysWild
16. The British Beekeeping Association: Member's Handbook (2012)
17. Devon Wildlife Trust: Exeter wild city (2018). https://www.devonwildlifetrust.org/what-we-do/our-projects/exeter-wild-city
18. Packham, C.: The people's walk for wildlife Saturday 22nd September 2018 (2018). https://www.chrispackham.co.uk/the-peoples-walk-for-wildlife
19. The Natural History Museum: Wildlife photographer of the year (2018). http://www.nhm.ac.uk/visit/wpy.html
20. British Bird Lovers: Bird watching apps for iPhone and iPad (2018). https://www.britishbirdlovers.co.uk/multimedia/bird-watching-iphone-apps
21. Cooney, R., et al.: From poachers to protectors: engaging local communities in solutions to illegal wildlife trade. Conserv. Lett. **10**(3), 367–374 (2017)
22. Carrington, D., Taylor, M.: Air pollution is the 'new tobacco', warns WHO head (2018). https://www.theguardian.com/environment/2018/oct/27/air-pollution-is-the-new-tobacco-warns-who-head?CMP=twt_a-environment_b-gdneco
23. Natural England: Access to nature: Inspiring people to engage with their natural environment (No. A2N). Icarus, Enabling Positive Change, England (2014). http://Publications.naturalengland.org.uk/category
24. Charny, D.: The power of Making. Exhibition the Victoria and Albert Museum. Victoria and Albert Museum, London (2011)
25. Carson, K.A.: The homebrew industrial revolution. Center for a Stateless Society Paper No (2009)
26. Frayling, C.: On Craftsmanship. Towards a New Bauhaus. Oberon Books Ltd., Great Britain (2011)
27. Open Glasgow: 2014 ideas for hackathons (2014). http://open.glasgow.gov.uk/2014-ideas-for-hackathons/
28. Tooze, J., Baurley, S., Phillips, R., Smith, P., Foote, E., Silve, S.: Open design: contribution, solutions, processes and projects. Des. J. **17**, 538–559 (2014)
29. Coughlan, S.: Surgery students 'losing dexterity to stitch patients' (2018). https://www.bbc.co.uk/news/education-46019429

30. House of Lords: The Make or Break: The UK's Digital Future (No. HL paper 111). The Stationary Office Ltd., London (2015)
31. Blackwood, N.: Digital skills crisis: second report of session 2016–17: report, together with formal minutes relating to the report: ordered by the House of Commons to be printed 7 June 2016 (No. HC 270). UK Parliament, London (2016)
32. Raspberry Pi: A credit card sized computer that plugs into your TV and a keyboard (2013). http://www.raspberrypi.org/
33. BBC: Mending our disposable culture (2018). https://www.bbc.co.uk/programmes/p06mpb1d
34. Mari, E.: Autoprogettazione?, 1st edn. Corraini, Mantova (2002)
35. van Abel, B.: Open Design Now: Why Design Cannot Remain Exclusive. Bis, Amsterdam (2011)
36. Ratto, M., Boler, M.: DIY Citizenship: Critical Making and Social Media. MIT Press, Cambridge (2014)
37. Haw, K., Hornigold, K.: Wood Wise NATURE INSPIRES EDUCATION Woodland Conservation News, Autumn 2017. Woodland Trust, United Kingdom (2017)
38. Davies, Z.G., Fuller, R.A., Loram, A., Irvine, K.N., Sims, V., Gaston, K.J.: A national scale inventory of resource provision for biodiversity within domestic gardens. Biol. Conserv. **142** (4), 761–771 (2009)
39. Cox, D.T.C., Gaston, K.J.: Human-nature interactions and the consequences and drivers of provisioning wildlife. Philos. Trans. Roy. Soc. Lond. Ser. B Biol. Sci. **373** (1745), 20170092 (2018). https://doi.org/10.1098/rstb.2017.0092 [pii]
40. Robinson, R.A., et al.: Emerging infectious disease leads to rapid population declines of common British birds. PLoS ONE **5**(8), e12215 (2010)
41. BBC: Birdsong phone apps 'harmful' to birds, say Dorset experts (2013). https://www.bbc.co.uk/news/uk-england-dorset-22863383
42. Heller, S., Vienne, V.: Citizen Designer: Perspectives on Design Responsibility, 1st edn. Skyhorse Publishing Inc., New York (2003)
43. Vaajakallio, K., Mattelmäki, T.: Collaborative design exploration: envisioning future practices with make tools. In: Proceedings of the 2007 Conference on Designing Pleasurable Products and Interfaces, pp. 223–238 (2007)
44. Björgvinsson, E.B.: Open-ended participatory design as prototypical practice. Co-Design **4** (2), 85–99 (2008)
45. Murphy, E., Hands, D.: Wisdom of the crowd: how participatory design has evolved design briefing. Des. Res. J. **8**, 28–37 (2012)
46. Suri, J.F.: Inclusive design through individual insight. In: Proceedings of the Human Factors and Ergonomics Society Annual Meeting, vol. 44, no. 38, pp. 897–900 (2000)
47. Chapman, J.: Design for (emotional) durability. Des. Issues **25**(4), 29–35 (2009)
48. Lofthouse, V., Lilley, D.: What they really, really want: user centred research methods for design (2006)
49. Lindo, D.: The urban birder (2018). https://theurbanbirder.com/
50. Lumber, R., Richardson, M., Sheffield, D.: Beyond knowing nature: contact, emotion, compassion, meaning, and beauty are pathways to nature connection. PloS ONE **12**(5), e0177186 (2017)
51. Hecker, S., Haklay, M., Bowser, A., Makuch, Z., Vogel, J., Bonn, A.: Innovation in open science, society and policy–setting the agenda for citizen science. In: Citizen Science, vol. 1 (2018). https://doi.org/10.14324/111.9781787352339
52. Sussex Wildlife Trust: The Sussex wildlife trust is the leading nature conservation organisation covering east Sussex, west Sussex and Brighton and hove (2013). http://www.sussexwildlifetrust.org.uk/index.htm?id=default

53. Sorensen, A., van Beest, F.M., Brook, R.K.: Impacts of wildlife baiting and supplemental feeding on infectious disease transmission risk: a synthesis of knowledge. Prev. Vet. Med. **113**(4), 356–363 (2014)
54. Schumacher, E.F.: Small is Beautiful: A Study of Economics as if People Mattered, 2nd edn. Random House, New York (2011)
55. Schumacher College: MA ecological design thinking (2018). https://www. schumachercollege.org.uk/courses/postgraduate-courses/ecological-design-thinking
56. Crilly, N., Moultrie, J., Clarkson, P.J.: Seeing things: consumer response to the visual domain in product design. Des. Stud. **25**(6), 547–577 (2004)
57. Kew: About Kew's seed collection, the millennium seed bank (2018). https://www.kew.org/ science/collections/seed-collection
58. National Trust: Botanical garden with the world's largest seed conservation project (2018). https://www.nationaltrust.org.uk/wakehurst#Overview
59. Board of Trustees of the Royal Botanic Gardens: Royal botanic gardens, Kew annual report and accounts for the year ended 31 march 2017 (No. HC 164). Printed in the UK by the Williams Lea Group on behalf of the Controller of Her Majesty's Stationery Office, UK (2017)
60. The National Trust: National Trust, Annual Report 2017/18. The National Trust, UK (2018). www.nationaltrust.org.uk/features/annual-reports
61. Transition Town Lewes: Transition Town Lewes (2018). https://www.transitiontownlewes. org/about.html
62. Depot: Depot is an independent community cinema and cafe-restaurant with education facilities, created and operated by the charity Lewes community screen (2018). https:// lewesdepot.org/about-us
63. Manzini, E., Coad, R.: Design, When Everybody Designs: An Introduction to Design for Social Innovation. MIT Press, Cambridge (2015)
64. Kilick, A.: Building a small cinema: resisting neoliberal colonization in Liverpool. Architecture_MPS **12**(3), 1–16 (2017)
65. Victoria and Albert Museum: Digital design weekend 2018 join artists, engineers and technologists for a weekend of free workshops, talks and demonstrations exploring the intersection of technology and design (2018). https://www.vam.ac.uk/event/6YVLW34q/ digital-design-weekend-2018-ldf
66. Association of Leading Visitor Attractions: Latest visitor figures visits made in 2017 to visitor attractions in membership with Alva (2017). http://www.alva.org.uk/details.cfm?p= 423
67. The Design Museum: The design museum, plan your visit (2018). https://designmuseum. org/plan-your-visit
68. Fairs, M.: Design museum beats annual visitor target after just 10 months, but only one fifth pay to visit exhibitions (2017). https://www.dezeen.com/2017/10/02/design-museum-london-beats-annual-visitor-target-only-one-fifth-pay-exhibitions/
69. Holland Park Ecology Centre: Wild life home, explore, discover be active in the royal borough (2018). https://www.rbkc.gov.uk/subsites/wildlife.aspx
70. Jordan, R.C., Gray, S.A., Howe, D.V., Brooks, W.R., Ehrenfeld, J.G.: Knowledge gain and behavioral change in citizen-science programs. Conserv. Biol. **25**(6), 1148 (2011)
71. Kuznetsov, S., Paulos, E.: Rise of the expert amateur: DIY projects, communities, and cultures. In: Proceedings of the 6th Nordic Conference on Human-Computer Interaction: Extending Boundaries, pp. 295–304(2010)
72. Leeson, G.W.: The growth, ageing and urbanisation of our world. J. Population Ageing **11** (2), 107–115-9 (2018)

73. Kalkanci, B., Rahmani, M., Toktay, L.B.: Social sustainability in emerging economies: the role of 'Inclusive innovation'. Georgia Tech Scheller College of Business Research Paper no. 18–24 (2018). https://doi.org/10.2139/ssrn.3192623. https://ssrn.com/abstract=3192623

74. Jackson, C.K., Bruegmann, E.: Teaching students and teaching each other: the importance of peer learning for teachers. Am. Econ. J. Appl. Econ. 1(4), 85–108 (2009)

75. Hess, K.: Community Technology. Harper and Row, New York (1979)

76. Clary, E.G., Snyder, M.: The motivations to volunteer theoretical and practical considerations. Curr. Dir. Psychol. Sci. 8(5), 156–159 (1999)

77. Roy, H.E., Popcock, M.J.O., Preston, C.D., Roy, D.B., Savage, J.: Understanding Citizen Science and Environmental Monitoring. Centre for Ecology & Hydrology, Natural Environment Research Council, London (2012)

78. Heiman, M.K.: Science by the people: grassroots environmental monitoring and the debate over scientific expertise. J. Plan. Educ. Res. 16(4), 291–299 (1997)

79. Gaver, W.: What should we expect from research through design? In: Proceedings of the SIGCHI Conference on Human Factors in Computing Systems, pp. 937–946 (2012)

80. King, S.: Nature Watch, How to Track and Observe Wildlife, 1st edn. Quadrille, London (2016)

81. Buckley, R., Pannell, J.: Environmental impacts of tourism and recreation in national parks and conservation reserves. J. Tour. Stud. 1(1), 24–32 (1990)

82. IDEO: The Little Book of Design Ethics, 1st edn. IDEO, London (2015)

83. Child Protection Resource: Child protection resource (2018). http://childprotectionresource.online/category/taking-photographs-of-children/

84. Wallach, A.D., Bekoff, M., Batavia, C., Nelson, M.P., Ramp, D.: Summoning compassion to address the challenges of conservation. Conserv. Biol. 32, 1255–1265 (2018)

85. Whatmore, S., Thorne, L.: Wild (er) ness: reconfiguring the geographies of wildlife. Trans. Inst. Br. Geograph. 23(4), 435–454 (1998)

86. Cutler, T.L., Swann, D.E.: Using remote photography in wildlife ecology: a review. Wildlife Soc. Bull. 27(3), 571–581 (1999). Autumn

87. Sousa, M.J., Rocha, Á.: Skills for disruptive digital business. J. Bus. Res. 94, 257–263 (2019)

88. Hartig, T., et al.: Health benefits of nature experience: psychological, social and cultural processes. In: Nilsson, K., Sangster, M., Gallis, C., Hartig, T., de Vries, S., Seeland, K. (eds.) Forests, Trees and Human Health, 1st edn, pp. 127–168. Springer, Dordrecht (2011). https://doi.org/10.1007/978-90-481-9806-1_5

89. NHS England: Social prescribing (2018). https://www.england.nhs.uk/contact-us/privacy-notice/how-we-use-your-information/public-and-partners/social-prescribing/

90. BBC: Dance lessons for the lonely (2018). https://www.bbc.co.uk/news/health-45861468

91. Foster, L.: Active ageing, pensions and retirement in the UK. J. Population Ageing 11(2), 117–132 (2018)

92. PokemonGo: Pokemon go (2018). https://www.pokemon.com/uk/pokemon-video-games/pokemon-go/

93. Althoff, T., White, R.W., Horvitz, E.: Influence of Pokemon go on physical activity: study and implications. J. Med. Internet Res. 18(12), e315 (2016). https://doi.org/10.2196/jmir.6759 [pii]

94. Colley, A., et al.: The geography of Pokémon Go: beneficial and problematic effects on places and movement. In: Proceedings of the 2017 CHI Conference on Human Factors in Computing Systems, pp. 1179–1192 (2017)

95. Tateno, M., Skokauskas, N., Kato, T.A., Teo, A.R., Guerrero, A.P.S.: New game software (Pokemon Go) may help youth with severe social withdrawal, hikikomori. Psychiatry Res. 246, 848–849 (2016). S0165-1781(16)31298-7 [pii]

96. Andrews, C.G.: Smartphone apps pinpoint wildlife sightings in yellowstone, but is that a good idea? http://goodnature.nathab.com/smartphone-apps-pinpoint-wildlife-sightings-in-yellowstone-but-is-that-a-good-idea/

97. Lester, C.: Public engagement (2018). https://webarchive.nationalarchives.gov.uk/20180319121326/. http://www.hefce.ac.uk/rsrch/publicengage/

Digital Memorialization in Death-Ridden Societies: How HCI Could Contribute to Death Rituals in Taiwan and Japan

Daisuke Uriu[1(✉)], Ju-Chun Ko[2], Bing-Yu Chen[3], Atsushi Hiyama[1], and Masahiko Inami[1]

[1] Research Center for Advanced Science and Technology, The University of Tokyo, Meguro-ku, Japan
{uriu,hiyama,inami}@star.rcast.u-tokyo.ac.jp
[2] Department of Interaction Design, National Taipei University of Technology, Taipei, Taiwan
dablog@gmail.com
[3] National Taiwan University, Taipei, Taiwan
robin@ntu.edu.tw

Abstract. Both Taiwan and Japan are entering an area of hyper aged and death-ridden society. The death rituals in both countries are rapidly changing due to urbanization and secularization, although both cultures have long histories and traditions for funeral and memorialization. Furthermore, some digital technologies have already been adopted in both countries, providing alternative changes for some occasions. This paper principally reports contemporary funeral and memorialization practices in Taipei and Tokyo by introducing insights from our fieldworks and interviews in both cities. These also include examples of digital technology adoption. Comprehensively understanding phenomena being caused by local faiths and traditions, we will discuss how ICT/HCI designers could contribute to the realm of local memorializations and more generally around the world, and what kind of design opportunities for the future death rituals they could be involved in.

Keywords: Death and HCI · Technology · Mourning · Funeral · Memorialization · Remembrance · Thanatosensitive design · Taiwan · Japan

1 Introduction

Both Taiwan and Japan are becoming hyper aged societies. This means that not only the population of elderly people, but also the number of deaths are rapidly increasing. Around 2040, it is said that the annual number of death in Japan will be the highest since after the WWII.[1] While although Taiwan is little bit

---

[1] In 2016, the number of death was around 1.3 million, but it is estimated to be 1.68 million in 2039 [1].

© Springer Nature Switzerland AG 2019
J. Zhou and G. Salvendy (Eds.): HCII 2019, LNCS 11592, pp. 532–550, 2019.
https://doi.org/10.1007/978-3-030-22012-9_38

behind Japan on the aging, its crude death rate in 2050 will be almost twice than today.[2] With the coming of death-ridden societies in both countries, ritual practices and people's thoughts on memorialization are also rapidly shifting.

Each country is a small island and has intense density of population in the city area, particularly Taipei and Tokyo. Although Taiwan and Japan are geographically close and influence one another, the religious and local customs are slightly different (e.g. [3–6]). Funerals and the other memorialization rituals in Tokyo, mostly based on Japanese Buddhism, are becoming more and more simplified in the last decade (e.g. [4,6,7]). Japan has a relatively long history of cremation and today, where over 99.9% of bodies are cremated [7].

In contrast, Taiwanese people more rigorously follow traditions based on Taoism, Feng Shui, and some local traditions (e.g. [5,6,8]). Even though people historically have practiced traditional burial and reburial rituals, which in total takes 6 to 7 years, they have now adopted cremation in the last decade. Today, over 95% of Taiwanese are cremated.[3] With increased cremation and the urbanization of memorialization practices, Taiwanese funerals and subsequent memorial practices in the city area are also rapidly changing. Since the shift to cremation in Taiwan occurred over a relatively short period of less than 30 years, Taiwanese people are more conservative and still keep to tradition [6] compared to Japan, where rituals are becoming more diverse and even simplified. But Taiwan and Japan share some ritual artifacts in common such as flower, incense, the mortuary tablet, coffin, urn, photography, and etc.

On the other hand, people in both countries are rapidly adopting Information and Communication Technologies (hereafter 'ICTs') not only in their daily life, but also in their memorialization practices. For example, there have been digital photo frames on the altars in funeral halls in Taipei since almost 10 years ago, according to our fieldwork described below. There are several online memorialization web services produced in Taiwan.[4] Further, in some columbaria in Japan, digital displays show the deceased's photos and his/her life data [12]. The question of how to utilize technologies in designing memorialization experiences is becoming a key issue in both countries.

Addressing this situation, this paper focuses on seeking how the deceased's memory and presence could be digitally archived, utilized, and inherited by the next generation within a hyper aged and soon-to-be death-ridden society. After briefly introducing traditional death rituals in Taiwan and Japan, we first examine the existing academic and case reports on digital commemoration. We then examine several websites—mostly hosted by funeral companies—to analyze contemporary funerary rituals and practices. These provide instructive visuals, text, and videos for customers. To support this analysis, we visited practical sites in both countries including funeral halls, cemeteries, columbaria, and related

---

[2] While the crude death rate was 7.5% in 2018, it is estimated to be 15% in 2050 [2].

[3] In 1993, the percentage of cremation in Taiwan was 45%, but it was 96% in 2017 [9].

[4] For example, a "Cloud Remembrance Platform System" was launched by Kaohsiung City on January 16, 2018 [10]. In a columbarium, a similar service using QR code has been commercialized [11].

expos. Occasionally and whenever needed, we interviewed people who work at these sites in order to understand contemporary rituals in Taipei and Tokyo.

Reviewing and analyzing these data, we describe the basic scheme of funeral procedures each in Taipei and Tokyo, and what kind of both analog and digital objects—related to the deceased—have been adopted. Holistically addressing these phenomena, we will discuss what kind of design opportunities there are for either archiving or utilizing the digital remains for/in the memorialization practices. Especially, we focus on discussing how people in the death-ridden societies could prepare for their deaths and what kind of technology-enabled designs are required by those who will encounter a death-ridden society. Finally, we will argue how ICT/HCI designers and creators handle people's memories in the sensitive contexts especially related with the death rituals in general, by learning from this research.

2   Background and Related Works

2.1   Key Objects for Memorialization in Taiwan and Japan

Over hundreds of years in Japan, cremated remains (cremains) have been highly appreciated and protected. Since cremation became popular from the late of 19th Century to 20th Century, people have favored constructing family gravesites in which multiple urns were stored over generations (e.g. [3]).

On comparison, the cremation history of Taiwan is shorter than Japan. Traditionally, the Taiwanese have also appreciated the dead's bones through the unique burial custom known as bone washing (撿骨) ritual. However, due to rapid urbanization and limited land for gravesites, Taipei city local government has promoted cremation to its citizen and built many public columbaria in the last 30 years (e.g. [8,13]).

Since the 1990s, customs and rituals for burial and disposal in Japan rapidly begun to change. Natural burials, defined in Japan as a means of interring cremains, such as the tree burial (directly placing ashes in the ground) and the sea burial (scattering ashes at the sea) has spread through society, as people who are unmarried or without children faced difficulties in keeping and maintaining their family gravesites. (e.g. [14,15]) In recent years, cases of isolated death and unclaimed cremains have become well-known social problems [7], broadcasted by major newspapers and TV shows. Though the custom of natural burials has yet to spread throughout Japanese society, memorial rituals are gradually shifting toward natural burials and other alternatives.

In Taiwan, Taipei city local government has been promoting the natural burial methods: "tree burial," "flower burial," and "sea burial" as a means of the saving its limited land space [8,13]. However, a limited number of extremely wealthy people in Taipei still refuse to adopt cremation even though they have to pay a vast sum of money[5] in order to purchase a gravesite for burial [6].

---

[5] Over ten million TWD: about three hundred thousand USD.

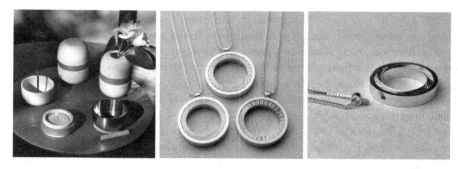

Fig. 1. *Temoto kuyo* products. Left: *"Mayudama"* [18], Middle & Right: "TORUS" [19]

In both Taiwan and Japan, the spirit tablet or mortuary tablet—*páiwèi* (牌位) in Taiwanese and *ihai* (位牌) in Japanese—has been interpreted as one of most important items involved in memorialization practices. Traditionally in Taiwan, *páiwèi* is initially made of paper by the Taoism master at the funeral, and after one year, is replaced by one made of wood for the bereaved family's home altar [5,6]. Contrastively, Japanese *ihai* is inscribed with a Buddhist posthumous name *kaimyo* (戒名)[6] and used at the funeral and domestic memorial customs at Buddhist altars (e.g. [3,16,17]). Similar to Taiwan, *ihai* is initially made of a light wood by the Buddhist priest, but 49 days after the dead, it is replaced by one formally made of wood stained with Japanese lacquer that is placed at the home altar. During the period when the deceased in Taiwan is represented by a paper tablet (one year), the bereaved family has to take care of him/her, offering incense and food every day. Otherwise, it is said the hungry ancestor will became a "ghost" who brings his/her decedents misfortunes and troubles [5,6]. In comparison to Taiwan, Japanese faiths and rituals for the spirit tablet *ihai* are relatively informal and becoming increasingly secularized especially for the younger generations.

2.2 Secularization, "Bodiless" Memorial, and Digitalization

According to contemporary research of Japan, several artifacts are taking over the *ihai* in ritual and informal settings. Suzuki [16] reports that many of Japanese families display framed photographs of the deceased or *iei* (遺影) instead of *ihai*. People who adopt *"temoto kuyo* (手元供養)"—a way of keeping ashes (cremains) stored in micro-containers or urns at home[7] —(e.g. [14]) usually display their

---

[6] Except the Buddhist school of *Jōdo-Sinshū* (浄土真宗) that gives the deceased a *hōmyo* (法名) or precept name during their lifetime, and does not make *ihai*.

[7] For example, a product—consisting of small urn and items for Japanese styled memorialization: incense tray, candle holder, *rin* (Buddhist instrument), and flower vase— has been marketed (Left on Fig. 1). Jewelry in which ashes can be inserted has been also produced by several Japanese companies (e.g. Middle and Right on Fig. 1).

temoto kuyo urns at home along with the deceased's portrait. Some still use *ihais* but some have thrown such traditional ritual items away.

Furthermore, in several cases photos used in memorialization practices have been digitalized, which can shift the meaning and value of such displays. New style columbaria known-as Automatic Conveyor-belt Columbaria (ACC) located in urbanized areas of Japan adopt digital displays of *iei* picture, *kaimyo*, and the other information about the deceased [12]. Gould et al. [17] describe contemporary secularizations of domestic memorialization rituals in Japan and introduce some digitalized Buddhist altar (*butsudan*) examples. An online *butsudan* service called Onra'in described in this article appears like a digitalized *butsudan* and virtually displays a family's *ihai*. Yet it also archives and shows pictures of/about the deceased, which technically more closely resembles online photo archiving services such as Google Photos [20].

Outside of Japan, death rituals including funeral, burial, disposal, and memorialization have been rapidly changed and secularized. Cann argues in her book [21] that memorial practices in the United States have been "bodiless," as people do not face the corpse or the nature of death given the rise of embalming and cremation throughout 20th Century. She claims people are now shifting to adopt "virtual afterlives" enabled by online memorial services and SNS on which the deceased could be represented again, although they are hidden from the rest of the (offline) world. Similarly, Arnold et al. [22] investigates how people mourn, commemorate, and interact with the dead through digital media, reviewing existing digital memorial platforms with a series of case studies drawn from North America, Europe, and Australia.

Of particular note are SNS such as Facebook and Instagram, which allow people to utilize several contents and services specialized for memorialization. Facebook provides "Memorialized Accounts" [23], a function that enables a particular user account belonging to the dead to be closed or changed to become an online memorial platform. (e.g. [24–27]) On Facebook, a service called "Legacy Contact" has been released. With it, a living user can appoint another as a Legacy Contact who has responsibility to manage the account in case of his/her death. [27] In another novel use of social media, Gibbs [25] surveyed photographs shared on Instagram public profiles tagged with "#funeral" and revealed how the users have already invented new but vernacular rituals for the context of death, mourning, and memorialization.

Especially in the West, several scholars have begun to study how digital technologies shape the presence of the dead in the society. (e.g. [21,22,24–26]) As Cann [21] pointed out, the presence of the dead has represented online while traditional death rituals (mostly based on religious thought) are simplified and secularized. Notably in the urbanized regions including Taipei and Tokyo, physical spaces for graveyard has been almost exhausted. This is the realm in which digital technology has already intervened and emerging technologies may contribute.

2.3   Death and HCI

Especially within the HCI (Human Computer Interaction) research community, there has been growing interest in how interactive technology intersects with experiences of bereavement and memorialization. For example, some systems working on smart phones have been installed in cemeteries or graveyards. Gotved [28] surveyed QR codes on gravestones in Denmark and revealed how people adopt a digital memorial culture as provided by the QR code cemeteries which connect physical sites with virtual memories. Now both in Japan (e.g. [29]) and Taiwan (e.g. [11]), there are also commercialized graveyards or columbaria utilizing QR code identification. Simultaneously, Häkkilä et al. [30] designed a location-aware navigation application at a graveyard. Also in Japan, similar smart phone applications have been released (e.g. [31]).

Massimi and others [32] argue "thanatosensitive design"—design that engages with the many issues bound to mortality, dying, and death through the creation of interactive systems—is a critical emerging area for HCI research and practice. Foong and Kera [33] adopt a reflective design lens [34] to interpreting experiences of digital memorials. The first author in this paper Uriu et al. [35] proposed a digital family shrine concept for people to remember deceased relatives. Following this work, Uriu and Okude [36] describe an interactive altar with the candle flame called "ThanatoFenestra" for supporting ritual prayer for one's ancestors. Applying and evolving its concept, Uriu and Odom [37] proposed an interactive altar called "Fenestra" and conducted deployment studies in domestic environments. They and others [38] are also trying to utilize incense smoke for memorialization practices. Wallace et al. [39] suggested digital locket jewelry that enables a digital legacy to be archived along with particular narratives about the deceased.

Reviewing these examples and many others, Moncur and Kirk [40] offer a framework for designing digital memorials. They articulate the need for future research to explore how interactive systems shape practices related to the post-self—how the identity of the departed is socially constructed. They [41] actually designed "Story Shell" an interactive sound player working with a sound-gathering system, which is specialized for archiving and playing back stories about the deceased. Odom et al. [42] model the design of future technologies aimed at supporting a relationship between the living and the dead, reviewing the process of their works Fenestra [37] and Timecard [43]. Pitsillides [44] proposes how to create new forms of agency for the dead by arranging the digital legacies the deceased leaves. In order to make digital legacies have agencies or keep the dead's presence in the society, she points out how designers can combine digital legacies with physical and digital materialities such as ThanatoFenestra [36], Story Shell [41], digital locket [39], and etc.

As we described above, Taiwan and Japan share some of objects for funeral and memorialization rituals. However, due to limitations on land and secularization in cities, each country's traditions and rituals are shifting. Faster than in Taiwan, some alternative products such as *temoto kuyo* (e.g. [14]) and ACC [12] have already discovered new markets in Japan. In the West, digital/online

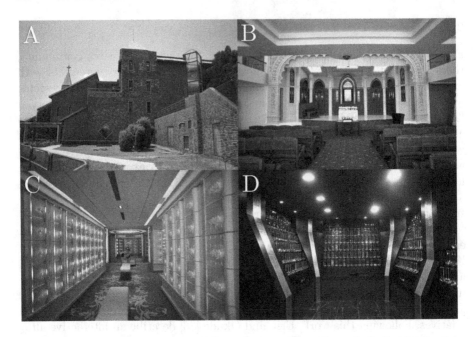

Fig. 2. Sunshine Life Memorial Hall (A: appearance, B: ceremony hall, C: columbarium floor, D: spirit tablet hall)

memorials are swiftly penetrating society, which illustrates existing ICTs have already been utilized for death related designs. We are now at the stage of exploring how emerging technologies within HCI could contribute to this realm.

Exploring contemporary cases in Taipei and Tokyo, this paper provides insight into multiple important topics of interdisciplinary concerns, identifying some design opportunities where ICT/HCI could successfully contribute. It proposes a set of future design directions to both Taiwanese and Japanese industries for funeral and memorial services, as well as what kind of topics the death related scholars should investigate, and how designers and engineers in the HCI community could collaborate with them.

3   Contemporary Funeral and Memorialization Practices

3.1   Methodology

This section consists of data captured in our field studies and interviews in both Taipei and Tokyo. In Taiwan, we had an opportunity to contact and visit Chin-PaoSan (金寶山) [45], established in 1977, which is one of the largest companies for memorial services in the country. It owns a huge region for cemeteries and columbaria in the north Taiwan area, and also provides funeral services in Taipei city at their funeral hall called ChinPaoXuan (金寶軒). The first field study, visiting their columbaria located in the north Taiwan area and ChinPaoXuan, was

Fig. 3. The funeral altars in the ChinPaoXuan hall.

conducted in 2016. After that, we had several opportunities to interview with their staff up until 2019. To understand Japanese landscape in 2019, we interviewed an individual working at funeral halls in Tokyo who actually conducts an array of funeral practices, including deciding funeral procedures with bereaved families, coordinating with Buddhist priests to hold rituals, and finally, working as an emcee at the funeral ceremonies. In addition to capturing these examples, we received some pictures taken at a funeral by a person who lost her grandmother in 2015. To comprehensively describe the situations in each city, we also refer to Web articles, films, media, and so on as necessary.

3.2   Taipei, Taiwan

Contemporary Funeral Procedure

One of ChinPaoSan's columbaria called "Sunshine Life Memorial Hall (日光苑)," architecturally resembles a Christian church and its interior is completely modern (Fig. 2). It holds memorial services within any religious and cultural backgrounds, such as Taoism, Buddhism, Christianity, and even none-religious. Before ChinPaoSan began to make columbaria in the latter part of 20th Century, Taiwanese columbaria were known to have a dark atmosphere with interiors that resembled simple storage facilities. Public columbaria today retain this design, but are available to everybody. Following the emergence of ChinPaoSan's columbaria, other companies also produced modern style columbaria in Taiwan, marketed especially to the wealthier people.

According to their website, the contemporary funeral service in Taipei is roughly divided into eight procedures, as below.[8]

(1) Hospice care
(2) Transport of the deceased
(3) Setting-up of the funeral hall
(4) Funeral coordination

---

[8] https://www.memory.com.tw/en/education.php#process. The introduction video (Taiwanese) is also available on https://www.youtube.com/watch?v=i_l8lz8V1Ts.

Fig. 4. Left: An urn specially designed for Sunshine Life Memorial Hall (Fig. 2) produced by ChinPaoSan, Right: an urn prepared at an urn shop in Taipei city

(5) Encoffinment
(6) Offering ceremony
(7) Cremation, columbarium (Installment/Interment)
(8) Follow up care

In phase (1), when funeral staff are informed a person is dying soon, they begin to prepare a whole package for the funeral ceremony. Just after the person dies in phase (2), they collect the deceased's body and move it to a public mortuary facility. Then the (Taoism or Buddhist[9]) priest holds a ritual to transfer "the deceased's spirit" to a spirit tablet, while the body is frozen and kept until the day for encoffinment (5). Simultaneously, the funeral staff talk with the bereaved family to decide the details of the funeral plan (3). In Taiwan, the day for encoffinment (5) and the day for the offering (departure) ceremony (6) and the cremation/burial date (7) do not occur on a fixed timeline. These dates are individually decided according to "the good days" following Feng Shui and Taoism. In phase (4), the spirit tablet is placed on the altar in the funeral hall such as in Figs. 3 and 5. During the days leading up to for final offering (farewell) ceremony (6), the bereaved family and any guests may to visit the altar, which is usually approximately one week. The bereaved finally reencounter—the first time after it got frozen (2)—the deceased's body at the public funeral hall when the corpse is cremated in the encoffinment (5) and the final ceremony (6). It takes a few days during phases (5) and (6), accompanied with some religious and local rituals with priests. In phase (7), cremains in an urn are installed in the columbarium such as Sunshine Life Memorial Hall after a ceremony at the hall (e.g. Fig. 2B). Urns in Taiwan are normally made of stone[10] and engraved with the deceased's name, portrait, his/her birth place, and dates of his/her

---

[9] In Taiwan, Catholic Christians also adopt the custom of spirit tablets, but Protestants do not.

[10] Commodity and cheaper one is made of marble stone but more expensive and highest quality one is made of jade stone.

Fig. 5. An actual example of a funeral altar layout (A: digital photo portrait, B: spirit tablet, C: offerings, D: messages and letters to the deceased, E: flower petals for visitors to be offered on the altar)

birth and death (Right of Fig. 4). After the package of funeral procedure, Chin-PaoSan focuses on following up with the bereaved family including grief care practices. The average duration from phase (2) to (7) is twenty days.

Rituals in Front of Funeral Altar
As shown in Fig. 5, the funeral altar consists of many objects. The digital monitor shows the portrait of the deceased in which multiple pictures can be stored and played as a slideshow. The spirit tablet is placed on the altar centrally with small dolls as servants to the deceased. Some offerings such as foods, drinks, snacks, flowers etc. are placed around it. Traditionally in Taiwan, during the period between death and the main ceremony, bereaved family members hold many local rituals (e.g. constantly offering incense sticks, performing "crying" whenever visitors come, and etc.)[11]. But nowadays in Taipei city, funeral companies have largely taken over these traditional rituals, corresponding with contemporary changes to people's working lives in the city area. At ChinPaoXuan, the staff offer foods and maintain the altars everyday, so the bereaved do not have to do anything. Yet, some of them frequently visit the altar and want to spend time with the deceased. For those visitors who would like to do something for the deceased, flower petals (Fig. 5B) and materials for writing letters (Fig. 5D)

---

[11] A Taiwanese movie called "Seven Days in Heaven (父後七日)" illustrates these traditional rituals [46].

Fig. 6. A funeral altar layout at the hall located in near Tokyo

are available in the hall. Traditionally, Taiwanese people pray for or "talk" with the deceased via the incense sticks, but today the use of fire is prohibited inside the newer buildings by the law. During the days the altar is set up in the hall, normally 100–200 people visit the altar. However, there is rarely an encounter with the corpse in the contemporary funerals in Taipei city.

3.3   Tokyo, Japan

Contemporary Funeral Procedure

Japanese funeral procedure is shorter than in Taiwan, basically as a result of differences in local religious faiths and ritual traditions. Memorialization practices in Japan are mostly derived from Buddhism, but some local rituals appear more vernacular. As a reference, we will introduce the procedure described on a website by a funeral association group called Bellco [47]. Since funerals in Japan are becoming simplified especially in the city area, traditional rituals are sometimes shorten or skipped [4]. But the procedure below is still standard in Japan, even in Tokyo.[12]

  (i) Death and Transport of the deceased
 (ii) Consulting with bereaved family and funeral coordination
(iii) Encoffinment

---

[12] Here is a set of explanations about Japanese funerals in English [48].

Fig. 7. Urns made of ceramic, commonly used in Japan

(iv) Night wake/memorial vigil
(v) Farewell funeral ceremony and cremation
(vi) Follow up care

In phase (i), when a person dies, the bereaved family call the funeral company. Sooner than later, the staff from the company transport the body to the funeral hall.[13] In phase (ii), the staff introduce their funeral package plans to the bereaved, who have to decide on a plan, choosing from options. Then, the company and the deceased decide dates for the night wake (iv), the farewell ceremony, and cremation (v); by checking the crematorium's availability, the bereaved's schedule, the Japanese calendar's six labels called *rokuyo*[14], and availability of a Buddhist priest who holds a set of rituals. While in Taiwan the encoffinment (5) is scheduled at least one week later than death, in Japan the body is encoffined at the same day of night wake (iv) usually just a few days after death.[15] The funeral altar is set up in the funeral hall (e.g. Fig. 6) before the beginning of the wake (iv). At the same time, the encoffined body is placed in front of the altar. At the night wake, the priest comes and holds a set of rituals with the bereaved family and guests related with the deceased. All visitors burn incense chips for the deceased.[16] As with Taiwan, a white wooden spirit tablet called *ihai* (位牌) is commonly placed on the funeral altar, which is engraved with the deceased's

---

[13] It was popular that the body is moved back to his or her home once from the hospital though final funeral ceremonies are held at the funeral hall. But today about 75% dead bodies are directly moved to the funeral hall.

[14] One of *rokuyo* labels *tomobiki* (友引) literally translates to "pulling a friend." Due to it's name, it is considered bad luck to schedule any funerals on these days. [49].

[15] A Japanese film called "*Okuribito*" [50] focused on the encoffinment specialist called *nokanshi* (納棺師). *Nokanshi* cleanses the body, lets it wear the burial outfit, and makes up the face, and encoffins it to the coffin with the bereaved family.

[16] The Japanese wake ritual originally means "the last night" with the deceased, hence the close relatives spend time together with the body until the morning. Nowadays in the city area, the night wake ends at 9pm.

Fig. 8. Left: a portrait of the deceased *iei* on the funeral altar, Right: Photos reminding of the deceased's memories displayed on an another altar in the funeral hall

posthumous name called "*kaimyo* (戒名)" given by the Buddhist priest. In phase (v), the final funeral ceremony is scheduled for 1.5–2 h prior to cremation. The priest holds some rituals and all visitors including the bereaved holds the incense ceremony again. After that, the bereaved family see the deceased for the last time. Then the body is moved to the crematorium and is cremated. After the cremation, the bereaved family members collaboratively pick up cremated bones and place them into an urn, usually made of white ceramics (Fig. 7). In Japan, installing the urn into the cemetery or columbarium should be scheduled for 49 days after death. Between the cremation and installation, the urn is generally stored at the bereaved's home. At the installation of the urn, the bereaved prepares a formal spirit tablet with the posthumous name engraved on it and asks the priest to hold a ritual to enshrine the spirit of the dead into the tablet.

Portrait of the Deceased, Use of Photos

A photographic portrait of the deceased is one of most important objects in a Japanese funeral. It is placed on the funeral altar throughout the night wake (iv) and the farewell ceremony (v). When the bereaved family accompany the deceased for cremation at the crematorium, one deceased family member brings this picture, called *iei* (遺影) (e.g. shown in the left of Fig. 8) as well as the *ihai* tablet. Both before and after the cremation, the *iei* portrait takes a key role in representing the deceased as an iconic presence. However, bereaved families have to find a photo of the deceased for an *iei* right after the death, despite being shocked and saddened by the loss. The *iei* picture—the image is cropped to the face and the original photo background is generally erased—has to be prepared for setting up the funeral altar before the night wake (iv) begins.

Corresponding to this need today, many *iei* portraits are systematically produced by on-demand workflows. Asukanet [51]—a pioneer company providing a remote *iei* production service—holds almost 30% of the market share in Japan. The bereaved family prepared a photo and pass it to the funeral staff. Then, the photo will be scanned and its data remotely sent to one of the photo editing centers run by Asukanet. A professional operator immediately edits the image, produces an *iei* picture, and sends it back to the funeral company. Finally, at the funeral hall, the *iei* picture will be printed automatically. In some of funeral halls in Japan, digital monitors for displaying *iei* pictures are installed, but this is still not popular in Japan.

In contemporary funeral ceremonies in Japan, not only the *iei* picture but also other photos (snapshots) are displayed in the funeral hall. For example, shown on the left of Fig. 8, some photos are displayed on another altar close to the main funeral altar (Fig. 6) by the hall staff. These consist of photos of the deceased, ones taken with her family and relatives, ones of her last days taken by staff in a care home, and etc. Interestingly, in this case, another *iei* picture frame of her husband who had passed away previously was also displayed (to the right of the right image, Fig. 8).

4   Design Opportunities in Death-Ridden Societies

4.1   Presence of Spirit

People both in Taiwan and Japan have traditional faiths with rituals for honoring the "spirit" of the deceased. Although the details of the rituals are different between the two countries, spirit is mutually "installed" in the spirit tablet that is appreciated and inherited by the bereaved and their descendants. (e.g. [3,5,6]) While Taiwanese rituals around the tablet—and how to treat the dead spirit—are still relatively strict and there remains strong belief levels in its society [6], Japanese rites are gradually secularized with newer rituals (e.g. [14,16]). We cannot predict whether both traditions of spirit tablet rituals will continue or disappear in the future, but we might forecast that there will be something representing the dead's spirit in each country. Today, both Taiwanese and Japanese people believe in the presences (spirits) of the deceased and the ancestors, and perform memorial rituals for them (e.g. [3,6]).

In the West, some digital memorials on the Web have already been adopted by a number of people (e.g. [21,22]). But Cann [21] pointed out that the backgrounds of contemporary death rituals—secularized, simplified, and even artificially faded in the last decades—has ironically caused the rise of digital memorials. She emphasized how people in the West have reclaimed death rituals online.

This situation is different from Taiwan and Japan, having long histories of death rituals that appreciate the dead's spirit. It is possible that emerging new technologies will be adopted by both countries but existing rituals will not simply be digitalized nor replaced by the current online memorials. Both in Taiwan and Japan, some online memorials have already been commercialized (e.g. [10,11,29, 31]) but these are not the main rite for physical gravesites and columbaria, yet rather additional services. According to domestic reports in Taiwan, although the government is promoting online memorial services, which has not been accepted by elderly people while relatively approved by youth [52,53].

4.2   Alternative Rituals Required

Considering what kind of memorialization practices both Taiwanese and Japanese people need, one of key issues that emerges is the use of images. On the funeral altar in ChinPaoXuan, there is a large digital monitor that displays portraits and snapshots of the deceased as slideshow (Fig. 5). These digital pictures in Taipei invoke the deceased's life memories, but do not have the strong presence of the deceased's spirit, which Japanese *iei* pictures (e.g. Left on Fig. 8) do. The *Iei* has come to occupy almost the same position as the spirit tablet in contemporary Japan—or even sometimes more important than the tablet [16]— during the funeral and following memorial practices. Displaying snapshots at the funeral such as shown in the right of Fig. 8, is a recent trend in Japan, that can be interpreted as similar to the digital slideshow at ChinPaoXuan.

As Pitsillides [44] has claimed, not only do images of the dead naturally remind the bereaved of the dead, but they could also assume a key role in manifesting the strong presence or agency of the deceased, with proper design. Particularly, emerging HCI technologies and their digital materialities (e.g. [36, 39, 41]) can be connected to digital legacies such as photographs. This integration would enable the realization of the agency or strong presence of the deceased.

4.3 What to Prepare for Your Death

Any digital legacies about a deceased person must be prepared before his/her death (though this may be changed through virtual modeling or realization technologies for/in Virtual Reality environment). Obviously, no one can support his/herself after your death. According to ChinPaoXuan staff, while some of the digital photo frames show a lot of pictures provided by the bereaved, some have only one or just a few, depending on the bereaved family. This suggests the importance of people in the digital age to store their life memories and package them in a way that can be inherited by their descendants. To this end, Asukanet [51] (the remote *iei* production pioneer) has an online photo archiving platform called "*Iei* Bank (遺影バンク)" [54]. It is designed for anyone who wants to choose a good portrait for *iei* by themselves and have it stored on the site. In addition to SNS such as Facebook, specialized services for memorialization are required that fit to local customs and rituals when preparing for death.

In the situation where traditional customs and rituals are shifting like in Japan, people are required to make decisions preparing for death; you have to choose your plans for the funeral, burial or disposal, and how the things you will leave should be treated. The term "*shū-katsu* (終活)"—activities of preparing your own death—is widely used especially amongst elderly people in Japan in recent years [55]. In *shū-katsu*, filling out the specially made templates called "*Ending Note*" is common. It consists of your wishes surrounding your death including the funeral, gravesite, legacies, and any other things which are not covered by legal will. In death-ridden society in general, the government or city cannot manage the performance of traditional death rituals due to limited space and secularization caused by changes to people's lives and working styles. The Japanese elderly have already begun to prepare for their own deaths within a context of diverse death rituals. With the increasing options of death rituals in the next decade, this shall also be a requirement for Taiwanese people. In the digital age, these activities for preparing for one's death also provides design opportunities with/on ICT/HCI.

5 Conclusion

Within our contemporary lives in urban areas, traditional death rituals held by local community previously are transferred to commercial memorialization companies. In the US, in the last few decades, local death rituals have faded away and the presence of death itself has become hidden from the society [21]. Both in Taipei and Tokyo, no bereaved family or relatives arrange funeral rituals by hand, as this is completely supported by the industry.

However, when participating in these fully supported and urbanized death rituals, some bereaved people might protest that there is nothing left to do by their own hands. Meeting these needs, ChinPaoXuan provides visitors with flower petal offering (Fig. 5B) and letter forms (Fig. 5D). In Japan, the common practice of the bereaved—filling the coffin with flower petals and inserting letters to the deceased—happens in the last minutes before moving to the crematorium phase (v). In addition, traditional fire rituals that involve candles and incenses are prohibited inside buildings by the local law, especially in the city area. We believe that emerging digital technologies could provide alternative rituals for people who want to do something for the deceased; at the funeral and also in the daily memorialization practices.

In this paper, we started with the question of how to utilize HCI technologies to support memorial practices, focused on contemporary funeral and memorialization rituals in (and preparing for) death-ridden societies, and reviewed examples in Taipei and Tokyo—more broadly Taiwan and Japan. Both countries have strong traditions of death rituals but have encountered situations that force them to change due to urbanization, secularization, and changes to living and working styles. Though people are forced to modify and sometimes simplify the traditions, there remain beliefs about the deceased and ancestors' spirits and its strong presences and agencies [44] in the daily life and culture. In death ridden societies in the digital age, designers and engineers have to engage with and support the local contexts and particular faiths behind the rituals, when utilizing emerging technologies.

Acknowledgement. We thank the ChinPaoXuan Group, Tomoetogyo Co., Ltd., and Amico Uriu for cooperating with us in our field studies, interviews, and feedback on this research. We also thank Hannah Gould for revising this paper's English expression, and Chihiro Sato for providing photos.

This research is supported by the Japan Science and Technology Agency and the Ministry of Science and Technology of Taiwan as part of the Japan-Taiwan Collaborative Research Program (MOST106-2923-E-002-013-MY3), respectively.

References

1. Ministry of Health, Labour and Welfare, Japan: White Paper & Reports. https://www.mhlw.go.jp/english/wp/
2. National Development Council, Taiwan: Population Projections for the R.O.C. https://pop-proj.ndc.gov.tw/main_en/

3. Smith, R.J.: Ancestor Worship in Contemporary Japan. Stanford University Press, Palo Alto (1974)
4. Shimane, K.: The experience of death in Japan's urban societies. Invisible Population: The Place of the Dead in East-Asian Megacities, pp. 29–49 (2013)
5. Wolf, A. (ed.) Religion and Ritual in Chinese Society (Study in Chinese Society). Stanford University Press (1974)
6. Lazzarotti, M.: Modern life traditional death. Tradition and modernization of funeral rites in Taiwan. Fu Jen Int. Religious Stud. **8**(1), 108–126 (2014)
7. Kim, J.: Necrosociality: isolated death and unclaimed cremains in Japan. J. R. Anthropol. Inst. **22**(4), 843–863 (2016)
8. Tremlett, P.F.: Death-scapes in Taipei and Manila: a postmodern necrography. Taiwan Comp. Perspect. **1**, 23–36 (2007)
9. 内政部全國殯葬資訊入口網. https://mort.moi.gov.tw/
10. Kaohsiung City Government: Mortuary services office Kaohsiung City (高雄市殯葬管理處). https://mentality.kcg.gov.tw/
11. 中天快點 TV: 雲端追思系統 掃墓祭拜聽線上遺言 (2017). http://gotv.ctitv.com.tw/2017/03/416535.htm
12. Uriu, D., Odom, W., Gould, H.: Understanding automatic conveyor-belt columbaria: emerging sites of interactive memorialization in Japan. In: Proceedings of the 2018 Designing Interactive Systems Conference, pp. 747–752 (2018)
13. Kong, L.: No place, new places: death and its rituals in urban Asia. Urban Stud. **49**(2), 415–433 (2011)
14. Duteil-Ogata, F.: Emerging burial spaces and rituals in urban Japan. Invisible Population: The Place of the Dead in East-Asian Megacities, pp. 50–73 (2013)
15. Inoue, H.: Contemporary transformation of Japanese death ceremonies, pp. 123–137 (2013)
16. Suzuki, I.: Beyond ancestor worship: continued relationship with significant others, p. 141 (2013)
17. Gould, H., Kohn, T., Gibbs, M.: Uploading the ancestors: experiments with digital Buddhist altars in contemporary Japan. Death Stud. 1–10 (2018, to be published)
18. Tomoetogyo Co., Ltd. (トモエ陶業株式会社): Mayudama (繭環). http://mayudama.hanatofumi.jp
19. Tomoetogyo Co., Ltd. (トモエ陶業株式会社): TORUS. http://torus.hanatofumi.jp
20. Google: Google photos. https://photos.google.com/
21. Cann, C.K.: Virtual Afterlives: Grieving the Dead in the Twenty-First Century (Material Worlds Series). University Press of Kentucky (2015)
22. Arnold, M., Gibbs, M., Kohn, T., Meese, J., Nansen, B.: Death and Digital Media. Routledge, Abingdon (2017)
23. Facebook: About Memorialized Accounts, Facebook Help Center. https://www.facebook.com/help/1017717331640041/
24. Graham, C., Arnold, M., Kohn, T., Gibbs, M.R.: Gravesites and websites: a comparison of memorialisation. Vis. Stud. **30**(1), 37–53 (2015)
25. Gibbs, M., Meese, J., Arnold, M., Nansen, B., Carter, M.: #funeral and instagram: death, social media, and platform vernacular. Inf. Commun. Soc. **18**(3), 255–268 (2015)
26. Walter, T.: Communication media and the dead: from the stone age to Facebook. Mortality **20**(3), 215–232 (2015)
27. Brubaker, J.R., Callison-Burch, V.: Legacy contact: designing and implementing post-mortem stewardship at Facebook. In: Proceedings of the 2016 CHI Conference on Human Factors in Computing Systems CHI 2016, pp. 2908–2919 (2016)

28. Gotved, S.: Privacy with public access: digital memorials on quick response codes. Inf. Commun. Soc. **18**(3), 269–280 (2015)
29. Bodaiju (菩提樹): Digital *kakocho* (デジタル過去帳). http://dejikako.com/
30. Häkkilä, J., Forsman, M.T., Colley, A.: Navigating the graveyard: designing technology for deathscapes, pp. 199–204 (2018)
31. Okiseki Co., Ltd. (株式会社沖セキ): *Ohaka-Mairu* (お墓マイル). http://www.okiseki.com/app/
32. Massimi, M., Charise, A.: Dying, death, and mortality: towards thanatosensitivity in HCI. In: Proceedings of the 27th International Conference Extended Abstracts on Human Factors in Computing Systems, CHI EA 2009, pp. 2459–2468 (2009)
33. Foong, P.S., Kera, D.: Applying reflective design to digital memorials. In: Proceedings of International Workshop on Social and Mundane Technologies, SIMTech 2008 (2008)
34. Sengers, P., Boehner, K., David, S., Kaye, J.J.: Reflective design. In: Proceedings of the 4th Decennial Conference on Critical Computing, CC 2005, pp. 49–58 (2005)
35. Uriu, D., Ogasawara, T., Shimizu, N., Okude, N.: MASTABA: the household shrine in the future archived digital pictures. In: ACM SIGGRAPH 2006 Sketches (2006)
36. Uriu, D., Okude, N.: ThanatoFenestra: photographic family altar supporting a ritual to pray for the deceased. In: Proceedings of DIS 2010, pp. 422–425 (2010)
37. Uriu, D., Odom, W.: Designing for domestic memorialization and remembrance: a field study of fenestra in Japan. In: Proceedings of the 2016 CHI Conference on Human Factors in Computing Systems, CHI 2016, pp. 5945–5957 (2016)
38. Uriu, D., Odom, W., Lai, M.K., Taoka, S., Inami, M.: SenseCenser: an interactive device for sensing incense smoke & supporting memorialization rituals in Japan. In: Proceedings of the 2018 ACM Conference Companion Publication on Designing Interactive Systems, pp. 315–318 (2018)
39. Wallace, J., Thomas, J., Anderson, D., Olivier, P.: Mortality as framed by ongoingness in digital design. Des. Issues **34**(1), 95–107 (2018)
40. Moncur, W., Kirk, D.: An emergent framework for digital memorials. In: Proceedings of the 2014 Conference on Designing Interactive Systems, DIS 2014, pp. 965–965 (2014)
41. Wendy, M., Julius, M., van den Hoven, E., Kirk, D.: Story shell: the participatory design of a bespoke digital memorial, pp. 470–477 (2015)
42. Odom, W., Uriu, D., Kirk, D., Banks, R., Wakkary, R.: Experiences in designing technologies for honoring deceased loved ones. Des. Issues **34**(1), 54–66 (2018)
43. Odom, W., Banks, R., Kirk, D., Harper, R., Lindley, S., Sellen, A.: Technology heirlooms?: considerations for passing down and inheriting digital materials. In: Proceedings of the 2012 ACM Annual Conference on Human Factors in Computing Systems, CHI 2012, pp. 337–337 (2012)
44. Pitsillides, S.: Digital legacy: designing with things. Death Stud. (2019, to be published)
45. ChinPaoSan Group (金寶山集團). https://www.memory.com.tw/en/
46. Wang, Y.L., Liu, E.: Seven Days in Heaven (父後七日) (2010)
47. Bellco (ベルコ): お葬式の流れ: (procedure of funeral). https://www.bellco.co.jp/sougi/flow/
48. Wiren, A.: Japanese Funerals, Japan Visitor. https://www.japanvisitor.com/japanese-culture/japanese-funerals
49. Dexter, K.: The many Japanese calendars and the ways Japan tells time (2014). https://www.tofugu.com/Japan/Japanese-calendar/

50. Takita, Y.: Departures (in English)/おくりびと Okuribito (in Japanese) (2008). https://en.wikipedia.org/wiki/Departures_(2008_film)

51. Asukanet Co., Ltd. (株式会社アスカネット): Memorial service division. https://www.mds.ne.jp/

52. Tsai, M.C.: A study on online memorial services and model construction. Master thesis at Department of Life and Death, Nanhua University (2010)

53. NCTU CastNet: 線上祭祀 科技與文化衝突 (2018). http://castnet.nctu.edu.tw/castnet/article/1594

54. Asukanet Co., Ltd. (株式会社アスカネット): Iei bank (遺影バンク). https://ieibank.com/

55. Nokosu Kioku.com (のこす記憶.com): What is Shu-katsu? https://nokosukioku.com/note/?page_id=818

Requirements for Gesture-Controlled Remote Operation to Facilitate Human-Technology Interaction in the Living Environment of Elderly People

Susan Vorwerg[1]([⊠]), Cornelia Eicher[1], Heinrich Ruser[2], Felix Piela[3], Felix Obée[3], André Kaltenbach[4], and Lars Mechold[4]

[1] Charité – Universitätsmedizin Berlin, Reinickendorferstr. 61, 13347 Berlin, Germany
{susan.vorwerg, cornelia.eicher}@charite.de

[2] Universität der Bundeswehr München, W.-Heisenberg-Weg 39, 85577 Neubiberg, Germany
heinrich.ruser@unibw.de

[3] August & Piela Konstruktiv GbR, Tempelhofer Weg 11, 10829 Berlin, Germany
{piela, obee}@konstruktiv-berlin.de

[4] Laser Components GmbH, Werner-von-Siemens-Str. 15, 82140 Olching, Germany
{a.kaltenbach, l.mechold}@lasercomponents.com

Abstract. The "SmartPointer" (SP) technology comprises a universal button-less gesture-controlled handheld remote device with a simple quasi-intuitive operating structure. With this handset, elderly people will be able to control various household devices in their living environment. In order to develop an age-appropriate SP system, the aim of the study was to determine the requirements of elderly people and people with tremor. For this purpose, a mixed-method design, involving several assessments, a guideline-based interview, a task-based investigation and a questionnaire using a gesture catalog, was applied. The whole sample included 20 seniors being 60 years and older. In the process, qualitative requirements were collected on the topics of device use, operating problems, desired devices for gesture control, receiver unit, gestures, feedback and safety. The interview results emphasized the elderly participants' needs to an easy and intuitive system use. Furthermore, concerns should be prioritized in order to the development of the system. In the quantitative evaluation, the use of various technical devices was analyzed and the frequency of used gestures was determined based the gesture catalog and the task-based investigation. The most frequently used gestures were horizontal, vertical, circular and targeting gestures. In summary, the elderly people were very interested in, and open-minded towards, the SP-system. In a comparison between healthy persons and persons with tremor, the results demonstrated only minimal differences regarding the requirements.

Keywords: Gesture and eye-gaze-based interaction · SmartPointer · Gesture control · Remote · Human-technology interaction · Elderly people

© Springer Nature Switzerland AG 2019
J. Zhou and G. Salvendy (Eds.): HCII 2019, LNCS 11592, pp. 551–569, 2019.
https://doi.org/10.1007/978-3-030-22012-9_39

1 Introduction

1.1 Age and Technology

In 2018, the proportion of people aged 65 and above in Germany was 22% of the country's total population. Up to 2040, the number of people over 65 is expected to rise from 17.9 million to 23.2 million (+9%) [1]. With increasing life expectancy, the majority of people in this population group are characterized by deficits such as mobility impairments, cognitive impairments and reduction in vision and hearing [2]. Despite existing illnesses and deficits, older people strive for an independent life, especially in their own living environment. According to statistics, almost 93% of people over 65 in Germany still live in private homes [3]. Technical devices and functions such as assistive technologies (AT) can provide great support in coping with everyday life and maintaining independence [4]. These techniques can be summarized under the concept of Ambient Assisted Living (AAL), where strategies include orientation, support and assistance services for older people. The aim of AAL is to combine new technologies and the social environment in order to improve people's quality of life [5, 6]. AAL services also include smart home solutions, which are becoming increasingly important in maintaining independence in old age. A smart home means a private home in which household technologies (such as heating, lighting, ventilation, consumer electronics and communication equipment) become intelligent objects [5]. However, technological progress may comprise challenges for people over 70 years of age, and therefore it is important that innovative smart home solutions are adapted to the requirements and limitations of older people. On the one hand, technical devices have different functions and complex operating modes. On the other hand, they are usually controlled via computers or mobile devices such as smartphones and iPads. In this context, it should be noted that less than half (45%) of people over 70 living in Germany use the Internet [7]. The use of terminals for this purpose is also low in this age group (26% laptop, 25% PC, 22% smartphone, 13% tablet) [8, 9]. Consequently, if smart home controls are connected to mobile devices, this can lead to uncertainties and avoidance of technical support among older people, since comprehensive understanding of such technologies is not yet established in the current generation of older people.

Furthermore considerable research activities have been directed to buttonless controls based on the recognition of gestures. Many of these systems use images from video cameras to determine the relative positions of the fingers of one or both hands. However, changing backgrounds, occlusions and different directions the gesture is pointed to still make video-based gesture recognition difficult [10–12]. Moreover, considerable hardware costs are involved and camera applications are often controversially discussed due to data privacy issues. In addition, hand-held devices equipped with tilt and acceleration sensors similar to the famous "Wii" game console are also considered too costly and complex for our purpose [13, 14].

Considering all the aforementioned, new smart home technologies should provide comprehensible operating possibilities, which are simple, small, inexpensive and lightweight, in order to ensure a smooth human-technology interaction. The research and development project "SmartPointer", pursues this goal.

1.2 "SmartPointer" (SP)

"SmartPointer" is a collaborative project funded by the Federal Ministry of Education and Research (BMBF) in the KMU-Innovative-Announcement Human-Technology Interaction program. As part of the project, a universal system with a simple quasi-intuitive operating structure is to be developed. By means of a buttonless gesture-controlled handheld remote device with a long battery lifetime, elderly people will be able to control various household appliances such as lights, heating, blinds, windows or TV in their living environment.

Technology

The new "SmartPointer" system consists of:

(1) a handheld battery-operated and buttonless "SmartPointer", similar to a small flashlight, which emits visible light to select a particular device and spatially structured, invisible infrared (IR) light to operate the device (see Fig. 1),
(2) an optoelectronic receiving unit (photosensors) in, on or near the device to be remotely controlled and
(3) a decoding and communication unit for reconstruction and recognition of the performed gestures and their conversion into the respective device-specific control commands, together with connection to the device to be operated.

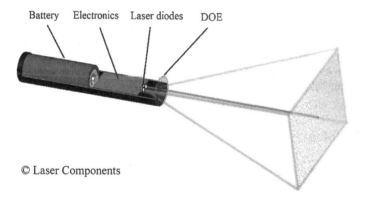

© Laser Components

Fig. 1. Schematic view of the SmartPointer (own illustration: Laser Components, 2019)

Functionality

With a handheld, buttonless and particularly user-friendly light pointer ("SmartPointer"), the user carries out typical intuitive pointing and operating gestures in the direction of the device to be operated, in order to select and switch it or adjust it continuously. A light-sensitive receiver on the device detects the trajectory of the emitted, specially structured light in the invisible IR wavelength range and converts the identified gesture into device-specific control signals. Preliminary studies by Ruser et al. [35] showed the feasibility and potential of this approach. Throughout all development phases, the user perspective of elderly and mobility-impaired people will be consistently considered. The intuitive, buttonless remote is intended to make a significant contribution to supporting independent living.

1.3 Tremor Symptoms

Essential tremor is a symptom that occurs in about 1% of the total population and about 5% of the population over 60 years. As prevalence increases with age, as many as 10–15% of those over 70 and 50% of those over 90 suffer from more or less severe tremor, which can significantly reduce the quality of life of those concerned. Routine activities such as writing, holding an object, dealing with buttons and drinking are usually affected at a very early stage and may no longer be possible with serious forms of the disease. This can have a negative influence on the social life of those affected, and they may withdraw more and more, due to shame and inability to manage their daily lives successfully [15, 16].

Against a background of tremor symptoms causing problems with the accuracy of gestures, we consider the question of how the SP system can overcome these problems. In order to be able to deduce conclusions for the system development, this group of people was included in the study. The evaluations of the reproduced trajectories will be used to determine whether certain algorithms can be developed to enable smooth gesture recognition, even with the disturbance variable "tremor". Although this question is essential for the project and the development of the system, it cannot yet be answered as only the requirements analysis has so far been undertaken.

1.4 Aim of the Study

Many studies in the field of gesture control in the past have concentrated on the target group of younger people. In contrast, the "SmartPointer" project focuses on seniors over the age of 60. The aim of the study was to determine the age-related requirements of older people and people with tremor for an SP system, using qualitative and quantitative methods. Furthermore, the study participants were asked about their concerns about, and expectations towards an SP system, in order to assess the level of acceptance for such an innovative system among the target group.

2 Methodology

In order to answer the questions, a mixed-method design consisting of a guideline-based interview, a task-based part and a questionnaire using a gesture catalog, was used. The survey was conducted once in individual interviews with 20 seniors over 60 years of age. A total of 16 subjects consisting of 10 healthy elderly persons and six elderly persons with tremor, completed the study. In the cases of four of the participants, we performed only the assessments, the task-based part and the gesture catalog. The interviews were conducted in German. All the described investigations were carried out with the approval of the responsible ethics committee (EA4/134/18). A declaration of consent was obtained from all involved persons.

2.1 Study Procedure

The study covered a survey period of two months (October to November 2018). In advance, interested respondents were informed and educated about the study via a telephone interview, and checked against inclusion and exclusion criteria. After signing the agreement on the survey day, the seniors completed three assessments.

1. To test their cognitive abilities, the subjects performed the Mini-Mental State Examination (MMSE) with 30 items, in a digital version. This test was also used as a screening test to exclude persons with cognitive impairments from the study (MMSE < 25). With regard to statistical quality criteria, this instrument has good to very good results (reliability coefficient .96 and retest reliability .89; validity .78) [17].

2. The hand force of the dominant hand was measured using a hand dynamometer. This was mainly used to highlight differences between healthy subjects and subjects with tremor. In this test, reliability coefficients of .89 to .96 are considered very good [18]. The content and construct validity can be assumed to be given [19].

3. The Grooved Pegboard Test was used to determine the coordinative abilities or fine-motor abilities of the dominant hand, in order to investigate the influence of tremor on gestures (test-retest reliability .69 to .76 for the dominant hand) [20].

Subsequently, the interviews and the analysis of the requirements for the SP system were conducted. The interview guideline was divided into five phases. In the first interview phase, the topics of sociodemographic data, domesticity, use of technical devices in the household and handling of technical devices and associated problems were covered. In the second part of the interview, a short explanatory video clip was shown to the test participants for a better understanding of the SP system. The subsequent survey focused on the requirements for the handheld device to be developed (design) and the associated gestures (desired functions of the devices to be controlled). In the third phase, the task-based investigation took place. Here, the test participants were asked to use their imaginations to demonstrate 32 intuitive gestures for particular operating functions of various technical devices (see Table 1).

Table 1. Devices and functions of the demonstrate gestures

Devices	Functions
TV	On/off
	Volume higher/lower
	Program forward/back
	Program selection
Music system/radio	On/off
	Volume higher/lower
	Song forward/back
	Function selection
Telephone	Answer/finish phone call
	Volume higher/lower
Heating	On/off
	Warmer/colder
Light	On/off
	Brighter/darker
Blinds	Up/down
Door	Open/close
	Unlock/lock

The intuitive gestures were demonstrated on a screen (1.20 × 1.50 m) using a standard laser pointer in sitting position. The distance to the screen was 1.50 m. Both the point projections of the pointer on the screen (see Fig. 2) and the arm or hand movements (see Fig. 3) were filmed. In these first experiments we used a video camera (frame rate 30 fps) with a resolution of 850 × 480 pixels.

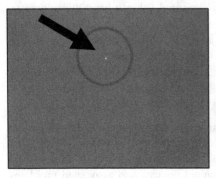
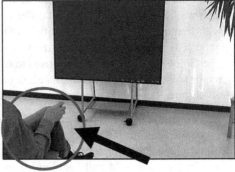

Fig. 2. Pointer on the canvas   **Fig. 3.** Gesture

The video material was subsequently evaluated with special software, which makes it possible to reconstruct the trajectories and derive the gesture recognition from them. Two examples are shown in Figs. 4 and 5, which also clarify the differences between the two groups.

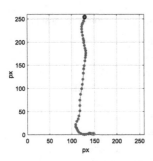
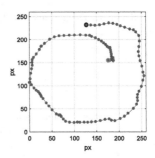

Fig. 4. Examples for recorded gesture trajectories. Participant P01 without tremor, gestures "UP" (left), "CIRCLE LEFT" (right)

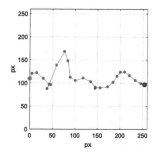 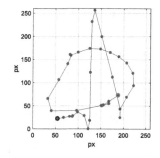

Fig. 5. Examples for recorded gesture trajectories. Participants T01 with tremor, gestures "RIGHT" (left), "CIRCLE RIGHT" (right)

In the fourth phase, the same devices with the corresponding functions were assessed using a gesture catalog. This time, the participants received suggestions and were asked to tick the gesture they thought appropriate for controlling the respective device or function. The gestures to be selected from were full circle, "A", "X", tick, swipe right/left, swipe up/down, clockwise/counterclockwise circle, wave and number. In the last part, the participants were asked about the requirements for the overall system (receiver unit, gestures and concerns).

2.2   Sample

The entire sample comprised 20 seniors aged 60 and over. Among them were 14 healthy seniors (seven male and seven female) aged 74.8 ± 3.3 years and six seniors (three male and three female) with tremor, aged 74.5 ± 8.7 years. The results are presented in Table 2. Based on the results of the MMSE, all recruited subjects were able to participate in the study (MMSE $\geq$ 25 points). The values showed only a small difference between healthy subjects (MMSE: 29.07 ± 1.12 points) and subjects with tremor (MMSE: 28.83 ± 1.17 points). In addition, finger coordination was measured using the Grooved Pegboard Test. The results show significant differences between the two groups in this test (U-test, $p = 0.011$). When measuring the hand force with a hand dynamometer, there are appreciable differences of approximately 9 kg between the groups, but no relevance could be determined when testing for significance (U-test, $p = 0.117$).

Table 2. Assessment results

	N	$\bar{x}$	SD	Sig.
MMSE_points	**20**	**29.00**	**1.124**	
Healthy	14	29.07	1.141	$p = 0.600$
Tremor	6	28.83	1.169	
Pegboard_min.	**20**	**01:45**	**00:54**	
Healthy	14	01:24	00:15	$p = 0.011*$
Tremor	6	02:34	01:21	
Hand force_kg	**20**	**25.415**	**10.576**	
Healthy	14	28.129	9.375	$p = 0.117$
Tremor	6	19.083	11.304	

Base: Mann-Whitney U-test, * $p < 0.05$

2.3 Data Analysis

The qualitative content analysis of the interviews was conducted by the moderators based on a systematic protocol. In order to ensure the correctness of the evaluation, the four-eyes principle was applied. The protocols for all 16 test participants were subsequently digitized and subjected to computer-aided evaluation using ATLAS.ti. The aim of the content analysis was to reduce the material from the interviews and to create an overview through abstractions. Therefore, the analysis was based on a category system of 42 codes. These codes were strongly oriented to the guidelines of the interview. For the final evaluation of the results, the contents of the codes were checked for similarities, from which the reduction was formulated in the form of requirements. For illustration purposes in the results evaluation, important requirements were documented with transcribed quotations from the tape recordings. Quantitative methods (descriptive and inductive) using Excel and IBM SPSS Statistics 25 were used to evaluate the sociodemographic data, the assessments, the task-based part and the gesture catalog.

3 Results

3.1 Qualitative Results

The following paragraph presents the results from the qualitative part of the study, using quotations from the interviews for illustration.

Use of Technology
The results of the qualitative part of the study show that technical devices within the households of seniors mainly consist of entertainments electronics. The most commonly used devices were PCs or laptops, TVs and radios.

Technology Operating Issues
The questioned seniors identified two main issues relating to system operation: firstly, the large number of choices within the operating menu and secondly, the large selection of buttons with unclear functionalities, constituting a high potential for operation errors. *"There is the potential that I hit the wrong button"* (P01, female, 79y).[1]

The long periods required for adaptation to new operation systems were mentioned and described as being problematic. Here, seniors mainly referred to the wiping gestures for smartphones or tablets. Seniors with tremor symptoms especially criticized small buttons, as their accuracy in pressing buttons is considerably reduced, and this leads to operating errors. *"Yes, sometimes it hardly works. The smaller the buttons, the worse the situation, because my hands, because they shake a lot"* (T02, female, 84y). In addition, seniors with tremor mentioned their problems with holding things. *"When I'm shaking badly, I could just throw it into the corner, because absolutely nothing works then"* (T06, female, 60y).

---

[1] All quotations were translated from German into English. A "P" stands for a healthy senior, a "T" stands for a senior with tremor symptoms.

Desired Devices for Gesture Control

Gesture control for TVs (n = 13), lights (n = 6), hi-fi systems/radios (n = 5) and doors (front door and room doors) (n = 3) were the most frequently desired by the interviewees. The majority of the study participants rejected gesture-based control of devices within close proximity of the user for reasons of pointlessness. Examples were washing machines and stoves or ovens. *"Perhaps an automatic system for automatically switching off the device, but otherwise you have to stand in front of the oven anyway" (P04, male, 76y).*

Apart from the control of devices, the seniors expressed requirements regarding the operation of functionalities for each device. Desired functionalities included, but were not limited to, switching the device on and off, adjusting the volume, switching TV and radio channels and directly choosing the channel, dimming the lights and opening/closing and locking/unlocking doors. Additional features were selected for heating, window blinds, telephones and mobile phones, TV media libraries and Internet boxes.

Receiver Unit

The study participants made diverse statements regarding the system setup. For the array and location of the receiver units especially, no general statements could be derived from the interviews. However, the seniors described two main possible concepts: (1) a central receiver unit combining all operable devices or (2) one receiver unit per device. According to the participants, a central receiver unit makes sense when a user wants to control devices outside the room that he or she currently occupies. *"A central receiver unit which can be extended to a random number of devices" (P08, male, 78y).* However, a central unit was also associated with complex handling. Therefore, many participants preferred one unit per device. *"Definitely one receiver unit per device. Otherwise, I would need a whole lot of different gestures" (P01, female, 79y).* One unit per device additionally offers safety-related benefits. *"It [the device control] is more direct, [...] maybe I cannot slip and trigger something [an action or function] I don't want to" (T04, female, 72y).*

Gestures

The interviewed seniors made clear statements regarding the gesture-control of various household devices. To some extent, these statements were linked to the participants' experiences with their current technology use and showed their great need for security and safety. The seniors asked for the use of consistent and uniform gestures for the same functionalities, regardless of the device. For example, the same gesture for volume control of TV and radio. *"It should be easy, clear, always the same. It may be boring for young people, but here it absolutely makes sense" (P09, male, 71y).* A great concern among the seniors was the possibility of forgetting the control gestures and consequently losing the power to control their devices. A catalog listing the gestures and corresponding functions was perceived as helpful by the majority of participants. *"Well, [...] if you forget that [gesture] – you forget things when you are old – then you can look it up" (T02, female, 84y).* The choice of whether to use their own invented gestures or gestures provided by the developing company, was dependent on the participants' trust in technology and their own perceived technical understanding. Seniors who rated their own perceived technology understanding rather high would prefer to invent their own gestures. In contrast, participants who stated they preferred gestures provided by the developing company also stated that they trusted the developing company to choose appropriate gestures, rather than themselves. *"No, I would rather trust the provided gestures because they have been evaluated and I would adapt myself, but I would also like to have a catalog listing the gestures" (P02, female, 81y).*

Feedback

All interviewed participants required feedback from the system indicating a successful or unsuccessful connection between the remote and the device. Two main types of feedback requirements could be derived from the interviews: (1) audible feedback and (2) visual feedback. According to the seniors, audible feedback should be unique and clearly assigned to a function and visual feedback should be clearly visible and differentiable from other light sources. Another idea from the participants was to have audible feedback via voice output. However, the best solution, according to the study participants, was a combination of visual and audible feedback, in order to allow distinct feedback for persons with either visual or hearing impairments. *"Well, I would prefer a visual feedback. For the time when I cannot see very well anymore, then an audible feedback should be implemented" (T04, female, 72y).* The seniors rejected a tactile feedback such as vibration, due to a potentially negative impact on the operation and handling of the system. Participants with tremor symptoms especially, expressed skepticism, but healthy seniors were also concerned about the potential impact. *"Well, [...] especially as vibrations or similar are present in various diseases anyway, and maybe affected persons experience it [a tactile feedback] as unpleasant or maybe it even triggers or amplifies symptoms. So maybe it would be helpful for a specific group of users, e.g., visually impaired people, but not in general for all users" (P02, female, 81y).*

Safety and Security

Many statements from the interviews revealed a high level of safety and security needs among the participating seniors. Their concerns included data protection, safety of people and potential operating errors. The interviewees frequently discussed the potential risk of system access by third parties. In the context of data transfer in the system, the participants wondered whether unauthorized third parties might be able to control devices from outside if, for example, neighbors owned the same system. They discussed whether they could control, for example, the unlocking mechanisms of a front door and gain access to the living environment. *"Well, I have that concern, that my neighbor or somebody with malicious intent, if he has access to my system [...], he could do anything with it: he could switch on my oven and when I am not home, he could wreak havoc, so it must be ensured that security programs similar to my computer program prevent access from outside" (P08, male, 78y).* An additional concern expressed by the seniors was related to people's safety in the context of the infrared lamps in the system. *"I have a great-grandson, he just turned six, and what if a child like him gets his hands on the remote and fumbles with it, what happens then? [...] You can see how I fumble around with that remote and what if my great-grandson is sitting there and the infrared lamps meet his face or his body, maybe you need to take that into consideration" (T03, male, 82y).*

3.2   Quantitative Results

The following paragraph presents the results from the quantitative part of the study.

Use of Technology
In the quantitative evaluation, the use of various technical devices such as TVs, radios, telephones, smartphones, mobile phones or PCs/notebooks/tablets was also evaluated (n = 16). The following results were determined for the use of smartphones. In the group of healthy seniors, two thirds of the respondents used their smartphones regularly, but in the group with tremor symptoms only half did so. Four of the test participants still used a conventional mobile phone (two seniors from each group). It was surprising that 14 out of 16 subjects owned a PC. Only six seniors had a Notebook and four had a tablet. Use of a television or the telephone was reported by all the respondents.

Evaluation of Task-Based Investigation and Gesture Catalog
The task-based part and the gesture catalog were also quantitatively evaluated (n = 20) for a comparison between gestures invented by participants and given gestures. The frequency of used gestures was examined as a priority. Altogether, 417 gestures invented by participants and 330 gestures from the gesture catalog were evaluated. Gestures that occurred only rarely or were mentioned or shown only once were not taken into account. As shown in Fig. 6, gestures such as horizontal (right/left) or vertical (up/down) lines and circular movements (circle, either clockwise or counter-clockwise) were the most frequently used gestures of the interviewed participants.

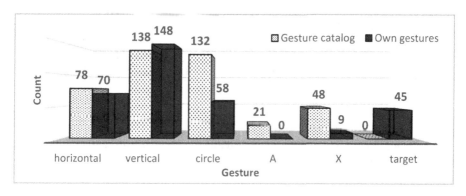

Fig. 6. Comparison between gesture catalog and participants' gestures for the most frequently used gestures for all functions

A comparison between healthy seniors and seniors with tremor showed clear differences in the task-based investigation for the gesture denoted "targeting" or "pointing to the device". Almost exclusively, tremor patients indicated this gesture as a control option (see Fig. 7). Almost 50% of healthy volunteers, on the contrary, preferred vertical pointing patterns.

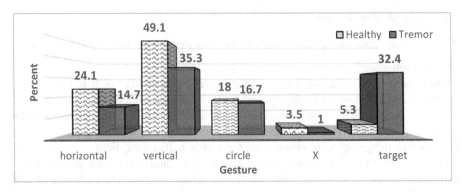

Fig. 7. Task based investigation: comparison of participants' invented gestures for healthy seniors and seniors with tremor

From the overall survey of the gestures used in the gesture catalog, it can be seen that there are only minor differences (approximately 5%) between the two groups (see Fig. 8), except that circular movement patterns seem to play a greater role in healthy seniors.

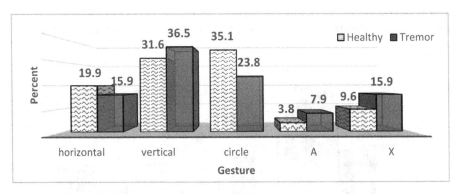

Fig. 8. Gesture catalog: Comparison of the indicated gestures between healthy seniors and seniors with tremor

In general, it could be observed that the gestures are oriented to existing patterns and that there are tendencies towards the use of certain gestures. As there were no serious differences in the gestures used between the two groups, the same functions for the different technical devices for all seniors were combined and are illustrated below.

Switching on and off occurs in the following devices: televisions, music systems, telephones, heating and lights. From the gesture catalog, it emerged that circular movements (60%) are the preferred gestures for switching on devices or systems (see Fig. 10). With regard to the participants' own gestures, the targeting gesture is somewhat favored (26%), although the circle pattern (20%) is also a relevant gesture (see Fig. 9).

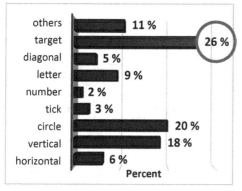

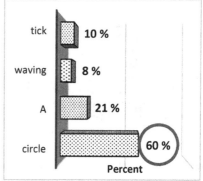

Fig. 9. Participants' own gestures – switch on   **Fig. 10.** Gesture catalog – switch on

The results for the switch off function are very similar. Seniors also prefer targeting (25%) for this function (see Fig. 11). Regarding the gesture catalog, the questioned participants disagreed. The gestures "circle" and "X" show an almost identical result, at 50% and 49% respectively (see Fig. 12).

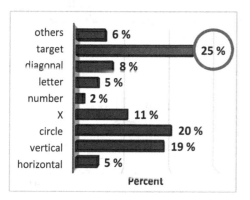

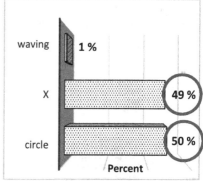

Fig. 11. Participants' own gestures – switch off   **Fig. 12.** Gesture catalog – switch off

The function for increasing or reducing volume was requested for televisions, telephones and music systems. Concerning this function, the participants were also divided in their opinion about whether vertical or horizontal gestures were more appropriate (see Fig. 13). The interviewed persons did not agree with regard to the gesture catalog, but the tendency towards vertical or horizontal patterns is still discernible (see Fig. 14).

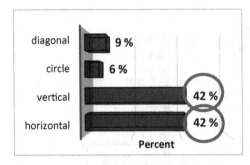 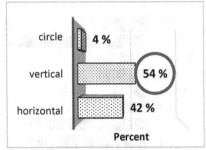

Fig. 13. Participants' gestures – volume up/down **Fig. 14.** Gesture catalog – volume up/down

Back and forth were functions that occurred either for the television, in switching programs back and forth or for music systems, in switching songs/channels back and forth. Interestingly, for this function there were different opinions for individual gestures and catalog gestures. For individual gestures, the preference was for vertical movements, i.e., upwards or downwards (see Fig. 15), whereas for the gesture catalog, the preference was for horizontal movements to the right and left (see Fig. 16).

In contrast to the back and forth function, the test participants agreed on the up and down function for controlling the temperature, the dimmer or the blinds. In this case, the majority voted for vertical up and down movement patterns both in their own gestures and in the gesture catalog (Figs. 17 and 18).

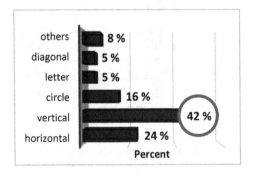 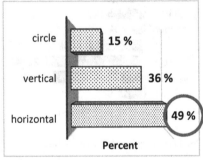

Fig. 15. Participants' own gestures – forward/back   **Fig. 16.** Gesture catalog – forward/back

The last function evaluated was opening and closing doors and windows. As shown in Figs. 19, 20, 21 and 22, the majority of the participants' own gestures were different from those taken from the gesture catalog. On the one hand, vertical movements were dominant in the participants' own gestures, and on the other hand, circular movements were preferred from the gesture catalog. The large number of gesture variations indicates a rather inconsistent opinion.

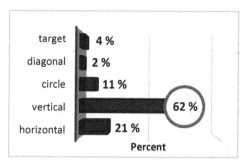

Fig. 17. Participants' own gestures – up/down

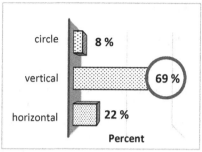

Fig. 18. Gesture catalog – up/down

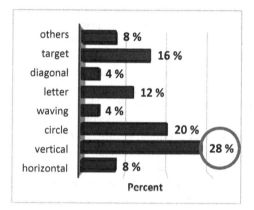

Fig. 19. Participants' own gestures – open

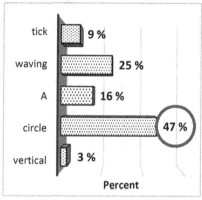

Fig. 20. Gesture catalog – open

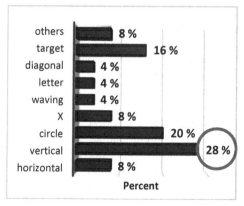

Fig. 21. Participants' own gestures – close

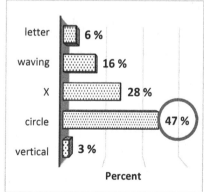

Fig. 22. Gesture catalog – close

4 Discussion

New human-technology interactions, which should contribute to an independent life into advanced age, increase the need for corresponding research in the geriatric field [21]. However, a review by Kühnel et al. in 2011 [22] concluded that only very few studies include age-specific user opinions in the design process for gesture-based interactions. This observation is still valid today. Therefore, this project has the goal of developing a technical solution especially for seniors. The emphasis was on older people and older people with tremor who were actively involved in the development process in order to identify requirements as well as expectations and concerns about an SP system. Through the 16 qualitative interviews, a multitude of age-appropriate requirements for the development of the SP system could be identified. These will be discussed in detail below. They are of central importance in the entire development process. Furthermore, studies prove the high importance of user-centered approaches, as there is a large gap between the requirements of younger and older people [21]. The use of technology constitutes an evidence of the solemn differences between the generations. Whereas over 90% of people in the age group up to 50 use a smartphone, only 41% of people over 65 do so [23]. Although the results of this study show that the interviewed persons used smartphones (60%) or tablets (25%), problems occurred with regard to device operation. According to the respondents with tremor, this difficulty can increase many times over, as the accuracy of gesture execution becomes impaired. Nevertheless, more complex tasks such as rotating or zooming, are also a challenge for healthy elderly people [24]. Against this background, gesture-in-mid-air systems can be a real relief for elderly people. The results of the present study also show that they are interested in the new gesture-based operating system. This type of system is especially popular since small buttons or applications such as those on a smartphone or tablet do not have to be hit accurately. These results were also confirmed in a study by Bobeth et al. [25]. Gesture-in-mid-air operation requires more practice in this age group, but study participants showed a higher interest in this compared to a control with mobile devices. Gerling et al. [26] also pointed out that handheld control devices such as controllers or remote controls facilitate the execution of a gesture, compared to hands-free control. This represents a further advantage for the SP system.

According to the test participants, visual or acoustic feedback or a combination of both would increase operating safety. The necessity for optical, acoustic or tactile feedback in gesture control has also been confirmed in various studies [27, 28]. Most of the surveyed seniors were in agreement about the doubtful usefulness of tactile feedback. They supported the opinion of Hwangbo et al. [28], that acoustic feedback makes more sense than haptic feedback, especially for older people. Sáenz-de-Urturi et al. [29] also recommended acoustic feedback, especially for gesture-in-mid-air systems.

The interviewed seniors mentioned concerns about forgetting operating gestures and operating the system incorrectly. According to Pages [30], operating errors are the result of lack of knowledge and experience in technology use, as well as cognitive impairment. Considering this, it is essential to prevent concerns about avoiding operating errors. According to the literature, a clear and easy operation procedure as well as intuitive and simple gestures, can counteract concerns about operating errors [25, 31–

33]. Additionally, users should receive a comprehensive training on the system. Seniors especially, could benefit from relevant information about the quality of safety-related measures intended to ensure personal and data protection.

As shown in the quantitative results, there were only a few differences between the two groups in terms of chosen gestures. With regard to one gesture, i.e., "targeting", there was an evident difference between the two groups and between the task-based investigation and the gesture catalog. The reason for the discrepancy might be explained by tremor symptoms. People with tremor might automatically choose gestures requiring little physical effort, in order to minimize movements. The gesture catalog did not list the "targeting" gesture. However, it listed a circle, which was interpreted by the seniors to be a pointing gesture and therefore chosen more frequently. A further outcome of the study was that the participants repeatedly chose the same, mainly simple, gestures, for the same functionality, regardless of the type of device. Generally, the chosen gestures were similar to the gestures defined for household technology in a study by Ouchi et al. [34], namely, straight up and down, straight left and right and a clockwise and counterclockwise circle.

5 Conclusion

In conclusion, it was shown that older people were highly interested in, and receptive to, the SP system. Existing problems with conventional technical devices, such as buttons which are too small and too numerous, often generate an overload for seniors, which can be minimized by an intuitive gesture-controlled and buttonless interaction. Although the seniors recognized the benefits of the system for themselves and for the most part could exactly describe the desired functionalities, they also expressed concerns regarding malfunctioning, system failure, forgetting gestures and data and personal security. A comparison of the requirements of healthy older persons and persons with tremor showed only a few differences in the types of gestures, feedback and concerns. However, the gestures of participants with tremor were performed less clearly. Preliminary studies by Ruser et al. [35] have already shown that a satisfactory performance of this innovative approach based on test trajectories with 29 gestures was achieved in healthy participants, with an average recognition rate of almost 94%. Considering only six fundamental quasi-intuitive gesture ('UP', 'DOWN', 'LEFT', 'RIGHT', 'CIRCLE LEFT', 'CIRCLE RIGHT'), the average recognition rate was above 98%. In this respect, it will be important in the further course of the project to determine the suitability of the system for people with tremor, and to develop technical solutions for gesture recognition in cases of tremor.

References

1. Statistisches Bundesamt: 13th Coordinated Population Projection for Germany (2015). https://service.destatis.de/bevoelkerungspyramide/index.html#!y=2030&l=en&b=1948. Accessed 26 Feb 2019

2. RKI: Health in Germany – the most important developments (2015). https://www.rki.de/EN/Content/Health_Monitoring/Health_Reporting/HealthInGermany/health_germany_node.html. Accessed 27 Feb 2019

3. Kremer-Preiß, U.: Aktuelle und zukunftsträchtige Wohnformen für das Alter. In: Wahl, H.-W., Tesch-Römer, C., Ziegelmann, J. (eds.) Angewandte Gerontologie: Interventionen für ein gutes Altern in 100 Schlüsselbegriffen, pp. 554–561. Kohlhammer, Stuttgart (2012)

4. Oswald, F., Wahl, H.-W.: Alte und neue Umwelten des Alterns – Zur Bedeutung von Wohnen und Technologie für Teilhabe in der späten Lebensphase. In: Naegele, G., et al. (eds.) Teilhabe im Alter gestalten – Aktuelle Themen der sozialen Gerontologie, pp. 113–129. Springer VS. Wiesbaden (2016)

5. Strese, H., Seidel, U., Knape, T., Botthof, A.: Smart Home in Deutschland – Untersuchung im Rahmen der wissenschaftlichen Begleitung zum Programm Next Generation Media (NGM) des Bundesministeriums für Wirtschaft und Technologie (2010). Institut für Innovation und Technik (iit). https://www.iit-berlin.de/de/publikationen/smart-home-in-deutschland. Accessed 08 Feb 2019

6. Meyer, S.: Technische Unterstützung im Alter - was ist möglich, was ist sinnvoll? Expertise zum Siebten Altenbericht der Bundesregierung (2016). Deutsches Zentrum für Altersfragen. https://nbn-resolving.org/urn:nbn:de:0168-ssoar-49980-9. Accessed 07 Feb 2019

7. Statista: Share of Internet users in Germany from 2014 to 2018, by age (2019). https://www.statista.com/statistics/790407/internet-usage-by-age-germany/. Accessed 27 Feb 2019

8. Statista: Anteil der Internetnutzer nach Endgeräten und Altersgruppen in Deutschland im Jahr 2016 (2019). https://de.statista.com/statistik/daten/studie/222917/umfrage/genutzte-internetzugaenge-in-deutschland-nach-alter/. Accessed 12 Feb 2019

9. Frees, B., Koch, W.: ARD/ZDF-Onlinestudie 2018: Zuwachs bei medialer Internetnutzung und Kommunikation. Media Perspektiven 9, 398–413 (2018)

10. Al-Shamayleh, A., Ahmad, R., Abushariah, M., et al.: A systematic literature review on vision based gesture recognition techniques. J. Multimed. Tools Appl. 77(21), 28121–28184 (2018)

11. Rautaray, S., Agrawal, A.: Vision based hand gesture recognition for human computer interaction: a survey. Artif. Intell. Rev. 43(1), 1–54 (2015)

12. Bachmann, D., Weichert, F., Rinkenauer, G.: Review of three-dimensional human-computer interaction with focus on the leap motion controller. Sensors 18(7), 2194 (2018)

13. Liu, H., Wang, L.: Gesture recognition for human-robot collaboration: a review. Int. J. Ind. Ergon. 68, 355–367 (2018)

14. Schlömer, T., Poppinga, B., Henze, N., Boll, S.: Gesture recognition with a Wii controller. In: Proceedings of the 2nd International Conference on Tangible and Embedded Interaction (TEI 2008), pp. 11–14 (2008)

15. Louis, E.D., Ottman, R.: How Many People in the USA Have Essential Tremor? Deriving a Population Estimate Based on Epidemiological Data. Tremor and Other Hyperkinetic Movements, 4 (2014). https://doi.org/10.7916/D8TT4P4B. Accessed 27 Feb 2019

16. Deuschl, G., Berg, D.: Essenzieller Tremor: State of the Art der Nervenarzt 4(89), 394–399 (2018)

17. McDowell, I.: Measuring Health - A Guide to Rating Scales and Questionnaires. Oxford University Press, New York (2006)

18. Fetz, F., Kornexl, E.: Sportmotorische Tests: praktische Anleitung zu sportmotorischen Tests in Schule und Verein. ÖBV, Wien (1993)

19. Bös, K.: Handbuch Motorische Tests - Sportmotorische Tets, Motorische Funktionstests, Fragebögen zur körperlich-sportlichen Aktivität und sportpsychologische Diagnoseverfahren (3. überarbeitete und erweiterte Ausg.). Hogrefe Verlag GmbH & Co. KG., Göttingen (2017)
20. Ruff, R.M., Parker, S.B.: Gender- and age-specific changes in motor speed and eye-hand coordination in adults: normative values for the finger tapping and grooved pegboard tests. Percept. Motor Skills, **76**(3_Suppl.), 1219–1230 (1993). https://doi.org/10.2466/pms.1993. 76.3c.1219. Accessed 08 Feb 2019
21. Chen, W.: Gesture-based applications for elderly people. In: Kurosu, M. (ed.) HCI 2013. LNCS, vol. 8007, pp. 186–195. Springer, Heidelberg (2013). https://doi.org/10.1007/978-3-642-39330-3_20
22. Kühnel, C., Westermann, T., Hemmert, F., Kratz, S., Müller, A., Möller, S.: I'm home: defining and evaluating a gesture set for smart-home control. Int. J. Hum Comput Stud. **69**, 693–704 (2011)
23. Statista: Share of smartphone users in Germany in 2017, by age group (2019). https://www. statista.com/statistics/469969/share-of-smartphone-users-in-germany-by-age-group/. Accessed 27 Feb 2019
24. Liang, S.-F.M., Lee, Y.-J.B.: Control with hand gestures by older users: a review. In: Zhou, J., Salvendy, G. (eds.) ITAP 2016. LNCS, vol. 9754, pp. 350–359. Springer, Cham (2016). https://doi.org/10.1007/978-3-319-39943-0_34
25. Bobeth, J., et al.: Tablet, gestures, remote control? Influence of age on performance and user experience with iTV applications. In: Proceedings of 2014 ACM International Conference on Interactive Experiences for TV and Online Video, Newcastle Upon Tyne, United Kingdom, 25–27 June, pp. 139–146 (2014)
26. Gerling, K.M., Dergousoff, K.K., Mandryk, R.L.: Is movement better? Comparing sedentary and motion-based game controls for older adults. In: Proceedings of Graphics Interface 2013, pp. 133–140. Canadian Information Processing Society (2013)
27. Chung, M.K., Kim, D., Na, S., Lee, D.: Usability evaluation of numeric entry tasks on keypad type and age. Int. J. Ind. Ergon. **40**(1), 97–105 (2010)
28. Hwangbo, H., Yoon, S.H., Jin, B.S., Han, Y.S., Ji, Y.G.: A study of pointing performance of elderly users on smartphones. Int. J. Hum.-Comput. Interact. **29**(9), 604–618 (2013)
29. Sáenz-de-Urturi, Z., García Zapirain, B., Méndez Zorrilla, A.: Elderly user experience to improve a Kinect-based game playability. Behav. Inf. Technol. **34**(11), 1040–1051 (2015)
30. Page, T.: Touchscreen mobile devices and older adults: a usability study. Int. J. Hum. Factors Ergon. **3**(1), 65–85 (2014)
31. Bobeth, J., Schmehl, S., Kruijff, E., Deutsch, S., Tscheligi, M.: Evaluating performance and acceptance of older adults using freehand gestures for TV menu control. In: Proceedings of 10th European conference on Interactive TV and Video, Berlin, Germany, 04–06 July, pp. 35–44. ACM (2012)
32. Gerling, K., Livingston, I., Nacke, L., Mandryk, R.: Full-body motion-based game interaction for older adults. In: Proceedings of SIGCHI Conference on Human Factors in Computing Systems, Austin, TX, USA, 05–10 May, pp. 1873–1882. ACM (2012)
33. Ferron, M., Mana, N., Mich, O.: Mobile for older adults: towards designing multimodal interaction. In: Proceedings of 14th International Conference on Mobile and Ubiquitous Multimedia, Linz, Austria, 30 November–02 December, pp. 373–378. ACM (2015)
34. Ouchi, K., Esaka, N., Tamura, Y., Hirahara, M., Doi, M.: Magic wand: an intuitive gesture remote control for home appliances. In: International Conference on Active Media Technology, Kagawa, Japan, 19–21 May (2005)
35. Ruser, H., Kosterski, Sz., Kargel, Ch.: Gesture-based universal optical remote control: concept, reconstruction principle and recognition results. In: IEEE International Instrumentation and Measurement Technology Conference (I2MTC), Pisa (2015)

Author Index

Printed in the United States
By Bookmasters